THE PLAYERS IN A DEADLY GAME

COLIN THATCHER—Tory cabinet minister and son of a prominent Canadian family, moody, powerful, and extremely clever . . .

JOANN THATCHER—The terrified wife whose ex-husband had already bungled one murder attempt and was about to try again . . .

TONY MERCHANT—Mercurial lawyer for the defense, his alibi for Thatcher was Colin's strongest hope . . .

GARRY ANDERSON—Hitman turned informer, his taped conversation with Colin contained a shocking revelation . . .

LYNNE MENDELL—Thatcher's glamorous California lover, her testimony could damn him or save him . . .

SERGE KUJAWA—Veteran Crown attorney, tough, angry, and determined to convict Colin Thatcher for murder . . .

A CANADIAN TRAGEDY

"Combining the zeal of an investigative reporter with the tenacity of a Crown prosecutor, Maggie Siggins reconstructs the case against Thatcher with an elaborate web of evidence gathered from the courtroom and her own extensive research. . . . By accumulating those extraordinary facts, A CANADIAN TRAGEDY turns from document to thriller."

—*Macleans*

"A CANADIAN TRAGEDY is cast in the tradition of Truman Capote's *In Cold Blood*."

—*Quill & Quire*

A CANADIAN TRAGEDY

JoAnn and Colin Thatcher: A Story of Love and Hate

MAGGIE SIGGINS

SEAL BOOKS
McClelland-Bantam, Inc.
Toronto

A CANADIAN TRAGEDY
*A Seal Book / published by arrangement with
Macmillan of Canada*

PRINTING HISTORY
Macmillan edition published October 1985
Seal edition / December 1986

Excerpts from *Blooming: A Small Town in Girlhood* (Little, Brown and Company, 1978) are rèprinted by kind permission of the author, Susan Allen Toth.

*Seal Books are published by McClelland-Bantam, Inc. Its
trademark, consisting of the words "Seal Books" and the portrayal of a seal, is the property of McClelland-Bantam, Inc.,
105 Bond Street, Toronto, Ontario M5B 1Y3, Canada. This
trademark has been duly registered in the Trademark Office of
Canada. The trademark consisting of the words "Bantam
Books" and the portrayal of a rooster is the property of and is
used with the consent of Bantam Books, 666 Fifth Avenue, New
York, New York 10103. This trademark has been duly registered in the Trademark Office of Canada and elsewhere.*

PRINTED IN CANADA
COVER PRINTED IN U.S.A.

U   11   10   9   8   7   6   5   4   3

For my mother, Elizabeth Siggins

ACKNOWLEDGMENTS

I am greatly indebted to the skill and dedication of my researcher, Sandra Bartlett. Without her perseverance, excellent journalistic sense, and good humour, this book would not have been possible in its present form. I also wish to express appreciation to Gerry Sperling for his never-failing inspiration and enthusiasm. Thanks also, for their encouragement, to Gail and Ted Bowen, who read the manuscript with insight. Last, but certainly not least, I am grateful to Doug Gibson, whose editing added a special dimension to this project.

Many people interviewed for this book, especially those living near Moose Jaw, did not want to be identified because they felt there might be further ramifications in the Thatcher affair. I have complied with their wishes.

Maggie Siggins
Regina
June, 1985

CONTENTS

CHAPTER ONE

STRANGE ENCOUNTER

MAY 1, 1984

To avoid alarming the neighbouring farmers, the four members of Regina's crack SWAT (Special Weapons and Tactics) squad arrived under cover of darkness at 3 a.m. Constables Jim McKee, Ray Golemba, and Ron Seiferling and Sergeant Ron Strassburger wore bush-green battle fatigues, and each carried a survival knife and a .38 revolver; the two group leaders were armed with M16-A1 rifles, the others, the snipers, with Remington .243 rifles. Their faces and hands blackened with camouflage paint, the four huddled together in the dark for a last-minute conference. It was chilly and wet—it had snowed only yesterday—and they had to speak above the whine of the wind sweeping across the abandoned farm. Quickly they laid their plans. two of the men would take up position on the cold soggy ground at the hedges near the front of the property, the other two would dig in at the rear of the farmhouse.

As yet there were no leaves on the trees, and little grass was growing. Some scrub bush and a few pieces of ancient rusting farm equipment were the only cover available. The policemen knew there was a chance that Colin Thatcher might spot them and a carefully rehearsed scenario had been worked out for that situation. Sergeant Strassburger would jump up and introduce himself: "Mr. Thatcher, don't be startled. You have stumbled into one of the largest cocaine busts in Saskatchewan history. Please leave the area immediately. My commanding officer is waiting to speak with you just up the road." If they were lucky, Thatcher would believe them, and the anxious Regina police would not have to watch fifteen months of painstaking investigative work go up in smoke. But it was not a perfect plan, and the SWAT team prayed they would not have to use it.

Five hours later, exactly as planned, Garry Anderson drove up in his half-ton truck. With his neatly trimmed jet-black beard and his hawk nose, he might have been considered handsome, except for the shifty look that always made a local teacher think of Iago whenever she saw him. At six-foot-two and 235 pounds, Garry was a hefty, macho-looking man, and in recent years he had developed a paunch. This was somewhat exaggerated today; for this morning beneath his shirt Garry Anderson was wearing a bullet-proof vest.

Under the vest was a body pack, a portable tape recorder placed there to preserve the conversation he hoped to have with his neighbour Colin Thatcher. The tape had already been running for some fifteen minutes, and it testified to the fact that Garry Anderson was a very nervous man. A Crown prosecutor would later say that the sharp intake of Anderson's breath was so exaggerated that he was close to hyperventilating.

While the four SWAT team members waited anxiously, Anderson paced up and down outside the ramshackle barn. The sun was bright, but spring had yet to grace the province of Saskatchewan, and only the odd touch of green could be seen here and there. This gave the old Bergren homestead a forsaken, sullen façade. Built in 1904, this had once been a prosperous place, and the rambling farmhouse retained remnants of pride and grandeur even in its present ruin. In summer when the fields were golden, grasshoppers swarmed around the barn in great clouds, and hawks perched in nearby trees, screaming and swooping low at human approach. Surrounded by the vast sweep of prairie, the deserted homestead stood as a symbol of man's determination to cultivate these plains, and indeed the rich land produced some of the finest grain grown anywhere in the world. Colin Thatcher had bought this farm for his sons, Gregory and Regan, in the hope that, whatever happened to him, his children would uphold the Thatcher reputation as prosperous and successful farmers.

The five men tensed as they heard the sound of an approaching car. A small grey Mayfair (owned by Sandra Sparks, the secretary of the nearby Caron Rural Municipality and one of the future organizers of the Colin Thatcher Defence Fund) turned off the grid road and halted in the yard. Colin Thatcher got out, explaining that the battery in his three-quarter-ton truck was dead. As he and Anderson stood talking, all four SWAT members trained their rifles on Thatcher. The cops felt that if he discovered the stakeout, or Anderson's body pack, Colin Thatcher could turn ugly very fast. Constable McKee was listening to every word of the conversation on an FM receiver so that he could give the signal to the others the instant something went wrong.

Thatcher asked Anderson if he wanted to go for a ride, but Garry prudently replied no, he preferred to stick around. "Have to be awfully cautious. One never knows," urged Thatcher. It was the first of many times during the conversation that he would warn Anderson about the danger of being overheard, revealing his terrible fear of police bugging. The two men chatted about everyday topics—farming, their travels—until Thatcher suddenly asked, "Have you been hassled?" Anderson understood right away that he meant hassled by the police. "Well, they came once and talked to me and just asked me about the Chev car, and that was about it. Other than that, nothing at all. How about you?"

"Just the once, the day after ... there's been some attempts to put us together and we should not be seen together."

The two men continued to talk intensely, walking about the yard as they did so. They discussed the "cheap stunts" pulled by the police to entrap Thatcher; the whereabouts of two men with whom Anderson and Thatcher had carried on shady business dealings a couple of years ago; and Thatcher's desire to get even with certain individuals who had crossed him. They also discussed the interesting matter of a car that Anderson had disposed of for Thatcher. "I had a bitch of a time getting the blood and stuff off," Anderson complained.

"Yeah. Is there no chance that it can ever surface? There is a chance it can surface?" asked Thatcher. "No," responded Anderson. "The car was cleaned."

At one point Thatcher asked, "Do you need some bread?" "Yeah, I can use some," Anderson replied. "I can use some for that car." Thatcher admitted he was strapped for cash at the moment, but he promised to round up some money. The two men agreed he would put it in a white envelope, which would be placed in a green garbage bag and then stuck under a weathered board near the abandoned farm's red Quonset hut. The date agreed upon for this drop-off was the following Friday, two days later.

After twenty minutes the conversation wound down. "Next time I see you, just give me that same sign," said Thatcher. "And there is no problem unless you do something stupid." "Okay," replied Anderson. "I'm glad you got her," he called out. "Okay," said Thatcher. The two men then got into their vehicles and went their separate ways.

As the sounds of the car and truck died away, Constable Jim McKee got up and walked over to the exact spot where Thatcher had been standing. He then turned and looked back at his hiding place; he could see the impression that his body had left on the ground. Colin had come within fifty feet of the policeman—so close that McKee feared Thatcher might step on him. "I was scared shitless," he told his colleagues, as they stood around shaking the stiffness and tension out of their limbs.

FRIDAY, MAY 4

Colin Thatcher didn't realize it, but when he left his house at about 7:15 a.m. he was the target of an intricate police surveillance system. Corporal Fred Waelz, head of the RCMP's Special O Section, started tagging Thatcher's brown half-ton truck at 7:31 as it turned west onto Caribou Street in Moose Jaw. At 7:40 Waelz came into radio contact with Constable Robert Britton, who was flying an aircraft overhead. The two police officers followed Thatcher and his truck to his farm some twenty-one kilometers west of Moose Jaw. As Constable Britton continued to circle overhead, Thatcher talked to two of his ranch hands about some sick calves and other business. After about an hour Thatcher, still followed by the two police officers, travelled to the nearby nuisance grounds, a local euphemism for the garbage dump, and dropped off some trash. As was his habit, Thatcher then dropped into the Caronport restaurant owned by the Briercrest Bible College and had a coffee. Half an hour later, Constable Britton watched from his plane as Thatcher drove into the abandoned farm. When Thatcher got out, Britton, realizing that the noisy aircraft might make Thatcher suspicious, left the area. Later that evening, Sergeant Jim Street of the Regina police force went to the abandoned farm, where he found $550 in cash in a garbage bag behind the ancient four-by-six plank.

MAY 7, 1984

As he left home at about 7:45 a.m. and set out once again for the Caron area, life must have seemed brighter for Colin Thatcher than it had for a year: the weather was a little warmer, seeding operations on his farm were under way, and, most important, a lawsuit that had nagged at him for fifteen months had been decided mostly in his favour. He drove his pick-up through the old Moose Jaw neighbourhood where he had grown up, and out to the main street, which would lead to the Trans-Canada Highway. As he neared the major intersection, he saw a Royal Canadian Mounted Police cruiser, lights flashing, waving him down. Assuming he was being stopped for not having his seat belt buckled, Thatcher screeched to a halt. Almost immediately a second unmarked police car pulled up alongside the first. Sergeant Street of the Regina city police jumped out, strode quickly to Thatcher's truck, opened the door, and told him to get out. Meanwhile two of Regina's most experienced and wily policemen, Inspector Ed Swayze and Detective Wally Beaton, had arrived. As the two unflappable cops walked slowly towards him, Thatcher glanced around in a manner that seemed to Swayze like "an animal trapped in a cage." Out of nowhere police cars had materialized to block the three other streets at the intersection. Other police in the vicinity had cordoned off the area to keep motorists away. There were even some Moose Jaw cops who had nothing whatsoever to do with the operation; they had come to watch history being made.

"Wilbert Colin Thatcher, I have an information here charging you with the first-degree murder of JoAnn Kay Wilson," barked Swayze. "Do you wish to say anything in answer to the charge? You need not say anything. Anything you do say may be used against you as evidence. You are entitled to consult counsel without delay. You will be transported back to Regina in the company of Detective Beaton." Swayze noticed that Thatcher's tongue had turned white and he kept swallowing as though the saliva had dried in his mouth. "He's in a state of shock," thought the policeman. Sergeant Street then snapped handcuffs on Thatcher. As he was being led to the police car, Thatcher whined, "Jeez, can't I even take my coffee?"

This was a man with a vivid, exaggerated reputation: a tough and wealthy rancher, a powerful, intimidating politician, a debonair man-about-town, and the cops arresting him were just a little awed by their prize catch. They were also extremely curious. For the last eighteen months they had listened to his telephone conversations, which had been legally wire-tapped, and they had talked to anybody who had the remotest connection to him, including many beautiful and fascinating past and present lovers. They knew that this was a man who played entirely by his own rules.

The police had been informed that Thatcher had a loaded gun in his house and they were determined to avoid a shootout where he, a member of his family, or one of them might be killed. So they had put off his arrest for three days, waiting for the moment when he left his house alone and headed for his farm. They wanted to approach him at the edge of town, so that he would be out in the open but not in a place so secluded that he would prematurely catch sight of police officers approaching. And it had worked; they now had Thatcher under arrest and were taking him to the provincial capital, Regina, seventy kilometres to the east along the almost arrow-straight, four-lane Trans-Canada Highway. On the way, Thatcher chatted for a few moments with Sergeants Street and Beaton about his seeding operation.

Meanwhile, ten Regina police officers armed with a search warrant arrived in Moose Jaw at the Thatchers' Redland Avenue residence. Their mission was to comb through every cupboard, every drawer, every corner, searching for incriminating evidence. One of their most significant discoveries was a box that had once contained a toy shower for long-legged "Cindy," a Barbie doll clone. The box was now filled with old editions of the *Los Angeles Times* and had been stashed in the upper cupboard shelf of Colin Thatcher's bedroom. it would prove a most vital piece of evidence at the trial.

Before everybody piled into the house, Sergeant Gene Stusek and Constable Sharon Fettes approached the children. The officers were amazed at the nonchalance of eighteen-year-old Gregory, fifteen-year-old Regan, and ten-year-old Stephanie after they heard the news of their father's arrest. One huge cop would later entertain his colleagues by coyly skipping around the house, humming away and smiling—his imitation of Stephanie Thatcher collecting her belongings as if in preparation for a perfectly normal visit with her grandmother in Regina.

In fact, Gregory had been following his father that morning in his own pick-up and had watched the bizarre episode unfold. He had rushed to a phone and contacted Tony Merchant, the family's solicitor and friend. Merchant responded briskly, "Don't worry. We'll get your father out of there this afternoon." He then pushed aside his mountain of work, left his rabbit warren of an office on Broad Street, and rushed to the courthouse, where he was able to set up a bail application hearing in the Court of Queen's Bench for early that afternoon.

Merchant approached that hearing with an attitude that many thought was a remarkable display of overconfidence. "Merchant assumed there would be no opposition," recalled Serge Kujawa, the chief prosecutor in the case, "that this fellow was just going to be let out on bail, sort of like walking up and getting your driver's license."

Indeed, so anxious was the defence lawyer to hasten the procedure that he agreed that the prosecutor would not have to call witnesses to put forth the Crown's case; it could be done through the submissions of the Crown attorney. Serge Kujawa considered this to be a suicidal move on Merchant's part. "If I can't tell the story more effectively than the police can, I shouldn't be here," he thought to himself. As well, Kujawa was considered a highly experienced and respected officer of the court and thus would be free of any taint of personal involvement that a cop, long embroiled in an extensive investigation, might be considered to have.

Merchant had decided to make such accommodation for expediency's sake because he was sure that bail would not be denied a man of Thatcher's influence and prestige in the community. "If this accused is not going to be released on bail, then I suggest it's tantamount to saying virtually no murder accused would ever be released on bail. And of course, they frequently and normally are, unless there's some reason not to do so," Merchant told the judge.

Kujawa, however, argued strenuously that neither he nor the defence could possibly be ready for a full bail hearing that afternoon. And although Merchant finally agreed that an appropriate time for the hearing would be the next afternoon, he was upset that Colin Thatcher would have to spend a night in jail.

* * *

At thirty-nine, E.F. Anthony Merchant already held celebrity status, as an enigmatic and controversial character in a province that traditionally nurtured the eccentric. The scion of a prominent Saskatchewan family, he practised law in a manner so unorthodox that the mere mention of his name among the judiciary resulted in the snapping of teeth and hissing of breath. "He is bright but he plays by his own rules," says an appeal court judge. "He's always applying the rules to you, but they are not supposed to be applied to him." But there were those who appreciated his gusty, belligerent approach, and he could boast of a thriving law practise consisting mainly of matrimonial and other civil cases. He was also a political figure of note, having once been a member of the Saskatchewan Legislative Assembly, and had come close to winning the leadership of the provincial Liberal party in 1976. Otto Lang, the former federal cabinet minister who for many years distributed patronage on the prairies the way other people do cattle feed, was Tony's brother-in-law. This fact alone ensured Merchant influence and power in his community.

That evening he had volunteered to pour drinks at the Montessori College of Western Canada's annual fundraising dinner held at Campion College, and he chatted with the stylish guests primarily about his latest achievement, a degree in business administration that he had recently earned from the University of Regina. He did not seem the least bit nervous about defending his old friend and political colleague the next day, but then early in his legal career he had practised criminal law almost exclusively and had been involved in three to four hundred bail hearings. In his experience, people charged with the most grisly murders often got out on bail, and he simply assumed that a man of Colin Thatcher's distinction would be no exception.

While the drinks flowed, the guests gossiped, and the speeches on progressive education were made, Thatcher grimly settled down for his first bleak night behind bars.

MAY 8, 1984

Thatcher liked to brag that he felt just as much at home in banker's apparel as he did in a pair of jeans and cowboy boots, and on the occasion of his bail hearing he decided that the urbane Colin Thatcher would be more likely to impress the judge. He wore a proper royal-blue suit, a crisp white shirt, and a silk striped tie. As was fitting for a proud man of influence, his emotions remained invisible. Indeed, during his many court appearances Thatcher seldom lost his composure. His face seemed set in porcelain, like the tragic twin of Thespis's famous dramatic masks, an image reinforced by the extreme downward turn of his mouth. Even when he smiled he appeared on the edge of a snarl.

Despite his controlled façade, Colin Thatcher seemed nervous, even frightened, as Crown attorney Serge Kujawa began outlining the bare bones of his case. Most of the spectators in the airy Regina courtroom were profoundly shocked at what they heard. For eighteen-year-old Gregory Thatcher, leaning against the wall, shoulder to shoulder with the overflow of curiosity-seekers, it was the beginning of an excruciating ordeal.

After JoAnn Wilson was murdered in the garage of her elegant Regina home in January of 1983, police had released a composite sketch of the suspect, and that drawing had been publicized across the country. The wanted man was described as about thirty years old, between five-foot-nine and five-foot-eleven, slim to medium build, with a heavy dark-brown or black beard. Certainly Thatcher who was forty-five, heavyset, about six feet tall, and clean-shaven, looked nothing like the individual on the wanted poster. People assumed that if he was to be accused of anything, it would be of *hiring* someone to kill his ex-wife. And yet here was the Crown prosecutor claiming that Colin Thatcher had actually pulled the trigger himself. For two long years he planned the killing, which, the prosecutor barked, "shows a very long, very sustained and persistent hate, vindictiveness, determination."

It was true, Serge Kujawa told the astonished courtroom, that Thatcher had tried to hire other people to commit the crime, but all of these deals had fallen through. And now, as the accused's terrible nemesis, one of these conspirators had revealed all to the police. Garry Anderson had woven a tale of intrigue and murder for the police investigators; the tape recording verified everything he said, and from Colin Thatcher's own lips. The entire conversation between Thatcher and

Anderson had been recorded. It was this tape that Kujawa called his "clincher, the binder" that pulled all the other evidence together and that made the Crown's case so strong.

Crown prosecutor Kujawa was determined that Colin Thatcher would not be released under any conditions. He insisted that the accused, with his vast wealth, would be sorely tempted to flee the country to avoid standing trial for first-degree murder. And the community must be protected: on the tape Thatcher had threatened at least three people, said the prosecutor, and when the police had searched his home after his arrest, they had found a loaded, unregistered snub-nosed .38 handgun that Thatcher had bought in California and smuggled into Canada. The ammunition for the gun had been found in the garage. Kujawa went on, "I think the fact that the gun was there, loaded and unregistered, is significant. It's pretty hard for someone in his position to say that 'I couldn't get a gun and register it.' After all, much lesser lights get registration for such firearms. This one was there. It was unregistered."

The Crown's argument stunned the defence. Merchant had received no warning that Thatcher was being accused of performing the actual deed himself, nor did he have any inkling that the tape recording existed. He had been caught off guard, but he fought back as best he could.

For most of Canada's judicial history, it had been up to the Crown prosecutor to show why an individual who was awaiting his trial should be detained in custody. By the mid-Seventies, however, there were growing complaints that far too many serious crimes were being committed by people out on bail. Buckling under the pressure, Parliament amended the Criminal Code so that the onus was reversed; an accused person such as Colin Thatcher now had to convince a judge that there was good reason why he should not remain in jail. Merchant went at the task of convincing Mr. Justice Maurice from several angles.

First, in broad strokes he painted a picture of Colin Thatcher as an exemplary citizen, a man whose roots were fixed deep in Saskatchewan history. This was a man, said Merchant, who was the head of a family with a distinguished tradition, his father having been a renowned premier of the province. The accused himself was a Member of the Legislative Assembly for Thunder Creek, and former energy minister in the current Conservative government. He controlled vast land holdings. And he was the proud father of three successful children, all of whom were going to the very schools that he himself had attended in the picturesque town of Moose Jaw. Most of his close friends lived in the province. Surely, Merchant pleaded, this man had too much to lose to flee before his trial.

Merchant then moved on to attack the specific charges. The Crown's case was anything but ironclad, he insisted. Indeed the charges against Thatcher were based on nothing but circumstantial evidence. There was no smoking gun. Certainly the word of the so-called accomplice would have to be viewed with grave suspicion, since he was probably tempted by the $50,000 reward that had been offered to anyone providing information leading to the killer's conviction. "I don't mean to be facetious about such a serious matter," he told the court, "but I understand that there was sort of an essay-writing contest, in the jails and penitentiaries, of various people trying to present different positions on how they could be of assistance to the Crown." Secondly, Thatcher looked nothing like the drawing of the murderer that police had been promoting across Canada for fifteen months. And thirdly, Merchant himself could personally provide information that would cut huge holes in the Crown's case. It was this final argument that was the most intriguing.

Sixteen months before JoAnn Wilson was murdered, she had been shot by a high-powered rifle as she stood washing the dishes at her kitchen sink late in the evening. The bullet, which had smashed into her shoulder, had come close to killing her. The assailant had never been arrested and now the Crown prosecutor was claiming that Thatcher had personally committed this crime as well. This information shocked Tony Merchant, he said, because he believed he could provide an airtight alibi for Thatcher on that evening. Merchant claimed that he had been informed about the wounding by the police shortly after it happened. He immediately talked to Thatcher by phone and then quickly drove to Thatcher's home in Moose Jaw some seventy kilometres away. According to this scenario Colin Thatcher simply could not have been at the Wilson home at the time of the crime. "This may result in my being a witness and not counsel," Merchant told the court.

In retrospect, what was most interesting about Merchant's comments was the information that he did *not* reveal at the bail hearing. At Thatcher's trial, some six months later, he would testify that fifteen minutes after JoAnn Wilson was killed in January of 1983, he phoned Moose Jaw and talked to Thatcher, thereby establishing an alibi for the murder. Yet during the bail hearing for that same murder, he mentioned not a word about this, only recalling what had occurred a year and a half before, on the occasion of the wounding. "That was the very first time it had ever crossed my mind that he was being accused of having committed the murder himself. . . . I was taken aback," remembers Merchant, to explain this surprising oversight. It is equally interesting to note that the lawyer did not call any of the witnesses who would later claim that Thatcher had been eating Hamburger Helper and watching the sports news at his home in Moose Jaw at the time of the murder.

Justice Eugene Maurice had been a Swift Current lawyer; he was a former president of the Liberal constituency association who had run twice as a federal candidate for the Liberals in the nearly unwinnable seat of Swift Current–Maple Creek. He was appointed a Queen's Bench judge in October, 1981. Merchant, who had an influential say in the selection of judges, thought that this justice would have at least some sympathy towards his case. Near the end of the hearing Mr. Justice Maurice, a youngish, balding, bespectacled man, asked counsel if they had any comments about conditions that should be imposed if Thatcher were given bail, a turn of events that further reinforced Tony Merchant's belief that Colin would soon be out of jail. At the question Kujawa jumped to his feet. "My Lord, if we get to conditions, the Crown has no concern about conditions." "I'm not sure I follow you, Mr. Kujawa," the judge replied. "The Crown will agree to any conditions whatsoever if we ever get to that point," said Kujawa in disgust, "having totally given up." It was a petulant remark for the province's special prosecutor to make, but it demonstrated his frustration at the very thought of Colin Thatcher walking the streets free. "When you've been around a great deal longer than the judge, there's

nothing wrong in letting him know how strongly you feel,"
Kujawa says.

But if Kujawa was taking a chance, so was Tony Merchant.
The usual bail restrictions would have required Thatcher to
report to the police once a week, live in Moose Jaw, stay
within an eighty-kilometre radius of that town, and give up
his passport. But Merchant argued that none of this should
apply to his client. After all he was not a "run-of-the-mill sort
of person." Thatcher could possibly live with the first two
conditions, admitted the lawyer, but he did need to travel.
"He has a second home in Palm Springs where he and his
family go quite frequently," Merchant pointed out. "It's my
hope that Your Lordship would permit him simply to go to
Palm Springs, and it could be restricted to that. There's no
need to go to other [states], just California."

It took Mr. Justice Maurice forty-five minutes to decide
that Colin Thatcher would not be going anywhere. He denied
him bail.

Thatcher was placed in the police station's holding tank to
await his transport to the Regina Correctional Institute. There
he was approached by a tall, burly Indian who had been
picked up for disorderly conduct. "Hey, Thatcher," he
whispered, "how much you charge, eh? I got an old lady I'd
just love to axe." He broke into loud guffaws. Thatcher said
not a word in reply but simply turned his back.

The prison in which Colin Thatcher was incarcerated was
considered so monstrous that some judges counted every day
an inmate spent there awaiting trial as two, and reduced the
sentence accordingly. The Regina Correctional Institute, built
in 1913, had suffered a long history of prison breaks, riots,
and hostage-takings. Inmates regularly complained about the
appalling quality of the food, about the rats and cockroaches
found in the cells, and about the strip searches that their
visitors had to undergo. In the early 1960s Ross Thatcher,
then premier of Saskatchewan, toured the prison, called it "a
disgusting place," and immediately promised reform. A few
modern additions had been constructed and some penal
reform had been implemented, but the place still reeked of
harshness and oppression. Thatcher's son, there for a different reason, considered it unfit for human habitation, "a hell
hole."

Except for a half-hour of outside exercise a day, remand prisoners who were considered to be in danger from other inmates were locked in their cells around the clock. Personal phone calls were limited to one a day. Business communications were permitted only as prison officials saw fit, and visits were allowed only during Saturday afternoons and one other hour per week. Such restrictions were terribly oppressive for the MLA from Thunder Creek, and he complained bitterly about the confinement, claiming that it made him feel claustrophobic. It didn't help when one day he returned to his cell to find a copy of *Playboy* magazine on the bed. In the centrefold lay a homemade cigarette, rolled like a marijuana joint, and a razor blade. In prison parlance the message was clear: he should smoke the joint, masturbate with the help of the Playmate, and then slit his wrists.

Shortly after his arrival at the ancient jail, Thatcher began having severe problems with his stomach and his nerves. "What I need," the accused man told a doctor, "is a couple of shots of good Scotch every night." The physician replied that he would prescribe that if he could, but a mild tranquillizer would have the same effect. Thatcher declined the medication, saying he was afraid of the effect of such drugs. After a psychiatric evaluation that indicated that he might indeed have suicidal tendencies, he was dispatched to the relative comfort of the medical wing. No guards were stationed there, only psychiatric and other nurses who allowed him out of his cell at about eight o'clock in the morning, often until eleven at night.

Now it was possible for Greg Thatcher, who suddenly found himself in charge of the ranching operation, to phone his dad as often as three times a day. The Thunder Creek constituency president, Lyle Stewart, also talked to the MLA many times during the week, and of course Thatcher had long conversations with his lawyers and with a variety of supporters who called to offer their condolences. Prison officials were equally generous in allowing him to see visitors. Greg would come three to four times a week; the two younger children, Regan and Stephanie, would spend Saturday afternoons with their father, although how much the ten-year-old girl enjoyed this was questionable. (Guards noticed that she would wander off by herself, daydreaming, while the others chatted with Colin.) And equally comforting was the constant and loyal presence of Diane Stoner.

In his mature years Colin Thatcher had developed an uncanny talent for charming women who were not only attractive and tastefully dressed, but also intelligent and interesting. Diane Stoner was no exception. Twenty-nine years old, blonde, and rather more curvaceous than many of Thatcher's women, she dressed beautifully. Many of her colleagues at Regina's Plains Health Centre raved about her ability as a nurse; she was particularly caring and kind towards patients, they said. She started going out with Colin in January of 1984, not realizing that he was also dating one of her nursing colleagues. After Thatcher was arrested, her competition bowed out, and Diane Stoner was inexorably sucked into the family's tragedy. The day Colin was imprisoned she moved into his Redland Avenue home in Moose Jaw to help care for Regan and Stephanie, undeterred by the fact that she would have to drive seventy kilometres back and forth to work every day. She remained loyal to Colin, bearing with grace the public scrutiny she would undergo in the coming months.

Thatcher's ability to attract beautiful women was an aspect of his personality that fascinated police and prosecutors who investigated the murder case. Says one, "When things went badly, when Thatcher was down, he had five to seven girlfriends to call in various parts of the world at all times. He'd call one in California 'Oh hi, I just got in from Paris, tired, just wanted to say hi and hear the sound of your voice. It was just three days, not enough time for fun. Good to hear from you. Glad I called. Good night.' He hung up. Zoom, zoom, zoom, another one in a different part of the land. 'I just got in from Germany. Doing some business there, dead tired. Just glad to hear your voice. That's why I called you. Bye.' Another one somewhere else. 'I'm sitting in the Minister of Finance's office in London. Only got five minutes but wanted to hear your voice.' And the guy hadn't been out of Moose Jaw for three weeks. And of course the girls didn't know he wasn't telling the truth." Thatcher also often *pretended* to be engaged in phone conversations. Obviously somebody nearby was meant to hear the important business deal and the important person he was talking to. The wire-tap, of course, revealed that only a dial tone was on the other end of the line. "Colin Thatcher lived in his own little world," says a close friend. "He could be so charming when he wanted....Few people, especially of the opposite sex, could resist him. And he worked his charm to his benefit in prison."

Tony Merchant believed that Thatcher was receiving "special treatment" at the correctional institute because both inmates and prison officials alike considered that he was being unfairly treated by the police. "Criminals don't mind police doing their job, but they don't expect them to go out of their way to single out a particular individual and 'overdo' their job," he theorized. Merchant claimed that during one visit, a prison guard told him that it was unfair that "Mr. Thatcher" had been refused bail when people who were found holding the axe with blood on it commonly were released on bail. And although Thatcher would talk with the guards only when it was necessary—to answer or ask a question—he was very polite when he did communicate with them. He was also civil with his fellow inmates. At one point there were rumblings of discontent throughout the prison because of the supposedly unique treatment Thatcher was receiving. This quickly ceased, however, after prisoners who talked with him reported that he was an all-right guy—for instance he was overheard promising several inmates that he would find them jobs when they got out of jail.

Despite his "soft" treatment, Thatcher was traumatized by his imprisonment, and he pleaded with his family and lawyers to somehow get him out. Then on May 15, Chief Justice E.D. Bayda of the Saskatchewan Court of Appeal granted Thatcher leave to appeal the decision of Mr. Justice Maurice. There was still a chance.

By this time Tony Merchant had bowed out and Thatcher had retained Gerry Allbright, a prominent criminal lawyer from Saskatoon. The choice was not surprising. Allbright had defended Thatcher once before, after he had been charged with the abduction of his daughter Stephanie. Those accusations had been thrown out of court, and Thatcher had acquired a high regard for the talents of the clever young lawyer. And Allbright liked his client. "I had had no unpleasant dealing with Colin. I saw him in a different light than the one everyone else painted." (Asked later if he felt that Thatcher was an innocent man, Allbright responded, "It

would be unfair of me to comment in that regard, but I have
no hesitation saying as a lawyer, I don't think there was
enough evidence to convict him.")

Now thirty-seven, Gerry Allbright was considered one of
the leading lights of Saskatchewan's closely knit legal community. A Queen's Counsel, former director of the province's
legal aid plan, and past president of the Law Society of
Saskatchewan (the youngest in that august body's history), in
his thirteen-year career Allbright had spent an impressive
amount of time in the courtroom. With his beautifully coiffured
hair and compact boyish looks he was handsome in the
refined way of the Kennedy sons. he was also exceedingly
articulate, and his manner in the courtroom was as courteous
and soft-spoken as Tony Merchant's was aggressive and abrasive.
Indeed, some Saskatchewan appeal court justices had unkind-
ly nicknamed Allbright "Mr. Goo," so slavish and ingratiating
was his manner towards them. "He was like a lap dog licking
your face all over," one appeal court judge commented.

In 1980 Allbright married a striking young woman from
Prince Albert who had been "born again in Christ." They
joined a Pentecostal Church in Saskatoon and remained devoted parishioners—so devoted, in fact, that Allbright would
astonish his sophisticated, rather cynical colleagues with the
line "Jesus was the greatest defence counsel of them all." In
fact, fundamentalist religion was something the defence lawyer shared with his client.

Before his arrest, Thatcher had not exactly been an enthusiastic churchgoer. JoAnn had been a staunch member of St.
Andrew's United Church in Moose Jaw, but Colin attended
only on rare occasions. After JoAnn was murdered, Gerald
Muirhead, a long-time friend and Tory MLA for Arm River,
sent Colin a letter expressing his sympathy. "Whenever I'm
troubled or sad," wrote Muirhead, "I turn to the Holy Spirit
and scriptures and I suggest it might work for you too." The
next time Thatcher ran into Muirhead he said, with a tear in
his eye, "Thank you very much for the letter. It means a great
deal to know I have a friend." After Thatcher was arrested,
Muirhead sent him a Bible with a list of appropriate passages
dealing with marital problems, revenge, and "dozens of things
you can look to for comfort."

One day Ray Matheson, an official of the Canadian Bible
College, was doing his rounds in the Regina Correctional

Institute and wandered over to talk to Thatcher. He noticed that the prisoner was reading a new Gideon Bible. Matheson asked him where he got it and Thatcher responded, "My best friend sent me this Bible." The two men began to discuss religion and after that Matheson visited the accused man often. In June, several months before his trial, Thatcher revealed that he had "found God and would be born again in Christ."

Allbright's most critical and difficult task at the May 24 bail appeal hearing was to convince the three Court of Appeal justices to consider vital new evidence. Since the original bail application had been heard two weeks before, a series of affidavits had been filed that claimed that Colin Thatcher could not have been anywhere near the Wilson residence the night JoAnn was murdered, at about 6 p.m. His sons, Gregory and Regan, claimed that on January 21, 1983, Thatcher, after working at his ranch all day, arrived at the Moose Jaw house at about 5:30 p.m., ate supper at 6 p.m., and then remained at home the entire evening. The family's housekeeper, Sandra Silversides, confirmed this, saying that she arrived at the Thatcher residence at 5 p.m. to prepare Hamburger Helper and then dined with Colin and the children at 6 p.m. Her brother Pat Hammond swore that he saw Thatcher's truck in Moose Jaw between 5:00 and 5:50 p.m. Barbara Wright, the wife of Colin's ranch hand, said she spotted Thatcher at the ranch at about 5:15 p.m. And Tony Merchant finally remembered that he had phoned Thatcher some time before 6:30 p.m. Surely, Allbright told the three judges, if such information had been available at the time of the original bail hearing, Colin Thatcher would not be in jail.

Since the Court of Appeal does not usually consider any evidence that was available at the time of the initial bail hearing, the justices were most interested in why this information had not been brought forth at that time. Why, they wondered, were these people not called as witnesses? Allbright explained that Merchant was so taken aback at the Crown's theory that Thatcher himself had pulled the trigger that he had not been prepared to present alibi evidence. Why, then, the justices asked, did Mr. Merchant not ask for an adjournment? Allbright agreed that in retrospect that might have been the proper decision, but Merchant had thought it would be a tactical blunder. Although he was shocked at the Crown's evidence, he didn't want to over-react.

It took the three justices only a short time to decide that they could not consider the affidavits. At that point, Colin Thatcher, dressed in his pin-striped banker's suit, turned towards Gregory, seated with the other spectators, and gave his son a look of such anguish that those who saw it were shaken.

Allbright was then forced to deal only with the arguments that Merchant had already offered, emphasizing Thatcher's substantial achievements. But Allbright had quite a different attitude about bail conditions than did Tony Merchant. Any conditions that the court might wish to impose would be just fine with his client, said the lawyer, including twice-daily reporting to the RCMP, depositing his passport, and staying near Moose Jaw.

For his part, the Crown attorney simply recounted once again the prosecution's strong case. And Allbright realized that without Thatcher's alibi to act as a shield, he would find Serge Kujawa a deadly opponent.

Indeed, the two counsels made a remarkable study in contrasts that would grow more vivid the longer they parried. Allbright, fresh-faced and preppy, was a smooth talker but rather verbose, his sentences tending to wind around each other like some intricate flowering vine. On the other hand, Serge Kujawa's trademark was his habit of presenting only the bare bones of a case, eliminating any information that smacked of the extraneous. He addressed the court quietly but emphatically, now and then making his point by purposefully pumping an extended left arm. There was drama in this gesture because the two middle fingers of his large and bony hand were missing. His barrel chest and slim waist—a result of daily weight-lifting sessions—and his craggy, flat-nosed face did nothing to belie his Ukranian peasant origins. Fifty-nine years old, he was the dean of Saskatchewan's prosecutors and a much-respected character in the province.

Kujawa liked the old-fashioned "sensible" way of carrying on business, where lawyers were considered good ol' boys and talked things out. "What would normally happen in a case of this magnitude—and I'm talking about what I hope is not a lost era—the defence lawyer would phone me and say, 'Serge, I'm acting for Colin. Got to see you right now. Can you come down here?' Then he'd tell me he's got these people who say the guy wasn't there. 'How the hell could he have committed the murder? I have all this alibi evidence and it's above board. Do I have to call these people or are you going to admit I have an alibi in court?' And I'd answer yes or no. He'd tell me what he had, and I'd tell him what I had, right off the bat. There was no game-playing at all and then we'd make our preparations [for court] on that basis.

"When you come up with a Tony Merchant type of attitude ... it colours the whole proceedings. So this was more adversarial, more antagonistic than it would have been. Then when Allbright came on the scene, it got worse."

What made Kujawa bristle was a comment that Allbright made during the appeal. When asked about the infamous tape recording between Thatcher and Anderson, Allbright responded, "It is non-existent, inaudible or garbled." That indicated to Kujawa that the defence considered the Crown's case a conspiracy, in which the police had fabricated evidence in a desperate bid to ensnare someone for a well-publicized unsolved crime. The statement marked the beginning of an antagonism between the two lawyers that would mushroom.

It was late in the afternoon by the time the defence and Crown had finished arguing their cases, and the three appeal court judges decided to reserve their judgment. The next day Colin Thatcher was informed that he had again been denied bail. There was, however, still a glimmer of hope. In accordance with normal Canadian legal practice, there would be a preliminary hearing to establish if the Crown had a case strong enough to go to trial. If Thatcher were to have another opportunity for a bail hearing after the preliminary hearing, the full weight of the Crown's case could be more adequately judged.

The preliminary inquiry was set for September 18 but Allbright began pushing hard for an earlier date. His client was suffering dreadfully in jail, he said. What was equally regrettable was the attitude of the Crown. "I had never in my life experienced such stonewalling," says the defence lawyer. "I never got anything voluntarily out of the Crown. I wrote letter after letter asking for disclosure, any kind of disclosure. And I'd get a letter back saying we're not ready to tell you anything." Finally Allbright resorted to holding an informal press conference on the steps of the courthouse. "I think that they are hiding something. They've had sixteen months to prepare this case and indeed they are not even sure, from what I can see, what theory they are going to adopt," he said. At the preliminary the Crown would be required to lay out neatly all the essential evidence. And the defence lawyer felt confident that at that point the case against his flamboyant client would collapse.

Allbright's comments to reporters infuriated Serge Kujawa, who later insisted, "We told him every damn thing we could have told him," Still, he agreed to move the preliminary hearing up by two months; it would begin in June.

A few days before the preliminary began, Allbright, accompanied by Tony Merchant, finally was given an opportunity to listen to the tape. The police officer watching the proceedings said Merchant "went stark white" when he heard the conversation between Anderson and Thatcher. Allbright, however, was furious when he heard it. He felt that the Crown had wildly exaggerated the significance of its contents. Kujawa had suggested that there was a kind of confession on the tape and he had insisted that Colin had threatened three people during the conversation. In the tape, Thatcher and Anderson talked about a person who Anderson claimed was asked to kill JoAnn Wilson. Thatcher said, "You know, should go just visit that son of a bitch some day, but not right now, not right..." The second alleged threat was a reference to JoAnn's lawyer. Anderson said, "How's your feelings with your old buddy Gerry..." Thatcher laughed and Anderson continued, "...Gerry Gerrand." "Well..." said Thatcher. Anderson asked, "Kind of mellow to him?" Thatcher responded, "No. A guy I could do. That guy I could do." Finally, the Crown contended that Thatcher was threatening Anderson himself when he said, "Next time I see you, just give me that same sign and there is no problem unless you do something stupid."

"I didn't see any threats at all," says Allbright. "I think you had to use a fair amount of ingenuity to conjure up threats to at least three people on the tape.... To me that was one of the very, very unfortunate things about the whole proceeding. It got everybody off on the wrong track, certainly got us off on the wrong track. Because you see a confession is a pretty serious thing. It's a suspicious tape but there's no confession on it. And there are not threats to at least three people." The Crown responded that although the language was coded and obscure, the people who were being threatened took it very seriously indeed.

JUNE 25, 1984

By 6:45 a.m., on a mild June day, sixty people were lined up outside Regina's modern, utilitarian courtroom on Victoria Avenue. Ten minutes after the doors opened at 9 a.m. all eighty of the seats reserved for the public were filled. This public presence only hinted at the widespread interest in Colin Thatcher. The saga of his downfall and the horrible deed he was accused of committing had gripped the entire province, and millions beyond its borders. The fascination would continue unabated.

Thatcher himself would arrive each day in the back seat of a cruiser. At first he shied away from the media, attempting to hide his handcuffs from the cameramen and photographers gathered in a large intimidating knot at the courtroom entrance. But when this proved impossible he grew more defiant, shouting out retorts in answer to reporters' questions. For the next four days he would be forced to listen to twenty-five witnesses testifying against him, without the opportunity to tell his side of the story. it would be an excruciating test of strength for anybody; not once did Colin Thatcher lose his composure. Indeed hardly an emotion flickered across his set, grey face as each of the Crown's witnesses appeared and told his or her mournful but compelling story, each symbolizing a different aspect of Colin Thatcher's turbulent life.

There was Tony Wilson, JoAnn's dapper and coldly intelligent second husband. In the courtroom he would represent the violent matrimonial battle fought between JoAnn and Colin Thatcher. Wilson could barely contain his contempt for the accused, a man he considered a phoney, a bully, and a liar. "As long as I have known JoAnn," he told the court, "she has been, or she was, subject to a constant terrorization by her ex-husband. . . . Any relations, any transactions that took place between JoAnn and Mr. Thatcher were the subject of extreme duress, constant pressure, constant harassment." Wilson had been called to provide a motive for the murder: he testified that as a result of JoAnn's death, Thatcher was able to postpone the payment of debt to his ex-wife. That, said Wilson, was the prime reason he killed her.

After he stepped down from the witness stand, Wilson stopped for a few moments in front of Thatcher's seat. There, for endless seconds, he glared at the accused with such ferocious hatred that time seemed to halt and everybody in the court froze in horror.

Glamorous Lynne Mendell, petite, blonde, and as thoroughly tanned as only a permanent resident of a southern clime could be, would symbolize Thatcher's taste for the fast-lane life of Palm Springs, California, where streets are named after Bob Hope, Gene Autry, and Frank Sinatra. Thatcher's lover for two years, Mendell had lived in his Cathedral Canyon condominium, had travelled with him on government business to Europe, and had provided him an opportunity for catharsis. Now here she was, nervously revealing all she knew about Colin Thatcher. She testifed that when she asked him about his ex-wife's murder, he replied, "Well, it's a very strange feeling to blow your wife away." Every pair of eyes in the courtroom was riveted on her at that moment, as everyone wondered if she could possibly be telling the truth. Gregory and fifteen-year-old Regan, both in attendance, looked particularly aghast.

Garry Anderson lived with his mother on a farm near the town of Caron, and his very poverty highlighted the vast wealth of the nearby Thatcher farm. Anderson had always been in awe of his big-shot neighbour, and he was surprised when Colin suddenly had become so friendly. And now here he was, the prime police informer, slowly, methodically, revealing the plot concocted by Thatcher to kill JoAnn and describing, in his own unimaginative way, the criminals and punks involved.

But there was one witness who, although called by the Crown, might prove that Colin Thatcher could not personally have murdered his wife. Craig Dotson, a slender, moustached civil servant, was the only person to spot the killer coming out of the Wilson's garage. Although it was 6 p.m. and quite dark, and although he saw the suspect only for a moment, he had been able to give a description to the police. Now he testified that the individual he had described looked nothing like Thatcher. This helpful testimony was ironic because Craig Dotson was director of research for Saskatchewan's

New Democratic Party. If there was one type of political animal that Colin Thatcher had despised with a passion—indeed he had built his political career around this hatred—it was the wretched socialist. And yet the testimony of this truthful NDPer might prove to be his only hope.

On the fourth and last day of the preliminary hearing Thatcher abandoned his businesslike apparel and dressed in his version of country—plaid shirt, designer jeans, expensive suede jacket, cowboy boots—almost as if this persona would bolster his spirits the most. Once the evidence of the twenty-five witnesses had been concluded, the lawyers made their final arguments. Kujawa's, typically, was so short as to seem non-existent, and Allbright's, also typically, was a lattice-work of sentences, which formed a final attempt to have his client discharged. Marion Wedge, an elegant and effective provincial court judge, did not even adjourn to consider the evidence. She simply said to the accused man standing before her, "I find that there is sufficient evidence to commit you for trial."

As he was led away, a policeman on each arm, Colin Thatcher yelled at the gathered media, "Eventually I'll be exonerated."

CHAPTER TWO

THE THATCHERS OF MOOSE JAW

SEPTEMBER, 1946

The boy said later that he liked the feel of the grain sliding along his skin, which was why he didn't scream for help earlier. He had been standing in the hopper as the newly threshed wheat flowed into it from the combine's clean grain elevator, something farm children liked to do. But most kids had enough sense to tramp the grain down as it poured in around them, thereby rising to the top as the container filled. This lad just stood there as the dusty material engulfed him. The farmer driving the tractor had completely forgotten about the kid, and when at last he looked around, all he saw was two small arms waving desperately from the top of the hopper. No amount of pulling would free the buried child, and so as quickly as possible the grain was dumped. The eight-year-old was saved from asphyxiation by only a few minutes.

The only person in the vicinity who did not rush to help and comfort the terrified, sobbing child was Ross Thatcher. Laughing his head off he pointed his thumb at his son and snorted, "Maybe that'll teach the little bugger a lesson."

The farmer and his wife were shocked by the incident, although when they talked about it later they realized that perhaps they shouldn't have been. It was so typical of the abominable manner in which Ross treated Colin. The wife saw it all the time. She was a tireless campaign worker for Ross Thatcher, often travelling with him on the dusty back roads of Moose Jaw, a federal riding that covered a vast amount of territory. Sometimes the small boy would come for the ride. "Look, Dad, look at the bulls," the six-year-old would cry. "For pity's sakes those aren't bulls, they're cows, you nitwit," Ross would snap at him. His lack of patience and his sarcasm towards the child would make the women wince. Finally she couldn't stand it any longer and although her two children and her husband considered Colin a nuisance—"he was a big, awkward booby of a kid"—she insisted on leaving him at her farm while she went campaigning.

Once while Ross was doing his rounds, chatting up his constituents, his wife Peggy visited at one farmhouse for a cup of tea. The farmer watched through the window while Colin fooled with every piece of dangerous material in the yard that he had been told not to touch. "As soon as it rains, Peggy," the farmer joked, "I'm going to do you a big favour. I'm going to take that kid of yours and I'm gonna drown him in the nearest slough." Everyone in the room laughed except Peggy.

Colin Thatcher was the type of seven-year-old who would—and once did—spit in a neighbour's face after she told him how nice he looked. "I suppose he was something of a brat," remembers the neighbour, "and he certainly didn't endear himself to me on that occasion. But I always felt that there was something pathetic about him. He seemed so lonely, so desperate for attention." Like many people who watched Colin grow up, this woman concluded that he had experienced the worst of both worlds: a mother who spoiled him and seemed unable to control him, and a father who dominated everybody and was almost impossible to please. Even his most devoted followers talked about Ross Thatcher's niggardliness in handing out praise. "Whether it was his grades in school or roping a calf, Colin could never do well enough for his father. I think he tried desperately to please him all his life."

This combination of having no boundaries set on acceptable behaviour, yet never being able to do anything that pleased, resulted in a deep insecurity and an obsessive urge to always prove himself better than the next guy. This compulsion for one-upmanship remained prevalent in Colin Thatcher's mature years. "I think much of the arrogance and bluster which Colin was so good at displaying in his adult years was a result of a deep-rooted insecurity," says Don McDonald, a veterinarian and close friend of the Thatchers.

Ross expected a great deal of his only child; after all, it would be up to Colin to promote the family name, which was growing more illustrious each year. It wasn't always renowned. Like so many success stories in Saskatchewan, the family connection between scratching for a living and enjoying respect and good fortune was remarkably short.

There is some confusion as to when Wilbert Thatcher actually joined the flood of homesteaders from the east who were determined to find prosperity on the prairies. His newspaper obituary claims he came to Swift Current from the village of Arthur, Ontario, in 1912. Colin Thatcher, however, writing about his grandfather in the official history book of Caron, says he arrived in 1905 and homesteaded in the Caron-Mortlach area; this version would have young Wilbert homesteading impressively early for the area—and at the unusually tender age of seventeen. Whatever the case, Wilbert Thatcher obviously did not like farming or was not any good at it, for he soon moved into other lines of work. He was employed by International Harvester, then ended up as a printer for the Caron newspaper.

Caron was then a much more prosperous town than the reduced place it is at present. There was a thriving hardware store, a three-room school, a grocery shop, a busy grain elevator, all ghosts of the past now. Most important, the Canadian Pacific Railway stopped there. When the railway decided to ignore it in the 1950s, like so many small prairie communities, it lost its raison d'être and began to stagnate. But when Wilbert Thatcher moved there around 1914 at age twenty-six, Caron was still a town full of bustle and enthusiasm. Wilbert quickly got to know the music teacher at the local school, Miss Marjorie Price, a pretty young woman who had also migrated from Ontario. They were married the following year.

In the course of his printing career, Wilbert had discovered that he had a head for business. With a small nest egg of savings, he and his bride moved to the village of Neville, population 179, in the southwesterly part of the province, and there opened a hardware store.

On May 24, 1917, the first and the most ambitious of their four children was born. Even as a small child, Wilbert Ross Thatcher was described as "quiet, serious, intense." After the family moved to another small town, Limerick, Saskatchewan (so named because the first homesteader was so desperately homesick for his Irish roots), and there opened another hardware store, Ross started elementary school. From the beginning he was a dedicated and brilliant student. "Getting good grades always seemed to matter to Ross," recalls an old acquaintance who knew him as a child, "but then he had a schoolteacher mother who placed great emphasis on education." About the only time anybody could remember Ross doing something naughty was when he joined a bunch of kids on Hallowe'en night in tumbling a huge pile of wood owned by a retired lumber dealer. The next day the school's principal insisted the four boys pile the wood neatly back just as it had been, a long and tedious job.

By 1928, with his young family growing, and four or five successful hardware stores to his credit, Wilbert Thatcher decided he was ready to establish himself in the big time. He opened another hardware store on Main Street in Moose Jaw.

From the beginning the prominent citizens of Moose Jaw thought the name of their town was most undignified and petitions were circulated to have it changed. There were those, however, who realized that such an unusual appellation would give any town character, might even bring it fame. And indeed the refrain "Is Anybody Here from Moose Jaw?" became a kind of comforting, homey joke when Canadian troops met in Europe during World War Two.

There is some controversy as to how the town actually acquired its peculiar name. The most popular theory has it as a derivation of an Indian name that means "the place where the white man mended the car wheel with the jaw of the moose." Leaving aside the mechanical improbabilities, the trouble with this proposition is that Annie L. Wallis, one of the town's first residents, reported that nobody had ever seen a moose within two hundred kilometres of the place. Another theory involves the weather; and since this is a subject to which Saskatchewan residents devote an impressive amount of time and thought, there is a certain plausibility to this one. Because Moose Jaw is situated in a sheltered area—a veritable oasis of water and trees in the vast dry plain—it is always slightly warmer than other areas. So the Indians supposedly named the area "Moosgaw," which loosely translated means warm breezes. The first settlers simply misunderstood them. Finally, the name may refer to the landscape at the confluence of the Moose Jaw River and the Qu'Appelle River, which the natives imagined looked like a jaw of a moose.

The town was established in 1881. Not untypically for that day, the founding fathers were two land developers, James Hamilton Ross and Hector Sutherland of Winnipeg. They guessed that the soon-to-arrive CPR would probably choose such an attractive place, located exactly midway between Winnipeg and the Rockies, as a divisional point, the juncture where train crews changed. They were right. The railway arrived in 1882, and with it came a swarm of settlers.

Annie Hoburg, an entrepreneur of great originality, was one of the first to smell prosperity in the wind. In 1883 she opened the Railroad Restaurant on Main Street, which immediately became the hub of one of the most ingenious and thriving whiskey outlets in the west. Many others followed her lead. Even a fire in 1891 that left the entire Main Street a smouldering heap did not dampen spirits for long. Between 1900 and 1915, over a million settlers arrived on the prairies, and many of them were unattached young men. Moose Jaw boomed. Brothels and boozeries, gambling dives and opium dens thrived there; of all the wide-open prairie towns, it bore the dubious distinction of being the place whose wickedness was the most accessible. River Street, notorious for its dens of iniquity, intersected with Main Street close to the CPR station. It supposedly took a determined young farm hand only three minutes to rush from the train to a River Street bed.

Prohibition began in Saskatchewan in December, 1916. For a short time the new laws put a damper on the more overt forms of sinful behaviour—but only for a short time. When the United States began its "noble experiment" with Prohibition in 1920, Moose Jaw became one of the larger outlets of Harry Bronfman's incredible whiskey export business and thus a base for the fabled rum-rummers of the prairies. These hombres with their souped-up cars were always ready to race across the undefended border on unpatrolled grid roads with a load of liquor for thirsty—and very grateful—Americans. They were not, however, prepared to give up their women, booze, and craps just because some government told them. to. And it helped that they had a friend in one of the most notorious police chiefs in the west. Chief Walter Johnson's practice was to turn a blind eye to the improprieties, all the while collecting a weekly fee from those who plied their trade in the red-light district. By 1925, River Street was bustling as it never had before.

The good burghers of Moose Jaw tended to ignore that seedy part of town, probably because so many of them were making money, either directly or indirectly, from the booze export trade. In any case, the citizens who patronized Temple Gardens, the most elegant dance hall in the west, seldom rubbed shoulders with the denizens of River Street.

From the beginning, Moose Jaw citizens had harboured great expectations for their town. The visions of grandeur were illustrated by the wide boulevards and the solid and impressive buildings: City Hall, St. John's Anglican Church, the Dominion Bank, the Empress Hotel, and even the brick public washrooms that were built after the fire of 1891. To this day one can sense that this is a vigorous and free-wheeling western town that has been tightly corseted by the God-fearing ruling class, who are WASPs, almost to a man.

After Moose Jaw was incorporated as a city in 1903, the influential citizens launched a campaign to make it the capital of Saskatchewan, rightly claiming that its geography was much more attractive and interesting than that of old Pile o' Bones, sometimes known as Regina, the leading contender. When they lost that battle, they attempted to persuade the provincial government to establish the University of Saskatchewan there. Saskatoon won that one. The CPR did, however, make it a divisional point and built major marshalling yards there, which gave Moose Jaw a head start as the province's major industrial city.

When Wilbert Thatcher opened his hardware store on Main Street in 1928, one of the strangest political movements Saskatchewan would ever experience was at its peak. On June 7, 1927, between seven and ten thousand people had crowded into a vacant field in Moose Jaw to listen to "spellbinding" orators insist, among other things, that there should be a ban on marriage between white women and black, Chinese, and Japanese men. Two hours of this hysteria was followed by the burning of a sixty-foot fiery cross at the top of Caribou Street. It was the first and largest Ku Klux Klan Konclave ever held in Canada and the organizers were so encouraged by the huge turnout that they made Moose Jaw their provincial headquarters.

The Klan had moved from the southern states north to eastern Canada in the early 1920s and had reached Saskatchewan by 1926. The organizers were two shysters, Hugh F. Emmons and L.A. Scott, both of whom had been involved in violent Klan activities in the southern United States. The black population in the province was very small—"About all they'd have to kick around was a couple of coloured train porters, and that surely wasn't going to satisfy them," said a commentator at the time—so they turned their hatred and bigotry to Catholics, who made up about 27 percent of the population, and French Canadians, who made up about 5 percent. Another important part of their appeal was their attack on the immoral activities in the red-light districts. River Street must be cleaned up, they cried, and Moose Jaw made a sanctuary for white Anglo-Saxon Protestants and those devoted to protecting "One flag, One language, One race, One religion, Race purity and Moral rectitude."

How Wilbert Thatcher felt about this phenomenon remains unclear, although he must have had ambivalent views about the KKK. He was a staunch monarchist and was to become a grand master of a Masonic Lodge. Both organizations hated the Church of Rome and considered the Pope the devil incarnate, and many of their members supported the Klan. Even his beloved United Church (or at least some of its clergy) was accused of Klan sympathies. On the other hand, Wilbert was a dedicated Liberal, and it was Jimmy Gardiner, Liberal premier of the province, who vigorously and unrelentingly attacked the Klan, while the Conservatives were said to be ingloriously enlisting the support of the KKK to stir up anti-French feeling. By the end of 1928, however, the KKK leaders had abandoned "moral rectitude" and run off with the funds. The organization died a quick death in Saskatchewan. The incident did reveal, however, a vein of bigotry and a sense of WASP superiority that would surface in many forms among Moose Jaw's élite. (A cabinet minister in Ross Thatcher's government once quipped to a group of reporters, "Ross isn't a bigot. He just can't stand Hebes.")

Ross Thatcher was eleven when his family moved to Moose Jaw. He was enrolled at Ross School and at Central Collegiate, performing so brilliantly that he was sent to Queen's University in Kingston, Ontario, when he was still in his mid-teens. He earned a Bachelor of Commerce degree when he was barely nineteen, the youngest graduate in the university's distinguished history at that time. "He never let me forget that he had graduated at such a young age," his son would later say. Of Colin's degree in animal husbandry, obtained when he was twenty-three, Ross Thatcher would comment, "He was the best-educated manure spreader there ever was."

The Dirty Thirties hit Saskatchewan harder than any other place in Canada. A glut of wheat on the international market, which caused prices to plunge, was only one part of the tragedy. The drought that went on for five long years was the worst villain. Indeed, God seemed to be seeking revenge on the "golden" province. Grasshoppers, hail, Russian thistle, and early frost all descended on Saskatchewan farmers during those years. And as the earth dried, ghastly dust storms blew the valuable topsoil away forever; bitter jokes had gophers being blown through the air, still burrowing away at the soil around them. Many families gave up in despair and, packing all their belongings in the Model T, moved to the nearest city or out of the province. But it was not only the farmers who were hit; workers suffered badly as well. Saskatchewan residents suffered a worse decline in wages during the years 1928–33 than did workers in any other part of the country. yet, while business for the entrepreneurs in Moose Jaw was not as good as it could be, life for these citizens went on pretty much as usual. The young people danced at Temple gardens, drank tea at the Grant Hall Hotel, and watched the latest Shirley Temple movie at the Capitol.

The Thatchers were among the lucky ones. While they were aware of the suffering—it would have been impossible not to be—the hardware business still provided a comfortable living. In the heart of the Depression, Wilbert Thatcher had even been able to send his oldest son away to university.

People who knew Ross in the mid-1930s remember him as being almost too good to be true. He didn't drink, gamble, or tell lewd stories. He certainly didn't spend much time on River Street. He taught Sunday school at St. Andrew's United Church and was president of the Monarch Club, a Bible-study group for young men that was very popular at the time.

Even at this young age Thatcher had a self-assurance that amazed his elders. "He was as nice and polite as could be. But you got the sense he was already in middle age when he was still only a kid," says Moose Jaw resident who knew Ross then. The young man's only vice was a passion for badminton.

Apart from Temple Gardens, social activities in the city centred on the Moose Jaw Badminton Club, considered a "palatial" place with its five fine courts, its glass-enclosed spectators' gallery, and its elegant dining room. During the Thirties young people developed a passion for the sport, and tournaments were played continually in Regina, Saskatoon, and Moose Jaw. In 1935 at the tenth annual provincial tournament, the excitement was such that the final matches were broadcast live, play by play, on CHAB radio. it was on the Moose Jaw courts that Ross Thatcher, himself not a bad player, got to know someone who could play much better than he. As early as 1934, Ross was pairing with Peggy McNaughton in the mixed doubles. She and her sister Leslie were so good at the sport that from 1933 to 1938 they won many provincial and city championships, in both the Ladies Singles and the Doubles events. Ross sometimes got to the semi-finals, but rarely beyond, though not for lack of effort. In 1937 the Regina *Leader-Post* reported, "Thatcher was on the verge of collapse at the end of the three-game set." -

Adrah Leone (Peggy) McNaughton was born September 11, 1915, in Worthing, a picturesque Sussex town situated on the English Channel. The McNaughtons immigrated to Canada when Peggy was a very young child and eventually established themselves in business, setting up the Western Ice Company in Moose Jaw. Peggy was a slender, attractive, raven-haired young woman. Both she and her sister Leslie were popular, and many people, especially farmers who lived in the area, believed that they were very interested in "society." "They had a habit of thinking they were kinda classy," recalls one old friend. "Her people were considered in the upper crust of Moose Jaw, if you can imagine anything as silly as that." Peggy even contributed for a short while to the social and personal columns of the Moose Jaw *Times Herald*. Although she was not remembered for her insight into deep political matters, she was a charming but most shy young woman. In years to come she would polish and hone her graciousness until many people considered her to be the best political wife an ambitious man could have.

Immediately after New Year's, 1938, Mr. and Mrs. C.G. McNaughton announced the engagement of their eldest daughter to W. Ross Thatcher. A whirl of bridal showers followed. On January 8, the guests played bridge and Peggy received a Kenwood blanket as a gift. Later that day a towel shower was held at the Moose Jaw Badminton Club. On January 11, a tea yielded "attractive gifts in the colour scheme of cream and blue" that Peggy had chosen for her kitchen. The whirl went on and on and Peggy received as much silver as any young bride could hope for. On January 17 there was a tea presided over by Mrs. McNaughton at Grant Hall for her daughter, a buffet supper for all her friends, and finally, early in the morning, a concluding breakfast party. "Breakfast was a hilarious time with newspapers taking the place of table linen . . ." reported the *Times-Herald*. Later that day Peggy left with her mother for Toronto, where her fiancé had taken a job.

The couple were married on January 20, 1938, at Bloor Street United Church. It was a small wedding attended by only a few close friends and relatives. The bride was dressed in a frock of cloud-blue crêpe. A smart poke bonnet, an heirloom locket of silver worn by Peggy's great-grandmother, and a corsage of American Beauty roses completed her outfit. Peggy was twenty-three years old; Ross was twenty-one.

Seven months later, on August 25, 1938, their son, Wilbert Colin Thatcher, was born.

Ross Thatcher later told friends that a serious dose of mumps he contracted just after Colin's birth determined that the family would be limited to one child. Many people felt this was a tragedy for Colin, that siblings might have saved him from a life of loneliness and self-centredness and that his father might not have demanded so much.

The couple were living in Toronto because Ross had taken a job at $22.50 a week as secretary to J.S. McLean, chairman of the board of Canada Packers. In later years he would tell different tales about his experience, depending on the political slant of his listener. To his free-enterprise buddies, he would say that he should have paid Canada Packers for working there, so valuable was the experience. To his socialist friends he would relate how certain practices—the injection of water into the meat to make it heavier, the exploitation of the workers, the filth of the place—had turned him off capitalism forever.

The Thatchers returned to Moose Jaw in 1940 so that Ross could enlist. Four times he tried, and four times he was turned down; even at this young age his blood pressure was dangerously high. This rejection was a serious blow for the patriotic young men, one it would take him a long time to get over. In the meantime he unleashed his considerable energy on selling hardware and acquiring real estate.

Thatcher Senior had built up a thriving hardware business on Main Street. Ross became sales manager and then president of the company, and with his younger brothers, Ron and Clarke, expanded that store. He opened another in Moose Jaw on River Street (now a much tamer place, thanks to the Depression), and new stores in Regina and Saskatoon. Thatcher's Hardware was not just a place to buy a washer or a screw; it was more like a large department store with three sections—china, hardware, and furniture and appliances. "When we got married in '46, that's where we bought our furniture," remembers Rynold Gleim, a Chaplin farmer. "You could buy anything in there but groceries and machinery. He had a terrific stock so that you could hardly walk about that place.

"Ross must have employed fifteen people at the time. He sat upstairs in that little glass-enclosed office. He had his eye on everything. He could see the entire store."

Ross quickly developed a reputation among his employees as a hard taskmaster and something of a Scrooge with a dollar. A former manager of the hardware section recalls that it was Thatcher's practice to give out bonuses on Christmas Eve based on the year's business and the employee's effort. Ross would sign the cheques as everyone stood around nervously sipping coffee. One year he had distributed all the bonuses except the one for the packer who worked down in the basement. Thatcher pulled out that cheque and tore it up. He was offended at something the man had done earlier; the fact that he had four kids and made little money didn't matter.

Milly Sentis, who worked there for a while as a clerk, recalls the time a fellow clerk was opening a carton containing a recently shipped walnut table. The knife slipped and marked the costly piece of furniture. When Ross found out, he was furious and demanded to know who did it. When there was no response, he locked the door and said nobody would leave until the guilty party came forward. Somebody finally confessed and he was bawled out by Ross in front of everyone. "Even though he was very young, there was a kind of master-slave relationship," she recalled.

There was a great deal of internal theft at Thatcher's Hardware and it was assumed the staff was getting even with Ross by swiping his stuff. Still, there were employees who remained devoted to Ross Thatcher for years, who considered his careful money management simply that, a key to his success as a businessman. And they were often rewarded for their efforts. For example, when Thatcher became premier of the province, the long-time manager of.the hardware store was given a key appointment in the newly created Indian and Métis Affairs branch.

But a hardware store could not satisfy the ambitions of such an energetic and clever young man as Ross Thatcher. Politics was the way to get ahead in the world.

"Ross Thatcher went to a Liberal nominating meeting," recalls Rynold Gleim, himself a strong Liberal supporter, "and they just ignored him. Said he was too young, just a kid and had no business at a political meeting. That hurt him pretty badly. So he joined the CCF."

Scoop Lewry, a newspaper reporter in Moose Jaw and later an outspoken mayor of that city, was astonished to receive a call from Ross one day in 1941 asking him to set up a meeting with CCF brass. Lewry was surprised at Ross's intentions, for several reasons. Just as he was a pillar of the United Church, Wilbert Thatcher was a dyed-in-the-wool Liberal and he expected his sons to carry on the tradition. Ron and Clarke were Liberals and indeed Ross had been the president of the Young Liberal Association of Moose Jaw. Yet here he was telling his father that he intended to cast his lot with the hated socialists.

There was no question that Ross Thatcher knew what he was getting into when he joined the CCF; for one thing, the socialist party's roots were deeply implanted in Saskatchewan's soil. This was where the movement had started. And CCFers felt that they were not so much members of a political party as they were followers of a religious cult. "We were out to change the world for the better, pure and simple," says farmer George Dault. "We had suffered too much during the

Depression." When the party officially came into being in 1933 it adopted the Regina Manifesto as its creed. One clause read, "No CCF government will rest content until it has eradicated capitalism and put into operation the full programme of socialized planning which leads to the establishment in Canada of the Co-operative Commonwealth." Ross Thatcher would later tell an interviewer, "I joined the CCF for the same reasons hundreds of thousands of others joined—as a protest against unemployment and because of the promise of a better future which they so convincingly offered. But I never was a real CCFer, even in the early days." He would, however, be active in the socialist party for fifteen years, a longer time than he would be a member of the Liberals.

According to political allies at the time, what Ross told his father was, "Look, there's only one ladder that's gonna get me anywhere right now and that's the CCF." (Despite Ross's argument, Thatcher Senior was said to be so upset at his son's decision to join the socialists that he retired in 1946 at age fifty-eight and moved to British Columbia.) One didn't exactly have to be a tactical genius to arrive at that conclusion. First, there was little room in provincial politics for a newcomer. Provincially, the Co-operative Commonwealth Federation would form the government on June 15, 1944, and Moose Jaw would elect two well-known social democrats, John W. Corman and Dempster H.R. Heming, who would win the seat with ease for years to come. A Liberal wouldn't stand a chance of capturing either of those seats. Federally, J. Gordon Ross, who had sat as the Liberal Member of Parliament since 1930, was a scion of the city's founding family, and a young upstart like Ross Thatcher wasn't going to wrest the nomination away from him. The only opening left up for grabs was the CCF nomination in the federal riding of Moose Jaw. First, however, Ross Thatcher would have to become a name in Moose Jaw. He would get his political feet wet at the municipal level.

On November 21, 1941, at age twenty-five, Ross was elected one of the youngest aldermen in Moose Jaw's history. He received 1,275 votes and placed fifth in a slate of fifteen, which meant that he was elected to a two-year term. He was part of a reform caucus that was loosely associated with the CCF and determined to tweak the whiskers of the old guard. From the beginning, Thatcher was a vociferous, energetic debater at City Hall, complaining loudly about such issues as the poor working conditions and low wages the city's nurses suffered. When he ran again in 1943, he received more votes but placed only sixth in the rankings, which meant that his term was for one year only.

In 1942 Thatcher was elected vice-president of the Moose Jaw provincial CCF and in 1943 president of the federal organization. He was now in an excellent position to seek the nomination in the federal riding of Moose Jaw.

There were three others after the seat, a schoolteacher, a farmer, and a young housewife, but none was as well known or as impressive as young Ross. For one thing, Thatcher's Hardware was looked upon very favourably by CCF farmers. The Moose Jaw Co-op had recently formed but it could not, of course, offer the wide selection of merchandise that Thatcher's could. Ross worked out a deal whereby the co-op members got a small percentage off the price of goods sold at his store and appreciative farmers thronged to the firm in increasing numbers.

That such a young man—Ross was only twenty-eight—should not be engaged in active service overseas might have seemed a disadvantage. But Thatcher could point out that he had left the rather comfortable job of managing the hardware store to join the National Selective Service and was working as a brakeman for the CPR. Thatcher would only perform this service for a few months but it did help injured pride at not being able to enlist. And Wilbert Thatcher was at this point still involved with the store.

People had also appreciated Ross's performance as a vocal and effective alderman. And he possessed a most charming personality. "He was there smiling and talking and shaking hands and patting you on the back. And he always, always remembered your name," recalls Sandy Anderson, a retired farmer. Even though he came from a prominent Liberal family, Thatcher was able to readily convince the CCF members of Moose Jaw that he would serve them well as their MP.

There were those who did not trust him from the start. "He didn't ring clear at all, he wasn't sincere in his dedication to socialism like so many of us were. But when the majority decided, there was nothing much you could do. We just pitched in and worked like dogs for him," recalls a former schoolteacher.

While many people recall how hard Ross worked, how he drove himself during the campaign, they also recall his stinginess. "He was just awful. he would never spend one red cent on anything political," recalls a former campaign manager. She was the person who arranged the myriad of small-town meetings and spent hours on the road with Thatcher, attending them. "One day we were in an awful hurry and Ross said, 'You come in early and we'll have dinner, then we'll go to Brownlee.' I thought, 'That will be kinda nice. We'll have a nice dinner at the restaurant and we'll go on out and that will be just fine.' So I stopped at Ross's house and he yelled out of the bedroom, "There's bread and peanut butter on the kitchen table. Make yourself a sandwich.' Never once in ten years did Ross Thatcher buy me so much as a sandwich or a cup of coffee. Never once." Still, like so many others she never once flagged in her devotion to the cause. "But then I was working for the CCF, not Thatcher."

On June 11, 1945, Ross Thatcher was elected a Member of Parliament for Moose Jaw. Although the Moose Jaw *Times-Herald* had seldom mentioned that Thatcher was even running but had given many, many columns of space to his prominent Liberal opponent, he quite handily beat J. Gordon Ross by 3,000 votes.

Saskatchewan had voted heavily for the CCF, electing 18 socialist MPs. But federally the results were disappointing for the party. The CCF had elected only 28 members in all, compared with the Liberals' 125 and the Progressive Conservatives' 67, and so would remain a third party, albeit a vociferous and influential one, but not the official Opposition as they had hoped. Certainly it was not what Ross Thatcher had anticipated.

The train journey to Ottawa was a tedious one and the House of Commons sessions proved to be long and exhausting. For the eleven and a half years that Ross Thatcher served as a Member of Parliament he found himself in the capital, away from Moose Jaw and his young son, for many months a year. It was left to Peggy to raise Colin, but even she spent long periods in Ottawa with her husband. Colin did attend school there for six months of grade seven and grade eight. But for the most part he was left alone with a housekeeper back in Moose Jaw. Later he would tell his wife JoAnn how desperately lonely and unhappy he had been as a child.

Ross Thatcher himself would later admit that he hadn't spent enough time with his son, hadn't shown him enough affection. "That's why when his grandson Gregory arrived on the scene, Ross was just crazy about him," a friend of the family explained. "I always felt that if only he could have shown Colin just a little of the love he lavished on Greg, things would have turned out differently. And Peggy, while I'm sure she loved Colin, she wasn't very demonstrative towards him either. She was a very shy and reserved person."

Moose Jaw was a wonderful place for a child to grow up in. "It was not so large, with a population of about thirty thousand, that you'd get lost in it, yet not a town so small that people knew your every move. It was a place you could choose your friends, yet enjoy a nodding acquaintance with many," recalls broadcaster Elwood Glover, who was born in Moose Jaw. There was hockey and figure skating in the auditorium in the winter and in the summer a wooden floor was laid down and it was turned into a roller-skating rink. There was swimming and piano lessons and, most important, Sunday school.

In 1948 the Thatchers bought a large, rambling home on Redland Avenue, situated in the north end but also very close to downtown. Although the bedrooms were small and the lot size modest, it was a comfortable and attractive place. The neighbours were doctors, lawyers, and successful business-men. As Ross became more prominent in politics, the Thatchers became the focal point of Moose Jaw's society; they were considered among the leading families. A block of buildings on Main Street was named after them; and in later years Rose Avenue was renamed Thatcher Drive. As a young man Colin was continuously reminded of how important, how powerful, the Thatcher name was.

Even in the months when Ross Thatcher was in Moose Jaw, he had little time or patience for his only child. A boyhood friend of Colin's remembers that the Thatchers were the first family in town to set up a rumpus room in the basement for the kids. "One day Colin invited a group of boys over there. We'd be about nine years old. Things got a little out of hand—Colin was always a kind of rough, crazy kid anyway—when all of a sudden the old man descended. He was just in a frenzy, just livid with rage, calling Colin every name in the book. I thought it was unbelievable and went home and told my dad I wouldn't trade him for anything. When I look back I would call it extreme verbal abuse. And, of course, then I never wanted to go back to that house again. That happened with a lot of kids."

Colin always seemed to have one or two close buddies with whom he hung around, but for the most part kids his age considered him something of an oddball, someone to be avoided. Since Thatcher Senior had been a president of the Moose Jaw Canucks, he always had rinkside tickets to the hockey games, which he gave to his son. Says an acquaintance of the time, "We were always torn over whether we should take a ticket and get stuck sitting with Colin or go in the cheap seats and have fun with our friends. It got so that Colin was afraid to ask us to go with him. 'I got a couple of tickets but I don't wanna use them. Want them?' And you just knew he was dying to go but was afraid of being turned down. He would have been much better off in the Pigpen [behind the net, where the children congregated] with the rest of us. But he always seemed to have to appear better than the gang, had to somehow be more important than the rest of us. I felt really sorry for him."

Colin did fairly well at King George Elementary School, on 5th Street North West in Moose Jaw. His teachers regarded him as a bright but somewhat surly, arrogant kid. Once when he was being reprimanded for a misdemeanour he asked, "Do you know who my father is?" The teacher just laughed, realizing that if Ross Thatcher knew what his son had been up to he'd punish him harder than she had.

When Colin was thirteen, his father came home one day and out of the blue announced that he had bought a grain farm at Tuxford, north of Moose Jaw. "We were surprised because farming was not his cup of tea," Colin later said. "Although he bought the Bill Knox grain farm, it was cattle he wanted to keep." As it turned out he had bought an excellent property. Says Tuxford farmer Carl Wells, "Bill Knox was known throughout the whole of Saskatchewan as being an outstanding farmer and a registered seed-grain owner. I think Ross bought it because it was one of the best farms in the community. He liked the name, he liked the prestige."

Ross hired the Vanderaadt family to look after the place, a mother and father and five children who had recently immigrated from Holland. They lived in the drafty, cold fieldstone house. Peter Vanderaadt remembers it well. "He paid me forty dollars a week for working on his ranch and in his hardware store six days a week. And then he took four dollars off for using his Model A to get back and forth. By the time winter was well on the way there was forty-five head of cattle. I looked after them before I left to go to work and after I came back."

Vanderaart thought young Thatcher was a spoiled brat. "Colin was not entitled to drive because he wasn't old enough and he didn't have a licence. Ross had given him a car to drive back and forth in the backyard. When Colin rammed it into the garage, Ross said, 'Ah, it's okay, it can be fixed.'" Vanderaadt didn't approve.

Ross admittedly did not know much about farming or cattle ranching but he quickly developed a passion for it. "He'd be out there dressed in his old overalls and rubber boots working like crazy," remembers Slim Longhurst, who used to do odd jobs for him. "And Peggy got involved, too. I used to think she was pretty cool and snooty until one day I saw her in pants on the floor of the farmhouse trying to feed a bottle to a little sick calf." Vanderaadt remembers that Thatcher's enthusiasm was excessive. "He used to get mad because we wanted to go to church on Sunday. He had nothing to do, so he wanted to put up fencing on Sundays. After six months, that was enough of that." Vanderaadt quit.

One of the first things Ross did was build a few corrals and buy a half-dozen ordinary cows from the slaughteryards. In a short while, however, he was specializing in purebred Herefords—he wasn't interested in the more mundane commercial cattle at all. He began travelling all over the province to various dispersal sales to gather a breeding stock. On many occasions he would take Andy Linton, a rancher whose knowledge of cattle was famous in the district. Linton, a dedicated CCFer, went as a favour to Ross; he was never paid a cent. On one such occasion, Andy urged Thatcher not to buy thirty head of cattle he had his eye on. "I knew Ross was going to get a trimmin' and I didn't want to be responsible for it. He didn't pay much heed to me. He was leaving for Ottawa the next day and I knew he wanted to tell the fellows there about the cattle he had bought."

By 1954 Ross had acquired a herd of about a hundred

animals but wasn't entirely satisfied that they were the best cattle available. He asked Andy Linton if he'd attend a sale in Dickinson, North Dakota, with him. "I said no, there's just as many good cattle around here."

Ross went away, and the story drifted back to Andy Linton. "From what he told me I guess things got out of hand. There'd been a big banquet thrown for Ross and things got a little rough. Too much liquor all around. Anyway Ross took just so much money with him and he had to go to the bank to borrow more." Thatcher had paid $7,300 for "PHR Astermix the 12th," supposedly the tenth most valuable bull in the United States. It was believed to be the highest price ever recorded in Saskatchewan's history to that point. He also bought another eighteen heifers that weekend.

Andy was called to examine the animals as soon as they arrived. "There was only one decent one in the bunch. I said, 'You didn't need to go down to the States to get them lot.'" "What's wrong with them?" Thatcher asked. "There's dwarf in them." "No, no," Ross responded. "Look at the size of their feet and head." "That's just what happens, big head and feet. I wouldn't give a dollar for them," said Linton. In years to come Ross's Herefords developed serious genetic problems; it was only after Colin took over the management of the herd that it was finally cleaned out.

With the arrival of the North Dakota cattle, the Tuxford farm was no longer large enough to accommodate the herd. Ross bought a full half-section, primarily grazing land, from the estate of A.B. Borgeson in Caron. In the years to come more and more land would be added to the family empire until by 1979 Colin Thatcher would own 4,811 acres of land. he was considered one of the largest landowners in the province. The hobby became big business. "Ross discovered that he not only liked it but you could make a fair buck on it, so that added to his pleasure," recalls Rynold Gleim.

Colin was enthralled with the ranch as well, and he spent his summer and other holidays working there. He bought his first cow when he was fourteen years old. He would later say, "I can remember the old cow very well. She was a huge Hereford with a great set of horns. At that time we had just a few old commercial cattle around and I would buy the odd cow with some money that I earned, and sometimes my

father would help me with them. Then an ordinary cow
would sell for seventy or eighty dollars."

But over the years the ranch would also prove to be a bone
of contention between father and son. Linton remembers that
Colin would spend hour upon hour with a lariat lassoing a
fence post when he should have been doing some chores.
One day Ross said to Andy, "What the hell am I going to do
with that kid?" Linton replied, "I'd send him down the road,"
meaning he'd tell him to leave home. The antagonism between Colin and his father increased over the years. "They
argued so much I just stayed away," said Andy Linton. One
day Colin got so angry at his father's criticism that he came
after him with a pitchfork. Ross had to make a run for his car.

Living just outside the village of Caron was an older couple
whose hobby it was to devise nicknames for people in the
community. They put a lot of thought into this process,
priding themselves on the fact that their nicknames had real
significance. They called the young Colin Thatcher "the
twin," because they thought they could perceive a deeply
divided personality. "We never met anybody that young who
was so two-faced," they said.

Socially Moose Jaw was neatly divided in two: South Hill (or
Garlic Heights), home of the ethnic and working class, and
North Hill (or Mortgage Heights), where the business and
professional people lived. The teenagers of North Hill and
South Hill were natural rivals, and sporting events and even
casual meetings between the two groups could be vicious and
contemptuous. Most of the South Hill crowd attended Technical High School (now Peacock High), which tended to
graduate plumbers and auto mechanics. The North Side
offspring usually went to Central High School and then to
university. There was some crossover of the two groups,
however, as the smarter South Hill kids were sent to academic
high school.

Colin Thatcher, of course, went to Central High, which
was situated on Oxford Street, only a block away from his
home. He was assured of a place in the North Hill clique by
virtue of his father's prominence in the community, but he
was far from popular. "He wasn't well liked. In fact I don't
remember him ever dating a girl at high school. The kids just
didn't have anything to do with him because he was different,

so pompous and arrogant. They shunned him," says a close friend of JoAnn's who went to school with Colin. His teachers remember that he usually got decent grades but he was not a top student nor did he participate in many extracurricular activities. This was quite unlike the experience of his great friend of later years, Ron Graham, who was a good scholar, a famed basketball player, and outstandingly popular with students and teachers alike. Colin did curl and he played football for the Central High Cyclones. Ken Mitchell, the playwright and novelist, who went to Central at the same time, remembers that Colin was a very aggressive football player but he wasn't a star. "He wouldn't have been successful politically if he had run for any of the social offices at the school because he was so aloof and was considered a bully."

His graduating picture in the 1955-56 *Cyclone* yearbook shows a smiling sixteen-year-old with an Elvis Presley haircut, stylish for the day, and an open squarish face. He is a good-looking teenager; the surly droop of the mouth so prevalent in his later years has not yet developed. "As centre of the Cyclone's big, powerful line Colin found himself at a post he could handle; but his football tactics seemed to overlap into basketball with obvious results. 'Le Gros T' can create quite a stir in French class when he gives his imitation of Elvis Presley," wrote the editor of the yearbook.

During the spring of 1956 Colin did date one young woman a few times. She didn't like him much and wanted to call it quits. He started to harass her endlessly. "I was living in Saskatoon, going to university there, and he would phone again and again, demanding that I tell him who I was going out with," she says. "That summer he showed up on my doorstep and started yelling at me. I finally told him to get lost, but it was really creepy."

During his third year of high school, something happened that caused him to be even more socially ostracized and involved him in several bloody fist fights. On April 22, 1955, Ross Thatcher announced that he was bolting the CCF to sit as an independent in the House of Commons. Thatcher laid out his reasons at a dramatic press conference covered by newspapers and broadcasters across Canada. When he returned home during the Easter recess, he claimed, he had been horrified to discover that the Moose Jaw CCF organization had been infiltrated by Communists and extreme leftwingers. That was the last straw; he had decided to quit the CCF.

Members of the CCF executive in Moose Jaw–Lake Centre claimed this charge was nonsense, the worst kind of red-baiting. "Of course it's not true," Scoop Lewry commented at the time, and "Mr. Thatcher knows it." Remembers farmer Len Donnelly, "There were many people who believed in the CCF as they believed in the gospel. They had worked very hard for Ross during three elections, given the party every little bit of extra money they could scrape together. And then he turns his back on them. They considered him an out-and-out traitor." (Interestingly, when Colin Thatcher was writing about his family for the official history of Caron, he pointed out that his father had been a Member of Parliament for twelve years but mentioned not a word about the fact that he had been a member of the CCF.)

Colin Thatcher still bears the scars he suffered from the intense resentment towards his father. Twenty years later he would say, "There are still people in Moose Jaw who supported Dad in the CCF who won't talk to me because my name is Thatcher."

In fact Ross Thatcher had been something of a maverick from the moment he was first elected, although during his first election campaign he had said, "The CCF has accomplished more in one year [as the government of Saskatchewan] than the Liberals had in the previous twenty," a statement that would come back to haunt him later. On various occasions, he defied the party. He announced in the House of Commons that he was opposed to the nationalization of banks. He stated that he favoured a means test in welfare payments. He urged the government to reduce corporate taxes. All were policies diametrically opposed to what the party stood for, and naturally many CCFers began to resent his contrariness. By 1949 he was attending very few caucus meetings. "His main concern was to grab off a headline, which of course he was able to do as the fellow who was making statements contrary to the party line," says Gordon Snyder, a former NDP member of the Saskatchewan Legislative Assembly and a cabinet minister from 1971 to 1981. "His favourite expression used to be, 'Sure got good mileage out of that one.'"

Thatcher formed a rump of the party called the Commonwealth Club, which put forth policies more right-wing than any the Liberals or Conservatives were advocating. He would later say that he was shocked when more and more radical leftists, particularly from British Columbia, joined the CCF. These people, he claimed, were turning the party into a languishing arm of the labour movement. "There's nothing wrong with socialism except that it doesn't work," he said. This sentiment would become his leitmotif.

By the mid-Fifties Thatcher's disenchantment with the CCF was complete. For one thing the party was not the mighty force he thought it was going to be; in 1953 the CCF managed to elect members to only 23 of the 265 seats, and it looked as though it would be a long time before it would either form a government or be the official Opposition. Secondly, it was painfully obvious that there was nowhere for Ross Thatcher to go. He had alienated the leader, M.J. Coldwell, and Tommy Douglas, the CCF premier of Saskatchewan, was looming large on the national horizon. "Ross always wanted to be a big frog," explained a former CCF worker. "He wasn't happy being the underdog. They weren't using him, in his opinion, to his full ability. And they weren't because they were losing faith in him."

Still, Ross had worked hard for his constituents in Ottawa; no problem was too insignificant to command his attention. In the 1953 election he had captured 12,436 votes, a thousand more than his two opponents combined. And he was personally popular. He had taken to smoking ten-cent cigars and had put on weight. He had turned into a rotund bulldog of a man who liked to play a mean game of poker and was quick with a joke and a slap on the back. By this time, too, he had developed his dynamic, sometimes mesmerizing manner of public speaking. "If Ross Thatcher said, 'I eat fried eggs for breakfast,' everybody would cheer enthusiastically," remembers Sandy Anderson. He even studied French to the point where he was fluent enough to give a speech in that language. "You were always hearing about him, he was always saying something that got him publicity," says Jim Murdock, whose parents were Thatcher workers. "Some of the folks in the political organization had an inkling that it [Thatcher's defection] was coming. But I would have to say that to 99 percent of our people, it was a complete bombshell."

"I had been his secretary from the time he started, handled

all his correspondence, everything, and we had an executive meeting, a quick one while he was there. He did not tell any of us that he was going to cross the floor. I had to hear it over the radio. And that really hurt, that really hurt," recalls Olive Wells. "I think if he would have said, 'Now, I'm getting disenchanted with the CCF, I think I'm going Liberal,' I'd say, 'That's fine, go ahead, Ross. Do as you think best.' But it was the fact he didn't tell us. I was browned off completely because so many CCF people said to me, 'But you told me that Ross was a good CCFer,' that kind of thing. They seemed to hold me sort of responsible. I felt terribly disillusioned about the whole thing."

Thatcher sat out the remaining two years of the parliamentary session as an independent, and an attractive, wealthy widow would not have been wooed more persistently. British Columbia premier W.A.C. Bennett, who knew Thatcher's mother in Vancouver, put pressure on him to lead the Social Credit party in Saskatchewan. Thatcher, however, thought the Socreds' economic theories were a little screwy; even worse, the party had managed to get only 4 percent of the vote in the 1952 provincial election and could not claim one MLA. It would have been a risky gamble indeed. As for the Conservatives, their leader George Drew was the kind of eastern élitist whom Thatcher could not abide, and anyway federal Conservatives were about as popular as grasshoppers in Saskatchewan in those days. He finally made up his mind, Thatcher later told supporters, when Prime Minister Louis St. Laurent offered him a senior cabinet post in the next government. "He would have tried for the Liberal leadership, no question," says Rynold Gleim. "He was never satisfied with anything but the top job. Nothing wrong with that." All he had to do was get elected as a Liberal Member of Parliament.

Moose Jaw–Lake Centre was considered solid CCF territory— the mayor of Moose Jaw, Scoop Lewry, was running there— and so Thatcher sought and won the Liberal nomination in the nearby federal riding of Assiniboia. CCFers, still bitter and determined to seek revenge, rallied their forces. Hazen Argue, a former deskmate of Thatcher's who had also shared a room with him in Ottawa, was the incumbent. "He thought he could easily beat me," remembers Argue, "but we showed him."

At the beginning of the campaign, Thatcher claimed that he had received anonymous threatening letters that warned that his car tires would be slashed and he would be pelted with rotten eggs if he dared appear on a speaker's platform. As a result he approached the Moose Jaw Wrestling and Barbell Club and hired himself six husky bodyguards, which, if nothing else, impressed his teenaged son. CCF workers thought it was a lot of nonsense, just Thatcher's way of getting press and, he hoped, the sympathy of the electorate. And if there were an unusual number of CCFers working the riding, there were an equal number of Liberals plugging away for Thatcher. Indeed, so many big-name federal Liberals showed up that Hazen Argue retorted, "A cabinet meeting could have been held any time in Assiniboia." It was to no avail, for on June 10, 1957, Argue beat Thatcher by 1,527 votes.

A year later in the Diefenbaker sweep Thatcher ran third in the riding; his old friend and rival Hazen Argue walloped him by almost 3,000 votes. The Tory received 200 votes more than Ross. Ironically, four years later Argue, after he was defeated in the federal leadership race by Tommy Douglas, defected to the Liberals.

But the two election campaigns did not yield entirely negative results for Ross Thatcher.

Like a reformed drunk, once Thatcher had abandoned the CCF he developed into a rabid anti-socialist. Many in the CCF felt that Thatcher was reacting to a sense of shame he felt for double-crossing them. On several occasions he used his platform in the House to criticize the Saskatchewan government's Crown corporations. "I admit very frankly that at the outset I strongly supported the Crown corporation program in the hope that it would provide jobs for Saskatchewan citizens. Yet after twelve years I firmly believe that this experience with state socialism has been a costly and dismal failure."

Naturally Saskatchewan's premier, Tommy Douglas, took umbrage at this and during the 1957 election campaign challenged Ross Thatcher to a public debate. CCF supporters boasted that this would prove to be Thatcher's Waterloo. Douglas would wipe the floor with him and he would not be heard of again.

Despite a torrential downpour, on May 20 a thousand

people crowded into the six-hundred-seat Town Hall in the village of Mossbank; the rest of the province listened to the debate live on radio. By everyone's account the premier was not at his best that night, primarily because he could not engage in his famous flights of fancy, which often ended with a pointed barb stuck in his opponent. The moderator, Dr. Fred Wigmore, insisted he stick strictly to the topic of Crown corporations. CCFers had agreed to Wigmore, a Moose Jaw doctor, because he was a Conservative and therefore supposedly neutral. What many didn't realize was that he was one of Ross's best friends—he would deliver the three Thatcher grandchildren. Although he did not show overt favouritism to Ross, he gave no leeway at all to the flamboyant Douglas. The result was that Thatcher managed to hold his own in the debate, which was considered a great feat even by devoted CCFers. "He fought clean and broke clean in the clinches," reported the Moose Jaw *Times-Herald*.

Watching the contest with keen interest was a group of prominent Saskatchewan Liberals. They were looking for a strong leader who might pull the provincial party out of the doldrums and give it new life in time for the next election.

Except for a four-year hiatus (from 1929 to 1934) the mighty Saskatchewan Liberal party had ruled the province from its inception in 1905 until Tommy Douglas and the CCF swept to power in 1944. But after fifteen years in opposition, the Liberals were a tired and ineffective party. A series of leadership challenges had left it weak from infighting and dissension. In the 1956 election, only fourteen MLAs were elected, compared with thirty-six of the CCF, and the Liberal percentage of the popular vote had dropped nine points. most significantly, the Social Credit party had polled 21 percent of the vote and had grabbed three seats. The situation was rather desperate.

For a long time after the Liberals approached him, Thatcher played hard to get, insisting that he wasn't interested in provincial politics and that if he couldn't win a federal seat, he'd be a gentleman farmer. The pressure continued, until finally he agreed to run if certain conditions were met: an organizational drive to sign up new members would begin at once; money was to be made available to hire professional organizers; and, most important, Ross Thatcher was to be the boss. He would brook no serious dissension; his policy would be the Liberals' policy. In time the party would become such a fiefdom of Thatcher's that leadership material and new ideas died on the vine. Only a few years after he was gone, the provincial Liberal party collapsed completely.

There were three other candidates besides Thatcher who wanted the top job at the leadership convention, held in September, 1959. But only Alex Cameron, the Liberal finance critic in the Legislature and the party president, was any threat. He was soft-spoken, reasonable and polite, a marked contrast to Thatcher, who was abrasive, pugnacious, and dramatic. "We had been in the doldrums so long we needed someone flamboyant who was going to hammer the socialists. Thatcher was that man," says Rynold Gleim. But not only Ross Thatcher's public-speaking ability attracted delegates.

Saskatchewan was on the eve of introducing universal Medicare. The controversy that surrounded this momentous piece of legislation would tear the province apart and result in the bitter doctors' strike of 1962. It was rumoured that the province's physicians were supporting Ross Thatcher to the tune of some $50,000. With that kind of money, the Liberals would have an enormous advantage before election was even held.

Ross Thatcher won the leadership on the first ballot, receiving 424 of the 625 ballots cast.

The following year a provincial election was called. While Thatcher had not had time to rally his forces to a victory, the Liberals did win seventeen seats, three more than in the previous election. The Social Credit party was wiped out. Thatcher himself contested the election in Morse, a rural riding that included his Caron ranch, and beat his CCF opponent, although by only 162 votes.

Colin Thatcher was naturally affected by these tumultuous and highly publicized events in his father's career. He would later recall the painful taunting he had received from the kids whose parents were CCFers or even disapproving Liberals. This teasing would sometimes result in bloody fights. Although Colin was a big kid, he was often on the losing end, primarily because there were so many more against him than for him.

After graduating from high school he attended the Univer-

sity of Saskatchewan in Saskatoon, studying agriculture from
1956 to 1957. It was not a happy experience for him; he
received poor grades and took little part in university life. He
later claimed that he simply couldn't get a fair shake from the
professors because of his father's notoriety. But he would also
tell JoAnn that he left that university because he badly
injured his knee, which disqualified him for a hockey scholarship he had won. When she came to Moose Jaw she was
surprised to discover that the University of Saskatchewan had
never awarded sports scholarships of any kind.

At Ross's urging and with his help, Colin began looking at
universities in the United States where nobody would know
either him or his father. He considered Cornell but then
decided on Iowa State, which had a reputation as one of the
best agricultural colleges anywhere. It was closer to home
and the methods of farming were more compatible with those
in Saskatchewan. And it was agreed that his University of
Saskatchewan credits would serve as an equivalent of his
freshman year.

Early in the fall of 1957, Colin climbed into his 1955
Vauxhall, a present from his parents, and headed for Ames,
Iowa.

Iowa State College of Agriculture and Mechanic Arts (in 1959
the name was changed to Iowa State University of Science
and Technology) was a crowded, bustling place with a population of some nine thousand students, of whom about one-fifth
were women, enrolled primarily in the home economics
course. Founded in 1858, the college had grown topsy-turvy,
so that the campus was a hodge-podge of architectural styles.
But there was the impressive Memorial (student) Union,
which the more sophisticated undergrads liked to describe as
"neoclassical," where young men could take their dates dancing, and there was Lake Laverne to stroll around, and a
first-rate football team to cheer. Pete Seeger gave concerts,
Dr. Martin Luther King talked about "The Moral Challenges
of a New Age," and the St. Louis Symphony Orchestra came
to play Bach.

In his first year Colin Thatcher lived in the dormitories of
Godfrey House, one of the many student residences on campus. The innocence of the times was reflected in the chief

activities of the house: hot popcorn and cider on Sunday nights, a fall hay ride, and a bowling competition.

Thatcher specialized in animal husbandry. As well as the standard math, chemistry, and English, he studied livestock problems, principles of crop production, and farm insects. While he didn't win any prizes for his scholarship, he worked hard and earned decent grades. "We took genetics together," remembers John Cotten, "and he was much, much more intelligent than I was in that area. He helped me in that class." Another student remembers him writing a paper on swine production that was well received by the faculty.

Students were expected to participate in campus activities, but there is no record of Colin being involved in any that might have interested him—the Agricultural Business Club, the Agronomy Club, the Brock and Bridle Club, the Agricultural Council, the Dairy Husbandry Club—nor for that matter in any kinds of social groups. The one exception was his fraternity.

Iowa State's fraternities and sororities were, in many ways, the heart and soul of the university's social life. Thatcher chose Alpha Tau Omega. It was based at 2122 Lincoln Way, across from the university grounds, in a pleasant, square brick house with dormer windows and honeysuckle bushes outside. ATO was founded as a national fraternity in 1865, as an instrument to help reunite the north and the south after the Civil War; the Iowa State chapter was chartered in 1908 and the house was built in 1912. By 1959 various additions had been constructed to accommodate the swelling student population.

At first the fraternity brothers were undecided about inviting Colin to join them. They thought him something of a snob. "He was a likeable guy, he'd have a lot of fun, but he did have this superior attitude," recalls Michael Berard, who was president of the fraternity. They finally decided that punching holes in his pomposity might be an interesting challenge. They called him Moose Juice and Sir Winston. They asked him if he was related to the Queen, and mimicked his supposed British accent. A Canadian flag was proudly displayed in Thatcher's room, and occasionally one of the frat brothers would steal it. The same thing would happen to his picture of the Queen. "That would make him very, very mad," recalls Berard. "The whole idea was not to show disrespect to the flag or to the Queen, but to show that Colin was being a little too distant and not one of the guys. Eventually he caught on. he seemed to fit in better after a year in the fraternity."

"The only thing I remember about Colin," recalls Charles Klapf, "was that he was a little on the arrogant side. He tended to be a little loud or abusive, a little of a know-it-all. It was common knowledge that his family was pretty well off. He got away with saying things that others wouldn't have. He was a bit of a spoiled kid, I think."

This was the late Fifties and the housemother, Mrs. Tague, ruled with a velvet fist, ensuring that the house rules and proper etiquette were strictly observed. The young men were required to dress for dinner except on Saturdays, women were not allowed above the first floor, and alcohol of any kind was strictly verboten. The fraternity brothers thought up ingenious ways to break the rules, especially in regard to booze. But generally that atmosphere was wholesome, with calypso parties, harvest balls, and horseshoe tournaments dominating social life.

In his second year Colin was named the fraternity's pledge trainer. His job was to make sure the new guys were taught the same rules and regulations and the traditions of ATO. "The one thing we all had to learn very fast was how to spell Saskatchewan," recalls David Berger. Thatcher also participated in intramural sports, an important part of fraternity life, which included everything from golf to handball. But he wasn't outstanding. He liked to brag about his prowess as a junior hockey player, which had been fair to good, and he would insist that his friends watch the occasional hockey game that was aired on television. "He gave us the feeling that he was almost a pro," says John Cotten.

Among the fraternity brothers there was a great deal of girl talk in which Colin enthusiastically participated, but nobody can remember him dating much. For one thing, the men outnumbered the women so drastically on campus that fixing a date was a major undertaking. Secondly, Colin's father kept him on a shoestring budget; he didn't have a lot of money to spend on women. One spring day in 1960 he spotted a very attractive blonde girl walking through the Memorial Union. "I asked one of my friends who that was," Colin would later recall, "and he said it was JoAnn Geiger. And I somehow managed to find a way to be lined up with JoAnn Geiger on Saturday night, and went to pick her up at her sorority house. Someone came around the corner and said, 'Hello Colin,' and I said hello. Then I realized there's been a mistake, I'm picking up the wrong girl. But I went through with it. And obviously things went very well because I subsequently married her."

Twenty-four years later he would stand in a Saskatoon courtroom, accused of brutally beating and then murdering that same woman.

CHAPTER THREE

JOANN GEIGER, AMES, IOWA

AUGUST 12, 1962

The aisle pews of Collegiate United Methodist Church in Ames, Iowa, were decorated with white candles encircled by pink ribbon. The dresses of the two bridesmaids and the matron of honour were of slightly paler pink. And the pink stephanotis in the beautiful bride's bouquet were an even more delicate shade. Alas, when the bride and the groom cut through the icing of the multi-tiered wedding cake, the innards revealed a shocking raspberry colour. JoAnn gasped. She had been very specific in her instructions to the baker, had even given him a piece of ribbon exactly the correct pretty pink shade, and the result was this travesty.

She had wanted a perfect wedding. After all, Colin was an only child and she was determined that the Thatchers and their guests, who had come all the way from Saskatchewan for the occasion, would be pleased and impressed. For months she had planned and worried about every detail. She had designed the attendants' dresses so that they were practical as well as fashionable: a chiffon overlay could be removed and the peau-de-soie sheath could then be worn to less formal affairs. She had gently spread the word about exactly which crystal and silver she was collecting. And she had soothed the shock of a wedding reception without liquor (her father had insisted on it) by agreeing to a cocktail party for the Canadians at their hotel.

Colin and the guests laughed at her concern over the raspberry-coloured cake, told her that it was delicious and that the wedding was a thoroughly charming affair. Since

JoAnn had resolved that absolutely nothing was going to spoil this "happiest day in my life," she was quickly appeased.

For the twenty-three-year-old home economics graduate the wedding represented the ultimate showcase for her flair and style. Ironically, the event would also limit the professional development of that same flair and style that had shone brilliantly at college, and would hold back her career. Over twenty years later JoAnn would caution a young friend, Shevawn Desrosiers, who was considering marriage, "Don't make the same mistake that I did and be pressured by what's happening around you. Where I came from, you went to college, got your degree, married, and lived happily ever after. It doesn't work that way."

Susan Allen Toth, who grew up with JoAnn in Ames and later produced a beautifully written, often funny, book about the experience (*Blooming: A Small Town Girlhood*, published by Little, Brown and Company in 1978), put it this way. "The kind of woman we thought we would become was what Ames, Iowa, saw as the American ideal. She shimmered in our minds, familiar but removed as the glossy cover of the Sears, Roebuck catalogue. There she rolled snowballs with two smiling red-cheeked children, or unpacked a picnic lunch on emerald grass as an Irish setter lounged nearby, or led a cherubic toddler into blue water. Her tall handsome husband hovered close, perhaps with his hand protectively on her shoulder. Pretty and well-dressed, she laughed happily into the KodaColor sunshine that flooded her future.

"During the past twenty years, that gleaming ideal has become tarnished, scratched and blackened as deeply as the copper bottoms on the shiny saucepans we got as wedding presents." And nobody would suffer more from disillusionment than JoAnn Geiger.

She was raised in Norman Rockwell's benign and wholesome Midwest America, In a *Saturday Evening Post* cover, she would be the curly-headed little blonde girl, prissy in a frilly white dress, who looks down with mock disdain on a brother all scuffed and dirty. From babyhood, JoAnn displayed all the traits of a traditional lady-like little female. Recalls her mother, Betty Geiger, "I remember her grandmother saying that with beautiful brown eyes like that she will be able to get whatever she wants."

* * *

Harlan and Elizabeth Geiger both grew up on farms in the corn state of Iowa. He was of German stock, she of Scandinavian. Both had the wherewithal to make it to college in the mid-1930s, a not inconsiderable feat for the time. "A friend of mine was describing this cute little girl," recalls Geiger. "I had just been introduced to Betty, so I said to him if she's so great why don't you take her and I'll take Betty. We went to a 4-H Club meeting and that's where it all began." Harlan graduated in animal science and after he asked Betty to marry him, she dropped out of the home economics course in which she was enrolled. The wedding was held on November 8, 1936, and two months later the couple moved to Osage, Iowa, population 3,000. Harlan had landed a job as county extension director for Iowa State's 4-H Clubs, an organization dedicated to teaching farm children useful skills in home economics, livestock raising, and crop production. "What I remember about 4-H were the contests. You were always either making preserves, or quilts, or getting some calf ready to compete in some fair or other." remembers Betty Geiger. Harlan Geiger would spend his entire working life as an organizer and administrator for 4-H Clubs in Iowa, a job he found deeply satisfying.

In 1938, a son, Donald, was born, and eighteen months later on August 21, 1939, JoAnn Kay Geiger arrived. From the beginning she was a model child. "She was a very easy baby," remembers her mother, "always so bright and sweet." Of their stay in Osage the Geigers recall one incident. "We were living in half of a house and the landlady, who was an avid gardener, had built a goldfish and lily pool which she covered with a wire mesh. One fall morning we found the little children standing right up to their necks in cold water. The landlady drained it immediately."

When JoAnn was two the family moved to Newton, Iowa, home of the mammoth Maytag Appliances. During these war years the huge plant was producing more aluminum castings for guns' turrets than washing machines. "Things were really booming in terms of employment," recalls Harlan. "They drafted me to head the seventh war bond drive. We wanted a little more attention than we'd been getting so I went over to see the Maytag folks. Mr. Butler, an executive, picked up the phone and in an hour he had a big long parade all lined up. Nobody could say no to Maytag."

JoAnn started kindergarten in Newton and a third child, Carolyn, was born in 1944. Harlan did the same type of work there but was responsible for a larger area and supervised more staff. He excelled at it, attracting more members to his clubs than did any other county in the state, and he was soon promoted.

In 1945 Harlan got the job of Assistant State 4-H Leader. Since 4-H Clubs were officially under the auspices of the Iowa State University, the organization's head offices were located in Ames. The Geiger family moved to the idyllic university town where Harlan and Betty remain to this day.

In many ways Ames is a typical American college town. There's an atmosphere of perpetual youth, a never-never-land quality about the place, primarily because students make up half the population of 45,000. The vibrant life of the town is dedicated to youth—there's Lucky Q, specializing in rock'n'roll and ice-cold beer, Lucullan's with its good-time video dance bar, and Whiskey River, which draws crowds to its pool table and great food. The city's transportation system is called "Cy Ride" (after Iowa State's mascot, a cardinal called Cy), the taxi service is named after the football team and Michael's Cyclery, specializing in bicycles and skis, is one of the town's most thriving business.

But there is another Ames, one that is associated with the quieter spirit of scholarly pursuits and university tradition. Elegant sorority and fraternity houses dot the neighbourhood around the campus. White oak and black maple trees line the clean streets. And many of the town's fifty churches are architecturally grand. To grow up in such a town was to be protected against adversity or cruelty of any kind, to remain perpetually naive about a larger world. Susan Allen Toth writes: "In our particular crucible we were not seared by fierce poverty, racial tensions, drug abuse, street crime; we were cosseted, gently warmed, transmuted by slow degrees."

The Geigers thought it the perfect place to bring up their family. They found a lovely new, two-storey home on Hunt Street, a quiet tree-lined avenue only a few blocks from the university. Although Harlan's new job was considered a promotion, he had not received a salary increase. "We looked at the outside of this home and thought, man, that is too much money—it was 25 or 30 percent more than the house we had just sold in Newton. We wouldn't even go inside," recalls Betty Geiger. "Then we looked at other places and came back and got this one." With four kids (the youngest child, Nancy, was born in 1959) and a job with an educational organization—his academic rank was assistant professor—Harlan Geiger never made a fortune; but the Geigers were not extravagant people.

They quickly discovered that the entire neighbourhood consisted of young couples with small children. "There were twenty-six pre-school kids and forty-seven in school," recalls Betty. "My brother came home from service and he just shook his head at all the kids pouring into the basement playroom. Finally he said, 'Do you actually know most of these kids?' JoAnn and the others, they just had a ball."

One of the advantages of living in a college town was that so many parents were deeply interested in education. As a result Ames has one of the best public school systems in the United States. "Ames schools are consistently in the upper part, the 99th percentile, in the ratings of the national tests," says Harlan Geiger. "JoAnn just loved school," recalls Betty. "She just couldn't wait to get there; it just was very important in her mind. And she was always a very good student."

The Geiger children went to Louise Crawford Public School, an excellent small school four blocks away from their home, and at age twelve she started Welch Junior High. In 1978 JoAnn went back to visit the institution where she spent grades seven, eight, and nine. Because of declining student enrolment it had been torn down and replaced by an apartment complex. "I feel like a part of my past has just disappeared," she told her parents. At that point, faced with painful marital conflict, she was feeling sadly nostalgic, remembering the happiness and comfort of her childhood.

In the course of these happy years, the Geigers did experience one serious mishap. A couple of days before Christmas, their son Don and a friend were waiting for the Des Moines newspaper to arrive so they could deliver it. The two boys decided to go for a walk in the woods around Lake Laverne. They were chatting about organizing a hockey game when Don's friend struck a stick against a tree. A splinter pierced Don's right eye and it had to be removed that night. The friend's father was very concerned that the Geigers might sue. "We never considered doing that. We considered it an unfortunate accident and suing was not going to restore Don's eye," says Harlan Geiger.

Unlike the Geigers' other two daughters, who were addicted to reading and studying, JoAnn liked to be with people. "While she was a very good student, it was very important to be involved in social things," recalls her mother. "She was always outgoing. When she was a very little girl I remember people visiting us and they'd say, "My, you're cute. Why don't you come with us?" She was all ready to go, and her brother would grab her and hang on to her and say, 'No, no.' But she would think they were perfectly serious, and she'd visit with anybody."

During her married life in Moose Jaw, JoAnn would attract an astonishingly wide circle of women friends from all strata of society, who would provide vital support during her battles with Colin Thatcher. Cherishing close female friends was a habit she developed early on in her Ames childhood. Writes Susan Allen Toth about her group of friends, "We giggled together, knew each other's secret wishes and fears, but we used each other too. We needed to find our places, and we had only each other to measure ourselves by."

And yet paradoxically, both her childhood friends and those she acquired later on would remark on how she would put up barriers against real intimacy with people. "She didn't like to be real close with you," remembers childhood friend Celia Strayer. "She was much more independent than most of us." "Even as a child, she was very much a private person. She possessed that famous Mid-western reserve more than most of us did," says another friend.

Upon reaching grade seven, the children of the Collegiate United Methodist Church were invited to join the congregation. For JoAnn this meant that her social life expanded considerably. While she had been a member of the children's choir and Sunday school, she now moved up to the junior choir and she could join the Youth Fellowship group. This organization met Wednesday evenings and organized all kinds of exciting events—box supper socials, occasional parties, even special out-of-town trips to such places as Des Moines, fifty-six kilometres south, where the young people would admire the golden domes of the State Capital Building.

Adolescence was also a time for pyjama parties (where you could giggle for hours about boys), long sessions at the Rainbow Café predicting what kind of man you were apt to marry, and summer afternoons at Carr's pool, where you could sunbathe and stare at the roughhousing male swimmers. While she wasn't the most popular girl in the neighbourhood, JoAnn was an integral part of her group.

"She was the kind of girl who would drive a slob like me crazy with envy," remembers Donna Livingston, a friend. "The whites of her saddle shoes were always scuffless, she always had a little bouquet of cloth violets pinned on her collar, and her hair was always neat." Remembers Betty Geiger, "JoAnn wouldn't dream of going to school without pressing her blouse, even if there was only the tiniest wrinkle in it. She was quite a feminine young girl." "She wasn't great on sports," recalls Harlan Geiger. "I tried to teach her to bat a ball and things like that, with little success. She liked clothes and pretty things."

Despite her femininity, JoAnn early on displayed an independence and determination that quite astonished her parents. Recalls Harlan Geiger: "Most girls at some time or other are very keen on horses, and JoAnn read every book on the subject she could get ahold of. She used to like to go away in the summer with the Campfire Girls. When she was twelve, she got it into her mind that she wanted to go to a camp near Cedar Rapids, about a hundred miles east of here, which had a horseback riding program. Now all her friends were going to the camp near Ames and they coaxed her and coaxed her to go with them. And we weren't anxious to have her go either. She wouldn't listen. She went off all by herself, not knowing a soul. And you know, she had a very good time."

One time JoAnn's brother came across an advertisement from a bicycle manufacturer who was about to bring out a new model of bike and was holding a contest to name it. "Gee, I think 'Corner Clipper' would be a good name," said Don. "You going to send it?" JoAnn asked. "Nah, can't be bothered," said Don. So she submitted it instead. A few weeks later there was great excitement in the neighbourhood when a large truck pulled up and unloaded a crate addressed to JoAnn. She had won a wonderful new bike.

It was these qualities of strength and resoluteness that

would make JoAnn's struggles with Colin Thatcher so fierce and prolonged. Even when she was acutely afraid, she would not give up.

"I would have voted JoAnn the least likely person in my high-school class to be murdered," says Catherine Weingart, who grew up not far from the Geigers. "She got into a situation which was so different from her background. As I recall she was always very exacting and did things in such a methodical way. She was so serious." Don Geiger's memories of her as a teenager are similar. "I don't remember her as a terribly warm person. She always had that air of efficiency about her. As for her marks—she got As and high Bs—I don't think it came that easily. She had to really apply herself. She seemed to be able to organize and do a lot more things than most people. You know they say the busiest people always find more time. Well, she was certainly an example of that."

In high school she was the devoted business manager of the drama club, the publicity editor for the *Spirit*, a member of the student treasurers' organization, the treasurer for the Palm Club, the treasurer of the Girl Reserves. JoAnn's pictures in *Spirit, 1957*, the Ames Senior High School yearbook, reveal a rather reserved, even forbidding, young person. Not a hair on her neat head is out of place. Her glasses are rather severe, with great pointed wings that make her look schoolmarmish. While the rest of the group is obviously laughing in response to something the photographer has said, JoAnn's slight smile is prim, and just a little condescending. Her neat white blouse has not a wrinkle in it and a bouquet of cloth violets decorates her collar. Among the autographs in her yearbook wishing her well, one by a boy named Bernard pokes fun at JoAnn's prudishness. "Jo, a hot little pill, we've certainly played nice bridge together. Boy, what you and Evards have done. Scandal! I might have asked you for a date but as Evards said you're too damn hot. Scandal!" Most of the other autographs were instead along this line: "Jo—To one of the cutest girls I know. You're so efficient and brainy too. Envy! Best of everything to you always. Margie."

While most slumber parties at the Geigers were devoted to intense conversation about boys, JoAnn did not have a steady, at least not for very long. "She always had a date for the big dances and that sort of thing, but chances are someone different would be calling on her for the next one," recalls Harlan Geiger. "She was never serious about any one boy all the time she was in high school." "There were girls that were a lot more popular with the boys than we were," recalls Thiel Ramsbey, JoAnn's best friend in high school. "But we always seemed to come up with a date on special occasions. We sort of blundered through. We knew our time would come eventually." Thiel remembers that JoAnn took the blue garter ceremony particularly seriously. Susan Allen Toth writes about it: "Our senior year in high school, for our last round of birthday parties, we chose a blue satin garter with white lace in a padded white satin box. It was extravagant, from Carole's, an elegant store, and intended, as a fancily lettered card instructed us, to be 'something new and something blue' to wear at one's wedding. Though none of us had weddings in the offing we knew that at eighteen they were edging closer."

"One thing we all agreed on," remembers Donna Livingston, "is that we would remain virgins, no matter what, until God sent the man that was destined for us. It was supposedly a gift we were giving our husbands. And what is surprising is how many of our group stuck to this crazy notion." Colin Thatcher would later tell a lover that, despite his best efforts, JoAnn would remain "pure" until their wedding night.

JoAnn didn't develop steady boyfriends because she was too busy making money. All the kids in Ames worked, it was the thing to do, but none worked harder than Miss Geiger. Early on she developed a passion for clothes; *Mademoiselle* became her bible and she would spend hours flipping through the thick glossy magazine, oohing and aahing over Bermuda shorts and semi-formals. She had an allowance of ten dollars a month, which covered clothes and everything else, and she planned its expenditure very carefully, but of course it never went far enough. She would often walk through Campus Town and ogle all the beautifully dressed co-eds. "She was exposed to an awful lot of temptation," laughs Betty Geiger.

Her brother began delivering papers for the Ames *Daily Tribune* when he was only ten; a few years later he did the same thing for the *Des Moines Register*, a more profitable and prestigious job, and he passed on his *Daily Tribune* route to JoAnn. She was one of the few girls in Ames delivering papers at that time and her friends were all envious. They'd tag along and help her just for the novelty. At one point the *Register* launched a circulation drive; all the delivery boys (girls were not allowed routes) would receive fifty cents for each subscription they sold. "Don was much more reserved and timid than JoAnn," says Harlan Geiger. "He hated knocking on doors and trying to sell things. JoAnn loved it. So she went out and sold all kinds of subscriptions to the paper he was delivering."

JoAnn also babysat, like teenaged girls everywhere, but in summer, like a true Iowan, she detasseled corn. It was a job that plenty of thirteen- and fourteen-year-olds, mostly girls, suffered through. Although it lasted only three or four weeks, it was so exhausting and strenuous that many corn detasselers, when they grew into adulthood, wondered why no labour-standards functionary had ever intervened.

For the plants to crossbreed properly the tassels had to be pulled from the female cornstalks. The workers stood on a motor-driven platform and pulled the silky tassels from the cornstalks as the machine chugged along through endless columns of corn. At the end of the eight-hour day, the young girls were sunburned, caked with dirt, and aching in every muscle. The pay was fifty cents an hour—unless you stayed the entire season, when it was retroactively raised to sixty-five cents. JoAnn Geiger was one of the few who stuck it out to the end.

When the magic age of sixteen finally arrived, it meant that a "real job" was possible. JoAnn clerked in the bakery department of Hy-Vee Grocery Store but then got a job as a saleswoman at Bobby Rogers' Women's Wear. "She just loved it," says her mother. "She was surrounded by all those clothes." The next year, however, she landed a higher-paying position at Younker's, Iowa's largest, most prestigious department store. At first she worked in the accessories department, selling neckwear, jewellery, and sweaters. "While the older women were griping that their feet hurt, she was pushing sales," recalls her father. "'We got in a nice batch of sweaters today,' she'd insist. Her sales of the little things were right up around a hundred dollars a day, and back then that was a lot. The older women selling the bigger things weren't making any more."

"She never stopped looking for ways to make more money," says her father. At one point JoAnn persuaded her boss at

Younker's to allow her to leave work a half-hour early. That enabled her to get to a drive-in restaurant situated on the edge of town by 5:30, in time to work the night shift there. And she was on weekend call to waitress at the Memorial Union. "She worked weekends, evenings, and all summer while she was in high school. She never asked for a bigger allowance. Whatever she had was always okay. She never seemed to feel put upon." JoAnn even paid a large portion of her wedding costs.

One job had a most profound effect on her. When she was transferred to Younker's linen and drapery department, she proved to be so keen and so capable that she was soon ordering materials, setting up displays, and advising customers on the appropriate curtains or bedspreads for their homes. Her boss was so delighted with her that he wrote a letter to her parents commending her on her fine work. "That's where she acquired the enthusiasm for home decorating, working with all those lovely fabrics." Some of the warmest memories Betty Geiger has of her daughter are of the two of them poring over interior decorating magazines until 3 a.m., dreaming of how they would remodel their homes.

JoAnn was able to sew her own doll clothes when she was seven. In junior and senior high school she took every home economics course available and earned the highest marks possible. "When we were in high school I wanted to do some decorating in my bedroom," remembers Catherine Weingart. "JoAnn came over and showed me how to put piping around a pillow. I was so impressed. I was kind of a klutz and she was so good at that kind of thing." It was predictable that she would decide to follow in her mother's footsteps and take home economics at university. Many members of Ames Senior High School's graduating class of 1957 were planning "to escape the small town" by going to university elsewhere. JoAnn inquired about colleges all over the United States. Then one day she picked up some brochures at Iowa State's home economics department. "I hate to admit it, Dad, but Iowa State's got the best program of anywhere," she said. "And it's true," says Harlan Geiger. "On this campus home economics has always rated. It has always got top billing and girls could always get good jobs out of here." Before her lay a strenuous four-year course. The first few semesters were devoted to basics—chemistry, mathematics, physics, English.

The more specialized courses were offered—textiles, child development, nutrition, interior design. "I felt strongly that the students should prepare for a profession," says Helen LeBaron Hilton, who was dean of the division at the time. "We felt it was very short sighted to just come for homemaking. Unfortunately many did."

Catherine Weingart recalls having lunch with JoAnn and a friend who was also taking home economics at Iowa State. "To my complete amazement, JoAnn's friend told me in great seriousness that there were nineteen precise steps to doing the laundry. I thought, 'Oh my God, there's got to be more to life than this.' But JoAnn seemed to just love it."

Almost as important to JoAnn as the selection of the university was the choice of a sorority. As a young girl, she had watched the beautiful co-eds flit in and out of the elegant, mansion-like sorority houses, often into the waiting arms of handsome young men. To her they were the cream of society, her ideal of young womanhood, and she yearned to be among them.

"It was a very cruel, cruel thing," says Helen LeBaron Hilton. "There was never enough space for all who wanted to get into sorority life. Some of the young girls who didn't get chosen would go home and never return, or else their college lives were ruined for them."

At Iowa State the official rushing period occurred a week before a girl's freshman year began. She and her competitors were put up at one of the college dormitories so they would be readily available for an exhausting round of parties given by the dozen or so houses. As the week progressed both the rushes and the sororities narrowed their choices. "Of course the girls who might look great at a party might not be the ones who had the most going for them, or the most brains," says Betty Geiger

"It got down to where JoAnn had to pick three sororities and place them in the order she most wanted them. She said, 'It's an awful feeling. It seems like you're cutting your own throat every time you put down the name because if they don't pick you, you're out.' Fortunately she got bids from all three."

JoAnn chose Chi Omega, considered by many to be the most prestigious sorority on campus in terms of social prominence and academic achievement. Established at ISU in

1921, it was situated at 227 Gray Street, a few blocks south of the university, in a rather grand colonial-style house of red brick with three-storey-high white pillars and circular top windows. The downstairs living rooms were tastefully decorated in a pale green and white. A baby grand piano occupied one corner. Mrs. Stow, the residence director, presided over the activities of the forty sorority sisters who lived there. There were strict rules, which were seldom broken. "Once a girl was found drunk in the bathroom. But this was such an astonishing event, it was talked about for months," recalls Kay Lemmon, who lived at the house in 1960.

Pledges did not live in the house and so for her freshman year, JoAnn stayed at Welch Hall, a women's dormitory. After that she resided at Chi Omega whenever she could afford it. Sorority life, with its national dues and boarding fees, could be quite expensive. "We paid the basic college expenses, which included room and board at home," says Harlan Geiger. "All the extras she paid for." "It was too bad in a way," adds Betty, "because the girls asked her if she would be living in the house for her senior year. She said she wasn't sure if she could afford it. They told her later that if she had given a definite yes, they would have voted her president." She was elected vice-president, however.

JoAnn Geiger blossomed at university. A picture taken of her with her sorority sisters in the spring of 1959, her sophomore year, shows an astonishingly different young woman. The severe glasses are gone ("Jo was never happier than on the day she bought her contact lenses," says her mother), her hair is fluffier and much more flattering, and a soft cashmere sweater drapes her slim frame. There is a real resemblance here to the elegant and fashionable woman whose picture would so often be splashed across Canadian newspapers in years to come.

She earned straight As. "I didn't think she'd excel academically in college but she took an incredible number of courses and got better grades than most people who considered themselves scholars," recalls her brother. "I began to think she could succeed at anything." "She beat me by one-tenth of a grade point," remembers Thiel Ramsbey. "It made me kind of mad, because I thought I had done real well." JoAnn won several scholarships, and in the fall of 1960, she was selected as a member of Phi Kappa Phi, a national honorary society recognizing high scholastic achievement. At Iowa State, only the upper one-sixteenth of graduating seniors were admitted to its ranks. She was thrilled when she received her selection letter.

Indeed, her four years at university brought many awards and accolades for JoAnn Geiger; she would later tell friends that it was the happiest, most satisfying period of her life. She was chosen for Omicron Nu, a national home economics honorary society for women who achieved high scholastic standards, and for Phi Upsilon Omicron, the professional home economics honorary society, an even more select group that based membership on "scholarship, outstanding leadership, professional attitude." She was one of twelve students named to the Dean's Advisory Board, which served as a kind of sounding board for students. "I remember JoAnn very well," says former Dean Hilton. "You could always depend on her to carry everything through. She was aggressive but with a very pleasant manner; she wasn't obnoxious in any way. She was a pusher but a nice pusher. She'd just go ahead and get things done.

"She was not the beauty queen type. She wasn't beautiful but she was very attractive. I always felt that had she gone into a profession, she would have been one of our most successful graduates."

Writes Susan Allen Toth, "VEISHEA was what Ames celebrated instead of Fourth of July, presidents' holidays or founders' days. Although it was a college holiday, its acronym formed by the major divisions of Iowa State (Veterinary Medicine, Engineering, Industrial Science, Home Economics, Agriculture), the whole town turned out for the three days of VEISHEA." It was the university's open house, its formal gesture of hospitality towards the community. Each faculty would organize a lavish display to illustrate what was going on in its world, and to the delight of schoolchildren this included handouts—ice-cream cones from the Dairy Industry, miniature cherry pies from Home Economics, tiny evergreens planted in paper cups from Forestry. There was also a parade, a clever satirical revue, and many splendid social events.

JoAnn was determined to become involved in the extravaganza that she had enjoyed so much since childhood. In her sophomore year she was co-organizer of the Home Economics open house display; this proved so successful that she was asked to be co-chairman of the entire VEISHEA the following year. It took an enormous amount of time agonizing over details. "I don't know how she managed to do that and maintain her academic excellence. But she did," says her brother. Despite a downpour during one of the days, the event was considered such a success that the president of the university wrote her a letter thanking and praising her for a job well done.

On the first night of the 1960 VEISHEA, thousands of students were gathered in the park in front of Iowa State's Campanile. They were excited and happy, for this was a very special ceremony. Suddenly JoAnn Geiger felt a slap on her back, and a hat was placed on her head. A great cheer went up and her parents, who had been hiding in the crowd, rushed over to kiss her. She had been tapped for Mortar Board, the highest honour the university could bestow on a woman student. She and fifteen other seniors had been elected into this very exclusive honorary society on the basis of their academic excellence, their service to the university, and their popularity among the students. "It was the most thrilling thing anyone could ever receive," says Jane Baxter, JoAnn's close friend, who had been tapped the previous year. She would receive many congratulatory letters and cables, all much like this one: "Dear Jo, Welch Hall congratulates you, a former Welch girl, on being selected for Mortar Board. It is a great and wonderful honor and we know you will live up to it." From then on, one day a week she was required to wear the prestigious Mortar Board white blazer and skirt, a symbol that her career at college had been an overwhelming success.

The Geigers have, as cherished possessions, a collection of snapshots taken of JoAnn during her college years. Many are pictures of her at social events. Here she is, dressed in a beautiful floor-length gown she designed and made herself, on her way to Chi Omega's Carnation Christmas formal. Here she is doing the Charleston in a Roaring Twenties outfit at a fraternity dance. And here she's frying hamburgers in apron and Bermuda shorts at a barbecue at Larry Jo's ranch. In all of these photos, there is a different man hovering nearby.

"Just as in high school, she dated around. She was never

very serious about anyone," says her father. "There was one chap from southwest Iowa who badly wanted her to marry him. I remember she went down to meet his folks wearing this blue sack dress. She liked him—he was a good student, good-looking fellow, kind and considerate—but she thought he just didn't have enough self-assurance. He just didn't stand out enough. The last time she came to visit us, she said, 'I could have married him and things would have been so different.'"

The Geigers had heard nothing about Colin Thatcher until Easter weekend of 1960. "She was home and we had gotten up early to do some fancy Easter eggs, decorate them with sequins and flowers and things," recalls Betty Geiger. "She said, 'I hope you and Dad like this fellow, because we're pinned.' I nearly fell over."

Colin was invited for dinner that afternoon and the Geigers can remember nothing very memorable about that first meeting. "He was quiet, well groomed, nicely dressed, but you didn't feel terribly at ease with him. Of course he was a complete stranger," recalls Betty Geiger. Harlan did notice that he seemed well informed, particularly about American politics. "He mentioned that once he and his father had met the governor of California, Ronald Reagan. Apparently they were very impressed," recalls Harlan. Betty felt that Colin was pleasant-looking, quite handsome. "When we came to Regina for JoAnn's funeral I saw one of his pictures on television and I was really shocked. He had developed that terrible scowl."

Colin received very mixed reviews from JoAnn's friends. "Everybody was amazed at the match," recalls Amy St. Ives, who was a sorority sister of JoAnn's. "They were two completely different people. Here was this serious student who was popular and attractive and capable, who I'm sure could have attracted any number of eligible men walking around, and who does she choose? A guy we considered a playboy, who wasn't involved in university life at all and who talked all about his father's money."

"I never understood what she saw in him at all," says Jane Baxter. "He never seemed very sincere to me. It's sort of petty but I will never forget how he tricked me one time. We had quiet hours at our sorority when we had to study. One of us was assigned phone duty to take messages and we were not allowed to disturb people during the study time. One night I was on phone duty and Colin called. I can't remember exactly what it was but he said there was some emergency, some serious situation which needed JoAnn's immediate attention. Anyway, I went and got her. Later I found out there was nothing to it. He made me so mad."

But there were others who understood her attraction to him. "She thought he was very sophisticated," says her sister Carolyn. "He represented a different kind of life. Ours had been sheltered and his was flamboyant." "He was exotic, that was the thing," recalls Kay Lemmon. "He came from a place called Moose Jaw, Saskatchewan! To us that was as intriguing as Istanbul or Shanghai. Not only that, he was a rancher. We thought of all those pictures in the cigarette ads of this rugged he-man roping a calf. *Quelle aventure*." "He struck me as being very sombre but virile—tough but sexy-looking," remembers Susan Allen Toth, who attended JoAnn's wedding. "I remember being a little envious at the time."

"She told us once," says her mother, "that Colin was the first fellow she had dated that she couldn't just wrap around her finger, and I think that intrigued her. She felt the other fellows just weren't independent enough."

Friends who knew JoAnn at the time felt that there were other, underlying reasons for her involvement with Colin. "By the time JoAnn was in her junior year she had developed certain expectations, certain social pretensions," says a sorority friend. "And to be fair, so did many of the sorority sisters. I think she was impressed by the fact that Colin's father was an important politician and had some money. I can remember Colin talking about politics in a very knowledgeable way, and giving the very clear indication that he might someday be involved. I think she could see a future with great potential stretching ahead of her. Also, of course, if you weren't pinned by your junior year, things were getting pretty desperate."

"Every girl thought she had to be married immediately," recalls Helen LeBaron Hilton. "If she wasn't married or engaged by the time she graduated, she was considered a failure. That was a very, very distressing attitude. I think that's why so many made unfortunate choices." JoAnn herself would admit in later years that social pressure was a major reason she was so anxious to marry Colin Thatcher. "And anxious she was, there's no question about that," says Kay Lemmon.

Because of her excellent grades JoAnn had been selected to serve an apprenticeship for six weeks in the summer of 1960 at Stix Baer Fuller, a large department store in St. Louis. "She was the only person who was allowed to sell from any department in the whole store," recalls Harlan Geiger. "She would circulate and help people where she was needed. On her noon hour, she would visit other department stores so that when a customer asked her for something she could say, 'Well, we don't have it but such and such a store does.' She had a wonderful experience." Stix Baer Fuller thought so highly of her that they offered her a position as a junior buyer. But by this time she was writing letters to Canada.

In August JoAnn went to Moose Jaw for the first time, to meet Colin's parents. Ross would later tell friends that he couldn't believe that his raggedy-edged son could have snared such an accomplished, pretty young woman. Both Thatchers came to adore JoAnn and to regard her as their own daughter; the mutually warm relationship would continue until Ross died, and until Peggy sided with her son in the bitter marriage breakdown.

Colin had received his Bachelor of Science degree in animal husbandry that spring and had started working on his father's ranch. The day before JoAnn's twenty-first birthday, August 21, 1960, the young couple were out riding in the Caron area. A car suddenly came around a bend. Colin's horse bolted, throwing him onto the hood. He was hospitalized with a badly fractured arm and the doctor told him that he might not have the use of it again. Fortunately an operation was successful, a pin was installed, and he eventually recovered almost completely. But it was a long process. "Rather than lay around and do absolutely nothing, I made the decision to go back to Iowa State and get a Master's [degree]," Colin would later explain. "The fact that JoAnn was there was a factor, no question, but from a realistic point of view, to be accepted quickly it had to be Iowa State since my undergraduate work had been taken there."

During the 1960–61 term, Colin rented an apartment not far from the Geiger house and the two young people saw each other every day. She would tell her friend Shevawn Desrosiers, "He was such a charmer when I first met him. He was this wonderful, flattering young man." He cut the Geigers' grass, took JoAnn's little sister Nancy out for ice cream, and talked about hockey with Harlan. But he was particularly devoted to JoAnn. To their friends, they appeared to be madly in love.

"In a matter of a few weeks everything got turned around," laments Harlan Geiger. Her parents expected that after graduation she would head for St. Louis, Chicago, or New York and an important job in merchandising. But at Christmas, 1960, JoAnn visited the Thatchers in Moose Jaw and began looking at job possibilities there. She soon discovered that she was vastly over-qualified for anything in retail merchandising—about the only job she could get was clerking at Joyner's Department Store. However, the Moose Jaw Board of Education told her that she would be hired as a home economics teacher in the fall, if she had a teacher's certificate.

JoAnn had not been the slightest bit interested in teaching and had taken no courses in the field. She returned to Iowa State and asked the head of the department of education if she could take the eighteen hours of courses all at once. It would mean that she would be taking first-year courses with third-year and he flatly refused her. Undeterred, she pleaded with Dean LeBaron Hilton. Because of her high marks she had been eligible to enrol in the honours program, which allowed each student to do specialized individualized study. That gave her a certain leeway, and the dean overrode the department head. So during the spring and summer semesters of 1961, JoAnn not only managed to earn a Bachelor of Science degree in home economics, summa cum laude, she also received enough credits to qualify for a three-year teacher's certificate. On May 26, 1961, the Thatchers sent her a cable: "Our warmest love and congratulations on your graduation day. Peggy and Ross."

The Geigers did have some misgivings about their future son-in-law. "I told Betty one time, 'I sure hope they stay in love because if they ever fall out he could kill her.' A couple or three things Colin had said during that year made me think that he could be violent," recalls Harlan Geiger. "He told me this story one time about how during deer-hunting season, he was driving along in his pick-up and he saw a car parked on his property near the entrance to a field. He just concluded that they were hunting on his property without his permission. He took out his shotgun and blew holes into their radiator. He seemed quite proud of doing that.

"Another time he was waiting on JoAnn to finish working. The store clerks didn't know of any connection between him and Jo. He was picking stuff off the shelf, looking at it and putting it down. This one clerk convinced himself that Colin was shoplifting. He came up behind Colin and put his arms around him. Now I don't know whether he was reaching for Colin's pockets to see if he had anything, but Colin jerked loose and knocked him flying. 'Nobody puts their hands on me,' he yelled. Didn't ask the guy what he was doing or anything. Just punched him to the floor."

During his two years at graduate school, Colin shared an apartment with his good friend Joe Saviano. "Joe was one of the most popular guys on campus," recalls Mike Berard. He had a superb voice and sang with the Iowa State Singers, the men's Glee Club, and the Iowa State Festival Chorus. He belonged to a sub rosa organization, Pies Eyes, a group of young men whose main interest was poking hilarious fun at the university establishment. They published the satirical *Pixie Press*, dedicating to laughing at tradition and rituals of all kinds. "Joe was so much fun," recalls Richard Phelps. "He was a loving, screwball type of guy, good-looking and popular with the girls."

Saviano grew up in a working-class neighbourhood in Chicago's Little Italy. In 1954 he won a football scholarship to ISU, but he received a bad injury in his sophomore year. Thereafter he couldn't afford to attend university full-time and would work in construction during the summer and fall months, returning to ISU for a semester or two each year. As a result he did not receive his business administration degree until the fall of 1962.

"Colin just worshipped Joe," remembers Gene Ehlert. "I think Saviano was everything that Colin admired and wanted to be." The two men met in 1960 at the fraternity house. The next year they and another student rented a furnished apartment. Joe remembers their time together. "I think Colin and I were enough of a contrast that we enjoyed each other. We grew up in entirely different atmospheres. I grew up as a survivor and I was very self-sufficient—you know, having my own apartment, cooking my own meals was no problem for me. Colin grew up with a lot more affluence than I did. I don't think he had been on his own much; he was a little unworldly."

The young men had worked out an arrangement whereby Joe cooked and Colin cleaned up. "I remember him scraping a great big casserole of macaroni and cheese down the drain. That broke me up for two reasons. One, where I grew up you don't throw food away, and two, you wouldn't push it down the drain. It never occurred to Colin that we might not have a garbage disposal.

"I liked Colin. I really did. He was a different sort of person from me, and I enjoyed that." Joe thought that Colin was quiet, reserved, seldom revealing his emotions.

Joe took Colin Thatcher home to Chicago one Thanksgiving and showed him the sights. Colin was overwhelmed at Saviano's street smarts. "I was very aggressive and assertive, a very confident young man, and I think he looked up to me because of that." At university Joe was often teased about his Mafia connections; he himself would quip that he had been the rear gunner in Al Capone's Cadillac. In reality, however, he was quite sensitive about it. "If some guy wants to think that every husky, brown-eyed, dark-haired, Catholic Italian is a mafioso, that's his problem," he told Colin. Thatcher couldn't help but realize that it was something of a sore point with his good friend.

Neither of the two young men had much money, so they spent a lot of time in groups, talking, drinking beer, and watching television at the fraternity. And, of course, during his first year of graduate school Colin was busy wooing JoAnn Geiger.

"During the year they were going together, he was over every night," says Harlan Geiger. "We had a recreation room in the basement and he would watch television down there. Or they would study together." Betty Geiger never felt very comfortable, mainly because he did things to needle her. "Nancy was only three and he would stop by on the way to the grocery store and want to take her along. But he would always act as though he was treating her miserably, calling her a brat, giving her a real rough time. I don't think he was, because she wouldn't have wanted to go with him. He just wanted to make me feel uncomfortable, for some reason."

"One day I had spent the day putting a fence in our

backyard," says Harlan. "Colin showed up and in a belittling way asked me how long it took me. I said a couple of days. 'Ah, on the ranch we'd drove those posts out there in an hour.' He thought it was very funny, but of course he didn't offer to help me.

"From the time he drove away from here after the wedding, he had never once been back, until after Jo had left him and he came looking for her," Harlan says. "He was invited but he never came, not once. I just think he didn't have any use for us." Years later JoAnn would tell her second husband, Tony Wilson, that one of the things that hurt her the most was Colin's attitude towards her family. "Colin thought that her father was an old twerp," says Wilson, and Thatcher would often remind her of that fact.

In the summer of 1961, on JoAnn's twenty-second birthday, Colin presented her with a lovely diamond ring and the couple became officially engaged. Although Colin would spend another seven months in Ames completing his Master's, JoAnn remained in Moose Jaw and began teaching home economics at Technical High School, a job she did not relish at all.

Her first home was a small, two-room apartment on the third floor of a retail block on River Street. The block was owned by Ross Thatcher and so the apartment was made available to her for a very low rent. One of the first things she did socially was join Beta Sigma Phi, an international sorority that had an active chapter in Moose Jaw. "I didn't know who she was but I offered to give her a ride home from something we were at to do with the sorority," remembers a close friend. "I noticed she was wearing a diamond ring, so I said, 'Oh, I see you're engaged. Is it a fellow from home?' 'No,' she responded. 'He's from here.' When she said 'Colin Thatcher,' I just about fell out of the car. He was always so pompous and arrogant, and she seemed so completely different."

In May Colin returned from Ames and began working for his father at the ranch. For a wedding present, he gave his bride a beautiful palomino called Golden Girl. It was such a spirited, eccentric horse that JoAnn was nervous of her and eventually grew too afraid to ride her. In many ways her experience with Golden Girl would be symbolic of her marriage. In June of 1962, the Geigers drove to Moose Jaw and met

Ross Thatcher for the first time. (They had met Peggy earlier when she and a friend had visited Colin in Ames.) The in-laws became fast friends. "They were very pleasant, vivacious, outgoing. Peggy, particularly, always was a charmer," says Betty. Harlan Geiger was a dedicated Republican (although not a supporter of Ronald Reagan), so that his political philosophy was similar to Ross Thatcher's populist conservatism. It made the two men quite compatible. When the Geigers came to Saskatchewan for visits after Thatcher had been elected premier, Ross would invite Harlan into his office and they'd have long talks about the intricacies of Saskatchewan politics. "They were very, very nice to us, always," says Harlan Geiger.

After staying a few days in Moose Jaw, Harlan and Betty, their young daughter, Nancy, and JoAnn set out for Ames. It was a holiday for them all and before they returned they drove west across the prairies to Calgary, Banff, and Lake Louise. It was a happy and sad time for the Geigers; they were losing the daughter they loved dearly, and they had nagging misgivings about the man she had chosen. And yet she seemed so completely happy. "We never did discourage Jo from marrying Colin. We had the feeling that our kids had to live with the people they chose. If we objected we would only make trouble down the way. We just had to rely on their judgment."

Before Peggy and Ross departed for the wedding in Ames, they held a reception at their home in honour of JoAnn and Colin. Scoop Lewry, mayor of the town, was there. "Ross turned to me and said, 'I hope to God she can do something for him because I've never been able to.'" The Thatchers bought Colin and JoAnn a 1962 Plymouth as a wedding present. Friends of the Thatchers thought that perhaps this was a way for Ross to appease his conscience.

By the time JoAnn returned to Ames in 1962, most of her school pals had moved elsewhere, so many of the guests at the lovely wedding were old friends of the Geigers'. But JoAnn's close childhood chum Thiel Ramsbey, who had married the month before, was the matron of honour. Her sister Nancy and Joan McIntyre, a vivacious young woman she had met in Moose Jaw, served as bridesmaids. Joan's parents, friends of the Thatchers since their youth, were also in

hen I'll commit myself.' He was so afraid of
ple. His bluster is all crust." Eventually the
me the closest of friends. Indeed, McDonald
rrible injustice was committed when Colin
nd guilty of murdering his wife. "I have
for twenty-three years, and I believe that
not capable of committing such a crime."

JoAnn continued to teach home economics
School, a job she loathed. "I can recall
hove her out the door to go to work," Colin
d not enjoy her Mondays to Fridays and her
school. Part of that was because she was
r duties with a teacher whom she did not
was an offensive person." Another reason
as that teaching was far removed from the
dising for which she had been so thoroughly

made about $4,500 a year, Colin insisted
he head of the household, he should be the
didn't want to become accustomed to the
e we knew that I would eventually stay
amily," JoAnn said. So with her wages, she
vings Bonds. "We lived a very moderate
ld call it spartan," Colin once said. "We
then we weren't deprived." He was paid
a month by his father, which was more an
age. Ross felt free to withhold all or part of
ed mistakes or indiscretions committed by
h the young couple's rent was negligible,
sts were covered, there was little left over
r extravagances of any kind.

s, for example, were all the rage among
Moose Jaw in the early '60s. A friend of
"The most you put in was about twenty
u may lose a little on one share but you
other. So you never lost your money, but
rtune, either. The members of the group
to join and he kept saying, "I can't afford
. He didn't have any money. I thought it
ble of Ross to pay him so little. After all,
goddamn ranch."

attendance. And the gregarious Joe Saviano was Colin's best
man.

Saviano had not got to know JoAnn very well. Because she
was Mortar Board, he knew she must be very bright, very
special, but he had no idea whether she was a warm person.
It was only when he and a friend took a duck-hunting holiday
to Moose Jaw three years later that he came to appreciate
her. "She had two men come into her home and stay there for
a whole week. And not one moment during that whole trip
did she make us feel anything other than that she was really
happy to see us there. She was very gracious, and warm. I
thought her a very gentle person."

Saviano was astonished when twenty-two years later he was
grilled on two different occasions by an FBI agent who was
helping in the investigation of JoAnn's murder. By this time
he was a prosperous and successful senior executive for a
Chicago steel company. Since he hadn't seen or heard of
Colin Thatcher since a brief meeting in 1971, he wondered
how his information could help them. It emerged that the
FBI agent was there because over the years Thatcher had
bragged to many people about his important Mafia connection. The name he would always mention was Joe Saviano.

CHAPTER FOUR
THE PREMIER'S KIDS

During his trial for the first-degree murder of his wife, Colin Thatcher described the seventeen years lived with JoAnn: "We had the same strains and stresses that any other marriage has and we, I suppose, had the same trivial disagreements that any other couple would have that are married but we had an excellent marriage by, I think, any standard." Asked by his lawyer Gerry Allbright how long this blissful union lasted, Thatcher responded, "As far as I was concerned personally, for probably sixteen to sixteen and a half of those seventeen years."

While she was alive, JoAnn told a very different story. It was happy the first year, she said to her close friends. But after that she began to realize that she had married a tyrannical man who would brook no argument from his wife or children, a man with a "volatile" temper who, in fits of rage, would kick the kitchen cupboards so often that they bore permanent scars, a man who was emotionally unstable, who one moment could be cracking jokes and the next would sink into the darkest depression. Appeasing, catering, soothing, JoAnn Thatcher somehow maintained the appearance of normality. "As I began to know more about her situation, I was amazed that she could hold some semblance of a life together for as long as she did," says her sister Carolyn. "I asked her one time how she could put up with someone like Colin for seventeen years," recalls Shevawn Desrosiers, "and she replied, 'I came from a family where when you got married, you grinned and bore it. You made it work. It was a career, and it was your responsibility to make it a success.'"

The full unveiling of Colin Thatcher's turbulent personality did not occur all at once. Initially the couple were quite content. After the wedding Colin moved in with JoAnn, who

in the past year had
on River Street in M
once recalled those
marriage, our life-sty
economically. We di
go to a lot of places

At first JoAnn was
kick out of teaching
cattle business. She
tion and bull sales
keeping track of the
dealings that went
husband's rancher ac
was something abou
Anderson. "She wa

In Moose Jaw Jo
friends for them, a
"JoAnn phoned an
Don McDonald, a
and myself had rec
'Sure, we'd love to
he said, 'Hello, D
see, already he
apartment and sat
never met another
have a friend, if it's
was determined
Thatcher.

"A couple of we
'we're not going.'
well, JoAnn's bein
came out and sat i
we never ever hav
kept at it. Phoned
met Colin, I disli

McDonald has
meetings. "Colin
himself, 'Hey, is
whether or not t
to these people,
don't know if thi
out. I'm not gon

be nice to me. T
being hurt by pe
two men did bec
is convinced a te
Thatcher was fo
known this man
Colin Thatcher is

After her marriag
at Technical Hig
almost having to s
once said. "She di
time spent at the
forced to share h
care for, and who
for her aversion
career in merchan
prepared.

Although JoAnn
that since he was
breadwinner. "W
two salaries, sinc
home and raise a f
bought Canada Sa
existence. You cou
had no frills, but
about $200 to $250
allowance than a w
it for real or imagin
Colin. And althoug
after other basic co
for entertainment

Investment club
the young men of
Thatcher's recalls,
dollars a month. Y
make it back on an
you didn't make a f
always wanted Coli
it." And he couldn'
was very unreasona
he was running the

Early on in his ranching career, Ross had hired Abraham Neufeld as his chief herdsman. "Ab was excellent, a super kind of herdsman, looking after the cattle, feeding them, weaning at calving time, taking them to shows," recalls Don McDonald, who was the vet for the Thatcher ranch. "However, it was Ross who put together the herd, bought from all over. But the herd was a disaster. A nightmare—he had all sorts of genetic problems.

"When Colin came back he took over the management of the breeding herd, selecting and culling out the bad ones. He did the very important selection of the bulls. . . . He was excellent at that type of thing. His memory was good. He could remember lines and so on, which you have to do in cattle sales. You fit together genetic pieces in your mind and visualize what kind of a calf you want coming from that combination. He was extremely successful. I think he had one of the top two or three Hereford herds in Canada."

And yet if Colin wanted to paint a barn, buy a piece of equipment, or hire an extra hand he had to ask his father. Don McDonald recalls: "He was paid and treated like a ranch hand, but he had all this responsibility. It was really unfair." It was, however, partly his own fault.

A few years after Colin graduated, his father had handed the financial management of the ranch over to him. After a few months, the books were in utter chaos, with bills not paid and cheques not cashed; after a screaming match, Ross confiscated them and from then on he ran the business from his office in Regina. In 1959 Thatcher had sold his chain of hardware stores, thereby avoiding any conflict-of-interest accusations that might be levelled at the leader of the Liberal party. This meant that the ranch was the family's one large financial enterprise, and Ross was determined that it would be managed properly.

His father's tight grip on the purse strings naturally led to conflict over specific decisions—fundamental points such as the length of time a bull should be kept with cows to ensure the largest calf crop possible, or when the cattle should be moved from one pasture to another. Colin's biggest battles were with his father, but he would sometimes argue with the placid Ab Neufeld, and sometimes even threaten to fire the herdsman. Ross would tell Ab to ignore Colin's rantings. His job was in no danger as long as he, Ross, was around.

As Ross Thatcher grew more successful in politics and the pressures correspondingly increased, he came to rely more and more on the comfort and relaxation his ranch provided. "The big black Chrysler with No. 1 on the licence plate would come down the road," remembers Chuck Deagle, who owns a farm near the Thatchers "and he'd stop at farms all along the way and visit. He used to say it was a wonderful place to get away."

"Ross's only relaxation was sitting on a tractor out on the ranch. He'd do that all day," recalls Don McDonald. "And the other thing he absolutely had to do was go to the cattle auction sale. It was a special time for him."

One day Colin approached Don and asked if he would have a talk with Ross. "He said, 'Dad goes to the Johnstone Auction Mart every Saturday and he buys these damned orphan calves for fifty dollars. The darned things get sick and then our calves [which were extremely valuable, and would sell for thousands of dollars on maturity] get sick. And it's a tremendous amount of work for us. Ab and I talked to Dad about it, but he kept on doing it. Won't you talk to him for us?'

"That was an ordeal because it was Saturday, Ross's special day, and he didn't want to discuss business with me. Anyway he agreed to talk. Without saying anything, he gave me a few moments to make my point. He replied, 'I don't doubt for one second that it's true. It's a bad thing, it's costing us some money, and it's causing them a lot of work. But there's nothing I like more than going to that auction sale. My real reason is to mix with all those farmers and ranchers, get out among the ordinary people and just relax. But I have to have a purpose, and my purpose is to buy those calves. I realize what's happening, and I'm going to keep on doing it.' End of discussion."

Ross meddled in ranch affairs all the time, often to the frustration and rage of his son. Colin would later admit, "My father became distressed at me at many, many things and I often got angry at him. We got along fine as long as we were at opposite ends of the ranch." Peggy Thatcher added, "My husband was a very exacting, demanding individual. My son once said, 'When Dad gives us nine things to do at the ranch and he comes out to inspect all nine, he goes on to ten, eleven, twelve, thirteen.'" Ross Thatcher's executive assistant, the late Jack Harrington, idolized his boss except in one respect—the treatment of his son. He thought it was dreadful. On many occasions, in Harrington's presence, Ross railed at Colin, calling him "stupid, an ass, a jerk. You didn't do this and you didn't do that," Ross would rant and rave.

Part of the problem was that Colin had come home from college with ideas on how to modernize and transform the ranching operation. This took money, and Ross objected strenuously. The father would often voice his displeasure with the son by bawling him out in front of everybody, using the crudest possible language. A cabinet minister in Thatcher's government recalls how Ross asked him to drive out to the ranch with him one day. On the way they talked business quite normally. But the moment Thatcher spotted his son, he turned into a raving maniac and started screaming at Colin through the car window about some perceived error in judgment. A furious Colin jumped into his truck, revved up the motor, and raced at the black Chrysler at an unbelievably high speed. The cabinet minister began saying a prayer, sure that it was all over. Thatcher Junior, however, swerved at the very last minute and missed the car by inches.

The stories of the confrontations between the Thatchers, *fils et père,* became legendary in Saskatchewan. The most famous of these had Ross tongue-lashing his son so mercilessly that Colin went and castrated the prize bull. While this story seems to be apocryphal—as one rancher puts it, "There's not too many bulls would have stood there and let him cut their private parts off"—it illustrates how widespread was the myth.

But the ranch wasn't the only place where Ross would humiliate his son. "Ross never really treated Colin as an adult or an equal. He treated him like a little boy," says Don McDonald. "Colin and I would be sitting in Ross's house and Colin would be talking with his dad. Before the conversation was over, before Colin could finish what he was saying, Ross would turn and start talking to me. I think Ross was so quick that he knew what the end of the story was before it ended, and he wanted to get on with the next one, so he just cut his son off. It was very embarrassing for Colin."

One famous incident occurred in the early Sixties at a political reception in Regina. Ross's trademark was the ten-cent cigar that he seemed always to be puffing on. On this occasion Colin, now in his early twenties, walked into the fancy gathering with a fat cigar hanging out of his mouth. Ross strode over, snatched the cigar from his son's mouth, and stamped on it in front of the one hundred or so guests. "This was pretty humiliating for a big fellow like Colin," recalls a former Queen's Bench judge who was there. "Ross was impetuous and I think the fact his son looked so arrogant and cocky, coming in with that cigar, just got to him."

JoAnn would tell her parents on several occasions that despite the abuse he had suffered, her husband simply worshipped his father and craved his approval. By then, of course, the Thatcher name was perpetually in the limelight and the son couldn't help but revel in the glow.

Ross Thatcher became leader of the Saskatchewan Liberal party in September, 1959, and after only two months, he had pumped vigorous new life into the near-moribund organization. He stomped off tirelessly to one fundraising banquet after another. Stealing a trick from the CCF (the first of many strategies he would borrow from the despised socialists), he declared that henceforth membership in the party would be paid for. As a result the $10,000 deficit was soon replaced by an $18,000 surplus. (During his entire tenure Ross would ensure that the party's finances were in splendid shape, but he also insisted on keeping tight control over them.) This financial rejuvenation produced remarkable bolstering of party morale; for the first time in thirty years, thanks to the energy and grit of their new leader, Liberals felt that they were capable of walloping the hated socialists.

After the 1960 election the CCF members formed the provincial government with a twenty-one-seat majority, but their popular support had sunk to the lowest point since they came to power in 1944. Neither the Social Credit nor the Progressive Conservatives had captured a single seat. It was a promising foundation from which to launch a Liberal comeback.

And Ross Thatcher threw down the gauntlet as soon as he walked into Saskatchewan's grandiose Legislative Assembly chamber. "Ross was an able debater, I couldn't take that away from him," says Gordon Snyder, who was a CCF MLA during and after Thatcher's reign. "But bombastic! You could hear him all the way down the corridor, notwithstanding the padded walls. The doors of the Legislature would swing open and you'd hear Ross rumbling away. You always knew when he was speaking because there was lots of emphasis and lots of volume. He had a happy faculty for antagonizing the Opposition, and of course we usually rose to the bait." Some of these debates were so vicious and disorderly that the Speaker could barely control them. In March of 1963, Thatcher was suspended from the assembly (along with another Liberal) for the day; he had called a government decision "socialist dishonesty," which many people considered unparliamentary and inappropriate language for the leader of the Opposition. "He was showing his contempt for the parliamentary system," says Snyder. "He knew what the rules were. He did it for publicity purposes." A few years later his son would be ejected from the Legislature on several occasions for vitriolic remarks that he refused to retract.

Ross Thatcher took every opportunity he could get to promote his theory that government activity, particularly the creation of monopoly Crown corporations, had nipped the enterprising spirit of the province in the bud. Socialism, he said, was stifling growth and prosperity in Saskatchewan. But as political scientist David E. Smith has pointed out, Thatcher was much more consistent in his anti-socialist, pro-free-enterprise rhetoric than he was in practice. "He compromised his private enterprise commitment on more than one occasion to allay the fear of potential supporters that the Liberals would subvert the most popular policies of the socialists." (Smith, David E., *Prairie Liberalism, The Liberal Party in Saskatchewan 1905–1971*, University of Toronto Press, 1975.) His supporters called Thatcher a pragmatist, while his opponents labelled him an opportunist. Much the same thing would be said of Colin Thatcher thirteen years later.

And nowhere was Ross Thatcher's habit of remodeling policy as he saw fit more evident than during the vicious Medicare debate. In December, 1959, Premier Tommy Douglas announced that his government planned to implement North America's first universal, compulsory, pre-paid medical insurance plan. The Liberals at first opposed it, because of what Thatcher termed the "staggering costs involved and the unprecedented tax burden that will result." At the very least, he insisted, there should be a plebiscite before it was implemented.

Tommy Douglas considered the 1960 provincial election a kind of plebiscite; since the electorate had returned the CCF to power by a twenty-one-seat majority, Medicare was obviously popular. The Liberal opposition to the plan died down almost immediately; even the doctors at that time seemed to realize that the die was cast. But over the next two years, as the details of implementing the scheme were worked out, bitterness grew between the government and the medical profession (egged on, and partly financed, by the American Medical Association, which could see the same fearful thing happening some day south of the border). Taking advantage of this acrimony, the Liberals joined with citizens in Keep Our Doctors (KOD) committees, which were designed to embarrass and pressure the government into compromising its position. The CCF refused to back down, and on July 1, 1962, the day Medicare came into effect, the doctors in the province walked off the job.

Thatcher made the most of this potentially dangerous situation, joining and often inflaming those opposing Medicare. On July 11, some four thousand members of KOD committees from all over the province demonstrated outside the Legislature, which was not in session. They presented a petition to Premier Woodrow Lloyd and several cabinet ministers, then peacefully departed. Inside the Legislative Buildings, Thatcher urged Premier Lloyd to hold an emergency legislative session, then and there. When the premier refused, Thatcher and seventeen of the eighteen MLAs decided they'd have a parliamentary debate of their own. But when Thatcher attempted to throw open the chamber doors he discovered that they were locked. The next day, the front pages of Canadian newspapers showed a grim-faced leader of the Opposition kicking at the door of the hallowed legislative chambers like some spoiled little brat.

Twenty-three days later a compromise was reached between the government and the province's doctors that resulted in a few changes, but left the CCF's long-cherished plan basically intact. Two years later Medicare had become so popular with citizens, and even with most doctors, that the Liberals did a *volte-face*, not only singing the praises of Medicare but suggesting that a drug insurance scheme might be a good idea.

The Medicare controversy had taken its toll on the CCF, however. KOD committees had managed to solidify the opposition in each area into a tight anti-socialist, free-enterprise coalition. As well, the CCF's highly respected leader, Tommy

Douglas, had left provincial politics to enter the national arena; W.S. Lloyd, the man who succeded him, was sickly and away from the Legislature a great deal; and many of the remaining MLAs were tired older men. Ross Thatcher was able to punch home, time and again, that the bureaucracy had grown fat, lazy, and pig-headed under the socialists. It was time for a tough, business-minded government. With the help of a Toronto advertising firm, which advised Thatcher not to use profane language or kick legislative doors, the Liberals put together a slick, effective election campaign in the spring of 1964 emphasizing the supposed economic stagnation of the province. Ranting at the "reds" or "dirty socialists" was not part of it; indeed during the campaign Ross Thatcher behaved like a soft-spoken, dignified bank president.

On April 22, 1964, Ross and Peggy, Colin and JoAnn happily joined the mob at the Trianon Ballroom in Regina to celebrate the ousting of the socialists after twenty years in power. The Liberals had won thirty-two seats, the CCF twenty-six. It was not an overwhelming win, since the Liberals had captured only 0.1 percent more of the popular vote than the CCF. But Ross Thatcher thought it a great victory. As premier he would be able to strut his stuff and stomp the goddamn socialists into the dirt.

FEBRUARY 4, 1965

No one was prouder of the new premier of Saskatchewan than JoAnn Thatcher. Dressed absolutely appropriately in a slim deep-blue skimmer dress, white satin gloves, and a perky light-blue satin hat drawn to one side by a rose, she sat among the guests on the legislative floor as the throne speech was read. Peggy happily took her under her wing, as they attended the teas, dinners, and balls that accompanied the ceremony. JoAnn loved the prestige and the glamour.

She had grown very close to her in-laws in the last two years. To Ross and Peggy, JoAnn had become the daughter they had always longed for. Every Sunday the senior Thatchers would drive from Regina to Moose Jaw, and while Ross went out to inspect the ranch with Colin, JoAnn would entertain her mother-in-law. Often they would visit with friends. "Peggy's a rather shy lady," says Elsie Eade. "She's comfortable in small groups rather than large crowds. That's why it was so nice to visit her in JoAnn's home. She was very human, I mean she was just Peggy, even though she was the premier's wife." Both JoAnn and Peggy had a love of fashion, and occasionally they would go on shopping trips to Regina, Calgary, Vancouver, or even New York. Sometimes JoAnn would take her mother-in-law to Beta Sigma Phi luncheons or to Mother's Day teas. "JoAnn and Peggy were very good friends," says Tony Wilson. "JoAnn certainly enjoyed going around with her mother-in-law. That was one of the dreadful ironies of the whole marriage breakdown. JoAnn felt terribly betrayed by Peggy in the end."

JoAnn also enjoyed an extremely warm relationship with her father-in-law. "He treated her like a princess," says a friend of the family. JoAnn once remarked, "I don't believe that there was a Christmas went by that Ross didn't give me something in the way of stocks and bonds. He was very generous to me." He would give her, for example, twenty-five shares of Bank of Montreal stocks or bonds amounting to five hundred dollars. This went on year after year while he was alive; ironically, it was these savings that later enabled her to leave her husband.

JoAnn's ties with the Thatchers were strengthened by the birth of their first grandchild, Gregory Ross, on June 26, 1965. "I never saw anyone dote on a grandchild like Ross did on Greg," says Betty Geiger. "Ross always had time for him. he just adored that child."

"There used to be a saying: if ever you want anything from Ross, wait until his grandson has been to visit. Then you can get anything you want," remembers Chuck Deagle, who farmed near Caron. "On Saturdays he'd get Greg and they'd stop at Frank Zimmerman's Esso about nine o'clock. Ross would buy ice cream for Greg and then he and Frank would have some great arguments. They'd visit for about an hour and then head out to the ranch and be there until suppertime."

"I remember once JoAnn and I took Greg to see his grandfather at the Legislative Buildings," recalls Elsie Eade. "Ross was having meetings and he would come into this little room and play with Greg, and then he'd go back to another appointment, and then come back and visit Greg. That was a very human side of him. He just adored Greg."

It got to a point where the Geigers, who saw their grandchild a couple of times a year, were worried that he was being spoiled. "Greg was always in high gear, and a very energetic little boy," recalls Betty. "And since he was little the Thatchers never just visited with him, they were always entertaining him or showing him off. He couldn't just be a little boy." "I expressed concern to Betty that they were spoiling him," adds Harlan. "Everything he said was wonderful, everything he did was lauded, and actually they were encouraging him to be a little show-off. I was concerned because of what it would do to him as he moved out with other people."

Margaret Flynn, a neighbour and close friend of JoAnn's in Moose Jaw, remembers an incident when Greg was just three. A number of kids were playing in the Thatcher's basement playroom. Margaret could hear some arguing and then a loud shout: "My dad is Colin Thatcher, my grandpa's the premier, and you'd better let me do as I want!" JoAnn, however, would always tell Greg that he must behave correctly because the Thatchers took so much pride in him. At Ross's funeral the little boy, who was just six years old, stood very quiet and proper. Afterwards he said to his mother, "Do you think Grandpa would have been proud of me?"

Since Colin Thatcher both worshipped and feared, loved and hated his father, JoAnn took a terrible risk when she could not resist the temptation to trade on Ross's affection for her. "I think in a strange way JoAnn was digging her own grave," says Judge Joe Flynn.

Like other friends and neighbours who saw the Thatchers during the 1960s, the Flynns began to notice that JoAnn used Ross to get what she wanted from Colin. Remembers Judge Flynn, "JoAnn came over one day and she said, 'I'd like to have a swimming pool in the back but Colin doesn't want one of those blankety-blank pools because he'd always be raking leaves. I'll have to speak to Ross.' And she did. A few days later Ross called Bump Hudson [a contractor] who gave him an estimate. Ross okayed it and the pool went in—whether Colin liked it or not.

"On another occasion we were invited to the legislative ball and Margaret and JoAnn were talking about it. 'Colin refuses to wear a tux,' said JoAnn. 'I will have to speak to Ross.'" Margaret Flynn continues: "She called us Monday morning and said, 'Guess where Colin is? He's being measured for a tux.' Ross had put his foot down again." And, said the Flynns, when Colin wanted a new car, JoAnn talked to Ross and he got it.

"Ross trusted JoAnn," says Judge Flynn. "She did all the banking, not only for the ranch and for the Thatchers personally, but also for the Liberal Party. Colin wasn't allowed to have anything to do with the business end, he was just on a small salary. He saw that his wife was regarded as trustworthy and he wasn't. I'm sure JoAnn built up a resentment in Colin which he didn't dare speak about. He couldn't do anything, he had to keep it bottled up because Ross would be provoked with him if he did, and he didn't dare incur Ross's wrath."

Other friends uneasily watched the same pattern develop. "I think JoAnn used Ross as a shield against the slings and arrows which Colin began to hurl at her more and more," says another close friend. "And the more this happened the more he mistreated her. It was a vicious circle."

"I'd phone JoAnn up and say bring the kids over and I'll put the coffee pot on," recalls Margaret Flynn, "especially in the winter when the weather was miserable. She'd come over or I'd go to her house. One day we were sitting in the kitchen: Colin had already gone out to the ranch. The back door slammed and in he walked. He had forgotten some papers. She had her back to the door and he walked right up behind her and screamed. "Where the blankety-blank did you put those papers?' Just swore and cursed at her as if it was her fault that he forgot the papers. I just sat rigid in my chair because I was sure he was going to strike her. He was that angry. But he didn't. He walked past her still cursing. JoAnn hopped after him, pleading, 'Oh Colin, I'm so sorry.' To me she said, 'Colin's just in a bad mood.' He was so abusive. I was absolutely shocked and came home and told my husband. He was appalled."

In one of the many court cases that occurred after their marriage had disintegrated, JoAnn gave some idea of what it was like to live with Colin Thatcher. "My husband has a very volatile temper, and he uses very poor language. He does not care whether the children are present during these times.... He has attitudes towards other people that reflect basically, why should I do something for them. They never do anything for me. These are the things that I've tried to buffer in my home. Temper! The children have seen the results of his temper and

I'm talking in terms of plates of food broken against my kitchen cupboard. I'm talking about glasses smashed because he's annoyed suddenly. My kitchen cupboards are scarred from his kicking them so often. When he was particularly violent with me one evening, I locked myself in the downstairs bathroom. The door is still in splinters."

"I didn't think that JoAnn should have stayed with Colin from the beginning," says Marnie McDonald. "I don't think he treated her particularly well. And I wouldn't have stayed with him. But then I wouldn't have got married to Colin in the first place." "JoAnn catered to everybody in the whole world," says Don McDonald. "That was JoAnn. She catered to Ross, she catered to his constituents, she catered to Colin, that was her personality. She would grit her teeth and smile because it was necessary." Interestingly, the McDonalds agree that the marriage actually improved over the years, that Colin became more courteous and civil, at least until the violent end.

In a remarkable way JoAnn Thatcher was able to maintain the facade of a normal happy marriage to the outside world. "JoAnn struck me as an American débutante type when I first met her," recalls Wendy Garrett, who was part of her coffee klatsch. "A little bit affected—so, so, so sweet. Everything was just wonderful. She was so kind and everything was going very, very well. I began to think things weren't so wonderful when she told me how Colin came home filthy from the ranch every day. He would soak in the tub sometimes until late at night, then he would yell at JoAnn and she would have to go and clean the ring away."

Her friends would sometimes be disturbed by the subservient, pandering attitude she displayed towards her husband. "She was programmed," says Darla Spicer. "She would bring him his coffee, bring him his drink, bring him his sandwich if he was sitting watching television." It was the lesson learned in Ames from all those *Saturday Evening Posts* and home economics courses, and JoAnn had learned it well. She remained determined to play the role of dutiful, loving, obedient wife.

"One time Beta Sigma Phi organized a mixed-swimming function with husband and kids at the Natatorium," remembers Wendy Garrett. "We planned to have supper and play games upstairs afterwards and we had ordered in snacks, packs of Kentucky Fried Chicken. JoAnn got the boys' and Colin's all ready, got out the little plastic knives and forks and napkins. Now I don't know if Colin was in an argument with somebody or just bored. But just as JoAnn was sitting down to eat, Colin said, 'Let's go!' and he walked out the door. JoAnn dutifully stood up and followed. 'Oh, oh, okay, Colin.' No questions asked. I felt like telling her to give him a good kick in the behind."

"He was never very nice to her," recalls another close friend of the Thatchers. "He always seemed to be putting her down. . . . He'd come tramping in the house with the manure on his boots. 'JoAnn, where the hell are you, bitch?' Boorish, brash. If JoAnn and I were having coffee I always felt, Oh God, it's time to gather everybody up and go. Because Colin would blow in the door like the north wind. I don't know if she was trying to cater to him, or do whatever had to be done to keep the situation under control."

"She was absolutely terrified of the fuss Colin would make," says Margaret Flynn. "She would do everything in her power to prevent a scene. Everything in her power."

After Ross was elected premier in 1964 and he and Peggy had moved to Regina, JoAnn and Colin bought their Redland Avenue home. Originally the senior Thatchers asked $9,500 for the rambling old house but they then reduced that by $2,000, to make it a very reasonable price indeed. Colin and JoAnn were able to give them cash by putting up their bonds as collateral against a loan at the Bank of Montreal. The house needed some renovating; in particular the couple wanted a den built to serve as an office, and some carpentry work done in the living room. JoAnn paid for a large portion of it by withdrawing the pension benefits she had accumulated as a high-school teacher.

JoAnn did an outstanding job of decorating the Redland house. "She did her living room in an avocado green, which in those days was very fashionable. I remember she had a thick, pale-green shag rug and she used a rake to clean it. There were brass candlelights hanging on the wall and little round tables which were draped to the floor with these beautiful cloths which she made herself. It was really a lovely room, but very traditional," says Wendy Garrett.

The Redland home was a squarish, two-storey structure,

Ron Graham and JoAnn Thatcher became
passionate love affair.

0s, Colin was involved in community activi-
ion of a prominent Moose Jaw family was
He was a member of the Kinsmen's Club, a
r of the Canada Hereford Association, and a
ctor of the Saskatchewan Roughrider Football
love, however, was politics. He was a political
ed in the subject since he was old enough to
-room table. Chuck Deagle recalls: "When he
ng man, Colin would go to the Caron Rural
eetings and ask tough questions. The council-
heir homework because he had done his." In
without his father's knowledge, he ran for the
nd was soundly defeated. In June of 1970, he
n on the Moose Jaw Board of Education in a
lost. But this was small potatoes. His father
le Colin's involvement in politics on a larger
dn't even let Colin play a role, either organizing, in his own riding of Morse.
Ross was premier, Colin was becoming ambi-
and wanted to run," remembers Jack Wiebe,
ted Liberal and farmer who ran Ross's cam-
"I told Ross that Colin's name was being put
of people in the ridings of Moose Jaw North
only comment to me, and he said it in a very
One Thatcher in politics at a time is enough!'"
volved in the mayoralty race between Jack
oop Lewry [in 1963]," remembers a close
s. "About twenty people were sitting around
in the house on Redland and Ross walked in.
going on?' he demanded. Colin said it was a
lect Jack McCaig. Ross said, 'I told you to
it of politics. You get these so-and-sos out of
all left."

is not the only person subjected to Ross
, autocratic style. Because of his vast political
practice of hand-picking most of the people
ral MLAs, and his shrewd, strong, pugna-
y, the premier had a hammer-lock on his

probably built in the early 1900s. In the large foyer, an open
oak stairway curved down. On one side was a pleasant,
celery-green den with French doors, where JoAnn and her
friends liked to sit and have their morning coffee. On the
other side were the large elegant living and dining rooms. Off
the front room was a small, window-enclosed room that
served as the Thatcher's office. The knotty-pine kitchen led
to a spacious and airy family room. Sliding glass doors opened
onto the pool. Upstairs were four bedrooms, including a
good-sized master bedroom and a full bath. The entire house
was done in shades of green with touches of yellow.

After Greg was born in 1965, JoAnn suffered two difficult
miscarriages. In 1966, she carried the baby for about six
months, was hospitalized for nine days, but then lost it.
Eighteen months later she became pregnant again. The
Thatchers found out at three months that the fetus was dead
but JoAnn had to carry it another three months before she
finally aborted it. It was a painful time for everybody. "JoAnn
just felt terrible," remembers a friend. "She was physically ill
and very depressed. Yet she was so kind and patient with
little Greg that I bet he didn't know anything was wrong."

Finally in the summer of 1968 she became pregnant for a
fourth time. The family was apprehensive that she would lose
the baby, but on February 19, 1969, Regan Colin Thatcher
was born. He was a sickly infant. "For most of his first few
months, "JoAnn later said, "feeding was a very serious problem. We had a really traumatic hour to hour and a half every
evening with him being in intense pain, and finally it resulted
in a major operation for him when he was about five months
old. In that time period, I very rarely left the home. If I did
go out, I took him everywhere." JoAnn would later tell
friends she felt that those six turbulent months with the
crying infant had put Colin off the child. He never seemed
very fond of him, and JoAnn would later tell a judge, "My
husband flatly told me that he really didn't feel anything for
Regan and didn't particularly like him at that particular stage
of his development." Ironically it would be over the custody
of this child that the most bitter and devious legal battles
were later waged.

"I wish I could be as good a mother as JoAnn was," says
Darla Spicer. "I never once heard her raise her voice to her
children, never saw her ever lay a hand on them. But she

could discipline them. She would use a tone of voice and they knew she meant business. She could get her ideas across to them without being nasty. She never lost her cool or flew into a rage. I always admired her for that."

JoAnn Thatcher was what women's magazines call a "creative homemaker." She helped her children make intricately designed gingerbread cookies and she always had home-baked goods in her freezer in the event guests dropped in. She was handy with a hammer and able to do excellent carpentry work. A superb seamstress, she sewed slipcovers and curtains for various rooms in her house. She would decorate the house with delightful paper ghosts and witches at Hallowe'en. At Christmas, she made braided bread decorated with holly and ribbon and bells for all her friends. She also found time to jog and swim and play golf. "We played quite a bit," recalls Elsie Eade. "We weren't very good. It took us all day to play nine holes. And then of course we always had children to get home to."

But what JoAnn enjoyed most was talking to people. Her coffee klatsch was wide and various. "I used to pop in and see her two or three times a week," says Darla Spicer, who lives on a farm about twenty kilometres from Moose Jaw. "It didn't matter what she was doing, she always had time for her friends. I'd give her a call. 'I'm in town. What are you doing?' She'd reply, 'I'm painting but come on over, just don't mind the mess. I've always got time for coffee.' And she'd sit there and paint a cupboard while we visited."

After the Thatchers moved into their Redland Avenue home in 1964, they began to entertain more extensively—dinner parties, Saturday-night get-togethers, and occasional Saskatchewan Roughrider victory celebrations. As Colin matured, he learned to be extremely charming in social gatherings. And, of course, JoAnn's college education had emphasized the art of hospitality. Peggy, who was doing almost no entertaining herself, was delighted that her son and daughter-in-law were such gracious hosts. She gave JoAnn a set of Louis XV-style silverware, saying, "My mother bought it after my father's death, piece by piece, every week, and even to the sterling steak-knife and fork." JoAnn had understood that her mother-in-law wanted her granddaughter, Stephanie (born in 1974), to have it one day, so when she left Colin she took the silverware with her. Peggy was terribly upset and bitter

about this; it was one rea[...]
son after the marriage bre[...]

While a variety of pe[...]
occasions, there were cert[...]
both called close friends. [...]
McDonald, Dr. Roger Te[...]
much-liked wife, Rosema[...]
Motors and his wife, Joa[...]
Thatchers, though, than [...]

Ron and Colin had know[...]
had gone through King G[...]
Central High together. [...]
every Sunday morning, v[...]
sidered Ron his closest, [...]
high-school basketball sta[...]
kept him in shape. He wa[...]
and fun at parties, who s[...]
one. Women were fond [...]
interested in listening t[...]
father, Peter, had set up [...]
Company, and Ron joine[...]
university and prospered [...]

Jane Graham was just a[...]
in Saskatoon, she was the[...]
owner and had been a p[...]
beautiful, she was intense[...]
well organized. She took [...]
women's groups, the Mc[...]
Phi—and her schedule w[...]
executive's. "It was a big [...]
have to leave a dance at a[...]
be having a good time, as [...]
designated time, Jane w[...]
home.' Jane could be real[...]
her but she was obviously[...]
be out working." She a[...]
discussed their children—[...]
and together grew disillu[...]

The Grahams and the [...]
dined together every Fri[...]
away. It would shock the [...]

when, in 197[...]
embroiled in [...]

During the 19[...]
ties, as the s[...]
obliged to do. [...]
national direct[...]
Moose Jaw dir[...]
Club. His main[...]
animal, immer[...]
sit at the dinin[...]
was a very yo[...]
Municipality n[...]
lors had to do [...]
the early '60s, [...]
Caron council [...]
ran for a positi[...]
by-election an[...]
expressly forba[...]
scale. Ross wo[...]
ing or campaig[...]

"At the time[...]
tious in politic[...]
a highly respe[...]
paigns for year[...]
forward by a l[...]
or South. Ross [...]
loud voice, was[...]

"Colin got [...]
McCaig and [...]
friend of JoAn[...]
the living roon[...]
'What the hell [...]
committee to [...]
keep your ass [...]
this house.' W[...]

But his son [...]
Thatcher's cru[...]
experience, hi[...]
who ran as L[...]
cious personal[...]

political machine. "If Ross told the whole goddamn cabinet to line up and then jump, they'd ask how high in unison on the way up. They were terrified of him," says a former Liberal MIA. And rumours abound that in cabinet meetings he was so harsh with ministers who displeased him that some of them were reduced to tears.

Thatcher ran the Saskatchewan government as if he were the omnipotent chief executive of a large automobile manufacturer. He threw himself into his work with a frenzy, breaking his health in the process and expecting others to do likewise. His self-confidence was simply overwhelming; once he made a decision it was almost impossible to get him to change his mind.

Tony Merchant, who would himself run for the Liberal leadership some years after Thatcher's tenure, believes that Ross's self-assurance and tenacity was understandable. All the advice Ross had ever received from friends, relatives, and political colleagues about major decisions in his life had been utterly wrong. "He was told not to leave the CCF, that he would just wither, go nowhere politically. Then everybody told him not to take over the leadership of the Liberal party. It had been languishing for so long, he'd never do anything with it. And here he is, the premier of the province.

"He was told by everybody not to expand the hardware business. Ross tricked into the business just at the right time. He was able to buy hardware stores for almost nothing and turn them into financial successes.

"He was told not to go into cattle because everybody was losing money. Ross got into cattle just as red meat took off and sales to Japan took the pressure off the world market. He made a lot of money. So the three major decisions he made, against the advice of everybody, were dead on. He started to believe he knew more about everything than anybody else."

While the CCF had prided itself in introducing innovative social legislation, the Liberal government's main concern was to create an economic climate that would entice private enterprise into a frenzy of activity. Thatcher's administration was to be a tough, lean operation. Each cabinet minister selected in 1964 was required to sign a letter stating that he would resign if his ministry's budget had not been reduced by 10 percent in the next year. Financial matters were of such importance to Thatcher that he had taken on the provincial treasurer's portfolio himself. Indeed government policies became an extension of Thatcher's own personal philosophy. And he had been a penny-pincher from way back. "Ross handled every dollar of government money like it was his own," said Jack Harrington, Thatcher's executive assistant.

One day Harrington noticed a large hole in Ross's shoe. "You know, Premier, you need a new pair of shoes." "Oh yeah, Jack, go get me a pair, will you?" Harrington bought a pair of standard black brogues. When he returned, Thatcher handed him a ten-dollar bill. "But sir, the shoes cost twenty-eight dollars." "Jack, you're a bloody fool. the last pair cost me six dollars. I thought I was giving you something for your time. If you paid more than ten dollars then it comes out of your pocket." And he never did give Harrington the extra eighteen dollars.

A similar modus operandi applied to the administration of the provincial government. The ministry of health had one of the largest budgets, $240 million, in Thatcher's government. Yet the premier was perusing expenditures so carefully one day in 1966 that he called Gordon Grant, minister of health, with an angry question. "What's this $105 for ?" he asked. "I had a bunch of doctors in to talk about negotiating the fee schedule for next year," answered Grant. "They all support us, and I wanted to get it nailed down. I served them doughnuts and coffee."

"Well, let the blankety-blank doctors pay for their own blankety-blank coffee," snapped Thatcher.

There were many who admired Thatcher's fiscal responsibility. "He was fifteen years ahead of his time," says Cy MacDonald, a cabinet minister in Thatcher's government and a loyal devotee. "Everything that Ross Thatcher tried to do, every politician in every government in the world is trying to do today. They're tackling deficits, trying to control wage increases, inflation, Medicare, union power. He was the one Canadian who had the foresight to realize which way the country was going and what needed to be done to prevent it."

But MacDonald and other admirers wish Thatcher hadn't offended quite so many people while he was implementing his vision of good government. He was so arrogant and rude, many people who normally would have whole-heartedly approved of his policies turned against him. Ted Hughes, a former Queen's Bench justice and now deputy attorney general for British Columbia, describes a typical incident. As chairman of Saskatchewan's Hospital Association, Hughes headed a delegation of six members who had driven from many parts of Saskatchewan to talk to the premier about an important health-related problem. After keeping the group waiting for about an hour and a half, Thatcher briskly entered and said, "Gentlemen, I know why you're here. I know what the issue is and I know the problem. The answer is no. No use you wasting my time and me wasting your time."

"He got up to leave," continues Hughes. "But a fellow from the southern part of the province who knew him personally and had been a political supporter said, 'All right, Ross. You're not leaving here on that basis. We've driven from all across the province to see you. Just sit down in that chair, because we're going to tell you our side.' He sat down, we discussed the matter for a couple of hours and thrashed out a resolution. I wasn't in a position to talk to him the way his friend had. He could easily have walked away. That experience always put doubt in my mind about his ability."

If Thatcher was insensitive towards men, he was totally inept with women. "Ross was so scared of ladies," says Roy Nelson, a dedicated Liberal who in 1971 was elected an MLA. "He'd drop his drawers if a woman so much as looked at him." He could never remember the names of the wives of colleagues, even though he had known them for years. "He'd been at our place many, many times," says Kay Nelson. "Roy worked harder for the Liberal party than most people but he [Ross] never knew me. No matter how many times he came to my house, he used to say, 'And what's your name?'"

"At coffee parties or meetings, Ross would speak nicely to the women about weather or something and then go and discuss issues with the men," recalls Jack Wiebe. "In the Morse constituency in that day, it was the custom that women sat on one side of the room and the men on the other. Ross would always wind up a meeting with a short speech and a question period. He would always face the men and turn his back to the women. We used to joke, 'We'll never have to worry about Ross Thatcher having an affair.'"

People who worked politically for Colin Thatcher claim that he was the same, so nervous around women that he would literally break out in a sweat when confronted with a group of them. "I think it's easy for someone like Ross or Colin to get into a situation and totally take control," says Don McDonald, "to take over a meeting or an organization by their presence, their ability to speak, their power, almost to manhandle a group. But they just didn't feel that they could do that with women and so they lost their advantage and became uncomfortable."

In the first three years of Ross Thatcher's regime, the province enjoyed unprecedented prosperity. There were record wheat crops and the Liberal policy of handing out public subsidies to private enterprise had attracted seven new potash mines to the province, while an American firm, Parsons and Whittemore, was in the process of building a multi-million-dollar pulp and paper mill at Prince Albert.

Ross had become friendly with Carl Landegger, the head of Parsons and Whittemore. In fact, Mrs. Landegger liked Peggy Thatcher so much she presented her with a gift of fine jewellery. Peggy in turn passed on an exquisite piece of jade studded with pearls to JoAnn. When it was appraised for insurance purposes, the Thatchers were amazed at how valuable it was.

On one occasion Ross, another cabinet minister, and several government officials went to New York to talk business with Landegger. Thatcher took Colin so that he could experience the Big Apple for the first time. After business was concluded, several of the Canadians thought it would be a lark to tour the seamier side of New York. When they got to the Bowery, however, Colin refused to get out of the car; he was too frightened. Several of the older men guffawed at this, and off they went.

Because of "sound" business deals that Ross Thatcher had made with people like Parsons and Whittemore, he felt satisfied that his government was performing superbly. Jobs had been created, taxes had been cut, and farmers were prospering. Thatcher, who had always complained bitterly of his "razor-thin majority," decided that it was time for an election. "The CCF won't get more than five seats," he told a reporter. "We'll get back to a two-party system, Liberals and conservatives." It didn't quite turn out that way. In the election of October 11, 1967, the Liberals won three more seats, bringing their total to thirty-five. The New Democratic Party (the CCF had by this time changed its name) won twenty-four. The Conservatives were wiped out. Most important, the Liberals captured only 1.2 percent more of the popular vote than the socialists. Ross Thatcher was bewildered and personally hurt by the results.

Gloom and despondency hung over the Liberal administration after the election. In 1968 the economy took a sharp downturn, which soon devastated the province. With an increase in the world supply of wheat, farmers discovered that markets were drying up for their bonanza crops, and prices fell. In the first six months of 1969, their cash receipts dropped 40 percent from the previous year. To make matters worse, so many potash mines had been developed in Saskatchewan and elsewhere that the international market was glutted. Prices dropped and production was cut back.

As government revenues decreased, the Liberals decided on a policy of tight austerity. "Deficit was a four-letter word to Ross Thatcher," says Cy MacDonald, "so he wouldn't consider it no matter what the economic conditions." In the process of imposing stringent cutbacks, Thatcher infuriated large segments of the population. The university community, teachers, labour, the public service all waged mighty battles with the premier. "If there was anybody that wasn't mad at us," says Dave Steuart, the minister of health and Thatcher's close confidant, "it was because we hadn't contacted them."

It was the provincial budget of March, 1968, however, that sent the citizens of Saskatchewan into a collective rage. The provincial sales tax was raised, the purple-gas concept (tax-exempt gas for agricultural purposes) was abolished, and most damaging of all, deterrent fees for hospital and doctors' visits, which would save $5 million in a health budget of $240 million, were established. The NDP called the budget "Black Friday," after the day it was introduced, and the phrase caught on. As the *Leader-Post* reported, "Surprise, shock and anger was the major reaction of people to the 1968–69 budget." The Liberals never recovered from it.

As the criticism of his regime grew shriller, Thatcher became more alienated and even more high-handed and severe in his dealings with people. The frenzied temper tantrums laced with foul language that raged in the premier's office became legendary across the province. Now Colin Thatcher was not only the son of the autocratic premier of the province, he was the son of a premier who was both autocratic and unpopular, and their relationship suffered even more.

Dick Collver, who would later become the leader of the Progressive Conservative party in Saskatchewan and play an important role in Colin Thatcher's life, was at that time a successful young entrepreneur living in Saskatoon. Since he was known to be a devoted provincial Liberal, a group of doctors asked him if he would approach the premier and try to talk him out of the deterrent fees proposal. The doctors felt that the fees were more bother than they were worth and that Ross would commit political suicide by imposing them. Instead, they wanted the Liberals to impose an annual $100 deductible fee to be charged to each family.

"My appointment with Thatcher was for two o'clock and I got there at 1:49. At about two, his assistant told me that the premier was going to be tied up for a few minutes, but he would be with me soon. I sat there and sat there and sat there and at twenty minutes after five, Mr. Thatcher opened the door to his office, stormed out, walked past, turned and looked at me, and said, 'Oh, you must be Collver. Okay, come into my office. You've got two minutes.'

"There I was, a known Liberal, a known contributor, a serious person who had come to talk to him about a real concern that these thirty doctors had, and he gives me two lousy minutes? I didn't walk out. I had enough respect for him and his office to make the presentation. That took me about three minutes. He said to me, 'Those goddamn fucking doctors aren't gonna tell me how to run the province of Saskatchewan.' And then he went into a tirade for fifteen minutes. He finished and I said, 'Thank you very much for your time, Mr. Premier,' and walked off. And I ceased being affiliated with the Liberal party at that instant in time."

The full extent of Thatcher's erratic dictatorial style of government is most vividly illustrated in what came to be known as the Wilf Gardiner–Homecoming '71 fiasco. It also sheds light on Ross's relationship with his son.

Wilf Gardiner had long been a thorn in Ross Thatcher's side. Son of the scrappy Liberal premier who presided over Saskatchewan from 1926 to 1929 and in 1934–35 and then became an influential federal agriculture minister, Wilf had run against Thatcher in the 1959 leadership race. And although defeated, he had raised some pointed issues, especially Thatcher's habit of changing political philosophies in accordance with how the wind blew. This did not endear him to the premier, who did not want Gardiner in his 1964 cabinet of twelve men. But Thatcher was told that it would be politically unwise not to appoint him, and Wilf Gardiner was made minister of public works. "In the first term," Gardiner recalls, "Ross had some opposition from cabinet and caucus. Some people were prepared to speak up and take exception to some things he might want to do. But after he got rid of me and Sally Merchant in 1967, most of his opposition was gone. By the time 1971 rolled around, a lot of ministers didn't even bother going to cabinet meetings. they thought it was no use because Thatcher made all the decisions anyway." Sally Merchant, it should be noted, was the mother of Tony Merchant. A Liberal MLA from 1964 to 1967, she was considered a very able politician who should have been given a place in Thatcher's cabinet. Ross did not hide the fact that he did not select her because she was a woman.

When Gardiner was defeated in 1967, he was offered several government jobs but chose to be a deputy minister of cooperatives, a position he held for three and a half "enjoyable" years until he was asked to head up "Homecoming '71." This was a scheme invented by the Saskatchewan Tourist Association in 1966 to attract people back to the province for a series of celebrations. Municipalities were encouraged to develop projects such as new bandshells in parks, or new museums, swimming pools, or libraries. In each case, the province would match the municipalities' funding to a maximum of $125,000.

By 1970, it was clear that Homecoming '71 had not exactly captured the imagination of Saskatchewan citizens. The preparations for the celebration were languishing, and since an election was approaching Thatcher decided he needed an able administrator to head the affair. Wilf Gardiner was asked if he would take it on. Gardiner was reluctant, but after he had extracted a promise that there would be no interference and no shortage of money, he finally accepted.

Many of the province's cities and towns had chosen to develop several projects instead of one large one. Moose Jaw, for example, had decided on five: a new office building for the

Chamber of Commerce, a pool for the Wild Animal Park, maintenance work in Crescent and River Parks, a summer stage in Crescent Park, and a grand Moose Jaw Air Show, held on July 11, 1971. As long as the total for the grants didn't exceed $125,000, Gardiners office considered this acceptable, and plans were proceeding accordingly.

Suddenly on March 5, 1971, when the deadline for the grants had passed, Thatcher stood up in the Legislature and announced that municipalities were to be limited to only one project each. Gardiner was flabbergasted at the statement. He had drawn up the policy, passed by the cabinet, which had put no limitations on multiple projects. And the applications had already been submitted; many of the municipalities had worked hard on their proposals. So Gardiner refused to back down, claiming that what the premier was trying to do was simply "nuts." During a turbulent caucus meeting in which Thatcher reportedly said he would resign if he wasn't supported in his position, the embarrassed MLAs decided that Gardiner would have to be fired. Many people, particularly Wilf Gardiner, wondered at the time why the premier would make such a fuss about a matter that was not exactly of earth-shaking importance.

It had to do with the premier's son.

In May of 1970 Colin Thatcher had been named to the board of Moose Jaw's Civic Centre, which was the main ice rink used by the city's hockey players. There was a lot wrong with the modern facility—Colin considered it "a dark, dreary place." In 1971, he was appointed chairman of the Civic Centre board, declaring that he would improve the facility. On March 1, he asked city council for funds to put in a lighting system. He was turned down because the councillors had decided they wanted to put the money into Homecoming '71 projects. "We were led down the garden path to the slaughterhouse and our throats were cut with a dull knife," Colin Thatcher said, using rhetoric that seemed excessive for the occasion. But he was so enraged that he complained bitterly to his father. Ross decided that one way to solve the problem was to eliminate four of the five Moose Jaw proposals. So three days after the city council decision, Ross Thatcher rose in the Legislature and spelled out the policy of giving grants to single projects only.

Ross, however, hadn't counted on the obstinacy of Wilf

Gardiner; he could not believe that this underling would buck his wishes. And he was not prepared for the intense media coverage that followed. The party now desperately needed another administrator and approached Les Donnelly, who had been associated with Homecoming on a volunteer basis for years. "I spent a terrible hour or two in the premier's office while he negotiated with me. But I stuck to my guns and he finally agreed to my conditions." The main stipulation was that Wilf Gardiner's carefully planned policy of funding multiple projects be reinstated.

Gardiner was so infuriated at what he considered his unfair dismissal that he resolved to expose the workings of the Liberal party under Ross Thatcher. He purchased a half-hour of air time on CKRM Radio in Regina; among other tidbits, he accused the premier of holding back payments to contractors doing government work until they made significant contributions to the Liberal party.

Thatcher belittled Gardiner's charges, calling them sour grapes, and didn't bother to deny them until three weeks later. Other Liberals, however, did not take the incident so lightly. The province was on the eve of an election and they realized that such criticism could be very damaging. In fact, some members of the Liberal caucus pleaded with the premier not to call the election so soon. The government had at least another year left in its mandate—valuable time to soothe many ruffled feathers. But Thatcher, as usual, was impatient. Conditions to him seemed ideal. Canada's first lieutenant-governor of Ukrainian background had been appointed, so the Ukrainian community that he had wooed so assiduously would be feeling good about his government; the premier's hard work on behalf of the Indians and Métis in Saskatchewan seemed to be appreciated; Saskatoon had been awarded the 1971 Winter Games; Parsons and Whittemore had undertaken to build a second vast pulp and paper mill. Most important, 1971 promised to yield a bumper wheat crop.

The premier called an election for June 23, 1971, absolutely confident that he would be returned with a larger majority.

Thatcher went on the attack immediately, lashing out at the "Maoists, radicals, and super-left socialists" who could be found within the bosom of the NDP. As the campaign progressed, he became even more vitriolic, and even more out of touch with the sensitivities of the electorate. "Ross was not a pleasant person during that time," says Tony Merchant. Part of the reason for his unstable behaviour was his deteriorating health. For years Ross Thatcher had suffered from severe diabetes, which he had struggled to control. "I was emcee at a banquet once," recalls Roy Nelson, "and I was sitting between Ross and Peggy. She said to me, 'Roy, can you hand me Ross's dessert? If you can eat it go ahead, if you can't, replace it with an empty dish.' I replied, 'Can't he just leave it?' She said, 'No, he won't. He's afraid he'll insult the ladies. He'll eat it and it's too sweet. He shouldn't have it at all. But he does it all the time.'" Alcohol was supposedly verboten as well, but he couldn't resist a drink. Many people, including members of the Moose Jaw police force, claim to have seen Thatcher falling-down drunk; no one is sure whether this was the result of drinking too much alcohol or just drinking without taking the proper precautions for a diabetic. "He was hospitalized for his diabetes," related Peggy Thatcher. "Every three or four months he would have to go in. He should have stayed ten days but he would only stay three because he wanted to get out."

In 1969 he suffered a heart attack. "That heart attack was probably the best-kept secret in Saskatchewan," recalled Colin Thatcher. "Several rooms in the Regina General Hospital were virtually sealed off. I don't think his executive assistant even knew." Because of this background his doctor had not approved of Ross's participation in the 1971 campaign. As the pace of the campaign heated up, Colin and JoAnn were afraid that he might not survive to the end.

The NDP had recently elected a new leader, Allan Blakeney, an energetic, intelligent, and persuasive young lawyer. His was not so much a campaign of vitriolic rhetoric as it was a specific criticism of government policy. He had much to talk about: the redistribution of seats in 1970, which was blatant gerrymandering on the part of the Liberals; the supposed sellout of Saskatchewan's natural resources to American multinationals; and the grievances of the many segments of the population that Ross Thatcher had offended.

The election results of June 23, 1971, devastated Ross Thatcher. The Liberals had lost no fewer than twenty seats, their representation on the House falling from thirty-five MLAs to fifteen. Worse, the NDP captured forty-five seats and 55 percent of the popular vote. The Conservatives had collapsed, and almost all their votes had gone to the socialists.

Ross Thatcher told the doleful Liberal supporters who awaited his arrival in the Trianon Ballroom that the overwhelming defeat was entirely his fault. After that he chose to do a most extraordinary thing. He walked into the sweltering NDP headquarters situated in an abandoned supermarket and received a rousing cheer, as he graciously conceded defeat. "My friends, I came to your headquarters for one reason, to congratulate Allan Blakeney on a magnificent election." As he began to leave the stage, the crowd broke into "For He's a Jolly Good Fellow."

This was roughly the way the *Leader-Post* reported the event and the way most NDP supporters who were there that night remember it. But Colin Thatcher would later give an entirely different version to a journalist. "I was there the night my father suffered a very inglorious defeat. I will never forget when only five people would accompany him over to the NDP headquarters. I've never forgotten that night when he had to face those people. None of his cabinet were there. They all chose to be elsewhere. If there was ever, ever somebody alone, it was him. All of us [who went with him] went through the indignity and the ridicule we took from Allan Blakeney and the NDP that night. And I guess I'd like to be there when those people face that particular kind of evening." From that time on Colin Thatcher vowed he would seek revenge from the NDP for his father's defeat and the imagined "indignity and ridicule."

Ross was naturally disconsolate after the election. Worse, when the final Liberal council meeting was held not long after the election, Jim Snedker, the previous Speaker of the House, a colourful and well-liked character, interrupted Ross's speech with "Resign now! Resign now!" in as loud a voice as he could muster. Thatcher decided that he would indeed resign as leader within a year. He told his colleagues that he looked forward to becoming a gentleman farmer.

At 4 a.m. on Friday, July 23, 1971, Ross Thatcher died. During his trial, Colin described the events leading up to his father's death. "He had, he appeared to have come back very well from the election defeat. He was low after the election.

No question. And the day before his death, he was out at the ranch and we had him doing various things. He seemed in a little better health. He seemed, he seemed quite happy and he stopped at my place on his way back to Regina and I had put a pool in not very, not very long before and he was, he was swimming in the pool. It had been a very hot day in July. And I recall him saying so well, "Well, I had a physical. Had my heart checked out. And it got a clean bill of health.' And about ten hours later his heart blew apart in Regina."

An autopsy report indicates that Ross Thatcher died of natural causes. Yet JoAnn, who was considered the most scrupulously honest of people, distinctly told people close to her that Ross Thatcher had committed suicide, that her father-in-law had shot himself in the head.

CHAPTER FIVE

THATCHER OF THUNDER CREEK

JULY 25, 1971

Ross Thatcher's closed-casket funeral was held at St. Andrew's United Church in Moose Jaw. It was a stately and dignified affair, with 1,400 politicians and friends from all over Canada there to pay their respects. Prime Minister Pierre Trudeau, former Prime Minister John Diefenbaker, and many cabinet ministers and senators flew from Ottawa to attend, as well as Harry Strom, premier of Alberta, Walter Wier, former premier of Manitoba, and Allan Blakeney, the new premier of Saskatchewan. The mourners lined up to shake hands and commiserate with Peggy, JoAnn, Colin, and Ross's mother, Marjorie. At the end of the service, as the pallbearers marched slowly out of the church carrying the flag-draped casket trailed by a twenty-foot tribute of white daisies and tiger lilies, the one-hundred-member choir sang "The Battle Hymn of the Republic."

Afterwards, as Colin Thatcher was walking up the steps to his Redland Avenue home, he turned to a friend and said, "You know, this is the first time I really feel comfortable walking through the doorway of this house." It was an extraordinary statement. But while he would also say he never "felt so far down" as he did at that time, it is undeniably true that Ross's death enabled Colin, at thirty-two, to finally come of age.

If there had been antagonism between father and son in the past, it did not surface in Ross Thatcher's will. He left an estate that was conservatively calculated for the benefit of the tax department as being worth half a million dollars. Off the top, $10,000 in cash to each was bequeathed to Peggy, Colin, Greg, and Regan. JoAnn, Ross's brother Clarke, and his mother-in-law Mrs. C.G. McNaughton each received $2,000. A further $195,500 consisted of stocks and bonds, around which two trust funds were set up. The first trust consisted of $65,200; Colin was to receive half the income from that, and his mother the other half. The second trust was made up of the remaining $130,300 and all income from it went to Peggy. The trusts would yield Mrs. Thatcher $9,500 a year. As well, she would receive $12,000 a year from Thatcher's pension plan and $87,000 from a life insurance policy. She also owned the fine house on Academy Park Road in Regina, and under provisions of the will was able to encroach on the estate should she need extra cash. On her death, the trust funds would go to her son. Colin was left 2,419 acres of pasture and grain land and a hundred head of cattle with the option of buying the remaining 175 at a very low interest rate. In fact he purchased these with promissory notes that were never called by the trustees. It appears that it was never intended that he would pay real money; Ross had set it up this way to avoid estate duties.

From then on Colin Thatcher would make all the major financial decisions in connection with his ranch and personal investments. Most important, however, he was now free to pursue his passion for politics, and for power.

In fact Colin had played a role in the 1971 provincial election, not by participating in his father's campaign—which was forbidden—but by assisting his friend Don McDonald, who was running as a Liberal in Moose Jaw North. "He was very front and centre," says McDonald. "He asked, 'Should I be visibly involved?' He was concerned about people's perception of him as being brash and arrogant. I said, 'You bet. You're my friend and if people won't accept me because they don't like you, well, thats's just fine and dandy, I'm willing to live with that.' He took complete charge of the nomination. I was running against a long-time Liberal lawyer and it was tough. When it came to the campaign, he still did door-knocking and he still took a role, but he mostly became an adviser. He was the knowledgeable one, he knew the mechanics of politics." McDonald won by 275 votes against Thomas Gifco of the NDP.

But now it was time for Colin Thatcher to establish himself

as a politician in his own right. The quickest route was via the by-election that would be called to fill his father's seat in the Morse constituency.

Jack Wiebe, a thirty-five-year-old farmer from Main Centre, had managed Ross's campaigns in 1967 and 1971 in a most effective and thorough manner. He was a soft-spoken man admired and liked by people of all political stripes. A week before he died, Ross visited Jack Wiebe at his farm, told him he was stepping down as leader, and suggested that he run in his place. Jack decided he would, so after Thatcher's death he informed the riding executive that he wanted to run in the by-election that was thought to be imminent. Because Wiebe had an idea that Colin might be interested in the nomination, he and a supporter drove to Caron to tell him of his decision. "I'm happy to see you running," said Thatcher. "One thing I promise you. I won't do anything against you for the nomination." Two weeks after this encounter, Colin declared he was throwing his hat in the ring. The person who agreed to nominate him was Bernice Crosbie, a housewife whose in-laws had farmed in the area for years. (Thirteen years later she was to become the chairman of the Colin Thatcher Defence Fund, organized after his murder trial to raise money for his appeal.

SEPTEMBER 13, 1971

At Chaplin Community Hall before a packed audience of four hundred, Colin Thatcher gave his first major political speech. "Tonight, to say the very least, is a difficult time for all of us. We are here to select a replacement for one whom we can never completely replace." As he spoke, it quickly became apparent that his motive for running was not because he had a vision of society, but because he wanted to seek revenge against the NDP and Premier Allan Blakeney. He blamed the NDP's victory for his father's death. "At his last political rally, my father said that the voters had to choose between a construction crew and a wrecking crew. I don't think anyone had any idea how devastating that wrecking crew could be." From this point on, bashing socialists became an obsession for Thatcher, much as it had been for his father.

The Morse Liberals voted for Jack Wiebe in overwhelming

numbers. "I got massacred," Colin admitted. "He had nothing to lose," says Don McDonald. "Colin was very clever about that kind of thing. He knew you could lose and still win. It gave him a great deal of credibility, he established himself, he got up and made a speech, and all those ranchers were really surprised at how well he could speak." Peggy and JoAnn sat in the audience as a show of support for Colin, but after the results were announced, Peggy Thatcher walked up onto the platform, shook Wiebe's hand, and offered him congratulations. The audience gave her a standing ovation. She was particularly fond of Jack, and she told several friends she was angry at Colin for going back on his word and running against him.

Peggy Thatcher didn't want to run as a candidate in the 1972 federal election; she was talked into it by prominent provincial Liberals who thought the Thatcher name alone would work magic. The final push, however, came from Tony Merchant's brother-in-law, Otto Lang, the federal justice minister who was also in charge of the Wheat Board. He phoned her and persuaded her to allow her name to stand in the riding of Regina East where she lived. "It was a mistake, right off the bat," says a close friend of the Thatcher. "She was a sacrificial lamb."

Ross must have rolled over in his grave. For his entire period in office, he had wrestled with the Liberals in Ottawa; the squabbles had grown so intense that it was hard to believe that the provincial and federal parties bore the same name. To make the present situation even more ironic, Ross had always retained a particular dislike for Otto Lang, whom he called an "egghead" and a "communist." For ten years he fought with Lang on many fronts. And yet here was Peggy on the campaign trail singing the praises of the despised Otto. He had done a wonderful job for the Canadian farmer, she said. "The Liberal government's record in agriculture is a success story unparalleled in Canadian history," she claimed, showing more devotion to her party than to unvarnished truth.

In public Peggy had always been so reserved and had languished so much in her husband's shadow that her friends were amazed at her decision to run. "When my husband was in Opposition," she explained, "I was his chauffeur. I drove him for thousands of miles all over this province and attended all meetings with him. I guess a lot of his political interest rubbed off on me." In fact, Mrs. Thatcher had devoted her life to Mr. Thatcher. She tried to keep him on a diet when he got too heavy; she worried about his diabetes; she ensured that he was dressed appropriately for every occasion. She even stopped smoking in public because Ross felt it wasn't ladylike. It seemed to her friends that running for the federal Liberals was one more obligation she felt she had to undergo. "I don't think she wanted to win," said Rynold Gleim, a long-time supporter of the Thatchers. And indeed Peggy campaigned very little—she didn't even attend the two all-candidates meetings held in Regina and Fort San.

Peggy Thatcher was badly defeated. The Conservative candidate, Jim Balfour, received 17,781 votes, the NDP incumbent, John Burton, 15,175, Peggy Thatcher, 7,892. It was not by any means all Peggy Thatcher's fault. Almost without exception, Liberal candidates did poorly in western Canada that election; the party, campaigning on the sleep-walking slogan "The Land Is Strong," won only seven seats west of Ontario and only one in Saskatchewan.

On October 30, 1972, Peggy, accompanied by her son, went to the Legion Hall on Cornwall Street to graciously congratulate Balfour. Colin Thatcher felt that the federal Liberals had wooed his mother relentlessly and then in the middle of the campaign had dropped her. He was furious, and from that point on loathed "the feds" even more than his father had.

After the election, Peggy, embarrassed and exhausted, became something of a recluse. "I lived in four walls," she said some years later. "As a matter of fact my daughter-in-law for the first little while would drive over from Moose Jaw and get my groceries for me, bring them to the house. I just wouldn't go out and then after that I didn't want to go out. I had had the public for long enough. I guess that's what it was.

"I lived like that for a good four or four and a half years. Any time I had an invitation to a coffee party or a cocktail party, I just wrote and said no. I just closed myself in."

Her one comfort during this period was visiting her family. On Saturdays while Colin was at the ranch, JoAnn would have her over to the house and on Sundays she would stay for dinner. "JoAnn once told me that she envied me because I could do what I wanted," recalls a close friend. "She said,

'Every Saturday and Sunday we have to have Peggy. It's not that I don't enjoy having her, but some Sunday I would like to do something just on my own. But I would never, ever say anything. I will have her as long as she wants.'"

Meanwhile Colin was designing his own political future. "Nothing political happened that Colin and I weren't together on. That was one of our great joys, having something new politically to talk about," says Don McDonald. "Colin was kinda hanging on, not making up his mind, when Gary Lane decided he wanted Thunder Creek. 'That ain't Gary's spot,' Colin said and that got him going."

The 1974 electoral redistribution had created a new seat, Thunder Creek, which took in a portion of Ross Thatcher's former riding of Morse, including the Caron ranch. It was a vast sweep of a riding, 115 kilometres north to south, 140 east to west with eighteen villages and two towns. It surrounded Moose Jaw but did not include the city, which had two seats of its own. This was rancher-farmer country where people could appreciate the bluntness and aggressiveness of a Colin Thatcher. "Ross and Colin were my kind of men," says Rynold Gleim. "They didn't hold anything back. If they had anything to say, they spit it out. They didn't beat about the bushes." The ranchers and farmers of Thunder Creek were a rugged, individualistic lot, and although about 30 percent were dyed-in-the-wool NDPers, the rest could be counted on to vote for the anti-socialist party. "Thunder Creek is still the safest Liberal and/or Conservative seat in the province," says Jack Wiebe. And Thatcher of Thunder Creek had an undeniably dramatic ring to it.

Thatcher's first task was to see to it that Gary Lane was checkmated. Lane was a bright, handsome, politically ambitious young Regina lawyer who had been executive assistant to Darrel Heald, the attorney general in Ross Thatcher's cabinet. Lane had already made a name for himself as a politico of Machiavellian inclination. He had run as a Liberal MLA in 1971, winning the seat of Lumsden. But his riding had disappeared in the redistribution shuffle and now he was considering Thunder Creek as a possible alternative. Colin Thatcher quickly sent out a letter to Liberals saying in effect that the party really didn't need any more Regina lawyers in a farming constituency. It went a long way to discredit Lane as a candidate. "Gary just backed right off," remembers Rynold Gleim, "which was a good thing. Under no circumstances would he have got the nomination as long as there was a local man running." (Lane ran and won in the riding of Qu'Appelle as a Liberal in 1975 and as a Conservative in 1978 and 1982; at this point he was named attorney general of Saskatchewan, a post that would bring him into unexpected contact with Colin Thatcher.)

But even with Lane gone, it was clear that there would still be a fight for the Liberal nomination. Two well-known, well-liked farmers, Randy Devine and Percy Lambert, entered the race. Both men had been active in Liberal politics. Randy Devine (now deceased) was the brother of a politically promising man named Grant Devine, and vice-president of the Thunder Creek Liberals. Early on, Thatcher himself had approached Lambert and asked him if he wanted to run. "We don't need to import a lawyer out of Regina. We need a farmer," he said, but Percy Lambert replied that he wasn't interested.

"It wasn't long after that that Colin was campaigning for himself," recalls Lambert. "If I wasn't going to run he would. Quite a few people contacted me and said Colin couldn't win the seat because of his abrasive personality. They said, 'You're the best known, you run.' So I did."

Rynold Gleim, who was chairman of the Liberal election committee in Thunder Creek, had already taken both Devine and Lambert around to meet the constituents in his part of the riding when Thatcher first came to him. "All I'll do is introduce you, and the rest is up to you. I'm not favouring anyone," Gleim told him. Thatcher responded, "That's all I'm asking. I just want you to get me acquainted with the people."

The winter of 1973–74 was severe, which made campaigning especially difficult. "Percy had a bunch of cattle, so he was stuck on the farm looking after them," remembers Rynold Gleim. "He couldn't get out all winter to do any more campaigning. And Randy was never able to get around, either." Colin Thatcher, on the other hand, had hired hands to do the work and he drove a powerful four-wheel-drive truck. "He could get anywhere, even over those snowed-in back roads. He'd stop and visit and drink coffee with people, usually in their kitchens. He was a farmer and they were farmers; some of them had bought purebred stock from him. They had a lot in common right off the bat. And he'd go back and back to those who he knew weren't supporting him. And by golly, I bet he switched 60 to 70 percent of them. Of course, he wanted the nomination worse than the other two."

The nomination meeting was held at Peacock High School in Moose Jaw on February 23, 1974. It was a cold blustery night; Highway 42 was closed and much of the area was blocked with six feet of snow. Yet interest in the Thunder Creek nomination was so high that 450 Liberals turned out to hear the three candidates make speeches and then to vote. "On the platform Colin Thatcher was a good speaker," says Gerry Weckman, who became president of the Thunder Creek Liberal Association after Lambert stepped down to run. "He would be uptight and nervous before, but if he really wanted something he would knuckle down and do a good job. His nomination speech was just really classy compared to Percy Lambert's or Randy Devine's. He just demolished them." Many people thought that Colin would get the nomination, since Thatcher was still a revered name in that community, but there was general surprise that he so completely overwhelmed his opponents. Devine received 60 votes, Lambert 154, and Colin 236. "Quite a bit of Colin's support lived near Moose Jaw and could get in. My support didn't get there because of the roads," says Lambert.

Even though she was again pregnant, once Colin decided to run, JoAnn became deeply involved in his political life. "One night in January [1974], there was a cabaret in Rouleau, and some of our friends had gathered here at our home for cocktails before going to the dance," remembers Adelaide Weckman. "It was really a stormy night. The doorbell rang and I answered. There were Colin and JoAnn. I hadn't met either before. I said, 'Whatever are you doing here on a miserable night like tonight? Anyway, come on in, we're just having a drink and you can join us.' So that was great. He met some Rouleau people and we met JoAnn. She was pregnant [with Stephanie], just a week or so to term. I sat beside her that night and we talked as though we had known each other for ages." JoAnn became so close to Adelaide and Gerry Weckman that she turned to them for much-needed help during her matrimonial battles with Colin.

Over the years JoAnn had become involved in Moose Jaw's community activities. She belonged to a number of sororities, the Kinettes, the University Women's Club. She canvassed for the United Appeal and worked on the Canadian census. And in March 1973 she coordinated the Saskatchewan regional finals of the Dominion Drama Festival, held in Moose Jaw. It was a big organizational job, but she did it so expertly she was presented with a silver tray as a token of appreciation. She possessed all the qualities of an ideal political wife.

"JoAnn felt so strongly about roles," says Don McDonald. "The role of the premier's daughter-in-law is this and I will do it. The role of an MLA's wife is this and I will do it. Come hell or high water she would do what was expected. During Colin's campaigns, she'd go out to Bethune or wherever and knock on doors. She didn't like it, it was tough on her having to meet all those strangers, but she did it and did a beautiful job. She felt it was her duty.

"She gave Marnie [McDonald] a hard time because she didn't feel that Marnie was fulfilling the role of the MLA's wife properly. She took it upon herself to tell her what to do, what to wear. JoAnn got really upset because Marnie wasn't going to wear a hat to the opening of the Legislature. And the second opening of the Legislature, Marnie decided not to go at all because she would have to take a day off work. It didn't matter to me that she wasn't there, being on show. She had gone once before and she had her own career to look after. But JoAnn was really upset. You're in a role and you are supposed to perform."

"Colin would blast off about something," says a close friend. "He would open his mouth to change feet. JoAnn would come along and smooth all the ruffled feathers. In any of the political circles, I don't think you'd find anyone who didn't like her, because she was so gracious. She was a real asset to Colin." But while Colin Thatcher could count on his wife's support he could never count on her vote; JoAnn never became a Canadian citizen.

During 1974 and the early months of 1975, as rumours of an election floated about, the Thatcher household was absorbed in politics; the Redland house was the centre of action. Betty and Harlan Geiger and their daughter Nancy had come to Moose Jaw in August of 1974 for a visit, and one day the Geigers, JoAnn, and the four children drove north to Saskatoon to visit an agricultural museum. They returned in the evening to discover the house filled with partying people. JoAnn, who had been told that a small committee would be meeting, was surprised to find a crowd of forty, swimming and dancing and doing everything but holding a political meeting.

"She and Adelaide Weckman just pitched right in," recalls Betty. "They brought out pizzas and other stuff that Jo had made and then frozen for just such occasions and really put on a good spread. Colin was relaxing in the pool and he'd yell, 'Jo, bring me a drink.' I felt like saying, 'Oh, go get your own drink.' I kept thinking to myself, 'Jo, you're a fool to do this.' But she would do anything to keep him from making a scene. And he knew it."

The months of speculation came to an end when Premier Allan Blakeney finally called an election for June 11, 1975. The race in Thunder Creek was not the piece of cake that Colin Thatcher had been predicting. It turned into a tough three-way fight.

Jim Murdock, a large, sandy-haired farmer in Central Butte, could trace his socialist roots back even farther than the CCF; his father had been active in the Farmer–Labour Group back in the early 1930s. The CCF took power in Saskatchewan when Jim was only thirteen, and CCF leader Tommy Douglas became and remained his idol. In 1971 Murdock was heavily involved in politics, managing Paul Beach's NDP campaign against Ross Thatcher in Morse. "We ran a hell of a good campaign against the premier. We had a tremendous number of workers and enthusiasm, although deep down we realized that we couldn't beat him." Beach did, however, manage a surprising 2,783 votes against Thatcher's 3,502.

In the 1971 by-election, Murdock himself ran in Morse, losing to Jack Wiebe by 400 votes, not an ignominious defeat by any means since Wiebe was perceived as an anointed successor. Now Murdock was willing to run in Thunder Creek. "I was at the age when I was pretty gung-ho. Nobody seemed to want to get involved in Thunder Creek in the next election, so I agreed."

By 1975, the mood of Saskatchewan in general and of the cattle country of Thunder Creek in particular was growing more conservative. If Murdock of the NDP had been Thatcher's only opponent, the race might have been an easy entry into politics for the ex-premier's son. But the candidate for the Progressive Conservatives had developed into a surprisingly strong challenger. For one thing, everybody liked Don Swenson, a quiet spoken Baildon farmer who was well known for his experiments in irrigation and for his ability as a keeper of leaf-cutter bees. Don and his wife Dorothy were an unusual species of political animal in the province, dedicated Progressive Conservatives since their youth, they were among the few who did not desert that party as it faded from the provincial scene. As president of the provincial Progressive Conservative Association, Don insisted that the party field a full slate of candidates. "Thunder Creek was a brand-new riding and I couldn't very well shirk my responsibility and not run," he said.

During the winter and spring of 1975, the three candidates knocked on every door they could get to, drank gallons of coffee and ate pounds of homemade cookies. "We travelled over fifteen thousand miles," recalls Swenson. "I spent too much time talking to people. My people would tell me, 'Don't cross the doorstep.' Well, you can't go to a rural home without sitting down and having a cup of coffee. Anyhow, how are you supposed to find out what people believe if you don't talk to them?

"One time JoAnn Thatcher and I were campaigning in the same village at the same time. I didn't know that she and her team were there. I was in a house talking to the owner when JoAnn suddenly came up. I said, 'Gee, I'd better step in the other room for a sec.' So she came in, and as she was making her pitch, I walked into the room. It was very, very embarrassing for her. She said, 'Well, Don, we had a notion you were in town today because your stuff is in the mailbox. I have given instructions to my people *not* to lift it." It was common practice for Thatcher—and many other candidates—to steal opponents' campaign literature wherever possible and destroy it. "My opinion of JoAnn went up quite a bit," says Swenson.

The Thatchers decided to buy a trailer, set it up on Main Street in Moose Jaw so that it could serve as campaign headquarters, and sell it after the election. "JoAnn phoned me one day," recalls Adelaide Weckman," and said, 'Do you suppose you and Gerry could come in? There just isn't anything happening here.' She was at the trailer, didn't know what to do, and of course Colin wasn't any help at all." Eventually a young woman was hired to supervise the headquarters and Rynold Gleim served as campaign manager. "Sure, it was a good campaign," says Gleim. "I don't know if we were to do it over again what we would have done differently." The Thatchers both threw themselves into the job of getting Colin elected. "It was an all-day, every-day thing," JoAnn once said. "I remember one particular time when we met each other coming in the door at eleven o'clock at night and both had been on the road since eight that morning."

Some people thought, however, that Colin's abrasive personality was losing him votes. "He sometimes made enemies," recalls Adelaide Weckman, "and we would go behind and say, 'Never mind what he's like on the surface, he'd make a real good MLA.' We had to sell him in a much different way than we would do when we were trying to sell another candidate.

"One time we organized a cabaret in Rouleau for Colin. We went to a lot of work and I think when it was all over Colin had turned off as many people as he had impressed. We had hired a local orchestra, a great favourite around here. The first thing that happened was that Colin was going to ream them out because they hadn't set up their instruments on time. The next thing, the bartenders were too slow and Colin was going to clean house in that department. After that, we ran out of mix or something and according to Colin, someone else was going to get it in the neck. We finally said, 'Colin, please just go and make some friends. Never mind getting all upset. Everyone else is happy.'"

A debate before a packed audience at the Central Butte High School auditorium was by far the most exciting event of the campaign, especially when it turned into a verbal brawl between Thatcher and Murdock. Thatcher's speech, typically, was a biting, vicious attack on the NDP government and in particular on its land bank legislation, considered a cornerstone of the government's philosophy. Basically the plan allowed farmers, especially those who were retiring or ill, to sell their land to the government at market prices. Young, low-income family farmers with little capital to expand could then lease the land at reasonable prices. Another important objective of the land bank scheme was to allow a farmer to pass on his land to his son without hopelessly weighing the younger man down with debt. At the end of five years, the renter had the option of purchasing the land.

"Thatcher came out with both guns blazing like some dude in a grade-B cowboy movie. The government was going to end up owning all the valuable land in the province, we'd soon all be working for the state, it would be just like the Soviet Union," says Dennis Platt, a farmer in the area. "Nobody mentioned that he'd been left some fifteen sections by his father. He didn't have nightmares about how he was going to repay his bank loan."

Jim Murdock did mention, however, that the Liberals under Ross Thatcher never did a "damned thing for the young farmer." "All the time the Liberals were in power we never had one program to help the farmer, not one." He then recited a long list of NDP achievements. Thatcher's retort to that was more socialist bashing.

"I'd say Don Swenson was the winner of that debate," says Rynold Gleim. "He didn't say very much, he just followed on behind, talked common sense, and slipped right up the middle. If the campaign had been another week or ten days longer, Swenson would have won it for sure."

Since the Tories had been an almost non-existent party for so long, Swenson had only a skeleton organization when he started. As a further handicap, as the election grew near he had to get his spring seeding under way. "I felt that economically we still had to make a living on the farm. Maybe I would have been better politicking than farming." A couple of weeks before the election, Thatcher began to wage an intensive, expensive advertising campaign, primarily on radio, which warned over and over again. "Don't split the anti-socialist vote, don't throw your vote away. Vote Liberal." Swenson felt that the commercials hurt him badly.

On election night, June 11, 1975, the Thatchers and their friends gathered in a banquet room on the second floor of the genteel old Grant Hall Hotel in Moose Jaw to watch excitedly as first place see-sawed between Thatcher and Swenson, with Murdock occasionally grabbing the lead. It was a full two hours after the poll closed before Thatcher could say with some certainty that he had captured the seat; it wasn't until

11:30 that it was official. Thatcher had won by 292 votes. The final count: Colin Thatcher, 2,640, Don Swenson, 2,348, and Jim Murdock, 2,036.

It had been a tight three-way race, and it demonstrated dramatically just how serious Thunder Creek constituents were about their politics; a full 86 percent of those eligible turned out out·to vote. Thatcher won in the rural areas and the Canadian Armed Forces base, Swenson in the larger towns, and Murdock in the parts of the riding that had traditionally voted NDP. In the village of Caron, where the Thatcher ranch was located, Colin and Swenson each took fifty-seven votes while Murdock managed forty-one. Thatcher was upset when he discovered that he had lost the polls located directly around his ranch; he knew that his father had always won them. Adelaide Weckman recalls his reaction: "Now instead of his attitude being, 'Gee, I've done something wrong there, I'll have to sharpen up,' he ranted, 'I know what I'll do with those guys. I'll bring some manure and drop it on them.' He had a real get-even attitude."

The province-wide results must have seemed ominous to a newly elected Liberal MLA. Although the NDP had dropped a full 15 percent in the popular vote, the party maintained a healthy majority, taking thirty-nine of the sixty-one seats. The Liberals' strength dropped from 43 to 32 percent, though they remained the official Opposition with fifteen seats. But it was the Conservatives who had made impressive gains, their percentage of the popular vote soaring from 2 to 28 percent. As well, they captured seven seats. The Tories were obviously the party on the move. Colin Thatcher was impressed.

CHAPTER SIX

AN EXCELLENT MARRIAGE

Canada's emerging women's movement was not a subject that JoAnn and her friends in the North Hill coffee klatsch discussed a great deal. Yet each one of them would be directly and sometimes painfully affected by the revolutionary ideas of feminism. "For years the talk had been about children and recipes," says Wendy Garrett. "Then it was: you hit thirty and you have to do something with your life. So all the housewives turned into professional women, all of a sudden."

Elsie Eade went back to university, then taught high school. Rosemary Tessier, a nurse, began working in her husband's dentistry office, while Wendy Garrett returned to teaching grade two. And Jane Graham, the former physical education teacher, threw herself into the world of computers. "At one point Graham Construction had expanded, so they needed someone else in the family on the payroll," says a close friend. "Jane refused to go on the payroll unless she had a job. Ron said she couldn't have one because the only opening would occur when the company established a computer centre. So Jane went to Saskatchewan Technical Institute [in Moose Jaw] and learned about computers. And she became an absolute whiz."

But none of the women would experience more upheaval in their lives during the Seventies than JoAnn Thatcher.

After Regan had grown out of his difficult infancy, JoAnn began to think seriously about a professional career. Then in the spring of 1973, she found herself pregnant once again. She obviously wasn't overjoyed about it, because she told very few people. One of her closest friends noticed that her shape had changed. "Haven't you put on a lot of weight recently?" she teased. JoAnn replied, "I'll lose it all in a few months."

Stephanie Ann Thatcher was born on January 7, 1974. JoAnn was going on thirty-five and was just a little resentful. "She complained about it," recalls Don McDonald. "Not that the Thatchers didn't love Stephanie; they loved her, of course, she was a beautiful little girl. But it really cramped their style. JoAnn couldn't continue to do the things that other women her age were doing because she was tied down with a baby. It certainly limited her freedom, and it really put her into a depression."

"I think JoAnn was going through what a lot of women went through at that time," Colin said. "She indicated that she wanted to do some of her own things and that the boys were getting older and she wanted to prove that she could do some things for herself. She would say, 'You've got your ranch, and your farm. You've got your politics. I really haven't got anything and I want to do something for myself.'"

It didn't help that once Colin plunged into politics he took even less responsibility for rearing his children than he had previously. "Colin was gone entirely during the week," JoAnn once explained. "He was gone before the children were up. He did not come home for meals in the middle of the day unless the Legislature was sitting, in which case he would get something to eat quickly, change his clothes, and go to Regina. Sometimes he would come home for supper, but often he wouldn't.

"I never expected him or counted on him for anything in relation to the children. I did not count on him getting Regan to his hockey games or other things. It was expected of me. Colin mowed the grass, shovelled the walk when it snowed, and maintained the swimming pool in the summer. That was the sum total of his contribution."

Margaret Flynn concurs: "Colin never changed a diaper, never gave one of those kids a bottle, never did anything for them. I can tell you that with absolute certainty." Colin Thatcher may have felt able to swear at his murder trial that his was an excellent marriage; clearly JoAnn felt it hardly lived up to the dreams of her young womanhood. As years went by she felt she was not so much the happy young mother on the cover of the Sears, Roebuck catalogue as she was some character in an Edgar Allan Poe story.

* * *

During 1974–75, JoAnn took a university credit course in basic accounting at the Saskatchewan Technical Institute and received top marks. After that she handled the bookkeeping duties, including complicated tax returns, involving the ranch, the household expenses, Colin's political affairs, and R.T. Holdings, which managed Ross's estate; JoAnn was its secretary-treasurer. She was not exactly fascinated by the intricacies of ranching, however, a fact that her husband resented. "If there was a reason to come out, such as driving Greg, JoAnn would do it. But as far as coming around and just having a look at what we were doing, I would have to say she wasn't the least interested. She never did any work on the farm, manual or otherwise," Colin said. It was one of several sore points in the marriage that would develop into serious wounds as the Seventies progressed.

Ever since the happy college years back in Iowa, JoAnn's first love had always been interior design, so it was in this field that she decided to make a career for herself. Under her supervision, the Redland Avenue home had been beautifully renovated, a family room added, a swimming pool built, and the kitchen expanded. JoAnn not only planned the refurbishing but did much of the decorating herself, so that she was considered something of an arbiter of good taste in Moose Jaw. By 1971, she was giving lectures to groups like the United Church Women on the fundamentals of interior decorating. She took courses at the Saskatchewan Technical Institute on design. "She'd help anybody," says Darla Spicer. "I'd bring my wallpaper book and she'd say, 'Now, what look to you want? I think this would look best with what you have in your room.' She was very talented that way."

In the fall of 1976 she took out a business licence in the name of "Interiors by JoAnn." It was strictly a part-time affair, run out of the Redland home, and she only made between $2,000 and $3,000 a year after expenses. But by everyone's account she was a resounding success.

Ron Graham was her first client. The construction company was renovating its head office in Moose Jaw and JoAnn was asked to coordinate the interior. Before she received the assignment, however, Graham asked Colin Thatcher's permission, and Thatcher agreed, reluctantly. "I didn't think there was any market for interior decorating in Moose Jaw.

But she did an excellent job of decorating Graham Construction. She seemed very happy at this point. I was delighted with the way the situation was going," Colin said.

As the business developed JoAnn was consulted on the interior design of private homes; she furnished the model home in a new housing development; she chose the drapes, rugs, and other amenities for a senior citizens' residence. And in the fall of 1978, she created the interior of a posh new restaurant called the House of Oak. The building, formerly a beautiful old home, was situated on Langdon Crescent, which curls around Crescent Park and the city's main library, through one of the loveliest areas of Moose Jaw. The house had been owned by Ken Doraty, once a player for the Toronto Maple Leafs hockey team and a former coach of the Moose Jaw Canucks. When two friends of the Thatchers, Lorne Humphreys and Gord Eade, bought it in 1978, JoAnn was hired. She chose muted forest-green materials for the chairs and carpets and tastefully traditional Tudor-style furnishings that complemented the heavy oak woodwork found throughout the house.

"Classy" was the rather inelegant word most people used to describe her work and to describe JoAnn herself as she approached forty. "She wasn't beautiful, really," says a friend, "but she had a presence—people noticed her when she walked into a room. For one thing she was always so beautifully made up, so beautifully dressed." Some people had difficulty breaking through her aloofness, a natural reserve that she had possessed as a child but developed even more as a politician's wife. She was regularly accused of snobbery, pretentiousness, and putting on airs. "She always sat with her ankles neatly crossed, her hands placed in her lap, her back perfectly straight. She was just never the kind of person who sprawled. I can't imagine her lying on a couch with her feet up."

There were many, however, who saw beyond the cool facade. "JoAnn had a soft, gentle ladylikeness, a sense of grace, and this was reflected even in her voice," says Shevawn Desrosiers, who worked with her. "She was very precise in the way she spoke," says Betty Gooding, another friend. "You would almost expect that she would have been an English major, she was always so descriptive and flowery when she talked about things. It was a real joy just to sit and listen to her. She was one of the most pleasant people I have ever met."

of the world and it's a backwood. I am rotting in this town.'
She said she should never have stopped working and come to
Moose Jaw because it put her out of the mainstream." JoAnn
denied feeling so strongly about it. "I used to like Moose Jaw
very much," she said. "It's the people who make the
place. . . . What was suffocating me was my husband."

Colin Thatcher's personality was so overwhelming, his immediate personal needs so intense, that his life-style dominated
the Thatcher family. JoAnn was keenly aware of this. But it
was only later that she realized that despite her husband's
ability to manipulate the media into portraying him as a
Canadian version of J.R. Ewing, with all J.R.'s worldliness
and sophistication, he was a very provincial person, and so
was she. Tony Wilson, JoAnn's second husband, paints a
revealing protrait of Thatcher. "Ironically, he went around
telling everybody how rich he was, but he lived the most
impoverished spiritual and cultural life that one could imagine. He was the most parochial person. His food consisted of
roast beef or steak and two vegetables, always. He watched
television and he seldom read a book. If he did it was a novel,
some thriller. His education was pathetic. He knew nothing
about music or theatre or anything like that. He had never
travelled. And of course, JoAnn was the same."

But it was not Colin's perceived parochialism that alienated
his wife. There was something far more sinister. She realized
that without the restraint of his father, his arrogance was
becoming awesome, his skill at manipulating people more
accomplished, and his refusal to be hampered by any ethical
constraints more disturbing. "I had listened to him talking on
the phone about some of his ruthless business deals," says
JoAnn's sister Carolyn. "And I heard him say things like, 'Boy,
if I'd known they were going to say that, I would have done
this.' He would have manipulated whatever he had to manipulate to get the outcome he wanted. In business deals he was
very shrewd, and it didn't seem to matter if something was
ethical or not. I'm not saying it was illegal, but there was a
question of ethics. He would do whatever would get him
what he wanted."

Like his father before him, during the 1970s Colin Thatcher
could boast of success on many fronts—his political career, his

farm operation, and his personal wealth. Perhaps he began to feel that he too was omnipotent.

The 2,400 acres of land that Ross had left to Colin was primarily pasture for the grazing of the Thatcher herd. In 1972 Colin bought a half-section on which to grow oats as cattle feed. In 1974 two grain farms north of Caronport became available. Thatcher quickly raised a $313,000 mortgage with the Moose Jaw Credit Union and snatched up the two sections. Land prices, which had hit rock bottom during the early 1970s, suddenly took off. "In a few years, that property increased in value four or five times," says Chuck Deagle, a nearby farmer. The following year Thatcher purchased another quarter-section of grain land for both Regan and Gregory, partly with the money left to them by their grandfather. The grain operation, which consisted of some 986 acres of top-grade wheat, yielded ready cash that could either go back into the ranch-farm operation or provide the Thatcher family with a more affluent life-style.

The cattle business flourished as well. Thatcher estimated that in the early Seventies the size of his Hereford herd was in the top 10 percent in the country. "The Thatcher herd was one of the best in this province. Colin knows cattle and he wouldn't keep anything around that wasn't producing quality," said Harold Lees, general manager of the Saskatchewan Hereford Association. And in 1977 Thatcher Farms won not only the grand-champion horned Hereford bull, considered a great coup, but also the grand-champion pair of bulls. "It was an achievement that Ross Thatcher would have given his eye-teeth for," says Les Allen.

In 1971 Ross Thatcher had imported a few Simmentals from Switzerland, just in time to watch the market in exotic cattle explode. "It was a very short bubble, but fortunes were made and lost on exotic cattle in that period of time," said Colin Thatcher. His old college pal, Joe Saviano, remembers that Thatcher did very well from that bubble. "In the early 1970s Colin phoned and said he and JoAnn were coming to Louisville, Kentucky, where I was resident salesman for Inland Steel, to sell a bull. He explained these bulls were from Switzerland. The United States wouldn't allow them in without going through a lengthy quarantine, but this did not apply if the bulls came in through Canada. And the best breeders wanted the Canadian bulls. I felt that JoAnn and

Colin were prospering because I can remember those bulls sold from $75,000 to $100,000 each."

After 1976, Colin Thatcher himself made all the decisions, minor or major, pertaining to his ranch, for in that year he parted ways with Ab Neufeld, his father's loyal herdsman. The parting offers a telling glimpse of Colin Thatcher in action.

One evening after the Legislature had adjourned, Thatcher's Liberal colleague Roy Nelson was waiting for Colin to get off the phone so they could go to dinner. "He was yelling, 'Get your bags packed and get the hell out of there. I don't need anything from you, you son of a bitch, you be out of there when I come home.' Slam, he hung up. I asked, 'Colin, who were you talking to?' He said, 'The hired man. The bastard's been there for twenty years.' I responded, 'Do something for yourself. Get on the phone and tell him you'll talk it over with him tonight.' 'To hell with that,' he replied. 'That bastard thinks he's running the place. He's telling me what to do. I'll show him. Let's go and eat.' Ab Neufeld had a job the next morning. They said he was the best cattleman in all of Saskatchewan."

In February of 1978, Neufeld sued Thatcher for what he claimed was money owing him. Ross had never paid Ab much more than minimum wage, as well as providing a drafty farmhouse for his family to live in. But almost every year he had given Ab a bonus, depending on how much the ranching operation yielded. Neufeld claimed that he had an oral agreement with Colin Thatcher to receive a commission of 2.5 percent on the net proceeds from a large dispersal sale that Thatcher had conducted in October of 1976. Neufeld had received an accounting of neither the sale nor the commission. Thatcher admitted that Neufeld often received bonuses, but insisted these were "granted solely at my discretion." On this occasion, Thatcher arbitrarily decided that Neufeld would not get his bonus. The action fizzled out in May of 1978. By that time Neufeld was living in Medicine Hat, Alberta, and when Thatcher demanded that Neufeld put up security to cover his costs, Ab decided that the action wasn't worth the trouble and gave up.

"Colin was very hard to work for—his men got tired of his attitude," says Chuck Deagle. The most extreme example of this involved a twenty-year-old who worked for Thatcher as a hired hand. There wasn't room for the young man in the main ranch house, so he lived in a tiny rented home in the village of Caron. "He had an argument with Colin over wages. He wanted to go away for a weekend during harvesting to a relative's wedding," remembers Curly Dick, a resident of Caron. "Colin ordered him not to go, wouldn't give him his paycheque on the Friday, but he went anyway. While he was away, Colin went in and ransacked the kid's house, threw all his furnishings, his chesterfield, chairs, and belongings onto the lawn."

"Poor little bugger had a real hard time getting over that," says Sandy Anderson. The RCMP investigated, but the young man said he was too frightened of Thatcher to lay charges.

Stories of Colin's terrible temper became almost legendary during this time. "His fuse got shorter and shorter," JoAnn told friends, and his blow-ups would occur over the most minor of irritations. One night Colin took young Greg to play hockey at the Civic Centre, only to find that the ice time had been cancelled because an important function was scheduled for that evening. "I will never forget the sight of Colin Thatcher kicking the boards like some naughty little kid over that. It was embarrassing," says a father.

On occasion his tantrums could be much more serious. Once, at a bull sale in Swift Current, the stockyard manager rejected a couple of Thatcher's bulls. "Colin just hammered him, knocked him down," says Roy Nelson. The man was sixty-six years old

"In many respects in different areas, my husband thinks he's above the law, and the law is for someone else," JoAnn Thatcher once told a judge. Thatcher's contempt for the judicial system, indeed for any authority, would grow like a cancer over the years.

At first this contempt manifested itself in minor ways. "I don't think that there was any facet of his business that I wasn't aware of," said JoAnn. "I knew of his under-the-table negotiations and other things that he didn't want the income tax people to know." Thatcher himself admitted, "I have always had a fetish about not telling banks any more about me than was absolutely necessary and rightly or wrongly I proceeded on the philosophy the less they knew about you the better it is. Consequently I've always dealt with at least three financial institutions."

But it was Thatcher's pride in his mocking, irreverent attitude towards authority that truly upset his strait-laced wife. He would order Greg to fill the family's station wagon with purple gas (gas sold without provincial sales tax for use in farm vehicles only). "It's not even the fact that purple gas is being used," JoAnn said. "It's the fact that he involves his son in this process. It gives him that attitude: 'Well, if we don't get caught it's all right.'"

And even when Thatcher did get caught, little seemed to happen to him.

One winter day in 1976, Tom Jackson was heading along Highway 2, about 155 kilometres south of Moose Jaw, close to the American border. He was driving a tractor connected to a backhoe and was on his way to dig a grave for his sister-in-law, who had just died. It was about nine o'clock on a cold, foggy, damp morning. As he dipped over a hill, he saw Colin Thatcher standing on the road, waving him down. He and JoAnn were taking a bull to a sale in the United States and he explained to Jackson that the three-quarter-ton truck had swerved on the slippery roads and the attached animal trailer had spun into the ditch. "Colin convinced me to help him out of the ditch," says Jackson, recalling the incident vividly. "I had just hooked up the trailer to the truck and started to move when I was hit from behind by a school bus." Jackson was thrown into the air and landed on his back on the trailer.

Gus Lawrick was the man driving the bus, with thirteen children aboard. He had come up over the hill to find the truck and trailer straddled across the road. Realizing that he couldn't stop in time he quickly decided that since the ditch was thirty-five feet deep he had no choice but to plough into the backhoe. His bus rammed it, flipped over, and ended up in the ditch anyway. The force of the impact also knocked a wheel off the backhoe, split the back end in two, but, irony of ironies, knocked Thatcher's animal trailer out of the ditch unharmed.

Inside the flipped-over bus was pandemonium. The children were all crying and a few of them were hurt and bleeding. JoAnn ran over and asked Lawrick if there was anything she could do. The bus driver was about to reply when Thatcher yelled, "Come on, let's get the hell out of here." As he climbed into his truck and drove off, Thatcher promised that he would phone the RCMP from the nearest house.

Lawrick and Jackson waited for ten minutes or so and then realized that Thatcher had no intention of keeping his promise. Fortunately by this time someone else had come along in a camper truck and had taken the children to the hospital, where it was discovered that one had a chipped tooth and another a broken nose.

Thatcher was stopped at the border by the RCMP and ordered to return to Moose Jaw to give a full report. He was "mad as hell" at the inconvenience and told the RCMP so in no uncertain terms. Although the others involved thought he should be charged with failure to remain at the scene of an accident, Thatcher was never reprimanded. Gus Lawrick was charged with negligence for driving too fast for the road conditions and Jackson was also hauled into court. Both men felt strongly that the accident was Thatcher's fault, that he should have sent JoAnn up the hill to warn oncoming traffic of what was happening. But every time they started to tell of Thatcher's role in the incident, "the tape machine was shut off and we were told not to mention his name," says Lawrick. A year went by and finally the charges were dropped against Lawrick and Jackson.

Thatcher was often abusive and belligerent in his daily dealings with the Moose Jaw police and the RCMP, which had jurisdiction for the area surrounding the city. If he was approached by a policeman, his greeting often was, "What the hell do you want?" Thatcher would regularly park his various trucks and automobiles the wrong way on the street outside his house. He received many tickets, which he left unpaid, until one day the vehicles were towed away. "Fuckin' pigs," was the response of the Member of the Legislative Assembly to that. The fifty-seven-man Moose Jaw police department adopted an unofficial policy of sending experienced cops who wouldn't be frightened of Colin or over-react in dealing with him. "He was a funny guy," says a veteran Moose Jaw policeman. "Some days he would be charming as they come, and the next he'd be looking for a fight." But what bothered the cops the most was that Thatcher, when he met a policeman at a social function, which naturally happened quite often in such a small city would go out of his way to humiliate him with some sarcastic remark.

He received so many speeding tickets in his daily travels that he got to know the RCMP officers well. He would even phone and challenge them to try to catch him as he drove from one place to another. "One day he was driving Number 1 highway," remembers a retired RCMP officer, "drinking a bottle of beer. I looked in his Corvette. Anybody else would have made an attempt to hide the beer, but not Colin. It was as if he was saying, 'He won't give me a ticket. I am an important person.' And I didn't give him a ticket because I was on my way to something more important."

That Corvette, a ten-thousand-dollar 1977 model, complete with air conditioning and a top-line stereo system, was a 1979 Christmas present from Peggy to her son. More than anything else, the flashy canary-yellow sports car came to symbolize Thatcher's self-imposed persona of a worldly, wealthy cowboy entrepreneur, a Hugh Hefner in an expensive buckskin jacket and hand-tooled leather boots. After driving home in his dusty three-quarter-ton Ford pick-up with the Thatcher Ranch symbol on it, Colin would shed his worn jeans and plaid wool shirt and take a shower. Then he would don an expensive fawn-coloured ultra-suede jacket, or a royal-blue pin-striped suit, hop into the Corvette and speed to the Legislative Buildings some seventy kilometres away. "He seemed to be playing a role in a movie," says a neighbour. "I often wondered if he knew who he really was."

CHAPTER SEVEN
LONE-WOLF LIBERAL

The grandiose Saskatchewan Legislative Building dominates the quiet city of Regina. Designed by the architects Edward and W.S. Maxwell and completed in 1912, it is constructed of pale Manitoba stone, cross-shaped and surmounted by a majestic high dome. The Legislature itself is a regal, ornate place, replete with finely carved oak, Connemara marble, and red plush; Queen Victoria would have felt quite at home there. Its mannered elegance often seems at variance with the rough-and-tumble debate that traditionally goes on here. Indeed, perhaps because the dichotomy in the predominant political philosophies that evolved over the years has been so sharp, the Saskatchewan Legislature has long been the stage for the most raucous, free-wheeling political debate in Canada. Civility and good manners seldom raised their fearful heads here. MLAs would sit holding newspapers in front of their noses while someone opposite tried to make a point; speeches were interrupted by the most gratuitous personal remarks; and the Speaker was often ignored in his rulings or simply insulted outright. Debating points were made not by brilliant repartee, or clever analysis, or even well-researched facts, but by the force and viciousness of the insult being hurled.

In an assembly replete with individualists and eccentrics, his nine-and-a-half year political career gained Colin Thatcher a reputation as a maverick and a loner. "He was a swashbuckling westerner, a kind of free spirit, the master of his own kingdom," says John Brockelbank, who as Speaker had the unenviable job of trying to keep order in the Legislature. Thatcher was also considered one of the most devastating and effective critics in the entire Legislative Assembly. "He sure had the NDP running half the time," says Rynold Gleim.

138

"They shivered in their boots. He was a little off base sometimes, but they would have been happy if he never said anything."

His caustic style is amply illustrated in Hansard. For example:

MARCH 17, 1976:

MR. THATCHER: . . . When somebody wants to cut me to the bone marrow just call me a politician, because, frankly, I am not very proud to be one. I am not very proud about what is going on around here. It has simply been a farce this entire week.

MR. MOSTOWAY: You are living proof!

MR. THATCHER: Well now, Member for Saskatoon, if you weren't sitting on it you would trip over your I.Q.

MARCH 23, 1976:

MR. THATCHER: In the Legislature, a sophisticated Assembly, we have a yo-yo stand up and give a speech about the problems of the cattle industry, who wouldn't know the north end of a cow when she is heading south.

APRIL 14, 1976:

MR. THATCHER: . . . Mr. Speaker, I am not capable of theatrics in losing my temper. When I lose it, I lose it very genuinely. I wish I did have the capability for the theatrics that some of the Members across the way do, but I don't . . .

MR. SPEAKER: Order! Order! I am not going to allow the Member to continue. The record will show that the Member is debating the issue and not raising the Point of Order.

MR. THATCHER: Point of Order, Mr. Speaker, is that in this House we have a double standard, we have a set of rules for this side of the House, we have a set of rules for that side. . . .

MR. SPEAKER: Order! Order! The Member is debating the issue. He is not stating the Point of Order.

MR. THATCHER: You call the same set of rules over there that you do for here. I agree with you, questions should be brief and to the point. But you certainly don't enforce answers, brief and to the point.

MR. SPEAKER: Order! Order! The Member has to bring that up at the time that it occurs. You are getting into a general discussion.

MR. THATCHER: Mr. Speaker, I should like to refer to this business of a twenty-four-hour ruling. I asked a question yesterday and you said I will give you an answer tomorrow. That is like a referee calling back a touchdown pass and saying I will take a look at the video tape and see how it went. . . .

MR. SPEAKER: Order! That is not a point of Order. The Member is not making a Point of Order now.

NOVEMBER 30, 1976:

MR. THATCHER: It has been amusing the last couple of days to look across at the people on that side of the House with their leers, like rats peering out of a ship that hasn't started to sink, but they know full well it is going to sink. You've had it, you are finished, and it's down to the bottom of the ocean for all of you . . . unless some other NDP government might hire you as hacks in their particular government.

MARCH 14, 1977:

MR. THATCHER: It is for this reason that I choose to refer to this budget as the "Red Budget." It is red in philosophy and the pages of its documentation are red with the red ink of deficit.

SOME HON. MEMBERS: Hear, hear!

MR. THATCHER: It could have easily been termed the "Bankrupt Budget" because it is certainly bankrupt of ideas and is taking a gigantic step towards ultimately bankrupting this province. It could also be dubbed the "Budget of Cowardice" in the manner the Government refuses to face the Frankenstein it has created. It could be dubbed many other names, but I believe the "Red Budget" says it all.

APRIL 21, 1977:

MR. THATCHER: Mr. Speaker, I listened with interest to the Minister take his big gulps of air and suck his slough water. . . .

NOVEMBER 17, 1977:

MR. THATCHER: Now, Mr. Speaker, members from both sides of the House have sort of been treating you with kid gloves this morning, that you are above all this and how wonderfully neutral you are in the institution. . . . I have seen you biased, bigoted and prejudiced in the past and you are again today. Frankly, when you didn't call that Member, ask him to withdraw the word "liar" today, don't lecture me about what in blazes the calibre of what should be happening in this House is.

MARCH 17, 1978:

MR. THATCHER: Oh, Mr. Minister, that answer's a real winner. You remind me of a situation we have out on the ranches occasionally. We use quite a few bulls and because they're registered cattle we have them all in their own separate pasture. Now, when they're in their prime, they get pretty top-quality cows and a lot of cows and a great big pasture. As time goes on, they get a little bit slower and consequently, you've got to make the pastures a little bit smaller or else they have trouble keeping up with the cows.

Here we have a minister who has given excellent service to his party and I happen to think you're one of the better ones over there, but you're winding down. Let's say your pasture's being made a little bit smaller this time. Let's say they're not giving you quite as many cows. . . .

MAY 26, 1978:

MR. THATCHER: You know, to the Minister of Highways, if you were about twenty years younger I would make you pay for that one. I am sure that you think that is funny, don't you?

You are a pathetic individual that is nothing worse than scum. You are the rottenest individual, with the foulest mouth of anybody I have had the misfortune to meet in that Assembly and don't ask me to withdraw that! You are a scum!

Brockelbank recalls those debates wearily: "One thing I was unsuccessful as a Speaker in getting out of Colin Thatcher in the entire period of our co-existence [seven years] was an unqualified withdrawal of whatever was unparliamentary on his behalf. He would always qualify and apology. 'Well, if you say so' or 'Well, if you want it.'" Other politicians, however, applauded Thatcher for his recklessness. Recalls a veteran NDP observer, "Colin went that extra inch that they wouldn't dare go. He simply never worried about the consequences." "He could think on his feet," says Don Snyder, an NDP cabinet minister at the time. "He touched nerve centres. If an Opposition member makes you uncomfortable and embarrasses you, then he is functioning the way he is supposed to." Not everybody marvelled at his verbal parrying, however. Says Dick Collver, at that time the leader of the Progressive Conservatives, "If you took the sixty-one MLAs in that House and you graded them on their ability to debate, Colin would have been in the top ten. But he wasn't in the top three. He wasn't incisive, he couldn't pinpoint, he couldn't be exact. He could say a phrase that the press would pick up, but that's not being a debater."

And his opponents could also give it back to him. Paul Mostoway, the NDP's party whip, took special pleasure in needling Thatcher. "Colin, you look like you've been sucking lemons" was one of his favourite retorts, referring to Thatcher's famous scowl. They called him a spoiled brat, or the silver spoon kid, referring to his father's wealth, or the bandit from Thunder Creek.

A strange legislative donnybrook that came to be known as the "son of a bitch" debate spoke volumes about Colin Thatcher. During the question period of March 30, 1978, Thatcher was refused a supplementary question by Speaker Brockelbank. Thatcher threw his papers on his desk and then in a loud voice heard by many MLAs called Brockelbank a "son of a bitch." Hansard, however, did not record the remark, probably because Thatcher was already sitting down when he said it.

Some moments later, Bill Allen, an NDP MLA, brought the incident to the Speaker's attention and said, "I think that this is highly unparliamentary language and I ask the Honourable Member to withdraw the remark and to apologize to the House." Thatcher's reply at that point was jocular and mocking. "I am rather a little bit shocked on the allegation made by the Member for Regina Rosemont [Allen]. Obviously, Mr. Speaker, the Member for Rosemont or myself run in different circles when he hears language like this. I can only suggest he was hearing somebody referring to the Minister of Finance."

Four days later Thatcher raised the matter himself. But this time he was deadly serious and pointed out that there was no record of the "son of a bitch" pejorative. He demanded that Allen withdraw the charge. Eiling Kramer, the minister of highways, a man Thatcher detested, intervened at that point to say that he had heard the remark as well. "By this time Thatcher had turned white and his hands were shaking," recalls a colleague who sat near him. "He was getting madder and madder at being accused of this. I watched him for a few minutes and I decided that in his own mind he hadn't made the remark, although all of us had heard him, and he had more or less admitted it a couple of days before." The ability to create his own reality at any particular time and in any circumstance was a quality that was becoming noticeable in the mature Colin Thatcher.

Thatcher could also be an articulate and serious debater in the House, especially on agricultural and energy issues. MLAs, including many NDPers, looked forward to his often-perceptive analysis of throne speeches or budget debates. And his popularity among his own constituents soared. "People got to like Colin as a politician more and more," says Don McDonald. "He might not bother to solve their constituency problems, but he said what had to be said, and he did it forcibly. 'He's a voice for me in the Legislature,' they would say. 'Here's somebody willing to fight for me. Whether I like him or whether I don't, he's got the guts to stand up and say something.'" This admiring perception of Thatcher would stick with him over the years, in some cases even after he was convicted of murdering his wife.

From the start, Colin's political philosophy and his modus operandi were moulded by the still-pervasive influence of

Ross Thatcher. In his maiden speech to the Legislative Assembly, on November 25, 1975, he made reference to his father as he chided the socialists for spending too much money. "Some years ago, after graduating from college with a couple of degrees after my name, I returned to the family operation and proceeded to revolutionize and change everything. Finally in exasperation, my father said to me, 'It doesn't take any brains to spend money. Any idiot can do that. It is quite something else to make it.'"

And the ghost of Ross Thatcher might have been at Colin's back when in April, 1977, he decided to take on fellow Liberal Eugene Whelan, the flamboyant federal minister of agriculture. Thatcher, by this time, had developed an extreme right-wing, free-enterprise political philosophy and approved of almost no government interference in the cattle industry. He had no time at all for Whelan, whom he habitually called an "absolute disaster." He ridiculed such measures as Whelan's cash advance program for calves, which was an attempt to help ranchers in short-term financial difficulties. When Whelan was supposed to have commented that "eating too much beef makes you ferocious," Thatcher demanded his resignation. But it was Whelan's proposal to set up a beef marketing board that truly enraged Colin. When Whelan challenged opponents of marketing boards to a public debate, Thatcher threw down the gauntlet. Negotiations for this extravaganza, which was to be telecast by the CBC, went on for several months, until Whelan finally backed down in August of 1977. "Colin really wanted that one," says a political colleague. "He knew that his father's famous debate with Tommy Douglas pretty well made his reputation as a provincial politician. He could see the same thing happening to him if he could demolish Eugene."

Colin Thatcher obviously believed that his job as an MLA included protecting the financial interests of his friends, in particular Ron Graham. His first political controversy, which blew up when he was very much a rookie politician in the fall of 1975, involved Graham Construction. The company had been the lowest bidder on a $1.1-million construction project at the Poplar River power project, but because it was not unionized, other workers at the site threatened to walk off the job. To avoid a work stoppage, the Saskatchewan Power

Corporation awarded the contract to the second-lowest bidder, Peter Leach of Winnipeg. In the Legislature, Thatcher claimed that the Power Corporation had condoned the "Mafia tactics" of the trade union and that "the government of Saskatchewan has allowed and... participated in a scheme of blackmail. In so participating, the minister responsible for the SPC is condoning gangster-like tactics... The NDP government has chosen to look the other way as these tactics are imported to Saskatchewan." Thatcher then let loose a stinging tirade in the Legislature against the union movement generally, insisting that the public sector should lose the right to strike, and calling workers lazy and lacking in initiative. The Liberals, who were trying to shake off the anti-labour reputation they had acquired during the Ross Thatcher years, were embarrassed and angered by the speech.

In the spring of 1978, Thatcher sent a letter to Hewitt Helmsing, the chairman of the Saskatchewan Housing Authority, threatening to "blow you wide open in the Legislative Assembly." The menacing letter was the culmination of a political war Thatcher had been waging for some months, again on behalf of Graham Construction. The Moose Jaw company had been the lowest bidder in a $4-million senior citizens' apartment project in Regina, but the contract had gone to MBS, a Winnipeg construction company. Thatcher declared the award "stinks to high heaven. Here is a firm with a poor track record given a contract contrasted with a firm that has an excellent track record and which had done work for the government before." It didn't seem to matter to Thatcher that officials for the Regina Housing Authority, the Saskatchewan Housing Corporation, and the federal Central Mortgage and Housing Corporation were unanimous in agreeing that the MBS design was vastly superior to that proposed by Graham Construction.

He was not averse to promoting his own interests in the Legislature, either. In 1979 he purchased 160 shares in Prairie Co-Ax TV Limited, the company that provided cable service in Moose Jaw. Donald McDonald and Ron Graham were directors. From then on Colin displayed a noticeably keen interest in cable television. On December 11, 1980, and on March 12, May 5, and May 7, 1981, he rose in the House to criticize the government for forcing cable operators, at some expense, to remove American beer and liquor ads. Not once did he mention the reason for his sudden fascination with the subject.

It was appropriate for Colin Thatcher to use his position in the House to embarrass the government; it was less appropriate to fight for his friends' and his own financial interests. But what was worse was his habit of using his power as a legislator, in particular his immunity against the laws of libel and slander for comments made in the House, to abuse and humiliate people with whom he differed. Judge Gerry King was a significant case in point.

Judge King sat on the provincial court in Moose Jaw. In the fall of 1980, while fining a young man from Caron for possession of marijuana, the judge remarked that tremendous quantities of drugs were emanating from Caron, Mortlach, and Parkbeg, three small communities in Thunder Creek. Judge King later said that he made the remark for two reasons: to inform the people who lived in these places of an illicit drug operation, and "to warn the people involved in the operation that I was aware of it." He added that he had obtained this information from people he knew, not from the police.

Thatcher flew into a rage over what he considered a slur on his constituents. He wrote to Attorney General Roy Romanow asking for an investigation into the judge's comments. Romanow responded that he had asked the RCMP to investigate not the judge's conduct, but the seriousness of drug activity in the three villages. The disciplining of judges, said Romanow, was certainly not up to him, but was the prerogative of the chief judge of the provincial court. "Judges are autonomous; they are independent from me and that's the way it should be," he said in the Legislature.

On December 1, 1980, Thatcher responded by asking Romanow, "Are you telling me in this case, where three communities and all the residents within it have been slandered by an individual—outright slander—that the person who has committed this slander is completely above everything else. In other words, in this case . . . the slander had been committed by an individual who is a blatant, willful liar. Are you telling me that he's above reproach? You can't be serious."

The Speaker interjected and reminded Thatcher that certain language was not permitted in the Legislature. "Well," he retorted, "I'll rephrase the words blatant willful liar to a total lack of precision as it pertains to the truth, if that would suffice."

The next day the Moose Jaw *Times-Herald* carried the story, with pictures of both Judge King and Colin Thatcher, on the front page so that the citizens of Moose Jaw could read in detail what an MLA thought of a member of the judiciary in their town.

But Thatcher, as was his practice, did not let the matter rest there. Three months later the RCMP reported that they had found no sign of a drug ring in Mortlach, Parkbeg, or Caron. Judge King responded that the operation had disappeared once he brought it to public light. Thatcher, however, went on the attack again. On March 23, 1981, he told the Legislature, "Mr. Attorney General . . . it would appear that none of Judge King's comments have been substantiated or validated. In other words the term which I referred to him as [blatant, willful liar] would appear to be accurate. I note that Judge King is still on the bench in Moose Jaw: in light of the fact that he has been proven at the very least to be grossly, grossly inaccurate, may I ask when this individual will be removed from the bench?"

Attorney General Romanow lamely responded that the chief judge of the provincial court, after looking at the accusations, had decided that there was no impropriety on the part of Judge King and that the matter should rest.

Thatcher then asked, 'Would the Attorney General tell me, so that I may convey to the people in my constituency who have to face this judge, how a judge who has been called a liar and confirmed as one by the investigation of your department—how these people can respect that individual and the institution of law and order? . . . Is the reason why you are defending Judge King because you know very well you made a bad appointment, and that basically we have an NDP activist on the bench and you are afraid of him?" If Romanow would not fire King, Thatcher concluded, then he should at least be transferred to Saskatoon.

Romanow answered, "I regret very much the personal attack on Judge King mounted by the Honourable Member of Thunder Creek in a forum where the judge is unable to defend himself. . . ."

"It was a very mean thing for Colin to do to Gerry King," says a long-time Moose Jaw resident. "The *Times Herald* played up all the accusations and insults that Thatcher spewed out, but said little about Romanow's defence. And, being a judge, there was no way for him to retaliate. How was anybody in the community supposed to have respected Gerry after that? It showed Thatcher's utter disregard for fair play and his contempt for our system."

Thatcher's criticism of Judge King seems somewhat hypocritical to at least one person. Lynne Mendell says she and Thatcher used to smoke marijuana on occasion. "Afterwards, I'd do Jane Fonda's workout and Colin would watch me. He used to tell me about this Indian that would make up a blend of high-grade pot and a little hash and he [Thatcher] would smoke it in a pipe while riding around his ranch." Mendell adds, jokingly, "I don't know how many times he fell off his horse."

Colin Thatcher may have made an impression in the Legislature, but looking after his constituents was not his strong point. "Colin was a completely different kind of political animal than someone like myself or Jack Wiebe was," says Don McDonald. "He wasn't good at constituency work. Jack Wiebe would never fail to go to somebody's fiftieth wedding anniversary because he knew it was important to the people. Colin wouldn't do that kind of thing. Jack would help people with immigration, income tax problems, that federal stuff, Colin would just tell them to go see their MP."

"He was the worst MLA we ever had in this area," says Gerry Weckman. "If you had a welfare problem or a school problem, you might as well be talking to the wall." "Colin couldn't be bothered with little problems or little people," says Jim Murdock. "A lot of people called me and said, 'Where the hell can we get in touch with MLA?' The only place I knew of was his home number in Moose Jaw or his office in the Legislature. I'd meet them some time later and ask them if they had got any satisfaction. 'Never did get ahold of him,' they'd say. 'Tried two or three times but no luck.'"

Although Hansard records that Thatcher claimed he had a constituency office and therefore received the permitted allowance of $538 (in 1980) for such an office, he did all of his business out of his Redland Avenue home. If he or JoAnn didn't happen to be there, the phone would go unanswered. It was a system that infuriated many of his constituents.

* * *

While Colin Thatcher was fashioning a reputation in the Legislature as a shoot-from-the-hip, acerbic maverick, inside the Liberal caucus he was establishing himself as a difficult and surly individual. "Colin pouted through every caucus meeting," says a former Liberal MLA. "He gave us the feeling that we were all inadequate, just trifles wandering around and as Liberals we were a lost cause." Part of the problem was Colin's intense dislike of Dave Steuart, Ross's long-time confidant who was now leader of the party. Colin once gave Steuart an imaginatively back-handed compliment. "Dave Steuart is the best number-two man a number-one man could ever have." Steuart believed that Ross Thatcher's autocratic and isolated rule was the major reason the Liberals lost to the NDP in 1971, and he was determined to seek the advice of the rank and file. His style during a caucus meeting was to let everyone have his say and not force his opinions down anyone's throat. Some MLAs, including Colin Thatcher, thought this was a trademark of weakness. "I think Colin was looking for a tough leader like his father, and he didn't see me in that role, Steuart said. I think he resented the fact that I healed the breach between the provincial and federal Liberals that existed when Ross was premier."

"He would sit and glower at Davey," says a former MLA. "When he did speak he was rude and insensitive." He would also indulge in bitter screaming matches over Liberal party policy and on five separate occasions Steuart had to threaten to throw Thatcher out of caucus meetings.

Still, his colleagues realized that the Thatcher name remained a revered, almost mystical one, in some Liberal circles so they became determined to appease and tame the lone wolf. The man they chose for the job was Colin's desk-mate in the Legislature, a lanky, good-natured rancher who sounded like Andy Griffiths.

Since the late 1950s, Roy Nelson had been a devoted servant of the Liberal party and he had worshipped Ross Thatcher as a politician. From 1964 to 1973 he was president of his riding association in south-central Saskatchewan, and in 1975 he won the seat of Assiniboia–Gravelbourg. While not always swift or concise in debates, Nelson took his job as MLA very seriously, and spent hour after hour digging up dirt about the NDP. He was very popular among the MLAs.

"I don't think there was a person who didn't like Roy," says a colleague, "even those he attacked with his great piles of facts."

"During a period of time we were all trying to figure Colin out," Nelson recalls. "I think it was Ted Malone said to me, 'Roy, you can get to know people as quick as any of us. Try to befriend Colin. Get him out to dinner with you.' The other guys kind of made a point of getting out real quick and leaving me with him. But I tried to feel him out. How could we get him part of the group?"

But being part of the Liberal caucus group seemed not to appeal to Thatcher at all. "We had a Christmas party," recalls Nelson, " and Colin was telling us how judges measure the size of the scrotums to determine which bull would become champion. I got on the secretary's dictaphone, and said something like, 'I wonder how Thatcher would stack up on this particular measurement.' Well, when Colin found out he was furious, he was just vicious around here. 'I'm going to find out who did that,' he screamed at the secretaries. I went over and said, 'I did that, Colin. What the hell's the matter with you? It was only a joke.' 'Well I don't appreciate it,' he said. 'Erase it then. It's no big deal, forget it,' I said. There was no fun in the man at all, though he could be tremendously sarcastic."

Nelson quickly discovered the key to Thatcher's modus operandi in politics. "One afternoon Colin had stood up in the question period and challenged Eugene Whelan to a debate. The next evening we had a caucus meeting planned in Moose Jaw. When I arrived he was standing at the desk at the Harwood Hotel. The caucus was upstairs and I wondered why Colin is standing down here. The action's upstairs, people are upstairs, it's the first meeting in Moose Jaw near his constituency and Colin is standing at the hotel desk. He had ahold of this paper and he barked, 'Nelson, I want to see you. Come here.' I went over and he showed me the Moose Jaw *Times-Herald*. His picture was right on the front page with the headline THATCHER CHALLENGES WHELAN TO A DEBATE. He said, 'Just like I've been telling you all the time, Nelson. You bust your ass but you don't know nothing about politics. You do all the work and I get all the headlines.'" Roy Nelson soon found out how far Thatcher would go to grab a headline. On at least two occasions, Nelson believes, Thatcher stole documents and research material out of his desk, photo-copied them, returned them, and then used them for his own purposes.

"I more or less covered all the Crown corporations for the Liberal party and SEDCO [Saskatchewan Economic Development Corporation] was my deal," says Nelson. "I loved it because I had enough crap on the NDP I could have pelted them with questions for weeks. One day I was sitting in the Crown Corporations Committee asking questions about a Golden Acres Motel in Moose Jaw which SEDCO had funded. I had all my research papers with me. Colin was back about four chairs from me. He came up with a remark about Golden Acres, and it was an obscure little bit of information that I had dug up and had written on the side of my papers. I turned around and said, 'You son of a bitch, you stole that right out of my desk.' Colin said, 'Yeah, Roy. I make better use of it than you.'"

Another incident involved the nuts-and-bolts issue of load limits. the NDP wanted to restrict truck weights for loads hauled on grid roads, primarily to save the roads from damage. Nelson had done a great deal of research on the issue, much of it very technical. He planned to ask a question in the House on a particular day in March of 1977 but time ran out. The next day he had promised to do some electioneering in the riding of Pelly. While Nelson was away from the House, Colin Thatcher asked a question about load limits.

"I had talked to Thatcher only a day or so before and he knew nothing about the subject. When I confronted him with stealing my material he just smiled, and certainly didn't deny it," says Roy.

Colin Thatcher went much farther with the issue than Nelson would have, and once again he saw his name prominently displayed in Saskatchewan papers for weeks on end. In a news conference outside the Legislature, he insisted that the law was a political one and advised farmers to break it. "I think the highway traffic board would be well advised to send their people around in trios because there are some pretty big, tough, mean farmers out there." He was immediately criticized by the president of the union that represented highway traffic officers, who expressed surprise "that an elected representative who takes part in making laws in the Legislature would actually solicit citizens to break them." The next week Thatcher apologized—in his own manner. "I suppose it was irresponsible of me to advocate breaking the law, a law-maker shouldn't do that," he said. "But you have to consider the context those remarks were made in.... It's a biased political law." This was only one of many indications that Colin Thatcher held the law of the land in contempt and considered that he, for one, was certainly above it.

Two days after the 1975 election Dave Steuart had announced formally that he was stepping down as Liberal leader. "It is much nicer to walk away from something than to be pushed away," he said. The leadership convention, however, did not take place until some fifteen months later. In the meantime, the party suffered from internal bickering and jostling as potential leaders jockeyed for position.

The first candidates to announce that they were off and running were three Regina lawyers: Gary Lane, Ted Malone, and Tony Merchant. But only two weeks into the campaign, Lane unexpectedly announced that he was dropping out. As a former aide in the Ross Thatcher government, he had been identified with the provincial arm of the party, as opposed to Tony Merchant, who as brother-in-law to Otto Lang was connected with the federal arm. Lane had decided that the Merchant-Lang forces were ganging up against him and he wouldn't have a chance. After that, Lane developed a severe case of sour grapes, and on October 25, 1976, he announced that he was defecting to the Progressive Conservative party.

His withdrawal left Edward C. Malone, thirty-nine, and Everett Francis Anthony Merchant, thirty-one, in the race, representing a contest between the affluent establishment and the party's young rebels.

Malone's gentlemanly demeanour and soft-spoken manner revealed his pedigreed roots. A tall, handsome man (now a judge of the Court of Queen's Bench), he was born into one of Regina's wealthy old families. His grandfather had been the mayor of that city, while his father, a manager of a brewery, had been a Liberal backbencher of some influence. Malone graduated from University of Saskatchewan law school in 1962 when Otto Lang was its dean. He was one of the bright young men chosen by Lang to organize federal ridings, but he also worked in provincial campaigns, so that he was considered something of a neutral as far as the provincial-federal dichotomy was concerned. Malone's power base was Regina Lakeview, a riding of stately homes, tree-lined streets, and a profound quietude, inhabited by provincial bureaucrats, university professors, and other professionals. It was in the heart of this pleasant area that JoAnn Wilson was brutally beaten and murdered.

Tony Merchant was to play a major role in the legal battles around that murder. Nine years earlier he was engaged in another important battle, the fight for the Liberal leadership. Like Malone, his roots were deep in Saskatchewan soil but he was certainly not predictably traditional. His father, a lawyer, was killed during the war just prior to Tony's birth, and his mother returned from Halifax to her home town of Yorkton, Saskatchewan. When her father, a district court judge, moved to Saskatoon, the young widow and her two young children followed.

Tony was a peculiar child. He once told a young journalist, "I modelled my childhood on a very spartan kind of existence. When I was fourteen I always kept my eyes below the horizon. I always disciplined myself in every way I could. I tried not to laugh and I tried not to cry, from the time of eight on. I was always very specific and inward-looking. I was always examining myself and my motives.

"I didn't go to school very much. My top year of attendance was 102 days out of 200. I just didn't go. I thought it was boring, that the teachers were stupid. I spent a lot of time reading, consuming my own thoughts on my own."

Merchant took law at the University of Saskatchewan, graduating in 1967. "Tony was a very eccentric, very odd student," recalls a lawyer who was a classmate of Merchant's. "For example, he would do crazy things, like come to class without any shoes on in the middle of winter." In the middle of winter in Saskatchewan, the temperature rarely, if ever, rises above the freezing mark.

"I was twenty-one, almost two years younger than other graduates," said Merchant. "I was an impish human being. Everyone in Saskatoon knew me well but they didn't know me to be a particularly respectful person. so the theory was that if I left Saskatoon for a year—Sally Merchant's son, Judge D.R. Smith's grandson, Otto Lang's brother-in-law [his sister Adrian had married Lang in 1962]—in my absence they would forget that I was a boy and even though I was a little too young, I would come back as a lawyer. People would look at me again and assess me again. I felt some pressure but I didn't have any doubts that I would perform well, particularly if I stayed in Saskatchewan."

Merchant articled at the law firm of Pedersen, Norman, McLeod & Todd, where he is now a senior partner. In 1970 he took on an added job as a host of a daily hot-line radio program on CJME, dispensing legal advice. It was this very public activity that got him into hot water with his colleagues, in particular the Law Society of Saskatchewan's committee investigating breaches of ethics. On two occasions Merchant was publicly reprimanded by this group.

Although he had been heavily involved in Liberal politics from his university days, and by 1971 was president of a Liberal constituency, he told his radio audience not to vote for the Liberals under Ross Thatcher, but to vote NDP instead. "I justified that by acknowledging that there has to be a certain capacity to divorce oneself from what you are by birth and choice and what your thinking may be at a particular moment."

In the early Seventies Merchant and some friends decided that the Liberal establishment was ineffectual and that they would take over a number of constituencies. Merchant chose Regina Wascana. "I negotiated with the incumbent executive and ultimately I got mad at them. They were prepared to give me and my friends a minority position on the executive. I told them I would accept that only if I became the president. The alternative was that I would be the vice-president but my friends would make up the majority on the executive. The existing president came to me and said, 'Well, we've decided that you'll be vice-president, and you'll have four members on the executive—which was a minority of eleven or twelve. I said, 'Well, Martin, I have news for you. I will be president and every single man jack will be mine. I will be at a meeting at such-and-such a date with enough people to take over the seat.' Then I hung up. He phoned back and said, 'Okay, but let's leave a few old guys on.' I ended up running the constituency and working about thirty hours a week. So I thought, what the hell, if I'm going to do all the work, I might as well be the MLA."

He was elected in 1975 and immediately gained a reputation as one of the sharpest and hardest-working members of the Legislature. During his year and a half in the House he presented more private member's bills than any other MLA, becoming an outspoken advocate of the rights of women and natives. He was also an extremely effective debater. "In those days the best of the bunch for attacking me was Tony Merchant," says PC leader Dick Collver. "He was a son of a bitch. And tough. And vicious. He had a sense of the kinds of things that would get you. I'd say, 'Oh, no, not again! Tony's on me.'"

Merchant had started campaigning for the Liberal leadership long before Steuart announced the time and place of the convention. "I had to criss-cross the province. I travelled some seventy or eighty thousand miles, often by automobiles. I drive a car at 110 or 120 miles per hour when I'm in a hurry. But people would also fly me. We'd land on highways and we'd land in fields. I remember arriving at one place where my pilot said, 'Gee, we just can't land there.' I said we had to. He had a tremendous plane and he was doing all this for nothing. We landed down near Moosomin and two guys who were there to meet us just rushed by me and went and shook the pilot's hand and congratulated him. They were both flyers and they hadn't believed that it was possible to land a plane there." Not surprisingly, Tony's daring, energy, and zeal attracted many young people to his side.

There were many Liberals, however, who thought that Malone was too staid and Merchant too "flashy." They were urging others to run.

For a few months during the summer and fall of 1976 Colin Thatcher had considered throwing his hat into the leadership ring. In October, he said that he would run if Malone and Merchant had not obtained the confidence of party members in rural areas by the end of the month. At the beginning of November he announced that he was again postponing his decision. Finally, however, Thatcher bowed out, saying that he was backing Gerry Fraser, a former executive assistant to Ross Thatcher and now a Saskatoon businessman. In the end Fraser decided not to seek the leadership. "I think Colin was waiting for a group of us to come and beg him to run," says a former Liberal MLA. "Nobody did. We could see that Colin felt that he was a little above most of us. This leadership was beneath him, and he wasn't going to be troubled by it."

He also was not openly going to support either contestant. Tony Merchant recalls: "He told me he wasn't going to be a part of the preservation of the Liberal party if all that did was make it more difficult for someone to defeat the NDP. I suppose giving his complete support to someone would mean that he was making a commitment to stay with the ship."

After some thought, Roy Nelson had become a dedicated supporter of Ted Malone. "We kept after Colin, saying, 'Look, are you going to commit yourself to Malone?' He'd reply, 'No, not publicly, but you'll get my vote, don't worry about that.' Then we heard rumours that he was going to support Tony and we approached him again. 'No damn way,' he said. 'Look,' we said 'we have a confirmed rumour that you are in a commercial for Merchant.' 'Hah,' he replied, 'I was just sitting there. No damn way they'll ever use that.' 'Have we got your word on that?' we asked. 'Absolutely,' he replied. 'Don't worry about me. I'm just going to put in a quiet word for Malone.'"

The final showdown took place in the crowded, smoky convention hall of the Regina Centre of the Arts on December 11, 1976. "The lights went out," says Nelson, "and the film about Tony came on. There was Colin loud and clear, supporting Merchant. We were all sitting towards the front with Ted, and Linda [Clifford, MLA for Wilkie] said, 'That dirty double-crossing so-and-so.' She marched over and confronted Colin and he said, 'Don't worry about me. I didn't know they were playing that.' Linda responded, 'You said you would support us. Now get up there and sit with Malone.' Colin replied that no, he was comfortable where he was. In the end he voted for Tony."

Merchant had gathered so much momentum in his campaign, and had spent so much money, that many Liberals presumed that he had victory in the bag. In the end, however, the establishment player was victorious: the final count was Malone, 628; Merchant, 521. Political pundits claimed that Merchant lost for two reasons. First, over four hundred elibible voters had not turned up at the convention; most of these were young, greenhorn supporters of Tony's and they either had lost interest or did not have the cash to spend several days in Regina. And then there was Tony's extravagant, noisy, American-style convention campaign, replete with bands, cheerleaders, and press-the-flesh workers. Such a flamboyant exhibition offended many of the middle-class, older Liberals, who in the end voted for the comfortable traditionalism of Malone.

Almost immediately the new leader ran into trouble. Two by-elections, in Prince Albert-Duck Lake and Saskatoon Sutherland, were called for March 2, 1977. Both seats had been held by the Liberals and Malone staked his reputation on retaining them. But as hard as he worked, the Liberal presence remained ephemeral; the real battle was fought between the two other parties and in the end, the up-and-coming Tories under Dick Collver took both.

Recriminations reverberated through the Liberal ranks. "They were absolutely intent on cutting their own throats. We just watched them self-destruct," says Dick Collver. Tony Merchant was particularly bitter and became a biting back-room critic of Malone's. Colin Thatcher was heard to say that he admired Ted Malone about as much as he was infatuated with Dave Steuart.

During the spring session of 1977, Thatcher served as the Liberal finance critic. He was in fine fettle, flailing away at his pet dragons—big bureaucracy, big unions, and big deficits. On one occasion he served up to the astonished Assembly a modernized version of the Twenty-Third Psalm as he saw it relating to Saskatchewan.

> The state is my shepherd,
> I need not work.
> It alloweth me to lie down on good jobs
> It leadeth me beside still factories
> It destroyeth mine initiative
> It taketh me on the paths of a parasite for
>   politic's sake,
> Yea though I walk through the valley of laziness
>   and depths of spending
> I will fear no evil
> For the Government is with me
> Out of the earnings of my grandchildren
> It filleth my head with security
> My inefficiency runneth over.
> Surely the state shall care for me all the days of
>   my life
> And I shall dwell in a fool's paradise forever.

* * *

Thatcher's budget speeches were extremely censorious of Prime Minister Pierre Trudeau and the federal Liberal government's financial policies, especially as they pertained to controlling inflation. This stinging criticism embarrassed many members of his caucus; although they might privately agree with Thatcher, they reasoned that the two Liberal parties did, after all, have the same name, and their dirty laundry should not be hung out in public.

By the spring of 1977, Thatcher's relationship with his colleagues was deteriorating quickly. "Colin figured the Liberal party was a lost cause, that there was a greater beyond for him," says Roy Nelson. "He was using us every day for his own purposes." "I always knew he was going to quit the party," said Dave Steuart. "He always wanted to break ranks because his dad did with the CCF."

The Pelly by-election, held on June 8, 1977, was the last straw for the renegade. Everybody knew the NDP would retain the seat—the fight was for second place. The race became symbolically very important, for if the Liberals did well they could claim that they had regained lost momentum and were on their way to recovery. Ted Malone urged every member of his caucus to campaign in the riding as frequently as he or she could. He also invited some federal big guns to participate, including Otto Lang, Jack Horner (who had recently defected from the PCs), and Warren Allmand, minister of Indian affairs and northern development. The federal presence in Pelly sent Thatcher into a rage; he declared that he was certainly not going to participate. When the Liberals not only placed third but received so few votes that they lost their deposit, Thatcher told a friend he was "embarrassed to be associated with the Liberal party."

Then the hated socialists rubbed salt in the wound. It is a fact of political life in Saskatchewan that the CCF-NDP has a base of between 35 and 40 percent of the vote. The two right-wing parties together customarily receive 45 to 55 percent. And there is a shifting vote of between 5 and 20 percent. This means that the NDP stands a better chance of winning if there are two strong opposition parties to split the vote and allow the socialists to come up the middle. The NDP, therefore, became very concerned that the Liberals were rapidly sliding in opinion polls. As a result the party took it upon itself to try to bolster Liberal spirits by making public noises designed to give that party credibility. Receiving condescending praise from the dreaded socialists was a humiliating blow to Thatcher's ego. For days he seethed with anger.

But there was another more important reason for Thatcher's disenchantment with the Liberals. He felt the gritty, spirited Tories were doing everything right while his party was getting everything wrong. "The Liberals were concentrating on giving beautiful speeches and preparing research materials, all that crap, while we were concentrating on getting visibility, grabbing newspaper headlines, and it worked," says a Conservative fundraiser who was an MLA at the time. And the person primarily responsible for the phenomenal Tory resurgence was someone whom Colin Thatcher had already grown to admire profoundly, Dick Collver, the very man who was to be an important hostile witness at his murder trial.

CHAPTER EIGHT

BORN-AGAIN TORY

"To Colin I was the father that he lost, probably never had. I wasn't vicious to him like his dad was, I wasn't cruel to him. And he could be a real lone wolf, a real crazy guy," says Dick Collver. Other Tory MLAs who watched the two men together agreed that Collver was certainly a father figure to Thatcher. Although the PC leader was only three years older than Thatcher, he was so overbearing, so much in command, at times so obnoxious and at other times so charming, that he must have indeed reminded Colin of Ross.

In a province that has produced an amazing number of unique politicians, none was more fascinating than this Anglo-Saxon Duddy Kravitz. Dick Collver was born in Toronto on February 13, 1936. His father was an itinerant salesman, flogging such items as seat covers, men's socks, and ballpoint pens. "You could write one line and blob three," recalls Collver. "This was a very family-oriented business. My father would go and peddle them, and then we'd come back and package up some more in the basement. That was the first money I ever earned. I was nine."

The family moved to Windsor and then Calgary, which was where Collver went to high school. Eventually he attended university, graduating with a degree in economics. In summers and on weekends he worked, laying lino, selling shoes, icing refrigerator railway cars, painting barrels in the Norman Wells oil fields, and serving as a barker at the Calgary Stampede. He articled at the prestigious firm of Price Waterhouse and eventually qualified as an accountant, but after two and a half years the dynamic young entrepreneur decided to go into business for himself. To raise the cash for this new plan, he took a job as a travelling salesman of veterinary supplies, primarily drugs for chickens, pigs, horses,

160

and cows in the northern prairies. "In the ten months I worked for that company, I outdid every one of their salesmen in Canada, and I had the worst territory," he says.

In some obscure way that experience amply qualified him to run a medical clinic in Edmonton; he was the business manager there for the next five years. "The guy whose name was on the clinic and I had a difference of opinion as to what should happen to the assets. I won, and it's not a good thing for the business manager to win against the senior partner. We agreed to part," recalls Collver.

At that time, free-enterpriser Ross Thatcher had just gained power and Collver, like many other entrepreneurs, thought Saskatchewan was about to boom. He moved to Saskatoon in 1965 and started up Management Associates Limited. His major clients were three internal specialists, Doctors Marcel, Donald, and Richard Baltzan, who were involved in kidney dialysis. They had made what one wag called "a piss-pot full of money" and wanted to make more. In a few years Collver's management company had offices in Thunder Bay, Regina, Calgary, and Edmonton as well as Saskatoon and employed some 2,500 people. Money was invested in a myriad of business ventures, including the old castle-like Bessborough Hotel in Saskatoon, which was restored to something approaching its previous glamour and elegance.

The Baltzans were influential Liberals and Collver himself was a substantial supporter of the provincial party, in terms of both cash donations and hard work for various candidates. Today Collver is quick to point out that he never supported the party federally. "I was never a Canadian Liberal, never, not in my entire life."

In the early '70s he got into a fight with Saskatoon Mayor Sid Buckwold and some senior councillors over the assessment of city land. When Buckwold announced his resignation near Christmas in 1972, a group of young people, primarily Liberals, told Collver he should run for mayor. "I came home and talked to my wife Eleanor [they were married in 1958] and she said, 'If you don't run for office when you have the opportunity, I won't want to hear you shooting your mouth off about politics at cocktail parties or screaming at the television ever again.'" Collver ran the most expensive mayoralty campaign, in the shortest period of time—the election was called on December 19 and was held on January 5, 1972—in the history of Saskatoon. Citizens grew a little tired of Dick's happily smiling face beaming down at them from what seemed like every billboard in the city. He placed third, losing by over 6,500 votes.

Among those who had tried so hard to get him elected was a Conservative, Kay McKormick, the sister of Jack Horner. She and Don Swenson (Colin Thatcher's future opponent in Thunder Creek in 1975) were serving on a provincial Progressive Conservative search committee trying to find a new leader for their party. Kay mentioned to Don, the provincial president, that Collver might be just the bright young energetic man they were seeking. "Collver said that it would cost a lot of money to get the party on its feet and he indicated that he would want control of the party if he decided to run. But he said he might be interested," recalls Don Swenson.

Collver's motivation in considering the job was peculiar, to say the least, and reveals much about politics in Saskatchewan. After the Tories approached him, Collver held long discussions with his Liberal friends. By looking at election statistics going back years, they reached the conclusion that about 20 percent of the people who voted NDP were in reality populist Conservatives who would prefer to vote for the Tories provincially if there were a realistic chance for them to win. If Collver took on the Tory leadership and revitalized the Conservatives to the point where he could carve out that 20 percent of the socialist vote, the Liberals would gain power.

"Mark Paulson was an interesting guy who had been active in provincial politics in Saskatchewan for a long time," says Collver. "He had been involved in the KOD (Keep Our Doctor) committee in '62 so he was a hard-core Liberal supporter. Paulson put in a call to his Liberal buddies, to Otto Lang, and asked them what they thought of our idea. They said, 'Sure, go ahead.' So at the beginning, I decided to take over the Tory party so the Liberals could get elected. Absolutely no question. We simply had to get the socialists out of there."

The Saskatchewan Conservative leadership convention took place on March 17 and 18, 1973, at a Regina hotel called the Vagabond Motor Inn. It was not an auspicious location for the renaissance of a moribund party. To add drama to the event, Swenson had persuaded Roy Bailey, the district superintendent of the Eston–Elrose School Unit, to run so that there would at least appear to be a contest. According to Collver it was not a close fight. "There were 375 ballots cast and of those, 230 were people I had brought myself." Collver might have won the contest in a walk, but it was a poor sickly party he had inherited. When Martin Pederson was elected in the riding of Arm River in 1964 it was the first time the Conservatives had won a seat in the province since 1929, and it was to be the last time until 1975. In the 1971 election only 2.13 per cent of the votes cast went to the PCs.

Collver was determined that the Conservatives would field a full slate of sixty-one candidates in the upcoming election, which was eventually held in 1975. "We dragged dogs out of broom closets and made them run," says a former Tory MlA, remembering those desperate days. "In my wife's home constituency, Saltcoats, we were holding a nominating meeting," remembers Collver. "It had been called for two weeks, we had put the ads in the paper, had done all the necessary things. Eleven people showed up, and of those, three were my staff. We had a guy all ready to be nominated but he stands up and says, 'I'm not gonna run 'cause I don't think we should run a candidate in this constituency at all.' I start looking around—who's going to run? 'You don't want me to run,' says one fellow, 'I'm the funeral director.' And the next guy says, 'I'm not going to run,' and the next and the next. A man walks in, everybody eyes him and says, 'We've got our candidate!' I yell, 'That's my wife's father come to visit his daughter.' I told them, 'One of you is going to run. We are coming out of here with a candidate for Saltcoats constituency. Nobody is leaving until we do.'

"The constituency secretary, Wilf Walker, was in the corner taking down notes. He was the local druggist and very well liked by everyone. I grabbed Wilf and I took him into another room and I worked on him for three-quarters of an hour. I worked on his patriotism, his dedication to his family, his love of the land, his drugstore. Finally he says, 'For heavens' sakes, oh, okay.' I grabbed him and announced to everybody that we finally had a candidate. And he came within a whisker of winning the seat."

In February of 1975, just before the election, Collver held a meeting for his sixty-one candidates. "It was actually one of the most moving experiences of my life to see these people who were given no chance of winning, none of them. I got stupid, I got mushy—that's when I said to myself, 'I can't let these people down.'" His deal with the Liberals was finished; now he was in the race to win.

During the June election campaign a spark was ignited and the PCs took off. To convince that 20 percent of renegades NDP voters who were considered pink Tories that Collver and his party were not very different from what they were used to, Collver grew a beard and his election signs were painted a bright purple. The campaign went so well that Dick actually began to think his party was going to win. Collver was running for the first time himself in the riding of Nipawin. "On election night I was getting off the plane in Regina from Nipawin and somebody asked me what was the worst thing that could happen. I replied that we elected only six other guys and one of them is a certain X whom I couldn't stand. And that is exactly what happened."

Dick Collver might have been disappointed that he hadn't formed the next government, but most other people were astounded at his success. The Progressive Conservatives' percentage of the popular vote went from 2 percent to 28 percent; his representation in the House from no seats to seven. And Collver handily won his own seat of Nipawin. "It was an astonishing showing, considering the leader had been in place less than two years," says Jim Eager, an NDP worker.

The veteran debaters of the other two parties were lying in wait for the new Tory rump when the Legislature reconvened in the fall of 1975. "I was totally inexperienced," recalls Collver. "It took me until 1976–77 to find my feet, which is why the first little while I reacted so badly. Some guy yells across the floor, 'Your old lady's a so-and-so.' I responded in shock, 'I'm not going to take that, Mr. Speaker. Why aren't you shutting him up? He's not supposed to say things like that in this august body.'

"I said to my caucus, We are going to be different. We're going to wear business suits, we're going to look professional, we're going to look dignified. The first day we're in the Legislature, Ralph Katzman [MLA for Rosthern] walks in wearing an absolutely filthy shirt—he had a big belly and he had spilled something down the front of it—and rubber boots. I said, 'What are you doing here like that?' He replied, 'What's the matter?' I said, 'You can't walk into the legislative chamber of the province of Saskatchewan in rubber boots.' He said, 'You're right, Dick. You're right.' He runs back and takes off his rubber boots and he walks into the Legislature in his goddamn socks!"

It did not take the nervy, energetic Tories long, however, to indicate that although they were fewer in number than the Liberals and therefore not the official Opposition, they were indeed the Opposition in spirit. Dick Collver immediately mounted a far from discreet campaign to lure "any warm body," be it Liberal or NDP, to the Tory camp. The first to succumb to his promises was none other than the disgruntled Liberal leadership contender Gary Lane. At the time Lane made his move Colin Thatcher told a group of reporters that he was "very disappointed at the way he did this . . . I would never leave the party in the fashion Mr. Lane did."

Ironically it was Gary Lane who first passed along news of Thatcher's disenchantment with the Liberal party. Says Collver, "Lane came to me and said Thatcher's mad at this, Thatcher's mad at that. Thatcher was mad always. He had left the Liberal caucus, at least in spirit, by this time, and he was like a lone wolf."

Collver realized what a catch someone with a name like Thatcher would be for his fledgeling party, and so he began a campaign of persuasion. "These conversations were all to be held in complete confidentiality," remembers Collver. "No way could Dick Collver be seen with Colin Thatcher. " One night Dick and Eleanor were invited to a discreet dinner by Colin and JoAnn at the Redland Avenue home. "We tried to keep it all as secret as possible. But as we were leaving I backed into a neighbour's car."

Naturally, word soon reached the Liberals that Thatcher was thinking of bolting the party. Several people confronted him with the rumours, but he always denied them. Finally on June 13, 1977, a story appeared in the Regina *Leader-Post*, stating in no uncertain terms that Thatcher was indeed "mulling his future as a Liberal." A caucus meeting was called to deal with the crisis.

Everybody at the meeting sat around tables in a square except for Thatcher, who chose to sit by himself at the back. Roy Nelson, for one, was furious at him. He addressed Ted Malone, loud and clear: "This guy's betraying us, he's an absolute scoundrel. He's leading us down the garden path. If you can't see that, Ted, then I had better leave this organization. I'm not going to put up with this crap." Then he turned and looked directly at Thatcher and said, "I don't want you in this party."

Several people were upset at Nelson for being so outspoken. They valued the Thatcher name, and Colin's contribution. "Colin was one of the very brightest ones in that caucus," says Cy MacDonald, who had been a cabinet minister in Ross's government. "Because his name was Thatcher and because I was the most experienced in the party, I felt a very major effort should be made to retain him. I told Ted Malone, 'That's your job. You try and convince him there's a role for him in the Liberal party.'"

Nelson tells this version of what happened next: "Ted said, 'There's no way we can have a party and not everybody work together. What are your thoughts, Colin?' Colin said, 'Oh, you fellows are taking me to task wrongly. I'm still one of you. I want to be part of the caucus and cooperate.'

"'Then what's wrong, Colin?' Ted asked. 'What's your problem?' He replied. 'You have no policy. You just stray all over the place.' Ted said, 'Okay, Colin, let's have a policy conference. We'll go someplace out of the city where we won't be interrupted and we'll thrash out policy. We're overdue on that and I'm the first to admit it.' Colin said, 'If you do that, I'll guarantee you that I'll stay right with you until such time as I disagree with the policies we formulate.'" The caucus then decided they would get together at Waskiesu Resort in a couple of months and thrash out policy. Everyone relaxed; Colin Thatcher was back in the Liberal fold, at least for the time being.

A few days later, on Thursday, June 23, Colin drove out to see Rynold Gleim, his former campaign manager. "We sat on the bale wagon and talked for an hour. He said, 'You've just got to come to that executive meeting tonight.'" But Thatcher did not say why. Later he would tell Rynold. "I just didn't have the heart to tell you." Gleim was deeply hurt.

That night the executive meeting was held at the Thatcher's Redland home. "Ted Malone had got wind that Thatcher was going to switch parties," remembers Adelaide Weckman. "He came [with party president John Embury] and wanted to address the meeting. Colin said no. It was an embarrassing situation, because it was Colin's house. If it had been a more neutral place it would have been different. Malone sat in the den for a while as we discussed it. Finally we suggested he go across the street to [prominent Liberal] Emmett Reidy's house and wait." The executive finally agreed that Malone could address them, but it was over Colin's objections.

It didn't matter, anyway. By this time Thatcher was determined to defect to the Conservative party, and in a highly charged atmosphere he flatly made that announcement, going on to plead with executive members to come with him. Many did; they tended to be anti-NDP in philosophy, and it didn't matter to them if they voted for the Tories or the Liberals. The majority of the people in the room, however, were dedicated Liberals and they were deeply upset at Thatcher's decision to switch parties. The secretary-treasurer of the executive, Rosalie Marcil, a quiet young housewife who had known Colin all her life, remembers her reaction that night: "I didn't support him and I didn't make any pretence about it. I was somewhat disgusted that we had worked that hard— put our time and money in—to elect him. I felt that his switching parties was opportunism. But I happen to value loyalty maybe more than a person should in this day and age."

Executive members noticed that JoAnn Thatcher was visibly nervous, even distraught during the meeting. Later as she said goodbye to her husband's former supporters, many of whom were good friends of hers, there were tears in her eyes.

The next day at a press conference called by Collver to gloat over his latest acquisition. Thatcher told the media that the Thunder Creek Liberal executive had given its blessings to his move. This infuriated president Gerry Weckman, because in fact the motion that had been passed had urged Thatcher not to switch parties. But no one could deny that Colin Thatcher's version of the truth suited him much better.

Since the election, the Conservatives had gained four seats through by-elections and defections from the Liberals: both parties now had eleven members. But then on September 30, 1977, Tony Merchant, still smarting from the leadership race, and Stuart Cameron, another Liberal MLA, announced that they were leaving provincial politics to run federally. Collver was delighted at this news. Surely now the two Liberal MLAs would have to resign their seats, leaving his Conservatives as the official Opposition with eleven seats to the Liberals' nine

Collver had long hungered for official Opposition status for some very good reasons. The first was money. In 1976, the Liberals had received some $16,000 more for research and staff. Secondly, the official Opposition was able to ask the first question in question period, thereby setting the pace in commenting on any controversy, and invariably this resulted in more publicity. Most important, a trend would be clearly established—the PCs were on the upswing, the Liberals were declining. The Liberals' response, however, was to argue that although Merchant and Cameron were nominated in federal seats, they need not submit their resignations from the Legislature until a federal election had been called. What followed was a battle of epic proportions.

On the day the Legislature opened, Eric Berntson, a Tory MLA and the party whip, sent a letter to the Speaker, John Brockelbank, in which he charged that there was collusion between the Liberals and the NDP to prevent the Tories from taking their rightful positions as the official Opposition. "I was very upset at receiving that letter. I felt it was a slur on my impartiality," says Brockelbank.

The House, faced with an unusual controversy, voted to resurrect the special committee on rules and privileges to look into possible impropriety in Berntson's remarks. The Conservatives boycotted the committee, noting that it had not met since 1917, and claiming that it was simply an instrument to punish them. To reporters outside the Legislature, Colin Thatcher, now a Conservative die-hard, described the committee as a "kangaroo court." A day or two later, Gary Lane, interviewed on television, repeated Thatcher's remarks. A heated debate raged for days over the affair until finally on December 19, the House voted to suspend Thatcher and Lane from the Legislature for five days, the most severe penalty that had ever been imposed on an MLA in Saskatchewan's history.

(The account of Colin Thatcher's political career is important because of what it tells about the development of his extraordinary personality. But this particular story is worth a detailed examination because of the part it played in Colin Thatcher's trial. While Dick Collver was testifying against Thatcher, Thatcher's lawyer Gerry Allbright tried to cast aspersions on Collver's ethics. He suggested that at the time of the "kangaroo court" controversy, Collver went to Gary Lane and Thatcher and said, "You guys will have to say that there was an agreement between the Liberals and the NDP to conspire against the Conservatives, and you will have to do whatever you have to do to tell the story." Collver denied that he had asked anybody to lie.)

The "kangaroo court" débâcle was only one controversy in a legislative session that will go down in the province's history as being among the ugliest and most vitriolic. "The two most difficult people to get along with at that time were Colin Thatcher and Gary Lane," recalls John Brockelbank, the Speaker. "They were both retreaded Liberals and were very, very aggressive. They were the senior members of the Conservative caucus—they had more seniority than the leader— and they took a leading role. They were eager to score marks on the government. And any time the Speaker got in the way, they attacked the Speaker."

"Instead of defending and attacking, Collver's tactic was to stir an issue up and then let it hang out there, make everbody wonder what the hell we were doing, and then back off," says a Tory bagman who was an MLA at the time. "So you were constantly caught in these awkward situations. The House was absolutely venomous. Everybody hated us with a passion. They would shout obscenities across the aisle. It was real tough stuff, and hard for a thin-skinned person to take."

In the fall of 1976, two troublesome business deals involving Dick Collver came to light and the Opposition played them for all they were worth.

First the brothers Baltzan, the Saskatoon doctors who had backed Collver's investment company, claimed that they had an oral trust agreement with him, which stipulated that each of the four partners would have an equal 25-percent interest in any assets acquired after 1965. Collver therefore owed them a substantial amount of money, and the Baltzans asked the courts to tie up his assets until the matter could be resolved. Collver claimed it was all nonsense, that no such agreement ever existed. The feud was settled out of court in April of 1978, but for two years the details of the case filled the newspaper columns and airwaves of the province's media and did Collver's political career irreparable harm. Today Collver is convinced that the Liberal Baltzans were trying to force him off the political scene and thereby weaken the Tories. To back up his claim he points to the fact that the settlement reached in 1978 was exactly, to the penny, the one he offered before the matter went to court.

The damaging Baltzan affair was barely settled when other storm clouds gathered. In the spring of 1978, the Saskatchewan Government Insurance Office named Collver in a $1.1-million lawsuit. He was a former part-owner of Buildall Construction Company, which had run into problems completing government projects in 1976; SGIO took over the company, and heavy losses ensued. Now, the Crown corporation claimed that Collver was personally liable for some of the debt. The matter was not resolved until 1983, when the PC government dropped the suit against the former Progressive Conservative leader. But the affair received an enormous amount of media attention and further tarnished Collver's reputation. Collver knew that with all the bad publicity surrounding his affairs, the NDP would be sorely tempted to call an early election. He warned his troops to prepare. And yet he remained confident that his party would win the next election. A former senior bureaucrat recalls how he attended a federal constitutional conference at which Premier Blakeney and Dick Collver were present, "Collver talked as if there was no question at all that he would be the next premier. It was somewhat embarrassing."

As election rumours began to spread, Colin Thatcher was shocked to discover that the Conservative nomination in Thunder Creek was not going to be handed to him on a platter, as Dick Collver had promised. Don Swenson, the Conservative who had lost against Thatcher by only 292 votes in the last election, the man who had "discovered" Collver and persuaded him to run, had decided that he too would seek the nomination.

"Collver was so desperate to stop Don that he personally drove out to our farm and tried to persuade him to run elsewhere," recalls Dorothy Swenson. Swenson told Collver that he thought Thatcher's image of a "hard, right-wing, knock-the-other-guy-down" politician was hurting the Conservative party. "And the more that I see Thatcher's influence in the caucus, the more I can't buy him. If he doesn't get his own way he kicks the chairs." Collver told Swenson that if he insisted in pursuing the nomination in Thunder Creek he would not sign his nomination papers. "I'm trying to attract Liberals to the Conservative party," says Collver. "And the son of the former premier who died a martyr to the Liberal cause is suddenly rejected by my guys... forget it."

Don Swenson contested the nomination anyway, and Colin Thatcher used every political trick in the book to beat him. Swenson worked hard at selling memberships, all of which he handed into the PC office so that the new members would receive their party cards. "Colin sold memberships, too, but he kept them all until just before the nomination. That meant he had access to my new supporters, but I didn't to his," Swenson says.

Premier Blakeney announced a snap election for October 18, 1978, and the Conservative nomination meeting for Thunder Creek was called in forty-eight hours. The election committee decided that there would be an advance poll, ostensibly so that farmers could come in, vote, and return to harvesting. A veteran scrutineer was puzzled by the decision; he had never run across an advance poll in a nominating convention in his lifetime. "It was absolutely ridiculous," says Don Swenson. "There had been no cut-off on nominations, and while the convention was being held, there was still a possibility that someone else could have come forward. Yet here was the ballot box already half full. And, of course, there were still the nomination speeches to be heard."

In due course, Swenson and his supporters discovered the real reason for the advance poll. "Colin's old Liberal friends, who didn't dare show up at a PC meeting, could whip in and vote without ever entering the hall."

Swenson also found that, through a genuine error, a large number of his supporters had been left off the computerized membership list. "Many of these people had held a PC membership for years and years," recalls Swenson. "We contacted Colin's representatives and they said, 'There's no way you can put those names on now.' I then phoned Colin. JoAnn transferred me to his mobile. I said to him, 'You know all these people who have been left off.' He barked back. 'That's not in my hands. My campaign manager's looking after that. Goodbye, I'm working on my speech.'"

Swenson threatened to resign, thereby creating a scandal, unless the old-time Tories were reinstated. He finally won the point. "But by that time, those people had come, found their names weren't on the list, and then left," says Swenson.

"During the nomination meeting, I got up and said what I had to say, and then sat on the stage. Colin gave his speech. then he just left. Didn't stay around at all." Whether this reflected Colin's petulance at being forced to fight for a nomination he considered his by right or whether he was afraid to face the questions of Swenson's supporters who were furious at the proceedings is not clear. Swenson's people had good reason to be upset. "They kept the votes separate," says Don, "and of the ones in the hall, we won. But we lost the advance poll by at least two to one." Thatcher had retained the nomination, but only by the skin of his teeth.

He won the seat handily, however, beating the New Democrat by 935 votes and the Liberal by 1,089 votes. He had successfully switched parties, just as his father had done twenty years before.

The election in 1978 was a sad one for the Liberal party; they were completely wiped out, winning no seats and only 14 percent of the popular vote. When JoAnn Thatcher ran into the defeated Roy Nelson. who like all his colleagues had lost his seat, she looked at him sadly and said, "Why do the good ones always lose?" The New Democrats had surged back, capturing forty-four seats and 48 percent of the vote. The Conservatives had jumped from seven seats to seventeen and from 27 percent of the popular vote to 38 percent. It appeared to be an astonishing gain for the Tories, but Dick Collver was deeply disappointed. He had fully expected to form the next government.

Six months after the election Collver announced that he was resigning as leader. "I realized that I had attracted every hard-core free-enterpriser out there. In order to win we would have to attract more Liberals, we'd have to start talking and acting like Liberals. And I didn't want any part of that." "Because of Collver's brilliant organization and his far-out ideas he was able to zip up to 38 percent," says a former Tory MLA. "But then he stalled. He recognized that he would never move from there. His image was too badly tarnished."

A PC leadership race was called for November 8, 1979. The Tories of Thunder Creek were extremely interested in the race, and since many, including Don and Dorothy Swenson, wanted to participate, a meeting was held to elect the ten delegates and three alternates who would represent the constituency at the convention. Neil Seaman, who was president of the constituency, chaired the meeting and Colin Thatcher, as the sitting MLA, was there as well. Colin volunteered to help in the proceedings and so while everyone else was drinking coffee, he and Seaman counted the ballots.

"I knew that my figures and Colin's figures should have been within the realm of norms," says Seaman. "They weren't. And I was surprised that all of my ballots had Don's name on it, and most of Colin's didn't. It bothered me. The ballots were left with me to destroy [there had been a motion to that effect] but I didn't destroy them. I took them home. My wife Colleen and I sat down and counted them all. We were quite shocked." Thatcher had given a false total. "He was just trying to ensure that some of the people who supported him would be delegates. And he disliked Don, so he wanted to see if he could do something about him."

Thatcher's rigging of the ballots meant that the order of the delegates changed. Don Swenson was listed as number seven rather than number one, but as long as he was a delegate it didn't matter very much. Seaman was relieved that only one person was directly affected; with a fair count Dorothy Swenson would have been a delegate rather than an alternate. Seaman thought about it for a while, and then decided to do nothing, since "it would have done terrible damage to the Conservative party." He adds, "The end will always justify the means. Colin believes that, no two ways about it."

CHAPTER NINE
PLAYGROUND OF THE RICH

"It's really peculiar that you won't listen to any newscasts or pick up any paper without finding a story about Colin Thatcher, the millionaire rancher," muses Don McDonald. "Every single time, it never fails. And Colin is not wealthy. . . . I suspect that I could name ten people in Moose Jaw who are wealthier than he is. I think it was Colin and JoAnn who were promoting that image to an extent. But it really isn't true. . . . I've never heard Ron Graham referred to as Ron Graham the millionaire, and his name pops up on the news all the time. And Ron's wealth is so much greater than Colin Thatcher's."

Ron Graham's grandfather, Philip, had started the family business in 1919, opening up a shop on Main Street in Moose Jaw. In 1967 the company had opened a branch in Saskatoon, and in the early Seventies it had grown dramatically, expanding to Regina, Edmonton, Calgary, and Vancouver. In 1978 Graham Construction began testing the waters in the United States, particularly Colorado, Texas, and Arizona, with such remarkable results that by 1980 Ron Graham was doing about $75 million worth of contract work annually and had spun off a string of subsidiary companies from Landsdowne Development Limited to Graco Masonry. Graham expertise developed and built such projects as Trinity Place, a $12.5-million, 215,000-square-foot office complex in Denver, and an $8.3-million office building in Seattle. For practical reasons Ron Graham became a genuine jet-setter.

Colin Thatcher was awed by Ron's business acumen and he valued the regular advice that Graham gave him about his own personal financial affairs. The men remained the closest of friends, playing golf as often as they were able, Ron talking

174

about the construction business, Colin about the cattle industry. Thatcher once told JoAnn that he had never before had a male friend with whom he could be so intimate and open.

The two families were close as well. The Grahams' three sons were best friends with the Thatcher boys, and Greg and Regan went on holiday trips with the Grahams to Minot and Calgary. Regan and Stephanie called Graham "Uncle Ron," although interestingly the Graham boys never called Thatcher "Uncle Colin." JoAnn and Jane not only chatted over coffee, they went on out-of-town shopping trips together. And it was the Grahams who introduced the Thatchers to Palm Springs.

"Palm Springs is my playground," Colin Thatcher would often say. "I live a very conservative life in Canada and Palm Springs is where I've always gone, where nobody knows who I am or, more important, cares."

Palm Springs, California, is not a flashy place like the Miami strip or Las Vegas. It's much like the tasteful emerald or topaz rings its residents wear; you have to know something about wealth to realize how much real wealth is there. Its appeal to the rich and famous is obvious—there's the (Charles) Farrell Road, the Gene Autry Hotel, the Alan Ladd Hardware & Gifts. A tourist who wanders into a men's apparel shop will find himself surrounded by autographed pictures of Dean Martin and Jackie Gleason, as he forks out fifty dollars for a shirt. A two-hour drive inland from Los Angeles, the desert town with a population of about 40,000 (which swells to more than 100,000 at the height of tourist season) includes many retired doctors, businessmen, and generals, and enjoys one of the highest per capita incomes in the entire United States.

Even the original natives, at least those few who survived the scourge of white man's diseases, got rich off the place. For hundreds of years the Cahuilla Indians gathered beneath the wild palm grove in the oasis at the base of Mount San Jacinto. They would ease their aches and pains in the mineral springs found there, believing, like future generations, in their magical healing powers. In 1891 Congress passed the Mission Indian Relief Act, which allotted the Cahuillas some 32,000 acres of reserve land, of which close to 7,000 is situated within Palm Springs. The Indian band remains the largest landowner in the area and its 150 members are among the richest native peoples in the United States.

During the late nineteenth and early twentieth centuries various hotels were built there; the primary attraction was the still-soothing powers of the mineral waters. The dry clear climate was also appealing, at least in fall, winter, and spring; it rained only fifteen or twenty days a year. But it was in the 1930s that Palm Springs became the mecca for vacationing Hollywood stars that it remains to this day. In 1932 Janet Gaynor convinced Charlie Farrell and Ralph Bellamy to buy some two hundred acres of land in Palm Springs at thirty dollars an acre, to build themselves a tennis court. They decided to build two, so guilty did they feel about "hogging" a single court to themselves. A small clubhouse and showers were added. This became the fabled Racquet Club at Palm Springs. After it opened its doors on Christmas Day, 1933, it quickly became the top vacationing spot for the glitter set. Marlene Dietrich, Greta Garbo, Ginger Rogers, Barbara Stanwyck, Joan Crawford, Mary Pickford, Lucille Ball, Greer Garson, Carole Lombard, Douglas Fairbanks, Spencer Tracy, Humphrey Bogart, Henry Fonda, William Powell, and Dick Powell all joined. It wasn't long before show-biz legends were made there. Norma Jean Baker, a young actress who had just been fired from Twentieth-Century-Fox, asked the famous photographer Dr. Bruno, "Bernard of Hollywood," for a job. He told her that he was about to do a magazine article called "The Racquet Club—Playground of the Stars" and invited her to come along. As she sunned herself by the club's famous pool, she was spotted by Johnny Hyde, a talent agent, who eventually moulded her into the superstar Marilyn Monroe.

As well as tennis, golf became the rage among the rich and famous at Palm Springs. The Bob Hope Desert Classic and the Nabisco–Dinah Shore Invitational are televised from there every year and golfers of the western world can turn on their televisions and drool over the lush surroundings. The handsomely manicured courses, preserved from the desert by constant irrigation, were one of the main drawing cards of Palm Springs for visitors like Ron Graham and Colin Thatcher.

Both men were keen golfers and had developed respectable handicaps. In fact the sport became something of an obsession with Colin. "He loved it. He'd play at least once a day and even when it was getting dark, he'd shoot an extra nine holes," recalls Lynne Mendell. "He'd get up at 6 a.m. I'd say, 'Come on, Colin, stay in bed.' He'd reply, 'No, Lynne, as attractive as that proposition is, I have my priorities.'"

Jane and Ron Graham bought a condominium that was part of the Cathedral Canyon Country Club golf course located in Cathedral City, a satellite community about sixteen kilometres southeast of Palm springs. JoAnn and Colin came for a holiday, were impressed, and decided to purchase in the same complex on Passeo Real Drive. R.T. Holdings duly bought the furnished white-stucco, adobe-style condominium with its two bedrooms, small den, kitchen, and living room. The cost was $82,500, and Colin took out a bank loan to cover $10,000 of the purchase price. Just a two-minute walk away, along a secluded road bordered by huge palm trees, was a lush green golf course and a luxurious club-house with tennis courts. Small swimming pools were everywhere. And uniformed guards were stationed to protect the residents from the revenge of the Palm Springs underclass, which is anything but wealthy.

Colin often said that he had bought the condominium for JoAnn. "JoAnn's primary complaint in earlier years was that we never went anywhere, and it was true. I was locked into a very difficult operation. We were always short of cash. We were like many other agricultural people—we were big on paper but never had cash. And basically I didn't have my operation organized well enough to get away very often and then part of it was psychological. You always think that nobody else can do the job that you're doing and you're absolutely irreplaceable." By 1977 his $21,000 annual salary as an MLA gave him some ready cash and his farming operation was becoming more and more mechanized. Once they bought the condominium, the Thatchers would consider Palm Springs their second home.

At Christmas of 1978 the entire Thatcher family vacationed there for over a month. JoAnn's sister Carolyn joined them for two weeks. She was a little shocked at what she found. "It was all partying down there. People were constantly coming in and going out. There was a lot of drinking. There was very little time for any quiet family life. I don't think either JoAnn or Colin wanted to be with the other at that point. Their time together was very difficult."

During this period JoAnn, who was usually a frugal person, went on the one extravagant binge of her life. She and Carolyn went shopping at Edith Morre Fashions, one of the most exclusive, expensive women's clothing shops in Palm Desert, and she spent somewhere between $1,500 and $3,000 on elegant women's fashions. Colin had to use two credit cards to pay the bill. JoAnn felt guilty about it, however, and paid part of the Visa charge with her savings. "Colin did not begrudge me buying the clothes," she said. "He had a very extensive wardrobe himself, but I'm not accustomed to spending that kind of money. I was uncomfortable about it and felt that it was wasteful."

"I don't know how many times the Grahams invited me to go down to Palm Springs," says Don McDonald. "They had their own private plane. They said, 'Come on, we'll just go for a weekend and it won't cost you anything.' But I said no. I've never been to Palm Springs. I really didn't like what it was doing to Ron and Jane and to Colin and JoAnn. They were changing, and Palm Springs was the focus. I resented it— what was happening to them.

"There was one thing that upset me most about JoAnn. I'll never forget and I couldn't believe it at the time. We hired a new manager for Prairie Co-Ax TV, and I invited him and all the shareholders, including Colin and Ron and their wives, to my house. This manager and his wife had just moved to Moose Jaw from Calgary. JoAnn sat beside the young woman and she said, 'Of course you can't buy clothes here. In fact, you can't even do it in Calgary or Vancouver. You pretty well have to go to Los Angeles.' I thought, Jesus, Moose Jaw was so bad that you couldn't even find a pair of jeans to wear. I couldn't believe that somebody could be that snobbish, especially when she had never been snobbish at all before. And I blamed it on Palm Springs."

But if JoAnn had developed certain pretensions, Colin had acquired a much more objectionable trait. Thatcher had become a womanizer of classic proportions.

"He was so open about it," says a close friend of JoAnn's. "We were in Regina one night with a friend from Vancouver— we had taken her out for dinner at the Cellar in the Sheraton Centre. I heard this voice in the booth at a level below us. He was throwing quite a line, going on how gorgeous his companion was and how she should go to California for the weekend with him. I said to my husband, 'That sounds like Colin.' I looked down and sure enough it was him, with some young woman."

JoAnn became suspicious that her husband was fooling around in the fall of 1977. As she later testified, "What distressed me the most was the fact that I had a husband who came home very late at night many times during the week, when the Legislature was sitting in Regina, but he was particularly late home on Wednesday night when the Legislature wasn't sitting at all. And by very late, I'm talking about two or three in the morning; and I can recall occasions as late as four o'clock, and these were not planned party occasions or anything like that." When she asked Colin about his late nights, he answered that since he had been drinking, he was afraid of being stopped on the highway by the police. He had to drink lots of coffee before he could leave Regina, he said.

"When he was home on weekends we were arguing because I was upset that he was out so late. We'd go out to an old friend's for just a weekend Saturday night and by eleven he was bored and wanted to go home. He was tired. Our company was not interesting enough any more," complained JoAnn.

She grew even more perturbed when Dick Collver told her that he had reprimanded Colin for missing so many caucus meetings and House sessions. These were the very evenings that Thatcher had insisted that he had been so busy with legislative business that he couldn't make it home until the wee hours of the morning.

On a couple of occasions JoAnn waited up for her husband and accused him of running around with other women. "If you don't like it, you know what you can do," he would scream. "You haven't got the guts to leave me anyway!" JoAnn claimed that twice he punched her with his fist, blacking her eye badly on both occasions. Thatcher had a different recollection of one of these incidents: "We had been arguing about something. The argument had taken place while we were in bed and I turned over quickly and caught her on the bridge of her nose with my elbow. It was accidental though I was turning in anger. I certainly did not intend to strike her and felt very badly about it after." He denied hitting her a second time. JoAnn did not consider these assaults accidents, however. She began to think of divorce. But for almost two years she kept her idea to herself.

One day Dorothy Yakiwchuk dropped in unexpectedly. JoAnn quickly reached for her dark glasses but before she could get them on, Dorothy noticed her ugly black eye.

"JoAnn would always cover up for Colin," says a close friend. "She said, 'Oh, I walked into the cupboard door, which is how I got this black eye.' That's why so few people in Moose Jaw would believe these things when they heard them later. She covered everything up."

In political circles, however, Thatcher's reputation as a philanderer was growing. Some of the secretarial staff at the Legislative Buildings grew so tired of his lascivious innuendoes and advances that they complained to their bosses. Not unexpectedly, nothing was ever done about it. A fair amount of gossip was generated when Colin and Bonnie Donison, Ross Thatcher's former personal secretary who had been a friend for fifteen years, were seen often together. They would dine at Golf's restaurant or the Sheraton and would attend social occasions at the Legislature together. Colin admitted he often went out with Bonnie but remained adamant that they were never romantically involved. "Our relationship is nothing more than brother and sister and has never been anything else."

But there were other liaisons that Thatcher later conceded were adulterous affairs. In court he admitted that he had taken Lorna Jackson, an attractive CBC news reader, away with him to Laguna Beach, a playground for the rich in southern California, in June of 1978. He would later say, "I felt absolutely disgusted and sick and everything else out of it. I came back just thoroughly repulsed with myself."

At about the same time he began to suspect that JoAnn was having an affair. The heavy emotional load of guilt and rage led to some very erratic behaviour. "Two weeks after he had been in California with another woman he accused me of giving him venereal disease," JoAnn once told a court. "I was in my bed—he came home from Regina. He came right upstairs to the bedroom. He hauled me physically out of bed and tried to push me out the front door. I broke away from him as he was trying to unlock the door. I ran down into the family room and at this point I didn't even know what was wrong. He kept accusing me. He called me every name you can imagine. It finally came out that he was a accusing me of having given him venereal disease. He said he couldn't go to a doctor. He might as well shoot himself because this was the end. I pleaded with him to go to a physician." Finally, two days later, he sought medical attention, and was told he had a slight infection that was not a result of sexual intercourse. He apologized to JoAnn, but she remained bitter about the incident.

It didn't help when he made sexual advances towards her sister when Carolyn was visiting their Moose Jaw home. "JoAnn had gone to bed and Colin had been drinking," remembers Carolyn. "He made this heavy pass. I told Jo later but she didn't seem to be surprised at all." The marriage had deteriorated even further.

"He locked me out of the house many, many times..." JoAnn once recalled. "On one occasion I simply had not been conversational on the way back from Regina. By the time we got to Moose Jaw, he'd gotten himself into such a stew and he never even indicated that he was upset. We walked to the door in silence. He stepped in first and slammed the door in my face."

A similar incident occurred when they were in Palm Springs in October, 1978. Colin and JoAnn had been dining with friends and were given a ride home with them afterwards. As usual the Thatchers got into a heated argument about something insignificant. Thatcher marched into the condominium first, locking the door behind him and leaving his wife stranded outside. "On that particular occasion, I went out and sat in a lounge chair by the pool," remembered JoAnn, "and he dumped me out of the chair, just like that."

After scenes like these, JoAnn would simply walk away from the house and head for the nearest friendly neighbour. Colin would usually come after her and say, "Oh I didn't mean it. Come back." Sometimes, however, he would escalate the emotional war. In November of 1978, Colin told JoAnn that he had gone to see Jack Rushford, a Moose Jaw lawyer, about getting a divorce. "I'll drive you down to sign the papers," he offered. Rushford later confronted Thatcher during a court hearing, claiming he had never been approached by him about a divorce, and Thatcher replied, "It was an unfortunate incident. As I walked out of the house, yes, I was going to go down and see you. I got over that one very quickly and I suppose I decided to let my wife stew a while before I contacted her later on in the day."

What bothered JoAnn even more than the physical violence she suffered were Colin's sudden, unpredictable flashes of anger. She felt that he was beginning to lose control of himself. "His distress was not related solely to his wife," says Gerry Gerrand, who as JoAnn's lawyer came to understand more than most people about Thatcher's motivation. "He was very unhappy with himself. From time to time he had feelings of inadequacy about how things were going, how people were treating him, which resulted in these displays of dark emotion." Thatcher himself often was a victim of severe emotional turmoil. One night JoAnn walked into his study and found him fondling a gun. He was seriously considering suicide. She talked him out of it.

JoAnn's friends began to wonder if there wasn't something dreadfully wrong with her marriage. During the 1978 election campaign, for example, the Thatchers visited Gerald and Adelaide Weckman in Rouleau. Since the Weckmans had remained staunch Liberals, Adelaide had not seen that much of JoAnn after Colin defected to the Tories. She observed a marked change in her. "She had lost a lot of weight and when I mentioned it she said she hadn't been sleeping very well. She also said that at her age it was time to take stock. I got the feeling that she was disturbed."

JoAnn would later tell a court, "By this time I was physically afraid of my husband. I had been abused, and I don't mean just a punch in the eye. I was very nervous when he came home because I never knew what kind of a mood or temperament he would be in. I was very much afraid that he would lock me out of the house as he had done on other occasions and keep the children inside and charge me with desertion."

During the spring of 1979, Colin realized that his marriage had soured, perhaps beyond redemption, and that there was a good chance JoAnn might leave him. He tried as hard as Colin Thatcher could to save it. He went jogging with JoAnn, socialized with the people she particularly liked, came home at a respectable hour, took the children on a short trip, even cleaned up the dishes once. To no avail. "It was not uncommon for me to find her crying in her room and I would go in and try to comfort her," said Thatcher. "I would say what can I do for you? How can I help you? She would say, nobody can help me. I'd ask what is the matter? It's nothing, I'll get over it, she'd say. I knew she was approaching her fortieth birthday and I knew this was bothering her."

In fact her despondency had little to do with her birthday,

and a great deal to do with her marriage, which she considered finished. She told her parents that she felt rather apologetic about not being more appreciative of his efforts to be nice to her, but it was too late, and she just didn't give a damn any more. "If only he had done that when I still cared," she said. It was too late, because by this time JoAnn was deeply, romantically involved with Ron Graham.

JoAnn had proven such a success at renovating Graham Construction's head office in Moose Jaw that she was hired to decorate the offices of their new branch plants as the company expanded. She designed the Vancouver office first, followed by the Edmonton branch. Although she travelled with Graham to these cities, there was no romantic involvement at that point. Indeed, on the occasion she went to Edmonton with him, the two met Jane there and went to a social affair. But early in 1979, JoAnn met Ron in Calgary to consult on the decorating of new offices there. They went out to dinner and a dance, and the sexual relationship began.

"We always felt that Ron and JoAnn would have made a marvelous couple if they had known each other before they were married," says a close friend. "They were both the same kind of warm, likeable people. Actually, though, I think it could have been anyone that would have been understanding and supportive of JoAnn. She was terribly vulnerable and Ron happened to be in the right place at the right time."

The Grahams were having difficulties with their marriage and Jane Graham suspected that Ron and JoAnn were having an affair as early as June, 1978. "The first time that that situation ever arose," Colin recalled, "Jane had indicated to me that she felt something was going on between them, and I scoffed at it. I didn't believe it and I told her so." But that summer JoAnn and the children visited the Geigers in Ames. She met Ron Graham in Des Moines and spent the day with him. "The phone rang and Jo answered it," recalls Betty Geiger. "Then she did a very strange thing. I was sitting in the living room and she in the dining room. She turned and said, 'Mom, this is a private call.' Afterwards she told us it wasn't Colin. And that was the first inkling we had that something was wrong with her marriage." JoAnn insisted in court, however, that her relationship with Graham was not sexual at that point.

The following Easter, April of 1979, JoAnn returned again to Iowa, and this time she spent three days with Ron Graham. "Colin phoned and asked for JoAnn," recalls Betty Geiger. "We told him she was shopping. 'Shopping at this hour?' he exclaimed. We reminded him that her brother Don lived in Des Moines. Colin called back three times. He was obviously very upset."

The Geigers liked Ron Graham. "He was very nice and treated us politely. We didn't criticize. It was her life and we never interfered, because it wasn't the way we did things," says Betty.

"I asked her one question about her relationship with Graham and it was in June," said Thatcher. "His wife had shown me a phone bill off Graham's credit card going back to when JoAnn had been in Iowa in April. During that interval— which was Easter—the Grahams were in Palm Springs, and according to Jane, Ron had disappeared for four days or she didn't know where he was for four days. She showed me a phone bill that he had apparently phoned JoAnn in Ames, Iowa."

Colin also was perplexed when Ron would call the Thatcher home at strange times of the day. "It was ostensibly for me. But it would seem to me to be times when he should not have expected me to be home. His wife kept telling me that they had a relationship, but I kept telling her that I thought she was wrong and that I couldn't believe it." When Colin confronted JoAnn with these allegations, she denied her involvement with Graham. "And Colin believed her," says a close friend. "He is so arrogant that despite all the signs to the contrary, he couldn't allow himself to believe that his wife was having an affair with his best friend. That simply couldn't be in the cards as far as he was concerned."

During June of 1979, JoAnn's crying spells intensified. "It wasn't uncommon for her to be that way three or four times a week," said Thatcher. One day JoAnn was so upset that Colin drove Stephanie, now a bright, mop-headed little girl of five, to school. She got out on the wrong side of the street and was hit by an oncoming car. Her thigh bone was fractured just below the hip. A cast was placed on her entire leg and she was confined to bed for many weeks. JoAnn blamed the accident on Colin's carelessness. It was one more serious wound to the already dying marriage.

Early in the summer JoAnn pleaded with Colin to allow her to take the children away on a holiday. She felt she needed time to be alone with them. He absolutely refused.

In July of 1979, JoAnn flew to Brampton, near Toronto, to visit her friends John and Mary Lee Sullivan. From 1971 to 1977, John had been the minister at St. Andrew's Church in Moose Jaw, where JoAnn was a devoted parishioner, and he had baptized Stephanie. JoAnn and Mary Lee had become the closest of friends. She found the warm and unpretentious minister's wife a welcome relief from the Moose Jaw and Palm Springs upper crust. Mary Lee had been born and brought up in Wyoming and the two "exiles" shared plenty in common, including children of the same age. "We were kindred spirits," says Mary Lee. But the two women seldom mentioned their problems. "She never, ever said a word against Colin, not once, in all the time we were together." On the last Sunday that the Sullivans were in church in Moose Jaw before their move to Brampton, Mary Lee caught sight of her friend; realizing how much she would miss Mary Lee, JoAnn had tears in her eyes. The visit to Brampton, however, was more than a reunion with old and valued friends. After long conversations with John Sullivan, JoAnn resolved to leave Colin. She signed an agreement to purchase a bungalow near the Sullivans' house for $72,000.

On her return to Moose Jaw, she summoned up her courage to talk to Colin about a possible separation. "He told me that there was no way he would ever let me have the children. He said he would fight me to the end of his resources. And that if I didn't shape up as his wife that he would bring another woman into the home and embarrass me out. I firmly believed that he would do this." JoAnn later told her lawyer that Thatcher ended the conversation by screaming at her, "If you take my kids, I'll kill you."

JoAnn decided that if she was ever to escape, she and the children would have to disappear without a trace.

CHAPTER TEN
LOVE, COLIN

AUGUST 13, 1979

Exactly one day after the Thatchers' seventeenth wedding anniversary, JoAnn packed some belongings and the two youngest children into her 1973 Ford station wagon and headed east. She had no fear of being stopped by her husband because she knew that Colin was once again vacationing in Laguna Beach with a twenty-year-old woman. She knew these details because Ron Graham had told her.

Her departure had been carefully planned. She had returned ten-year-old Regan's baseball sweater to his coach, she had taken back the library books, and she had ensured that her freezer was stocked with meals and baked goods for those she left behind. She also took certain documents pertaining to the Thatcher family's financial affairs. JoAnn later insisted that she had commandeered a small bundle of papers, including one quarterly report pertaining to the ranch and R.T. Holdings. Colin claimed that the entire estate file was gone, including the journal entries for the years 1974 to 1978.

These documents were important not only in subsequent court cases, but in drawing family battle lines. Peggy Thatcher was terribly angry after she learned, from Colin, that JoAnn had taken a copy of Ross's will. "I felt that that was personal property and I didn't think it should be tossed around as it had been," she said. "I really was upset at that. It was perhaps only a little thing but to me it meant a lot." That was one reason why Peggy chose to side with her son. Yet since she had loved JoAnn and been close to her, she was placed in a most unenviable position from this moment on as the marital wars began.

JoAnn paid what were, in fact, farewell visits to her many

friends, although she told no one except Dorothy Yakiwchuk that she was leaving. The possession of that knowledge would later put Dorothy in a highly vulnerable position.

JoAnn had given her oldest child's situation long and careful thought. Greg by this time was a tall, slender, good-looking fourteen-year-old about to enter high school. "Gregory was like his father in temperament—not a smiley, happy kind of kid, but a laid-back, very serious kind of person," recalls Wendy Garrett, who had a son the same age. "At birthday parties Greg would sit back and watch while the others fooled around. Even as a child he had a low, commanding voice which reminded me of his father."

Greg had always done well at school. His grade two teacher, Maxine Amer, described him as "my best student, a model student, very well mannered and fairly bright." By the time he reached adolescence, he seemed mature and responsible beyond his years. "The last time Greg was down he was delightful," says Betty Geiger. "He helped us so much, took responsibility for looking after Stephanie a great deal of the time. At the airport, he got the luggage off the carousel. We thought he was developing into a real nice boy."

Greg was only four when his two-year-old bull won grand championship at an agricultural show. From that point on he loved the ranch and everything to do with cattle. His father would brag that by the time he was thirteen "he could do almost anything on the ranch. He could drive any vehicle." Typically, when JoAnn decided to leave Colin, Greg was working hard out at Caron. "I didn't feel it was fair to take Greg out of the home at that time," JoAnn later explained. "He had done a lot of maturing in the last year. For the first time he was closer to his friends and he didn't jump into friendships easily. He was happy. He was looking forward to starting high school. I felt it was unfair to disrupt him from that. And he had a closer rapport with his father in that he worked on the farm. . . . And if things didn't work out and he wanted to come to me later, then he could do so." JoAnn also told her parents that there was another reason for leaving Greg in Moose Jaw. "She certainly did not want to hurt Colin too badly," says Betty Geiger. "That's why she thought it was best that Greg stay. Colin needed him." Gregory never forgave his mother; he always felt that she had abandoned him—and with his father's best friend.

On August 13, JoAnn explained to Greg that she, Stephanie, and Regan were going on a short vacation to a provincial park in southwestern Saskatchewan, and then she headed in the opposite direction. The first leg of the journey ended at Winnipeg, 625 kilometres east of Moose Jaw. JoAnn stayed there for two days, taking the kids to the zoo and on picnics, waiting for Ron Graham to arrive from Laguna Beach.

Thatcher and Graham had flown to Los Angeles on August 10, three days before JoAnn left Moose Jaw. Waiting for them was a special friend of Thatcher's, Janis Gardiner, who was the Tory press secretary in Regina, and another twenty-year-old from Saskatoon who was to be Graham's "date" for the five days they were together. They drove south to Laguna Beach, where they stayed in a luxurious condominium owned by a wealthy Calgary friend of Graham's.

Laguna Beach can best be described as a very private hideaway of the rich. A story that illustrates the neurotic local concern for security involves a maid whose identification card had expired. The next morning she was not allowed past the gate because her card had not been renewed. It was a simple oversight on the part of her employer; the guards had known the woman for years, knew that she was still working for the same people, knew that she was totally reliable. But still they would not allow her entrance. In Laguna Beach the rich could play in complete secrecy.

Graham, Thatcher, and the two women golfed, dined out, and sunbathed. Both men admitted to having sexual relations with one of the young women. In the middle of the week, the group flew to Palm Springs in a neighbour's private plane. Colin and Janis stayed in the Thatcher condominium and then flew back to Laguna Beach.

What with Palm Springs, Laguna Beach, the ocean, and the golf courses, it was a very pleasant vacation and Colin was surprised when Ron announced that he had to leave early. Thatcher drove him to L.A. International Airport in the belief that his unfortunate friend was rushing back to Vancouver on pressing business matters. When he later discovered the real reason for Graham's sudden departure—to meet JoAnn in Winnipeg—Colin became convinced that Ron had set him up.

He later explained how the holiday plans had developed. "That spring [1979], during the Legislature, [Janis] was Press

Secretary to our caucus and it was a common thing between 5 and 7p.m. for us to go down to the Press Club, or some place, and we would have a drink in that time interval. She was often with us, not specifically with me but with a variety of MLAs. I suppose that's really where it started, although not in a physical fashion. And I guess when the plan was made for California it was during the prorogation party of that spring." The trip was originally to begin August 3 but Graham delayed it a week, claiming that his friend's condominium was not available. Thatcher felt that Graham was toying with him, and this manipulation was the major reason why Thatcher's hatred of his old friend Graham took such a vicious twist.

Ron, JoAnn, and the two children left Winnipeg for Toronto on August 16. It was a long drive, and along the way they stopped at motels. While JoAnn insisted that she and the children be assigned one room and Graham another, she later admitted to having sexual relations with him. That she could do so after knowing he had just left the Californian embraces of another woman was something her friends could not fathom. "She was so ladylike and dignified. I think she was so desperate that she was just using him," says a close friend. JoAnn hinted at this herself. Her car was six years old, she had never driven more than 250 kilometres alone on the highway, and she felt she needed Graham's help. "It was the end of our relationship—I told him that. At that time I knew that he had spent the last few days before he helped me with another woman in California, as my husband had, and I accepted his help as an extension of friendship."

When they arrived in Brampton, JoAnn walked into her newly purchased house to find clothing and furniture still there; to her dismay she discovered that it could not be occupied until the end of the month. She also found that the Sullivans had just gone away on a family vacation to Wyoming. Where were they to go? At Ron Graham's invitation, and at his expense, JoAnn and the two children flew to Dallas for a three-day holiday. "Ron was away on business all day and I spent my time totally with the children, taking them out for lunch and to an amusement park." During the evening, however, and despite "the end of our relationship," Ron and JoAnn's lovemaking continued unabated.

JoAnn, Stephanie, and Regan then flew to Ames to visit the Geigers. "We knew she was coming but we had no idea that she had left Colin." says Betty Geiger "When we found out, we were very sympathetic, because by that time we realized that it was just a hopeless situation She told us that she couldn't have physically left if Colin had been there. He would have beaten her."

Ron Graham joined them in Des Moines and the foursome then flew back to Brampton, arriving the afternoon the Sullivans returned from their vacation. JoAnn's house was not available yet since certain renovations still had to be done, so she and the children spent an awkward few days at the Sullivans'. "By having her here, it meant we took sides against Peggy, whom I had been very friendly with. But there was nothing we could do. She was our close friend," says Mary Lee.

JoAnn had taken out a $52,000 mortgage, and had borrowed $20,000 from the Canadian Imperial Bank for the down payment on the house. Before returning to Moose Jaw, Ron Graham guaranteed the loan so JoAnn was able to obtain a far more favourable interest rate She had assets of some $32,000 in stocks and bonds—money that Ross Thatcher had given her—and felt she could live off that for two years, during which time she planned to take interior design courses. She had already registered at Ryerson Polytechnical Institute in Toronto, but then decided to postpone her classes until at least January. "I quickly concluded that I could not go back and forth as a regular commuter and look after my children adequately. My daughter was having difficulty crossing the street [because of her accident] and I felt that I needed to be there."

Both children were enrolled in the nearby Parkway Public School. They began Sunday school and Regan signed up for a hockey camp. "They never once asked to go home," said JoAnn. "They were so totally settled in. The little boy next door asked my son, 'Where are your toys?' and Regan simply said, 'I brought the ones that were important to me' Stephanie brought up her father two or three times. Regan never once asked for his father. They never asked for their brother after they were into the house. They totally accepted their move and, I think, in a remarkable fashion."

* * *

Meanwhile Colin Thatcher was in a frenzy. He had arrived home from Laguna Beach on August 15. At first he believed the story that JoAnn had told Gregory, primarily because he had not noticed that she was in any distress when he left for California. In fact, he claimed that they had experienced a glorious night of lovemaking on the eve of his departure. "If I had known she was leaving, I would not have been away," he said. "Consequently I sat and waited for the phone to ring.... I became very concerned when she didn't phone that first night because that was so unlike her. Greg had been left with a young lad, a terrific young lad, but still I had been so positive that she would phone to make sure that I had gotten home to take over with Greg. No phone call came, and I became very, very concerned that something drastic had happened to her."

The next morning promptly at eight Thatcher called the RCMP, but they had heard nothing. "It wasn't until that evening and I thought, my God, it isn't possible is it?" Thatcher ran upstairs and looked in her closet. "All of her pertinent clothes were gone, and then I looked at a few other things, and it was obvious that she had gone." Thatcher immediately phoned Jack Rushford, only to be told that the lawyer no longer acted for him. But for his wife, and that he was not prepared to reveal JoAnn's whereabouts. "That was a shock in itself," said Thatcher.

That night he also called his mother and the Graham household, hoping that Ron would be there. He wasn't but Jane announced that she would stop by later and have a drink with him.

"I'll really never forget her coming through the door," Thatcher recalled in court. "It was dark and I guess I didn't have the lights on in the house and she came in without knocking. It was almost eerie because, and I remember this so well, she was sort of illuminated by the lights of the street light behind her and I couldn't see her except her silhouette. I will never forget her words. She said, 'She's in Texas with my husband and I've told you before that they have been having an affair. She's with my husband in Texas.' I said, 'You're wrong. You are mistaken.' I was quite sharp with her. I didn't believe it."

The next day Thatcher phoned a business associate of Graham's and asked if he knew where Ron was staying in Dallas. The man was vague, couldn't give him the name of a hotel, but said he would relate the message. The following day Graham phoned and Thatcher told him everything, and asked if he had any idea where JoAnn might be. According to Thatcher, Graham expressed sympathy and shock, said he couldn't believe it and that he had no idea where she could be. If he could think of anything he'd phone Colin immediately, he added. Thatcher would later learn that Graham's call came from Brampton, Ontario.

"It was perhaps, outside of my father's death, the only time in my life that I have ever been that far down. And I don't know whether anything that I felt at that time would accurately reflect anything except the terrible misery and remorse that I felt, wanting my wife and two children to return and willing to pay almost any price to get them back."

Thatcher contacted Rushford and asked the lawyer to forward letters to JoAnn. He wrote three on Province of Saskatchewan, Legislative Assembly letterhead;

8/18 [79]

My dearest JoAnn,

Words cannot describe the agony, emptiness and grief inside me. Greg figured things out yesterday and he is heartbroken. I almost break down every time I look at him.

I beg you to communicate with me by phone. It is the not knowing that is so terribly difficult. I cannot eat, I cannot sleep, I cannot go very far in case you should phone.

Life has no meaning without you. You are my love and I will always love you. I beg you not to do this to our kids. Greg's face tells it all.

I am too grief-striken to be angry at your actions. I blame myself for being so intransigent about your desire for seclusion. I respect the manner in which you have withdrawn to your seclusion.

I pray your reflection will cause you to decide to

return to us. I have no terms or conditions—only an insatiable desire for you and the kids.

I have many questions about Stephanie and Regan. Please allow me to ask them soon.

I have always respected you, your actions in this case have increased this respect. You have done it with class. I know that you too hurt inside and feel much the same way I do.

I cannot imagine a life without you and the kids. *Please come home*. We both love you and need you.

Love
Colin

8/19

My Dearest,

I am writing this second letter because Jack [Rushford] is away until tomorrow and I cannot get it mailed until his return. It feels so strange to communicate in this fashion.

I deserve what you have done. Since I can do nothing except feel sorry for myself, by necessity I have also been reflecting. I feel guilty about many things, especially for the poor quality husband I have been for the vast majority of 17 years. However, I do feel I have been a good husband and father this past year. you have been a marvellous wife for 16 of our 17 years.

I again ask you to consider the positive aspects of our marriage and there are many. I have learned a lesson from this experience—a lesson I feel would be helpful in continuing our marriage.

While I yearn to know your plans and talk to the kids. I know better than to interfere with your seclusion. Even if I knew your whereabouts I would not come. I miss you all so desperately. I *learned* from this.

Come home.

Love
Colin

8/20

My darling Jo,

Time passes so slowly. It is terrible to wake up wishing this day was over.

Our son has become a man. I am amazed in the manner he has matured these past few days. I am very proud of him.

As I am proud of Greg, I ache for Stephanie and Regan. For their mother, I would pay any price to have her back.

A death in the family would be easier to handle than this. Still, I take all the blame for my intransigence in forcing this course of action upon you.

It is most repetitive in saying "I love you and need you." The lessons of this experience have given those words a much broader dimension than they have ever meant.

Please come home.

Love
Colin

"At the time I wrote those letters," Thatcher would later say, "I was absolutely destroyed. I did not know where she was. I was in the depths of remorse."

The letters brought on a weeping spell for JoAnn. But she had been subjected to Thatcher's manipulations and chicanery so often in the past that she realized that they may have been written either to pressure her into revealing her whereabouts so that he could snatch the children, or else to lure her back to Moose Jaw where the cycle of abuse would start all over again.

Thatcher, meanwhile, was desperately trying to find out where she was. He confronted her close friends, pumping them for information. Darla Spicer called one night to ask if JoAnn was back from her vacation yet. "Next time you're in town would you like to stop around," Colin asked. "I'd like to talk to you." Darla avoided his invitation, not only because she knew he would question her about JoAnn but because she felt he would make derogatory remarks about her good friend.

Thatcher realized that Dorothy Yakiwchuk was likely to know where JoAnn was. On several occasions, he stormed up to her house and loudly and angrily demanded to know the whereabouts of his wife. "He continued to harass our home and not only that, he did it with my children present. He had no consideration whatever about my children being there. I had to ask him to discontinue what he was saying and excuse my children to the downstairs or outside. He just—that was just not one consideration he had at all." Once he began throwing chairs around, so determined was he to pry the information from Dorothy. She refused to tell him anything. "JoAnn was physically afraid of Colin, and I knew that, and my loyalties lay with JoAnn, and I could not tell him, I could not." Thatcher finally gave up, but Dorothy remained terrified of the man.

Adelaide Weckman was also very concerned about her close friend and she went to the Thatcher residence to discover what she could. "I remember standing in the driveway talking to Peggy. She said to me, 'I can't understand why JoAnn would leave all of this,' and she pointed to the house and the cars, all the material things. And it went through my mind, 'My God, there's got to be something else in life. JoAnn can't stand living with that person [Colin].' That's more important than 'all of this,' the big Thatcher house, the swimming pool and so on. And you know, that was my turning point. I thought, 'Gee, this woman [Peggy] is on track two. She's not on the same track I am.'"

The week before JoAnn left, Gregory had noticed Mary Lee Sullivan's name on several parcels which his mother was mailing. Thatcher called a neighbour and old friend of the family's, Susan Beesley, and asked for the Sullivans' address and telephone number. He did not tell her why he wanted it and so naturally she gave it to him, something she regrets to this day. Thatcher phoned Mary Lee and while she did not tell him JoAnn was there, something she said made him suspicious. Peggy Thatcher, who had been close to the Sullivans, then phoned John Sullivan, who agreed to talk to Colin. "I phoned John Sullivan directly," recalled Thatcher, "and he let enough out which indicated to me that JoAnn had been in the company of Ron Graham."

Meanwhile Ron Graham was still periodically phoning Moose Jaw, supposedly from Texas. Thatcher played along; he was now lying in wait for Graham.

On August 25, Ron Graham returned to Moose Jaw and

Colin made a date with him to play golf the next day. What happened next is best told in the exact words Thatcher used at his trial for first-degree murder. "We were both reasonably good golfers and he was about to tee off on the fourth hole. I said, 'Usually I birdie this hole and when I sink this putt if you haven't told me where my wife and children are, I'm going to give you the embarrassment of your life in front of all these people.' He scuffed his drive and we rode the rest of the way basically in silence. And after I sunk my putt, I turned to him and started to walk towards him and he said, 'You know, you don't really need this.' I said I didn't believe him. And, we said some other words and he said, 'I don't know exactly where she is right at this .time. I think I can arrange for her to call you.' That really wasn't as much as I was looking for, but it was the first, the first, shall I say straw that I had in, in ten days to grab hold of, and I agreed." What Ron Graham later told the police was that on the fourth hole, as he sank his putt and birdied the hole, Thatcher snarled at him, "If you don't cough up where my wife and children are, I will kill you."

During Thatcher's trial for the first-degree murder of his wife, Crown attorney Serge Kujawa indicated that Thatcher had told Garry Anderson that he had threatened to kill Ron Graham. Thatcher responded. "I never threatened to kill Ron Graham."

KUJAWA: Right.

THATCHER: Where did I do that? That's a new one.

KUJAWA: It's new to who?

THATCHER: Me threaten to kill Ron Graham? I have never done that.

KUJAWA: You've never done that?

THATCHER: No.

KUJAWA: Of course, you haven't killed JoAnn Wilson either?

THATCHER: No, I most certainly did not.

JoAnn phoned Thatcher that afternoon from a pay telephone. At this point she was still visiting her parents in Iowa and had not yet returned to Brampton. "I talked to him briefly. I told him the children were all right, that I was all right. I refused to tell him where I was. I said, please don't come. I don't want to see you. I just told him that we were all right and not to worry about us. I told him the reason I wouldn't tell him where we were was because I was afraid that he would come and take the children. . . . He said I shouldn't be afraid of him. He said that there's no way he would take the children." JoAnn agreed to call him again.

While Colin was talking to JoAnn he could hear an echo from another conversation and he spotted what he suspected was a distinct Iowan accent. It was only a hunch, but he decided that JoAnn must be at her parents' place. He and Greg jumped on a plane to Des Moines the next day and then drove to Ames.

"They arrived unannounced just before supper," recalls Betty Geiger. "I invited them in and asked them to join us. Colin kept asking, 'Are you sure she isn't here?' I said, 'No. She was here earlier in the week.' But I could see he didn't believe me. He said, 'I've brought Greg along and he's close to his brother and sister. So if the kids are here, they can all stay and go to school here.' We knew that was just another one of his lies, just a front.

"And I'll tell you, that house was thoroughly searched from top to bottom on one pretence or another. He suddenly wanted to use the bathroom and up the stairs he went. Later he wanted to see the basement, then the family room. I knew he was looking for a phone number or address. And actually her phone number had been on a table. I slipped upstairs just as he came in and put it away where he couldn't find it.

"Then he coached us all evening and the next morning trying to get information out of us. He was ever so nice and polite. But Jo had warned me, 'He'll be talking about one subject and then in the middle of the sentence he'll switch suddenly on you and you'll have answered the question without ever realizing it.' That stood me in good stead, because he did exactly that.

"Finally the next day we were alone in the house and I said to him, 'This isn't getting us anywhere. I'm not going to tell you. I promised Jo I wouldn't. If I made a promise to you I would do the same thing. So you are just wasting your time.' After that they left."

Thatcher had a suspicion of where JoAnn and the children were. "And for about the next week or ten days I guess I just stumbled around suspecting they were in the Toronto area, but not knowing."

As she had promised, JoAnn phoned a few days later. "Colin told me that Greg wanted to come and look over the Toronto area. He put Greg on the telephone. I asked my son, 'Are you saying that you'd like to come to school here?' He replied, 'I want to come and look it over.' He wouldn't say he wanted to live here. I asked, 'Greg, is this something you want or is this something that your father wants?' It was obviously a ploy by Colin."

Thatcher asked her to call again. "He promised me that he had quit looking for me. He said, 'Don't worry. I understand that you need time.' He said he would not come to Toronto until I would come and meet his plane. Shortly thereafter the school phoned and said they had an inquiry as to whether my children were enrolled at that school. This terrified me. I called and got a hold of Colin. I was very upset. I told him I didn't trust him, that I was going to proceed with a divorce. He asked me if I would please wait a week. He said they were harvesting and that he didn't have a lawyer. He kept asking me over and over again, 'Don't do anything permanent. Don't do anything legal.' And I promised him that I wouldn't do anything. . . . Every time I believed in Colin I was the loser."

In early September, Jane Graham found a phone number in her husband's handwriting in "a place where it shouldn't have been." It had no area code. Colin persuaded a friend to dial the Toronto area code and the number and then carry on a phoney conversation while he listened in on the extension. He recognized JoAnn's voice. He was then able to convince someone he knew at the Saskatchewan Telephone Company to find—for a fee—an address that corresponded with the number.

On Tuesday, September 11, in Brampton, Regan and Stephanie set out for Parkway Public School. As they approached the schoolyard, they heard someone calling them. They were astonished to see their father and Sandra Hammond, their freckle-faced, seventeen-year-old babysitter, waving from a car. "Hi, kids, hop in!" their father yelled. Colin drove them to Niagara Falls. It was a sight that Regan had long awaited, and he was impressed. "Stick with me, kid," his father said.

Later that day they drove to Buffalo and then flew to Moose Jaw.

At 9:20 that morning the principal phoned JoAnn and told her the children were missing. In a panic she drove to Toronto International Airport. With her high heels clicking on the marble floor, she ran through Terminal Two asking this person and then that if they had seen a man with two children. She later told her parents that it had been an awful feeling but she had simply put aside her shyness and pride in her desperation to find the children.

Immediately she called Jack Rushford, who advised her to phone the police. "I did that. Then I called their grandmother and told her the children were missing. She simply said, 'I'm sorry.'" JoAnn then contacted Greg, who said he thought his dad was out at the ranch. JoAnn later discovered that Thatcher had told not only his son, but everybody she might contact, that they were to say he was harvesting "whether it was rain or shine."

Thatcher phoned her in Brampton at five the next morning, three o'clock Saskatchewan time. "Just as I picked up the phone, he said very coldly, 'Your children are safe and where you will never find them.' I was very upset." Later that day Thatcher phoned back and said he had enrolled the children at King George School in Moose Jaw. I packed the children's clothes and flew back to Moose Jaw that afternoon. Since she had asked Dorothy Yakiwchuk to meet her at the airport, she was surprised to find Colin waiting for her as well. She talked with him for about an hour but refused all attempts at reconciliation. She insisted on driving to Moose Jaw with Dorothy.

That night Colin phoned JoAnn at the Yakiwchuks and asked her if she would like to see the children. She said yes and walked over to the Redland house for a visit that evening. As she sat in the den, Colin riddled her with questions. Where had she been? With whom? What were her plans? JoAnn refused to answer and as she realized that he was growing more and more volcanically angry, she told him she'd like to go back to Dorothy's. Then, JoAnn later testified, they walked into the garage and suddenly Thatcher's temper flared. He kicked at her, hard, catching the knuckles on her hand. "I went back into the house and put my hand under cold water. Then I proceeded to walk home. By the time I walked back to Yakiwchuks', my hand was black-and-blue, and my knuckles were swollen."

Thatcher's version of events that night was very different. "I did not kick my wife, the thing is absurd. Shortly after she had returned from Brampton, we were leaving and I think we were just about to get in the car and she said I'm going to walk, and it was quite late and I said don't be silly, it's too late, and she started to walk about and I slapped her on the backside, which I often do...."

The next evening, Thatcher called again and asked if she wanted to see the children. Again JoAnn went to the Redland house and again they had a screaming session in the den. This time he informed her that he had obtained interim custody of the children, and threw the court document at her. "From now on you will not be allowed to see the children except under my close supervision," he spat at her.

JoAnn asked him if she could take the children out the next Friday night for dinner. He refused, but said she could bring in Kentucky Fried Chicken. When JoAnn went to buy the dinner she discovered that she didn't have her purse and spent time returning home to get it, which made her late. "Colin was standing in the driveway when I got there. He wasn't going to let me into the house because I was late. He was very abusive. I went to the front door and rang the doorbell and got in that way. He then snatched the car keys out of my hand yelling, 'If you're going to be here with the kids, I'm going to take your vehicle.' I protested, saying it wasn't mine, I had borrowed it. He finally gave the keys to me, left and came back in a more reasonable mood."

From that point on she always had to get his permission to see the children.

In Moose Jaw JoAnn temporarily moved in with her friends Gord and Elsie Eade, although at that point Elsie still was unaware that JoAnn had left Colin; she thought she and the children had been away on vacation. But JoAnn immediately confessed her affair with Ron Graham. "That really, really shocked me," says Elsie. "Of all the people I know I would have suspected it least of her and second least of him. they did not seem to be the kind of people to ever get involved in a situation like that."

Indeed, all of Moose Jaw was shocked. It was the talk of

the town for months. "Colin was telling everyone that JoAnn ran off with another man," says Adelaide Weckman. "No one ever knew that he was in Palm Springs with another woman at the time. That didn't come out. JoAnn wouldn't say anything, she didn't want to embarrass him." Moose Jaw would prove even more of a fish-bowl for JoAnn in the coming months, although more like a fish-bowl inhabited by sharks, eager to tear her reputation to shreds.

One of the worst lies Thatcher told JoAnn's friends was that his wife had agreed that he could have custody of the children for a million dollars, or "as much money as he could raise."

After Gord and Elsie had gone to work in the morning, Thatcher would barge into their home unannounced, ostensibly to talk reconciliation with JoAnn. Many of these meetings turned into verbal bullying sessions. He told JoAnn that since she wasn't a Canadian citizen she didn't stand a chance of gaining custody. He suggested that she should leave town (without the kids or a property settlement) before the situation became more difficult and embarrassing for her. He boasted that he was experienced in public speaking and that her lawyer could not make him say anything he didn't want to. "My lawyer will make mincemeat out of you. He's a real crackerjack," Colin insisted. The man he had chosen for the job was his sharp-tongued former colleague in the Legislature, Tony Merchant.

"Colin told me that he asked around, that he had asked Roy Romanow, Saskatchewan's attorney general, and was told, rightly or wrongly, that I was the best marital lawyer in the province," says Merchant. On September 12, the day of the children's return, Merchant had obtained an *ex parte* order for interim custody from Mr. Justice R.A. MacDonald on Thatcher's behalf. This was meant to maintain the status quo, to prevent the children from being grabbed back and forth by the parents, until a motion for permanent custody could be heard. But because he had once been an associate of Ross Thatcher's Mr. Justice MacDonald disqualified himself from any further proceedings regarding the Thatchers.

Merchant then had the opportunity to sniff out a Queen's Bench justice who he thought would be sympathetic to Colin Thatcher. "Tony came into my chambers without an appointment," says M.A. (Sandy) Macpherson, who is now retired. "'Can I see you, My Lord?' he said. he told me that he was acting for Colin Thatcher, that there'd been a split-up, that his wife had run off with another guy. He then led me to believe that all my colleagues down the corridor had disqualified themselves because of some political connection with either Ross or Colin. So I said, "If everybody is disqualified down this corridor, it's got to be me.' Subsequently several of them told me that they wouldn't have disqualified themselves. Tony gave me a line there, and by the time I found out I was into the thing."

"I picked out MacPherson," says Merchant, "because I think over the years he was the best marital judge in the province. He had an ability to listen, he took very strong opinions and he tended to jump to conclusions, but he would listen and jump back." Merchant also concluded that MacPherson, because of his family's prominence in the province, would have an understanding of the importance of the Thatcher family name and reputation.

CHAPTER ELEVEN
CUSTODY

Judge M.A. MacPherson's father grew up in Cape Breton, the youngest in a poor Scottish immigrant family and the only one of six siblings to be educated. Murdoch MacPherson fought his way through to a law degree from Dalhousie University in Halifax and then went west to the land of prosperity, arriving just in time to sign up for the Great War. Since the possibility of his emerging from the trenches alive seemed remote, his first-born was given the family name in toto—Murdoch Alexander MacPherson. He never used it, however, preferring the formal "M.A." or informal "Sandy."

Murdoch Senior survived the war, albeit with a badly shattered leg, and returned to Saskatchewan to work as a lawyer, first for the civil service and then in private practice. In 1925 he won a seat in the provincial legislature as a Conservative, representing the riding of Regina City; he was named attorney general in the Co-operative government, a strange mixture of Conservatives, Progressives, and Independents that somehow managed to stay in office from 1929 to 1934. After his political career ended, MacPherson Senior continued to thrive as a lawyer in the firm MacPherson, Leslie & Tyerman, which to this day remains a pillar of Saskatchewan's legal establishment.

Sandy MacPherson followed in his father's footsteps in almost every way. At the age of sixteen he was sent back east to Dalhousie, but when the Depression resulted in a shortage of funds for even a prosperous lawyer's family, he completed his final two years at the University of Saskatchewan, receiving a law degree there in 1938. The family pattern continued, for once again a European war interfered with MacPherson plans: the next year he too enlisted.

The war years were exciting and educational for the

handsome young MacPherson. For a time he served as a court-martial officer, prosecuting the randy young soldiers who had gone AWL for long periods. Unhappy with the justice that was being handed out—"it was pretty bloody awful"—he asked for a transfer. He was trained as a supply officer, and three months before D-Day he was named Staff Captain of supplies and petrol of the 2nd Canadian Corps. In that capacity he travelled across France, as part of the liberation forces. In early 1944 he and two other soldiers in a jeep wandered into the coastal town of Le Touquet. When MacPherson spotted a very pretty eighteen-year-old with long blonde hair, jumping up and down and yelling at them, they stopped the jeep and she came running and gave Sandy a hearty kiss. It was a clichéd scene from the liberation, and yet... they talked. Her name was Dorothy Borutti. Her parents had operated an exquisite hotel in the charming resort town but the family had suffered terribly during the war, and her father had died only months before. MacPherson and company were the first members of the Allied forces to reach them.

Sandy and Dorothy were married a few months later by the mayor of Le Touquet. Over the years the two would return often to France and MacPherson would develop a reputation as a superb photographer, noted for his portraits of European faces. All of this gave Mr. Justice MacPherson a sophistication, worldliness, and self-confidence that marked his performance as a judge.

After the war MacPherson joined his father's law firm, where his specialty was civil and criminal litigation. "I didn't want to do corporate law," he says. "But as the oil business came, and the firm started to grow, I was being squeezed out of the money." In 1955 he started his own law practice, which quickly thrived. "There was a time after I left my father's firm when I seemed to be acting for every used-car dealer in Regina. This was great fun. I was not only their solicitor but also their conscience."

Like his father before him, MacPherson remained a devoted Progressive Conservative and a supporter and friend of John Diefenbaker. "After the change of government in 1957, I had the patronage of Regina in my hand. I said, 'Take this away from me and don't give me any of the legal work.' I wanted to be clean." In 1962, Diefenbaker phoned him and said, "Sandy, wonder if you would like to go to the appeal court?" MacPherson replied, "I'm honoured, Mr. Prime Minister, but there's a vacancy on the Court of Queen's Bench and I would prefer that. You were a trial lawyer. Would you at age forty-four like to spend the rest of your working life on the Court of Appeal?" Diefenbaker agreed that the Court of Queen's Bench it would be. MacPherson would remain an odd animal in the corridors of Regina's courthouse—one of the very few judges who was not a liberal or beholden to that party's patronage machine.

During his twenty years on the bench, Mr. Justice MacPherson tried every kind of case, from murders to contested elections. But he developed an expertise for trials that involved massive amounts of detailed information. "I've always felt that MacPherson was, if not the best, one of the best, trial judges during the past decades," says Gerry Gerrand. "However, he was not without his faults. He should have been born a country gentleman with a big house in the Cotswolds, with lots of books, and things to do." "Sandy was an excellent judge," says a justice of the Court of Appeal, "but he certainly was arrogant. If you didn't invite him to a party, he would be pleased because if he wasn't invited the party was not worth attending anyway." MacPherson was considered something of an eccentric, so outspoken was he during deliberations in the courtroom and in his judgments afterwards. He was also considered a superb writer. "I used to read his judgments because he had a very good command of the language," says Fred Johnson, Lieutenant-Governor of Saskatchewan and a former chief justice. "He was one of the best writers we've ever had on the bench." All of these qualities were about to be tested in the fire of the Thatcher custody case.

Both sides expected that the hearing for permanent custody of the three Thatcher children would go ahead on October 10, 1979. But MacPherson felt strongly that both parties needed time to cool off, to think rationally, and perhaps even come up with a solution of their own. "I gave them what I call my standard Ann Landers talk. 'You've got your duties to the children. I want you to think practically and not emotionally.' I went on for twenty minutes to half an hour. I told them that if I did try the case it would not be on the basis of who is the good guy and who is the bad guy. The issue was the welfare of the children, plain and simple."

Peggy Thatcher was in the courtroom that day. Mr. Justice MacPherson looked directly at her and told her that she had a responsibility as a grandmother to act as a go-between and not to be biased. He then adjourned the case for a month. "There's no reason why you people can't sort out the problems yourselves," he said. MacPherson did, however, give JoAnn access to the children three days a week. Colin was to leave the Redland home on Saturday morning and not return until the following Monday evening; it was an order Thatcher strongly resented.

That evening he called JoAnn to tell her that he was unhappy with the arrangement and that he wanted access to the house on the weekends to shower and change. "It's very obvious the judge is going to give me the children because of the way he's come down on this," Colin said. "Let's make a deal. I'll give you generous visiting time and I'll pay for airline tickets and other expenses, if you just drop the case at this point and go away." JoAnn told him she wasn't interested and that he would not be welcome in the house on weekends.

The next Saturday, JoAnn arrived at the Redland home to find that Thatcher had taken his two sons goose hunting. They arrived home at 11 a.m. and she ran out to greet them. "Colin was very abusive," said JoAnn. "He screamed at me, 'If you're going to be miserable and not bend the rules this is all you're going to get.' Then he called me all sorts of names in front of Greg and Regan. I went into the house and when I was talking to Greg, I was in tears and I said, 'Greg, your father's not perfect either.'" Greg's cold retort was "My father told me that you would try and turn me against him." That afternoon the fourteen-year-old was playing in a collegiate football game in Regina. JoAnn had been planning to take the two younger children to watch their big brother in action but she discovered that the only available vehicle had been taken to the garage for a tune-up. To make matters worse, that night Colin had given Greg permission to go to a party. He spent Sunday with his friends. "The only time Greg was in the home the entire weekend was that Sunday night," said JoAnn. And he was very cool, almost rude to his mother.

The next weekend was a similar story until finally on the Monday morning Greg told his mother that he would not be

staying with her any other weekends. "I asked him if this was
his choice," said JoAnn. "He indicated that it was. He said he
was fourteen years old and he didn't have to go or stay
anywhere he didn't wish." Colin later remarked jeeringly that
the court order did not say how many children were supposed to be in the home when JoAnn was there. "When I
came home from Brampton, Greg was a very warm boy," said
JoAnn. "Very warm to me. And I was glad to see him, and I
felt compassion and warmth with him. Our conversations up
to that time on the telephone had been very positive. The
change came the day that this court put in the weekend
ruling, and I feel that Colin went directly home and by his
influence and his pressure . . . he turned Greg against me." It
was the beginning of Thatcher's long and insidious campaign
to poison the children's minds against their mother. Outside
of her actual physical injuries, nothing would prove more
nerve-wracking or heartbreaking to a woman who had dedicated so much of her life to the rearing of her children.

On November 9, 1979, at nine on a clear, cool morning,
JoAnn, Darla Spicer, and Dorothy Yakiwchuk gathered at the
Redland home. They were planning to drive together to
attend the custody hearing in Regina scheduled for ten that
morning. Since JoAnn wanted to read over some documents,
she asked Darla to drive, but when her friend turned the
ignition of the 1973 Ford LTD station wagon, nothing happened.
She tried again, without success. JoAnn was surprised because she had driven the car the night before and there was
no sign then of a mechanical problem. Dorothy's husband
was called and he discovered that the distributor cap was
missing. It was the first of a long series of automobile mishaps
that would occur over the next year and a half, many of them
serious and life-threatening.

The three women arrived at the Regina courthouse to find
Colin in a jovial mood. "He thought it was all a big joke," said
Darla Spicer. "He smirked at us when we went into the
courtroom. 'You're just wasting your time. I'm going to win
this hands down.' Merchant was the same way. JoAnn was
very worried and upset, thinking that she wasn't going to
win."

The strategy of her lawyer, Jack Rushford, was simply to let
JoAnn tell her story of how and why the marriage broke

down. She did not try to hide her affair with Graham, but claimed that it was over, that she had not seen him since her return from Ontario. "I deeply regret any involvement I had with him," she told the court.

In cross-examination, Merchant's approach was to show that JoAnn had no intention of staying in Moose Jaw if she was given custody of the children, and that she would uproot them. Merchant questioned her: "You had always complained about Moose Jaw. Indeed you said once to Colin that if you lived there, you supposed Stephanie would grow up and marry one of these cruddy Moose Jaw types?" "No," JoAnn answered. "That doesn't sound like my language." Merchant responded, "Well, I made up the word 'cruddy'. As a matter of fact, I think the word you used was 'labourer-type', one of these Moose Jaw labour-types." "No, I don't believe I would have said that," retorted JoAnn. She pointed out that she had already sold the house in Brampton and had decided to remain in Moose Jaw with her children.

Four of JoAnn's best friends, Elsie Eade, Darla Spicer, Adelaide Weckman, and Dorothy Yakiwchuk, took the stand to point out what a superb mother and homemaker JoAnn had been. Of Colin, they remarked that he had seldom been home over the years and that he had had very little to do with the raising of his children.

Thatcher's and Merchant's strategy was obvious from the beginning. They believed that as long as they could show that the children were well looked after, the Thatcher name and prestige would be enough of an ace in the hole that MacPherson would certainly give Colin custody. To that end they called as witnesses Beverley Hammond and her daughter, Sandra.

The Hammonds, whose lives would become so tightly intertwined with Colin Thatcher's, and with his court cases, lived on 3rd Avenue, about four blocks away from the Redland house. Ron Hammond was an instructor of electronics at the Saskatchewan Technical Institute. Beverley was a homemaker caring for her three children. In 1975 she began babysitting the Thatcher kids and as JoAnn began to work at her interior design business, her services were needed often. By 1979, her daughter Sandra had taken over the babysitting duties.

Sandra was then a plump, fair, freckled girl of seventeen, a grade twelve student at Central High School. After JoAnn left Colin, Sandra came into the Thatcher home every day and supervised the lunch hour. She picked Stephanie up after school, made the supper, did the dishes, put the little girl to bed, and laid out the children's clothes for the morning. For that she received five hundred dollars a month, and the occasional use of Colin's yellow Corvette.

The Hammonds had taken sides in the Thatcher marital battles very early on. Colin had asked Beverley if Sandra could go with him to get the children in Brampton. After some thought, for she realized the significance of this action, Mrs. Hammond agreed, and her daughter Sandra was with Thatcher when he snatched Regan and Stephanie on their way to school. From then on the entire Hammond family would be sucked into the bizarre and tragic events that would beset the Thatchers over the next half-dozen years.

There were two other witnesses called by Merchant. Dr. Fred Wigmore, the very man who long ago had chaired the famous debate between Tommy Douglas and Ross Thatcher, said about Colin, "I've known him since he was eighteen months old, I believe, and I've always had a very high regard for his ability, his conduct and his ideals." But Wigmore did not indicate whether he thought JoAnn or Colin was the better parent. Wayne Ralph, principal of King George School, simply testified that the Thatcher children did well at school.

There was someone else, however, waiting in the corridors of the Regina Court House, who was anxious to take the stand. Thatcher had decided that his fourteen-year-old son should testify against his mother. When JoAnn learned that Greg might give evidence, she felt as though she had been punched in the stomach. He was not called, however, because Mr. Justice MacPherson was dead set against it. "I think it would be dreadful on a child of that age, a terribly impressive, sensitive age, to go back and tell his brother and sister what he saw here, what was asked, and to tell his friends. And for the rest of his life to remember that he testified in this case. It's bad enough for him to know that his parents can't get along, without him having to participate in the determination." Greg was furious when he learned that MacPherson wouldn't hear him. He refused to speak to Tony Merchant for some time, claiming that he hadn't tried hard enough to convince the judge.

One piece of evidence that emerged disturbed MacPherson

greatly and would indeed prove to be an omen of things to come. Before the hearing, Colin had placed a newspaper clipping from the Moose Jaw *Times-Herald* on the door of the refrigerator. It was headed: "Man ordered to pay $80,000 for affair with friend's wife."

The story was date-lined Warwick, R.I. (AP).

> A superior court jury has ordered a West Warwick man to pay $80,000 to a former friend for having an affair with the friend's wife.
> "This is like something out of the Dark Ages," Joseph McGair, lawyer for defendant Sidney Robinson, said after the verdict Monday. "It's as if people have been in closets for the past 40 years."...

"I felt it was most cruel for Thatcher to do that," says MacPherson. "He left it up while she was there. He said it was a joke, but it wasn't a joke to her. He wanted to show the kids that their mother was an adulteress, that's why he put it up. It was most evil."

Both JoAnn and Colin were asked why they should be given custody of their children. Their answers reflected strikingly different values. JoAnn said, "I feel that they'll have a much more emotional upbringing. I think they'll feel much more secure. I think they'll have more self-esteem. I can give them a more personal confidence. I think they will get along better with people. I can offer them a wider, warmer range of friendship in terms of family. They have been really segregated from most relations with other family members."

Colin said, "There is a stability factor that I can perhaps offer that she cannot. I'm established where I am; I have roots. I have an operation in place, which enables me to have time to devote to them through this difficult period.... I can give my children a little bit of both worlds, urban and rural.... My children can get a taste of what it's like to go out among the cattle, see the calves born and watch us wean them. At the same time, we come back into town, we clean up and step right into an urban existence... I suggest very few children have that sort of an option."

In his closing argument to MacPherson, Merchant enlarged on this theme. "I tried to communicate what seemed so obvious to me—that there is a great benefit for these children to grow up as Thatchers in Saskatchewan, to grow up as people with a reputation hanging over their heads, a reputation to live up to. . . . In part I felt that because Mr. Justice MacPherson had grown up with this same millstone around his neck as I had and Colin had, he would appreciate that being mentioned in the final arguments." In fact MacPherson was furious that Merchant would bring up his personal background. "This was a classic example of Tony's, if not bad judgment, bad taste," says MacPherson. "You don't bring the judge's personality into it. It was disgusting." MacPherson reserved his judgment to further study the evidence.

That evening Thatcher phoned his wife and demanded that she return the family's 1973 Ford station wagon, which she had driven to Brampton. A young man had been paid to return it to Moose Jaw; he had done so, and she had been driving it ever since. She said she would bring the car over if he would replace it with one of the family's six vehicles. He flatly refused to do so. Five minutes later the station wagon disappeared from in front of the Yakiwchuks' house where JoAnn was staying. Thatcher later told her he had taken her keys that day, and that the Ford had been driven to Palm Springs by this same young man. That left JoAnn without transportation until she was able to purchase a 1978 Thunderbird in January of 1980.

On November 27, MacPherson brought down his decision. Colin was awarded the custody of Greg, JoAnn the custody of Regan and Stephanie.

"There are several positive reasons for awarding custody of Regan and Stephanie to the wife. She is a much warmer, more affectionate and sympathetic person than the husband. I venture the thought that his lack of these qualities, his failure to appreciate the wife, caused the marriage breakdown. Adultery is rarely the cause, it is the result."

Of Gregory, the judge had this to say: "It is hard to accept that Greg adopted this [negative] attitude to his mother without his father's interference. The news item on the refrigerator shows how far the husband, carelessly or deliberately, is prepared to go.

"But Greg's preference is real. I cannot order him to live with his mother while he possesses it. He is too old, at fourteen, for that. The order would be either unenforceable or disruptive."

Thatcher had not allowed himself to even consider the possibility of the judge failing to award him the two youngest children, so when he heard the news he was "crushed". JoAnn came over to talk to him the same night, a Tuesday, that the decision came down. She asked her husband if he would allow her to move into the Redland house with Stephanie and Regan, pointing out that the home was registered in her name. His reply was a bellowed "No!" Since she was then living with the Yakiwchuks, she asked if Stephanie and Regan could remain here until the weekend, by which time she would have found accommodation for them all. "I would be delighted if you would leave them forever," was his reply. It was the biggest mistake JoAnn could have made. By Friday Tony Merchant had filed a motion to appeal MacPherson's judgment; with it came an automatic stay of the custody order, which meant that the children would remain where they were, living with their father, until the appeal could be heard several months later.

Not only that, JoAnn suddenly found herself without a lawyer. At the beginning of the custody hearing, Merchant had popped up and asked Justice MacPherson to disqualify Rushford from acting for JoAnn. Thatcher claimed that while Rushford had not done all of his legal work, he still considered him his personal solicitor and he pointed to the Ab Neufeld lawsuit as an example. He insisted that Rushford had access to personal financial information that could prove detrimental to him in a matrimonial property trial. Rushford had denied that he had any such information or that he was Thatcher's solicitor and MacPherson had dismissed Merchant's request. Still, Rushford felt he had to bow out of the case, although he says it had nothing to do with Thatcher's attempt to intimidate him. "I could see that the custody and matrimonial matters would probably take all one's time and attention for many months," says Rushford. "I had a general practice and simply couldn't spend the time." He phoned a friend in Regina who recommended two lawyers who specialized in family law. One was Tony Merchant, the other had already been retained by Thatcher for one of his sons. Rushford then recommended Nick Sherstobitoff of Saskatoon. Sherstobitoff told JoAnn that there was still one means left by which she could get custody of Stephanie and Regan immediately; she could try to get an order lifting the stay of judgment pending an appeal. This would require the intervention of an appeal court judge.

The application to set aside the stay was considered on December 5, 1979, by Mr. Justice Mervyn Woods. He concluded that it would be better for the children if they remained in their Redland home. Of the twenty-nine court appearances the Thatchers would undergo during their marital struggle, this was one of only two times JoAnn would lose. But it would prove to be a disastrous decision for her. "I have constantly, and I am not alone in this, believed that if Woods had not ordered a stay of my judgment a great deal would not have happened that did happen," says MacPherson. "This was a great judicial error."

JoAnn continued to exercise her access to the Redland house and the children on weekends. Thatcher's harassment and dirty tricks continued unabated, although he would later insist that these confrontations were attempts at reconciliation. "I very much wanted my wife to come back and see if we could sort things out. As a matter of fact, I made a fool of myself for several months trying to put it together at all costs," said Thatcher.

Thatcher asked his old friend and mentor Dick Collver to act as a mediator. By this time Collver had stepped down as leader of the Conservative party and had been replaced by Grant Devine, but he was still sitting as a Tory MLA. Dick agreed to intervene, and he and his wife, Eleanor, took JoAnn out to dinner at the elegant Upstairs Downstairs restaurant in Regina. "She kept repeating over and over, during the course of the evening, that she would not return [to Colin] because she was afraid, and that she was afraid for herself and she was afraid for her children." In fact, JoAnn was so nervous and upset that she became sick to her stomach and had to be helped to the washroom by Eleanor. The Collvers then took her home.

"She was afraid of Colin, she really was," says Darla Spicer. "She told me, 'If I am ever killed you will know who will have done it.' I said, 'Don't ever think that, JoAnn, that will never happen.' Because at that point I never thought it would."

Despite her fear, JoAnn became more and more determined to fight her husband, although she already had some idea what the cost might be. Her close friends noticed that she was losing weight rapidly. She was taking sleeping pills, which weren't helping much, and dark circles ringed her eyes. She was also in a very confused and troubled state of mind. Two months earlier, in October, she had visited a young psychic, Susan Roberts, who had arrived in Moose Jaw the year before to discover there was a thriving market for her talents. Roberts developed a large clientele, gave courses in psychic development at the community college, and delivered guest lectures at the University of Regina. Today, she remembers JoAnn well. "One of my clients, a dentist, came in one day and handed me a ring. I said, 'This isn't your wife's or anybody's like that. Whoever owns this ring is in a legal battle and is also in trouble. I'm not prepared to discuss it with you. If she wants to come in, fine.'

"Not long afterwards this lady drove up in a battered old car. She was dressed very plainly in jeans and a T-shirt and no jewellery. I had no idea who she was at that point. I said, 'You're the lady who gave my client the ring.' She was very vague about it, would give me very little personal information, because she was testing me." During that first reading, Roberts said among other things that a yellow Corvette was involved, that JoAnn had been experiencing marriage problems for a good seven years, and that her husband was a tremendously strong, domineering individual. JoAnn was impressed with her insights, and for the several months before Roberts moved to Edmonton, JoAnn saw her almost every day.

"She had a tremendous fear of her husband, no doubt about that. She kept saying, 'Am I safe, am I okay?' I kept saying, 'Yes, but there are certain steps you have to take to ensure that.' But even at that point I was very concerned for her. I said this is not the end of the struggle, this is the beginning."

For months Thatcher had been pressuring his wife to go to Palm Springs for Christmas. "It was getting very late and very difficult to get reservations but I had been able to piece one together and I was trying very hard to get her to come," said Colin. "Her return ticket would be open-ended with the agreement that if it wasn't working out she could come north when she chose." At this point such suggestions were something of a joke to JoAnn. She chose to spend Christmas with her sister Carolyn in Anchorage, Alaska, although she did not object to the children going, since they had been looking forward to it for some months.

On December 15, Thatcher, the three children, Sandra Hammond, and Sandra's boyfriend Blaine Mathieson (who had been given JoAnn's ticket) were boarding a plane in Regina when Colin was handed a divorce petition. It was a lengthy document, and he read it with anger and dismay on his way to Palm Springs. After Christmas Colin phoned Dick Collver and asked if they could all come and visit him in Arizona. During the fall, Thatcher had done a lot of crying on Dick's shoulder. "He was obsessed with his marriage problems," says Collver. "He couldn't think about politics or anything else. As a result I said to him in passing one evening, Why don't you come to the ranch between Christmas and New Year's, which is exactly what he did."

Dick had bought an old dude ranch in Wickenburg, Arizona. It was complete with a schoolhouse, sumptuous western lodgings, a small rodeo grounds, stables, and a grand old ranch house with a huge circular fireplace. Visitors (and they were many) expected to see Roy Rogers or Gene Autry come riding up at any moment. What they usually saw was Dick Collver holding court. He and his family lived in a large house perched on a hill, with a spectacular view of the Arizona desert.

"Dick's plan for the ranch was both ingenious and a bit off the wall," says one guest. Curiously, in the large state of Arizona most of the land is taken up by Indian reserves or federal parks, or is owned by the state, so there is very little left for real estate development. Collver was planning on developing largish plots of at least five acres each, upon which million-dollar houses would be built for those Americans fleeing to the sunbelt. And, as an added attraction, Phoenix was only a hundred kilometres away.

The Thatchers, Sandra, and Blaine made the four-hour drive from Palm Springs to Wickenburg a few days after Christmas. (The exact date remains unclear.) Dick and Eleanor were not home when they arrived but the Thatchers made themselves comfortable looking at the horses and wandering around until the Collvers got back at six. During the dinner Colin talked continuously about his marital problems. Whenever he or young Sandra Hammond mentioned JoAnn, they called her "the bitch"—a slur they would use repeatedly throughout their stay. Dick and Eleanor were upset by this, and appalled by the effect this would have on the children, who were hearing their mother described in this way all the time.

The next day Collver got up early to do some work around the place. At about ten, Colin suggested to him that they have a chat over coffee and orange juice. Collver later testified: "He opened up by saying, 'I have only one solution for the bitch.' 'What is that, Colin?' I asked. 'I've got to hire somebody to kill her. Now in the past we've talked about lawyers you knew in Alberta'—and it's true a good friend of mine, Ken Harkness, had many, many bad people as clients— 'Will you please call them and find out who will do the job?' I was horrified and I protested, 'No, don't even talk to me about this. I don't wish to discuss it. You're embarrassing me. As a matter of fact you're going beyond friendship by even discussing this with me.'"

Collver contends that on three occasions, once in the morning, once shortly after noon, and once in the evening, Colin pleaded with him to find a hit man to kill JoAnn. "And I kept saying to him, 'Colin, you're obsessed! Stop it. Get on with your life.'" Collver was outraged by what was happening, and he was even more furious when he found out that Colin and Sandra had spent hours teaching Greg and Stephanie to play "Let's Get Ron Graham." Thatcher had somehow obtained a Graham Construction Company credit card and now the children were placing long-distance calls on it all over the world. "This was supposed to get back at Ron Graham for the terrible things he had done to them," says Collver. "What kind of person would do that in a friend's house?"

Finally Collver got angry and told Thatcher, "Until you're rid of this obsession, I'm going to ask you to leave my ranch." The Thatchers left early the next morning.

Collver immediately phoned Ron Barclay, his lawyer in Regina, to tell him that Thatcher had asked for his help in having JoAnn murdered. Collver needed advice on what to do. "Do I have an obligation? Should I come forward? Should I go to JoAnn? What should I do about it?" Barclay's reply was, "Do what you think is right, but you have no legal obligation." Collver says now, "I thought at the time that perhaps it would pass and that perhaps Colin would get better, and I let it slide." That decision was to become part of a pattern involving many other good citizens. If any one of them had decided to intervene in the Thatcher wars, JoAnn might still be alive.

JoAnn's prospects brightened considerably in the New Year when she decided to move to Regina to put some distance between Colin and herself. "He won't feel so free just to walk in on me," she told Adelaide Weckman. Fortunately, the Weckmans had come across a Regina banker who was about to take his family on a three-month sojourn to Victoria, British Columbia. During that time, JoAnn was able to live in their lovely home in the south end of Regina, and it cost her only a hundred dollars a month for utilities. She grew to like the city and from that point it was her home, until she was murdered there.

In 1979 Regina was a pleasant, prosperous city with a population of 160,000 and an offbeat history, summarized in its original name, "Pile O' Bones". The city's flat location had been ideal for the Cree Indians, who would kill huge herds of bison nearby, then camp and prepare the carcasses. The buffalo bones were then placed atop one another until a gigantic pile, six feet high and forty feet in diameter, had been erected—hence the name Pile O' Bones. The newly arrived settlers thought it lacking in elegance, and in 1882 the small settlement was rechristened Regina—the Queen City of the Plains, after Queen Victoria. Governor Edgar Dewdney must have been impressed, for the next year it was designated the territorial capital. From 1908 to 1911, the appropriately stately Legislative Buildings were constructed, to serve the newly created province of Saskatchewan.

The city grew, the hub of a thriving agricultural economy, but when the Dirty Thirties hit, naturally the Queen City was directly affected. It was here that in June of 1935, the long-suffering army of unemployed, who had been riding the freight trains to protest to Ottawa, ran into trouble. The Regina Riot between the police and the "trekkers" resulted in the death of one policeman and injuries to eighty-two other people. It made national headlines, which further blackened Prime Minister Bennett's tarnished image, and the Riot became the city's unwelcome trademark of sorts. After the war, Regina benefitted from the exploration of oil and gas in Saskatchewan; between 1964 and 1967 Regina and Saskatoon were the fastest-growing cities in Canada. While the downtown would remain uninspired, Regina had one major amenity—a 2,300-acre water and park system called Wascana Centre, which curled along the city's backbone and helped make it an agreeable place to live, at least in the spring, summer, and fall.

After she moved there, JoAnn found a job that was ideal for her. She was hired by Willson Business Environments as a salesperson specializing in office furniture. At first she took a training program, for which the salary was $1,300 a month before taxes. After that she would become a commissioned salesperson and would more than double her earnings. She enjoyed immediate success. "She was very professional in her outlook, very efficient, energetic, and capable," says one client. "She was also very cool and aloof."

Interprovincial Steel Corporation (Ipsco), western Canada's only steel mill, was in the process of building and renovating a large office complex in Regina, at a cost of over $100,000. The Willson firm was contracted to furnish the office interiors, and JoAnn was the chief sales representative on the job. She interviewed the staff to find out what their daily needs were, worked with the designer, and generally organized the installations. One of the people she found it necessary to consult with was Ipsco's vice-president of planning and development, who was overseeing the entire renovation. His name was Anthony Wilson.

The evening after Tony Wilson first met JoAnn he phoned her. "Would you like to go out for dinner?" he said. "Or have you got something better to do?" Wilson can't recall what restaurant they went to, but he does remember that he found her "attractive, well dressed, and interesting." "I had never been out with an American woman before, not like her. She was a sort of Norman Rockwell type, a little old-fashioned, which I felt was cute. She was not exactly a caricature, but typical of someone from the Midwest who had been to university and been involved with American football and sororities and all that stuff. We were very different in many respects in our experiences, but nevertheless we found each other interesting." So interesting, in fact, that they began to see each other regularly from then on.

JoAnn's friends were delighted by the romance and marvelled that Tony seemed to be the very antithesis of Colin Thatcher. He was sophistocated, widely travelled, interested in the arts, soft-spoken and reserved. He was also a good-looking, muscular man with an interest in hiking, camping, and mountain climbing. "Tony was just everything Colin wasn't," says Darla Spicer. "He was a perfect gentleman, always thoughtful of her. JoAnn always came first with him, instead of last." To JoAnn Thatcher he must have seemed like somebody from another world.

Anthony Wilson was born in 1935 in the charming seacoast town of Poole in Dorset, England. During the war, his family moved to Blackpool, where Tony attended Arnold's, a school for boys. He had been accepted for officer's training in the Royal Navy when he briefly developed a skin rash that resulted in his flunking the medical. He then decided to study at the world-famous London School of Economics.

Tony was very active in sports—soccer, cricket, rugby, tennis, and particularly rowing. At a party for the rowers, he met a young au pair who had come from Germany to learn English. A romance quickly developed, and Ruth and Tony were married in 1955 while he was in his second year of university. Wilson graduated in 1956 with a commerce degree. There followed two years of compulsory national service, during which time the Wilsons were stationed at a senior officers' headquarters. Among other duties, Tony counselled pilots and other career officers on how to adapt to civilian life; the armed forces in Britain were shrinking. The Wilsons had their first child, Willie, during this time.

After his military duty was completed, Tony joined Esso Petroleums as a middle-management trainee and became interested in computer systems. During this time the couple had another son, Alex. In 1963, when Northern Electric was looking for knowledgeable people to set up a large computer centre in Montreal, Wilson was given the contract. "One day, out of the blue, Tony came home and said, 'How'd you like to go to Canada?'" Ruth Wilson remembers. "We said, 'Sure, we'd love to.'"

The Wilsons had lived in Montreal for only about a year

when Massey Ferguson lured Tony to Toronto. He stayed there just for a short time before he was hired away again, this time by Stevenson & Kellogg, a management consulting firm. This was a job Wilson loved. It offered diversity and challenge as he travelled all over the country solving thorny management problems. When Tony was asked by Stevenson & Kellogg in 1967 to open a branch office in Calgary, the Wilson family moved there. It was a city Ruth loathed. "People there didn't have anywhere near the courtesy or friendliness we had expected." As well, Tony was away much of the time and Ruth was tired of raising two children practically on her own. Tony had been doing steady consulting work for Ipsco, and so in 1968, when he was presented with "an offer I couldn't refuse" as executive assistant to the Ipsco president, he grabbed it. Ruth, seven-year-old Alex, and ten-year-old Willie moved to Regina to settle down at last. "It was beautiful. We felt right at home," remembers Ruth.

At that time Ross Thatcher's government had initiated a campaign to encourage people to adopt Métis and Indian children. The First Baptist Church, which Tony and Ruth had joined immediately on their arrival in Regina, showed a propaganda film about the program. It made the Wilsons think that raising another family might be the Christian thing to do. "I was at the point where I was either going to go to university or out to work," recalls Ruth. Instead, the Wilsons adopted two Métis girls, Donna, four, and Carol, five. "I was very unfair," says Ruth. "The kids came from a farm atmosphere and I put them into little white gloves and white stockings. And they were so boyish. They could climb a tree in two seconds flat." The Wilsons tried hard to help the children adjust. They provided private tutors to help them at school, gave them sewing and drama lessons, took them on a vacation to Europe. When the two girls showed a real talent for competitive swimming, they were encouraged to join a swim club. "I used to get up every day at 5 a.m. to drive them there," recalls Tony. "I got quite good at getting up, driving, and coming back without ever waking up, so I could go back to sleep." And they were successful in some areas: "They became quite accomplished socially," says Tony. But they did poorly at school. They failed a number of times, which did not help their self-image. When they reached adolescence they became very interested in boys. "Our daughter announced that she wanted to leave and have her own apartment—at age twelve," recalls Tony. "From then on it was a disaster." (By the time they reached their twenties, the two young women had undergone many unwanted pregnancies and had been involved in prostitution and drug addiction.) As the girls approached their mid-teens, the experience was putting unbearable stress on the marriage, and as well, the Wilsons had developed markedly divergent interests. Ruth and Tony were divorced in 1978.

Colin Thatcher later made use of this family tragedy. In the summer of 1984, after Thatcher had been arrested for the first-degree murder of JoAnn, Tony Wilson, realizing that Stephanie might suffer from so much publicity, applied for interim custody of the child. His plan was to send her to the Geigers in Ames, Iowa, while the trial was on. Thatcher responded by hiring a private detective to dig up all the dirt he could on Wilson. In an affidavit, Thatcher revealed many of the problems the Wilson girls had encountered, to illustrate that Tony was not a fit father. Nowhere in the document did he mention that Carol and Donna were adopted and nowhere did he indicate the near-heroic efforts the Wilsons had made to try to integrate them into their family.

After the divorce Tony remained in the family home, a handsome sprawling house of white stucco with red-shingled roof, French windows, and large, airy rooms. It was situated on Albert Street, one of Regina's main thoroughfares, on a corner lot directly across from the Legislative Buildings and the magnificent Wascana Centre. "I can remember the first time I took JoAnn home," says Wilson. "She and I had dinner and we were sitting around having a drink when these two fellows showed up. A good friend of mine, Timothy Vernon, who had been the conductor of the Regina Symphony Orchestra and the Canadian Opera Company, dropped in, and another friend of mine, an electric-furnace designer from Czechoslovakia. We had a hilarious time. And she was just sort of sitting there with her eyes wide open, listening enthralled to the conversation." This was indeed another world, and for JoAnn it offered the chance of a new beginning.

After she moved to Regina, JoAnn quickly realized that it would be too awkward to retain a solicitor in Saskatoon so she began looking for a Regina lawyer who was tough and experienced. On the advice of Ed Odishaw, an old friend and former executive assistant to Ross Thatcher, she approached Gerry Gerrand, a rotund, distinguished-looking man of forty-nine, with greying hair and a twinkle in his one good eye. JoAnn and he would fight side by side in the bloody litigation wars, and in the process would develop a deep respect and admiration for each other.

Gerrand's father, Ernest, was also a lawyer, a graduate of the University of Manitoba. In 1915 he moved to Melville, in the southeastern part of Saskatchewan, and set up his law practice there. Ernest Gerrand sat as a Liberal Member of the Legislative Assembly from 1935 to 1938, and in 1940 he moved his law practice to Regina. There Gerry Gerrand practised law with his father from the time he graduated in 1954 from the University of Saskatchewan to the older man's death at age eighty-one in 1970. Gerry's son David now works in the same firm.

Over the years Gerrand built a distinguished reputation, primarily as a civil litigation lawyer. "Product liability, contract disputes, torts generally, a strange set of circumstances that give rise to significant damages and pose real problems in solving—those are the cases I find interesting." Gerrand cites as an example the instance of a huge Simpsons-Sears warehouse with computerized bays in which articles by the millions were stored. "A couple of years ago they were replacing the roof. After the workmen left, the whole thing caught fire, the roof burned, and there was great damage done to the building. Who is to blame? Why did the fire start? Was it by reason of electrical failure? Was it because of the equipment used by the roofers? That's the kind of complex litigation I find fascinating." What Gerrand did not enjoy very much was family law. "I felt that over the years I had done my share, because it is not the most pleasant work to do."

Consequently, when he was first approached by Ed Odishaw in February of 1980, he didn't want to take JoAnn's case. "I could see that it would have all kinds of ramifications, that it would go on for some time and that it would be strenuously litigated. And I was not enthusiastic about becoming involved in a matrimonial matter. That was my first reason.

"My second was the husband involved. . . . I had never met

him, but I had seen him on television and read about him
and he seemed a hard-nosed, difficult gentleman, and this
would not make for happy litigation. Not that that turns me
off, I have never been reluctant to meet challenges, get in the
battle of the courtroom, but it was one ingredient.

"And the third one was that the lawyer for Mr. Thatcher
was Tony Merchant. I had dealt with a great number of the
one hundred or so practitioners in this province and I've
never had any difficulty getting along with them. But I just
didn't get along with Mr. Merchant." The antagonism between Merchant and Gerrand went back ten years to the
time when Tony was hosting a hot-line radio show. "I didn't
think it was good for the profession or good for him," says
Gerrand. "I told him he should make a choice—either be a
broadcaster or be a lawyer. You can't be both, because it's
demeaning to the profession."

"He didn't like me giving free legal advice over the radio,"
says Merchant. "The big prosperous firms didn't mind. There
wasn't any legal aid in those days, and they thought that if I
was prepared to look after all that—in their words, the
grubby, poor problems—super. The little firms that were
scratching around for money, some of those didn't like it. Also
the younger lawyers overwhelmingly thought that what I was
doing was fine and the older lawyers thought that what I was
doing was not. Mr. Gerrand was older and from a small law
firm. But I don't think the radio was why he disliked me. It
must have been my style."

In fact there was a far more deep-rooted reason for the
animosity between the two men. Gerrand had once been
president of the Regina Young Liberal Association, and although he had had little to do with politics over the years he
was still regarded as a Liberal supporter. As his reputation as
a lawyer grew, it was assumed by many that he would be
appointed to the bench; because of his ability with complex
legal matters it was expected that he would be appointed to
the Court of Appeal. It was an honour he would have
relished. "Gerrand was one of the most able lawyers," says a
former chief justice. "Not a high-profile man, but a very able,
sound lawyer. And I know that on a list of potential judges
kept in the Department of Justice in Ottawa, his name was
high. . . . And, of course, Tony Merchant, being the brother-
in-law of Otto Lang [who for a time was justice minister and

for even longer was in control of all Saskatchewan federal patronage], continuously fed information into the system in Ottawa that was derogatory to Gerrand. It was terrible, just terrible. It's a shocker, really." When Merchant was asked whether he had prevented Gerrand from being appointed to the Court of Appeal, he said, "I think that's a good guess. I didn't think he would be a good judge."

For all these reasons Gerrand was hesitant about taking JoAnn's case and tried to explain his reluctance to her. "She said, 'Are you telling me that I can't have my free choice of counsel just because he would prefer not to become involved with Mr. Merchant on the other side?' I looked at her and about five seconds went by. 'Of course, I can't say that,' I exclaimed. I took her case and I never, never regretted it."

JoAnn continued to drive to Moose Jaw every weekend to follow through on her access to the children and the Redland home. After their return from Palm Springs, Regan and Stephanie were glad to see her, but already she could perceive the effects of Thatcher's campaign to discredit her. Shortly after New Year's she had bought a 1978 Thunderbird. The children were out looking at it when Stephanie piped up, "Sandra says you didn't pay for it, Mom." "She told me that, too," said Regan. "Well, who do you think did?" asked JoAnn. "Uncle Ron [Graham]!" they chorused.

JoAnn had always been particularly close to her middle child. Regan was a much more gregarious, fun-loving kid than his older brother: he was not the student Greg was, although he was considered bright and well disciplined. He loved hockey and baseball and would much rather watch the Saturday-morning cartoons than go with his father to the ranch, which may explain why he was not Colin's favourite. JoAnn said that at one point her husband admitted that he didn't feel anything for Regan and didn't particularly like him. What distinguished this child, however, was his sense of humour. "There was nothing that that kid liked better than a joke, and the cornier the better," says a friend of the family.

JoAnn described her younger son this way: "From the time he was little if he didn't wish to do something that I asked him to do he didn't argue about it and put up a big fuss, he just quietly never did it. He didn't rock the boat. If he were hurt or distressed, he would remove himself. He would go to his room. He could be quite stoic." She noted, however, that "he still liked to be cuddled and loved. He didn't ask for these things, but he needed them very much. And if we were watching television and eating, he liked to come and put his head on my lap. Things like that mean a lot when little boys try to be grown up."

In the coming months, JoAnn would watch in dismay as her relationship with Regan began to disintegrate under the pressure exerted by his father, who waged a relentless campaign to destroy her son's affection for her. At first the warning signals were dim. "I remember giving him a bathrobe on the couch while we were watching television one Saturday night," said JoAnn. "He liked to get a bathrobe and put his head in my lap while he watched television. Sandy [Hammond] and Blaine [Mathieson, her boyfriend] walked into the house and he quickly jumped up from the couch and moved off to the La-Z-Boy as if he was ashamed."

Just before this incident Sandra, Greg, and Regan had been chatting about marriage when Regan suddenly said, "Well, that's nothing. I saw my mom with Mr. Graham on the couch in Brampton." He explained that he was supposed to be sleeping but he got up to get a glass of water. "My mother was dressed and Mr. Graham just had his underwear on and they were kissing." Greg yelled at his father, who was reading the newspaper in the family room, "Come up here, come up here, quick!" For the next couple of hours Colin grilled Regan about the incident until the young boy felt like quite a hero, reporting on his mother's illicit relationships. Both JoAnn and Ron Graham denied that anything of the sort had happened.

In March Thatcher began plotting to get Regan out of the house and away from JoAnn on the weekends, in defiance of the court order. One Saturday he took him to a Canuck hockey game, the first time he had ever done so that JoAnn could remember. The next Saturday he arranged a shopping trip with Peggy. "The following weekend it was the same sort of thing. They called at suppertime and Regan wanted to stay overnight because he wanted to go to a movie with his dad. I hardly had any time with him at all." Greg, meanwhile, was staying each weekend with the Hammonds, four blocks away.

Thatcher deeply resented having to vacate the Redland home every weekend. "I confess to detesting the weekends in Regina," he said "And they were very lonely weekends, extremely lonely, in fact, the loneliest time of my life." Colin would escape by occasionally flying to Palm Springs. He would leave Friday evening, stay for a week and return the next Monday. He had a good time; for one thing it was a great place to meet beautiful single women. Thatcher's little black book was soon swollen with names. "Down here, Colin could divorce himself from the reality of Moose Jaw or Caron," says Lynne Mendell. "Palm Springs is the kind of place where you can have any kind of story you want 'cause no one knows where you came from. Colin liked the feeling of being a big fish in a little pond."

He was often absent from the Legislature during that spring session. On one of the days when he did put in an appearance, John Skoberg, a New Democratic member from Moose Jaw, stood up and said, "Mr. Speaker, we have a very important person here today. And this person has travelled a great distance to be here today. He has made a very special effort to join us. And I know all Members will join me in welcoming the Member from Thunder Creek." Everyone broke into ironic applause.

Because Thatcher was so obsessed with his marital problems, he constantly talked about them, until most members of the Conservative caucus became painfully aware of the deep animosity he held for JoAnn. In fact Dick Collver believes that "several of the [present] sitting cabinet ministers were approached [by Thatcher to find a hit man]." He recalls, "It was much subsequent to the event of Thatcher appearing at my ranch that we sat around the Legislature, several of us, and discussed the insane behaviour of Mr. Thatcher." Yet nobody saw fit to report this conversation to the police—and another opportunity to save JoAnn's life was lost.

As the appeal date approached, Thatcher became even more vindictive towards JoAnn. On Sunday, March 24, he marched into the Redland home uninvited, something that by court order he was not supposed to do. He was in a particularly sour mood. When he saw that the Grahams' son John was visiting Greg, Colin snapped at JoAnn in the presence of the children, "You shouldn't be in the same room as John Graham after you ran off with his father." He then told JoAnn that if he lost the appeal, he would cut Stephanie and Regan out of his will. Then Thatcher stomped into the kitchen. JoAnn had invited Gerald and Adelaide Weckman for a barbecue supper that evening and had taken four steaks out of the freezer to defrost. When Thatcher saw them he flew into a rage. "You goddamn fucking bitch," he roared. "You're not eating my food." Grabbing the steaks, he threw them out the back door into the snow. He turned to Gregory and said, "This is why Regan calls your mother a hooker." Then Colin and Greg left, and JoAnn retrieved the steaks.

The Weckmans arrived shortly after. "The Thatchers had a gas barbecue and JoAnn asked me if I knew how to get it started," says Gerry Weckman. "I said sure. I rolled out the barbecue so that it was just under the big double garage door. I went out to check the steaks and all of a sudden the garage door came crashing down on the barbecue. There was a big scramble because I didn't even know where the button was that made it go up. The only explanation was that someone drove by with the automatic garage-door-closer. I came out of it swearing at Colin."

On another occasion, at about this time, JoAnn was driving back to Regina from a Moose Jaw visit with the children. As she approached the overpass at Belle Plaine, she stepped on the brakes to slow down. Nothing happened. She pumped harder and harder. Nothing. Terrified at finding the car out of control, she finally managed to bring the Thunderbird to a halt by swerving into the ditch. A mechanic who later looked at the car said the brakes had been tampered with; JoAnn had no doubt who was responsible for the tampering, just as she was sure how the distributor cap had previously gone missing. "What bothers me," JoAnn told a friend, "is that I could have had Stephanie or Regan in the car, and he could have killed them, too." After that frightening incident, JoAnn was always nervous about driving.

The custody appeal was heard on March 26, 1980, by Chief Justice E.M. Culliton and Justices R.N. Hall and E.D. Bayda. Tony Merchant argued that MacPherson had made four errors in his judgment. He had erred in not allowing Gregory to testify; he was wrong in separating the siblings, awarding Greg to the father and Regan and Stephanie to the mother; he had not put sufficient weight on the possibility that JoAnn might move from Moose Jaw; and he had failed to issue an order requiring that the children remain residents of that city.

By this time Gregory had retained his own independent counsel. He was Ron Barclay, the same Ron Barclay who three months previously had given Dick Collver such memorable legal advice when Collver told him that Thatcher had asked him for a hit man. Now Barclay made an unusual demand of the appeal court judges: he asked that Greg be allowed to testify before them. The justices quickly dismissed this request. They noted that they might have considered it if Gregory's preference had been ignored. But he had wanted to stay with his father and that was what MacPherson had ordered.

At the end of the proceedings, Gerrand went over to Merchant and asked him if Thatcher would allow JoAnn to move into the Redland home, which was registered in her name, if Thatcher's appeal was dismissed. Merchant's only answer to that was a scowl and a shake of the head.

The judgment, written by Chief Justice Culliton, came down twelve days later. The appeal was dismissed on all four grounds. "In arriving at his conclusions, it cannot be said he disregarded material evidence," wrote Culliton. "I would go further and say the careful and detailed analysis of the evidence which he made, fully supported both his reasoning and his conclusions." The court order stood: Greg was to remain with his father, Regan and Stephanie with their mother.

CHAPTER TWELVE

"PUT A PRICE ON THE KID"

Colin Thatcher, the children, and Sandra Hammond were in Palm Springs during the Easter break when the appeal court decision was released. Merchant phoned to break the bad news. The two men talked for a while and then decided that they would take the case to the Supreme Court of Canada. Soon after, a neighbour of the Thatchers in Palm Springs was shocked at a conversation she overheard involving Colin, Greg, and Sandra. "The mother was referred to as the fucking bitch this or the goddamn whore that. They were going to do this and that to her—real violent expressions. And in front of the two younger children. I was appalled."

Meanwhile JoAnn had been sharing a two-room apartment in Regina with the young daughter of a friend. It was an uncomfortable situation but she was waiting for the next step in the judicial process. Since she had promised in court that she would raise the children in Moose Jaw, she was determined to do just that. So Gerry Gerrand petitioned the court on behalf of JoAnn for possession of the Redland home.

That he was actually in danger of losing the Redland home had simply never occurred to Thatcher before, and he flew into a rage, instructing his lawyer to oppose it at all costs. Merchant argued strenuously before Mr. Justice K.R. Halvorson that the hearing regarding the possession of the house should be put off until May 5, when the Supreme Court of Canada would decide whether it would hear Thatcher's case or not. Justice Halvorson denied the request for adjournment. On April 18 he ruled that JoAnn should have exclusive possession of the Redland home, at least until the entire matrimonial property issue between the Thatchers was resolved. This was to take effect April 27, although Thatcher would have until May 7 to remove his personal and business effects. JoAnn prudently decided to wait until May 8 before moving into the house.

Meanwhile JoAnn was having problems gaining access not only to the children but to the house. While the others were in Palm Springs at Easter, she had gone to the Redland home to pick up some spring clothing. She found Sandra Hammond's boyfriend, Blaine Mathieson, guarding the door. "Colin gave me orders that I can't let you in," he said. JoAnn left without further fuss. It turned out that Thatcher, on Merchant's advice, had arbitrarily decided after the Court of Appeal decision that JoAnn could no longer have access to the Redland home on the weekends. Merchant sent her a letter saying so. When Mr. Justice MacPherson heard about this he was furious. "You chose to ignore it [the order]," he berated Merchant. "That's not the first time in your career that you have chosen to advise your clients to ignore my orders."

JoAnn persevered, however. She drove to Moose Jaw on April 19, the Saturday after the Thatchers returned. When she saw Greg, he snarled at her, "You are trying to take this fucking house and bleed Dad dry. You are trying to take everything we have." Colin wasn't there, but Sandra Hammond had been assigned to watch JoAnn while she visited with the children; she found this humiliating and soon left. She returned after supper, however, gave Stephanie a bath, and watched television for a little while with Regan. When she left she discovered that two keys were missing from her purse, one to her post office box and the other to her office at Willson's.

JoAnn returned to Redland the next day. Colin had reluctantly agreed that JoAnn could take Stephanie out of the house, but as they were leaving, he yelled, "I want her back here by 5 p.m. and that doesn't mean five after." This was infuriating for JoAnn; not only had her legal custody of the two youngest been confirmed at this point but she had also been awarded exclusive possession of the Redland home. Worse, however, was to follow.

When JoAnn returned to Moose Jaw the following Saturday morning, she arrived at 9:45. Sandra Hammond had just finished preparing scrambled eggs for the children and Colin was at the ranch. JoAnn asked Stephanie if she would like to visit Dorothy Yakiwchuk and her children for a while and the little girl said sure. While JoAnn went up and got her clothes, Sandra ran to Greg's bedroom, woke him, and told him to get up quickly. JoAnn helped Stephanie dress and the two walked into the family room to find Greg sitting there. As they moved towards the side door leading to the garage, Sandra grabbed JoAnn by the wrist and said, "Mrs. Thatcher, you're not to take Stephanie." Greg then jumped up from the couch saying, "Dad said you're not to take her out."

"I have custody of Stephanie and I can take her," JoAnn stated firmly, picking Stephanie up and heading towards the side door. Greg blocked her way. When she turned to go out the front door, he blocked her again. Then he grabbed Stephanie, pulling her from JoAnn's arms, and JoAnn, fearing that the little girl might get hurt, let her go. JoAnn told a court what happened next when she tried to pick her up again: "He pushed me and I flew into the rocking chair and hit my jaw on the seat of the chair and knocked the rocking chair over." What she told her friends, however, was that Greg had punched her in the jaw, cracking it, which caused her to fall into the chair. She said she was afraid to tell the court the true story, for fear that her son might be charged with assault.

The battle continued until Sandra yelled, "Greg, let them go." At that moment out of the corner of her eye, JoAnn noticed Regan, who had been watching the whole episode, run up the stairs of the kitchen and disappear. JoAnn again tried to take Stephanie from Greg. Screaming "you goddamn fucking woman," the fourteen-year-old again shoved his mother and again she fell, this time into the closet. Stephanie was crying, "I want to go with my mommy. I love my mommy," but Greg picked her up and ran out into the garage. JoAnn raced after him and again a scuffle occurred. Greg handed Stephanie to Sandra and the three ran back into the family room, locking all the doors to the house. Standing in the garage, exhausted and profoundly shocked at Greg, JoAnn finally realized that it was hopeless, and gave up and left.

Immediately she phoned Gerry Gerrand. Fearing for her physical safety, he told her not to go near the Redland house again until she took full custody of the children and occupancy of the house on May 8.

Colin Thatcher would make much of the incident in the coming legal battles, claiming that JoAnn had assaulted Gregory.

Colin said that the boy had been dressed only in jeans, and his mother had scratched him on his bare back and shoulders until blood flowed. He also claimed that she repeatedly kicked her son with her high-heeled shoes. Sandra Hammond, however, testified that Greg was wearing a T-shirt throughout the encounter. Because of such contradictions it was easier to believe JoAnn's version. She admitted that she may have scratched Greg and stepped on his bare feet in her high-heeled shoes but she said it was entirely accidental and she could not remember doing so. And there can be no doubt that JoAnn received treatment from both a doctor and a dentist for her badly injured jaw.

One night around this time Colin asked Dick Collver to meet with JoAnn and work out a settlement. "You're a good negotiator," he told him. While he accepted the task, Collver insisted on knowing one thing: "What's your bottom line? Because you're being bled to death by the lawyers and by the courts." Thatcher responded, "Four hundred thousand dollars and I must have the boys."

That same evening Collver met JoAnn for dinner at the Mediterranean Restaurant in Regina and for several hours they discussed various aspects of Colin's proposal. Then JoAnn asked him if Tony Wilson, a person she described as knowledgeable about finances, could join them. Ten minutes later Wilson arrived. "The upshot of the meeting was that she agreed that she would settle for $230,000," says Collver. "She wanted custody of the little girl... but she agreed that Colin would get custody of the two boys. I was ecstatic. I thought the matter was settled.

"I contacted Colin and told him what happened. I told him that she was ready to settle. I told him that her current friend was there and that he had approved of this settlement. And I said, 'Colin, it's a terrific deal. It's tremendous. Take it.' His answer to me was, 'The bitch isn't going to get anything.'" His reaction reinforced the theory that Colin Thatcher wasn't the least bit interested in settling with JoAnn: he wanted only revenge.

The incident highlights Thatcher's attitude and style, but it should be noted that the deal was unlikely to go through in any case. Tony Wilson says that Collver misunderstood JoAnn's position; she had only agreed to consider the proposal at that point. She later decided that under no condition would she give up custody of Regan.

Meanwhile, Tony Merchant was busy entangling the case in further judicial machinations. He flew to Ottawa on April 21 to ask the Chief Justice of Canada, Bora Laskin, to grant an interim stay of the custody decision until May 5, when the Supreme Court would decide if the case would be heard. Laskin told Merchant he would not grant an interim stay and suggested he go to the Chief Justice of the Saskatchewan Court of Appeal. Merchant took his advice but his options were quickly running out. On May 5 leave to appeal the custody order to the Supreme Court of Canada was denied Thatcher. The law had spoken. JoAnn had to be given the Redland Avenue home and custody of Regan and Stephanie.

That day Colin Thatcher finalized the purchase of a $100,000 house, a white stucco, Spanish-style affair with swimming pool and fireplace. It was in every respect but one a fine new residence for Greg and him. But the one drawback made his friend Don McDonald groan with embarrassment when he heard about it. The house was located on Simcoe Avenue at the point where it formed an exclusive little crescent. Not only would Don McDonald be a new neighbour of Colin's but so would Ron Graham; Thatcher's new house was directly kitty-corner from the Graham residence. Every time Ron opened his front door and looked out the window he could feel Colin's eyes glaring at him. Ron Graham did not appreciate the proximity, since Thatcher had already threatened to kill him. It became a kind of joke among the Moose Jaw police force that never before had so many cops enjoyed such wonderful vacations—they all had made so much extra money guarding Ron Graham in their off-duty hours.

THURSDAY, MAY 8, 1980

JoAnn took official custody of her two children and possession of the Redland house. The moving van arrived about the same time that Stephanie and Regan got home from school. Regan was excited because his mother had bought him an expensive Moto Cross bike while they were in Brampton, and it was there along with the other furniture. He immediately climbed on the bike and rode over to the Hammonds.

Beverley Hammond called out to Regan, "My, that's a nice bike." The child replied, "Yeah, Mr. Graham bought it for me in Brampton," trying to further promote the idea that Graham and his mother had had an illicit affair in Brampton. In fact, JoAnn had purchased the bicycle at Simpsons for $149 and she had the receipt to prove it.

Alerted by Beverley Hammond, Thatcher soon arrived and took Regan and Greg out for dinner and a little pep talk, in the course of which Regan assured his father that he had no intention of living with his mother. When Colin told him he had to go back that night, the boy loyally insisted, "Well, I'll run away tomorrow morning." Thatcher then returned him to the Redland house. That evening Stephanie told her mother that she had overheard Colin and Regan talking in the home's office before JoAnn moved in. "Daddy said, 'Regan, run away three times, and the first two times I'll bring you back and the third time I won't, I'll keep you.'" It occurred to JoAnn that she would have to endure a struggle over her middle child, but she did not yet realize how fierce, devious, or bitter it would become.

FRIDAY, MAY 9

Regan came home for lunch but failed to show up after school. He had once again gone to the Hammonds'. Sandra drove him from there out to Caronport, where his father was working at the grain farm. Colin stopped JoAnn and told her he was giving the boy supper.

That evening Tony Wilson came to visit JoAnn at the Redland Avenue house that was now hers. He was playing bingo with Stephanie in the family room when Thatcher, Regan, and Greg walked in through the side door. Abruptly Thatcher said to JoAnn in front of the children, "So this is the man you've been living with." JoAnn replied, "You know where I've been living for the last month," and she told Colin that she no longer wanted him walking into the house unannounced. When he asked if he could have the two children on Saturday and Sunday, JoAnn curtly replied, "No, talk to my lawyer."

JoAnn went up to the bedroom with Regan and they chatted for half an hour. Here, for the first time, Regan told his mother that he didn't want to live with her, that he wanted to stay with his dad. JoAnn felt hurt and upset by this admission but Tony reassured her that if she could spend some time alone with her son, his once-strong affection for his mother would resurface.

That evening JoAnn called Beverley Hammond and angrily told her that she no longer wanted either her or Sandra interfering with Regan, and then threatened her with legal action. JoAnn did not know that during the conversation Colin Thatcher was at the Hammonds', listening in on an extension.

SATURDAY, MAY 10

At three in the morning Regan sneaked out of his bedroom, hopped on his bike, and rode to the Matador Motel three blocks away. His father was staying there until the Simcoe Street house was available. When he encountered Regan, Thatcher recalled, "He was very upset. He was shaking. I could not settle him down in the motel room." Thatcher told a court that Regan was so distraught because he had seen his mother with another man, Tony Wilson. "He was thinking about the incident in Brampton where he saw his mother in a state of undress with Ron Graham who was only wearing his underwear." JoAnn insisted that the episode in Brampton never occurred, just as Graham had never bought a bike for Regan. She believed that Colin knew that Regan was lying, primarily to garner his father's approval. Thatcher not only accepted it as the truth but used it as an instrument to further poison the boy's mind.

Early in the morning, Colin left the hotel with Regan and drove with him to Peggy's place in Regina. Regan kept reassuring his father, "I'll never go back, you can't make me go back. I'll just keep running away." Greg joined them and they all went fishing at their grandmother's Katepwa cottage.

Regan had left secretly in the middle of the night and JoAnn was in a panic when she discovered upon awakening that the boy was not there. She phoned the Hammonds at about eight to see if they knew where he was. Greg was staying there until he and his father could move into the new house, and he answered the phone. JoAnn demanded to know where Regan was, and when he wouldn't answer her, she said she wanted to speak to Beverley Hammond. Mrs. Hammond refused to come to the phone. "Tell her if she won't come to the telephone, I'll be there in five minutes," JoAnn yelled. Beverley's husband, Ron, responded that he would call the police. JoAnn quickly got Stephanie up and dressed and was driving towards the Hammond house when she spotted Sandra and Greg in the Thatcher station wagon, heading out of town. She was certain that they were on their way to meet Colin and Regan.

By this time it was 8:30 a.m. and JoAnn went to the Moose Jaw city police, who told her they could only help if she would fill out a missing person's form. JoAnn talked this over with Gerry Gerrand, who said it was inappropriate for her to do because she knew where Regan was, or least whom he was with. At noon Colin finally phoned JoAnn and told her he was not going to bring Regan back, nor would he tell her where he was.

While JoAnn was out that evening, someone broke into the Redland home. Many of the shipping cartons, which she had not yet emptied, were opened and their contents of dishes, bedding, and clothing were scattered all over the living room. The day she moved in she had changed the locks on the house and had put one of the keys on the top of the china cabinet. That was stolen. She called the Moose Jaw police, and they discovered that someone had slipped in through the dining-room window. The intruder had not stolen anything but the key.

SUNDAY, MAY 11

At 6:30 the next morning JoAnn woke to a loud pounding on the door. It was Thatcher, belligerent as usual. They talked for an hour or two but he refused to tell her where Regan was and insisted that he was not prepared to hand over the child at that time. He suggested that she could gradually gain custody of the boy, beginning with brief visits weekly, extending to longer periods. "Are you kidding?" JoAnn said in disbelief. She knew that such an arrangement would only further serve Colin's designs of turning the child against her. "You can stop Regan from running away by refusing to allow him in your house," she said angrily. He retorted, "Just because you've

lost both of your sons, I'm not going to lose them as well."
JoAnn snapped back, "If I had my way you would never see
the children."

That evening JoAnn and Tony Wilson took Stephanie swimming. While they were gone, the house was once again
broken into and boxes were overturned and their contents
searched. This time an extra set of keys to her car were
taken. (Since the intruder was never caught, it is interesting
to note that Charlie Wilde would testify at Thatcher's murder
trial that seven months later he was given keys to the 1978
Thunderbird by Garry Anderson. Anderson had obtained
them from Thatcher.)

MONDAY, MAY 12

Thatcher and Greg were busy moving their furniture from
the Hammonds' house to their new Simcoe Street home
when Regan showed up on his bike. Colin told him he could
help with the unloading. At about 6:45 Regan went to visit a
neighbour, a lawyer and city alderman named Kerry Chow,
with whom Thatcher had gone to high school. The lawyer
advised the boy to return to his mother and offered to go with
him. "If you don't want to stay with your mother, I'll bring
you back," he said. When they got there JoAnn took her son
into the den and for the first time tried to tell him her side of
the story. "I have made mistakes and I have admitted them,"
JoAnn told the boy. "Your dad isn't perfect either. Do you
know where he was when I left?" Regan replied that he
didn't. "He was with another lady," JoAnn said. "I don't
believe you," retorted Regan. "You're just trying to turn me
against Dad, just as he said you would."

Regan went upstairs, grabbed a baseball mitt and a skate-
board, and ran out of the house, en route to his father's
house. JoAnn didn't try to stop him. She had decided instead
to take further legal action.

TUESDAY, MAY 13

In the morning Gerrand appeared before Chief Justice F.W.
Johnson, of the Court of Queen's Bench, and told him the

sorry story of what had occurred since JoAnn obtained custody of Regan. Merchant was also there to put forward Thatcher's side of the story—that the child simply refused to live with his mother despite his father's pleas to the contrary. Johnson's fiat was short and to the point. "The court will not tolerate its order being flouted any longer. An order will go directing Colin Thatcher to forthwith deliver up to JoAnn Thatcher the child Regan Colin Thatcher. An order will also go that failing compliance by 12:00 p.m. [noon], May 14, 1980, an order will go that any sheriff, deputy sheriff, or peace officer having jurisdiction shall do all such acts as may be necessary to cause the child Regan Colin Thatcher to be delivered up forthwith into the custody of the parent JoAnn Thatcher.

"It is forthwith ordered that Colin Thatcher and anyone having notice of this order be restrained and enjoined from interfering with the care, custody and control, by JoAnn Thatcher of Regan Colin Thatcher."

JoAnn did not see Regan that day.

WEDNESDAY, MAY 14

The order was served not only on Colin Thatcher but on Beverley and Sandra Hammond, Blaine Mathieson, Kerry Chow, and Gregory. The noon deadline passed.

That evening Colin phoned his old friend Don McDonald. "I've been instructed to physically return Regan to the Redland home, and that I really should have a witness that I'm complying. Will you come?" McDonald said he would.

"Regan was very reluctant to go," recalls McDonald. "Colin said, 'Regan, you're going back to Redland.' Regan answered, 'I'm not going back to Redland. I don't want to go.' 'You have to go,' replied Colin. 'I won't stay there anyways,' the boy exclaimed."

On the way over in McDonald's car, Colin broke down and began to sob. "He was in a pretty bad emotional state, as one can imagine," said McDonald. "I had never seen Colin cry, but he did, he cried all the way from Simcoe to Redland and it disturbed me." Don felt deeply sorry for his old friend.

When he got there, Thatcher told JoAnn, "I am complying with the court order. Regan, you are to stay with your mother." The boy walked quickly past his mother into the house, and just as quickly walked out the side door.

Colin asked McDonald back to his new house and they had just poured themselves a coffee when Greg yelled, "Dad, Regan is back again." Colin walked downstairs just as JoAnn drove up in the driveway. She reclaimed Regan, but as she was helping him into the car, Colin yelled, "When are you going to leave this poor kid alone?"

JoAnn now decided that if she was ever to have any control over Regan she would have to get him out of Moose Jaw. She packed clothes for him, Stephanie, and herself and drove to Adelaide and Gerry Weckman's farm in Rouleau, some forty kilometres away.

THURSDAY, MAY 15

Despite the distance, JoAnn took Regan and Stephanie to King George School in Moose Jaw that morning. As soon as she drove away, however, Colin pulled up in his half-ton truck, which had been parked around the block. He then had a talk with his son, in defiance of Chief Justice Johnson's order prohibiting him from doing so. At lunch hour JoAnn returned to the school to pick up the two children but Regan did not appear. She phoned the Hammonds and Thatcher and asked if they had seen him. Both replied that they hadn't and Colin added, "If you were any kind of mother your son would stay at home." Later that day she learned from Regan that for lunch he had eaten left-over Kentucky Fried Chicken at his father's place.

After school JoAnn met Regan at the Natatorium where he had a swimming lesson, and drove him back to the Redland house. As they were coming in the house Stephanie asked her mother if they were going to Rouleau that night, at which Regan announced, "I'm not going!" JoAnn replied, "Yes you are!" At that Regan lunged toward the front door. JoAnn pushed it shut and Regan's elbow got caught in it. "Regan started to cry," said JoAnn. "Stephanie at the same time became distressed and I turned to attend to her. At this point, Regan dashed out the door and was gone without a sound."

Colin had his own version of this episode. As he related in

an affidavit to the Court of Queen's Bench, "Tony Wilson was with my wife.... At between 4 and 4:15 Regan tried to get out of the house and my wife screamed 'God damn you' at Regan and cracked a large oak door on Regan's elbow. Regan went back into the house and was in considerable pain. My wife stomped away and the man [Wilson] said something to Regan, but almost immediately Regan was able to get out of the house and ran through exactly the same door; he ran between houses for five or six blocks and then ran over to 1170 Simcoe."

Thatcher feared that Regan's elbow might be badly injured, so he took him to see Dr. Wigmore at the Union Hospital's emergency ward. The doctor found there was some bruising but no fracture and he bandaged the arm. Meanwhile, JoAnn had called the Moose Jaw police. When they went to retrieve Regan from Thatcher's home, the boy told them that his mother had purposely injured his arm. After they brought him back, JoAnn and her good friend Allan Gooding drove him to Rouleau.

Gooding was a pilot at the Canadian Forces Base near Moose Jaw but, in planning his retirement, he had discovered the lucrative business of selling Amway products. He had first met JoAnn at an Amway social function—she had been there with a woman friend. He had just gone through a divorce and so the two had a lot in common. He might have become interested romantically in JoAnn except for the fact that early in 1980 she had met Tony Wilson and he had met his present wife, Betty. The Goodings would remain close friends of JoAnn's through some trying and even dangerous situations.

That evening JoAnn asked Gooding if he would mind helping her transport Regan to Rouleau because he had become so wild and unmanageable at that point. While Allan and JoAnn sat in the front, the boy was placed in the back seat so he could not unlock the doors and jump out. From that vantage point Regan told his mother a revealing story. He said his father had sent him to see a child psychiatrist, and Sandra had been talking about this to Tony Merchant that day. "The psychiatrist told Tony that it would make your mind sick to live with your mother," said Sandra.

By this time JoAnn was beside herself with anger. She had already decided that there was no way she and the children could live peacefully in Moose Jaw under the dark shadow of Colin Thatcher.

FRIDAY, MAY 16

There wasn't much for Regan to do at Rouleau since all the other children were at school. Most of the time he sat in his bedroom reading while the Weckmans kept a close eye on him in case he bolted. "He did try and run away and I followed him in the four-wheel-drive truck," recalls Gerry Weckman. "I realized that there was no way I could grab him and put him in the truck, so I just drove along beside him. He said, 'I'm going to walk to Moose Jaw; and I said, 'Fine, I'll go along with you.' Finally when we got out by the school grounds, he said, 'Well, maybe I'll come back.' So he jumped in the truck." The Weckmans and several of their neighbours had seen Colin Thatcher driving around the small town in his half-ton truck on several occasions. And many times over the five days the Thatchers stayed with them, the telephone would ring. "We'd pick it up and nobody was there, although you could hear the person breathing on the other end."

That afternoon Dr. D.E. Walter of Regina examined Regan's bruised arm. "He doesn't need that," he said of the bandage and took it off. Regan spent the evening swinging on a long rope. His arm had made an excellent recovery in only one day.

Just over a week after she moved into the Redland house, JoAnn decided to move out. She realized that to remain in Moose Jaw would be to subject herself and her children to an unrelenting campaign of harassment and terror. She was very frightened of Thatcher, she told her close friends. Her house had been broken into, her telephone had never stopped ringing, her mail had been stolen. Most important, she knew that Colin would do anything, pull any dirty trick, to keep control of Regan.

She planned now to move to Regina. Tony Wilson had helped her find an unfurnished house for rent on Qu'Appelle Drive, which was close to the Wascana park complex and a block away from Athabasca Public School. She decided to move immediately.

SATURDAY, MAY 17

When she arrived at the Redland house that morning to move out her belongings, she had a copy of the court order giving her possession of the home and custody of the children. She left it on the front seat of her car before going into the house. Three friends, Allan Gooding, his fiancée, Betty Patrick, and Darla Spicer, arrived to help JoAnn finish packing the crates. A large truck with ACE MOVERS lettered on the side drove up and the men quickly began loading the cartons and furniture. When they were about three-quarters finished, Allan heard Thatcher's truck arrive and saw him go over and talk to the movers.

Thatcher then marched into the house and screamed at the top of his voice, "Nothing is leaving this house without my permission." He took one look at Allan Gooding, whom he had never met and, pointing his finger at him, barked, "You! Get out of my house." Allan could tell that JoAnn was very frightened and didn't want him to leave. "We're staying," Gooding said.

"That's when he threatened me," Gooding recalls. "He took off his wrist watch and started shaking his fist at me. He came up so close I could smell his bad breath." "Are you going to get out or am I going to have to throw you out," he screamed. "Get lost!" Gooding responded. Surprised at the other man's resistance, Thatcher backed down, put his watch back on, and went to talk to JoAnn. Gooding noticed that Thatcher was shaking badly, and seemed unable to control himself.

JoAnn told him she had every right to remove the belongings. "Get out of this house," she demanded. When he insisted that everything, including the furniture she had bought in Brampton, be taken out of the van and unpacked, she called the Moose Jaw police. Unfortunately, because of a long-simmering labour dispute the police were holding a study session that day and answering only emergency calls. They considered this request a mere domestic dispute, and they refused to come to the Redland house.

Colin then phoned Tony Merchant and on his advice insisted that the head mover drive to the police station with him. There he announced that he would charge the Ace man with theft if they did not return all the loaded items to the house; the police told the mover that they would have no choice but to confiscate the van if Thatcher did so. The man then informed JoAnn that there was nothing he could do but unload the truck. "But I have a court order giving me possession of this home," JoAnn protested. Colin yelled, "If that's so, show it!" She ran out to her car to get it, only to discover that it had been stolen.

While Thatcher was out of the house, JoAnn grew more and more concerned that Regan might be abducted and asked Allan to drive to Rouleau to ensure the child was safe. Since Darla had to go home, that left only Betty and JoAnn at the Redland house to deal with Thatcher when he returned. They were about to take Stephanie's beloved cat, Bandit, out to the car, when Thatcher, snapping his fingers, said, "You, leave that cat here." JoAnn quickly handed the cat to Betty. "Get in the car and lock the door," she ordered, and blocked Thatcher's way as he made a lunge for the startled animal. As she stood in the doorway, Colin grabbed hold of the door and raked it over JoAnn's sandalled foot. Betty heard a loud scream and turned around to see blood gushing from her friend's ripped foot. She was about to drop the cat and go to her when JoAnn yelled, "Betty, get in the car." Betty made it to the Thunderbird and locked the door just as Colin ran up screaming at her, smashing his fists on the window again and again. "I just sat there and prayed that JoAnn would some-how make it to the car." JoAnn had gone in the house to get some Kleenex to wrap around her bleeding toes. Now she came limping out, tears welling in her eyes, and got into the car.

At first Colin just stood there, but as the women left he jumped into his truck and followed them. "JoAnn was trying to drive down streets where he wouldn't find us," says Betty Gooding. "But he always ended up behind us with that sick smile on his face." The two women finally decided to stop for a coffee at a doughnut shop. When they returned to their car, Thatcher had disappeared.

Allan Gooding was outraged that Thatcher could get away with such bullying tactics. "He was doing so many things and getting away with them legally, I thought this incident was the last straw." Gooding went to the Crown prosecutor in Moose Jaw the next day and described what had happened. The prosecutor said, "Yes, there's definite grounds for assault whether he actually hit you or not. He threatened you with words and with physical gestures, and either one was sufficient grounds." Gooding felt he was being encouraged by the Crown and Moose Jaw detectives to lay charges, and so he went ahead.

After the charges were laid, Gooding was sitting in his car near the Redland house when Thatcher came up to him and threatened, "You can continue this if you like, but if you do I'll sue you for defamation of character." Shortly after, Tony Merchant wrote a letter to Gooding's commanding officer claiming that there were no grounds for the assault charge and that Gooding was harassing his client. Merchant went on to ask the base commander to exert his influence on his subordinate to get him to withdraw the charges. "So I was called into the Colonel's office," says Allan. "He asked me what the situation was and I told him. He said to me, 'Well, go get him.'"

"In court it basically boiled down to my word against Thatcher's, and the judge believed him," says Gooding. Colin's defence was that when he drove up to the Redland house, he saw that the door was open. He didn't know the movers were there and didn't see JoAnn, so he thought Betty and Allan Gooding were thieves. "All I could think was—here are two people I have never seen before and they're stripping my house. There's no question I was prepared to stop them from removing any articles." He told the court that he saw no need for violence because "it was pretty obvious that I could handle him [Gooding] physically." Judge E.A. Lewchuk bought Colin's story, and the Goodings were furious. "For one thing he parked right beside the van which had ACE MOVERS written in huge letters across it," said Betty. "And secondly he stopped and talked to the movers. We saw him. Thirdly he saw JoAnn in the house before he saw Allan." At the break, Gooding went running up to the prosecutor and said, "Listen, it's a simple matter. Find the two movers and get them to testify. Tell the court about the name on the moving van. Call JoAnn to the stand." But none of this was done, and Colin was acquitted. "We lost a great deal of confidence in the judicial system," says Betty.

Colin gloated over his victory. The Moose Jaw *Times-Herald* ran a headline across the top of the page: "Thatcher says NDP will go to any lengths to embarrass enemies." The story read:

> An angry Colin Thatcher, Conservative MLA for Thunder Creek, said Tuesday that the New Democratic government of Saskatchewan would go to any lengths to embarrass a political enemy....
>
> "My general reaction is one of complete contempt, complete scorn for the department of the Attorney General of this province."
>
> He said the charge was a phony, trumped-up and "had my name been Skoberg, Snyder or Messer [NDP MLAs], it would never have seen the light of day."

Allan Gooding choked when he saw that story. He had been a dedicated Progressive Conservative longer than Thatcher and he knew that the NDP government had nothing to do with the laying of charges. But the political dragon-slaying in the local press was to have an important effect; fear of similar charges of "political harassment" may well have been one reason why in the months to come the NDP Attorney General's department was so timid in its actions towards Thatcher as he broke the law time and again.

SUNDAY, MAY 18

It was a beautiful, sunny, and warm weekend, and the Weckmans decided to open their cottage at Regina Beach some twenty kilometres away from the capital. JoAnn and her children, the Weckmans and their children, and some friends had a marvellous day. JoAnn noticed that Regan, who played all day in the water with Stephanie, seemed to be more his usual happy, spontaneous self.

MONDAY, MAY 19

In an affidavit signed that day, JoAnn said, "I can say that Stephanie and Regan are relaxed and enjoying their stay at the beach.... Regan has made no mention of running away or being unhappy except a brief reference at noon. I had been sleeping with him and last night he cuddled up to me and slept peacefully through the entire night, which has not been the case recently. I believe that if I have some reasonable time with my son in the absence of his father, I can re-establish the loving mother-son relationship that I had with my child for ten years. On the other hand, if access is granted to Colin Thatcher, I am certain he will continue to adversely influence Regan and that I will never be able to redeem the situation."

That evening as the group were finishing their supper, Adelaide Weckman yelled, "That's Colin, isn't it?" She had spotted a truck with the Thatcher Farms insignia on it. "We had decided then that since he was keeping track of us we would leave the area the next day and go to Lumsden Beach," recalls Adelaide.

TUESDAY, MAY 20

Before they could leave the cottage, Regan disappeared. He walked to Haus Groceries in Regina Beach and there placed several telephone calls. The only number that answered was the Legislative Buildings. Informed that his father wasn't in, Regan asked to speak to Gerald Muirhead, a Conservative MLA who was a close friend of Thatcher's. Obviously distraught, Regan told Muirhead that he was being held captive at Regina Beach and that his mother had severely beaten him. The MLA promised to contact either his father or Tony Merchant.

By this time JoAnn had called the RCMP. They picked the young boy up in the grocery store and delivered him to the Weckmans' cottage. The police told JoAnn tht Regan had been overheard recounting how his mother had badly beaten him. When JoAnn confronted him with this, he let loose a tirade of invective, telling her she was a "rotten mother", that she was a "whore who took money from men," and other similar accusations. When JoAnn argued, he said, "You're just upset because you don't like hearing the truth." At that JoAnn turned him over and spanked him half a dozen times on his backside. Asked if she regretted doing this, JoAnn replied, "As a matter of fact he straightened around and was a much nicer kid after that."

In the course of all this, a piece of paper had fallen out of Regan's jeans, and JoAnn picked it up. It was a list of phone numbers—in Colin's handwriting—of Tony Merchant, Kerry Chow, and Colin Thatcher. "Phone me any time you get a chance, Regan, and I will come and get you," Colin had told him when he gave it to him.

WEDNESDAY, MAY 21

Before her second attempt to move out of the Redland home, JoAnn obtained a court order allowing her to take specific items out of the house. A plainclothes policeman was on hand to assist her in the house, while two uniformed officers sat in a cruiser outside. When JoAnn arrived she discovered that all the things she had packed four days before had been unpacked. She phoned her friends for help. Betty arrived once again, along with Darla Spicer and her daughter Dana and another friend, Sharon Krueger. Thatcher was there, of course, as well. "Everything we packed, he unpacked right behind us, claiming he wanted to make sure JoAnn wasn't taking something she shouldn't," recalls Darla. "He would come and just upset things in the middle of the floor. He was just a general pain in the ass. He was so childish that I just wanted to give him a good shake. I think he felt that with JoAnn leaving town, he was losing control, and that scared him.

"We had police protection and I'm so glad we did because I don't think any of us would have been here today if we hadn't. I was scared even with the policeman there."

Gregory arrived at noon. "Greg would block our entry as we were carrying packages to the van," says Darla. "He stood in the doorway, leaning up against the wall, bumping his mother every time she passed, just being miserable, mimicking his father."

"I was out in the garage," says Betty, "and Greg came in and he and his Dad had a little tête-à-tête for a minute. Then Greg said, 'I'd better look on this truck and make sure there's nothing of mine on it.' The movers yelled, 'You get off that truck. This is our territory.' Colin responded, 'He can get onto that truck if he wants to.' Then JoAnn intervened, 'Why would I want to take anything of yours, Greg?' Greg's response to that was a loud 'Shut up, you fucking bitch!' The police officer flung around and said, 'Who is that?' JoAnn responded, 'That, Officer, is my son.' The policeman just shook his head. All of us were very shocked." Peggy Thatcher was watching all this and she reprimanded Greg. "Don't talk to your mother like that," she said. The caution had no effect. About half an hour later, Greg was overheard saying to JoAnn, in a low voice full of venom, "If you lay a hand on Regan again, I will kill you."

He continued to make the moving process as difficult as he could. "Greg hauled off a carpet cleaner, which the detective subsequently said should go back on the van. And he pulled off an old, old stereo record player of Regan's," said JoAnn. As a chest of drawers was put on the truck, Greg would go through the drawers pulling out toys and clothes, supposedly to ensure that his mother wasn't taking anything of his. Colin Thatcher would later say that Greg was upset and angry because his mother had refused to allow him into the house to feed his fish and he had just discovered that some of them had died. JoAnn said she would have gladly let him in the house. "All he had to do was ask," she said.

Meanwhile Colin Thatcher was being as obnoxious as possible. Once he snarled at Darla, "Why the hell don't you get out of here? I never asked you to come." Darla responded, "Colin, I'm not here because you asked me, I'm here because JoAnn asked me." At that point Darla's seventeen-year-old daughter yelled at Thatcher, "Oh, fuck off!" This intervention startled Darla: "I never heard my daughter use that kind of language before. She was upset because at that point both of us were sure that he was going to strike me. I was just shaking because he was so furious."

Finally, after what seemed like an excruciatingly long three hours, the van was loaded and JoAnn took off for Regina, where Stephanie and Regan were waiting.

FRIDAY, MAY 23

JoAnn drove Regan to Regina's Athabasca Public School where he was now enrolled in grade five. At recess he disappeared and the principal phoned his mother. Later, when Regan turned up in Moose Jaw, Colin said that the boy had hitch-hiked; JoAnn always suspected that Colin had been lying in wait for the ten-year-old and had driven him back himself.

SATURDAY, MAY 24

JoAnn phoned Colin and told him to bring Regan to Regina. Thatcher refused, saying that he was exercising his visiting privileges and intended to keep Regan for the weekend. "Put a price on the kid," he said to her, "and I'll attempt to raise the money."

SUNDAY, MAY 25

Regan was due to be returned in the evening to his mother in Regina, but he did not appear. At 10:30 p.m. JoAnn drove to Moose Jaw and knocked on Colin's door. He answered and told her that Regan wasn't there, that he was spending the night with friends. JoAnn responded, "Colin, if you don't get Regan, I'm calling the police. You are in contempt of court." For fifteen minutes JoAnn stood outside the house waiting, until finally Regan came to the door. His mother asked him to get another pair of jeans to bring with him. "He just folded his arms and said no," JoAnn recalled. "I asked him twice and he still said no, so I decided that I wouldn't push it any further. I said, 'Okay, come on Regan, let's get in the car.' He just stood there. As I said it again, I reached out to take his hand. Greg was standing between Regan and me and he slapped his hand down on my wrist and I said, 'Are you going to let Greg do this?' Colin said nothing." JoAnn tried again to reach for Regan, and Greg caught her wrist again. At that point Regan ran away. His father just stood there, grinning.

Soon afterwards JoAnn appealed to the courts once again to enforce the order giving her custody of Regan. She also asked that Colin be charged with contempt of court. By that time, however, Tony Merchant had convinced Chief Justice Johnson that there had been a significant change in the circumstances of the case—notably Regan's apparent determination not to

live with his mother—and the judge ordered that a new
custody hearing take place. Another Queen's Bench judge,
Mr. Justice Sirois, decided that until that hearing occurred,
which was likely to be some time in the summer, Regan
should remain with his father and finish the year at his Moose
Jaw school. It gave Colin Thatcher the opportunity of completing the job he had started. So far his campaign to turn
Regan against his mother could be considered an overwhelming success.

CHAPTER THIRTEEN
BEYOND BITTERNESS

JUNE 17, 1980

During June and July the red-hot Thatcher wars were fought in the cool, air-conditioned Regina courthouse. These were battles so bizarre and so charged with emotion that they would be talked about in Saskatchewan legal circles for years.

The first round involved the division of the matrimonial property, and in this JoAnn would prove lucky. Just five and a half months before, "An Act Respecting the Possession and Distribution of Property Between Spouses" had become law. *Thatcher* vs *Thatcher* was the first major case under the new provincial legislation, which had vastly improved farm women's financial position on the break-up of a marriage. Some people found it ironic that it should involve an MLA.

There were further ironies. The politicians had been pressured into action after several instances of gross injustice to farm women had come to light during the early 1970s. In Saskatchewan the most highly publicized case was that of Helen Rathwell, who despite raising four children and labouring for twenty years on the family farm, worth $200,000 to $250,000, was told by a Queen's Bench judge that in the divorce settlement she had no claim on it whatever. An appeal court eventually found in her favour because she had contributed a small amount to the original down payment, but clearly the law needed to be revised. While in the Legislature, Tony Merchant had been an avid supporter of women's rights. In 1978 it was he who managed to get an amendment to the Married Women's Property Act through the House, a not inconsiderable feat for an Opposition member. The amendment appropriately changed the name of the act to the Married Persons' Property Act and permitted

251

judges much more leeway in distributing property; they were to do so in a "fair and equitable" manner. But women's groups felt that farm wives were still at the mercy of the whims and prejudices of old-fashioned, male judges, so in the fall of 1979 the NDP introduced new legislation that specifically and clearly spelled out the married person's property rights. Approved unanimously by the House—Colin Thatcher's vote included—it was one of the most favourable such acts to women in all of Canada.

At the heart of the new legislation was the concept that the wife's care of the children and her management of the household were to be considered equal in value to her husband's tending of crops and cattle. Colin's protests, therefore, that JoAnn was not interested in the agricultural operation, and outside of the bookkeeping had performed no labour on the ranch, meant nothing in the context of the new law. And the fact that the titles of the ten sections of agricultural lands were in Colin's name, not JoAnn's, was also irrelevant.

There was another aspect of the act that would prove tremendously beneficial to JoAnn's case—property inherited after the marriage was also subject to equal distribution. All that had to be shown was that the benefactor, in this case Ross Thatcher, had wanted both Colin and JoAnn to share equally in his largesse. A one-line note from Ross dated December 17, 1962, and addressed to Colin and JoAnn, giving title to a quarter-section of land was all the evidence the judge needed to prove that Thatcher Senior had the interests of both his son and daughter-in-law at heart.

This would be the last case that Mr. Justice E.N. (Ted) Hughes would hear before he left Saskatchewan to work in the British Columbia Attorney General's department. Hughes was appointed to the district court in 1962 by John Diefenbaker, and then promoted to the Court of Queen's Bench in 1974. Despite a reputation as a highly capable judge, he was another victim of the political struggles that seemed to rage continuously among the judiciary in Saskatchewan. He had been told that he was to be named chief justice, only to find out that his former political affiliation prevented any such honour. He quit the bench in anger, with the dramatic case between the Thatchers—whom he did not know—as his swan song.

The trial took place in a large courtroom on the second floor of the Victoria Avenue courthouse in the centre of Regina. Seating in the courtroom was like a bizarre version of a wedding. Thatcher and his entourage were stationed at the extreme left-hand side of the room, JoAnn and her people on the extreme right-hand. "One could sense the unpleasantness and intense feelings of discord," says Hughes. "It was a long, expensive, and bitter trial." For one thing, neither lawyer could stand the client on the other side. "I disliked JoAnn," says Merchant. "I thought she was a phoney, terribly phoney, terribly prepared, contrived, very contrived. Her best friend told me once that JoAnn had never walked into a room since she was sixteen without setting her face. The only genuine thing I ever remember her saying throughout the entire trial was when she got mad at me in cross-examination and shouted, 'Well, I voted for you too.'" Gerrand simply considered Thatcher a despicable bully. In addition the two lawyers disliked each other so intensely that communication between them was practically nonexistent. There was, therefore, no hope for an out-of-court settlement. Indeed, before the hearing Merchant, on behalf of Thatcher, would make no admissions at all, refusing even to provide the court with simple information such as how many cattle Colin owned.

Lawrence Welcher of Mortlach was called as a witness by Gerry Gerrand for this purpose. Welcher (now deceased) had been forced to retire by Thatcher in 1979; he was then seventy-five years old, having worked at the Thatcher ranch for ten years. Gerrand recalls thinking "about that man and his qualities and his honesty, his simple means of living and his big fingers from hard work all the years of his life, thinking how superior an individual he was in every way compared to the man he testified against." Part of Welcher's job each day had been to count the cattle scattered in various pastures around the Caron area to ensure that none were sick or missing. He estimated the herd at 281 cattle. Thatcher, in his testimony, portrayed Welcher as a befuddled old man. "Lawrence's eyesight has been going badly for a couple of years and he gets things...confused. It was not uncommon for Lawrence to completely ball up the number of cows and the number of calves," he said. Thatcher insisted that he owned only 180 cattle. Interestingly, in calculating the worth of the cattle ($200,000), Mr. Justice Hughes believed Welcher, not Thatcher.

Since the most valuable part of the Thatcher holdings was made up of the 4,800 acres of pasture and grain-growing land, Gerry Gerrand hired the most experienced appraiser he could find, Art Hosie of Regina. Hosie phoned Merchant and asked if he might inspect the farm lands. Merchant said no, and hung up the phone. Because inspection of Thatcher's vast land holdings from the road was difficult and Thatcher had warned Hosie that he didn't like trespassers, Gerrand was then forced to get a court order that directed that Hosie should have access to the property at any reasonable time and specifically be allowed to inspect the interiors of buildings on Saturday, May 3, 1980. Hosie arrived at the Thatcher farm on the specified day and Colin was fairly polite to him; they went to the Caronport restaurant for lunch.

The politeness was misleading. Hosie's wife, Paula, was the secretary to the Conservative caucus at the Legislative Buildings. On the following Monday, Thatcher walked into the office of Grant Devine, the PC leader, and said, "Either Paula Hosie goes or I quit." Mrs. Hosie lost her job.

Gerry Gerrand heard about it on a golfing trip, from an old friend, a Conservative MLA from Estevan. He decided that the obvious vindictiveness of that one act would cast a shadow on much of Thatcher's evidence, so he had Grant Devine subpoenaed. "But the trial was developing so badly for Thatcher," says Gerrand, "I didn't think it was necessary to call him. So after talking it over with JoAnn—she was much more a political animal than I was—we phoned Devine and said, 'Disregard the subpoena.'" Those in the Tory caucus who knew about the episode sighed with relief—but Colin Thatcher had tried one more bullying tactic and had won because nobody stood up to him.

To establish the extent of the Thatcher wealth, Gerrand called fourteen witnesses, including Ron Graham. The purpose of Graham's testimony was twofold: to show that by holidaying at Laguna Beach with other women Colin had dissipated his and JoAnn's assets; and to indicate that the shares Thatcher owned in Prairie Co-Ax Cable Ltd. were worth $40,000.

JoAnn also gave evidence. Mr. Justice Hughes could see that she was in a very distressed emotional state. "But she had the appearance about her of being a very pleasant person."

Six and a half days into the trial, Colin Thatcher took the stand. Merchant was questioning Thatcher about his background and assets, when Gerrand's ears suddenly perked up. Colin was claiming that because of "a verbal secret trust," much of the property JoAnn thought he owned was really his mother's. Gerrand looked over at his son David, who was helping him in the case, and whispered, "Secret trust—last time I heard that expression was when I was in law school twenty years ago." Mr. Justice Hughes admitted he had to refresh himself on the legalities of such a thing, and so he decided to put aside the part of Thatcher's testimony until the next day. Gerry and David Gerrand spent that evening in their law firm's library plumbing the mysteries of "secret trusts."

The next morning Colin told the story. In 1969 Ross Thatcher had suffered a heart attack and afterwards had changed his will. Instead of leaving most of his agricultural lands to his estate, as he had originally planned, he signed a codicil on December 19, 1969, transferring to his son all farm lands, buildings, and equipment. According to Colin, Ross took him aside and asked for his agreement never to transfer the title of those lands from the estate to his name. "He was attempting to provide in the most even-handed fashion for both my mother and myself. He did not want to unduly restrict me, yet at the same time he was adamant that my mother must certainly be protected during her lifetime." And indeed the lands had never been transferred from the estate to Colin Thatcher and now because of this "secret trust" between father and son, JoAnn had no claim to the 2,400 acres of land that Ross had accumulated. "There was not even the slightest suggestion [of such an arrangement]," JoAnn countered. "He always talked about it in terms of his land or our land and he never separated one parcel of land from another. It was all lumped together when he talked about how many sections or quarters he had. It was never called estate land."

Stanley Sheppard, a supervisor with Permanent Trust, one of three executors of Ross Thatcher's estate, had given other reasons as to why the transfer from the estate to Colin Thatcher had not taken place. "Colin said that he was thinking of setting up a private company for tax purposes and therefore requested that the transfer of the land titles be held off for a while." Other witnesses, including Ed Odishaw, Ross's lawyer at the time of his death, confirmed that this had been Colin's intention.

Intrigued by this novel explanation, Garrand asked Thatcher, "When did you first hear of the expression 'secret trust'?" "It was a very recent thing," Colin responded. "I'm trying to think whether it was in this courtroom. I think it was in Mr. Merchant's office. . . ." Gerrand smiled in satisfaction.

Thatcher claimed that his mother knew about the secret trust, and so Peggy Thatcher was called as a witness. It was obviously a very uncomfortable and difficult situation for her. Peggy told the court that the half-hour discussion between her husband and son took place in the den of the Thatchers' Regina home in the early fall of 1969. "I was in and out of this conversation. I heard half of it, but I did not like listening to Ross talk about his will . . . but I did hear him tell Colin this, that he was leaving the land to him, but he did not wish the title taken out of the estate until my death."

While giving evidence, Peggy Thatcher revealed that her life-style had changed quite remarkably over the last four months. In the eight years since Ross's death she had lived quietly, well within her means. Under questioning from Gerrand she said, "I tried to save money. I also was very conscious of giving things to my family. I felt this way, Mr. Gerrand, that I would sooner see happy, happy faces on my family while I was living than when I died." In February of 1980, however—after it became clear that JoAnn would be seeking a share of the estate—a surprising change came over her purchasing patterns and life-style. She bought a $140,000 (U.S.) house in Palm Springs not far from Thatcher's condominium. It had a swimming pool, a Jacuzzi, and extensive gardens. "I have to have a gardener and a pool man, which costs close to $230 a month," she said. And, she added, she was planning to spend about $60,000 (U.S.) furnishing the place. At the same time she had purchased the house, she had bought a $40,000 Mercedes Benz, even though she already owned a $14,000 1979 Cadillac Eldorado. She said her son had encouraged her to buy both cars, pointing out that they were good investments.

All of these added expenses meant that Peggy Thatcher

would for the first time, have to encroach on the estate left by Ross Thatcher. And that, of course, would diminish the estate funds—and JoAnn's share in it should a judge award her any part of it.

Gerrand was successful in revealing to the court that Colin Thatcher had picked out the model and the colour of the Mercedes, that he had bought it (with his mother's money), and that he was the one who drove it. "Would it be surprising to know that the registration to that car remains in the name of your son?" Gerrand asked Peggy Thatcher. "No, the registration is my name, Mr. Gerrand," she replied. "Well, I've had it searched, Mrs. Thatcher. I had it searched today and here's a Xeroxed copy of the only registration that appears with the Saskatchewan Highway Traffic Board." "Well, you'll have to ask my son about it," Peggy responded. "I haven't got my glasses. I can't read it, I'm sorry." The name on the registration was that of Colin Thatcher.

Nothing upset JoAnn more during the legal battles than Peggy Thatcher's testimony. "I can't believe that she would lie for Colin," she told Tony Wilson.

The drastic change in Peggy's life-style following the break-up of Colin and JoAnn's marriage was one of the points that Mr. Justice Hughes weighed in deciding if the witnesses were telling the truth about the secret trust. The judge also wondered why Ross, who was the most meticulous of men, especially in business affairs, would leave such an important part of his will unrecorded. And he questioned why neither Colin nor Peggy had mentioned the existence of this arrangement to anyone, including JoAnn, for seven or eight years. Finally he concluded that the secret trust did not exist. He awarded JoAnn a half-share of the estate lands, which were valued altogether at $359,000.

In his closing remarks to Mr. Justice Hughes, Tony Merchant had placed great emphasis on Peggy Thatcher's prestige and respect in the community, saying, "The court must either find the secret trust to exist or find Colin and Peggy Thatcher to be complete liars." Hughes was upset over Merchant's black-and-white approach. The judge felt that there could have been a grey area: Ross could have said something like, "I'm leaving the lands to Colin but I expect him to look after you," and Peggy might have misinterpreted it.

There was one other strange twist in the matrimonial property trial. When JoAnn left Moose Jaw and her marriage in September, 1979, the Thatchers were in an enviable financial situation. The vehicles, land, cattle, and the rest, was valued at just over $2 million. Their debt to the Moose Jaw Credit Union and various banks was about $365,000, which was not a bad ratio considering the plight of many farmer-ranchers. By the time the property trial occurred ten months later, Thatcher's debt had risen by $700,000, to over $1 million. Merchant argued that the astonishing jump in the amount of debt was a result of normal ranch business and that JoAnn should shoulder half of it, despite the fact that it had all been incurred after she left Moose Jaw and after her involvement in the operation had ceased.

About $200,000 of it was an operating loan. Another $50,000 was a loan made to a Palm Springs businessman, Owen Klein, when Thatcher made the trip to Palm Springs while holidaying in Laguna Beach. "The gentleman involved, at thirty-seven, suffered a crippling heart attack," said Thatcher, and "has been in default on the payments for quite some time. . . . I think those funds are in a great deal of jeopardy because of the tragic accident that he went through." Questioned by Gerrand, Thatcher said Klein had signed a promissory note, but he was not able to produce it. Nor did he have the bank draft obtained when he sent the money to Palm Springs, or any correspondence relating to the mysterious loan.

By far the largest portion of the new debt—$429,000—was for the purchase of two sections of grain-growing land. According to Thatcher, he decided some time previously to buy two quarter-sections owned by a neighbour, Gerry English, for $224,000. "Gerry English is probably the best farmer in the Greyburn area, and I've been attempting to purchase his land since 1974," Colin said. Thatcher claimed the deal had been worked out in November of 1979, but payment had not been made until May 1, 1980. On December 2, 1979, Thatcher also made another deal, this time with Tom Bergren, to buy a half-section of Bergren's land. Again the payment of $205,000 was not made until April of 1980. "If God ever made a perfect half-section, it is that one. It is flawless," Colin enthused. Significantly, the English and Bergren properties were placed in trust for Gregory and Regan, and therefore they could not be sold until the boys reached maturity; Thatcher, meanwhile, had mortgaged his own lands to raise the needed amount. "Didn't you tell your wife some months ago that she would share in one-half of your debts," Gerrand demanded, "and that's all you'd have and that your children would be rich?" "No," responded Thatcher.

It was generally assumed that Thatcher had taken on such a heavy debt load after his separation because he believed the extra $700,000 would be included in the matrimonial property division, and so he would be punishing JoAnn. Merchant, of course, tried to convince Mr. Justice Hughes to include the new debt in dividing up the property. But the judge ruled that since JoAnn was not consulted about any of these deals, she would not be burdened by any resulting financial obligation.

Indeed, the new act was so clear on that point that Thatcher surely must have realized that he was in grave danger of shouldering the full debt load, and thus would be seriously encumbering his portion of the land. As well, he knew that costly and bitter legal battles were looming. Why then did he buy the land? He might have been so determined to win his sons' allegiance that he was trying to woo them with the gift of valuable farm land; but by this time the boys were so much under their father's sway that such drastic action would have seemed unnecessary. It is possible that Thatcher suspected that financial ruin was around the corner and so was taking care of his sons' futures by providing both of them with excellent farms, totally unencumbered by debt.

These questions were less important than the one that hung over the court when, after ten days of testimony, the trial finally ended on July 29, 1980. But Mr. Justice Hughes reserved his judgment, so that he could study the complex and often contradictory evidence. It would take him two and a half months to write his judgment.

The matrimonial property trial had been heard in two stages, five days in June and five in July. Sandwiched in between, from July 2 to July 16, was the second custody battle fought over Regan. Mr. Justice MacPherson would say of it, "In my twenty years on the bench, this is the worst matrimonial case that has come into the court, the most interminable, the most bitterly fought, and the most expensive."

MacPherson had been involved in a long, difficult trial during May and June of 1980 and he was under the impression that the Thatcher matter was to be heard by Judge Hughes. "I didn't want to take the second trial. I had had one kick at the can and I thought someone else should do it. Furthermore I had heard that I was being criticized by Thatcher, and I didn't want any more acrimony." One day, after MacPherson had adjourned his court late in the afternoon, he got a call from Chief Justice Fred Johnson (now Lieutenant-Governor of Saskatchewan). Ted Hughes was in his office. "They had decided between them that I, not Hughes, should take the Thatcher custody trial, which had already been set. Well, about this time Hughes was on the way out and there was a great deal of bitterness among the judges and I was trying to alleviate that as well. At any rate, Hughes and Johnson told me that, in their opinion, it was my duty to take the second trial. I was arguing that I didn't want to. Finally I said, 'Oh hell, I'll take it, if that's what you want.'"

The first item MacPherson had to address was the divorce. A very reluctant Ron Graham testified that Colin Thatcher had committed adultery with Janis Gardiner, and he had done the same with JoAnn Thatcher. Mr. Justice MacPherson thought Graham's evidence "a real shocker." "I got the impression... that although this wasn't an unpremeditated roll in the hay, that this was something that happens to people who live too well, too richly, with too much booze and too much gaiety, a life-style in which promiscuity isn't a sin. Graham seemed to be terribly ashamed of what he had done.... He was dreadfully unhappy to be there, and I kind of hoped it was the evidence of a man who had learned his lesson."

Back home in the Graham household, this seemed to be true. After Ron had returned from his tryst with JoAnn, his wife had served him with a divorce petition. "By this time Jane had taken over Graham Construction's computers," says an old friend, "and she knew exactly how much to ask for in a divorce settlement. Ron realized that he couldn't divorce her without ruining the company." As well, Ron's father had entered the scene, pointing out to his son a few home truths. The Grahams had long enjoyed an impeccable reputation in their community and they resented the scandal their son had caused. Jane and Ron Graham were reconciled.

At his trial for first-degree murder, Colin Thatcher would

remark, "JoAnn never forgave me for breaking up her plans, which were to become Mrs. Ron Graham. And when I brought my children back from Brampton, everything was exposed. Graham was served with a divorce petition. Graham then had to move to consolidate his own position at home because he couldn't afford a divorce any more than I could. In the process, JoAnn was lost in the shuffle. She never forgave me for her not being Mrs. Ron Graham."

MacPherson granted JoAnn a decree nisi right then. "I had reason to believe that she wanted to marry Tony Wilson. I thought possibly he [Thatcher] might get married again, too. And the sooner this got settled with the other two spouses, the sooner the custody thing would straighten itself out. One lives in hope. Very rarely does the judge hear the end of the story—but this one I sure as hell did."

Since it was Tony Merchant who pushed for the custody hearing, it was up to him to convince MacPherson that it would be in Regan's best interests if he reversed his order and gave custody of the child to Thatcher. To this end, the eleven-year-old boy had been examined by a battery of psychiatrists, most of whom saw him once for less than an hour, had never met JoAnn, and knew nothing of the tactics used by Colin Thatcher, but who had no hesitation in making firm recommendations about the child's fate.

Thatcher had arranged for Regan to see Dr. Peter Matthews, a psychiatrist specializing in children and adolescents at the University of Saskatchewan, on April 29. After talking to the boy for forty-five minutes to an hour, Matthews felt that Regan was "a very bright youngster, able well to appreciate what's going on." Dr. Matthews reported that Regan felt his mother "was not behaving in a way that he liked to see her behaving." "If he was forced and he really hadn't a good say in what was going to happen, then I think this would be damaging for him and I would see him as becoming a rather bitter and angry person." Dr. Matthews concluded, "It would be in Regan's best interests and probably the best interests of society as a whole for him to go with his father at this time." Matthews admitted, however, that he had not talked to JoAnn.

JoAnn's family doctor had recommended that Regan be psychiatrically assessed as well. The child met with Dr.

Joseph Benjamin on May 15 and May 20. A psychiatrist with a general practice, Dr. Benjamin also interviewed JoAnn, whom he described as "an adequate woman, a very strong woman, I would say, mature in most ways, a good mother, a homemaker, carried a tremendous amount of responsibility through her years of marriage, well educated, superior intelligence, and with a great deal of warmth towards her children." Dr. Benjamin felt that Regan's running away was "partly instigated, that it was not entirely his own idea. That he was getting rewarded for that.... I understand that the boy was not given much attention prior to the difficulties that came about in 1979. The older child was favoured by the father. After Regan was taken back by the father from the custody of his mother and provided with trips to Palm Springs and apparently told certain amounts of land and such were to be placed in his name, I felt that those kinds of rewards would be reinforcing of his wanting to be with the father." He concluded, "I think that if Regan is placed with his mother she should have complete control of him, that it would be best if he did not have contact with his older brother or his father for a reasonable period of time—I would estimate no less than six months—during which time I feel that the mother would be capable of re-establishing a good relationship with him, given no interference." Dr. Benjamin had not met Colin Thatcher.

Dr. Roderick MacLeod, another child and adolescent psychiatrist connected to the University Hospital in Saskatoon, was asked by Thatcher and Tony Merchant to see Regan, and he met with him for about fifty minutes on June 2. He recommended that custody of Regan be given to Colin Thatcher. "As I picked up from him [Regan], I think that he would be a real risk of beginning to become more physically aggressive against property and also making comments and trying to embarrass and anger his mother and make her, I guess, desperate enough to say, okay go." Regan told the doctor that one of the reasons he was upset at his mother was that he had seen her "petting" with a boyfriend in Brampton. MacLeod had not asked JoAnn if there was any truth to this allegation because—according to the depressing pattern—he had never met her.

Dr. Ronald Gabriel, a child psychiatrist practising in Regina, had been asked by the court to examine the child and he met with him on June 25. "He doesn't know what's going to be happening to him and although he's presenting a pretty tough exterior—he's a proud young man—there were signs from time to time that he was hurting and I think he tended to look upon the paternal home as being a symbol of strength, wealth, his future, power," Gabriel reported. "He is very, very negative and angry towards his mother." Mr. Justice MacPherson asked the psychiatrist if giving Regan his way and allowing him to live with his father might not spoil the child. Dr. Gabriel responded, "I think, My Lord, that we're really beyond spoiling this child. I feel that the situation has been really very, very damaging to the child to now and that the most that can be aimed for is to reduce the tensions in the child, by letting him have his way and be spoiled. That is the position I would find myself moving towards and feeling very unhappy about it." Gabriel commented that, not surprisingly, Regan was becoming rather sophisticated in his ability to handle psychiatrists and their questions.

Mr. Justice MacPherson summed up his feelings on this testimony very precisely: "However eminent and competent Doctors Matthews, MacLeod and Gabriel are, there is one weakness in their evidence and that is that they do not know the facts as I do. Their conclusions within the limits of their knowledge were unquestionably correct but as each said, he was unable to judge the parents. It is not surprising that their opinions are what they are. They were entitled to assume a degree of normalcy and reasonableness in the father and his home. From this prominent and wealthy and articulate father they had no reason to expect the extent of wrongful attitudes and activity that I have [become aware of and come to expect]."

Dr. Peter Matthews had suffered a detached retina and had undergone two serious eye operations, which meant that he could not testify at the trial. So Merchant and Gerrand flew to Saskatoon to take commissioned evidence at the doctor's house four weeks before the trial began. When it was over, Merchant said to Gerrand, "Could you lend me twenty dollars, Gerry?" "Why?" Gerrand wanted to know. "Well, I never carry any money," said Tony. "Everybody knows that. I need a taxi to get to the airport." Gerrand gave him the money. A couple of weeks into the trial, Gerry asked Merchant for his twenty bucks. "It's dictated," said Tony. "I have three series of dictations, urgent, important, and not important. That letter to you with your twenty dollars is in the non-important pile. It will get out in a week or two." Gerrand took it as a joke and laughed. It was one of the few times there was any levity in this deadly serious trial.

Colin was able to persuade many of the Thatcher's old friends—Murray and Sharon Barrett, Donald McDonald, Rosemary and Roger Tessier, and Beverly and John Patterson—to testify on his behalf. But it had been a difficult decision for all of them. Indeed, the Thatcher battles had split the upper crust in Moose Jaw very badly. Many had taken Colin's side, especially those who were fond of Jane Graham, because they felt that JoAnn was a "gold-digger" and a "home-breaker," who was only after Ron's money and prestige. And since JoAnn, who hated gossip, had avoided saying anything derogatory about her husband, few people knew that he had been involved in far more illicit affairs than she. Nor had they any idea of the harrassment, even terror, that she had undergone since leaving her husband. After choosing sides it is always hard to change; even after Colin was found guilty of the first-degree murder of JoAnn, many of those who had come down on his side in the custody question refused to believe that he had committed the crime.

Thatcher's witnesses all testified that Colin had become a born-again father. Sure, they admitted, he had had little to do with raising the children while JoAnn was in the home. Now, however, he was a responsible, devoted father. "Certainly since last year at this time there has been quite a significant change in Mr. Thatcher," Don McDonald said. "I think he started to see things like his home, his backyard, his children, his ranch as being a lot more important.... Colin hadn't had too many bad bumps along life's road. He has been successful in business and politics and in most things and, all of a sudden, he has had a pretty traumatic experience and he has finally had to take a look at himself and to realize that things like his family are important."

Sandra Hammond, the young housekeeper, once again testified on Thatcher's behalf. Merchant asked her, "Is there a lot of talk in the home about the court cases, the situation?" She replied, "Yes, there is. Regan and Greg are constantly asking their dad how things are going." MacPherson considered that a significant statement. He would later write,

"Considering the extent of the proceedings, custody, divorce, under the Matrimonial Property Act, the innumerable chamber applications and appeals, this must have occurred almost every evening over several months. All three, the father and the two sons, talked of good days, bad days, what 'we' are doing or planning. Mr. Thatcher made his sons participants and indeed parties throughout. They could not have been other than biased against their mother. They share their father's purpose to defeat her."

During the fourth day of the trial, MacPherson blurted out, "I hope that somewhere there is a heaven for exhausted and confused judges. I am absolutely beside myself in this case." What had upset him was the fact that Tony Merchant was presenting the evidence "backsideways." Instead of calling Colin Thatcher at the start and asking him to explain what had gone on with Regan since the fall of 1979, Merchant called his other witnesses, who presented bits and pieces of the story, first. It seriously undermined Thatcher's case. "I've always felt that one is entitled to question the reliability of evidence where the corroboration comes before the substance," says MacPherson. "It would have made Colin considerably more credible if he testified first and then the others came and backed him up." MacPherson warned Merchant of this danger a number of times. The lawyer ignored him. Indeed for some reason, throughout the trial, Merchant decided to play the part of Peck's Bad Boy. "I grew progressively more impatient with Merchant," recalls MacPherson. "He would not accept my rulings. I felt Merchant and Thatcher were trying to take over my courtroom. And I run a very tight court."

MacPherson's irritation with Merchant was curious, because Tony was considered one of his pets. MacPherson had been at Dalhousie with Merchant's father and he knew Tony's mother, Sally, quite well. When Tony graduated from law school and was about to practise in Regina, she asked her friend the judge to keep an eye on him. "I took this quite seriously," says MacPherson. "As time went on, he became a smart-ass and required fatherly discipline, which I gave to him. He was acting strangely and I began to get complaints from the other judges, both district court and our court. I used to call him into my office and on at least one occasion

I had him crying because of his irresponsibility in court. I gave him hell because his mother had asked me to...I was tough. I told him he had to smarten up or he was going to get in real trouble. I suppose I was trying to shake the constantly immature Merchant into mature judgment." Yet in many ways MacPherson appreciated Merchant's drive and unorthodoxy. "Tony is a tremendous worker and a very clever man. What he lacks sometimes is judgment."

That Merchant was "a tremendous worker" was demonstrated by one surprising incident. Near the beginning of the trial, MacPherson came back to his office one night at about 9:30. It was located just opposite Courtroom Number Four, where the Thatcher hearing was being held. MacPherson noticed the light was on in the courtroom and he discreetly looked in the window of the door. "There was Merchant at the counsel table and Thatcher in the witness box. I suppose Tony was trying to make him feel comfortable as a witness. The caretaker came by and told me that they had been in there ever since we'd adjourned at about 4:30 or so. I had never seen that happen before in all the years I had been on the bench." What was astonishing about this was that Merchant and Thatcher would work so hard, and yet seem to have no idea of how completely they were alienating the judge.

MacPherson became particularly infuriated when Merchant insisted on putting Greg Thatcher in the witness box.

THE COURT: I'm just thinking of this family as a family. If you bring that child... he's got to describe among other things the dreadful incident in which he must have struck his mother.

THE COURT: He's going to try to blame it on her.

MR. MERCHANT: Yes.

THE COURT: And immediately there's a conflict when the mother testifies in the other direction. I have to resolve the conflict of interest between a mother and a fifteen-year-old boy and call one of them a liar, or mistaken.

MR. MERCHANT: Yes.

THE COURT: Now this trial is going to go down in the life of that child, for his whole life, but your instructions are nevertheless to bring him in here, to call his mother names, in the sense of she's the one who broke up the home.

MR. MERCHANT: Well...

THE COURT: If I were acting for Mrs. Thatcher and you put that boy in the box I would be interested to know how much he knows about the peccadillos of his father, inasmuch as he is so concerned about the chastity of his mother. If Mr. Gerrand were to ask him, well, "Who are you talking about, your mother and her boyfriends. What do you know about the girlfriends of your father?" Isn't that nice?

MR. MERCHANT: Well...

THE COURT: Isn't that lovely to raise with a fifteen-year-old?...And I think it is absolutely abhorrent for a father who claims to have the best interest of that child at heart to want to bring that child into this dreadful piece of litigation.

Tony Merchant called Gregory as a witness anyway. "I had to have Greg testify because of Regan," says Merchant. "There's a principle of law that says you don't separate siblings, so if I could, through Gregory, make Judge MacPherson realize that Regan was very determined [to stay with his father] then I could say to him, You've got to give the two boys to the father, and you shouldn't separate the siblings, you should give him all three.

"MacPherson was a judge who jumped [to one side or the other]," continues Merchant. "I don't say that in a particularly negative way. I liked him as a judge because I knew what he was thinking. . . . I want to know what my guy is thinking up there and then I can deal with his concerns. . . . So if I said I know the guy has jumped [to the other side] so I don't want to antagonize him, well, hell, that's just saying I am going to lose. I have to keep piling up these things—every one will antagonize him—until maybe he'll jump back."

On the stand Gregory told his version of the physical fight he had with his mother. He said that his father had instructed him to let JoAnn visit with Stephanie but not to let her out of the house. The fourteen-year-old told his mother this and when she persisted in taking her daughter, Greg blocked her way. "I had bare feet on and she had these wooden sandals with high heels and she started to stomp on my toes and kick me. At first I didn't do anything. I just jumped out of the way. Then she started scratching me with one hand and I just sort of pushed her away from me. And she came up again and she started scratching me and I got some blood on my arm and I just pushed her away again. And by this time Stephanie had been put down and I just picked Stephanie up and I went outside, into the garage, because I wanted Mom to come out of the house. She came after me and I put Stephanie down. And Mom got behind me and she had her teeth in the back of my neck so I just pushed her away and I grabbed Stephanie and went inside and locked the door. . . . She was always chasing me, yelling 'God damn you' and 'damn you'."

MacPherson thought the allegation by Greg that his mother had tried to stomp on his toes and bite his neck was absolute nonsense. "That loving mother doing a thing like that—ridiculous." The judge was so appalled by Greg's story, in fact, that he had to knock back a couple of drinks that night to help him sleep.

Gerrand realized that Greg's evidence was hurting Colin Thatcher's case far more than it was helping it. "In cross-examination, I tried to have Greg develop how he felt and what he did in a very polite way. I was very polite to him," recalls Gerrand. "I did not in any way try to trip him up. I just wanted him to talk more, because I knew the more he would talk, the more the judge would come to the conclusion that he did come to—and that was that this young boy was being developed in the same mould as his father. It was a tragic thing. I felt bloody bad about it, and I still get tears in my eyes when I think of that young man and his brother and sister."

MacPherson's picture of Gregory after his testimony is sharply etched. "He is a tall, handsome, and intelligent boy. He testified for well over a half-day. He said nothing at all critical about his father. He rejects the mere suggestion of wrongdoing on his father's part. In many ways he reflected his father's personality—arrogant, proud, vain, even belligerent. For his mother he showed scorn, contempt, and disrespect. His professed love for her was, I felt, insincere. He had no regret for the force he had used upon her. He was simply obeying his father's orders, which was his justification."

After Greg had testified for three hours, Merchant asked that Regan be allowed to take the stand. MacPherson once again was appalled.

*   *   *

THE COURT: Are you going to destroy this family utterly? The purpose of the father, as I understand it, is to keep the family together.

MR. MERCHANT: Yes, My Lord.

THE COURT: It seems to me that I'm shocked enough by what I heard from this boy today. Now, am I going to hear more of it?

MR. MERCHANT: Well frankly, My Lord, I will be content, I suspect, with your decision on whether you hear him, and I hope I don't change my mind two months hence and have to explain these words to the Court of Appeal.

THE COURT: I don't care. I don't care. I'll run my court within the law, as I see it, and you can threaten me with appeal until the cows come home and I don't care whose cows they are.

MR. MERCHANT: I wasn't. I was making a bad joke.

THE COURT: No, you were threatening me with appeal and I don't care.

The next morning the witnesses and counsel gathered before the session and Colin walked over to Gerrand. "Boy, did that young fellow ever stand up to your cross-examination yesterday." Gerrand knew how damaging to Thatcher Greg's testimony had really been and he replied, "That reminds me of the story of the soldier in the Second World War who was engaged in a battle of bayonets with a German. The German said after the American had taken a swipe at him, 'You missed me!' The American replied, 'Wait till you try and turn your head.' Thatcher blanched and said something sneeringly to me, and perhaps threatening. I said, 'Your utterances are fatuous and feckless. I don't propose to discuss this matter with you and I don't have to. You get away from me or I'm going to get an order in court requiring you to.' Then I told Merchant to keep his client away from me."

As he heard the full story of what had occurred since JoAnn had first been awarded custody of Regan, MacPherson became more and more alarmed. "With his domineering personality and his determination to win at all costs, Thatcher sought to control the court and me and the result of the trial. . . . You can't imagine the atmosphere in that courtroom of hatred, of oppression, of distrust, I could go into my thesaurus and find all sorts of dreadful epithets but I think oppression is the word I would favour. I can't recall any other trial while I was at the bar or on the court in which I felt the same. It was beyond bitterness—I'm used to bitterness in the courtroom—it was the exercise of force, the feeling of violence. The clouds were low, so low that I had to lean down to look under them."

MacPherson took three and a half weeks to write his judgment. "I was afraid that what I had written was a diatribe and not a judgment. I nearly tore it up and started again." Darla Hunter, a young articling law student who was doing some work for the judges on the rules of court, wandered by. MacPherson called her in and asked her to read it. "Tell me if it's a diatribe or a judgment." She came back in less than an hour with tears in her eyes. "That is the way a judgment is supposed to read," she said. The Chief Justice also read it. "I thought it was an excellent judgment. I think Sandy's choice of words was accurate."

The judgment was a searing indictment of Colin Thatcher. MacPherson wrote, "I have no doubt that the cause of the breakdown of the marriage and of the lengthy and expensive litigation was, and is, the personality, actions and attitude of Mr. Thatcher. He is forty-two years of age, very large of stature. . . . He is articulate, domineering and intimidating. As the evidence developed in this trial, it became more and more apparent to me, indeed it was overwhelming, that he was determined to win custody of the son, Regan, by any means at all.

"At the time I wrote my earlier judgment I possessed the hope that this prominent and intelligent and wealthy and well-educated couple would try to find a way to solve their problems. It was for that reason that I did not treat the husband as critically as I then felt was justified. So much for the Judge as social worker. That [trial] was only two days in length. This one consumed eleven days. I know Mr. Thatcher much better now. His methods and purposes have been to destroy his wife in the minds of their children. In so doing, he has gone a long way towards destroying the children themselves.

"Another result of the second trial is that I have more respect and sympathy for Mrs. Thatcher. . . ." MacPherson then briefly summarized improprieties on the part of both partners. "The foregoing is only the bare bones of a long and dreadful story of interference, contempt of court and downright deception by Mr. Thatcher.

"In a normal home with children in our society it is the mother who is the mainstay, the planner of everything. The mother has always been the object of love because of her devotion and sacrifice to her family. When, therefore, a mother suddenly abandons her home, particularly with another man, it is easy for a man such as Mr. Thatcher to destroy her in the minds of her immature and impressionable children. The natural love for the mother evaporates because in their minds she has become unworthy. She gets no second chance because she presents her case to closed minds.

"This is exactly what happened in the Thatcher family. This foolish man did so much in such a diabolical fashion that it all becomes almost unbelievable. The sons closed ranks about their father and excluded her. Stephanie, it seems, remained constantly affectionate to her mother. It is important to note here that Mr. Thatcher left his sons in complete ignorance of his own adultery which was the precipitating factor but not by any means the sole cause of the breakdown of the marriage. . . .

"If the child [Regan] is to be saved from becoming the image of his father, only his mother can do it. She wants to try. She has had no chance. That has been denied her for nearly a year by the actions of her husband and Gregory. . . ."

MacPherson not only awarded custody of Regan to his mother, but he ruled that neither Colin nor Greg were to have any communication with the boy for an entire year. He also ruled that anyone having knowledge of the order would be prohibited from interfering in any way.

CHAPTER FOURTEEN

ABOVE THE LAW

AUGUST 11, 1980

On the advice of Gerry Gerrand, JoAnn's parents drove from Ames, Iowa, to assist their daughter in taking custody of Regan: JoAnn could not formally serve the court orders, but either of the Geigers could. The formal Judgment Roll was issued in Regina at 3:30 p.m. on August 11, 1980. At 6:20 that evening JoAnn and Harlan Geiger drove to Moose Jaw. When they knocked on the front door of the Redland home, no one answered. They could hear the television blasting in the background, so they walked in the house. Greg and Colin were eating their supper in front of the TV. "How'd you get in?" Colin demanded roughly. "The door was unlocked, Colin," said Harlan. He promptly handed him the court order and then pressed one on Greg. "That's when he hit the ceiling," recalls Harlan. "He had heard about the custody decision, but he didn't know about the actual court order." Colin said that Regan wasn't there and anyway, he insisted, he had no intention of giving up custody until he had talked with his solicitor.

JoAnn immediately drove over to the Hammonds and spoke to Sandra's young brother Patrick, who told them that Regan was staying with his mother and father at their Jackfish Lake cottage in northern Saskatechewan until August 22.

Harlan and JoAnn got back to Regina at about nine. Tony Wilson gallantly offered to drive the 415 kilometres and the three set out northwards, leaving Stephanie in the care of Betty Geiger. After travelling all night, they arrived at Jackfish Lake about nine the next morning and asked the proprietor of a small grocery store for directions. The proprietor feigned ignorance of the Hammonds and their cottage—JoAnn sur-

mised that the Hammonds had warned the man that they
might arrive—but a clerk overheard the conversation and
piped up, "Oh I know where they are," and helpfully gave
directions.

"We drove over there and knocked on the door," remembers Harlan. "They were obviously expecting us, and they
told us that Regan had already left." Despite the court order
prohibiting him from doing so, Colin had contacted the
Hammonds the night before and Sandra had left immediately
for Moose Jaw with Regan, presumably passing JoAnn's north-
bound car in the middle of the night. Now Beverley Hammond
talked to JoAnn and Harlan through the screen door of the
cottage but she refused to unlock it. Since the Hammonds
were clearly involved in the case to the hilt, Harlan was
determined to serve her with the court order prohibiting her
from interfering with Regan—so determined, in fact, that he
smashed his fist through the screen, touching her with the
legal document and thereby formally serving her. Harlan and
JoAnn quickly returned to the waiting car. The Hammonds
rushed out, screaming that Geiger had destroyed their door.
"Send me the bill," Harlan yelled. "They did send it, too,
and, boy, was it padded. He was a handyman and all they had
to get was a piece of screen. But they charged mileage for
trips to town, so many hours of labour, cost of materials. I
would have paid it anyway, but Jo said, 'If you do, I will
never forgive you. After all the things they've done to me.'"
(When JoAnn's brother, Don, heard about the incident he
was flabbergasted, because the action was so uncharacteristic
of his father. Harlan Geiger was five-foot-six and sixty-seven
years old, had a heart condition, and was the most gentle and
pacific of men.)

JoAnn, Harlan, and Tony quickly drove back to Moose Jaw.
They went first to the Redland home and then to the Hammond
residence. They found nobody at home and the doors locked
at both houses.

That same day, August 12, Merchant filed a notice of
appeal on behalf of Thatcher, which meant an automatic stay
of MacPherson's judgment. Two days later, however, the
Chief Justice of the Court of Appeal ruled that the stay be set
aside: MacPherson's judgment once again prevailed. Gerald
Kraus, Regan's lawyer, phoned Gerrand that day at about 4

p.m. and told him that the boy was ready to go with his mother.

About an hour later, JoAnn and Harlan once again set out for Moose Jaw. By this time JoAnn was worried that Colin might react violently, and Allan Gooding had volunteered to act as a protective escort. He joined them at the Redland house. Blaine Mathieson, Sandra Hammond's boyfriend, answered the door. "Regan's not here," said Mathieson, "he's at the Caron ranch." JoAnn said she wanted to use the telephone, and eighteen-year-old Blaine told her he had been instructed not to allow her entry into the house. JoAnn pushed her way past him, went in, and collected Regan's belongings.

The threesome then stood outside the Redland house until about 6:15, but neither Colin nor Regan showed up. They went to Allan's for a cup of coffee and returned an hour later. JoAnn and her father walked up to the porch and Allan Gooding stood outside on the sidewalk. This time Thatcher himself came to the door and said that Regan had to collect his things but would be out in a minute. He refused to let JoAnn and her father into the house, although he himself went in, locking the door behind him. Five minutes later Colin and Greg came out the side door, followed by Regan some five or ten steps behind. Harlan yelled to his grandson, "Hi, Regan!" The child hesitated for a moment and then he took off at a gallop for the nearby coulee behind the house. JoAnn started after him but was prevented from doing so; Colin and Greg blocked her on one side, and two vehicles parked in front of the garage blocked her on the other. Colin called after his son, "Come on back here, Regan," but it was not convincing. Everybody realized that the whole escape had been carefully orchestrated by Colin, Greg, and Regan. "Colin had wanted to appear as though he was complying with the court order, but the whole thing had been staged," says Harlan Geiger.

Allan Gooding stepped forward to take off after the boy but Thatcher immediately confronted him. "Colin came up to me nose to nose," says Allan, "and snarled, 'You take one step on my property to go after him and I will kill you.'" The next day Gooding once again laid a charge against Thatcher, this time of threatening. Several months later, it was dismissed in court on a legal technicality.

It may have seemed another small, sad, unimportant little scuffle, one of Regan's many runaways engineered by his father. But JoAnn did not see the boy again for over a year, and she never did take custody of her son. After he ran away, he hung around the ranch for a week or two and then flew to Palm Springs on a ticket that his father had bought. He was enrolled in a private boys' school called Palm Valley School in Cathedral City, and he lived with his grandmother in her new house, not far from the school. Colin came down often that year to visit his son. The boy was registered at the school as Regan Erickson by a woman who posed as his mother. Cindy Erickson, a tall, leggy blonde, very flashy and very Californian, was Thatcher's mistress at the time.

"JoAnn's friends and her family and everybody were so frustrated at this point, because we felt such a sense of injustice," says Betty Gooding. "We kept asking, why was Colin getting away with everything and she was being brutalized? We couldn't understand how the judicial system could allow this to happen." JoAnn herself felt as though she were sinking into a judicial quagmire with no bottom. But she refused to give up.

From the time that Regan bolted, JoAnn was in close contact with the Moose Jaw police. When Sergeant Richard Baum and Constable Jim Dykes questioned Colin Thatcher about the matter, he said he didn't know where Regan was; the police were astonished that Thatcher was so nonchalant about the disappearance of his eleven-year-old son. They also talked to Peggy Thatcher and several of Colin's ranch hands. No one had the slightest idea of where the boy might be.

On September 3, Colin brazenly phoned JoAnn and demanded that he be allowed to take Stephanie to Moose Jaw for the weekend. JoAnn, who was furious at him over the Regan shenanigans, said, "You will not see her in the foreseeable future." On September 10, Tony Merchant brought a motion before Mr. Justice MacPherson asking that Thatcher have access to Stephanie. That gave Gerry Gerrand an opportunity to tell the judge about recent events.

Sandy MacPherson couldn't believe his ears when he was told of Regan's disappearance: "I along with everybody else was overwhelmed with suspicion as to who had caused the child to go missing." Gerrand pointed out that in court in England it is a practice for judges to call the media into the courtroom and to ask their assistance in locating a missing child. "I thought that was eminently sensible," says MacPherson. He adjourned the case until the following morning and told a *Leader-Post* court reporter to round up as many journalists as he could find. He also ensured that copies of his twenty-page custody judgment were available. "Thatcher might have considered himself above the law," says MacPherson, "but I thought that if he wasn't sensitive to the law, he might be sensitive to what the public thought about him."

The next morning MacPherson held what Thatcher would later term his "press conference." "For about three weeks, Mr. Thatcher tells the police that he doesn't know where Regan is," said MacPherson, "but he is not concerned. The matter obviously requires the widest publicity so that the child may be found and delivered to the mother in accordance with the Order of this Court. . . . In the present circumstances the mother requires the assistance of the media, and of the public, to find her child. . . .

"If Mr. Thatcher is the author of this disappearance of Regan, he may be guilty of contempt of court, because my Order of the 11th of August provided that he would not interfere with his wife's custody for a period of a year.

"It is also possible that anybody who is assisting Mr. Thatcher in the disappearance of the child may be guilty of contempt of Court. And I must emphasize that if it can be established there is contempt of Court that this Court will not hesitate to punish."

The next day the Saskatoon, Regina, and Moose Jaw papers published reports on MacPherson's statement. None of them, however, mentioned the scathing criticism the judge had made of Thatcher in his August 11 judgment, even though its text had been made available to them. "The media thought Sandy was grandstanding, so they didn't publish very much about the affair," says a Queen's Bench justice. "It's too bad, because it might have had some effect, at least on the Attorney General's department."

The day MacPherson made his appeal to the media, Thatcher was in Palm Springs, ensuring, among other things, that Regan was settled in. When he returned to Moose Jaw on September 26, 1980, he held his own press conference. It was something of a spectacle. Tony Merchant, who orchestrated the affair, rented a room at the Hotel Saskatchewan for the event, and cameramen, radio reporters, and many members of the press all crowded in. Thatcher spoke in his usual self-assured, pugnacious manner. "Unfortunately you were all but ordered to report the matter when requested on behalf of the court to be present and were told twice by the judge that his judgment was available." Thatcher then outlined his version of the marriage breakdown and the custody trial. He detailed JoAnn's "adulterous affair" but somehow neglected to mention anything about his own dalliance with a twenty-year-old. He emphasized that "Regan's lawyer and three leading child psychologists urged the court to allow Regan to stay with me." Thatcher insisted that the many court actions only strengthened his son's determination to remain with him, "and talk of contempt by Judge MacPherson or the continuing vendetta of my wife will not make me let my family down." He added that time would tell if he was in trouble politically because the judge had made the situation public but "I will not be threatened into betraying those close to me."

The next day the Moose Jaw *Times-Herald* gave his press conference generous space on page one, and other media played the story up as well. Dale Eisler, a political columnist for the Regina *Leader-Post*, wrote an account of the event that was notably sympathetic towards Colin: "As Thatcher read his five-page prepared statement, outlining details of his personal life that no one else should have the right to hear, the horrid side of political life seemed to hang heavy in the room. The strange fact was that no one wanted to be there— not Thatcher, his lawyer, party aides or even the media. There is an unspoken rule that profoundly personal matters that affect only those in an immediate family are not trotted out by the media for public perusal. It is a question of dignity and the knowledge that the same could happen to anyone else."

The notion that Thatcher's outrageous flouting of the law was somehow his own private business, not to be scrutinized or punished, was prevalent not only in the media, but also among the province's law-makers, as they ignored Thatcher's contemptuous disregard for the legal system. In retrospect, it was another missed opportunity. This unfortunate reaction to his defence merely strengthened Thatcher's already firm belief that he was indeed above the law.

Meanwhile, JoAnn had been fighting back in the only legal way she could. On September 16 Gerrand filed a notice of motion with the Court of Queen's Bench asking that Thatcher be found guilty of contempt of court, and MacPherson had ordered Thatcher to undergo an examination in aid of execution. This occurred on September 26. Thatcher was arrogantly uncooperative.

GERRAND: Did you see Regan the day following your discussion with Mrs. Thatcher when Regan disappeared from your yard premises?

THATCHER: I don't recall any specifics about that day at all. There's nothing about that day that makes me recall very much.

GERRAND: When was the last time you saw your son Regan?

THATCHER: I don't know. I think I will decline that question.

GERRAND: Do you decline to answer it?

THATCHER: Yes, and also say I believe that I have complied with the judgment.

GERRAND: Do you know if Regan is going to school or not? It's a very simple question, Mr. Thatcher. Do you know if Regan is going to school or not?

MERCHANT: Wait!

GERRAND: I want the record to show Mr. Merchant has written something down and handed it to Mr. Thatcher to read.

THATCHER: I think I'll decline that answer and say that I believe I have complied with the judgment.

GERRAND: I'm going to repeat the question, Mr. Thatcher. Do you know whether or not Regan is presently going to school?

MERCHANT: You have given your answer to that question.

THATCHER: I have answered.

GERRAND: What was Regan wearing the last time you saw him?

MERCHANT: Give the same answer.

THATCHER: I would have to decline.

GERRAND: I don't want counsel telling the witness that he

doesn't remember when the subject has never been raised before.

MERCHANT: When I see the witness pondering and nodding his head...

GERRAND: Don't be telling him to answer he doesn't remember, Mr. Merchant. Let the witness answer himself truthfully.

All other questions pertaining to Regan were answered in a similar vein.

Four days later Gerrand asked Mr. Justice K.R. Halvorson to order Thatcher to answer the questions. He did so. What followed was like an episode from the Keystone Kops as various sheriffs and other officials attempted to serve Thatcher with Halvorson's order. On September 30, process-server Donald Anderson went to the Redland home in Moose Jaw in search of Thatcher. According to Anderson, Sandra Hammond answered the door and asked him into the hallway. "He's home. I'll just let him know you're here," she said, and then called up to Colin. Anderson waited for about ten minutes until Hammond told him that Thatcher had gone out the back door. The station wagon that had been in the driveway was gone. "I believe Colin Thatcher was on this occasion attempting to evade service by me of the court document," Anderson swore in an affidavit.

Sandra Hammond, whose sworn testimony was to prove helpful to Colin Thatcher's case on future occasions, gave a quite different account of this event. In an affidavit sworn on December 13, 1980, she said that Thatcher had been upstairs showering and shaving in preparation for a constituency meeting when the server arrived. "I told Mr. Thatcher that though I had asked what the man's name was, he had refused to give his name at the door. I asked Mr. Thatcher if I should invite the man in, and Mr. Thatcher told me that I shouldn't since the man had declined to give his name." Hammond claimed that she told Donald Anderson that Colin was in the shower and would be quite a while. According to her, Anderson then left, saying he'd be back in a little while, but by the time her returned Thatcher was gone. Anderson, an officer of the court with no apparent reason to lie, denies Sandra's version of the story. The incident seems to demonstrate how far the young girl was willing to go to help her employer even in 1980.

Thatcher also played cat and mouse with Denis Paquin, a Moose Jaw sheriff, and after many attempts he, too, failed to serve Colin with the order. Finally, however, Thatcher agreed to undergo a second examination in aid of execution, which was set for October 27, 1980.

In the meantime Merchant had appealed Halvorson's order directing Thatcher to answer the questions. On October 8, the three appeal court justices ordered that Thatcher must answer all but one of the twelve questions in dispute and any other questions which were relevant to the proceedings. That judgment did not affect the way that Thatcher, on Merchant's advice, handled the October 27 examination.

GERRAND: When did you last see Regan?

THATCHER: I refuse to answer on the grounds it may incriminate me.

GERRAND: Have you made arrangements with any person, Mr. Thatcher, to take care of Regan, during the last two months?

GERRAND: Where was the last place you saw your son, Regan?

THATCHER: I refuse to answer on the grounds it may incriminate me. . . .

GERRAND: Have you taken any steps to locate your son?

THATCHER: I refuse to answer on the advice of counsel.

All forty questions were answered in a similar manner.

Gerrand was livid with Thatcher, and with Merchant, and with how the law was being defied. "That was really quite a morning," recalls Gerrand. "I found the whole thing offensive. . . . As a person who believes in the rule of law, I couldn't believe what I was observing. There were people who were assisting Thatcher very overtly at that point who should believe in the rule of law. I was mad, I was angry. I didn't strike out and hit people. I didn't call people names. I thought that eventually justice would prevail, but I was mad at what had happened and how it could have happened in our justice system."

During the fall of 1980, JoAnn was still being subjected to the most blatant harassment. During the summer Stephanie's cat—the object of the moving-day altercation—disappeared from the home on Qu'Appelle Drive. Bandit later showed up in Moose Jaw at the Redland house and Colin told his daughter that its feet were terribly sore from walking the seventy kilometres from Regina. The theory that it had hitch-hiked was not put forward.

At the end of the summer, the Qu'Appelle Drive home was sold and JoAnn and Stephanie moved to a rented townhouse at the corner of Gordon and Pasqua Streets. Although she shared a common garage with several neighbours, it was only JoAnn's car that was vandalized. After her Thunderbird failed to start on two occasions, a mechanic found sugar in her gas tank. Not only were the tires on her vehicle slashed but once when Tony Wilson came to visit, he found his tires hacked at as well, even though he had parked a good block and a half away. Her phone rang continuously, and once the caller warned that a bomb had been placed in a parcel; the police were called but found no explosives. And her house was broken into at least once. One of JoAnn's friends was very concerned that one ground-level window facing north was totally unprotected by curtains or blinds. "You know he could sit out there and pop you off right through the window," she told JoAnn, who replied, "Oh, you don't think he would do anything like that." "I wouldn't put it past him," said the friend.

In October of 1980 Colin Thatcher met with his neighbour Garry Anderson. Four years later Anderson was to stun a courtroom with his testimony that at that encounter Thatcher asked him to kill JoAnn for a substantial fee.

The Andersons were a well-known clan around the Caron area. As often happens, one side of the family worked hard and thrived, and the other side languished in poverty. William Anderson, the great progenitor, had come to Saskatchewan from Collingwood, Ontario, in 1902. After running a livery stable and homesteading near Drinkwater for fifteen years, he and his wife, Christina, moved to a farm near Caron. The couple had nine children, including Garry's father, Bill.

Bill Anderson was very bright at school. "He could read a page of a book and then recite it word for word," remembers his brother, Sandy Anderson. But with so many siblings and a farm that barely yielded a living, there was no opportunity for a "scholar" to pursue his talents. So Bill became a farmer like everyone else and indulged his passion for words through conversation. "Bill never shut up," says Chuck Deagle, "and he talked fast. You could hear him coming 'cause when he was all alone, he was still talking and arguing about something." He was a strong CCFer and attending political rallies was among his favourite recreations. Despite this, he was to get along pretty well with his neighbour, Ross Thatcher, when Ross bought property in Caron.

In 1946 Bill married Katie Harder, a pretty young woman from a Mennonite family who farmed at McMahon, south of Swift Current, Saskatchewan. The couple would eventually have five children, two boys and three girls. While Sandy Anderson took over the family farm, Bill bought land a half mile north. It was a farm of poor, sandy soil best suited to a livestock operation. Katie and Bill were both industrious, and they managed to build a fairly prosperous dairy farm, but it was a tough life for the family, and the children as well as the adults had to work very hard just to make a go of it. When Bill died in 1966 at age fifty-four, the dairy operation collapsed and the family eventually disintegrated into painful poverty.

Interestingly, a teacher of Garry's who was also a long-time friend of the family could see a striking similarity in the way Colin Thatcher and Garry Anderson were brought up. "I could see where those two would be friends," she says. "Garry had a tough life. His dad bullied him and it was only natural that he should bully others. And his mother, because his dad was so hard on him, tried to make it easy on him by saying that anything Garry did was just fine. That's a poor combination, and it was very similar to Colin's background. Colin's dad never thought he did anything right. He never spared his feelings and he told him in front of everybody. The same with Garry."

Garry and the other Anderson kids started grade one in the rural, one-room Breadalbane school. When it closed in 1961, the students were bussed fourteen kilometres to the village of Mortlach. There Garry was considered a good student, fairly bright, and hard working. "I don't remember him causing any problems at all," says an English teacher. "He was never late, always had his homework done. And I felt sorry for him because he had no place to do his homework. He had to do his work sitting on a bed with a board over his knees. I would have said that was a fellow, when he got away from home, that would succeed and make something of himself."

"I had the impression that if he was better educated, he might have become a lawyer because he was always so argumentative," recalls Rosalie Marcil, who rode the same school bus with Garry for years. Rosalie's father, Bill Towriss, was a good friend of Ross Thatcher's, so when he became party leader, Towriss abandoned the CCF and voted Liberal. The Anderson clan remained CCF devotees and resentful of the Towriss "traitors." "We were considered lower than low," remembers Rosalie. "They were cruel, they would beat us up, hit us, tell lies about us. The whole family and some cousins, too. It was probably the worst time of my life. Garry was mouthy and he would be just so mean."

Garry grew into a strong, hulking, emotional teenager who lost his temper frequently and got in some bloody fights as a result. "He talked with his hands," says a math teacher. "Never could get him to accept the idea that you could catch a lot more flies with sugar than vinegar." A friend says, "He reminded me of a farm dog. He would often go along with being kicked, but every once in a while he would turn and snarl." Once he was expelled for threatening a teacher. The man was on hall duty when Anderson backed him up against the wall and suggested he step outside to settle an argument. What Garry didn't realize was that this fellow, who weighed 98 pounds soaking wet, was an expert in karate and would have torn him apart. The teacher, wisely, refused the invitation. Garry was summoned to the principal's office and reprimanded.

And yet some students felt a certain compassion for him. "I always liked Garry," recalls one former classmate. "He talked a good line, but he was entertaining." But, say his teachers, he was usually alone. "I don't think Garry ever had one close friend," recalls one. To make things worse, Garry's younger brother Dale was very popular with his schoolmates.

Shortly after he graduated from high school an incident occurred that badly scarred Anderson. He was charged with raping a young woman with whom he had gone to high school. He was eventually cleared of the charge. "It was just a put-up job," says Sandy Anderson. "But it was an awful thing for him."

After Garry graduated from Mortlach High School in 1965.

he attended Aldersgate Bible College in Moose Jaw, taking one religious course and several general arts courses. He earned average grades and caused no problems. Over the next two years he studied business administration at Saskatchewan Technical Institute. By this time he was twenty-one, six-foot-three, handsome, and decently educated. He should have enjoyed a successful career of some kind. But something went wrong. Over the years he drifted from one place and one job to another. He worked as a farm hand, a bouncer in a Moose Jaw bar, and a collection agent, but he was always spinning big dreams about his future. "Everyone around here knows Garry," says Chuck Deagle. "He's one of our famous products. When you see Garry coming, you say, 'I wonder what story he's got for us today.'" He'd brag about the fights he'd been in, the money he was going to make, the people he was going to get even with. "I just let his stories go in one ear and out the other," remembers a neighbour who sometimes hired Garry to work on her farm. "We just let him talk and talk and talk. My brother came in one day and said he had run into Garry in the coffee shop. 'Boy, I can't believe this guy. I've got his whole life story in half an hour.' Still we liked Garry and he was a good worker as long as you let him keep his own hours."

A big part of Garry's problem was his uncontrollable temper. In the mid-Seventies he married a young bank teller. "He was very happy with his new wife," remembers a friend. "He brought her out to our farm to show her off." The couple had a little girl whom Garry adored. But he beat his wife on more than one occasion and she left, taking the child to Prince Albert with her. His marriage was gone, and it didn't help that he was drinking far too much and even (despite being one of Colin Thatcher's squeaky-clean Caron constituents) indulging in marijuana and more exotic drugs such as opium. He was convicted on various occasions of impaired driving, refusing to take a breathalyzer test, and driving while prohibited from doing so. In 1977 he was found guilty of assault causing bodily harm after he punched someone during an argument. He was sent to prison.

Marilyn Riendeau, a mother of three who had been separated from her husband for thirteen years, was working in a Moose Jaw restaurant when she met Garry Anderson in June 1979. Her romantic involvement with him would last four months;

it would prove to be a summer of violence. "He always seemed to have a fear that someone was going to get him. Like you'd go into a restaurant and he would never sit with his back towards people. Stupid." That summer Garry had lost his licence and since he was bailing hay, Marilyn was driving him around. One evening he and some buddies started drinking and horsing around. This developed into a fight between Garry and a young chap. He demanded that Marilyn drive him back to his truck. "I knew what he was going for—he had a gun behind the seat—so I just whipped the car around and went back and told them to get out of there." But Garry returned and waved his gun at the kid. He was charged with pointing a firearm.

Not long afterwards Marilyn told Anderson that she didn't want to see him any more. At about 1:30 that morning, a drunken, raving Anderson kicked open the door to Marilyn's trailer. "It was a real bad pounding he gave me. I resigned myself to the fact that this was it—he was going to kill me." The next-door neighbour, coming home from work, saw the light on in Riendeau's trailer and dropped in. "He just said, 'Come on Marilyn, get outta here,' and Garry just cowered in the corner." Marilyn Riendeau was hospitalized for her injuries.

That fall Anderson was sentenced to seven months in the provincial correctional institute for the two incidents—pointing a firearm and assault causing bodily harm. In November of 1979 he joined Alcoholics Anonymous, and he successfully quit drinking. But his trips to prison had clearly established his local reputation as a tough, violent man who had been on the wrong side of the law.

In September of 1980 Garry was working in Lethbridge, Alberta, when his mother phoned to tell him that Colin Thatcher had been over to see her and had said that he wanted to meet with Garry. The two men had known each other for a couple of years. They were neighbours—some Thatcher land abutted onto Katie Anderson's farm. At one point the Andersons had rented Thatcher some pasture land and sold him some hay. Garry would sometimes ask Colin's permission to hunt on his property . "Garry always looked up to Colin," says a cousin. "He thought Thatcher was a big shot, someone who could make things happen, make life exciting."

On a visit to Caron in early October, Anderson arranged to

meet Thatcher at an abandoned farm about a half mile north
of his mother's place. (Not to be confused with the abandoned
Bergren property, site of the famous tape recording between
Thatcher and Anderson.) It was a strange place for a friendly
meeting, but Thatcher had a strange proposition to make. As
Anderson later reconstructed it in the witness box, if he
would kill JoAnn, Thatcher would pay him $50,000—$10,000
to start, $10,000 on completion, and $10,000 a year for three
years thereafter. Anderson told him that he wasn't interested.
"Do you know anyone who might be interested?" Colin asked
him. Not offhand, Garry replied, but he agreed to keep the
problem in mind.

Anderson returned to Lethbridge but Thatcher called him
there two or three times, insisting that they meet again. On
numerous trips home to visit his mother, Anderson did just
that. "On those occasions, he still asked me if I was still
interested in doing it, or would do it, and I said no and he
asked if I had thought of anyone or found anyone who might
be interested."

Thatcher became even more persistent after October 20, the
day that Mr. Justice Hughes's long-awaited decision on the
matrimonial property trial was released. JoAnn was allotted
$849,648.90, one of the largest matrimonial property awards
ever made in Saskatchewan. The judge ordered that Thatcher
would have just over four months, until February 1, 1981, to
raise the cash. If he was unable to do so, some properties
would have to be sold to raise the required amount.

To Colin Thatcher, the judgment was a real "shocker." He
was fond of bragging that the Thatchers didn't sell land, they
bought it. And he wasn't prepared to have half of his agricultural empire, founded by his illustrious father, auctioned off
to please some damned judge. Tony Merchant filed a notice
of appeal immediately.

In November Garry Anderson finally thought of someone
who might be interested in Thatcher's job offer. The candidate was a curly-headed, cherub-faced drug addict by the
name of Charlie Wilde. Charlie had a criminal record as long
as his needle-marked arm, mostly for drug-related offences—
as Crown attorney Serge Kujawa once said, Wilde had a habit
of being found in drugstores after closing time. Anderson had

met Charlie some eight months before while both of them were doing time in the Regina Correctional Institute. Garry had liked the affable Charlie and remembered him.

Garry went to see Charlie at his house on York Street in Regina, and then the two men went for a drive. They chatted for a while and then Garry asked him if he needed money "What do I have to do?" Charlie asked. Anderson replied he was required to murder somebody. "And," recalls Charlie, "I said, 'No, I'm not interested myself and I don't know anybody.'" The two men parted.

But a few days later Garry returned and outlined the details of the proposition. The hired "hit man" was to receive $15,000 down, $10,000 on completion, and $25,000 in a year's time. Charlie's ears perked up at the $15,000 down, and he told Anderson he might indeed know somebody who would be interested. The man he had in mind was another pillar of Regina's criminal establishment, a man with the Dickensian name of Cody Crutcher. According to Charlie Wilde, he and Cody talked about the deal. "He said, 'Sure, introduce me to this guy and I'll take his bread.' He had no intention of doing the hit but he wanted to take the money."

They met Garry Anderson in the easy warmth of the Fireside Lounge in Regina's Sheraton Hotel, a week before Christmas. Charlie introduced Cody to Anderson as Jack Goldie. After they talked for a while about terms, Cody told Garry he was indeed interested in doing the murder. Thus encouraged, Garry passed on the information that the intended "hit" was Colin Thatcher's wife, JoAnn. He also specified that Thatcher's young daughter was not to be harmed in any way. Then the two men went to the washroom, where Garry passed Cody an envelope containing $7,500. Charlie gave Garry a ride to the bus depot and Cody returned to his job at the Chicago Food Company restaurant. Later that evening Cody and Charlie gleefully split the $7,500.

Several days later Anderson arranged to meet Wilde on Rose Street in Regina. Anderson first dropped into the Thatcher residence and, as pre-arranged, picked up two envelopes in the foyer. He gave these to Wilde and told him one contained $7,000, which was $500 short of the agreed-upon amount Anderson explained that he was keeping that for himself presumably as an agent's fee, and then left.

Wilde opened the envelopes at Cody's house. One con

tained the money, as Anderson had promised. The other held keys to a 1978 Thunderbird and a picture of JoAnn that had been cut in half. Cody eventually burned the picture, and the car keys disappeared when Cody himself prudently took off for Winnipeg. (The police were never sure that JoAnn's car keys had actually been stolen, and she had sold the Thunderbird in 1981. But during the murder investigation, investigators tracked the car down in Saskatoon and seized the lock. There was only one set of keys in existence rather than the customary two.)

Anderson was to testify that during the negotiations, with himself in the role of middleman, Thatcher had insisted that the murder should take place during the Christmas holidays of 1980, while he was in Palm Springs. He was concerned for Stephanie's safety, and he wanted to take her south with him. JoAnn would not allow her to go, however—a piece of inconvenient behaviour on her part that threatened to ruin Thatcher's plans. On November 7, Tony Merchant brought a motion before Mr. Justice MacPherson asking that Colin be allowed access to Stephanie for three weeks at Christmas. MacPherson replied on December 2, "It is impossible at this stage of the process of the Thatcher litigation to ignore the facts that Regan has not been delivered to his mother's custody, that he was last seen at Mr. Thatcher's home and that Mr. Thatcher is refusing to answer questions concerning Regan's whereabouts. . . . I consider it unsafe to allow Mr. Thatcher to have any unsupervised access to Stephanie until there is a satisfactory explanation of Regan's absence."

By now MacPherson, and a number of other judges, were concerned that criminal charges had not been laid against Colin Thatcher. For one thing, the Moose Jaw police force now knew where Regan was and knew that Thatcher knew where he was. Sergeant Bill Mitchell had obtained a search warrant to check Thatcher's phone records; the frequently called numbers in Palm Springs revealed that the boy was living with his grandmother in Cathedral City, California. "If one of us had been sent down to Palm Springs, it would have taken us exactly half a day to locate the child," says a Moose Jaw policeman. In California, Canadian police could not simply grab the child and return him to his mother in Saskatchewan; that would have been beyond their jurisdiction and therefore illegal. They could, however, have easily gathered evidence to prove that Colin Thatcher was in blatant contempt of court. The police didn't do this because the Attorney General's department indicated that they would refuse to prosecute Thatcher. "I pressed and pressed the Attorney General's department to lay criminal contempt charges," says Gerry Gerrand. "It's just unbelievable that steps were not taken in some way to penalize whoever caused the secreting of this child, and there was no doubt at all who was behind it."

While they were having their daily coffee in the Regina courthouse library, the justices of the Court of Queen's Bench discussed the Thatcher matter frequently and at length during the fall of 1980. Sandy MacPherson was particularly incensed about it, but so were the others. Finally he said to Chief Justice F.W. Johnson, "Fred, you've got to write to Romanow and tell him to lay criminal charges." The other judges agreed, saying, "Yes, it's about time." Johnson wrote Roy Romanow, attorney general of Saskatchewan, a strong letter, saying among other things that Thatcher, a Member of the Legislative Assembly, was flouting the law of the land. Johnson felt that Thatcher believed he was above the law and that this blatant disrespect by a legislator was an arrow directed right at the heart of the court system. He wrote that it was up to Romanow to do something about it, and suggested that criminal contempt charges be laid.

A journalist once wrote of Roy Romanow, "He should have been a movie star, not only because of his fabulous good looks, but because of his care before the cameras, ability to ham it up, and secretiveness about his age." Seldom has a politician with such "flash and dash" emerged from the farm province of Saskatchewan, and seldom has a ranking member of the NDP been touted as a possible future leader of the federal Liberal party. "A Canadian Jack Kennedy," they called Roy Romanow, and the people of Saskatchewan concurred, electing him four times, first in 1967, until he lost in 1982.

The son of a Ukrainian immigrant, a Canadian National Railways section man, he was raised primarily in Saskatoon and received his law degree from the University of Saskatchewan in 1963. In 1970 he lost the NDP leadership to Allan Blakeney by only fifty-eight votes, and it has always been assumed that he will ascend the throne when Blakeney decides to step down. He served as the province's attorney general from 1971 to 1982. As his knowledge and skill grew, so did his responsibility; he took on many jobs—House leader, intergovernmental affairs, and communications. "There's so many titles on his office door that it just about fell off," one official was quoted as saying.

But it was not until Canada's great constitutional patriation debate in the early 1980s that Romanow was thrust dramatically on the national stage. He was a most effective co-chairman of the federal constitutional review committee, and as it travelled across Canada hearing various views on the matter, Romanow's comely face was seen often in the media. His co-chairman, federal Attorney General Jean Chrétien, nicknamed the Saskatchewan politician "Count Romanow," and there was even speculation that the Count was about to defect to the Liberals—a rumour he claimed was always just that. It did indicate, however, that Romanow was hardly a socialist ideologue; indeed he was considered part of the NDP's right wing. "He was always very cautious about using his power as the attorney general," says a former senior bureaucrat, "which is why he was so careful about Colin Thatcher."

The Attorney General's department thoroughly studied the matter of laying criminal contempt charges against Thatcher; a large brief was prepared. "It was decided that it was not criminal contempt, it was civil contempt," says Ken MacKay, director of public prosecutions in Saskatchewan. "And I agree with that decision because it started as a dispute between the parties, and one of the parties refused to follow a lawful court order. That was civil contempt." The judges of the Court of Queen's Bench disagreed with this interpretation of the law, as did many other legal authorities.

Chief Justice Johnson met with Dr. Richard Gosse, the deputy attorney general, and talked with Romanow himself about the Thatcher affair. According to Johnson, Romanow told him that his department believed that it would be difficult to get a conviction on criminal contempt against Thatcher, and also that he would be placed in a difficult position if he initiated criminal proceedings against a member of the Legislature of an opposing party. In other words, according to Johnson, now Lieutenant Governor, politics played a role in the decision not to charge Thatcher. (Roy

Romanow declined to be interviewed for this book, on this point or any others, on the grounds that the Thatcher case is still before the courts. He did write, however, that it was his practice to leave such decisions as that relating to Thatcher to the director of public prosecutions. "In that way, prosecutorial decisions would be free of any suggestion that they were influenced by political considerations," Romanow wrote.)

MacPherson, for one, was furious when nothing was done. He feels that if Thatcher had had a taste of prison for six months or so he might have had second thoughts about murder. His feelings about this remained so strong that they resulted in an embarrassing and dramatic encounter. A few days after JoAnn was killed, MacPherson was a guest speaker at a luncheon of the Saskatchewan branch of the Canadian Bar Association. While the guests were having a pre-lunch drink, the deputy attorney general, Richard Gosse, went over to MacPherson. "Well, Sandy, what do you think of that?" he asked, referring to the murder. MacPherson looked him straight in the eye and said, "Do you realize that if you had done what the judges asked you to, this guy would not believe he was above the law—and this woman would still be alive?"

Gosse looked aghast and said nothing.

"Anyone but Thatcher would have been sent to jail," MacPherson insists. "Clearly this was proof that there was a separate law for the privileged. And the judges didn't like it."

CHAPTER FIFTEEN
THE FIRST SHOT

JANUARY 3, 1981

The Thatchers' divorce was finalized on December 22, 1980, and two weeks later JoAnn and Tony Wilson were married at First United Church in Brampton by John Sullivan. Timothy Vernon, at the time the conductor of the Canadian Opera Company in Toronto, was best man, and Mary Lee Sullivan was matron of honour. Seven-year-old Stephanie was at the wedding as well. The wedding party celebrated with a champagne dinner at a posh Toronto restaurant. On their return to Regina, the Wilsons held a reception for their many friends in their Albert Street home. "They were both very happy, you could tell," says Darla Spicer. "When I came home that day, I just felt terrific. I really did. I said to my husband, 'Well, finally JoAnn's going to have a happy life.' I thought, 'Now Colin will leave her alone.'"

Her friends had already noticed a change in JoAnn, a metamorphosis that would grow more pronounced during the short time she was married. "It was a wonderful marriage," said Dorothy Yakiwchuk. "She grew at a fantastic rate as a person. She no longer felt inhibited."

"She and I didn't have the same tastes when we first met," says Wilson. "I like Italian Modern and she had very traditional tastes. But gradually over the period we knew each other she ended up liking Italian Modern as well. She had had little exposure to the real world, she had never left the North American continent. She had gone occasionally to Vancouver with Peggy Thatcher and I think she went to Ottawa a couple of times but those were the only places in Canada. . . . And I think even in the States the only places she ever went were Ames and Palm Springs. We started to travel quite a bit." JoAnn accompanied Tony on several business trips to Toronto, Washington, and, at Easter of 1982, to Japan. They stayed at a resort hotel on the island of Kyushu that was designed for Japanese guests. "The room we had was sort of divided in half," recalls Tony. "There was a regular western bed and a Japanese-type bed on the floor with bean pillows. We slept on the floor." Relishing the Japanese culture like this was typical of their entire trip and of the change in JoAnn's character now that her confining first marriage was behind her.

Since Tony was something of a gourmet cook, one of their great pleasures was entertaining each other and friends. "I guess she never had a chance to do anything other than what he [Thatcher] wanted to do, so we started having food that she had never heard about, let alone eaten, and we used to joke about that. And she was open to these things. She wasn't prepared to eat liver, but she would eat fish and seafood that were quite unusual." Another of Wilson's passions was the arts, particularly symphonic music and theatre. "JoAnn got an undertaking from me that I would teach her all about classical music, which she knew nothing about. We started to go to the symphony and the Globe Theatre." Wilson says JoAnn thrived on this new exposure. "It was like being reborn, almost."

"Tony had a real influence on her," says Shevawn Desrosiers, a young interior designer who eventually worked for JoAnn. "One day I was over at her house, helping her clean out cupboards, and we came across this big pack of pictures. They had been taken while JoAnn was still married to Colin. I thought, this is not JoAnn's style, the JoAnn that I know. Under Tony's influence her wardrobe did a complete change-around. Tony loves silks, wools, and classic lines, very tasteful tailoring and good workmanship. He was the kind of person who likes to shop with his wife and help her select clothes and colours and things like that. He enjoys that, he enjoys having that kind of influence." Still, Desrosiers insists that this was not another Svengali or Pygmalion relationship. "I'm sure JoAnn always had that style, that class. That's not something you learn overnight, or by virtue of a marriage to a man. Tony just helped her refine it."

"JoAnn must have felt a little like Cinderella," says an old friend. "The prince was Tony, of course, and Colin Thatcher had been the ugly stepmother in drag. Too bad she didn't have a chance to live happily ever after."

The ugly stepmother had not exactly been living a celibate life since JoAnn left. For Colin Thatcher, Palm Springs had proved to be a bonanza of beautiful young women, many of whom considered him sexy and wealthy enough to be attractive. He now possessed a little black book that had swollen impressively since the fall of 1979. Then in the early fall of 1980 he met a petite, clever blonde, with green-blue eyes; she was relentlessly talkative and Californian to her core, and she would be his lover over the next two years. Thereafter she would be a devastating witness against him at his murder trial.

Lynne Dally (by the time of Thatcher's trial she had married and changed her name to Mendell) was raised in suburban affluence in Glendale, a satellite of Los Angeles. At eighteen, Lynne says, she had just been accepted into a small, private college when her father, a lawyer, came home one day in 1968 and said that he had bought a hotel, the Sheraton Oasis, in Palm Springs. "I said, 'Oh, terrific. Who would build a town in the middle of the desert? You gotta be crazy.' It took me six months to even come down and see it. Then he tricked me. I drove over one perfect weekend in March. He put me in the best room in the hotel. I ordered room service, laid out in the sun, and hung out at the health food store. Then I started bringing my things over. Once he saw that I'd gotten about 50 percent of my clothes moved, he kicked me across the street to two tiny rooms in the older buildings and put me to work." Among other tasks, she worked as the reservations manager at the hotel.

Dally did attend college in Palm Springs, but it was an occasional thing and she never did receive a degree. "My education was 'not complete' on paper. And one of the things Colin never understood about me was that I was reading when I was three and a half and I had read all the Greek philosophers, Socrates, Aristotle, Plato, and all the existentialists and Bertrand Russell, etc., on my own before I graduated from high school."

Until she went to Palm Springs in 1968, Lynne claims she was very involved in the Vietnam peace movement. "I was a flaming liberal and my father—whom I love dearly, he's a wonderful man—and I used to scream at each other. I once accused him: I said, 'You'd vote for Mickey Mouse if he were running Republican. He said, 'You're probably right.'" But after living in Palm Springs for about a year, she gave up that "unrealistic flaming liberal nonsense." "I realized I was beating my head against a brick wall for, capital letters, PEACE. I was always a bad hippie, anyway, because I had such a passion for new jeans." Still, her brush with the radical Sixties was one of the items that intrigued Colin Thatcher about the lippy Lynne Dally.

Lynne assumed that she'd probably be married by the time she was twenty-six or so, but she found that life in Palm Springs wasn't exactly conducive to settling down. She began to take more and expected to do the work of four people, ten times better than anybody else. I could work a ten-hour day, but if I wanted to take an hour and a half for lunch I'd hear about it. I'm the easiest person I know of to get along with, but the employees wanted to have something to talk about. They said, 'She's got to be a spoiled, rich-bitch brat. She's only got the job because her father owns the hotel.' Not true. I'm not ugly and I'm not dumb, and if I gained forty pounds and got my nose broken I might get some credibility."

Still, Lynne lived rent-free for eight years. "I never saved a nickel but I dressed very, very well." (Her future husband once asked her why she had four pairs of lavender-coloured canvas shoes. Her reply was, "You're lucky I'm not into expensive jewellery.") Palm Springs was not a great town for a single woman. "There's a lot of retired people, a lot of young waiters and desk clerks, some gay decorators, but very few interesting single men. And the interesting single men were usually attorneys and just getting over their first divorce." Attractive, well-dressed Lynne, however, managed to go out most nights, usually with young professionals—lawyers were her specialty—from L.A. or Beverly Hills. What she liked was a superb meal at an expensive restaurant, and fast and stimulating verbal repartee. Words were a passion for her. "I became the Scrabble champion of Palm Springs. Unofficially, I can't play any more, 'cause no one will play with me."

When Lynne met Colin Thatcher in the fall of 1980, she was living in a friend's condominium—"two bedrooms, two baths, furnished in a great combination of modern antique and Oriental"—in a complex called the Sunrise Oasis. After working hard for ten years at the hotel, she had been given a year off with pay. She was thirty and just a little bored, so when the Sheraton Oasis was short-staffed, Lynne would help out. One day in early October, 1980, she was filling in for the dining-room hostess when she ran into her friend Bob Gustav, a Palm Springs businessman. Gustav asked her if she was dating anybody seriously and she replied no. "When's the last time you had a blind date?" he asked her. "Never!" "There's someone coming into town who is a business associate. He's single and I'd like you to come out with him and my wife and me." Naturally Lynne asked, "What's he like?" "He's a wheat farmer from Moose Jaw," replied Gustav. "Don't do me any favours," Lynne groaned. Gustav explained this was a very unusual wheat farmer, a very interesting, rich, and powerful wheat farmer. "Since you're one of the nicest guys in town, I'll do it for you," she promised.

"Bob has a wife who talks a mile a minute, and she and I basically ended up chatting the entire evening. Colin and I didn't hit it off. Not at all." For one thing, she didn't think he was particularly handsome. "He looked like a football player, which he was. Funny," she muses, "because I always like men who are thin."

"Colin took me home and I invited him for an after-dinner drink. He made a move and I passed on that and said good-night." Thatcher called the next day and took her to Wally's, one of the most expensive restaurants in Palm Springs. "I had a nice time. He took me home, and it was again good-night. Then about the third or fourth date, I began to think he was pretty interesting. . . . He was very nice to me, a perfect gentleman."

At Thatcher's trial for first-degree murder, defence lawyer Gerry Allbright asked her, "The money, the trips, what you conceive to be the worldly possessions, the power, this was all part of the man's charm?" "Yes," Lynne agreed. "I don't think that Colin Thatcher would have even had the charm that he had without that power and money." "You wouldn't have been interested in him then, I take it, if he didn't have the power or money?" Allbright asked. Again Lynne agreed: "Initially, probably not."

But Lynne now stresses that she was used to going out with men of wealth. "I mean, Colin only had one Mercedes and it was not a four-door, and his condo in Palm Springs was definitely not the top fashion model."

Despite these drawbacks their relationship developed quickly, and Colin invited Lynne to Saskatchewan to attend the opening of the Legislature on November 27, 1980. Lynne had long blonde hair at that point, a slightly fuller figure than she displayed at Colin's trial, and, of course, a gorgeous California tan. "When Lynne showed up on Colin's arm," says a Tory MLA, "people's eyes just popped out of their head. Some people thought she was a real tart, and others that she was the most glamorous thing alive. There were all sorts of rumours floating around that Colin had been dating movie stars, particularly one of Charlie's Angels. So we all just assumed she was some exotic doll he had met in Tinseltown."

Colin had told Lynne that she would probably hate Moose Jaw: "It's 500 miles north of the end of the world," was how he described it to her. "I loved Moose Jaw, I just loved it. It reminded me of a northern Palm Springs, at least the way it used to be when I first went there. A mellow, peaceful, you could leave your door unlocked, kind of town. A nice place to raise kids. I could see that I would spend the three winter months in Palm Springs and the rest of the time in Moose Jaw."

Colin had complained bitterly to her that his former wife hadn't taken any interest in the ranching operation and Lynne was determined not to make the same mistake. When he asked her if she would like to go and look at the cattle, she said "Sure!" "Here I am in this four-wheel-drive truck, no roads, I'm bouncing, my head is hitting the ceiling, I'm bouncing all over, I feel sick to my stomach, I get a headache, I just want to go home, and Colin screeches to a halt just at the edge of a precipice. 'I'm just going to see if any cows wandered there,' he said. I'm sure we are going to fall over the edge and die."

Two days later Colin took Lynne to Agribition, Regina's huge agricultural show. "Here's me in my two-hundred-dollar camel-coloured suede boots, walking into this world of cows. The first thing out of my mouth was, 'Colin, I don't think I can stand the smell in here for more than the next horse.' 'Ah, you'll get used to it,' he said."

Lynne had been dating a Palm Springs lawyer when she

met Thatcher. "He was a very funny, sophisticated, polished-edges gentleman. Colin was very jealous, although he had no reason to be, 'cause we weren't involved in any kind of heavy relationship." After she returned from Moose Jaw to Palm Springs, however, she went with the lawyer and four other people to Puerto Vallarta, a ritzy Mexican resort town, by chartered plane. They stayed at Gringo Gulch, right across from Elizabeth Taylor's mansion. "Oh, Colin couldn't get over me doing that," says Lynne. "It was a point of contention for a year." Indeed they had such a disagreement about it that Thatcher hauled off and slapped her. Lynne slapped him right back. They were still not speaking to each other when Colin and Greg came to Palm Springs at Christmas. It was to become a typical pattern in their tumultuous relationship. "I was always angry at him," says Lynne. "He'd turn from the charming person I liked into this Mr. Hyde. His face would go into that deep scowl and his voice would turn hostile. I couldn't ever pinpoint when those changes would come. I always knew when I drove out to his place that the chances were fifty-fifty that I'd go home angry.

"If I did leave mad, I'd walk in the door and the phone would be ringing. It would be Colin. 'Honey, baby, darling, I love you. Come back to me.' Sometimes I would be furious at him and I'd just let the phone ring. It would ring on and on until finally he quit. The next morning the phone would be ringing either just before he went on the golf course or just after he got off. I'd pick it up and he'd say, 'Honey...' 'Colin, didn't I tell you last night, I don't want to see you again, you're a total idiot, I don't need to be treated this way, I know the difference, I've been loved, I know what love is, don't tell me you love me, get out of my life, I never want to see you again, get out your black book,' on and on and on. Then he would say, 'Does this mean we're not going out for dinner tonight?' And that would make me crack up, because that was part of his endearing self. I'd start laughing and he'd start laughing and I'd say, 'Oh, come on over. But just for five minutes.' And we'd end up having a lot of fun and being together for the whole night."

By the time the Christmas holidays were over in January, 1981, and Regan had been taken to Disneyland as a treat, Lynne and Colin had made up and were lovers once again. Colin gave her his Legislative Assembly credit card number and told her to telephone any time she wanted. He would call her as often as three times a day. (In fiscal year 1977–78 taxpayers paid Thatcher's long-distance bills to the tune of $800; the following year it had risen to $1,600; by 1980–81 it had jumped to $5,934, the second-highest in the Legislative Assembly. Lynne certainly played her part in raising that proud total.)

One trait of Colin's that particularly upset Lynne was his obsessive hatred of his former wife. "He kept saying over and over what a rotten bitch she was, that she had walked out on him for no reason. 'She gave up seventeen years of a first-class free ride,' that was his favourite phrase. He hated her. He was very, very bitter. He spent interminable hours describing the custody suit and the divorce settlement—all the trial procedures he had been through. I finally said to him, 'Colin, how would you like it if I never stopped talking about my ex-boyfriends?'" On many occasions, he told Lynne that no matter what it cost he was going to find somebody to kill "that bitch JoAnn."

Garry Anderson later testified that when JoAnn was not murdered during the Christmas holidays of 1980, Thatcher was upset that he had paid out $15,000 with no results. As soon as he arrived home from Palm Springs, he contacted Garry Anderson. "So what happened?' he asked. Garry was apologetic: "The hit didn't go down. I'll try and find out why." He immediately drove to Charlie Wilde's house in Regina. "Goldie [Cody Crutcher] got tied up in Winnipeg," Wilde explained. Anderson passed on the news that Thatcher was going to Palm Springs in February, so there would be another opportunity to kill her then. Charlie said that he would tell Goldie.

Meanwhile JoAnn had not given up on Regan. Although she had not seen the child since the day he ran away in August, she assumed that Colin had hidden him somewhere in Palm Springs. She had thought about hiring private detectives and lawyers in California—she would have to obtain a court order there to gain custody of Regan, a time-consuming and costly procedure. And money was becoming a problem for her. Although she had been awarded a very large amount of the matrimonial property, Merchant had appealed immediately, so the judgment was stayed and the funds sat still frozen. She also wanted to pay Gerrand, to whom she owed thousands upon thousands of dollars by this time. To that end, Gerrand had appeared before Mr. Justice Roy N. Hall of the Court of Appeal, asking that at least some of the $819,648.90 owed her by Thatcher be paid. The judge turned the request down, saying that he didn't want to set a precedent.

It was only the second time JoAnn had lost in her court battles with Thatcher, yet it would prove a most unhappy and crucial judgment. It not only stopped JoAnn from trying to find Regan in California, but it also meant that in the coming months she felt under pressure to settle the matrimonial property question for a much lower amount than the court had awarded her, rather than wait a year or two for the appeal to be heard.

JoAnn did, however, proceed with the civil contempt of court charges against Thatcher. These pertained to the fact that he had refused on two occasions to answer questions on the whereabouts of Regan, even though both the Court of Queen's Bench and the Court of Appeal had ordered him to do so. On February 5, Mr. Justice Noble considered whether Thatcher should be committed for contempt. Gerrand said that it was a straightforward matter—Thatcher's refusal amounted to nothing more or less than disobeying a valid court order. Merchant presented a much more elaborate legal argument, the main point of which was that Thatcher should not have to answer questions that might incriminate him or others. After listening to both sides, the judge found Thatcher guilty. But because it was a civil and not a criminal matter, he gave him two weeks to purge his contempt by complying with the terms of the previous court orders.

Merchant immediately began spinning another legal web. He appealed Noble's decision. The case was heard by three appeal court judges in early March, and they quickly dismissed it. However, since the deadline by which Thatcher was to have purged his contempt had already passed, the court gave him until March 20 to do so. Thatcher and Merchant came head to head with Gerrand once again on March 18 in yet another examination in aid of execution. Thatcher did answer a few questions this time. He admitted that since Regan ran away from his mother eight months before, he had met with the child in Moose Jaw, Caron, Mortlach, Saskatoon, Los Angeles, Anaheim, Santa Ana, San Francisco, Las Vegas,

Lethbridge, Swift Current, Portland, Great Falls, Minot, and, of course, Palm Springs. But he refused to tell Gerrand where the child was living, or who was taking care of him. In fact, he refused to answer most of the questions the lawyer asked him. Once again Gerrand pursued him like a bloodhound, and Thatcher was ordered to appear before Mr. Justice Noble on April 28.

Incredibly, Thatcher decided that he was not going to come to this particular judicial engagement; equally incredibly, his lawyer Tony Merchant would not even condescend to argue the case. While Gerrand carried on with the proceedings, Merchant sat in the back of the courtroom like a sullen schoolboy. "In our view launching this motion does not revive the contempt matter previously before the court and would not in general be a proper way to bring allegations of contempt before any court," Merchant wrote in a five-page memorandum to the judge. Mr. Justice Noble was furious at these antics. "While he [Merchant] is not about to come here and present his argument in the usual form, he seems to think he can take it in the back door in written form. I find this tactic highly improper and coming from counsel of Mr. Merchant's experience, an affront to the court," he wrote. "I have read the transcript of the questions asked and the answers given on March 18 with great care. An analysis reveals the extent to which Mr. Thatcher, with the active assistance of his counsel, is prepared to go to prevent the mother of Regan Thatcher from gaining lawful custody. For example I counted sixty-one answers in which the words, 'I cannot recall' or 'I do not recall specifics' or 'I have no recollection' were used in reply.... In my view the whole examination was a contrived attempt to be as evasive as possible...."

The judge did not mince words when he wrote about appropriate penalties. "Mr. Thatcher has an advantage many citizens could not claim. So, when he commits a contempt of a court order, it holds the law and the court up to ridicule, because many members of the public expect people who have attained his stature in society to obey the law.... I wish to make it clear that were it not for Section 28 of the Legislative Assembly Act, I would have sent[enced] Mr. Thatcher to a period of incarceration for his contempt. However Section 28 of the Legislative Assembly Act reads: 'No member may, during the session of the Legislature, be liable to arrest, detention, or molestation for any debt or any cause of a civil nature.' Because of that I feel I am unable to impose the sanction of a jail sentence on Mr. Thatcher. I must therefore look to other means of imposing a penalty on him." Noble fined Thatcher $6,000.

"In all due respect to Mr. Justice Noble," says Merchant, "it was a wrong finding of contempt. If he [Colin] had been asked proper questions such as 'Where is Regan?' and Colin had said, 'I won't tell you,' then that would be contempt. But he had a right not to answer the questions asked because they wanted to find out who took the child to Palm Springs. Mr. Justice Noble looked beyond that and found Colin in contempt for hiding the kid rather than dealing with the specific questions." Merchant appealed Noble's judgment.

The punishment was about as painful as a mosquito bite. In most places in Canada, a contempt-of-court finding against an MLA would be a major news story. The Regina *Leader-Post* gave the story only eight small paragraphs on page three. The Moose Jaw *Times-Herald*, which usually ran huge black front-page headlines if Thatcher cut a ribbon on a new gasoline station, gave it four paragraphs at the very bottom of page one. The electronic media did give the story more play, but only for half a day, and then it disappeared. That conviction certainly did not affect Thatcher's political career; in the next election his constituents voted for him in record numbers. But if Thatcher had gone to jail, a virtual certainty if he had been charged with criminal contempt (when he would *not* have been protected by his MLA status), the whole Colin Thatcher story might have been a different one. And JoAnn just might still be alive.

Meanwhile Thatcher had been dealing with his legal problems in his own malicious way. JoAnn was not killed while he was in Palm Springs in February, and on his return in March (according to Garry Anderson's sworn testimony) he again contacted Anderson and demanded to know what had gone wrong this time. Anderson again phoned Charlie Wilde.

Wilde and Anderson met this time in the neighbourhood of Peacock High School in Moose Jaw. "What happened?" asked Anderson. "Why wasn't the job done?" Wilde made up an excuse: "I don't know where Goldie is. Last I heard he was in

Vancouver." Anderson told Wilde that Thatcher wanted to talk to him about his misappropriated $15,000 and Wilde agreed to meet him when Anderson had made arrangements with Colin.

The next evening Anderson met Charlie Wilde at a Moose Jaw restaurant, and the two men headed for the Bergren property, the abandoned farm where the notorious recording session between Anderson and Thatcher would eventually take place, many months later. When they got there it was between seven and eight, and not yet dark. A half-ton truck drove up and Colin Thatcher emerged, was introduced to Wilde, and began to ask him anxiously about Goldie (alias Cody Crutcher). Charlie testified later that he understood Thatcher's anxiety: "At that time I guess he [Thatcher] realized that the money was gone but he wanted to get the keys and the pictures back because, as he said, if anything happened to JoAnn it would tie him into it," said Charlie. He told Colin, "Well, if I see him, I'll ask him about the keys."

Recovering his confidence, Thatcher then asked him, "Would you be willing to kill JoAnn?" "Not really, I wouldn't," said Charlie.

"But then," Charlie was to recall for the benefit of the jury, "he offered me $50,000 or $60,000 to do it and I said, well, maybe. But I said, you know I've got no money for transportation or a gun or anything like that." Colin then told him that JoAnn, Stephanie, and Tony were going to Ames, Iowa, for Easter and he suggested that Ames would be a good place for JoAnn to be murdered. Colin added that if Charlie was willing to accept the job he would give him $3,000 to $3,500 to buy a gun in the States. "So I was moving from Regina anyway," says Wilde, "so [I got] greedy a bit, I guess."

One evening the following week Colin Thatcher, MLA for Thunder Creek, met Charlie Wilde in front of the Saskatchewan Legislative Buildings at 9 p.m. The two men got into Thatcher's yellow Corvette and drove around the beautifully landscaped area. As they cruised, Thatcher gave Charlie an envelope containing $4,500—$1,500 in American money and $3,000 in Canadian. He asked Wilde if he knew where to get a gun. In Calgary, Charlie replied. Thatcher then gave him the Ames, Iowa, address of Betty and Harlan Geiger, described their house—Charlie was to testify that Thatcher told him, "They live a couple of blocks up from the university"—and told

Wilde the exact dates during the Easter holidays, April 15, 16, and 17, 1981, when the Wilsons would be there.

On Easter weekend Charlie Wilde was arrested in a Brandon, Manitoba, drugstore. He had borrowed a friend's medical card to obtain a prescription for a drug he greatly desired. He was given a thirty-month penitentiary term for impersonation to obtain a property. At the time he was picked up, the police found two $100 Canadian bills and $1,400 in American money. The money was confiscated, but later returned to him. In all, that meant that Wilde made somewhere over $11,750 for what he termed "the Thatcher caper." Indeed, it had become a profitable encounter for everyone but Colin Thatcher; with Crutcher's and Anderson's take added in, Thatcher had handed out $18,750 for nothing.

When JoAnn was not murdered during the Easter weekend, Thatcher once again contacted the confrère in crime, Garry Anderson. This time, Anderson swore, Thatcher asked him to buy a gun. From Lloyd Collier, a friend in Moose Jaw, Anderson purchased a .303 Enfield, an army-type rifle considered quite powerful. When Colin paid him for it, Garry suggested that he practise with it—"You know, to see how it feels, the recoil and that on it." Thatcher agreed he would try it out on some pasture lands.

On two occasions after that, Anderson and Thatcher secretly surveyed the Wilson property at 20th and Albert Street in Regina. "He showed me the residence and explained to me how easy it would be to get her," said Anderson. "He also showed where a person could come in, and how a person could leave from the house. He also showed me an approximate location where a person could stand to shoot the rifle." Garry remained adamant, however, that he would not kill JoAnn.

Finally Colin asked him if he would get him a car. Anderson rented a new model, a brownish orange Mustang with a white vinyl roof, from Scott Motors in Moose Jaw. As Thatcher had requested, Anderson left the car two or three blocks west of Thatcher's home in Moose Jaw some time during the weekend of May 15, 1981. Anderson can't remember exactly, but he left the keys either under the floor mat or in the ashtray.

Blaine Mathieson later told police that Sandra Hammond

knew about the orange Mustang and the rifle in the back seat;
in fact she ordered Mathieson not to go near the garage
where Thatcher, having retrieved the car, had parked it. She
also told him not to come anywhere near the Thatcher
residence on Sunday, May 17. Questioned by the Crown
prosecutor during Thatcher's trial for murder, Sandra was to
deny ever seeing a Mustang around the Redland property
during that time.

Unaware of the plans being woven around them, Tony and
JoAnn Wilson were settling into a marriage routine that was
both close and happy. JoAnn enjoyed her work at Willson's
and was learning enough about office interiors that by October of 1981, she was able to open her own business, Radius 2
Interiors. "My first wife was domesticated," says Wilson, "a
true German hausfrau. Although she was very socially outgoing, she never worked. JoAnn was a professional woman, and
it was quite stimulating to have a wife who was at the same
level as you were. You had things to talk about outside the
home. It was a complete change." JoAnn also brought some
order to Tony's sometimes disordered life. Marja Lahtinen, a
nineteen-year-old au pair who came to Regina from Finland
in the fall of 1981, says JoAnn was difficult to work for
because she wanted the house to be kept so perfectly. "She
was incredible herself," says Marja. "She got a million things
done during the day, she was so well organized. And she was
perfect in that she just didn't do things halfway, but finished
them up, too. She expected other people to do the same
thing. She could get really upset if there were fingerprints on
the salt and pepper shakers." And yet Marja and JoAnn
became good friends. For one thing, JoAnn was glad to have
company when Tony was away on business. "She was a little
like a big sister to me," says Marja.

By court order Colin Thatcher was allowed to visit Stephanie
in the Wilson home during the weekend. JoAnn, however,
usually permitted him to take the little girl out for the
afternoon. "He would come in occasionally and we would
argue about things," recalls Tony Wilson. "He would com-
plain about visiting rights and things like that. They were not
intellectual discussions or anything like that. They were
housekeeping things."

But by this stage, JoAnn and Tony felt that the situation

with Regan, who was still in California, was simply ridiculous, and they were upset that the matrimonial property matter was still in the courts. So they decided to bring a little pressure to bear.

MAY 9, 1981

Colin arrived as usual to take Stephanie out. This time, however, JoAnn and Tony insisted that he sit down and talk about a possible settlement before he was allowed to have the little girl. It was an uncomfortable confrontation—Colin felt that he was being blackmailed. According to the Wilsons, he spent most of the time railing against the MacPherson custody decision and the Hughes matrimonial property decision. (Colin, on the other hand, was later to claim that in the course of the conversation JoAnn agreed to give up custody of Regan if the matrimonial property matter was settled. Tony Wilson flatly denies that JoAnn was willing to give up Regan at this point.) The meeting ended in acrimony and Thatcher left, very angry.

MAY 17, 1981

Early spring brought a lovely, warm, but windy Sunday. The Wilsons had done some renovations to their house, remodelling their kitchen and back deck, and now they had begun working on their garden. JoAnn was painting a new fence when the telephone rang. It was her old friend Darla Spicer, who along with her husband and mother was in Regina attending a dog show. She wanted to know what the Wilsons were doing. "We're painting the fence," JoAnn said. "Come on over." "Oh, you don't need company," Darla replied. "No, no, we'd love to see you," JoAnn enthused, insisting they visit.

"We got there," says Darla Spicer, "and she was just covered in paint." "Who's getting the paint job, the fence or you?" Darla joked. Then JoAnn invited the Spicers for dinner but they politely refused, settling for a cup of coffee instead. They had so much to talk about, however, that the Spicers didn't leave until well into the evening.

It was late, therefore, when the Wilsons finished eating.

JoAnn got Stephanie into bed while Tony was upstairs taking a shower to remove the paint, she cleaned up. She had loaded the dishwasher and was scrubbing the pots, her back to the patio door. Suddenly there was a loud *crack*. Tony heard JoAnn scream and he came racing down the stairs. He found her sitting propped up against the wall in the hall, blood pouring from her shoulder. "The dishwasher exploded," she cried. It was as likely an explanation as any but Wilson could smell cordite, and when he examined the patio door, which had disintegrated like a car windshield in a bad accident, he realized what had happened. He phoned the police and yelled, "He's shot her!" Tony was certain that the assailant was either Colin Thatcher or a hit man he had hired.

When the ambulance attendants arrived at about 10:15 p.m. they found JoAnn sobbing with pain while Tony cradled her in his arms. They rushed her to Regina General Hospital. Although she had lost blood and was in great pain, her life was not in danger. But it had been a very close call. Only months before Tony had consulted Gerry Weckman about installing a new patio door. "Why don't you get a triple-glazed door with a wooden frame?" Gerry suggested. "It'll be a real energy saver." Wilson had taken his advice, and now that extra layer of glass had saved JoAnn's life. Not only was the bullet deflected by the glass—it was only a couple of inches away from striking her in the neck and killing her—but it shattered. Pieces of bullet are still lodged in the kitchen cupboards and walls of the house. One fragment grazed JoAnn's lip, scarring it sufficiently that thereafter she had to apply her lipstick carefully so that her mouth would not look lopsided.

The bullet had broken bones and ripped muscles in her right shoulder and the doctors were not sure what use she would have of her arm. "She had two choices," says Tony Wilson. "She could leave her arm down in a comfortable way, but then the muscles would heal in such a fashion that she wouldn't be able to lift it above a certain point. Or she could wear a steel brace, which held the arm up perpendicular to the shoulder, until it healed. But she was told she could never take it off, not even when she was sleeping. The doctor said, 'I would advise you to do this. But if it was me I'd have it down here, and to hell with not being able to use it at a later date.' We discussed it and I said, 'I think you should try the brace, because you're still a young person and you want to try all sorts of interesting things.' She agreed but it was a terribly onerous burden to have to go around like that. I'd take her out of it and wash her and put some powder underneath and then strap her in. It was really a trial." This ordeal lasted for three months.

While JoAnn was in the hospital Tony hired security guards to protect her, and they carefully screened her many visitors. "When I went to visit her in the hospital, I expected to see somebody who was horrified and shaken," remembers Betty Gooding. "There she was as composed as ever, with her arm up in this awful thing. She even got out of bed and sat on a chair. She just talked as normal as if she had fallen and bumped her knee. I said, 'JoAnn, aren't you just terrified for your life?' She said, 'The Lord's looking after me. Here I am alive. Maybe I'm not in the greatest shape I've ever been in but with physiotherapy, I understand I'll get the use of my arm back.'"

When Darla Spicer came to visit her, she too found her in amazingly good spirits, although Darla thought she looked terrible. JoAnn joked, "I came in covered with paint and the nurses didn't know what to think of me." "We talked about who would have done it," recalls Darla, "and she was quite sure it was Colin."

Another visitor was her lawyer Gerry Gerrand. But this was a different man from the tough, composed courtroom professional. As he looked at her, he became tearful and upset and mournfully said, "Things have come to a pretty pass, JoAnn. Here you are with your arm up in the air, and you came close to death. We won every application at court, with a couple of small insignificant exceptions. You don't have a five-cent piece from Mr. Justice Hughes's judgment. And your child Regan is nowhere to be seen. You know," he concluded miserably, "maybe you should get another lawyer. I'm not helping you much." JoAnn's reply was, "Gerry, you can't get out of it that easily."

While he was on trial for murder, Colin Thatcher swore that he, too, visited JoAnn at the hospital. It was an attempt to illustrate that their relationship was quite congenial at that point. "We were in the room alone and she showed me her wounds. She—it was far enough along that she no longer had a dressing on her wound, and she was showing it to me and the extent of it." Tony Wilson and her friends claim this is an outright lie. Wilson says that Thatcher phoned and asked if he could see her. Tony said no, but Thatcher showed up at JoAnn's hospital room anyway, where he was refused entry by the security guard.

The day after JoAnn was shot, Garry Anderson went to a prearranged place in Moose Jaw to pick up the rented Mustang. He noticed that the licence plates were smeared with mud. Anderson cleaned the car thoroughly inside and out and returned it to Scott Motors.

One week after JoAnn was shot, on May 26, Colin and Tony met at the Wilsons' residence. According to Tony Wilson the two men sat in the elegant grey-and-white living room sipping very expensive Scotch and conducting an extraordinary conversation. Thatcher politely asked Tony about JoAnn. Wilson coolly replied, "Colin, I'm satisfied that you somehow arranged the shooting of JoAnn." Thatcher looked blankly at Wilson. No emotion showed, but he did not deny the accusation. "It's easy enough to hire somebody to do such a job, Vietnam veterans, and that sort of person," Thatcher remarked. "Yeah, I guess I could do the same thing myself," Wilson agreed.

Both men remained calm and cool throughout this surrealistic conversation, although in Tony Wilson's words: "It got to the point where we were sort of threatening each other to have a little war in the streets of Regina." The discussion then turned to the property settlement. Wilson says that Thatcher proposed to pay JoAnn $1,000,000 over a period of twenty years, without interest. Wilson responded that the Court of Appeal would likely award JoAnn at least $600,000, to be paid almost immediately. "I think this is a more reasonable area to start our negotiations," said Wilson. "I'm not going to be bled dry!" exclaimed Thatcher, and headed towards the door. His parting shot was ominous: "If that is your position, you and JoAnn had better take steps to protect yourself."

Thatcher left behind a paperback called *The Bourne Identity*, by Robert Ludlum. The book is a violent thriller full of intricate plotting, in which one of the characters is shot through the neck with a rifle. Wilson was never sure whether Thatcher had left the book by accident or by design.

Thatcher's version of these events is quite different. In

affidavits, he maintained that he did not visit Wilson on May 26, but talked to him twice by telephone. He claimed that Wilson agreed that he could have custody of Regan if Wilson could adopt Stephanie. "It was an amicable conversation," said Thatcher. "My conversations with him usually are, but I couldn't agree to that and told him that."

When JoAnn had recovered enough to leave the hospital, she, Stephanie, and Tony went to British Columbia. "We left so the police could concentrate on finding out who shot her and not have to concentrate on protecting her," says Tony Wilson. They wanted nobody to know where they had gone, and so they told their friends that they had borrowed a yacht and would be sailing along the B.C. coast. In fact they went to White Rock, a community south of Vancouver where the president of Ipsco owned a summer home. When JoAnn returned to Regina, the first thing that Thatcher said to her was, "How'd you like White Rock?"

There were witnesses who had seen JoAnn's assailant. By a coincidence not permissible in fiction, Gerry Gerrand's daughter Pamela and her boyfriend, Terry Stewart, were attending a high-school graduation party that evening in the backyard of a house directly across the street from the Wilson residence. All evening the young people danced to rock-and-roll blaring over a loudspeaker. But a friend of Pamela's had forgotten her purse in Terry's car and Pam and Terry volunteered to walk back and get it. They were nearing the car when they heard the sharp crack of a rifle. A man came running through a yard, jumped into the car ahead of theirs, threw a rifle in the back seat, and took off. Terry yelled, "Pam, we'd better see if we can get a licence number!" They tried, but the plate was covered with mud—no letters or numbers were visible.

The two young people described the suspect as being in his twenties, about five-foot-eleven, medium build with dark hair and a bushy beard. They told the police that although they couldn't name the exact make of car the man jumped into, it was a new model, brownish orange in colour.

When Pam reached home two hours later, she woke her astonished father to tell him that his client had been shot and that his daughter was a chief witness. "I almost had a heart attack," says Gerrand. (Later there was a speculation that since the suspect she had described looked nothing like

Colin, Pam might be called as witness for the defence in Thatcher's murder trial. This would have provided an ironic twist, since her father was acting as an informal consultant to the Crown on matters pertaining to the divorce and custody questions. She was not asked to testify.)

The day after the shooting, Colin Thatcher and Gregory went to the Moose Jaw police station and signed separate statements. Greg said that he had spent the evening at a friend's house and arrived home at 10:30 p.m. Thatcher told the police that he and Regan—who, it turned out, was back from California—had been opening the swimming pool during the entire evening. It was about 11 p.m., Thatcher remembered, when Tony Merchant called to inform him that JoAnn had been shot. The police had already been to his house in Regina, Merchant said, and they would be likely to pick Colin up for questioning. "I'll leave immediately," Merchant said. Thatcher claimed that Merchant arrived at the Moose Jaw house about 11:45.

Merchant would also later relate how police officers arrived at his Regina house, told him that "Mrs. Wilson had been shot ten or twelve minutes earlier," and asked him where Thatcher was. He said he immediately called Colin. (During Thatcher's trial, it was revealed that JoAnn had been shot at 10:10 p.m., and Merchant's telephone records indicated that the call to Moose Jaw was made some time in the eleventh hour, that is between 11 and 12 p.m. Merchant's assumption that he telephoned Thatcher ten or fifteen minutes after the shooting, therefore, was not accurate.) Merchant said he drove very fast and arrived at Thatcher's home some thirty-five minutes later, at approximately 11 p.m. He had expected the police to be there already and was amazed to find they hadn't shown up. He claimed he stayed about an hour and left just after midnight.

The Moose Jaw police had a very different account of the comings and goings at the Thatcher house. They had been contacted by their colleagues in Regina shortly after the shooting took place. An officer went to the Redland home, but he did not feel that he had enough information from the Regina police to knock at the door, so he did what is termed in police parlance "a peek and sneak," looking in windows, the backyard, and the garage. As far as he could tell, nobody was home. He then hid in the rose bushes. From that vantage point, he saw Merchant arrive at 12:45 a.m. Sergeant Bernie Jeannotte, who was the investigator on the case, said that Merchant phoned him at 1:30 a.m. from Thatcher's residence. This was directly contrary to Merchant's account. He claimed that he arrived at the Redland Avenue house at about 11 p.m. and left just after midnight. He said he did not remember calling the Regina police that evening.

After the shooting the Moose Jaw police immediately set up roadblocks on Highway 1 and questioned people travelling from Regina. One of the police officers suggested to his dispatcher that Colin Thatcher was a suspect. A medical doctor in Regina, a short-wave radio ham, heard the remark and reported it to Tony Merchant. Merchant, on behalf of Thatcher, then threatened to sue the Moose Jaw police chief and the officer who had made the remark. He wrote a remarkable letter, pointing out both his and his client's distinguished positions in the community and demanding that the police officer be fired. The police chief ignored his request.

On the night of the wounding, Colin telephoned Lynne Dally at her condominium in Palm Springs. "Merchant's just called and said JoAnn has been shot. I don't know if she's dead or alive. Talk to you." A few days later, he arrived in Palm Springs and told her that he hadn't wanted to say anything on the telephone. "He had quite a fear of having his home and phones both in Canada and Palm Springs tapped and/or bugged," Lynne later testified. "He always told me his phone had been tapped . . . because of the divorce trial, the custody suits—they were trying to find Regan." He felt his Palm Springs home might also be bugged, so he and Lynne walked over to the Graham condominium (Thatcher still had a key from happier times). There, safe from prying ears, "he took forty-five minutes to tell me this hilarious story about how he practically didn't make it home because of the road-blocks," remembers Lynne. "He said he kind of panicked and drove out into the country a long way, circumventing the roadblocks, and drove back into Moose Jaw. He parked the car several blocks from his house and he knew he had lost a lot of time and the only thing that really saved him, quote unquote, 'was that the police had not come directly, physically, to his house.' He laughed his head off. He said, 'Jesus, I practise all this time with this gun and I didn't realize how thick the glass was. Boy, did I screw up.'"

Colin Thatcher would not have been laughing quite so loud had his return trip been a little different. Garry Anderson testified that Thatcher told him that if anyone had stopped him on his way back to Moose Jaw after the shooting, he would have killed that person and then committed suicide.

But now here he was, safe and sound in Palm Springs, hilariously telling Lynne all the details, including the fact that he had donned a disguise that night—a wig of red hair, black scraggly beard, and overalls. But that her lover had just tried to murder another woman in cold blood did not really "sink in" with Lynne; she continued her relationship with Colin Thatcher. "It's a little difficult to believe sometimes that things like this actually happen," she said while testifying at Thatcher's preliminary inquiry. "There's still an air of unreality. I didn't know JoAnn. I'd never met her. I had heard . . . only Colin's side of their relationship, and when she was shot, it was a strange feeling, but she wasn't killed. And it just didn't really sink in." She did feel some qualms of pity, however, when on a visit to Moose Jaw that summer, she saw a haggard JoAnn, her arm still in the uncomfortable brace, telling of her misfortune on television.

When the Wilsons returned from White Rock to find that the police could report little progress, they decided to give up custody of Regan. "We had a sort of tribal conference with Gerry Gerrand," says Wilson, "to decide what should be done to defuse the situation, because I had had this meeting with Colin, which was scary. We decided we had to do something to calm him down." "JoAnn thought that the custody issue was the obstacle which, if removed, would end the reign of terror," says Betty Gooding. "She was also terrified that she would be shot again and this time murdered." With great sadness the Wilsons also realized that Regan, having been so long under his father's sway, might well be incorrigible by now.

Negotiations started in late June at a time when Lynne Dally was visiting Moose Jaw. "He [Thatcher] visited their house several times . . . and he came back saying, 'Well, I'm in a position of greater strength now because they know I'm not playing around. They're scared.'" The campaign of uncivil disobedience and brutal terror had worked; with great reluctance and a heavy heart, JoAnn signed the consent form granting Thatcher legal custody of Regan and a judge formally approved it on July 8, 1981.

The next day the Moose Jaw *Times-Herald* published a front-page story headed: "THATCHER AWARDED CUSTODY OF REGAN AFTER LONG BATTLE." It was a deplorable piece of journalism.

> Thunder Creek MLA Colin Thatcher has been awarded permanent custody of his 12-year-old son, after a one-year battle to overcome a court decision originally giving custody to Thatcher's ex-wife, JoAnn Wilson. Justice R.H. McClelland made an order awarding Thatcher custody of his son Regan at an appeal hearing held Wednesday in Regina.... "Naturally I'm delighted about the decision," Thatcher said this morning. "It's been a very long uphill battle."

JoAnn was furious when she read the story. Any informed journalist must have known that Thatcher had been awarded custody of Regan only after an appalling series of events that had seen Thatcher convicted of contempt of court, and his ex-wife's shoulder smashed by a sniper's bullet. She clearly had reluctantly agreed to give up Regan because of fear of being shot again and perhaps murdered. To that point, partly on Gerrand's advice and partly because of her own natural reserve, JoAnn had never discussed her matrimonial problems with the media. But Thatcher's gloating, irresponsible remarks goaded her into calling a press conference.

MONDAY, JULY 13, 1981

The press conference was held in the Library Room of the old Hotel Saskatchewan on Victoria Street in Regina, one of those grandiose palaces built by the Canadian Pacific Railway to emphasize its presence on the prairies. The media, with all its apparatus and attendant bustle, turned out in full force. JoAnn looked strained from the pain she still suffered, her hair was limp, and the wound on her lip had not wholly healed. But her encounter with violence was most sharply demonstrated by the draconian-looking steel brace that still held her arm aloft. She began in a tense but firm voice, "Late last week, the news media made reference to litigious matters concerning myself, my former husband Colin Thatcher, and my son Regan. These media stories and utterances were misleading and inaccurate and I therefore must make a public statement to set out certain basic facts. . . .

"I decided that I would no longer pursue my claim to custody of Regan in the best interests of all persons, and having regard to the undercover existence and unhealthy influences that Regan has been subjected to during the past eighteen months. The fact that I have personally been terrorized during the past eight months was an ingredient of that decision. . . ."

Close to tears, she continued, "On Sunday, May 17, I was the victim of an attempted murder when I was shot by a bullet fired from a high-powered rifle. Needless to say, I am afraid for the well-being of myself and my family. Since that time, I have been unable to look after myself or attempt to give Regan the care and attention he needs and requires.

"Shortly following the shooting, I learned that Regan had been returned from the United States to Moose Jaw.

"I dearly love all of my children. I have fought for Regan for close to twenty-four months. No custody litigation in this province has been more prolonged or extensive. Regan can no longer be subjected to the manipulations that his father has orchestrated. My daughter Stephanie needs a healthy mother able to care for her. For these reasons, I have given up my fight for Regan and he will apparently be living with his father.

"Mr. Thatcher has lost all of his court battles regarding Regan because of damning evidence that was led against him. He now has custody of Regan solely by reason of my decision prompted for the reasons outlined. Mr. Justice MacPherson concluded ten months ago that Mr. Thatcher was trying to win by cheating. As a result of the events since that judgment, I must concede that Mr. Thatcher has succeeded. . . .

"I am puzzled by the apparent reluctance of the media to reproduce the actual court judgment and court proceedings as opposed to publishing the interpretive utterances of Mr.

Thatcher and his lawyer, Mr. E.F.A. Merchant. Therefore, I believe that I must set the record straight."

Under questioning, JoAnn said that she reported to police on numerous occasions during a period of several weeks in 1980 that her car tires were slashed, sugar was put in her car's gas tank, and she had received telephone calls "with no one on the other end." For JoAnn, facing the media was a demeaning, difficult task. The journalists sensed the terrible pathos of her ordeal, and that day and the next the event received wide coverage across the country.

Thatcher's response to JoAnn's press conference was to allow Regan to be interviewed on a Moose Jaw open line radio show. The twelve-year-old boy pontificated about the lack of children's rights in custody battles.

JoAnn had not been the only one offended by Thatcher's gloating in the press. The news story of July 9, reporting that he had been awarded custody of Regan, had included two explosive paragraphs: "He [Thatcher] said the fight to regain custody of Regan was an indictment of our entire system and said political differences played a part in the battle.

" 'I think Regan paid the price of some animosity on the part of some members of the judiciary against his grandfather (former Saskatchewan Premier Ross Thatcher) and myself,' Thatcher said."

A lawyer heard about the story at 10 a.m. and promptly telephoned Justice MacPherson. To say that MacPherson reacted angrily to this attack on his integrity would be a considerable understatement. "I could see him picking himself off the ceiling," recalls the lawyer. " 'I'll sue the bugger, I'm going to do this, I'm going to do that. I'm going to the Attorney General's department.' I said, 'Hold it, Sandy, just cool it. Finish your day in court and then see John Moss [a highly respected senior solicitor in Regina].' "

MacPherson was so upset at the statement that he adjourned the very complex trial he was presiding over at the lunch break. "I couldn't go on that afternoon, I was so hurt. Here at the end of my career having something like this said about me. Although my name hadn't been mentioned, there was no doubt that he was pointing the finger at me. I called up Richard Gosse [deputy attorney general] and I said, 'Drop everything, I am coming right over.' He said, 'Sandy, there will be proceedings undertaken within two weeks for contempt.'"

MacPherson then asked the advice of John Moss and some colleagues on the bench. They all said, "Don't sue him, Sandy, don't sue." So MacPherson decided to leave the matter up to the Attorney General's department. A few weeks later he ran into Gosse. "He said, 'Yeah, the charge is going to be laid within a few days.' Nothing was done and Thatcher got away with it again. This was appalling and I was deeply hurt. I felt that I had been seriously let down by the Attorney General's department by not punishing him for hiding the boy, by not punishing him for what he said about me."

Interestingly, the Attorney General's department hired a respected Saskatoon attorney, Tom Gauley, to investigate the situation. Even more interestingly, Gauley concluded that Thatcher had indeed committed criminal contempt. "But by that time, a lot of time had passed and it was decided not to press charges," says Ken MacKay, director of public prosecutions. Nobody seems to know why such a lengthy period had been allowed to elapse, or why in the face of such outrage from the bench it was decided not to press charges. Once again, the law had lost a chance to show Colin Thatcher that the same rules applied to him as to everyone else.

At the same time, the Attorney General's department was involved in another matter concerning Thatcher. Tony Merchant had immediately appealed his client's April, 1981, conviction for civil contempt of court. After Thatcher gained custody of Regan, Merchant began bargaining with the Attorney General's department to lower the $6,000 fine. Officials seriously considered acceding to Merchant's request, but ran the idea by Gerrand first. "How could you even think of such a thing?" he stormed. In the end the outraged Gerrand convinced them not to give in to Merchant and eventually the appeal was dropped, and the $6,000 fine was duly paid.

The custody of Regan had just been settled when the Thatcher wars flared up again. This time it was over Stephanie.

Although her arm was still in an "airplane" brace, JoAnn returned to work at Willson's during the latter part of July, after the press conference. "She was only coming in half-days because she was exhausted," recalls her colleague Shevawn

Desrosiers. "She of course had to write with her left hand and she was having a bitch of a time. One day she called me and said, 'Shevawn, would you mind coming over to my house and helping me with these accounts, because I am so tired.'" Desrosiers was leaning over her, helping her, when the telephone rang. It was Thatcher. JoAnn took notes as carefully as she could with her left hand. The message, as JoAnn wrote it down, was chilling. "If you think you had fun with Greg and Regan, just wait till I get to Stephanie." Shevawn remembers: "JoAnn took it to mean that if he didn't get Stephanie, he would do the same thing again."

"JoAnn became determined that no matter what happened, she would fight for the rest of her life to keep Stephanie," says Gerry Gerrand. She had already noticed the first telltale signs of an obvious campaign by Thatcher to woo the little seven-year-old. When he visited her, he would describe the toys, the ponies, the trips that he would be happy to provide for her. During his Saturday-afternoon outings with her, he would give her five dollars and let her loose in a shopping plaza. One day JoAnn discovered the child surreptitiously phoning her father. "I told Stephanie she could telephone her father any time at my expense but that she should tell me she wanted to do this first," she said. Once, as he was leaving, Thatcher flung a bitter comment at JoAnn that made his plans clear. "I still expect to pick Stephanie out of the gutter and have custody of her."

Over the summer of 1981, Thatcher asked the court to extend his visiting rights with his daughter. To that point, he had been allowed to see the little girl only on Saturday afternoons in the Wilson home. "It is impossible to have any sort of an organized communication with my daughter," he said. "Part of that is because of the influences in that house. When I go to see her, I don't know whether I'm going to be confined to the interior of the house or whether I'm going to be allowed to take her out, or whether I'm going to be confined there for an hour and then told I can take her out halfway through. In some ways two hours is too long and in other ways it's too short. My daughter is seven and it is difficult to communicate indefinitely with a seven-year-old and keep her interested time after time for two hours." Thatcher said he wanted to take her to Moose Jaw on the weekends so that she could "communicate with her brothers."

JoAnn was determined to fight this, and to that end Gerrand required that Thatcher once more undergo an examination in aid of execution. "We wanted to show that he should not be trusted with extended access because he had breached the law in regard to his rights to Regan. We wanted to see nothing happening that would result in Stephanie's disappearing," recalls Gerrand. This time Thatcher did answer most of the questions, which revealed, of course, that he had secreted Regan and disobeyed a myriad of court orders. The Attorney General's department again ignored his outright flouting of the law. Once again the excuse was that it was too late to do anything about it. The court, however, did refuse to grant more liberal access to Stephanie.

Meanwhile, Thatcher was also pressing for a property settlement. "We thought, what can we do to defuse the situation, because [we felt] it was getting to the point where he's going to shoot her again," says Tony Wilson. "The police hadn't done anything so we had to do it ourselves." So during the late summer of 1981, Wilson worked out a property agreement he thought would be acceptable to Thatcher. The total amount was $575,000, considerably less than the $819,000 the court had awarded. Of that, $200,000 was to be paid on signing, and the balance of $375,000 was to be paid in five equal instalments of $75,000 due on September 1 of 1982, 1983, 1984, 1985, and 1986. No interest would be charged on the unpaid balance, as long as the payments were not in arrears. This provided the bare bones of a settlement but since Gerrand and Merchant were now so antagonistic, they were not able to negotiate further with any civility. It was thought wise to hire a mediator to thrash out the final draft. The man chosen by both sides was William Elliott, QC, a highly respected lawyer in Regina.

From December to March, 1982, Elliott carried proposals back and forth between the parties, until finally an agreement was worked out that was acceptable to both sides. The total amount of the settlement was $500,000. Of that, $150,000 would be paid February 1, 1982, followed by four yearly instalments of $87,500, due each year on February 1, and a final payment of $99,250 on February 1, 1987, which was the interest outstanding at 10 percent per annum. Thatcher was to abandon the appeal and JoAnn was to hand over title to the

Redland house. (Thatcher, it should be noted, had been living in it since JoAnn had moved out.)

There were, however, two clauses that would prove of vital importance. One specified that if Thatcher fell in arrears with his payment at any time, JoAnn would have the option of demanding that the entire amount owing her be paid immediately. As well, the following clause was included: "In the event of the death of [JoAnn] Wilson prior to payment in full of the principal sum and interest, Thatcher, at his election is entitled to a one-year moratorium on payment with interest to continue as set out herein."

"I wanted to have a clause that said if JoAnn died then it would all become payable immediately," says Wilson. He believes that if this version of the clause had been accepted she would still be alive today. But Thatcher was adamant that the moratorium clause remain. "We discussed it, and in the end we decided that we'd better let it in and get it settled," says Tony Wilson. "We thought a one-year moratorium surely wasn't going to make him shoot her."

Bill Elliott, the mediator, was a senior partner in the law firm of MacPherson, Leslie & Tyerman (Sandy MacPherson's father's old law firm). Another senior partner was Ron Barclay. He became involved again immediately after JoAnn was shot, when Dick Collver phoned him and asked his advice regarding Thatcher's request that Collver find a hit man in December, 1979. A brief was written assuring Collver once more that he had no legal obligation to approach the police with this information. Elliott knew about the brief, and about Thatcher's attempt to hire a murderer. "But it didn't have any real part to play," says Elliott, "because Wilson had said from the onset that Thatcher was responsible for the first shooting. He reiterated this over and over. It was a very, very horrible thing. I thought if I could get this thing settled, I'd be doing a service to both of them." Elliott, too, thought no one would commit murder simply to get a twelve-month reprieve from payment.

On February 19, 1982, the agreement—including the strange clause about JoAnn's death—was signed, and Thatcher made the first payment of $150,000. Of that JoAnn was required to hand over $130,000 for legal and other expenses she had incurred from the beginning of the legal battles. Still, the Wilsons breathed a sigh of relief—for they thought that

Thatcher's terrible, evil antagonism would now surely have played itself out.

But even before the agreement had been signed, in late December and early January, Thatcher had begun searching for a gun specially designed for killing people. On several occasions he dropped into the Frontier Gun Shop in downtown Palm Springs. It was a clean, modern-looking store, displaying the very latest in weaponry used to combat the growing crime in wealthy Palm Springs. One of the hottest-selling items was a bumper sticker that shouted in bright red, "My Wife Yes, My Dog Maybe, MY GUN NEVER." On his visits to Frontier, Colin chatted with a husky Alberta-born salesman by the name of Ron Williams, who had been a cop for sixteen years before an injury forced him into early retirement. Williams was an authority on guns and owned twelve himself. "He [Thatcher] would drop in and we would talk about different types of firearms," says Williams. On January 29, 1982, Thatcher bought a revolver called a Ruger Security-Six .357 Magnum, for $247. By state law anyone purchasing such a firearm was required to fill out a form giving his California driver's licence, and then wait fifteen days before he actually received the gun. When Thatcher returned two weeks later to pick up the revolver, he bought two boxes of Winchester-Western silver-tip hollow-point bullets and two bags of .38 special reload to use in practice. Williams and Thatcher had discussed ammunition on several of Thatcher's previous visits. "I specifically directed him to the silver-tip hollow points as a good home defence round, a good stopping round," says Williams. As he told Thatcher, "It penetrates, but it also opens up as it penetrates. It was developed for killing a human being."

Lynne Dally said that for a long time Thatcher practised with his new gun in the desert, using empty Perrier bottles as targets.

While he was testifying during his trial for first-degree murder, Thatcher said he bought the gun after he received a death threat. "It was late January of 1982, and I had just gone golfing to catch a fast nine before dark. And when I got back, Lynne said, 'One of your girlfriends sent you some roses.' And we opened the box and there was seven roses in it and I just didn't know what the significance of seven roses; who would send me seven roses? There was no signature. We were mystified." The phone rang soon afterwards. Thatcher picked it up and a male voice said, "Just calling you, Colin, to let you know that whether you're in Saskatchewan or in California, we can get at you any time, any time that we want." "Who is this?" Thatcher demanded. The caller just laughed and hung up.

What Thatcher didn't know was that on that evening, about that time, the caller and a husky friend had stationed themselves outside his condominium until they sensed that the security guards were becoming suspicious. They had hoped that Thatcher would emerge because they had a plan worked out. By peppering him with insults, they thought they could get him to react, physically. They would then have an opportunity to retaliate; they weren't sure where the beating would stop. Fortunately for Thatcher, he remained in his condo the entire evening and the two thugs finally gave up and went away.

In one of the more bizarre twists in the entire Thatcher affair, Regina police later discovered that the men who had purchased the flowers—seven roses are a traditional Mafia death threat—from a Palm Springs florist shop and had stood outside Thatcher's condominium worked officially for the British Columbia sheriff's office. They had been hired by one Joe Yablonski to go to Palm Springs to harass Thatcher.

Yablonski had a fascinating history. As an RCMP officer for over twenty years, he had been an important member of the Security Service, masterminding many of the force's top-secret missions—the bugging of embassies, surreptitious entries, electronic lock-picking. He was close to RCMP Commissioner James Bennett; after his downfall Yablonski was shuffled out of Ottawa, and he quit the force in 1974. He then began a business called International Security Advisors. This company was in charge of security for Ipsco in Regina and it was through this link that he became a close friend and a business partner of Tony Wilson's. Eventually he met JoAnn, and he and his wife liked her very much; indeed, he would be a pallbearer at JoAnn's funeral. After the first shooting, he felt that if Thatcher had a good scare he might not do any further violence to JoAnn. About all he managed to do, however, was provide Thatcher with an excuse for his purchase of a gun. The police, of course, claimed that Thatcher later used the weapon to murder JoAnn Wilson.

And yet during 1982, as the Wilsons had hoped, Thatcher's terrible anger seemed to subside somewhat. There was no longer the constant harassment of the Wilsons, and Lynne Dally would say. "It was easier. I mean, he didn't talk with as much hostility... although there was never a time he didn't talk about it. It was just a degree of extremes." But now Colin Thatcher had something to distract him from hatred—his political career was blossoming.

CHAPTER SIXTEEN
"THE BEST MINISTER"

After Colin Thatcher crossed the floor to become a Conservative in 1977, he was made Tory finance critic. There he did an effective job analyzing NDP budgets, all the while spewing out anti-socialist rhetoric. Like his leader Dick Collver, Thatcher expected the Tories to win the 1978 election, so that when the NDP were returned with a far bigger majority, he became very despondent at the prospect of four more years in Opposition. "After 1978, he was a pain in the ass," says Collver. "He was always provoking the party, he wouldn't do anything, and he was always running down to Palm Springs. I thought that by making him House leader it might keep him quiet. It didn't."

"Right after the election he came to an executive meeting," says Neil Seaman, who was president of the Thunder Creek PC Association. " 'What do you think of the new crop [of Tory MLAs], Colin?' somebody asked. 'Well,' he said, 'there's a few in there that have promise, but there's lots of dummies.' He had utter contempt for some of the people who had been in the party longer than he had. Colin would say things about them all the time at executive meetings, but of course he expected it to be kept in confidence."

In 1979, as his marital problems grew more serious—JoAnn was despondent, weeping all the time and refusing his attempts to save the relationship—he became even more erratic. That summer there was talk that he might quit altogether. He told a Saskatoon *Star-Phoenix* reporter that his enthusiasm for politics was not at its peak, but he added, "Who knows, maybe we'll get a Messiah [at the leadership convention] who will get us all going again." There was some speculation, at least in the ever-loyal Moose Jaw *Times-Herald*, that Thatcher might run for the Conservative leadership in 1979.

He denied that he was interested. "I have a very young family and an ideal wife." One week later the ideal wife left him and the Thatchers were plunged into their matrimonial war. For months after that, political fights were of no interest to him, locked as he was in his obsessive battles with his wife.

Thatcher didn't have much appreciation for the new leader, concluding quickly that Grant Devine was weak and ineffectual. Devine was a thirty-five-year-old professor of economics at the University of Saskatchewan in Saskatoon who revelled in his rural roots. "There's nothing I like better," he once told a reporter, "than to go to summer fairs, watch the horses, and play horseshoes." He had never been a politician—he lost his one bid to win a legislative seat in Saskatoon Nutana in 1978—but that didn't bother the delegates gathered in Saskatoon's civic centre on November 11, 1979. He won easily on the first ballot, capturing 418 of the 693 votes cast.

But that left the Tories without a commander in the Legislature. To avoid being labelled as a lame-duck leader, Devine went searching for a Tory devotee who would step down to give him the opportunity of capturing a seat in a by-election. The Devine family farm was located near Lake Valley in Thunder Creek so it was perhaps natural—if ill advised—for him to approach Colin Thatcher. Whether Thatcher physically threw Devine out of his house or merely told him in no uncertain terms to get lost has never been confirmed. With astonishing frankness, Thatcher would later describe the leader of his party to a *Globe and Mail* reporter: "My personal assessment is that I liked him better six months ago when he was elected leader. I think his political judgment is suspect. . . . I think there's probably going to be a reassessment if there isn't a dramatic improvement in his judgment. I believe at this point in time he's more concerned about finding a safe seat to win than he is about winning a general election." (Devine ran in a by-election in Estevan, considered one of the safest Tory seats, in November, 1980, and lost to a New Democrat. He won that same seat in 1982.)

On September 5, 1980, the *Leader-Post*'s political columnist, Dale Eisler, wrote of Devine and Thatcher, "The real test for Devine is how he deals with Thatcher behind closed doors. The common rule in politics is that if you have a problem, first you shut the door before you begin lashing out at those you work with. . . . It is those sort of unwritten constraints that seem the most difficult for Thatcher to accept. He is too much an independent, a free spirit of the right to be able to feel comfortable within the straitjacket of party. . . . The man has incredible ability, a flair for politics and the art of aggravation in the Legislature unlike anyone else. . . . "

Not all his constituents appreciated his performance as an MLA. This was demonstrated when the Thunder Creek executive, who by this time were almost all Thatcher devotees, called a surprise nomination meeting in March of 1982. Those who were not Thatcher supporters cried dirty politics. "I was part of the executive [as past president]," says Neil Seaman, "and I was not aware that the nominating meeting had been called. It was just a bit more than I could take." With the help of Don Swenson, he persuaded a Boharm farmer, Don Hill, to run. Hill had been president of the riding association before Seaman but he had quit when Thatcher became a Conservative because he simply detested the man. He says the 1982 campaign to get the nomination was typical of Thatcher's dirty tricks: "We were trying to secretly gather up support for people to go up to the nomination meeting, but naturally they had to have a PC membership. Fourteen hours before the meeting we turned in our names—we had about 120 lined up—to Lyle Stewart [the constituency president and a supporter of Thatcher's]. Colin had managed to sign up about a hundred members. When we got to the nomination meeting, we found out that there were about thirty people there who didn't have memberships in Thunder Creek but who belonged to the Conservative party of Canada. They'd all been brought by Colin. The constitution said they could vote, so we knew the jig was up." Thatcher received about forty more votes than Hill. The vote was so close, in fact, that Thatcher tried to prevent the results from being made public. It was an embarrassing situation for Colin, particularly because Grant Devine was in attendance as a guest speaker. "Some of those people he had voting there were really not able to vote," says Hill. "He's not able to vote because he doesn't live in the constituency, but he voted, his two sons voted, his housekeeper voted, and four or five other people whom I knew all my life—they used to live in the constituency at one time, but they retired and moved to Moose Jaw. Immediately afterwards I wrote a letter complaining to the president of the provincial organization, but he just ignored me."

By the spring of 1982 polls taken by the Conservatives indicated that the NDP government was in very serious trouble. Opposition MLAs realized with glee that at last they were likely to form the next government and that realization did wonders for party loyalty. In Colin Thatcher's eyes, for example, Grant Devine had suddenly turned into a shining knight on a white horse. During a budget debate on March 23, 1982, Thatcher told those across the floor, "I've been out on the hustings and I'm confident of what's there. And what waits for you is the decimation of the New Democratic party. And you have helped us. . . . You have underestimated your opposition. And let me tell you, when you call it [the election], Grant Devine is going to blow Allan Blakeney right out of the water. . . . Let me tell you, Grant Devine is going to kick the blazes out of Allan Blakeney in rural Saskatchewan. He's just one heck of a good speaker up on the platform."

Thatcher was right. The NDP was decimated in the April 26, 1982, election. Devine's Progressive Conservatives managed the largest landslide victory in Saskatchewan's history. The PCs swept into office, winning fifty-six seats compared with the NDP's eight. The NDP's popular vote fell from 48 to 38 percent. As Saskatoon author Guy Vanderhaeghe quipped, "The electorate planned to give the government a slap on the wrist and ended up tearing its arm off."

Despite being cited for contempt of court and despite the persistent rumours that linked him with the shooting of JoAnn eleven months previously, Thatcher garnered far more votes in his own riding than he ever had before. He polled 4,412, the NDP 2,036, while the once mighty Liberals drew only 264. For Colin Thatcher there was only one bitter note in the campaign—the two huge NDP signs located directly across from the Legislative Building, on the lawn of Tony and JoAnn Wilson.

In the newly elected Conservative government, Thatcher was naturally cabinet material. There were only a few who had been in the Legislature as long as he, his political acumen and combative style had been major components in the impressive Tory sweep, and everyone knew that the squawk he would make if he wasn't chosen would be terrible. Some

Tories tried to block him from being appointed to a major cabinet post; they were still furious at his public criticism of Devine, they remembered him throwing chairs around in fits of rage in caucus meetings, and they were a trifle uneasy about the wounding of his former wife. But Thatcher's importance was underlined when he was named to the transitional team that planned the installation of the new government. Clearly he was going to get a cabinet post. His own keen preference was to become the minister of agriculture, but that post went to Eric Berntson, the burly MLA from Souris–Cannington, who had sat as House leader during the entire two years Devine was without a seat. Thatcher was offered the energy portfolio instead. "On the table at the time," says a colleague of Thatcher's, "were some very, very heavy negotiations involving upgraders—projects in the order of two and three billion dollars, the biggest in Saskatchewan's history. They needed somebody who could tough it out with the oil companies; they knew Thatcher had the guts, and, of course, a mind like a steel trap."

Although it was a most important ministry in Saskatchewan, a province of vast undeveloped natural resources, Thatcher balked at first at taking Energy. But after pouting for a bit, he grabbed it. One reason was that it was an impressive empire. Not only would he be responsible for government energy policy, but he would also control three important Crown corporations—Saskatchewan Mining Development Corporation, Saskatchewan Oil and Gas Corporation, and Saskatchewan Minerals. Once he made the decision to take the job, he tackled it with fierce enthusiasm. "He was fascinated at what he didn't know," remembers Lynne Dally. "He was fascinated at what he was learning. It was the first thing I saw him take a total intellectual interest in."

By most accounts he did a superb job as energy minister. "I think he was the best minister that government had," says Dick Collver. "He was extremely competent." Jerry Hammersmith, the MLA for Prince Albert–Duck Lake, was the NDP energy critic while Thatcher was minister. Although he certainly didn't agree with Conservative policy—"It's easy to reach agreements with the oil industry when you are handing them everything on a silver platter," he says—he has nothing but praise for Thatcher's personal performance. "I always had a great deal of respect for him as an individual, both as a member of the Opposition and the government," says Hammersmith. "He had a lot of natural, well-honed ability as a politician and was able to grasp issues and outline his view of them very quickly. He was highly intelligent. And certainly we often disagreed, Colin and I, on specific issues, but I always had a great deal of respect for his abilities and quite frankly enjoyed serving in the House with him. Colin didn't ask any quarter and didn't give any quarter, but you always knew where he stood and in that respect he reminded me a lot of his dad. I always respect that and I respected that in Colin."

Thatcher's initial priority was to restore the health of the sick and lagging oil and natural gas industries. Within two weeks of taking over he had raised natural gas prices, and within two months he had produced a new tax and royalty structure for the oil industry. Both had the effect of a dose of penicillin; by September Thatcher was able to brag that both of these resource industries were on their way to recovery. "He was a very candid individual," says Garry Priddy, then an executive with Getty Oil. "He spoke his mind, and when you're dealing with politicians that's pretty unusual."

"At first the oil men were cautious, very, very, cautious," says a former executive assistant of Thatcher's. "They were powerful men in their own right and they were sceptical of this high-flyer known throughout the land as the J.R. Ewing of Saskatchewan. However, he was very forthright and they respected that. And he was a force in the cabinet, certainly a force to be reckoned with."

It was only natural that when Colin Thatcher was sworn in as minister of energy on May 8, 1982, Lynne Dally would fly up for the ceremonies—because she felt very much part of his life. According to Lynne, Colin had asked her to marry him the first time she visited Moose Jaw, in the fall of 1980, and she fully expected him to follow through with the marriage plans.

They had a curious relationship: during the good times, it was predicated on fast quips and incessant, sometimes cruel, one-upmanship. "He's fast with his mouth," says Lynne. "But he wasn't fast enough the occasional time I'd get in my Joan Rivers words. He just sat there with it hanging open." Lynne knew him so well that she knew his weak spots, and knew that she would draw blood whenever she kidded him about two particularly sensitive areas—his age and his weight. "Colin always lied about his age. I mentioned to Greg and Regan one time that their father was forty-two. 'No, no,' they said, 'he's forty-four.' So when he was in the shower the next morning, I looked at his driver's licence and he was forty-four. I said, 'Colin, this is silly, why lie about two years?' He said, 'I'm not forty-four.' I replied, 'Your sons say you're forty-four.' 'They're wrong.' 'Your driver's licence says you're forty-four.' 'It's wrong.'" Lynne didn't let him get away with it; she teased him unmercifully for months, never pausing to consider the implications of this tendency to reorganize unwelcome reality.

On one occasion, Lynne had great difficulty zipping Colin into his chaps. "They've shrunk, Lynne, they've shrunk," he kept saying. She replied, "Colin, I don't think chaps shrink, I mean, when was the last time you put them in the dryer? It's your extra pounds, you jerk. You had a lazy summer." "No, no, they've shrunk, they've shrunk," he kept insisting.

Lynne was amazed by Colin's capacity for eating red meat. "Colin had custom-cut T-bones. They'd be two inches thick, big beautiful cuts that cost maybe fifteen dollars a steak. He would cook them to within an inch of their lives, until they were grey. He'd have those tri-tips cut into filets and he had a whole freezer full of back bacon," she recalls. When he got nasty, she used to say to him, "Why don't you cut out the red meat for a couple of weeks and see how your character turns." Lynne has a recurring dream: "I'm watching Colin walk away. In one hand he has a great big plastic bag full of steaks and a bottle of Chivas Regal, held by the neck. In the other arm he's holding a great big teddy bear."

Despite Thatcher's little quirks, not to mention his avowed attempt to kill his wife, Lynne found him interesting enough to want to marry. "Here's this horrible funky rancher, who comes home just grubby, he really puts his physical effort and time into cows. And when the Legislature was meeting, he'd come home at noon, he'd shower and change into a three-piece suit or ultra-suede jacket and go to work. That was fascinating to me. It was great, the best of both worlds."

Lynne had spent ten days in Moose Jaw in the summer of 1981. She thought the Redland house a "beautiful home, with large mouldings over the doorways, the funny little den with the French glass doors, and the spacious backyard." But she was appalled at JoAnn's decorating scheme, which, although shabby by this time, was still intact. "Green is not my favourite color. I thought, just let me get my hands on this place with one good decorator and we will make a showplace out of it."

Lynne met the Moose Jaw upper crust and liked them all. They had the Barretts and the McDonalds over for drinks. She and Colin went to see a version of the musical *A Chorus Line* in Regina with Rosemary and Roger Tessier. Lynne also attempted to bring a little culture into the lives of the two Thatcher boys. "I liked his kids. I tried to enrich their lives with a little tongue in cheek. I'd say, 'Okay, we're having culture corner. You will sit down and listen to me for five minutes, that's all I'm asking.' Once I asked them to watch twenty minutes of *My Fair Lady*. I explained to them the Greek myth of Pygmalion, and George Bernard Shaw, and how Leslie Howard and Wendy Hiller made the first movie in 1938, etc. I told them that if they didn't like it, they could leave. They left after twenty minutes." It hurt Lynne's feelings a little.

Lynne felt she had a special relationship with Regan, although it was expressed in a twelve-year-old boy's own way. "He would demonstrate karate moves on me. I'd be lying in the sun and he and his friends would turn the hose on me, and I'd pretend I didn't see it coming. We'd play cards a lot and sometimes we'd get into arguments. I'd get up afterwards and rub his back and say, 'You know, Regan, I'm not here to upset things, or disrupt your life or take your dad away.' Once he blurted out, 'Lynne, you've got to realize, my dad is just totally burnt.'"

The one person who could not abide the house guest was Sandra Hammond. Apparently she took one look at her boss's 100-pound, glamorous, mouthy girlfriend, and decided she couldn't stand her. Lynne was philosophical about it: "I can understand why she didn't like me—her exposure to life, the way she looked physically, her naiveté. I'm there to hate—what's to like?—and I understood that." Sandra was shocked that Colin and Lynne were sharing the same bed, since they weren't married, and she told her parents who, of course, were not so shocked.

Still, Lynne said, she tried to befriend the young girl. "We did have our rare, girl-to-girl, funny moments. One day she told me, 'Mr. Thatcher always puts Grecian Formula on his shopping list but he always denies using it. He says just in case we have company.' I just looked at her and said, 'How many overnight guests have you had in the last year? One? Two? How many wanted to dye their hair?' Both of us fell on the floor laughing."

One thing about Colin that really upset Lynne was his attitude to Bev Banbury, his mother's good friend. Several years after Ross's death, Peggy began seeing Banbury, and their relationship had developed into a warm one. "I used to tell Colin that Peggy was damned lucky to find someone like Bev. He was so nice. Colin hated him. 'I can't stand that SOB jerk,' he said all the time. I said, 'Colin stop and think. Your mother is alone. Widows her age are a drag on the market. Here is Bev, who is good-looking, has money of his own, is outgoing and gregarious and fun to be with. Colin, your mother lucked out.' Still Colin bitched about him. Finally, I said, 'Face it, anybody who isn't your father is not going to be acceptable.'"

After her 1981 visit to Moose Jaw, Lynne was sufficiently confident about their up-and-down relationship that she moved into the Thatcher condominium in Palm Springs. "It's a nice-size condo, two bedrooms, two baths, and a little den. But, oh God, it's God-awful Palm Springs-ten-years-ago decorated—yellow, white, and bright green. Colin admitted he bought it as a model, and models are not meant to be lived in." She didn't work; the arrangement was that he would support her. "I started my artwork, I lay in the sun, I read. I wasn't working, yet I wasn't married to Colin and the future was iffy. I was in limbo, really." Their relationship continued on its rocky road with not a week going by without some emotional upheaval. Lynne says that on at least four occasions, Colin struck her. "He had got me this beautiful outfit, white shot-silk pants, a red silk shirt, navy blue ultra-suede jacket. It's like seven hundred dollars for all this, and it fits. I was delighted and he couldn't believe that I was delighted because he told me, 'Of all the things I ever bought for JoAnn, they never fit and she didn't like them.' I remember he was driving me home and I don't know what happened—when he gives it to me verbally I give it back. So we had this fight. I remember him going around to the passenger side and dragging me out on the asphalt driveway. The only thing

I thought of was 'Colin, the goddamn pants, you're going to ruin them.' If I got nothing out of this relationship I wanted that outfit.

"The next day I said, 'Colin, you practically beat me up.' He said 'I did not. I've never hit a woman in my life.'"

Lynne became convinced that there was an imbalance in Colin's physiological make-up that brought on his violent, erratic behaviour. She was concerned about his red-meat-and-alcohol diet. "I kept telling him, 'Colin, get your blood sugar checked.' I'm still positive there was something wrong—his diet was so strange and he would often flare up after several cocktails."

After the May, 1982, swearing-in ceremonies, Lynne Dally stayed in Moose Jaw for several weeks. It would prove to be a tumultuous, violent visit. Lynne and Colin fought mostly about what she considered his reneging on a promise to marry her. "Before I left Palm Springs, he'd assured me, 'Yes, we're getting married. Tell your friends, tell your family. Taking you to Canada, my darling, and you can design your own house. Everything will be wonderful.'" She talked over her plans with Peggy, at a baseball game for MLAs she told Thatcher's old friend Gerald Muirhead that she wanted to marry Colin, and she discussed with Sandra and the boys what life would be like after she moved in.

"After I had been there several weeks, I really wanted to talk to him about it. I wanted to say, 'Oh gee, I have been up here and no move is being made to really fit me in as you had promised.'" When Lynne did approach him, she said Thatcher went a little crazy. "I won't go so far as to say he beat me up, because he didn't break any bones or blacken my jaw or eye. But I was on the floor of the den because he was hitting me. I was crying, very upset. And I recall I just told him, 'Just go upstairs, go to bed. Please just leave me alone.' I was hysterical."

Lynne said she walked into the kitchen and took about a dozen 292 pain-killers, a potentially lethal large dose. "I waited for half an hour or forty-five minutes until I felt them starting to take effect. I realized then that Colin Thatcher really wasn't worth killing myself for, that it was a pretty stupid thing to do and a pretty unstable thing to do." Lynne said she went upstairs and woke Colin up. He and Greg took her to Union Hospital in Moose Jaw. A nurse there gave her medicine that made her throw up, and she was released about an hour and a half later. "No matter how much out of it I was, I noticed the whole time that Colin was demonstrating great concern, great presence of mind, great speed. But in the back of my mind, I thought, 'He's just scared it's going to get in the papers.'" However, the next day the two made up once again and Lynne remained in Moose Jaw for several more weeks.

"By the end of the summer, before I left, I said to myself, I can see what my life would be. I'm not in love with him, I never was in love with him. But I said, okay, it's a fair trade. He gets the benefit of not being alone, of having me on his arm and not having to hustle for a date, having someone to share his bed—which, by the way, is not a thrill of a lifetime, because he's terrible. I can have a very nice life on my own because I'm pretty self-contained. I can do my art, go to the gym, lay in the sun. And when he comes home, all I have to do is be pretty and smile and share his bed. That's not very romantic, but at the time I thought he was a lot wealthier than he was. I thought, if I'm going to marry money, I'm going to marry big money, none of this $100,000-a-year nonsense. I want someone who can write a cheque for a million dollars. I mean, if you're going to cop out and marry for money and be cold about it, it might as well be something big."

After Lynne went back to Palm Springs, Garry Anderson popped up again. For the last year, he had been living in La Ronge, 770 kilometres north of Moose Jaw, working for a lumberyard, then for the City of La Ronge, and finally as a collector for the Department of Northern Saskatchewan. Anderson had just returned to Caron for a visit and he hadn't seen Thatcher for many months. Garry was to testify in detail about what happened next. Colin asked Garry to meet him at the abandoned farm where they had talked previously. "How the hell could you have missed?" Garry asked, referring to the 1981 shooting. Colin shrugged his shoulders and said he didn't know. He gave Anderson a Ruger .375 Magnum and asked him if he thought he could make a silencer for it. Anderson replied that he'd try, and indeed over the next few months Garry and a Moose Jaw friend, Dan Doyle, made no fewer than six. "We experimented with them," said Anderson.

"I believe at the last, the last one we had, we had it down to about three-quarters volume of sound." In the end Anderson never did give Thatcher the silencer, because Colin would not pay him the money he wanted for it.

Anderson and Thatcher saw each other periodically during this time. On one occasion in October, Colin asked Garry to get him a car, and Anderson rented a 1978 green Chevrolet from a Saskatoon car dealer. It was supposed to be returned on October 13, 1982, but Thatcher didn't get it back to Anderson until October 18. There was a bag containing a black wig and a tire iron in the car, Thatcher said. "Make sure you take that out before you give it back." (This information suggested to police investigators that the weapon used in JoAnn's murder, over a year later, may have been a tire iron with a very sharp point. Another interesting fact they later uncovered was that the Chev had been seized by the Wascana Centre police because it had been improperly parked on the Legislature's grounds and had mud smeared on the licence plates. While giving evidence at his murder trial, Colin Thatcher alluded to such a vehicle himself. But Thatcher said it had been Anderson who had illegally parked it before it was towed away, and claimed that he had simply been trying to help Garry when he phoned the Wascana police. All of this was part of the intricate story produced by Thatcher to explain the inconvenient tape recording of the conversation between himself and Anderson.)

Through all this time, Thatcher was busy looking after the energy concerns of Saskatchewan. The previous government had attempted to orchestrate what was considered the biggest single industrial project in the province's history—the Great Plains heavy-oil upgrader. It had invited five large oil companies to form a consortium to undertake the billion-dollar project. Although the Moose Jaw area had been chosen as the location for the upgrader, and months and millions had been spent on feasibility studies, the proposal was still on the drawing boards when the Tories took office. Thatcher didn't like it one bit. He called it a "shotgun marriage," and as a free-enterpriser he frowned at the oil companies' demands of almost blanket risk coverage in the form of government loan guarantees. So unimpressed was Thatcher with the proposal that he didn't even bother to take it to the cabinet. When one of the partners, Husky Oil, threatened to pull out and build an upgrader of its own in Lloydminster, Thatcher didn't beg the firm to stay, he "stood tough" and insisted that he himself would find other, more willing partners. In four months, Thatcher made five trips to Los Angeles (at a cost to the taxpayers of $6,500) to meet with officials of the giant Getty Oil. "Colin just loved jet-setting around, hob-nobbing with these executives of billion-dollar multi-nationals," says a Tory MLA. "But from what I understand he was quite brilliant at it." The television series *Dallas* was at the peak of its popularity and, more than ever, Thatcher's fans and enemies linked him with the colourful and scheming J.R. Ewing. To further add to the image, while he was in California, Thatcher could always drop in on Palm Springs for a couple of days of golf and dalliance with Lynne.

In November of 1982, Thatcher set off for Europe with the heavy-oil upgrader on his mind; but his primary aim was to find markets for Saskatchewan's vast uranium deposits. Lynne Dally went with him.

Their first stop was London. As Lynne remembers that visit, "We had a driver at our disposal who was right out of Central Casting—the John Gielgud of drivers—and he was very funny. Named Douglas, I wanted to see it all. As long as we're here for only four days, let's do the Tower of London, Buckingham Palace, Ascot, the countryside. We had very full days. The last night we were in London, I was tired and I went to bed. Colin started making it, and for the first and only, I hope, time in my life, I said, 'I'm so tired and I've got a headache.' It was real dark and all of a sudden, wham, I got knocked almost on the floor. I just wanted to go to sleep and suddenly half my head's coming off."

"Don't you know that the only reason I brought you to Europe was to fuck you?" Colin raged at her. Lynne replied, "'No, I didn't know that but you're out of luck tonight.' Wham, wham, 'You bitch, you.' I said, 'Okay, go ahead, and I'll just lay here.' And by God he did." "A Stompin' at the Savoy" was what Lynne would hereafter call that episode in her life.

Lynne then ran into the bathroom and phoned the front desk. "I had stopped smoking for Colin, something I have never done for anyone else. 'Get me another room,' I said, 'and a pack of any kind of cigarettes you can find.' They gave me a suite—at least I ripped him off for another suite—and this was the Savoy Hotel."

The next morning she called Thatcher and said, 'Hi Colin." He said, "You're on your own, kid." "And he was serious, too. I called Heathrow and got two different flights There was London to L.A. that afternoon at one. 'Shit,' I said to myself, 'I'll never see Paris.' I called Colin and said, 'The earliest flight I can get is nine tomorrow morning. And they won't accept my ticket without your signature, 'cause it's on your American Express card.' 'That's tough,' he said and hung up. I thought to myself, well if I'm going to be stuck it might as well be at the Savoy."

Lynne went to Thatcher's room and knocked on his door "Look, we've got to catch a plane for Paris," she told him "Stop being silly and let's get packing." "Oh, all right." he said, and they both started laughing.

They had a wonderful time in Paris. "I should be arrested if I buy myself any more clothes," says Lynne, "but Colin told me to pick out an outfit and he would pay for it. It was the year of Lady Di, all taffeta and ruffles, which I simply can't wear. Finally, after much searching, I found a pair of bright red, stitched down, pleated, 100-percent wool cu lottes, which fit like a glove and a sweater that was forest green, grey and red with a little silver thread running through it. I thought, 'Oh yeah, all right.'

"They cost about eight hundred dollars but the shop wouldn't take American Express. Colin panicked. He tried to tell me that he couldn't use his Master Card because that was a government card, and he didn't want to write off my clothes to the government. I was practically in tears because I had already tried it on. I'd fallen in love with it. Gritting my teeth, he finally put it on his Master Charge. I said, 'Why are you so upset? If it's a government card, you can just pay them back.'" (There is no public record of Thatcher's expenses for the trip. He went on behalf of the Saskatchewan Development Mining Corporation, a Crown corporation that refuses to release this information. Southam news reporter Don Sellar wrote in May of 1984 that Thatcher had $10,000 in disputed expense claims, many charged to his American Express card. Thatcher denies the allegation and is suing Sellar over the story.)

Thatcher was pleased with his European negotiations. But

what he had to confront, on returning to Moose Jaw, was sorting out the mess of his personal finances.

Thatcher had fallen behind in his payments on the $177,000 mortgage he had taken out on January 14, 1980, to purchase the English farm for his sons. In the summer of 1980, during the Thatchers' matrimonial property trial, he had explained some of the reasons for his difficulties. "Interest rates just suddenly lost all perspective and went crazy and my debt load just simply raised my cost of operation terribly dramatically. My personal difficulties have been expensive. I virtually had no cattle income at all this year." In August of 1982, the Moose Jaw Credit Union applied to the courts to commence foreclosure actions against three parcels of land that Thatcher had bought in 1974 and used as collateral for the lagging $177,000 mortgage. Not only did he have to find some cash to appease the credit union but the second payment to JoAnn, of $87,500, was due on February 1, 1983. And Thatcher knew that if he could not raise the money, the Wilsons could demand that the entire sum of $350,000, plus interest, be paid immediately.

His financial difficulties did not, however, prevent him from taking a month's holiday in Palm Springs over Christmas and New Year's. When he returned to Regina on January 9, 1983, he walked into what he termed "a hornet's nest." "I had a meeting with the premier at five o'clock [on January 10] and I basically spent the rest of the week fighting for my political life. I lost the fight."

From the beginning there were cracks in the façade of total government support for Colin Thatcher. Initially Thatcher had been appointed to the board of directors of the Crown Investment Corporation, the holding company and master planner for the province's seventeen Crown corporations. Before the board even had its first meeting in June, however, Thatcher had been replaced. Since he was responsible for three of the most important Crown corporations, this move was unexpected. According to Dale Eisler, the political columnist, Thatcher's blunt remarks that the Crown corporations should either face a massive purge at the senior levels or be cut back in size was what led to his removal. It was an indication that Premier Devine was not going to put up with Thatcher's shooting off his mouth.

The next month saw another Thatcher-instigated ballyhoo in the Legislature that caused Devine and his party some embarrassment. On July 8, 1982, after being questioned by the Opposition, Thatcher said he had never personally fired any employee in his department. A few days later New Democratic MLA Jerry Hammersmith—ironically, the very man who admired Thatcher so much—produced a letter signed by Thatcher, firing Shakir Alwarid as assistant deputy minister. "Thatcher has deliberately misled the House," said Hammersmith. On Tuesday, July 13, the Tory-appointed Speaker, Herb Swan, ruled that Thatcher had indeed misled the Legislature. Colin quickly apologized: "I give the assembly my assurance, in answering questions of the Opposition, I was at no time attempting to mislead the assembly deliberately or otherwise." He said while he had indeed signed the letter, someone else had done the actual firing.

Swan accepted Thatcher's apology, and if the matter had been dropped there, it would have vanished overnight. But as he left the chamber Thatcher, his blood boiling, flung out at reporters standing in the hallway, "When I got the knife from Brock [former Speaker John Brockelbank, under the NDP government], I got it from the front." He implied that he only apologized to Swan because he had to. This caused another uproar and the next day Thatcher said, "Mr. Speaker, last evening in the corridor I made an off-the-cuff remark that was stupid, inappropriate and inexcusable. Mr. Speaker, I have absolutely no excuses for this because someone with my experience knows better. I acknowledge full responsibility for it." Swan again accepted his apology and the matter was dropped. But since Swan had been appointed by the Tories, Devine was enraged that it was one of his own that had caused him his first real problem. Another black mark against Thatcher.

Although there was no question that most people thought Thatcher was doing a superb job as energy minister, he continued to earn the disapproval of his cabinet colleagues Tony Merchant talked to Thatcher about the reasons why he was fired from the cabinet. "Colin was surprised to find that being effective in his job didn't count very much, that it was a whole list of garbage little things that apparently was troubling his cabinet colleagues." Thatcher attended cabinet meetings sporadically, neglecting to show up even when he was personally invited by the premier. And he was less than enthusiastic about keeping them up to date on his activities in the energy department. Sometimes they had not the slightest idea where he was. There were some who disapproved when he brazenly took Lynne Dally to Europe. He had been warned against it before the trip, but he, of course, paid no attention. "All those politicians may have mistresses downtown," says a long-time Tory, "but when you go to an official function, you're not supposed to take anybody but your wife." Thatcher thumbed his nose at this axiom and introduced Lynne to high government officials and politicians as neither his wife nor his secretary, which could only have meant she was his mistress. There was criticism over the manner in which he treated his expense accounts. And he had a fierce argument with Patricia Smith, the MLA from Swift Current, over a patronage question. "He wanted to give a government contract to some Conservatives in Moose Jaw, and she wanted to give it to some Conservatives in Swift Current. So boy, did they clash," says a Tory fundraiser. (After Thatcher had been demoted to the backbenches, he kept a low profile. The one fracas, in April of 1984, that won him wide publicity involved Pat Smith, who was education minister. In the Legislature Thatcher asked his former colleague what policy changes had occurred under the Progressive Conservative government. "What's the difference. What else has changed? What's changed?" he kept goading her. Smith rose and unsmilingly retorted, "Maybe if the Member were around more often he would know what's changed." The clash fuelled rumours that Thatcher was thinking of switching back to the Liberals.)

Indeed, old-fashioned pork-barrelling was at the core of several items on the "garbage list." The only time the Conservatives had even tasted power in Saskatchewan was from 1929 to 1934 in a cooperative government. It was a long time to be denied the public trough in a province where so much business is done through government agencies. After April, 1982, Tory supporters felt that at last their turn had come. Consequently there were loud Tory complaints when Thatcher handed over oil and gas contracts to firms owned by supposedly non-Tory supporters near Estevan. Confronted with this, he promised that it wouldn't happen again. It wasn't long, however, before some powerful Tories found out about the government largesse he was passing on to his old Liberal friend Tony Merchant. George Hill was the man who finally had the axe brought down.

Hill, an Estevan lawyer and long-time supporter (appointed to the Court of Queen's Bench in December, 1984, by justice minister John Crosbie, shortly after the Conservatives took office in Ottawa), had been elected president of the provincial party in 1977. After the Conservatives came to power in 1982, Hill and an associate, Grant Armstrong, opened up a law office in Regina. In June, 1982, Devine appointed Hill vice-chairman of the Saskatchewan Power Corporation, and in November, when cabinet ministers were replaced by citizens on Crown corporation boards of directors, he was named chairman. It was Hill and other leading Tory lawyers, Ron Barclay included, who discovered that Thatcher, on behalf of the Saskatchewan Mining Development Corporation, was giving Tony Merchant's law firm thousands upon thousands of dollars of legal work. (SMDC, a Crown corporation, will not make public the exact amount paid to Pedersen, Norman, McLeod & Todd.) Hill and Barclay couldn't believe their ears when they found out that the man who had once almost won the Liberal leadership in Saskatchewan was being given lucrative government contracts. Hill complained bitterly to Eric Berntson, the deputy chairman and a good friend. Thatcher was confronted with this information and told to stop giving Merchant's firm business.

But some time later it was discovered that Thatcher had persisted in awarding government contracts to his personal lawyer. At this point, Berntson said to Devine, "Either he goes or I do." A former Tory MLA summarized the situation: "Devine certainly couldn't have the guy who had kept the party together for years leaving, so it had to be Thatcher." (Despite the fact that these details were confirmed by four important Conservatives, and parts of the story were brought out in court during Thatcher's murder trial, Eric Berntson says this account is "totally inaccurate." He will not, however, reveal why Thatcher was fired from the cabinet.)

The interesting question, of course, is why Thatcher would jeopardize his political career by giving Tony Merchant's law firm government work. The two men were friends and although they saw little of each other socially in Regina, Merchant stayed at Thatcher's condominium in Palm Springs. The two had fought long and costly legal battles together, and there was much speculation that Thatcher was paying off his lawyer's bill by providing him with government work. Merchant flatly denies this, pointing out that in as large a law firm as his, with a complicated and thoroughly inspected bookkeeping system, it would have been impossible to make such a deal with Thatcher. Merchant says that neither friendship nor previous professional involvement was the reason Thatcher handed Merchant's firm lucrative government contracts; it was a special service that Merchant could offer. "One important thing it did was to open some access to federal cabinet ministers," says Merchant. "He [Thatcher] and his Crowns [corporations] were able to get the sort of preferred status in Ottawa through me that wouldn't have been available without me."

Probably more than any single reason, however, Thatcher was fired because of his attitude. Tony Merchant looks at it from a historical perspective: "Colin Thatcher was probably the most effective cabinet minister they had at the time. And he appeared to the public to be effective. He was good for the government politically because he was a former Liberal that the old-time Liberals could respect, as they had respected his father. So for every reason, you'd think they would want to keep that man in the cabinet.

"But then you have a cabinet full of naive, green Conservatives who are all bubbly and enthusiastic about the fact that they're in power for the first time—most of them, including the premier, are elected for the first time. People are fawning over them because now they're cabinet ministers and they think they are doing wonderful things for the province while for Colin Thatcher—well, he was around when there was a similar government and it was his father's. He took all this enthusiasm with a certain degree of disdain. 'We're going to do a better job than the NDP but don't be so quick to pump yourselves up, guys,' he'd say. He wasn't bubbly and enthusiastic and delighted with this wonderful job that they would self-aggrandize themselves for doing. So the feeling was that he just wasn't a team player."

FRIDAY, JANUARY 14

Colin Thatcher met Grant Devine in the premier's office for one last vicious screaming match. It turned into a physical confrontation, with pushing and shoving. In the end, at 3 p.m. Thatcher was told he must either resign or be fired.

MONDAY, JANUARY 17

Grant Devine held a press conference just an hour before leaving on a five-day government trip to the United States. He said that Thatcher was quitting the cabinet for "family and financial reasons." It was a mutual decision, said the premier, before heading off for five days of being unavailable for comment.

Thatcher's "resignation" was a very big story in Saskatchewan and Tony Wilson heard it on the radio. He called JoAnn at work immediately and told her the news. When she got off the phone, she turned to her colleague Shevawn Desrosiers and said, "That makes me very nervous indeed."

CHAPTER SEVENTEEN
MURDER

MONDAY, JANUARY 17, 1983

Grant Devine announced Thatcher's resignation from the cabinet on the same day that the funeral for Don McDonald's father, Tom, was held at Lakeview United Church in Regina. Tom McDonald was a much-beloved man, and most of Moose Jaw's elite turned out to pay their last respects. Penny Livingston, an old Moose Jaw friend of JoAnn's and Colin's, was standing with the McDonald family when she glanced up the stairs. "There came Colin talking to Jane [Graham], the Pattersons were behind them, and then there was Ron. I was sure that that was the first time they had all been in the same room since the whole thing blew up."

At that moment reporters were searching everywhere for Thatcher for a comment on his resignation, so Colin prudently asked Bob Livingston if there was a back door. They started to chat and Colin suggested that they step into the church library where they would not be seen. They talked for some time and Colin kept repeating, "I want you to know that there is absolutely no personal scandal connected to my resignation." The Livingstons were surprised that he was so subdued; they expected Colin, in his usual manner, to be raving about the "stupid SOBs" who had forced him out of the cabinet.

Afterwards Thatcher returned to Moose Jaw and for the remainder of that week he claimed that he was "licking my political wounds. I was hanging around my ranch, [in] the Caron area, and not going very far, doing paperwork in my office at home, mainly, along the lines of cattle records and that, just doing odds and ends. I was not feeling particularly buoyant. Didn't really want to encounter any more people than I had to. I was not taking phone calls."

TUESDAY, JANUARY 18

As a housekeeper for Duane Adams and his family for the last ten years, Joan Hasz had her cleaning routine down pat, and as usual she began tidying up the living room at three that afternoon. Located at 20th and Angus, one block west of the Wilsons, the Adams residence was a lovely big house, white wood with a red tile roof, and a summer garden so beautifully manicured that it was the pride of the neighbourhood. While Mrs. Hasz was dusting she glanced out the south window onto 20th Avenue and caught sight of that blue car again. When she had first seen it, she thought it might belong to somebody visiting in the neighbourhood but "then it started to bother me. I don't know why but I started to feel like it seems it is always there and that's why on this particular Tuesday, I sort of took note," she said. When Adams arrived home at about five, the car was gone, but Mrs. Hasz mentioned it to him.

WEDNESDAY, JANUARY 19

At precisely 3 p.m. Mrs. Hasz noticed the blue, medium-sized Oldsmobile parked in the same spot again. "This time I got very upset and I thought, well, I'm just going to watch and just see why it seems to be out there." She saw a lone occupant in the car, a man of about thirty, slight to medium build, wearing a dark-coloured toque pulled right down to his eyebrows, and a dark-blue, down-filled jacket. He had a well-trimmed but full black beard which Mrs. Hasz said covered a large portion of his face. He was sitting "crunched down" in the driver's seat.

Duane Adams had been called at work about the car and so he came home early, at about 4 p.m. He spent some twenty minutes watching the figure carefully. His description matched that of Mrs. Hasz, except he added one important fact. "They [his hands] were stark white and the skin on his face was either heavily tanned or olive, but his hands were stark

white. And you could also see, even at this distance, that the
fingers were well outlined and I was quite surprised by the
hands." Adams surmised that the person might have been
wearing surgical gloves. About five o'clock the car circled
around the block once and then drove away.

THURSDAY, JANUARY 20

Mrs. Hasz, a small, compactly built woman in her sixties, was
not feeling too well and decided to go home early at about
4:30. She had not bothered to look out of the window to see if
the mystery car was there. Now, however, as she approached
her own vehicle she realized with a start that the Oldsmobile
was parked right in front of her. While she was scraping the
snow off her car, she thought, "Well, I should try and get the
licence number since it is upsetting me so." She discovered,
however, that there was mud covering much of the plate, and
she decided to scrape it off. At this point she caught a glance
of a "bump" in the driver's seat. "I thought, well, maybe now
there is someone in there. Maybe I hadn't better. Then I
happened to look up into his rear view mirror and I could see
his eyes glaring at me." In a panic, she drove away. Mrs. Hasz
had, however, been able to see three numbers and as she
drove she kept repeating to herself, "292, 292, 292." "I ran
into my house and I just grabbed a piece of paper and wrote
it down because my family said, 'What's wrong with you?'
And I just said, 'Be quiet. If anything happens, remember
these numbers.'" Mrs. Hasz also recalled seeing a bumper
sticker on the car. She hadn't been able to make out the
words but she thought it had black letters on an orange
background.

At the murder trial Garry Anderson testified that earlier
that day, Thatcher had told him that he had been stalking his
former wife that week. By coincidence Anderson had
encountered Colin Thatcher at the Caron service station. He
was still living up north in La Ronge and had not seen Colin
for three or four months, not since Thatcher had handed over
the .357 Magnum and asked him to concoct a silencer.
"How's it feel to be unemployed?" Garry teased now. Thatcher
told him about his firing, and about how he and Grant
Devine had engaged in a shoving match during their last

showdown. Then he asked, "Have you still got that gun I gave you?" Anderson replied that it was at his mother's farm. The two men agreed to meet the next morning at the same place.

Neither man saw Sergeant Ken Hagerty of the Moose Jaw police force, who happened to be at the service station, and who noticed them talking.

Late that evening JoAnn Wilson telephoned Adelaide Weckman at her farm in Rouleau. The two old friends hadn't talked to each other for a month and it took three-quarters of an hour to catch up on all the news. JoAnn said that Stephanie had been sick with the flu and she had been up several times during the previous night looking after her. "Stephanie was so precious," said JoAnn. "She looked at me and said, 'Mommy, I'm sorry to keep you up.'" She added that Tony had caught the bug as well. JoAnn joked about Thatcher resigning as energy minister. "Tony said, well, now Colin will have another target besides me."

FRIDAY, JANUARY 21, 1983

At 10 a.m. Anderson and Thatcher met once again at the abandoned farm. Anderson testified, "He told me that he had been down [to Regina] the previous night but he did not get her, and then he asked me if I would be able to get him a car. . . . I said, yes, I could." The two men agreed to meet later on that afternoon.

Dressed in a black ski jacket, blue jeans, and sunglasses, Thatcher was walking down a street just west of Redland Avenue in Moose Jaw when Anderson picked him up in a souped-up 1974 Mercury that Garry owned. This was a heavy, powerful vehicle with a 400-cubic-inch V-8 engine. Anderson swore that at this point he handed over the Ruger Security-Six and a bag of ammunition. Thatcher told him that he was to listen to the news, and if he heard that something had happened to JoAnn he could collect his car three blocks west of Thatcher's Redland home. Then he let Anderson off in downtown Moose Jaw and drove away.

It was an extremely busy day for Shevawn Desrosiers and JoAnn Wilson. In recent months their Radius 2 company had taken off. "We were on a roll," says Desrosiers. "We were an unusual group. Two women, both very aggressive in business, and we worked very well together. We clicked. People liked, I think, working with us."

JoAnn had established the company in the fall of 1981 after Willson's had announced that it was closing down. She started small, on her own, but by August of 1982 she was in a position to hire Shevawn full-time. Desrosiers was a qualified designer and handled that end of the business; JoAnn was the coordinator and salesperson, and she was superb at it. Among other accomplishments, Radius 2 had designed the offices of a law firm, a physiotherapist, and a business equipment outfit, and they had also done a few private homes. By January they were thinking of hiring another full-time designer because they had more business than they could handle.

"JoAnn was a very demanding person at all times and sometimes I felt that she wasn't being fair," recalls Shevawn. "But it got so that I would say, look, there's only so many hours in the day. And she really respected me for that. . . . She very rarely gave you credit for anything. But when you did a really excellent job she would say, 'Thanks, you did really well. Take a couple of weeks' holiday, have a gas, you deserve it.' She was very demanding, but very honest and sincere." By January the two women had worked out their differences and had become the closest of friends.

At Willson's their desks had been situated close together behind a plate-glass window; after the shooting, Shevawn, who was very similar in stature to JoAnn, was always very nervous that an assailant might take a shot at either one of them. But Radius 2 was located in Telsec, a business centre that provided secretarial support and a telephone answering service. "JoAnn felt safer there," says Desrosiers. "Nobody could barge in on her. There was always somebody covering for her." Shevawn and other friends were amazed that JoAnn had recovered so well psychologically from the first shooting. "She was never actively nervous, never looking around, that sort of thing. You had to have guts to go out and do some of the things she did, just being in the public eye with somebody like that lurking around. She was very brave."

On this particular Friday, the two women were especially busy because after months of twelve-hour days, Shevawn was leaving for a two-week holiday in Mexico. On her return the Wilsons were to take off on their own vacation in Guadalajara, Mexico. Shevawn had not had a chance to say farewell to JoAnn when she left the office at twelve, so the two women kept phoning, and missing, each other all afternoon. They never did connect and one of the things that Shevawn deeply regrets about that fateful day is that she never had a chance to say goodbye to her good friend.

At the end of the day, JoAnn dropped into the office of Bowering, Charbonneau & Associates, an interior design firm. JoAnn had commissioned the company to do some work for her, and she wanted to show Daphne Bowering some furniture materials. The two women had become quite friendly in the course of doing business, and they chatted over a glass of wine for about an hour. "JoAnn was, and I am, something of a workaholic. We both enjoyed our work and we spent a lot of time discussing and planning it," says Bowering. She felt that under JoAnn's influence, Radius 2 was on its way to becoming a very successful business.

JoAnn seemed especially happy on this particular day. She had just received some tourist brochures about Mexico, and she excitedly told Daphne all about their projected trip south. She also boasted about the beautiful fur jacket that Tony had given her for Christmas, which reminded her that she should get home because her husband was sick with flu. The last time Daphne saw her, "she went bouncing out the door."

Marja Lahtinen, the housekeeper, was expecting JoAnn at any moment and kept glancing out the window into the winter night. Finally she saw the familiar blue Audi coming along 20th Avenue and she waved and went to put the finishing touches on the dinner table. After a while, she realized that it was taking JoAnn an awfully long time to come into the house, and she guessed that perhaps she had been grocery shopping. She was on her way to the back door to help carry the parcels when she heard a loud bang. Marja thought that her meat loaf, cooking in the microwave oven, had exploded, and she ran back to rescue it.

The light in the Wilsons' garage was dead and as JoAnn was getting out of her car, she could see only vague shapes.

Suddenly, looming out of the dark came a man. With one hand he seized her by the collar of her new fur jacket. In the other he clutched a heavy, sharp weapon with which he began to hack feverishly at her head and face. Again, and again, and again. Screaming, she desperately raised her arms to stave off the blows but they continued to rain down on her head and hands until the baby finger on her right hand was almost severed. Although blood was flowing, bones were being crushed with each blow, and bits of skin were flying from her face, JoAnn put up a superhuman fight. Indeed, she was inching her way towards the open garage door when her attacker, sensing that his prey was on the verge of escape, took out a gun and shot her through the head. She died instantly.

Craig Dotson and five other NDP staff members had been duplicating and collating three hundred copies of a speech Allan Blakeney was giving to a party meeting the next day. By 5:45 p.m. Dotson had decided that he had done his stint for that week. His house was situated on Regina Avenue, about six blocks away, and he usually walked home from the Legislature along 20th and down Retallack Avenue. Regina sidewalks are seldom cleared of snow in the winter, so, as usual, Dotson was proceeding down the middle of the road. As he neared the Wilson house, he noticed an Audi pulling into the garage. A few seconds later he reached Angus Street, the next intersection. Behind him he heard a loud shrill scream, which was repeated over and over. "There were small children in that neighbourhood. I thought I was hearing the cries of a child in some modest distress. I continued walking, paying no particular attention to it except that I was hearing this noise. And I walked another thirty or forty or fifty paces, at a normal walking pace. . . . I continued to hear these cries of a child in distress and the longer I heard them, the more concerned I became." Dotson finally concluded that the child must have been badly hurt in some way. So he turned around and went back towards the Wilson home. "The cries suddenly intensified with a single particularly loud, particularly shrill cry and then I heard a single large, sharp noise and then I heard nothing else."

As Dotson approached the lane that ran beside the Wilson residence, a man emerged from the garage. "The person did nothing to attract my attention. I didn't dwell on looking at this person." Then Dotson looked into the garage and saw a body on the floor. He ran back to the laneway to see if he could spot the man again, but saw no trace of him; he had vanished. He would later tell the police that he had seen the suspect for only a second, he was thirty or forty feet away, and it was dark.

Dotson then ran into the garage. JoAnn was lying face down, and her head and shoulders were just under the car so that he could not see the bloody mess the assailant had inflicted, something he is grateful for to this day. He knelt down and in a gesture of comfort placed his hand on her head. "Mrs. Wilson, Mrs. Wilson," he said softly. When he drew his hand away, it was covered with blood. He realized then that she was dead, and had probably been shot.

Suddenly Craig Dotson was desperate to involve other people, but he chose not to go directly to the Wilson residence. "I did not want to go into the home of someone and say that your wife or mother has just been shot. I wanted the police to take care of it." He ran to a house across the street, instead, but nobody answered his frantic knocking. Finally Dotson summoned up his courage and ran to the Wilsons' patio door. Marja answered and Craig yelled something about Mrs. Wilson being shot. The young woman hurried with him to the garage, took one horrified look and, sobbing loudly, ran to get Tony Wilson, who came running down the stairs dressed only in his bathrobe. Rushing out to the garage, he bent down to his wife for only a moment, and then rushed in to phone the police.

The two men came back again to the dark garage where JoAnn lay. Tony knelt down and spoke quietly to his wife. He then took her pulse, hoping for any sign of life. He stayed there beside her for so long in the bitter cold that Dotson took his parka off and placed it around the shoudlers of the grieving man. Finally they returned to the house and in a state of shock sat silently in the kitchen until the police arrived.

Constable Joe Fraser, the first officer on the scene, came at 6:05. He took one look at the body and radioed for help. In a few moments, the area was swarming with officers. Sergeant Bob Murton of the Regina police force's Criminal Investigation

Division, the senior officer on the site at that point, was overseeing the activity when Constable Tom Shuck approached him. "Look what I found, Sergeant." It was a Visa receipt that had once been folded in four but had sprung open when it had fallen. Shuck had discovered it lying on the ground about four feet from the garage. Murton could make out "W.C. THATCH"; the rest of the signature was illegible.

At about seven that evening, Adelaide Weckman was told by a friend that she had seen police cars around the Wilson residence. Right away Adelaide phoned Tony Wilson and said, "Is everything all right, Tony?" "No, it isn't, Adelaide, JoAnn is dead." When the Weckmans arrived half an hour later, Tony was sitting in the front room alone. Although he weas obviously in deep shock, and grieving, he had remained composed throughout the entire ugly scene, with the legendary British stiff upper lip coming to his assistance. His twenty-two-year-old son Alex was upstairs reading Stephanie a story, in an attempt to shield her somewhat from the full impact of the horror. Adelaide tiptoed upstairs to see the little girl. "The previous summer we had taken her in the boat to a spot on the lake where we explored and searched for pretty shells and rocks. She asked me that night, 'Could we go again to that little hideaway place at the lake?'" "Of course," Adelaide replied.

More friends gathered at the Wilsons', all in shock and all saying the same thing. "She should not have had to endure the turmoil of her divorce. She should not have suffered the pain of the first attempt on her life. She should not have died. She deserved nothing but happiness." And all in that room felt they knew beyond a shadow of a doubt who was responsible for the murder.

They were not alone in their assumptions. Justice M.A. MacPherson's wife was in Vancouver that evening, so he was alone in their stately Regina home when his brother Donald phoned him, terribly upset, to tell him of JoAnn's murder. MacPherson hadn't gone hunting in ten years but he found his old shotgun and put it together. Then he laid out four rounds of ammunition in the middle of the living-room carpet. "If he was going to come after me, I would go down fighting. It was that old army training."

Gerry Gerrand placed a club under the seat of his car.

SATURDAY, JANUARY 22, 1983

Immediately after the murder, Thatcher had asked Tony
Merchant about his legal status in regard to Stephanie and
the lawyer had advised him, says Thatcher, "that I had every
legal right to take Stephanie to Moose Jaw." Early the next
morning, the day after JoAnn was killed, Colin drove to
Regina and knocked on Wilson's door. Marja was politely
telling him that Stephanie was somewhere in the neighbourhood
when Tony Wilson appeared. Wilson was totally convinced
that Thatcher was responsible for his wife's death and he
angrily told him that he couldn't see the child, before slam-
ming the door in his face. Thatcher then went to Tony
Merchant's residence, only a block away.

Stephanie had gone to play with her school chum Kristin
Kohli, the daughter of freelance journalist Susan Swedburg-
Kohli. According to Susan, just before 1 p.m. Tony Mer-
chant's wife Pana came to her door. Pana, her neighbour and
friend, asked Susan if Stephanie was there, and added that
Thatcher was at her house. When the two women finished
talking, Susan went inside and was astonished to discover
Thatcher, Merchant, Greg, Sandra Hammond, and Lyle Stewart,
the president of the Thunder Creek Progressive Conservative
Association and Colin's friend, standing inside her back door.
Susan said that she had not heard them knocking, and the
doorbell had not rung. Susan is not sure whether Tony
Merchant said "We have come to see Stephanie" or "We have
come to take Stephanie," but she responded, "That's fine,
but you will have to step outside my house so I can make
the phone call over to Wilsons' to make sure that it's
okay."

According to Susan, Merchant then replied, "Well, forget
that, he won't give her to us anyway, you might just as well
give her to us right now." Susan is a small woman but she
stoutly insisted, "Will you please leave until I phone." Thatcher
kept saying, "I want to see my daughter. I have a right to see
my daughter." Stephanie had been playing with Kristin in the
child's bedroom but the two girls came out to see what the
fracas was all about. Hearing her father, however, Stephanie
fled back into the bedroom. Susan's husband, Dave Kohli,

had been out grocery shopping and when he came into the hallway into the middle of this astonishing scene, Susan handed him a card with the Wilsons' phone number on it and asked him to make the call at a neighbour's.

Then, Susan says, Thatcher stepped right into her hallway. "At that time I was no longer speaking in reasonable tones and I started to scream, 'Get out of my house, get out of my house!'" Despite her small size she tried to stop Thatcher, who was a foot taller and a hundred pounds heavier. "I began pushing at them, and there was a struggle and he [Thatcher] was knocking over the groceries that were on the floor, and there was a coffee pot that got spilled. I was screaming, and I believe at one point I grabbed at his belt buckle to stop him from going into our bedroom, and I think I ripped one of his belt loops." The struggle between Susan and Thatcher continued. "He by then had ripped open the bedroom door and Stephanie had jumped into my arms and was yelling, 'No, Dad, please don't do this.'" Then Greg became involved. "Let her go, she is my sister," he yelled. Stephanie was hanging onto Susan, her arms tightly around her neck; the woman held on to the child equally fiercely until in Susan's words, Greg began to "push and shove. He grabbed at my neck, grabbed at my wrists, so then I was compelled to let the girl go." Greg then carried the child out of the house without her winter clothes on, and the other invaders quickly followed.

Susan's neck, wrists, and elbows were sore for days after the confrontation, but that was not the only after-effect of the ugly scene. During the following week, the tires on her car were flat three times, which she thought was odd since she hadn't had one flat tire in the previous six years. For a much longer time, her phone rang late at night and when she answered there was nobody at the other end.

But there was something else, something more frightening, that happened to Susan shortly after her run-in with Thatcher and friends. She was working as an editor at the *Women's Guide*, and that publication ran photos of its employees. One day a letter arrived for Susan; someone had cut out her picture and neatly fitted it into a card. Below the picture were the words, "Susan Swedburg-Kohli—Such a lovely girl." "I didn't think too much of it," says Susan, "but then I showed it to a couple of my journalism friends. They kind of looked funny at each other and said, 'Well, do you know what this is? It looks like one of those memorial books that you get at funerals.'" Susan took it to the police.

Tony Merchant would later explain why he went to the Kohli house with Thatcher. "I was concerned that something illegal might happen, that somebody might throw a punch or do something. And so I wanted to be there both to stop that from happening and secondly to be a witness that the court would believe. I believed then, and still believe, that Colin legally had every entitlement to go and take the child and indeed to use a certain amount of violence to take the child if that was necessary."

At Thatcher's trial for murder, Merchant gave the following account of the incident. "We knocked on the door, rang the doorbell. I knocked on the door. Mrs. Kohli did not answer the door. Subsequently I came to know that she had pincurlers and was taking out her pincurlers. I thought she perhaps hadn't heard. We opened the door and shouted in through the door. There is a porch and we were inside the porch." Merchant claimed that he asked Susan if he could come in and she said yes.

His explanation infuriated Swedburg-Kohli. For one thing, she says she never wears "pincurlers," ever.

During his murder trial, Thatcher said he had snatched his daughter in that manner because "I was concerned about Stephanie's safety in getting her out of Regina and out of that house." What bothered Wilson about this statement was that the previous night, when the danger must surely have been greatest, Thatcher made no direct attempt by phoning him to ascertain the well-being of the little girl.

Tony Wilson had been called in the midst of the fracas. Terribly distraught and upset, he ran out of his house, but, perhaps fortunately, the group had left by the time he got to the Kohli house. He then contacted Gerry Gerrand, who set in motion the legalities necessary to retrieve Stephanie. Gerrand was able to point to JoAnn's will, which stated, "In the event of my death I appoint my husband, Anthony Wilson, the guardian of the person of my daughter Stephanie." A few hours later Chief Justice F.W. Johnson, of the Court of Queen's Bench, after an unusual Saturday-afternoon hearing, gave Wilson interim custody of the child.

Early that evening, Sergeant Wally Beaton, a rumpled

veteran of many criminal investigations, drove to Moose Jaw
to arrest Thatcher on abduction charges and to pick up
Stephanie. Beaton and Thatcher engaged in a slight argument
over whether the sergeant needed an actual warrant for his
arrest or not, but Colin was cooperative and polite. "He was
prepared to come with me as soon as I walked in and told
him why I was there and gave him the usual warning."
Beaton mentioned that Stephanie would have to go to the
Regina police station, and Thatcher balked at that. But after
he phoned Tony Merchant, he agreed to cooperate. He
wanted to drive his own car so he could return to Moose Jaw,
and the police obliged him. Beaton drove Stephanie and
Colin in Thatcher's station wagon, and the other police
officers accompanying Beaton drove the cruiser. "Sergeant
Beaton is a gentleman," Thatcher would later say. Throughout the entire transaction, the sergeant was surprised by
Stephanie's complete lack of emotion. "I don't recall her
shedding tears or anything like that. She didn't say anything
as to what she wanted to do." That evening she was returned
to Tony Wilson.

After Thatcher had been photographed and fingerprinted at
the Regina police station in connection with the pending
abduction charges, he was also asked to give a statement
indicating where he had been the previous evening. He told
police he had been eating dinner with Greg and Regan and
Sandra Hammond in his Redland home at the time of the
murder.

Significantly, he made no mention of Tony Merchant making a phone call the previous evening. He did say that he had
received threatening phone calls some months before and
suggested to the police that Tony Wilson's son Willie was
probably the perpetrator of the threats. This was not the first
time Thatcher had indicated that he thought Wilson's sons
were capable of violence—even the wounding or murder of
JoAnn. It was malicious gossip based on no facts whatsoever.
Thatcher also mentioned in his statement that a blue government Oldsmobile, signed out by him, had been parked in
front of his house since the previous Monday, January 17. The
police then showed him the Visa receipt found at the site. He
admitted that it was his, but said he had no idea how it had
got there.

Tony Merchant had also been arrested and brought to the police station that afternoon. Police noticed that the lawyer was unusually subdued and looked frightened. He had every reason to be; being found guilty of such a serious criminal charge could well mean the end of his legal career. However, neither Merchant nor Thatcher was formally charged at that time. New provisions of the Criminal Code dealing with the abduction of children under fourteen had come into effect just weeks before, and these stipulated that the consent of the attorney general must be obtained before police could lay charges. After four days of long debating sessions involving various prosecutors and other officials, Saskatchewan's attorney general, Gary Lane (Thatcher's old political ally), authorized the police to go ahead. Thatcher and Merchant were jointly charged with abduction and mischief.

Six weeks later Merchant ran into Inspector Ed Swayze, with whom he'd always enjoyed a good relationship. The lawyer told the police officer there was no way the abduction charges would hold up in court—and in this, Merchant would prove accurate—and he wondered why the charges had been pressed. Merchant says Swayze admitted that since the police had quickly linked Thatcher to JoAnn's murder, they had been "jumpy" the day after, and had decided that something had to be done about his child-snatching. Merchant says that since the murder and the abduction seemed to be linked, he told Swayze that if the abduction charges were dropped, he would ask Colin Thatcher to take a lie-detector test. He contacted Colin and several days later, Merchant claims, Thatcher agreed to undergo the test. Swayze, however, was not successful in convincing the Department of Justice to drop the charges. According to Merchant, the question of Thatcher's taking a lie detector test did not come up again.

When nobody had been arrested for the murder by Saturday evening, Craig Dotson became more and more nervous. While he hadn't recognized the man coming out of the Wilsons' garage, he thought that the suspect might have seen him, might even have known who he was. At about nine o'clock, after the three children had gone to bed, Craig's wife, Kathy, said that since it was such a lovely night she wanted to test her new cross-country skis. The Dotsons' backyard faced onto the Wascana Creek, where there were lit ski trails. "When she wasn't home by ten, I went to the back sunroom," recalls Craig. "No sign of her. Then I saw shadows under the bushes. Oh Jesus, I thought, that's her body. Then I told myself that's stupid. I looked out the front window, and across the street there were shadows under a bush from the streetlamp. That's where she's lying, she's dead, I thought. Again I said that's dumb. I went on that way for half an hour. I just got myself into a complete state." Then the phone rang and it was Kathy telling her husband that she was having coffee at a neighbour's. "I just about collapsed. That was the worst hour of my life," says Dotson.

SUNDAY, JANUARY 23, 1983

Garry Anderson had read of JoAnn's murder in the Saturday *Leader-Post;* according to his testimony, that story signalled to him that it was time to reclaim the car he had lent Thatcher. He borrowed a truck from a friend in Regina and then picked up his brother-in-law, who then drove that vehicle while Anderson dealt with the Mercury. In the passenger seat he found a black ski jacket, a pair of faded jeans, some grey socks, and sunglasses. On the floor of the car he discovered some silver change, a credit card receipt, and tufts of hair that looked as though they came from a wig. After he drove out to his mother's farm, he took all these items and burned them in a barrel behind her house. He then cleaned the mud off the licence plates and vacuumed and scrubbed the car inside and out.

TUESDAY, JANUARY 25, 1983

Tony Wilson read the scripture from the Book of Wisdom, Chapter Three—"The happiness of the just, and the unhappiness of the wicked." "In the sight of the unwise they seemed to die; and their departure was taken for misery. And their going away from us, for utter destruction; but they are in peace," he intoned, looking at JoAnn's open casket as he did so. About two hundred people, including the dead woman's parents and brother and sisters, were in attendance. Stephanie cried throughout. School friends had brought her flowers and a teddy bear, hoping the gifts would ease her pain. There was a contingent of JoAnn's good friends from Moose Jaw, but it did not include those people who had sided with Colin in the custody dispute over Regan. Conspicuous by their absence were JoAnn's former husband and mother-in-law, and her two sons. Thatcher had phoned Tony Wilson and asked if he could come. "He wanted special privileges. He wanted to come in the side door to avoid the media. I said, no, I don't even want you there. Then he asked if the boys could come. I said yes, as long as they don't come in the side door." Wilson didn't want the embarrassment of a grand entrance. Instead of going to his mother's funeral, Greg wrote a grade twelve algebra exam; he achieved high marks.

By the time of the reception afterwards Stephanie had recovered somewhat. "Little Stephanie was right in there, almost as though she really didn't know what had happened," recalls Betty Gooding. "She'd say, 'Can I get you a coffee?' She was so kind, passing things around just like she had stepped right into her mother's shoes. It was eerie, but you could just see JoAnn in her."

Later that day Thatcher received seven more red roses, courtesy of Joe Yablonski.

THURSDAY, JANUARY 27, 1983

At the Regina airport, a CKRM radio reporter accosted Thatcher, who told him that he was disgusted with innuendoes in recent news stories linking him with his ex-wife and therefore by association with her murder. "They're sensationalized crap," he said as he flew off to Palm Springs.

When he arrived in California, he phoned Tony Wilson in Regina and said he wanted to make arrangements regarding access to Stephanie. Tony replied, "There is no way I am going to discuss this with the person who arranged for my wife's murder." Thatcher did not deny, nor did he confirm, the shocking accusation. Nor did he know that the conversation had been taped with equipment supplied by the Regina police.

According to Lynne Dally's testimony, when Thatcher walked into the condominium, she shook her head and said, "Well, you really did it, didn't you?" Although he scowled and pointed to the walls and ceiling, indicating to Lynne that wire-tap bugs might be installed there, Thatcher nodded yes. She was not surprised because for many weeks she had known that Colin was planning to kill his ex-wife.

While Colin had been in Palm Springs during Christmas of 1982, he had told Lynne he wanted to establish a nightly phone-call routine. She was to be available for phone calls in late afternoon, around supper, and later in the evening. Either one would call the other. "I assume he was establishing that he was at home certain times in the evening. He was going in [to Regina] every night to see if he could find an opportune time when JoAnn would be available."

According to Lynne, on the day of the killing, Colin phoned and said, "Well, I'm going now. This might be the night, stick around." Later he called and said, "Oh, my God, I've just been called. Apparently JoAnn has been shot in her home and has been killed." "I understood this to mean that Colin had gone in to Regina and was instrumental in that [her death]," Lynne Dally later told a court.

She could not remember exactly when these phone calls were made. Telephone records later disclosed that there were five calls made from Palm Springs to Moose Jaw or Moose Jaw to Palm Springs that day. One of these was placed at 6:24 p.m.

The first or second evening after Thatcher arrived in Palm Springs, Peggy Thatcher and her friend Bev came over to visit Lynne and Colin. They all read the account of the murder in the *Desert Sun*, the Palm Springs paper, which mentioned that JoAnn had been beaten as well as shot. Lynne told the court that a little later when she and Colin were alone, he said to her, "I don't know why they said she was beaten. I didn't beat her." "Now I don't know whether that was for my benefit or not, I don't know," Lynne said. Later while they were driving, a contemplative Colin said to her, "I have to admit it is a strange feeling to have blown your wife away."

As a result of JoAnn's death, Thatcher's financial problems eased somewhat. Under the matrimonial property agreement, he did not have to make the $87,500 payment on February 1. Under the terms of JoAnn's will, Stephanie was left a special bequest of $100,000 off the top. Of the remaining amount, 65 percent also went to Stephanie, 25 percent to Tony Wilson and 10 percent to Harlan and Elizabeth Geiger.

Thatcher was determined to win permanent custody of his daughter. On February 4, 1983, he signed an eight-page affidavit, which outlined in glowing terms his affection for his child. "My relationship with Stephanie was never affected by the disputes with my former wife...," he wrote. He also painted a cheerful picture of his encounters with JoAnn and Tony. "My relationship with my former wife had calmed and the necessary interchanges with her and with her husband prior to her death were as relaxed as they had ever been since the separation. At Christmas [1982] when I called to speak with Stephanie, JoAnn and I had the first amiable conversation we had had for a long time. My dealings with Mr. Wilson had always been good and they were getting better."

For once the law was on Thatcher's side; it stated quite clearly that as the natural father he would probably be awarded custody of Stephanie over Wilson, unless it could be proved that he was a totally unfit parent. Gerrand decided that drastic action was necessary. On February 21, 1983, Tony Wilson signed an affidavit that, in effect, accused Colin Thatcher of murdering JoAnn. It outlined the threats Colin had made to the Wilsons over a period of two years and suggested that Thatcher's motive for the killing was the moratorium on the $87,500 payment that would have been due February 1. It was an astounding document (although not so astonishing in retrospect), and the media, including the national press, seized on it, demonstrating that JoAnn's murder was now a huge national story.

Thatcher, of course, denied Wilson's accusations.

Shortly after this Mr. Justice MacPherson paid a friendly visit to Gerry Gerrand in his office. He suggested to the lawyer that he was now too emotionally involved in the case and that his judgment was being impaired as a result. While MacPherson waited in the library, Gerrand phoned Wilson and made an appointment with him for that afternoon. Then he told Wilson that he could no longer act effectively for him and suggested he retain Gordon Kuski, a Regina lawyer who was highly regarded in the legal community. It was an unhappy end to the most bitter and frustrating legal battle Gerry Gerrand had ever experienced.

* * *

After the murder, police officers had moved right into the Wilson home. They escorted Stephanie back and forth to school every day, and their very presence reminded the little girl, and everybody else, of the terrible tragedy. Tony Wilson decided that they needed to get away from Regina. At the end of February, he arranged a five-week trip to Japan for Stephanie, Marja, and himself.

Marja now played a very important role in Stephanie's life. A striking blonde-haired, blue-eyed immigrant from Finland, she had just turned twenty. She had tried to shield Stephanie from the bitterness of her parents' dreadful marital battles, but found that the child already seemed to have a strange sense of reality. One evening about five months after JoAnn had been shot the first time, Stephanie and Marja were watching *Dallas* on television. It was one of the soap opera's usual complicated, dramatic plots, this one involving J.R. Ewing's attempt to kidnap his own son. "Stephanie turned to me," Marja recalls, "and said of J.R., 'Is he the good guy or the bad guy?' I answered, 'He's an extremely bad guy. He's kidnapping the kid.' Stephanie said, 'No, you're wrong. I'm sure he's a good guy.' At that point she didn't know what was good or what was bad."

On the morning of their departure for Japan, Marja had to struggle to get the child ready. "She was scared to go. She was only eight, and with all the hassle with the police and everything, home life had been really weird." She was very upset and even after they boarded the plane she was still crying, so a stewardess gave her a colouring book. On the first page was a line that read, "This Book Belongs To" and then a blank line. The little girl wrote "Stephanie Wilson NOT Thatcher" and then underlined the word "NOT" many times.

When they returned from Japan, Tony's lawyer, Gordon Kuski, informed him that his chances of winning permanent custody of Stephanie were slim to non-existent. Kuski suggested that he work out an arrangement with Thatcher that would give him liberal access to the child. On May 5, 1983, Wilson signed an agreement giving Thatcher interim custody of Stephanie, and on November 25, a final settlement was completed. Wilson was to get Stephanie every second weekend, fourteen days in the summer holidays, and six at Easter school break, as well as reasonable telephone access to her. As time went by, Thatcher paid no more attention to this agreement than he had to any other legally binding obligation.

In July of 1983, the child moved back to Moose Jaw, changing her name from Stephanie Wilson to Stephanie Thatcher.

CHAPTER EIGHTEEN
CRACKING THE CASE

JANUARY 21, 1983

Although both had undergone the metamorphosis from naive farm boy to tough cop, the two sergeants were a study in contrasts. Bob Murton was a burly, open-faced, teddy bear of a man with a wide, boyish smile. He had walked the beat, handed out parking tickets, and escorted funerals for the Regina city police, until his dream finally came true and he ended up working full-time as a detective in the Criminal Investigation Division. His partner, a wiry, tense man who looked more like a croupier than a cop, had also worked his way up through the force. After eight years of investigating major crimes, murders, and armed robberies, Jim Street had developed a heavy dose of cynicism, one of the occupational hazards of constantly meeting the underworld.

At 6 p.m., the two partners were just sitting down to eat their supper in the police station's cafeteria when the dispatcher ran in with the news that there had been a shooting at the Wilson residence. Both men realized the significance of the Wilson name, and the connection to Colin Thatcher, and the news sent both Street and Murton racing out the door, their meal forgotten. They reached the Wilson residence in less than five minutes.

Street took one look at the mutilated body on the garage floor and realized that the seriousness of the crime, combined with the prominence of the victim, made this an especially sensitive case. Systematically he began to telephone his way through the police hierarchy, informing everyone up to the chief of police of what had occurred. He also lost no time in telling the Regina dispatcher to ask the Moose Jaw police to maintain a surveillance of Thatcher's Redland home.

It did not take investigators very long to conclude that Colin Thatcher had probably committed the crime in person. There were enough clues pointing in his direction. First of all, the terrible damage inflicted on the victim indicated that it was a savagely vindictive act perpetrated by somebody who hated JoAnn deeply. "If you had full intentions of walking in and shooting somebody, it's my opinion in investigating these things, that you go in and shoot them," says Murton. "You might shove them back or something if they try and get the gun, but you would shoot them. If you're going to beat them up and kill them that way, then you beat them up. You wouldn't do both unless you had a real grudge and you wanted to inflict real pain on that person." Very few hit men would take the time to murder their victim twice, the cops concluded.

(Saskatchewan-born novelist W.O. Mitchell provides interesting corroboration of this theory. In 1981, researching a scene for his novel *How I Spent My Summer Holidays*, he consulted an eminent American police pathologist, a doctor who had studied scores of murder victims. Mitchell wanted to know how an estranged husband would kill his attractive-looking wife. The pathologist advised him that in most such cases the murder would involve numerous frenzied blows to the head and face. Bella Motherwell died that way at the hands of her husband in Mitchell's 1981 novel. JoAnn Wilson's very similar death a year or so later eerily reminded Mitchell of the pathologist's theory.)

The police were also struck by the fact that the body was positioned at the rear of the bloodied cars parked front first in the Wilson garage. When Al Lyon, the lanky CID staff sergeant, arrived at the scene at 6:20, he noted the potential significance of the body's position. "You could see that she had got out of the driver's door and there had been quite a struggle, and when she was actually shot she was down behind her car, so she was almost out of the garage. She was putting up an awful struggle, I would imagine the adrenalin must have been pumping pretty bad. It may have been that the gun was never intended to be used, except as a last resort."

Garry Anderson would eventually reveal to the police, and to the court, that Thatcher had told him that he had been stalking his wife for a week, looking for an opportune moment to kill her. It was simply a coincidence that Thatcher ran into Garry the day before the murder; from that chance meeting came Garry's return of the gun to Thatcher, which made it a further coincidence that Thatcher happened to have the gun on him the night of the murder. The police surmised that Thatcher had been prepared to kill his wife by hacking her to death (and indeed JoAnn would probably have died from the extensive injuries to her head) but since the gun was available he finished off the job with it when he ran into unexpected difficulties.

Another piece of evidence that immediately pointed to Thatcher was his "calling card," in the incriminating shape of a Visa receipt found on top of the freshly fallen snow about four feet from the garage. There was a brisk wind that night and police surmised that the receipt must have dropped out of the assailant's pocket as he was pulling out his weapon at the garage door, but that it had then blown up against a clump of snow where it was found. The theory that the murderer had somehow acquired Thatcher's receipt and then planted it there to incriminate him did not make sense. "If someone was going to plant it, they would plant it close to the body [in the garage], because then you'd know it wouldn't blow away," says Murton. That evening Murton and another veteran investigator with CID, Gene Stusek, drove out to the J & M Shell station at Caronport. They were able to confirm that Colin Thatcher had indeed signed the Visa slip; he had used it to buy $29 worth of gas on January 18, three days before. He had, ironically, almost driven off without picking up his receipt.

The detectives placed appropriate importance on Craig Dotson's description of the suspect. He was taken to the police station, where he wrote out a statement and worked with a police artist to create a drawing that he felt was as close to the man he saw walking out of the garage as he could remember. He described a man approximately thirty years old, five-foot-nine to five-foot-eleven, medium to slim build, dark brown or black beard, collar-length straight hair, wearing a black jacket, three-quarter length, not bulky, with a button front and dark pants. The drawing illustrated the suspect with and without a beard. Without a beard, he had a long oval face with a long, narrow nose and looked nothing like Colin Thatcher—except for one feature. Dotson had described dark glowering eyes. Some investigators concluded that Thatcher had used the oldest trick in the book—he had donned a disguise. Still, because of Dotson's description, the police could not rule out a hitman, or someone totally unconnected to Thatcher, as the person who had committed the murder.

Inspector Ed Swayze, the burly, affable cop in charge of CID, was having a drink with some colleagues from Saskatoon at the Diplomat restaurant when he got an urgent call. Sergeant Street's telephoning was getting results fast, and it was only 6:25 when Swayze arrived at the murder scene. He was not entirely pleased by what he found. To start with, he was concerned by the number of police officers roaming around the site. "I don't like crime scenes cluttered up with people," Swayze says. "The less people you have there the better. I can't think of anything that was lost, but nevertheless I'm a stickler when it comes to managing a crime scene." He had noticed, for example, that the back lane behind the house wasn't protected, and he immediately ordered a police officer stationed there to stop anyone from using it. In fact, this precaution was too late; it had already been violated. A set of narrow automobile tracks belonging to a front-wheel drive were found. They ran from the edge of the Wilson garage, into the lane, then backed into a neighbouring yard, where they spun out and then ran north. The police thought that they might belong to the getaway car and so the tracks were carefully measured and photographed. Later investigators discovered that neighbours in the area had come out of their garage shortly after the murder; unaware that the area had been cordoned off by police, they had driven down the lane to the Wilson house, where they were stopped. The car then backed up in some deep snow, where it accelerated and then headed straight north.

Another potentially vital piece of evidence was a footprint of a running shoe found between the garage and the sidewalk. It also was photographed and measured with great care. For the longest time police searched for a size ten shoe, even as far away as Palm Springs. Eventually, however, they concluded that it belonged to a man in a Volkswagen who had driven into the lane, opened his car door, and stepped out for an instant. Then, perhaps seeing all the commotion, he had simply driven away.

Constable Bing Forbes and his police dog Chico were brought onto the scene in an attempt to pick up the assailant's scent. "In actual police work, people don't usually leave articles of clothing lying around, so the dogs are trained to pick up the freshest scent in a given area. A dog will also readily react to a fear scent, or the guilt scent, the mark that an involved person leaves." But there were so many people on the scene when he arrived that the dog had difficulty. To make things worse, it was cold and snowy so that any scent would readily disperse. Chico did, however, eventually sniff out a track that went north down the back lane to the rear of the second house which faced on to Angus Street. At that point the dog lost the scent. The police felt that the assailant had probably continued through that backyard to a getaway car on Angus, the street west of the Wilsons'. They had hoped that the dog would track down either or both of the murder weapons that had been used, or something else the assailant had dropped, but despite constant forays up and down the snowbanks Constable Forbes and Chico had no luck.

That night, of course, the area was searched for the murder weapons as thoroughly as possible in the dark. And the next day Sergeant Gene Stusek combed the surrounding area with a metal detector. He found nothing. For months after the murder the investigators continued to hunt for that gun; it became a kind of mirage hanging over the prairie flatlands. "I walked from here to Pense [a village thirty kilometres away] a couple of times and searched every bridge, culvert, weed, bush for days," says Sergeant Street. The gun was never found. The police never did determine conclusively what the other weapon was, and they never found any instrument that they thought might have been used.

On the evening of the murder, police quickly began knocking on doors in the neighbourhood. Sergeant Street interviewed someone who said he saw two people in the Wilson garage at about 6 p.m. Asked for a description, he volunteered a quick sketch. It proved to be the spitting image of Craig Dotson. A few weeks later, Dotson was in the police station when one of the investigators asked, with a straight face, if he would like to see the chief suspect. When Dotson was then shown the sketch of himself, he was furious that the police apparently had nothing better to do with their time than make fun of him by drawing funny pictures. He was somewhat appeased when he discovered it had been the work of an eyewitness trying to be helpful.

That night the police also found an eleven-year-old boy who had been delivering papers in the neighbourhood at the time of the murder. He remembered seeing a two-door, pea-green Chrysler Cordoba with a dark-green vinyl roof parked in the nearby 28 block on Angus. The police had assumed that the assailant had run out of the garage, gone down the back alley a short way, cut through the second backyard, and jumped into a getaway car parked on Angus. A wanted poster that was released to the public included the boy's description of the car he had seen in the area prior to the murder. Later, investigators came to believe that the child may have been confused. They found a woman who had been delivering Mary Kay cosmetics in the 29 block, one block south, with a car that precisely accorded with the boy's description. As well, in the first week of February, the child underwent a session with Sergeant Tom Barrow of the Calgary police force, who is an expert on memory recall. At that point, he remembered different details. From his description of the shape of the car, the police eventually concluded that he was talking about not a Chrysler but a Ford product, very much like Anderson's 1974 Mercury. He also described big, full-disc hub caps, exactly like the Mercury's.

During that evening the police knocked on the door of Duane Adams, and he told them how he and his housekeeper Joan Hasz had worried over the mysterious man in the blue Buick. Mrs. Hasz was contacted and she revealed that she had written down the number 292 from the licence plates. Now that a murder had occurred and her worst nightmares had been confirmed, Mrs. Hasz was upset—she had wanted to call the police but Duane Adams had discouraged her. His motives speak volumes about Saskatchewan politics. Adams was an able and dedicated career civil servant with the provincial government, and under the NDP had served as deputy minister of social services. When the Conservatives came to power in the spring of 1982, they fired hundreds of senior bureaucrats who were thought to have NDP sympathies, although very few of these people had been political appointees and many had no visible political affiliation at all. The purge caused great panic and fear in the civil service (which was hardly abated to this day). Adams quickly discovered that he was among those frowned on by the new government—eventually he left to take a senior post with the federal government. But at the time of the murder he was still employed by the Saskatchewan government and feeling vulnerable; so vulnerable, in fact, that he assumed that the mystery man in the car was spying on him, watching his comings and goings, and those of his friends, and reporting them to his Tory bosses. Because of this feeling of paranoia, Adams did not call the police. Some of the investigating officers were disturbed after they talked with Hasz and Adams. They felt that JoAnn Wilson's life might have been saved if they had been told earlier about the mysterious stalker.

For hours that night, police searched the city's airport, railway station, and bus depot, and they stopped cars travelling out of Regina. They were looking for someone who answered the description provided by Dotson, Adams, and Hasz. When by the wee hours of the morning no suspect had been found, Inspector Ed Swayze—aware of how quickly a murder trail grows cold—knew that it would not be an easy case to crack. But he had no idea how long and difficult the investigation would be, what a jigsaw puzzle of a thousand pieces it would prove, and how it would consume his life for fifteen long months—until an arrest could be made, and thousands of jeering tongues silenced.

A handsome man in a heavy-set owlish way, Swayze, at forty-two, was thoroughly liked by his subordinates, mainly because he never forgot what it was like to be an ordinary cop on the beat. "I always think that if you remember where you came from, you can't go too far wrong." He had joined the Regina police force when he was twenty, only a year out of high school, and he had walked a beat for five of the twenty-two years he had been a cop. The police force at that time was a military-like establishment with arbitrary, punitive rules, and Swayze was always in trouble. "In those days I was charged all the time for being off my beat, in other words having a coffee, walking my beat not according to the beat book, insubordination, idling, and gossiping. I stopped and talked to a retired detective one time and I was charged for that." Being charged with these offences often resulted in the loss of two or three days' pay. "When I started, policemen were really unjustly treated. They really were," recalls Swayze, and this sense of injustice was one reason why he became heavily involved in police associations. In 1972 he was elected president of the Saskatchewan Police Federation, an office he held for nine years. It was through that organization—and the local police association, which initiated a grievance procedure—that the policeman's lot improved vastly over the years. His activism was one of the reasons Swayze was so popular with the rank and file. And it did not hinder his career, not at all.

In March, 1968, he was sent to the Criminal Investigation Division. Over the years he would be transferred out of the unit to other duties, but invariably he was ordered back. "I guess they figured that there's not much point driving a square peg into a round hole or vice versa," he says. In truth, the authorities could not fail to recognize what a sharp investigator Swayze was. In 1972, he and his partner Wally Beaton were two of six people, Jim Street included, who formed a new major crime unit responsible for handling armed robberies and homicides. It was an amazing group of police officers. "One team would go as hard as they could for as long as they could—fourteen, sixteen, eighteen hours was not unusual. Then, about two or three hours before you totally exhausted yourself, the other team would come in and pick up. Our unit probably had the best record of any place in Canada."

In 1969 Regina was suffering an epidemic of armed robberies. A group of crack police officers, which civil libertarians would label the vigilante squad, was formed to combat the crime wave. Swayze was one of these and, as always, was a tough, no-nonsense cop. Along with three other police officers, he was once charged, on information provided by the RCMP, with assaulting a member of the Apollo motorcycle gang. Swayze claimed that, first, he wasn't even there when the supposed assault took place and, second, the victim of the supposed assault worked for him as an informer. The charges were thrown out of court, but the incident was played up in the media and bothered Swayze. "Those were tough times. We had death threats on us. There were all kinds of things that came about which were really hard on our families." It did not seem to hurt his career, however, because in 1973 he was made a sergeant and in 1980 he was made staff sergeant. In 1981 he became inspector and by 1983 he was in charge of the CID unit. (In 1984 he was named deputy chief.) A dapper man who indulged in ultra-suede jackets and a Mercedes-Benz, much as his prey Colin Thatcher did, Swayze might be gregarious and personable but he was also a deadly serious, dedicated investigator. The JoAnn Wilson murder became the ultimate challenge for him. As each month slipped by without an arrest, he became ever more determined to crack the case. And he was indefatigable.

The day after the murder, valuable manpower was siphoned off the investigation to deal with the astonishing matter of Stephanie's forcible removal from her friend's home. After Thatcher had been brought to the Regina police station and had given a statement about his whereabouts at the time of the murder, the investigators noticed something unusual about his alibi for that night. Thatcher stated that after he learned of JoAnn's death at about 7 p.m., he went out jogging. Police thought this was an odd thing to do after a wife of seventeen years had just been killed. The story seemed even odder when they learned from the Moose Jaw police, who had watched the Redland home from about 6:30 p.m. on, that Thatcher had not left the premises all evening. According to Garry Anderson, Thatcher told him he would leave the Mercury some four blocks away from the Redland house. Police surmised that Thatcher mentioned jogging to cover the possibility that someone might have seen him running from the car to his residence. Naturally the timing would be slightly off, but then most people tend not to remember precisely when they see someone jogging down their street.

The terrible damage done to the murder victim, the Visa receipt found at the scene, and the fact that the police felt he had lied about his activities that night made Colin Thatcher the prime suspect. And Thatcher remained the prime suspect in the investigation for the entire fifteen months until he was finally arrested. The arrest came as a complete surprise to him. He had no idea that the police, whom he considered a stupid lot and no match for his talents, had been circling closer and closer.

Mrs. Hasz had provided an invaluable clue by jotting down 292 from the muddy licence plate on the mystery car. On Saturday the police found a 1980 dark-blue Oldsmobile parked outside Thatcher's Redland home. Its licence plate was half covered with mud, but three numbers were visible. They read 292. There was also a black-and-orange bumper sticker on the rear bumper. The car was quickly traced to the Central Vehicle Agency, the Saskatchewan government's Supply and Services Branch. It had been signed out by Thatcher on January 10, 1983, before he had been fired from the cabinet. Still the investigators felt they could not say with certainty that it was this car that Mrs. Hasz and Duane Adams had seen. Every vehicle in Saskatchewan with licence number ending in 292 was checked by the police. And there were thousands of them. Not one other car matched Hasz's and Adams's descriptions. When the Oldsmobile was returned to Regina, the two witnesses were able to pick it out in a parking lot filled with twenty cars.

The police knew right away, however, that this was not the getaway car used on the night of the murder. There was some snow lying on it, which indicated that it had not been moved for a day or so. Thatcher's neighbors confirmed that they had seen it parked there at the time of the shooting. "In Garry Anderson's statement, it came out that he [Thatcher] felt that his car got burnt, that his car was hot, so he needed Garry's car," says Sergeant Murton. In Murton's opinion, "he had been seen the day before, when Mrs. Hasz wrote the license number down, so he was scared to use his [government] car."

On January 25, the police released a composite drawing based on Dotson's impressions of the killer, as well as descriptions of the Oldsmobile and the Cordoba that the paper-boy had seen. The public was also notified that a $50,000 reward would be given for "information leading to the arrest and conviction of the person or persons responsible for the murder of JoAnn Kay Wilson." The police commission had posted the reward and several senior police officers were angry at their decision. "It's something you do when you are backed into a corner, not when you're starting out an investigation," said one. They still feel that the reward did not help the investigation at all—the chief players would have had to talk in the end—and in court Allbright, of course, could imply in his defence of Thatcher that many of the witnesses were only testifying because of the money.

On February 10, a second updated circular was released. By this time, Mrs. Hasz and Duane Adams had added their impressions and the sketch was quite different. The suspect now had jet-black hair and a neatly trimmed beard. Indeed, he looked remarkably like Garry Anderson.

Sergeant Wally Beaton's job on the night of the murder had been to man the telephones. "We had to notify other police departments and then, of course, the phones started ringing and everybody's gonna tell us what happened. It got to be quite a nuisance talking to them," says Beaton. The phones continued to ring. A large number of people with beards were reported as looking like the wanted poster and the police had to check all of them out. "Some of them looked pretty good until we were able to eliminate them," says Swayze. One they did not eliminate was Garry Anderson. An anonymous phone call to the CID unit revealed that he had had something to do with the murder.

Anderson was about to board a bus in Moose Jaw to return to La Ronge when Sergeants Beaton and Stusek picked him up. They brought him to Regina for questioning, specifically about where he had been the night of the murder. Garry told them that on the afternoon of January 21, he went to the dentist and then got a haircut. At about 6 p.m. he visited Glen Crockett, a friend of his, for about twenty minutes and after that he went to a Moose Jaw hotel named the Grant Hall, where he had supper and chatted with two women friends. He gave police this information in great detail, but chose not to mention a word about his involvement with Thatcher. The police released him after about an hour. They then carefully checked out his alibi and satisfied themselves that he was telling the truth.

Yet they remained suspicious of him. For one thing they were professionals, and they thought his story just a little too pat. Bob Murton recalls that the alibi was a bit too detailed. "He went and talked to everybody and probably said, 'Hey, look, it's six o'clock. I'm here.' There were too many people whom he'd seen, and talked to, and had supper with." And since Anderson was considered something of a character around Moose Jaw, people remembered him, confirming the alibi. But the police did not like him or his story. "He was not a nice person to deal with even from the beginning," said one investigator. The police felt he might be hiding something and they began to ask questions to find out all they could about Garry Anderson and the people he knew.

In the early stages of the investigation, there were about twenty-eight police officers involved. The man who kept track of their daily activities was CID Staff Sergeant Al Lyon. After twenty-seven years with the Regina police department he was on the point of retiring, and the Thatcher affair would be his last big fling. Tall and thin, with a lined face, Al Lyon looked like the stereotype of the slow-moving farmer. In fact he had one of the sharpest minds on the force. With the help of a continuously updated flow chart, which he kept in his Regina office drawer, he methodically pieced together the mosaic of detail as it began to accumulate in the case.

Among the most interesting facts uncovered were Thatcher's long-distance telephone records, which the CID investigators acquired as soon as possible. They discovered a large number of calls placed to or from the Palm Springs condominium, including one at 6:24 on the night of the murder. Further conversations with people in Moose Jaw revealed that Thatcher had a live-in girlfriend in Palm Springs by the name of Lynne Dally. It was soft-spoken, avuncular Wally Beaton, a twenty-four-year veteran with the Regina police force, who was sent to Palm Springs in March of 1983 to speak with Lynne.

Beaton discovered that because she was "scared," Lynne Dally had moved out of Thatcher's condominium after he had left in January, and had moved in with her parents. Accompanied by a Palm Springs policeman named Mike Hall, Beaton arranged to meet with Lynne in an office at the Oasis Sheraton. But Dally's father was a solicitor and, realizing the possible consequences of her involvement in the case, he did not encourage her participation; at that meeting she said she knew nothing. Five minutes after they left, Lynne says, she changed her mind. "I had something to say and I figured I should say it." When she phoned Hall, he dryly said, "We were wondering when you were going to tell the truth." The two policemen interviewed her again and this time Lynne agreed to give a statement. At this point, however, she did not admit that Thatcher had told her directly that he had shot his wife in the shoulder and then murdered her. She did volunteer that he had bought a gun in Palm Springs and that in the summer of 1982, he had wrapped it in the *Los Angeles Times* newspaper, placed it in a box that had once contained a toy shower for a doll, and packed it in his suitcase when he was returning to Canada. Tony Wilson was asked to find out from Stephanie if she had ever received a "Cindy Shower" for a Christmas present. The little girl remembered that she had— the last time she was in Palm Springs for Christmas.

Beaton had not been overly impressed with Dally; he described her as a little strange. But in Regina Ed Swayze realized what an important witness she could eventually prove to be. "I talked to her on the phone at least once every week. I tried to keep some line of communication open, see that there was nothing bothering her, see if she remembered anything about certain evidence." This diligence would later prove to be invaluable.

Armed with the information provided by Lynne, the Palm Springs police began searching the records of the gun stores in the area. It was not long before they discovered that Thatcher had indeed bought a Ruger Security-Six .357 Magnum and two boxes of silver-tip, Winchester-Western hollow-point bullets in January, 1982.

After the remains of the bullet had been retrieved from JoAnn's skull during the autopsy, they were given to Staff Sergeant Arnold Somers, a forensic expert with the RCMP. The bullet had fragmented to such an extent that Somers had difficulty stating with absolute certainty what type of bullet and gun were used. In a report released on March 25, 1983, he felt able to conclude, however, the bullets were encased in an aluminum jacket, reporting that "Winchester were, or are, the only people who have used an aluminum jacket in this type of bullet." The fragments, Sergeant Somers concluded, were probably from a hollow-point bullet. "I was satisfied that it was the kind of bullets Thatcher bought in Palm Springs," says Swayze, "and that these bullets were not readily available in Canada." The availability of the bullets would become something of an issue at Thatcher's trial.

The police continued to talk to anybody they thought could give them even the smallest, most obscure, piece of information. One of the most distasteful and unfortunate trends that emerged from these conversations was the pervasive, malicious gossip that was spreading about JoAnn Wilson. Some investigators were shocked when people told them with great certainty that JoAnn had indulged in affairs with hundreds of men; that she was a drug addict; that she had neglected and beaten her children. "JoAnn was nothing but a tramp," was a comment the police heard over and over. A persistent rumour was that Radius 2 was a front for an escort service, that JoAnn was a madam and Shevawn Desrosiers the chief prostitute. Thatcher had initiated much of this gossip himself, but it had spread like sinister fog, particularly over Regina and Moose Jaw. It was a sad and unfair epitaph for a woman who had been so brave and, in many ways, so honourable.

As police traced the network of Thatcher's friends and acquaintances, like some strange personal grid map, they were astonished at the number of women—either friends or lovers, but mostly the latter—who had been involved with him. After listening to wiretaps on his phone they were staggered, first by the stories he made up to aggrandize himself, and second, by the number of gullible women all over the North American continent whom he frequently contacted and who believed his tales.

Thatcher had told a number of his former lovers and friends—a nurse, a real estate agent, a clothing store owner, and even a former page in the Saskatchewan legislature—bits and pieces of information about the wounding or the killing. After the police had discovered these details, the Crown attorney, Serge Kujawa, considered calling at least one of them as a witness at the trial, but the young woman was so terrified of Thatcher that he refrained from doing so.

Among the people the Regina investigators interviewed were Thatcher's colleagues and employees at the Legislative Buildings. "It was funny because people in the Legislature were rather evasive," says Sergeant Street. "Rather evasive" was in fact a euphemism that Street quickly discarded. "They were scared shitless to talk to us because they figured they'd get into trouble."

This lack of cooperation from Thatcher's political colleagues was one of the reasons Regina police did not send someone to talk with Dick Collver, even though they had heard through the grapevine that he had some knowledge of Thatcher's attempts to hire a hit man. Crown prosecutor Serge Kujawa understands their reluctance to pursue that distant lead.

"Collver's way out there in Wickenberg [Arizona], and the police have talked to a whole lot of other people here in the party, and we are reasonably sure they know something along the same lines, and they just got rebuffed and mistreated—and not even politely treated. They [the politicians] are not going to risk their little careers on something like this." Kujawa says he is "pretty sure" that two of the people who failed to cooperate with the police are now cabinet ministers in the Saskatchewan government.

By way of confirmation of this theory, the police learned that at a Conservative caucus meeting in Prince Albert, around the time of the 1982 election, Thatcher was overheard to ask, "Why do I have to pay the $819,000 divorce settlement when a bullet only costs a dollar?"

The police did, however, received some cooperation from people who had worked with Colin Thatcher. Vonda Croissant, Thatcher's former secretary, revealed that she had noticed a gun holster that had been brought into the office by Thatcher's executive assistant, Chuck Guillaume. In turn police questioned Guillaume, who told them that in October, 1982, he had found a holster under the front seat of a car that Thatcher had signed out of the government's Central Vehicle Agency; Guillaume had been asked by Thatcher to drive the car from Moose Jaw to Regina. When he showed his boss the holster he had found, Thatcher said, "Oh, really?" "He seemed very unconcerned," his assistant reported. The police retrieved the holster and later showed it to Ron Williams, the gun dealer in Palm Springs. He identified it as a 5 BHL holster manufactured by the Bianchi Leather Company of California, and confirmed that he had sold Colin Thatcher one exactly like it.

Naturally, with the $50,000 reward as a lure, all sorts of people came forward with information, some of it very strange indeed. One story that Ed Swayze initially took very seriously was told by Eddie Johnson, a Regina underworld figure. Johnson claimed that before JoAnn was shot the first time, a dinner meeting had been held at Golf's Steak House attended by himself, Colin Thatcher, and two others. The subject of polite dinner-table conversation was finding a hit man to murder Thatcher's former wife. Johnson took and passed a lie-detector test on his story, but the others flatly denied that they had attended any such meeting, and Swayze discarded the story.

* * *

Meanwhile the Regina investigators were continuing their extensive interviewing, concentrating particularly, of course, on the Moose Jaw and Caron area. They were bound to come across Blaine Mathieson sooner or later. Blaine had been Sandra Hammond's steady boyfriend for about two years, until he went to the University of Saskatchewan in Saskatoon in 1982. She went on to marry and change her name to Silversides, but she and Blaine remained friends. During their relationship, he had found himself drawn by Sandra deep into Colin Thatcher's affairs.

It was affable Sergeant Murton who talked to Blaine and thought him "a real nice kid." And the veteran cop raised a professional eyebrow at the story Blaine told. Mathieson claimed that Sandra once told him that Thatcher had arranged to have a hit man come to Saskatchewan from the United States to "do in JoAnn." Sandra told Blaine that during the latter part of April, 1981, before JoAnn was wounded the first time, she had learned from Thatcher that this hit man had been arrested in Calgary while attempting to enter Canada with a gun.

Blaine also reported that he had heard from Sandra that one thousand dollars in American money was placed in a bag and deposited in a fertilizer spreader in the alcove of the Redland home. The details of this story did not fit exactly with what Anderson, Charlie Wilde, and Cody Crutcher later told police, and for a while it confused matters. Sergeant Murton finally came to believe, however, that "he [Thatcher] didn't want Sandra and the others to think that he had pulled the trigger, so he was making up these stories that there were hit men caught here, and hit men caught there, and how he was hiring through the Mafia. You know, if you hire somebody to do something, it doesn't look as bad as if you do it yourself." Ed Swayze believed that there was another reason Thatcher talked so much about hit men. "Men like him don't do it themselves. Men like him pull strings. After all, he is who he is, a man with connections. Let everybody know, 'I can have this done.'"

Blaine Mathieson did give Murton one piece of information that proved to be a vital link. He said that one week before the first shooting, Sandra told him not to go into the Thatchers' garage because parked there was an orange-coloured Mustang car with a rifle in it. Blaine, however, had been curious and had taken a good look. He had seen the car, the rifle in the car, the cartridges, and the car rental agreement. Sergeant Murton and Superintendent Jim Kane, another key player in the investigation, paid a visit to Scott Motors in Moose Jaw and dug up the original vehicle rental slip made out to Garry Anderson. This was the first direct evidence they had linking the case with Anderson. If Garry knew nothing about all this, how had a car rented by him ended up in Thatcher's garage with a rifle in it? Lots of interesting questions stemmed from that car, and the police were determined to find it and nail down the evidence. The car had been sold, but the police managed to trace it through registrations to a car lot in Swift Current and then to a private individual in Medicine Hat, Alberta. One hot July day, Sergeants Murton and Street and Blaine Mathieson drove west to Medicine Hat. There Mathieson was able to identify the car, and the police took pictures of it. Garry Anderson did not know it, but he was now in serious trouble.

From the beginning the police had felt that Anderson was involved in the murder, that he might even have provided the getaway car. There was some confusion, however, since people they talked to about him said he drove a Ford, yet the only car registered in his name was a Dodge. Finally the police discovered that there were two cars and the Ford Mercury had been sold to J & M Service Station—the same service station where Thatcher bought gas with his Visa card three days before JoAnn's murder. "The day we stopped to question them [the owners] the car was parked right behind the service station," recalls Murton. "I seized it that day, brought it back to town, but of course this was the summer of '83 and a lot of time had elapsed between then and the murder and I didn't find anything." The RCMP crime lab inspected every inch of it and also found nothing. A month later the 1974 Mercury was towed back to the service station. The car didn't have a licence and it had never been registered in Saskatchewan.

About the same time, a girlfriend of Cody Crutcher's, a lady well known in Regina's underworld, went to the police. She said that Cody had told her about a big rip-off that had gone down in 1980 and 1981. As well as Crutcher, it involved

Charlie Wilde, Garry Anderson—and Colin Thatcher. "I didn't believe a word of the story at first," the informer said. "I thought Cody was bragging as usual." When JoAnn Wilson was murdered, however, she realized that it might not be just a tall tale. "The fact that she heard about it from Cody personally—and she was a reliable person—made it a little more than mere scuttlebutt off the street," says Swayze.

Although this was the first time Wilde and Crutcher had been connected to the crime, their names rang loud bells with most of the CID investigators. They had been arrested so many times it would have been difficult for any veteran Regina police officer not to have met them in a professional capacity.

Charlie Wilde was born in 1949 and raised in the small village of Silton, the home of author-illustrator R.D. Symons, whose last book, *Silton Seasons*, described the village. Charlie's father was the caretaker of the summer resources building at the nearby resort town of Regina Beach, and during the winter he maintained the local school, butchered, and worked as a handyman. There were five kids in Charlie's family and they lived in a small house where, in the words of Beverley Rolfe, who grew up in Silton, "their family life was rather loosely organised."

Charlie grew up clever but also lazy. "He was always the first out the door at recess and noon hour," remembers Rolfe. A teacher of his says it was difficult for any of the Wilde children to do their homework properly, their home was so small and cluttered: "But Charlie wasn't a bad kid. He was something of a show-off, maybe, but he always dressed well, and took care of himself. There were lots worse than him."

Because of his father's job, Charlie would hang around Regina Beach on the weekends. His elaborate expositions of what he had seen—the drinking in cars, the swearing, the necking, and more—made him the centre of attention with Silton kids on Monday mornings. Charlie just loved being the "big cheese" among his buddies.

Just before Charlie's sixteenth birthday, his parents went away on a short trip and when they returned he had disappeared. "So finally we heard from him. The beggar had gone to the coast," his father says. But he returned to Saskatchewan, took a job with Dominion Bridge in Regina, married, and had a child. That stability soon ended, however.

The marriage split up and he began drifting. His problem was an overwhelming addiction to drugs; as a young runaway in Vancouver, he had become hopelessly hooked on heroin. From 1968, when he was charged with breaking and entering to obtain illicit drugs, he was in and out of penitentiaries half a dozen times, and almost all his crimes were related to his addiction. By the summer of 1983 he had been released from Stony Mountain Penitentiary after having served time for the Brandon drugstore caper, and was living in Winnipeg.

Sergeants Murton and Stusek went to Winnipeg to talk to Charlie. When they walked into his fourplex, the landlord yelled, "Hey, aren't you two guys cops?" That served as a warning to Charlie and he didn't respond when Murton knocked on his door. "I think he thought we were Winnipeg city police looking to arrest him," says Murton. "I was sure he was in the apartment but we couldn't kick his door or anything." The investigators were in Winnipeg for two days but since Charlie did not wish to be found, they never did find him.

It was a much easier task to find Cody Crutcher; he was incarcerated in Drumheller Penitentiary near Edmonton. A well-built, handsome guy, Cody was also a doper, something of a con artist, and a great favourite among Regina's underworld. His criminal convictions dated back to 1965 and included possession of a narcotic for the purpose of trafficking, causing a disturbance, breaking and entering, and possession of a restricted weapon. But in the summer of 1981, Cody found himself in much more serious trouble.

At 2 a.m. on June 9, Constable David Scantlebury of the Regina Police SWAT team watched from the top of a building while Cody Crutcher, thirty-two, and his friend John Prangley, twenty-six, poured gasoline all over the ground directly in front of the College Park Apartments, struck a match, and set it on fire. "It lit up the whole area and the flames went approximately forty-five feet into the air," said Scantlebury. Police had been tipped off that the crime was to take place, so the fire department arrived quickly and no one was injured, although the building was damaged. Prangley was arrested at the site and Crutcher was grabbed the next day.

A year later at their trial for arson, the two men pleaded not guilty and told the following interesting story. Some time before the fire, they had completed "real estate" work for Dr.

V. Ivanovski, a Regina dentist who owned the ill-fated building. But all they received for their efforts was a bounced cheque. Dr. Ivanovski then promised to pay them with imported gold. Prangley said he was picking up the second batch of gold at the apartment building when he smelled gasoline and shortly after that saw the fire. Crutcher stated that he had not been anywhere near the place that evening. During the trial it was revealed that Ivanovski was in serious financial difficulty, but when Crutcher and Prangley were asked if the dentist had promised to pay them to set the fire, both said no. They were found guilty of arson and sentenced to five years. (After the Crown appealed, their sentence was jacked up to eight years.)

When Ed Swayze went to Drumheller Penitentiary, he didn't confront Crutcher himself. Instead he spoke to other inmates who had been dreaming about the $50,000 award and who had indicated that Cody was doing a lot of talking in prison. They said, "Gee, don't talk to him now, because he'll tie it in to us." "Rather than embarrass them, we just backed right off," says Swayze. "We knew he wasn't going any place."

Even before talking directly to Wilde or Crutcher, the police had pretty well pieced together the outline of what had happened before the first shooting. With that, and the hard-won information on various interesting cars, they felt they could now apply enough uncomfortable pressure on Garry Anderson to make him talk. Anderson would testify that he decided to talk to police "some time between February and June [1983], and mainly because [of] my conscience, and I knew that it was a wrong thing to have done and become involved in." Anderson first contacted his lawyer in June of 1983. But when Sergeants Murton and Stusek went to La Ronge to interview him that month, Anderson still refused to say a thing. "He was very nice and invited us into his suite," says Murton. "We talked about the nice weather and fishing." Anderson recognized Stusek because he and Wally Beaton had interviewed him in January, and Garry courteously asked the policeman how his old partner was. But then Anderson phoned his lawyer, Lloyd Balicki in Prince Albert, and the tenor of the conversation changed. "He says I don't have to talk with you. Will you please leave my suite," said Anderson. Murton later talked to Balicki but all the lawyer would say was: "We aren't willing to talk yet." "In this day and age, you can't threaten and you can't promise, so basically we drove to La Ronge for nothing," says Murton. On the second occasion Sergeants Murton and Street talked briefly with Anderson's girlfriend, who just told them that he was not home.

This was not promising. But then two RCMP officers offered their services to Swayze. Anderson had known Doug Anderson and Carl Monaghan, who had worked out of Moose Jaw, for almost twenty years and he considered them friends. They understood Garry's personality and how he would put a man like Thatcher "up on a pedestal." "He's the type who would probably do things to ingratiate himself with people whom he considered a power source, a type of hero," says Monaghan. "When it was over he realized that his hero had taken advantage of him, and that he was a fool."

The Regina police felt that an RCMP visit to Anderson certainly wouldn't hurt. As Swayze said, "Maybe he wouldn't shut them out as fast as he would some of our own investigators." So Doug Anderson and Carl Monaghan went to La Ronge on September 6, 1983. Garry was glad to see his old friends, in Doug Anderson's words, "for about seven seconds," and then he realized that something wasn't quite right. Garry didn't say much but he listened intently as the police officers talked to him in a firm but friendly manner for about an hour. "We explained to him that we were quite satisfied that he didn't have any direct involvement in the actual killing," recalls Carl Monaghan. "We realized that he was in a very difficult position but that he didn't have to be in that position, and if he would choose to cooperate with the authorities, he didn't have to be charged himself." While Garry Anderson didn't talk, the policemen felt that they "had planted a bug in his ear." And in several weeks, Swayze got word that Balicki was prepared to meet with the Regina police on behalf of Garry Anderson.

Balicki's practice was in Prince Albert, but since he was going to Saskatoon anyway, he agreed to meet Swayze and Al Lyon there on October 13, 1983. What Swayze said to the lawyer was very simple. "Your client can either be an accused or he can be a witness."

In January, 1984, Swayze and Wally Beaton travelled 333 kilometres north to Prince Albert to meet with Anderson personally, in the presence of his lawyer. The police promised him immunity from a charge of conspiracy to murder, but there was one fundamental condition. "He had to tell the truth. If he lied once, then prosecution would take place," says Swayze. Anderson stated in court that this was not the only reason for revealing all: "I believed that I had done wrong. I knew that I had done wrong. Certainly the fact that I may be charged certainly entered into it, but I had done wrong and there was no excuse for that." For whatever reason, at that meeting and on these terms, Anderson gave a brief written statement outlining what he knew.

The formal letter from Ken MacKay, the director of public prosecutions for the province, was signed on February 27, 1984. It read:

Dear Mr. Anderson:

Inspector E. Swayze of the Regina City Police has informed me that you have information pertaining to the wounding of JoAnn Wilson on May 17, 1982, and to her murder on January 21, 1983. Inspector Swayze further advises that you are willing to make a statement and to testify in court as to the person or persons responsible, and that you will so testify upon my assurance that:

1. You will not be charged in the connection with the wounding and/or murder,

2. The Saskatchewan Department of Justice will pay your lawyer's fees pertaining to this matter in the sum of [$- - -], and

3. The Saskatchewan Department of Justice will arrange with the R.C.M Police for the usual witness protection and change of identity.

On behalf of the Saskatchewan Department of Justice, I hereby agree to the above conditions provided that you were not personally involved in the actual wounding or murder, and that you give the statement to the police and testify in any legal proceedings that may ensue, as you have indicated you are willing to do, on the following understanding:

1. Your testimony is direct evidence implicating the

person or persons responsible for the wounding and murder, and

2. Your evidence is true.

Yours truly,

Kenneth W. MacKay, Q.C.
Director of Public Prosecutions

The CID investigators immediately set to work checking out his story. "Nothing Garry Anderson ever told us was a lie. Everything he told us was checked out by other evidence and found positive," says Murton. It was a distinct thrill for the CID men to watch the case finally fall into place so neatly. Interestingly, for one reason or another, little of this evidence was used at the trial, and has never been revealed until now.

The verification of Anderson's story was meticulous. For example, Anderson told the police that in the fall of 1982, on Thatcher's orders, he had rented a car from a Saskatoon dealership. When it was returned to Anderson, he found a paper bag containing a black wig and a tire iron in the car. Thatcher, he said, commented specifically on the tire iron, saying, "Make sure you take it out of the car before returning it." The police duly checked with the appropriate Saskatoon car rental agency. The car had been a 1978 green Chevrolet; its licence number was KXP 283; it was supposed to have been returned October 18, 1982, but Anderson finally brought it back on October 19. The police found that the vehicle had been illegally parked during that week at the Legislative Buildings and that the Wascana Police Authority had towed it away.

Checking another of Anderson's stories proved to be a dirty, painstaking job. Anderson told the police that when Thatcher gave him the gun in the fall of 1982 and asked him to make a silencer for it, Anderson took it out in a field and fired one bullet into a ditch near his farm. Murton and two other determined cops went out to the ditch one day with shovels and a metal detector. It took five or six hours of back-breaking work but, Murton recalls, "We just kept digging the side of the road out until we found the lead in the bullet." It proved to be exactly the kind of bullet that Anderson said it was.

Anderson also stated that on the day after JoAnn was killed, when he picked up his car three blocks from the

Redland residence, he found on the passenger seat "a black ski-type jacket, a pair of blue jeans, a pair of gray work socks. There was some loose change on the floor. There was a credit card receipt, and I believe a tuft of hair what I thought looked to be out of a wig. And there was a pair of sunglasses." He drove the car to his mother's farm where he took these objects and burned them in a barrel. He then placed a piece of junk wire on top.

Murton went to the Anderson farm and found the barrel. "It just looked to me like garbage, burnt ashes, so I just emptied the barrel contents into a box. But when the corporal with the RCMP told me what he had found, I returned with him and seized the rest of the barrel." Corporal Jack Cronkhite, a forensic expert with the RCMP crime lab in Regina, had phoned Murton after examining the ashes. "He said, 'There's a pair of runners, a coat, a pair of blue jeans, glasses.' I said, 'You're crazy.' But I went to look and he had little bottles of teeth from the jacket, and this told him what size the jacket was. He had so many cogs from the zipper of the pants, and he could tell the size of blue jeans. From the epaulets on the coat he could tell who the manufacturer was and what year the coat was manufactured." Corporal Cronkhite also found a fingerprint on a button that he thought might be Thatcher's. He was able to determine the prescription of the sunglasses and that seemed to match Thatcher's. And in the burnt residue he found a glob of plastic that was consistent with material used in wigs.

Yet none of this fascinating detective work was ever used as evidence in court. "If we had had just a smidgen more here and there, we would have definitely called it," says Serge Kujawa, the Crown attorney. "I spent a lot of time with the lab boys and we went through every damn thing. We found just about proof that the glass in there was from Thatcher's eyeglasses, just about proof that the button came from that jacket. The fingerprints were eight points' similarity, but we require ten in the usual practice or we don't call it. The corporal couldn't say, 'Yep, those were the same glasses.' All he could say was they were likely the same. And a dozen likelies does not make one fact beyond a reasonable doubt." All this information was, however, very useful. It convinced the investigators that Garry Anderson was telling the truth.

Anderson was also able to find one of the six silencers he

claimed he had made for Thatcher's gun. He met Murton and Stusek at the Vagabond Motor Inn on April 24, 1984, and handed over the gadget.

By now more than fifteen months had gone by since the murder, and the public in Saskatchewan and beyond had given up on the Regina police's ability (even, some said, their political will) to solve the case. Murton remembers the growing tension in the spring of '84. "At this point there were probably only five people who knew we were still working on the case. It was kept very quiet because we didn't want to be seen with Anderson at that time. We didn't want to place him in jeopardy. Anderson would come into town, book into a hotel, and we'd meet him there, instead of him coming to the police station, where he might run into the news media, or just anyone." Anderson told the police that he had thrown a couple of silencers out on his brother's farm. "He didn't really get along that well with his brother and he didn't want a whole lot of police in there—plus his brother's farm is right across the road from Thatcher's," says Murton. But Garry did slip in one night and find one. Anderson had finally concocted a silencer that worked very well. "But," says Murton, "he never received any money for it so he didn't give it to Thatcher. And he felt the silencer could be traced back to him."

Ever since the unsuccessful visit to Winnipeg the police, of course, had remained most anxious to talk with Charlie Wilde. There was a warrant out for his arrest on a minor breach-of-probation charge—he had been convicted of a crime, the Brandon drugstore caper, while still on probation. Meanwhile in Winnipeg, Charlie had been picked up for breaking and entering—another drugstore, of course—so that he was in custody. The Regina police managed to get the Saskatchewan warrant extended to a Canadawide one and on March 11, he was shipped back to Regina. The police suggested to him that what he had perpetrated on Thatcher was fraud for which he could be charged. Charlie told his story on March 14.

Cody Crutcher was already in Regina, for the appeal of his arson conviction. He too was persuaded to talk.

After Cody and Wilde had talked separately to police officers, the two old comrades in arms were allowed to chat with each other in the same holding cell. Afterwards they each signed a written statement. At the trial Allbright insinuated that while they were together, they had concocted their

stories. Swayze says they were only together for about five
minutes, not nearly enough time to fabricate such an elaborate plot. What was even more important, their stories
dovetailed with Anderson's, and the police were satisfied that
Garry had not met either man since before the first shooting
of JoAnn Wilson. And there was the other factor that encouraged honest confession. "They were all told the same thing,"
says Swayze. "One lie and they would be charged with
conspiracy to murder."

By early April 1984 the police felt that they had enough
evidence to lay charges. Through the entire fifteen months of
the investigation, the Regina police department had been
under enormous pressure to crack the case. They were
criticized and ridiculed by many citizens, some of them
prominent. "When no arrests were made, the question that
was often raised was 'Do you think you're capable of handling
this type of situation?'" says Vern New, the police chief at the
time. He was never officially approached to have outside
investigators come in. "But nevertheless I don't doubt that it
crossed the mind of some people [in authority] because
unofficially that question was posed to me from time to time."
The cops were naturally itching to show that they weren't
country bumpkins, that they didn't need the help of Scotland
Yard, or even the Toronto police force, that in fact they had
done what Kujawa would call "magical police work."

In early April, an important conference was held between
the police and the prosecutors. Ed Swayze, Wally Beaton,
and Al Lyon were there, as were Serge Kujawa, Al Johnson
(who would serve as the assistant Crown attorney helping
Kujawa), and Ken MacKay and Dough Britton from the
Crown attorney's office. They discussed the evidence in
detail. Everyone agreed that charges could certainly be laid
against Thatcher. But then Kujawa piped up. Okay, it's a
prima facie case, he said. But it just cannot be in the public
interest to charge a person of that calibre, or any person, with
first-degree murder when the chances of conviction were
almost non-existent. "When we get down to proving something beyond a reasonable doubt, we're just too damn thin,"
Kujawa said. The men then discussed laying second-degree
murder charges, or even simply charging Thatcher with the
first wounding. It was quickly agreed, however, that since

they all believed that he had committed the first-degree murder, he should be charged with nothing less. Kujawa remembers the next few seconds of conversation. "At that point, from the extremely long faces, Swayze said, 'What can we do? Where can we get more evidence?' I expressed the view that the only hope was to get some evidence out of the accused himself." Swayze said, "You talking tape?" Kujawa said, "Yeah. Body pack." "Anderson?" asked Swayze. "Anderson's got to be number one and if that doesn't go, try Charlie Wilde," advised Kujawa. While Swayze didn't say so at the time, he decided to try it.

Actually Swayze says he first talked to Anderson about the possibility of taping a conversation with Thatcher early in January. His lawyer didn't like it one bit, but Anderson didn't say no; he shrewdly recognized that the more evidence the police could gather, the greater the chance of Thatcher going to jail, and at this point that was of vital concern to him. So after Swayze decided to try the body-pack ruse, he found it easy to convince Anderson to participate. But because Thatcher was in Palm Springs, the operation was put on hold for about a week.

Perhaps the week's delay was useful, because the recording session was a major manoeuvre; at one point about twenty-five police officers, members of both the Regina city police and the RCMP, were involved. They did everything, from following Thatcher in airplanes to monitoring electronic equipment. The police decided that the most natural place for Anderson to have a conversation with Thatcher was the Bergren farm, where the two men had met on several previous occasions, once with Charlie Wilde.

Besant Trans-Canada campground, ten kilometres away from the Bergren farm, was selected as the police centre of operations. Since summer was approaching, work crews were in the park cleaning up, and many of the people involved were criminals who had, to their regret, been previously in touch with both the Regina police and the RCMP. This hampered the secret operation somewhat. "We had to keep a kind of low profile during the day," says Swayze. Two motor homes were rented discreetly, where the police officers could sleep and have a coffee. The real nerve centre, however, was located in the Regina police force's command trailer, where a network of electronic equipment and telephones was installed.

MAY 1, 1984

At 6:14 a.m. Anderson met Corporal Donald Domenie and Sergeant Bob Laporte of the RCMP's Special O squad in the command trailer. In court Gerry Allbright would later joke that Anderson must have looked like a walking advertisement for Radio Shack, and with some justice. Taped to Anderson's bullet-proof vest on the left side was a small Nagra tape recorder about three-quarters of an inch thick. A microphone connected to the tape recorder was taped in the hollow of his chest right below his throat. The recorder itself was a specialized machine used primarily by police. It was of excellent quality, very sensitive to sound, and could record about three full hours of conversation once it had been activated with a very simple start mechanism. It had no playback capacity at all, so nobody could tamper with the tape.

To Anderson's right side was taped a Bell and Howell FM transmitter about the size of a cigarette package, which would broadcast the conversation to two FM receivers. One of the receivers was given to Jim McKee of the Regina police SWAT team, one of four officers who would lie hidden on the site during the entire time the conversation was taking place. By listening to the conversation, McKee would know if Thatcher threatened Anderson in any way, and would be able to intervene quickly if he did. Another receiver was placed under the front seat of Anderson's truck. This device also recorded the conversation, and although the taping quality was much poorer than that of the body pack, it would be useful as a back-up, in the unlikely event the Nagra should fail. Rounding out the electronic arsenal was a second FM transmitter that had been installed surreptitiously in the barn a few days before the conversation took place. Thatcher and Anderson had always gone into the barn during their previous conversations so it was assumed that with this device, the SWAT member could continue to listen to the conversation if Anderson and Thatcher were hidden from sight.

Swayze and Anderson had discussions about how the recorded conversation with Thatcher would go. "I essentially told him to let Thatcher do the talking, not to ask point-blank questions because that would spook him. 'If he wants to talk, let him do the talking,' I said." Swayze felt that since Thatcher obviously knew that the police were questioning his friends and acquaintances about Anderson, he would naturally be curious to talk to Garry and find out what Anderson had told the police.

When Anderson drove off on his mission at about seven that morning, some police officers laid heavy odds against the plan's success. "I thought Anderson's chances of, first, getting Thatcher to meet him at the abandoned farm and, second, to get him to say anything other than screw off, were infinitesimal," said an RCMP officer. When Thatcher swallowed the bait right off, the police were amazed.

Since Anderson's conversation with Thatcher was not being broadcast to the command centre, there was little the police not stationed at the site could do but wait in high expectation at Besant Park. Immediately after the conversation took place, Garry had been told to drive to a nearby service station and contact Ed Swayze. When the phone rang, the inspector answered it in his usual calm, unexcited manner. In fact he was so calm that those who knew him well realized how excited he was. It must have been agony to wait the ten minutes or so it took Anderson to get to the command centre, but Swayze as usual gave no indication he was in any suspense.

When Anderson returned to Besant Park, however, he was disappointed that there was not a clear blanket confession by Thatcher on the tape. The closest thing to an admission was a remark made right at the end of the twenty-minute conversation. Anderson said, "I'm glad you got her," and Thatcher replied, "Okay." When Swayze listened to the tape through a pair of earphones in the command trailer, in his unflappable why he was very pleased. "Why should Thatcher tell you he murdered his wife when he knows you already know?" he told Anderson. Swayze immediately phoned Serge Kujawa and arranged to meet him at the RCMP headquarters in Regina at two that afternoon.

The two men listened to the tape together and both were astonished by what it revealed. Certainly there was no outright admission of guilt by Thatcher, but they had never expected one. Almost as important, in their minds, however, was the way the conversation seemed to tie all the various threads of evidence together like a neat bow or—more appropriately—an old-fashioned hangman's noose.

Three days later Thatcher was arrested on the outskirts of Moose Jaw and charged with first-degree murder.

But the police investigation did not stop once Thatcher was in custody. Warrants in Sergeant Stusek's name allowed the police to comb every inch of his ranch and farm properties and his home on Redland Avenue. Scuba divers arrived to scout the murky waters of the various dugouts on Thatcher's land in the hope of turning up the murder weapon. It was never found. Police did find the Cindy Shower box, and the June, 1984, *Los Angeles Times* newspaper stuffed inside it; both discoveries backed Lynne Dally's story of how Thatcher had brought the Palm Springs gun to Canada.

In the master bedroom of the Redland house, they also came across a surprise—an unregistered revolver. Ammunition for it was soon uncovered behind the woodshed in the garage. Further research revealed that Thatcher purchased this gun in California, in a small town some sixty kilometres from Palm Springs, telling the gun dealer that he was buying it for his own protection at the condominium. This would raise the question, Why did Thatcher not use this weapon to kill JoAnn, rather than rely on Anderson to return his Ruger? Swayze has his own theory as to why the unregistered gun played no part. "It's what is known in the industry as a Saturday-night special. It's not a very good weapon, especially compared to a Ruger. And Thatcher is a chap who does on occasion, when it suits him, seek out quality." But the very existence of this unregistered gun in Thatcher's house demonstrated to the police that he certainly was capable of smuggling firearms into Canada.

There was still one more essential, and exotic, fish to land. On a sunny June 4, 1984, Ed Swayze paid a visit to Serge Kujawa in his airy office on the fifteenth floor of the Regina City Hall building. "I want you to come to Palm Springs with me, Serge," Swayze said. "I got a search warrant and we can check out the gun matter and the prescription eyeglasses. And by no means least, we're gonna talk to Mendell—and you have a way with women." Kujawa could hardly refuse such an invitation.

Swayze, Kujawa, and Sergeant Gene Stusek flew from Regina early the next morning and arrived at the Sheraton Oasis in the afternoon. Eleven months before, on July 1,

1983, Lynne Dally had married a forty-year-old broadcast executive, Bill Mendell. It had been a case of old-fashioned love at first sight. Lynne recalls: "I think we agreed to get married on the third date but we had already decided on the first." She was now called Lynne Mendell. While she had never formally met Kujawa or Swayze, she had talked so many times on the phone with Ed that she had developed a rapport with him. Now, she agreed at least to discuss the matter, and the three sat down for a cup of coffee. "Before the coffee was brought, Lynne was all worked up and agitated and launched rather breathlessly into a tirade," remembers Kujawa. "'Look, I know why you guys are here. I wasn't born yesterday. I don't have an IQ measured at 150 because I'm stupid.'" Kujawa looked at her. "Relax, doll, you're with equals." They all laughed. But although that broke the ice a little, Mendell remained adamant. She was going to take her father's advice and refuse to testify.

Finally the two men realized that attempts at further persuasion were going to lead nowhere and they returned to their hotel room. They tried to call Lynne's father but he wouldn't talk to them. While they kept up a cheerful patter, talking about how good a witness Lynne would be, they felt anxious—suppose they couldn't get her to budge? Finally Swayze said he was going for a walk, but an hour later he was back. "Swayze is always cool, but when he's excited he's a little too cool, I could tell he was excited," says Kujawa. Now Swayze announced casually, "Lynne and her husband Bill will be here at four o'clock."

Kujawa asked an FBI agent to join them and by the time the Mendells arrived he was already there. The American policeman wasted no time but said, "I'm here to tell you these people have absolutely no rights over you at all. You don't have to talk to them, you don't have to say anything, you don't have to be here. Here is my card. Call me if they bother you." Then he left, and the four sat down to talk. "Bill Mendell cross-examined me. It was a damn good cross-examination maybe for over an hour," says Kujawa. "He asked me about our case, about our system, about assurances. I told him there were no assurances in this whole bloody thing." At last Bill turned to Lynne and said, "Well, I've found out everything I need to know. The decision is yours. And whichever way you decide, I will support you. But I think that you have to go [to testify]." Lynne went flying into his arms, saying, "You'll support me no matter what? Bill, you're wonderful." Swayze and Kujawa got up and had a good Canadian look out of the window at the palm trees until the couple disengaged. Lynne had still not definitely agreed to testify but as she was leaving the hotel room, Lynne turned and joked, "If I go to Regina, I want to be picked up by a handsome driver in a Mercedes-Benz." Kujawa and Swayze looked at each other; Lynne had no way of knowing that Ed Swayze was almost certainly the only cop in Saskatchewan who drove a Mercedes. "We can provide the car easy enough," said Kujawa, "but I don't know about the handsome driver."

While they were there, Swayze and Stusek, with the help of local police, thoroughly searched Thatcher's condominium and car. In the trunk of the Mercedes they found documents pertaining to a legal case involving Thatcher and Bob Gustav, the man who had introduced Lynne to Colin on their first blind date. Swayze was fascinated to learn even more about Thatcher's tangled financial dealings. It seemed that he, along with Gustav and one other person, was a major investor in a luxury Palm Springs condominium project called Palma de Majorca. Gustav was the "sole managing partner, with full authority to act on behalf of the partnership." The town was somewhat overbuilt by the time the project got off the ground and Gustav decided to cut the square footage per condo and thereby lessen the price per unit. He says the decision proved to be "100-percent accurate as far as the market conditions were concerned." But because of "a gut feeling," Thatcher decided to pull out, leaving Gustav and the other partner in near financial ruin. They named Thatcher in a million-dollar lawsuit.

After this was initiated, Gustav says, "A great deal of damage was done to my personal property by someone unknown." Gustav was terrified of Thatcher. The trial was set in Palm Springs for March, 1985, but after Gerry Allbright filed two affidavits, one immediately following Thatcher's murder trial and one in January, stating that it was likely that Thatcher would win a new trial, Gustav's suit was postponed. It is still outstanding.

Although he found no murder weapon or prescription lenses to fit the charcoaled remains in the barrel, Swayze did come across a couple of interesting items in Thatcher's condominium. There was a hat of the kind that the canine unit of Swayze's own Regina police force gave out as a public relations gesture. And carefully tucked away in a closet in Thatcher's bedroom was a cover story clipped from an old *Time* magazine. It was a report on capital punishment.

CHAPTER NINETEEN
A STRANGE FEELING

OCTOBER 15, 1984

By 6 a.m. Ted Bourree was sitting outside Saskatoon's very ordinary, very utilitarian courthouse opposite the baronial Bessborough Hotel. Bourree was a skinny, worn man with a drooping moustache and an "authentic" cowboy hat who looked as though he had spent most of his years roping cows; in fact he was a retired provincial safety inspector. He would become a kind of symbol for the province's—and indeed the country's—fascination with the Thatcher story. He would get up at the earliest hour, brave any weather, wait patiently for hours outside to enjoy "the greatest show in town." Having carefully read the preliminary hearing transcript, he already had a detailed knowledge of the Crown's case. As the trial progressed, he would be in a position to weigh the significance of every piece of evidence. His only problem was finding someone, anyone, to listen to him.

By nine that morning the crowd behind Bourree trailed down the steps of the courthouse and on to Spadina Crescent. Over the nineteen days of the trial, an *esprit de corps* would develop among the waiting spectators. They brought each other coffee, chatted about the trial, speculated and gossiped while they inched their way towards the courtroom. Occasionally raucous arguments broke out about what specific evidence meant or whether one witness of another was lying. Once somebody tried to butt into the line, fisticuffs resulted, and the RCMP was called. And every day, members of the Thatcher family were forced to run the gauntlet of these staring, morbidly curious eyes.

On the first morning, Greg sat alone in the half-dozen or so seats reserved for the Thatcher family. He was immaculate in a blue pin-striped suit and a red tie. To the surprise of the out-of-town media, who expected buckskin and a ten-gallon hat, Thatcher was also most elegantly attired in a well-tailored, greyish-brown pin-striped suit with a cream shirt and a brown-and-cream striped tie.

Although he was suffering from a bad case of grey-faced jailhouse pallor, he was still remarkably relaxed on this, the first day of his murder trial. As he waited for court proceedings to begin, he whistled to himself, smiled brightly at Gerry Allbright, and chatted with the RCMP officer who was guarding him. It was quite remarkable that he should appear to be so sanguine and composed, for already he had suffered major reversals during the pre-trial legal manoeuvres.

Try as he might, Allbright had not succeeded in getting Thatcher out on bail: Not only had Colin suffered during his twenty-three weeks in the Regina "hell hole" and the Saskatoon Correctional Institute, but Allbright had felt unable to prepare his case properly with his client in jail. There was no privacy, the defence lawyer complained. "If there's a cough you can hear it, or a scraping of the chair." There were other fears. Allbright had been sure that the telephone calls Thatcher was making at the Regina Correctional Institute were tapped by the police. "I'm convinced that they weren't with me. But they were with him and his family, and evidence was obtained [and used in the trial] as a result of that," Allbright maintains. As the trial progressed, Thatcher's lawyer would become even more convinced that information gleaned from illegal wire-taps was used against his client.

During the summer Thatcher had applied for bail as often as the court system would allow it. As a result there had been five major hearings and the media, naturally, played each one as a major news story so that there was hardly a person in Saskatchewan who was unaware that a whole gaggle of judges had turned him down many times. That these respected members of the judiciary had thought the evidence so damaging and the accused so potentially dangerous cast a dark shadow over Thatcher by the time the trial began. The rumour mills were hard at work, too, with Regina cab drivers assuring out-of-town visitors that Thatcher would never get bail because it was known that he had a "hit list."

In August Allbright had asked for a change in venue. He pointed out that no Saskatchewan case had drawn as much attention "since Mr. [Louis] Riel appeared on the scene some ninety-nine years ago," a remark that raised eyebrows since it implied that Thatcher, like the executed Métis leader of the 1885 rebellion, had also become a martyr in the public eye. Kujawa at first frowned at the idea of shifting the locale but then said he didn't have "a firm footing to oppose" it. Allbright had wanted the trial held in Prince Albert, 363 kilometres away from Regina, but when Kujawa said that was too far, he agreed to Saskatoon, 259 kilometres from the capital, as a compromise. Kujawa's opposition had been purely formal because, confidentially, he thought moving the trial to Saskatoon was a grave error on the part of the defence. He felt that the closer to Moose Jaw it was held, the more likely it would be to include one juror who would prove unshakeably loyal to "old man Thatcher" and refuse to convict his son, no matter how strong the evidence. And one holdout was all that was needed to prevent a guilty verdict from crashing down.

And there was one other vitally important legal question that had already been decided by the time the trial started. The indictment under which Thatcher was charged read that Thatcher "did unlawfully cause the death of JoAnn Kay Wilson and did thereby commit first-degree murder, contrary to Section 218 of the Criminal Code." The operative words were "cause the death of." They meant that Thatcher could be found guilty regardless of whether he had committed the crime personally or had persuaded somebody else to do it. On September 19, Allbright argued before the trial judge, Mr. Justice J. H. Maher, that the Crown should have to make a choice between the two. Allbright contended that his approach and manner of defence could vary depending on whether Thatcher was being accused of committing the act himself or arranging for the murder to be committed by persons unknown. Maher dismissed the application, ruling that it should be left up to the jury to decide which, if any, of the charges had been proved.

Although the Crown was not planning to call as evidence any of the tape recordings of Thatcher's telephone calls made over a period of eighteen months, Allbright had asked Mr. Justice Maher that he be allowed access to the tapes. "I didn't have a whole lot of police working for me and I needed to get leads where I could get them," says Allbright. "Another thing I needed those tapes for was this—it was obvious they had information about telephone calls between Colin and Lynne Mendell, and I wanted to find out what those conversations were." Kujawa opposed his request vigorously. Mr. Justice Maher's order was very convoluted and the Crown interpreted it to mean that any conversation that involved Thatcher need not be disclosed—which rule out almost everything of interest to Allbright.

On Friday, October 12, the usual pre-trial conference involving the defence lawyer, the Crown, and the judge was held to anticipate any legal problems that might hinder the smooth running of the trial. Towards the end of the conference, Kujawa joked, "Gerry, are you going to call the accused?" Allbright responded, "I don't know about that, but I can tell you right now we're calling a couple of experts on the tape recording." To Kujawa this could only mean one thing— that Thatcher was going to deny that it was his voice on the tape (between Anderson and Thatcher). Kujawa had already suspected that this was going to happen, because months earlier Allbright had revealed that he wanted a copy of the tape so that it could be examined by experts. Now, after consultation with Al Johnson, the other Crown attorney involved in the trial, Kujawa decided to add two police officers to the list of witnesses. These were members of the RCMP's Special O Section. One in a truck and one in an aircraft, they had followed Thatcher from his home to the abandoned farm for the meeting and would further verify that Thatcher had been with Anderson at the time of the conversation. "I called Gerry and told him we were calling these guys," says Johnson, "and he told me that he was going to object to their evidence. Well, it just confirmed my thought that Thatcher was going to deny that tape recording." About eight days into the trial, it became obvious that Allbright was not going to dispute that it was Thatcher's voice on the tape. The Crown remains convinced to this day that Thatcher changed his story during the two days between the pre-trial conference and the actual trial. And some very strange evidence that Thatcher gave while on the stand further confirmed this theory for both Kujawa and Johnson.

For his part, Allbright insists that Thatcher never planned to deny the tape; he maintains that Colin's explanation of it was consistent from the time he began to represent him. Concerning his remark about the tape expert, Allbright says,

"I guess my view of the whole thing was, I had the distinct
and clear feeling that the Crown had a way that they were
going to proceed with this prosecution, and that they would
get no help from me. That was a very pointed comment in
that regard." In his view the tape expert comment was never
intended to be more than a red herring that would confuse
the Crown.

By the time of the trial, antagonism between Kujawa and
Allbright had grown intense. "Someday there ought to be an
investigation into the investigation," says Allbright. "The
authorities under our law have a duty to prosecute someone
who they think has committed an offence, but that duty must
be exercised within the bounds of what is right, fair, and
proper. There are just a lot of troubling questions regarding
the investigation and the prosecution that are isolated from
the question of innocence or guilt, that really bother me, and
have left me with some very unresolved feelings."

Kujawa, too, had strong feelings about some strategy used
by the defence. At the last appeal regarding Thatcher's bail,
this annoyance was all too obvious. 'I was pretty nasty in the
last bail deal," says Kujawa, "and one of the reasons I was,
was because I wanted to show my displeasure at the court. . . . I
was pointing out [to the judges] that this guy [Allbright] who
is the new young leader of the bar is doing all sorts of
improper things right in front of your goddamn noses and you
don't stop him. He started off, just as he did before the jury,
sliding the kids in, pointing out that all of the Thatcher family
is here, Greg is here, Regan is here, and on and on, and his
mother would have been here, but unfortunately My Lord,
she's contracted flu. . . . He goes on, takes five minutes of the
court's time to explain about Peggy and goddamn flu."

In some ways it was natural that the old lion and the whiz
kid would develop an antipathy. One was thirty-seven and
determinedly carving out a distinguished career, while the
other was fifty-nine and enjoying the reputation that a distinguished career had earned. Although both were as much
products of Saskatchewan as Number One Hard Wheat, they
were as different as prairie lily and prickly pear.

Serge Kujawa was born in Poland, his ethnic origin was
Russian, and the language spoken most at home was Ukrainian.
His father served in the Tsarist army for eight years, until the

end of World War One. He was a poor, illiterate peasant who by the end of his military career had obtained the rank of "feldsher," a medic halfway between a nurse and a doctor, a highly respected occupation in Russia. Kujawa Senior was virulently anti-communist and just before the Depression, he, his wife, and four children immigrated to Canada. "It took a great deal of courage," says Serge. "Whether it was real courage of just insanity I don't know."

The Canadian government had been looking for strong-backed, hard-working, and above all unsuspecting peasants to open new bush lands. The Kujawa family was encouraged to head for St. Walburg, at the end of the railway in the northwest corner of Saskatchewan. It would prove an isolated, lonely existence for the family, exacerbated by the fact that most of the Ukrainian-speaking farmers lived on the west side of town, while the Kujawas ended up on the east side. They arrived just as the Depression hit. "It was a real no-shoes hard time," says Kujawa. Eventually the land would provide a prosperous living (Serge's brother still farms there), but it took many years of struggle merely to survive while the bush was being cleared, in the depths of a Depression that ruined even well-established farmers.

What was most difficult for the new immigrants, however, was the hard-core racial discrimination they experienced. "You know, 'dirty Russian lousy bohunk' was part of your name," remembers Kujawa. "To somebody like Colin Thatcher I was a nobody, worse than a nobody, a minus. To him a guy like me is a minus."

To Kujawa Senior, education was magic and could do magical things. Serge tells a story about a young girl in his town in the 1930s. "Well, the bohunk's daughter is going after high school, not to teach school or be a nurse, that in itself was a little presumptuous, but she's going to university, for Christ's sake. Nobody from that town ever went to university. Nobody, man, woman, or child. And a woman going to university from there? A DP woman. And top of all that what does she take—medicine. Unheard of." That young woman was Serge's sister, and she has practised medicine for years.

After high school, Serge Kujawa went to teacher's college and then taught forty or so kids in eight grades, a job he did not particularly relish. He spent a year and a half in the

Canadian army before the war ended. And for the next half-dozen years or so, he panned for gold in British Columbia, sold aerial photographs of farms, and farmed with his brother. One day he was cutting wood with a large circular saw when it slipped and the two middle fingers of his left hand were severed.

At what was then considered the ripe old age of twenty-eight, Kujawa went back to university and graduated from the University of Saskatchewan law school in 1957. From that point until 1961 he worked for the firm Davidson, Davidson and Blakeney. His only interest was courtroom law. "Some types of law like conveyancing and real estate trasactions, you're far better off sawing logs than doing that for a living," he says.

One day Kujawa was defending a fellow who he knew was "guilty as hell." Serge took advantage of one mistake the Crown had made and his client was let off. The lawyer was congratulated by one and all. "I remember driving home in my 1952 Chevrolet, on a beautiful spring evening and thinking, I left a farm in the boondocks to make something better of myself. I'm springing a thoroughly no-good guy. Is that what this great status is all about? I don't think I've risen anywhere in the world at all."

Kujawa pleaded with the Attorney General's department to hire him and he became a Crown prosecutor in 1961. "And I've not been sorry since," he adds. Five years later he was named director of public prosecutions for the province of Saskatchewan.

Over the years his reputation grew as he fought case after case in all the courts of Saskatchewan as well as before the Supreme Court of Canada. He was considered a blunt, outspoken, yet sincere individualist, an ethical and fair prosecutor. He developed as a specialty the legal concept of insanity, an offshoot of his interest in psychology. His peers held him in such high regard that he was the first Crown attorney in Saskatchewan to be appointed a bencher of the Law Society. "Serge is up-front, he won't pull anything sneaky on you like not revealing vital evidence," says a lawyer who has worked against him many times in the past. "But he is also a very enthusiastic prosecutor. Any weapon he thinks is necessary will be trotted out."

By 1983 he was associate deputy minister and general

counsel for the Attorney General, which meant that he acted as a special prosecutor, involving himself in cases that were difficult or unusual. It naturally fell to Kujawa to take the Thatcher case. He didn't hesitate. "Why would you want to be playing somewhere else when the World Series was in town?"

Gerry Allbright was brought up in Prince Albert, John Diefenbaker's home base. His father, Marshall, ran a grain elevator and flour mill, one of the few such privately owned operations in the province. When United Grain Growers bought it, Marshall Allbright opened an electronics store, which he ran for about fifteen years. His first love, however, was municipal politics, and he sat as an alderman for twenty-five consecutive years. "I used to wonder how he could put up with the constant telephone calls," recalls Allbright. "I remember going out with him and we'd look at somebody's sewer, somebody's lawn, somebody's road."

Gerry enjoyed a secure, wholesome childhood in the northern town, loved and "spoiled" by four sisters. He seldom got into any trouble as a kid and was a hard-working, popular student. "I really don't remember a time when I didn't want to be a lawyer," he says. "Probably it was the unconscious influence of people in my community like Diefenbaker and [Clyne] Harradence [a highly respected attorney]."

After graduating from University of Saskatchewan law school in 1970, Allbright worked for the Prince Albert lawyer Gordon Kirkby. Although he was in private practice, Kirkby was an agent for the Attorney General, which meant that he acted as a prosecutor as well as a defence lawyer. Allbright spent three years flying around northern Saskatchewan to places like La Loche, Buffalo Narrows, La Ronge, Uranium City, and Stony Rapids, conducting trials that most often involved native peoples. "Many times we'd run twenty-five trials in three days. And that went on month after month." Allbright conducted his first murder trial two months after he was admitted to the bar. 'I'd never seen a full Queen's Bench jury trial so I read as many books as I could." He was, perhaps fortunately, prosecuting and not defending on that occasion.

In 1973 and 1974 he worked for the Attorney General's department, primarily doing civil litigation work. One of his colleagues there was Serge Kujawa, whom he considered a good friend. After that he was appointed director of the newly created Regina Legal Aid Clinic and then spent a year and a half as provincial director. He had moved to Saskatoon, a city he grew to like very much. It was at that point he made his first contact with Colin Thatcher. "I didn't know him, although I realized he was Ross Thatcher's son. He wondered whether a constituent of his would be entitled to legal aid. He was very nice about it. In fact he was very different from this boisterous, arrogant guy whom I had heard about."

Allbright's next step was to go into private practice, first with a general law firm and then specializing in litigation with Silas Halyk, a highly respected criminal lawyer. By this time Allbright had gained a reputation as one of the rising young stars in the Saskatchewan bar, a fact confirmed when he was elected president of the law society at thirty-four, the youngest president in the province's history. By the time of the trial, Allbright had started his own law firm.

When they were selecting a defence lawyer for the murder trial, Tony Merchant and Colin Thatcher considered three possibilities: Doug Laidlaw, of Toronto (who was killed in an automobile accident shortly afterwards), Dave Brodsky, a criminal lawyer from Winnipeg, and Allbright. They finally decided on Gerry, primarily because he had impressed them in the abduction proceedings but also because they thought a jury might resent a hot-shot lawyer who was not from Saskatchewan.

Allbright says now that he had no idea of the impact the trial would have on him. "I knew from the abduction that it would receive a certain amount of publicity. But the abduction compared with the murder trial was like learning to swim and then swimming the English Channel. There was just no comparison. It started to take progressively all my time and had an impact on my life as a lawyer, and on my personal life. I don't think that unless a lawyer has lived through a case like this he could ever appreciate what a toll it would take. Without my faith it would have been a far harder ordeal for me." Although during the trial he never raised the fact that Thatcher and he were devout born-again Christians, there were hints of it in the way Allbright operated. For example, when reading a transcript of the tape, he refused to say the words "son of a bitch."

Such prissiness made Kujawa squirm.

* * *

When court was called to order with Mr. Justice J.H. Maher presiding, the first business, of course, was the selection of the jury. Considering the folklore that has arisen about the mysteries of jury selection, it was a remarkably uncomplicated affair. The jury panel of about fifty members were asked two questions. Were they related in any way to the accused or the witnesses? Had they read the transcript of the preliminary hearing? Nobody responded in the affirmative. As each member of the jury panel came forward, he or she was asked no questions but simply accepted or rejected at face value, a process that took only eighteen minutes. But it was not quite as simple as it looked. For about four weeks, Allbright had possessed the panel list, and it included ages and occupations of each potential juror. While it was considered highly unethical to approach any of these men or women directly, it was thought acceptable to talk to neighbours, relatives, or colleagues at work. As a result of some digging, Allbright knew a fair amount about each member of the jury panel before the proceedings began.

The final jury of five women and seven men was certainly a mixed bag in terms of age and occupation, although on the surface there seemed to be nothing very unusual about any of them. There was a secretary, an owner of a business machine outlet, a part-time laundress in a senior citizens' home, a farmer, a sheet-metal worker, a manager of a family confectionery store, a saleswoman in a card shop. Robert Hutchinson, a tall, handsome man in a beautifully tailored suit, was chosen jury foreman, and he took copious notes throughout the trial. He turned out to be the representative of General Motors products in Saskatoon.

Mr. Justice Maher began the proceedings with a short nuts-and-bolts address to the jury, outlining some elementary points of law. He had some good news; the jury would not be sequestered until deliberations began.

John Hayes Maher looked a little like a benevolent version of Mr. Magoo. Indeed he was famous for his wit, which could be devastatingly funny. He was very popular among his peers and a favourite with children, who loved his jokes and his tricks. He, too, like Kujawa and Allbright, was from northern Saskatchewan. In 1902 John Maher's father opened up the first store in North Battleford, a city 139 kilometres north of

Saskatoon. His brother, James, became the mayor of the city and he himself practised law there for twenty years. When he was made a judge in district court out of Humboldt in 1966, his was considered one of the few appointments without political overtones; he had been chosen strictly on his reputation as a fine criminal lawyer. In 1977 he was promoted to the Court of Queen's Bench in Saskatoon. Even the young feisty defence lawyers liked him. "He doesn't tolerate any tampering with evidence but he isn't volatile or tyrannical, and he's not likely to make unreasonable or unpredictable decisions," said one. Maher was noted for keeping tight control in his courtroom and for not permitting theatrics. On the other hand, he did not behave as if he felt he should be the star. With two experienced counsel like Allbright and Kujawa, he preferred to take a non-interventionist attitude. And in fact the trial would run very smoothly; there were few objections from Crown or defence, and little of the constant bobbing up and down and hysteria that afflicts so many criminal trials elsewhere.

In his opening address to the jury, Kujawa sketched briefly the Thatcher story of love and hate—the marriage, the children, the turbulent divorce, JoAnn's remarriage, the first shooting, and then the murder. He then talked briefly about the evidence the twenty-eight witnesses would bring forth. It was a typical example of Kujawa's bare-bones style—short, to the point, and remarkably simple.

Allbright did not give an opening address. "I wanted to see how our evidence went, and to see if some witnesses would or would not be called towards the end of the trial," he says.

By this time Peggy Thatcher had arrived, dressed in a beige trenchcoat with a red scarf. All eyes in the crowded courtroom were on her. It was impossible not to feel sorry for this woman who had once been the first lady of the province, who with her handsome young son and lovely, fresh daughter-in-law beside her had basked in the pomp and ceremony as her husband was sworn in as Saskatchewan's premier. She would attend every day of the trial as a show of support for Colin. For a woman so habitually shy and concerned with image, it must have been an excruciating and humiliating ordeal.

The first witness called by the assistant Crown attorney—Al Johnson, a quiet, bespectacled young man—was Constable

Walter Fryklund of the Regina police Identification Service. He had taken a series of photos of the area around the Wilsons' house, of the body lying under the cars, and of various cars involved in the murder. These were meant to help the jury view the evidence in concrete terms. What was not shown in court was a series of photos taken of JoAnn's mutilated and incredibly bloody face and skull. The beating had been so savage that Kujawa felt the pictures might turn the jurors' stomachs; also, they were so inflammatory that the judge would probably not have allowed them in as evidence. Fryklund had also tested the Visa slip located near the garage for fingerprints, and the only ones found were those of the two police officers who had handled the receipt after it was discovered. Allbright revealed, in cross-examining Fryklund, that the police had found a footprint of a size ten running shoe near the Visa receipt.

The next two witnesses were police officers, who testified that on the day Thatcher was arrested they found a box that had once contained a toy, a Cindy Shower, in a small closet. The only entrance to the closet was through Thatcher's bedroom. Inside the box was a copy of the *Los Angeles Times* dated June 25, 1982.

The final witness on the first day of the trial was Craig Dotson, a balding, soft-spoken man of forty. In precise and painful detail, he told his story of how he had heard the shrill screams, seen the assailant coming out of the garage, and notified Tony Wilson that his wife had been shot. Asked about his identification of the suspect, Dotson emphatically said, "What I saw was very dark and very vague and very brief."

It was of vital importance to the defence to establish that the man Dotson saw looked nothing like Thatcher, and neither did the drawing of the suspect the police created from Craig's description. Although he was soft-spoken and looked very nervous on the stand, Dotson was a hard nut to crack. Allbright asked him: "But that individual that's in the sketch, with that description, Mr. Dotson, to you as a citizen under oath in this court, that looks to you to the best of your ability, always remembering that, like the man you saw coming out of the garage?" Dotson: "Yes. If you will just permit the qualification again that when you show me the photograph, the drawing, the illumination is better and you ask me to pay attention to it and you show it to me for a long time, neither one of those things was true when I saw the person. But with those qualifications, my answer to your question, sir, is yes."

Secretly, Dotson was furious at Allbright's style of questioning. "I found him condescending, pompous, and obviously manipulative," he says. What bothered him most was that Allbright kept putting words in his mouth. In one example the lawyer said, "You appear to me to be meticulous, careful, not the kind of person to jump to conclusions. And this is not the time for modesty, Mr. Dotson, but would that in your opinion be a fair estimation of you?" In court Dotson replied, "I'm not certain, sir." Later, he fumed: "It didn't matter what I said because the jurors had already heard those words. There were other examples of this. I was offended and insulted that he could think he could put this over on me or the jurors."

TUESDAY, OCTOBER 16

The lovely sunny fall that had made this charming, riverside city golden had prematurely turned into winter. A raging blizzard had descended on Saskatoon and snow would fall all day; one reporter quipped that it was God showing his displeasure. But the miserable weather did not stop spectators from lining up outside the courtroom early. They brought sleeping bags and thermoses of coffee and they huddled companionably together for shelter.

The day's first witness was Constable Joe Fraser, the young official who had arrived first at the murder scene. He testified that the time was precisely 6:05 p.m. Allbright spent some time with this police officer, trying to establish that at 6 p.m. on a Friday it would take ten to fifteen minutes to reach the outskirts of Regina. "You don't agree with that?" asked Allbright. "No," answered Fraser, who maintained that it could be done faster. Allbright was trying to establish, with Fraser and other witnesses, that it would have been impossible for Thatcher to commit the murder and then drive back to Moose Jaw in time to telephone Lynne Mendell in Palm Springs at 6:24 p.m. Astonishingly, all of this would become irrelevant; the

6:24 p.m. phone call never did become hard evidence that the jury could consider in its deliberations.

The next couple of witnesses testified about the suspicious gas receipt. Constable Thomas Schuck described how he found the Visa slip four feet from the corner of the Wilson garage. He made out the word "THATCH" and then handed it over to Sergeant Murton. "Did you get the feeling that somebody had almost left a calling card, Witness?" Allbright asked. Schuck replied, "No."

Jack Janzen, who owned the J&M Shell station near Caron at the time of the murder, testified that he sold Thatcher the gas on January 18, 1983, three days before the murder. Allbright said to him, "I understand this happened about mid-afternoon on that date, that's what I'm advised of. Is that your understanding as well? Do you recall that?" Janzen answered, "I think it was. It was after dinner, yes." To him, dinner meant the midday meal. This was important evidence because Allbright would later claim that Thatcher could not have been stalking his wife at 3 p.m. that Tuesday as the Crown contended.

Margaret Johannsson, a young, well-dressed civil servant, described how she was walking home from her job at the Legislative Buildings at about 5:05 p.m. on Thursday, January 20, 1983, when she spotted a car parked on 20th Street between Albert Street and the alley that ran behind the Wilson house. "I noticed as I got to it that there was a person sitting in the car. I thought it was unusual because the car wasn't running and the lights weren't on." She noticed a fluorescent orange-and-black Government of Saskatchewan sticker on the bumper.

A serious and nervous Joan Hasz next took the stand. Nicely dressed in a blue-and-white flowered print dress, her hair freshly permed, she recited how she first spotted the blue Oldsmobile on Tuesday, January 18, and then observed it for the next two days. She recalled how on Thursday she decided to make a note of the licence but the plate was smeared with mud. She did, however, note the numbers 292. She also saw a "mustard yellow sticker with black letters" on the car's bumper.

Allbright handled Mrs. Hasz with great condescension. He quickly mentioned three numbers and then asked her if she remembered the first combination. The older woman had difficulty doing so. Allbright said, "We won't get into a guessing game, but suffice it for me to say to you that sometimes numbers are difficult to remember, but if this assists you, I said 838. And what happens is that when something else happens, you can forget what has gone before. Does that not happen to you as it does to me?" Mrs. Hasz replied, "Right." Nobody knew what the jury's reaction was to Allbright's numbers game, but many among the media observers felt it might have backfired; for one thing, few of them had remembered 838, either.

Mrs. Hasz's employer, Duane Adams, made a marvellous witness for the defence. He confirmed most of what Mrs. Hasz had said, but then insisted most emphatically that the man in the car looked nothing like Colin Thatcher. Allbright: "Approximately thirty years of age or less. That was an age estimation that came from you, sir?" Adams: "It was." Allbright: "By the way, would you not agree that Mr. Thatcher looks every one of his forty-six years?" Adams: "Well, I'm not going to judge Mr. Thatcher's age, but certainly the person we're talking about is a person younger than Mr. Thatcher." Allbright: "In fact to get to the point, the person you described in the vehicle doesn't look like Mr. Thatcher at all?" Adams: "No, it doesn't."

Thatcher was visibly happy and relieved with this testimony.

The court adjourned early at 3 p.m. so that the jurors could get home through the snowstorm. As he was leaving the courtroom, Colin turned and nodded at his mother. She was the only one of the family who had made it through the blizzard. All day she had sat alone in the courtroom as the evidence accusing her son had droned on.

WEDNESDAY, OCTOBER 17

Colin Thatcher was resplendent in a fawn-coloured ultra-suede jacket, a cream shirt, and a dark brown-and-beige striped silk tie. He would have been right at home on Canyon Drive in Palm Springs; perhaps he realized that the California part of his life would be dramatically on display during this day.

The judge and the Crown were set to proceed when Allbright piped up, "I wonder, My Lord, if we might get our jury." There was much laughter all around, especially from Mr. Justice Maher. "Ladies and gentlemen of the jury, we tried to start without you, but they would not let us," he said.

The morning began with two quick witnesses for the Crown. Sergeant Gene Stusek told the jury about finding the Oldsmobile with mud and the numbers 292 on its licence plate in front of Thatcher's Moose Jaw house. He said that the car had been covered with snow, indicating that it could not have been used on the night of the murder.

Charles Guillaume, Thatcher's former executive assistant and his 1982 campaign manager, described finding the holster under the seat of the government car Thatcher had used. Allbright asked him, "You found the holster and you showed it to Colin, asked if it was his, he couldn't be less concerned about this holster than he appeared to you, could he?" Guillaume answered, "No." This witness looked very uncomfortable on the stand, probably because he remained a staunch supporter of Thatcher's.

At last, the witness everybody had been waiting for floated into the courtroom. Lynne Mendell looked very Californian. Her hair was a bronze colour, styled very short and smoothed around her face. She was slender and small-boned with a perfect tan. She wore a tasteful blue wool skirt, quite full, a brown jersey sweater, a salt-and-pepper tweed jacket and the ever-present expensive grey suede boots. One reporter whispered that she looked like a jaded Mary Martin playing a coy Peter Pan.

In a serious, earnest manner, Mendell told of her "stormy" relationship with Colin Thatcher, how he hated his wife, how he had many times told Lynne he wanted to kill her; how fearful he was of his phone and condominium being bugged; how he told her that dressed in a disguise he had shot but only wounded JoAnn—"And I had to go out in the goddamn prairie, circumvent the whole thing and, boy, did I have to drive fast and I was sweating," he laughed—how their relationship continued but was more turbulent and violent than ever; how he had set up an alibi by establishing a phone pattern with her; how in January of 1983 he had said to her, "I have to admit it is a strange feeling to have blown your wife away." When Lynne spoke those words, several jurors visibly winced.

If the jury believed Mendell's story, Thatcher would have

to be found guilty of first-degree murder. That made it imperative that Allbright discredit her as a witness. Through two and a half hours of hard-hitting cross-examination, he was on the attack. Mendell had told Kujawa she was now a full-time artist, specializing in montages. Every word dripping with sarcasm, Allbright began his cross-examination: "Mrs. Mendell, I learned something today I didn't know at the preliminary. I take it it is new. You are an artist now, you tell us?"

MENDELL: Yes, I always have been. Not always full-time.
ALLBRIGHT: Now you are a full-time artist, is that it?
MENDELL: Yes.
ALLBRIGHT: And looking to make a bit of a name for yourself as an artist, are you?
MENDELL: I don't know.

Allbright's strategy was to lay bare the weaknesses not so much in Mendell's evidence as in her character. Why hadn't she warned the police that JoAnn was about to be murdered, for example?

ALLBRIGHT: You had no concern for the life of an individual that was about to be taken. It mattered not to you, Witness, is that it?
MENDELL: I didn't say I had no concern and I did not say it did not matter.
ALLBRIGHT: You had it in your power, Witness, if you chose, from what you tell us, if what you tell us is true, you had it in your power to save a human life. You just threw that chance away with a snap of a finger just like that, is that it?
MENDELL: If that's the way you want to put it. I don't really see it that way.
ALLBRIGHT: . . . In fact you didn't do anything even when you knew on January 21, 1983, even when you knew what you say you knew, you didn't take a step to tell anybody?
MENDELL: Perhaps this was a mistake on my part.
ALLBRIGHT: Perhaps this whole little bit this morning is a flight of fancy on your part, Witness. A little bit of imagination, would you agree with that?
MENDELL: Not at all.

* * *

Allbright was walking on eggs here, because if he was going
to fault Mendell for not going to the authorities, he was
basically admitting that his client must have committed the
murder. He quickly moved on to something else.

It was important to show that Lynne Mendell was untruth-
ful. Allbright pointed out that when the Regina police had
first contacted her she refused to tell them anything. "So at
the right occasion, at the right time, for the right reason, you
would be prepared to lie, Witness, is that correct?" demanded
Allbright. Mendell responded, "I don't think that's correct.
Under pressure from my father and in an age and era of
quote 'Let's not get involved' unquote, I believed him for the
few minutes it took him to convince me that my safety would
not be jeopardized if I just didn't get involved. I never really
lied. I just never told them what I knew."

While Allbright cross-examined Lynne, and indeed many
witnesses, he moved continuously around the room. One
moment he would be standing beside his seated client—as if
soliciting sympathy—a good thirty feet from the witness
stand; another moment he would be eyeball to eyeball with
the often intimidated person he was questioning; at other
times, if the evidence was dramatic or important, he would
do a pirouette in the middle of a sentence, turning his back
on his victim as he demanded, "Do you really believe that,
Witness, do you?" In his flowing court gown, he looked like a
handsome but menacing black butterfly, floating endlessly
from one spot to another.

Allbright's next ploy was to portray Mendell as emotionally
unstable. As ammunition he was able to point out her suicide
attempt after a bitter fight with Thatcher in the summer of
1982. Up until this point Allbright had managed to keep a
tight reign on his witness, sometimes asking her long-winded
questions designed to evoke responses of a few words. But
Mendell appealed to the judge, who allowed her to break
away and tell her side of the story: Thatcher had promised to
marry her and had reneged; they had had a violent fight and
he had hit her; after she had taken the drug she realized "that
Colin Thatcher wasn't worth killing myself for"; she had
awakened him and had received treatment at the hospital.
After Lynne Mendell was finished, Allbright said: "Witness,
this was a suicide attempt on you part and while we're

covering it with some very nice language, let's call it what it is. Would you not agree... it was a suicide attempt?"

MENDELL: Yes, it was fifteen minutes of that state of mind, of course.

ALLBRIGHT: And that is not, Witness, the action of a stable individual, would you agree?

MENDELL: I was rendered rather unstable at the time....

ALLBRIGHT: I suggest you weren't stable for about the last three years from what you have told us, Witness, is that a fair assessment of your character? Your mental state? Your emotional well-being?

MENDELL: I would not say that is a fair assessment at all.

Since Mendell could not be subpoenaed from the United States, she had voluntarily come to Saskatoon to testify. It was essential for Allbright to find a reason why she would give evidence against Thatcher.

ALLBRIGHT: Isn't the reason you became bitter towards Colin Thatcher is that you, Witness, spent, and as you viewed it, you wasted two years of your life on that man and when you realized he wasn't going to marry you, you got bitter and I mean bitter?

MENDELL: When did I say I was bitter? You said when I became bitter. You haven't established that I had become bitter because I didn't.

ALLBRIGHT: Oh, you didn't become bitter?

MENDELL: The one time in the summer, the summer up there when I took the pills, I was a little bitter, yes. There were so many lies. I was bitter then. Afterwards I wasn't. When I left him, I was not bitter at all. I was more just relieved.

ALLBRIGHT: We're talking, Witness, about the kind of bitterness I suggest to you that comes after two years of what you conceive to be giving this man your all and then he clearly doesn't want to marry you. Is that the kind of bitterness you might have felt?

MENDELL: No, no...

The defence lawyer tried another tack.

ALLBRIGHT: Is this a fine act for this jury?

MENDELL: My act?

ALLBRIGHT: Yeah, your act?

MENDELL: Not at all.

ALLBRIGHT: You enjoy this process.

MENDELL: Not at all.

ALLBRIGHT: Being here? Not enjoying the notoriety of being here as a witness in a major murder trial with such cogent evidence to give, Witness?

MENDELL: The life of my husband and myself has been threatened twice by telephone.

ALLBRIGHT: Oh, that's very convenient.

MENDELL: Do you think I would be here if I enjoy it? I'm sorry.

ALLBRIGHT: Very convenient.

The final punch that Allbright threw could have resulted in a knockout. The most important information the lawyer had at his disposal was that Mendell had continued to have sexual relations with Thatcher during the time he was in Palm Springs after JoAnn had been murdered. As well, she had visited with Colin and his sons on at least five occasions during 1983 and 1984 before his arrest.

ALLBRIGHT: Witness, what kind of woman sleeps with a man, she's not married to, when she knows in her mind, if what you tell us is true, that the man has just committed murder. What kind of a woman does that, Witness?

MENDELL: Someone who is very afraid that if she doesn't she, which it happened in the past, if you want an incident in London I can get that to you, that if she didn't she would get smacked around again.

ALLBRIGHT: I see. Of course there were never any witnesses to this smacking around, were there? Never any witnesses, Witness, were there?

MENDELL: You are right, there were not.

ALLBRIGHT: And of course that's the kind of thing that would come down to your word perhaps versus his. No independent witnesses. Convenient.

MENDELL: I don't like the picture it makes of me to admit that I stayed with someone who had hit me, even once. . . . I wouldn't make that up. That was a weakness. I had . . .

ALLBRIGHT: . . . Mrs. Mendell, the conscience of every soul in this room will I'm sure suggest to you as I do at this time, if you believe, if you believed that Colin Thatcher was a murderer, you would have put so much distance between you and he that the two thousand miles we earlier talked about would seem minuscule. You would have gotten so far away from him, Witness, that you would have nothing to do with him. But you didn't do that, did you?

MENDELL: I wanted to take everything I owned with me. I didn't get that far away. I just moved back with my parents. I don't understand what you are trying to say or ask me.

During much of this cross-examination, Kujawa was fuming. The police officers at the trial who sat in the prisoner's box behind him thought they could see smoke coming out of his ears. Finally he intervened. "My Lord, on that point, and I hesitate to rise with an objection of this kind, but My Learned Friend has been speaking sentences occasionally, but mostly paragraphs which I have difficulty following. He is supposed to ask questions when he is cross-examining. My Learned Friend is not supposed to state what everyone in the world has told him in paragraphs and then at the end ask if that's so. That's impossible to answer. . . . Let me register an objection to that line of cross-examination which has been improper from the word go."

Mr. Justice Maher gently chided Allbright. "In a trial like this of course we give all the rights we can to cross-examining counsel and hesitate to interfere, but witnesses find it difficult, and I would if I were a witness, when a question is put following a long dissertation. And the problem you have is whether the witness is answering the long dissertation or simply the last question phrased."

Allbright made much of the the fact when Thatcher had discussed the murder and the wounding with Mendell he had used oblique coded language, at least when he felt that he could be overheard by bugs. Lynne testified that after she had said, "Well, you really did it this time, didn't you?" meaning the murder, Colin nodded and then pointed to the ceiling and walls and said hush.

ALLBRIGHT: Can you tell me this, Witness, did you ever give Colin Thatcher the benefit of one doubt on one occasion in that when he said something to you it might have been

very innocent? You could have put an innocent interpretation on it as opposed to a guilty one. Did you ever do that?

MENDELL: I'm sure I have.

ALLBRIGHT: Would you agree with me that you certainly
haven't in any fashion today with anything we've talked
about today, have you?

MENDELL: No.

The Crown had only one point to make in re-examination.

KUJAWA: We've spent a long time here, Mrs. Mendell, on the
issue of your understanding the communications between
yourself and Colin Thatcher. If I said to you last week,
every time I say, "I have obtained the groceries," every
time I say that to you, it means that I have obtained some
heroin and I phone you and I say, "I have the groceries,
Lynne," what would it mean to you?

MENDELL: I have heroin.

KUJAWA: What would it mean to these people listening on the
side?

MENDELL: I have the groceries.

Colin Thatcher had sat through the ordeal stony-eyed, not
showing a flicker of emotion. When the cross-examination of
his former lover was over, almost everybody—the spectators,
the media, the lawyers, the jurors, the judge—felt as though
they had been put through the wringer of an old-fashioned
washing machine. Lynne Mendell, however, looked just fine.
She put on fresh lipstick and posed for a moment for the
hordes of photographers and cameramen outside the courtroom. That evening the picture of the Palm Springs golden
girl with the green eyes was flashed across the country to
appear on the front pages of Canadian newspapers from coast
to coast. For now there was no question; the Thatcher
murder trial was the biggest story in the country, and every
detail was being eagerly gobbled up by millions of readers
and viewers.

There was, however, one part of Allbright's cross-examination
that had puzzled and upset Lynne. He asked her if she had
ever had a stormy relationship with her husband and she said
no. Then he asked her if she knew a Palm Springs attorney
by the name of Bob Kramer. When she nodded yes, he

suggested that she had gone to Kramer to ask for the name of a good divorce lawyer. "I deny that. I deny the thought," she said.

Mendell says that she had indeed called Kramer but in order to ask for a good divorce lawyer for her husband's receptionist, whose marriage had just ended. "When I got back from Canada, I called Kramer and said, 'I've got a little bone to pick with you, kiddo.'" It turned out that Kramer had mentioned her call to his partner, who was the son-in-law of Thatcher's next-door neighbour at the condo. Mendell thought that line of questioning was a low blow; it was the one thing that truly upset her about the trial.

THURSDAY, OCTOBER 18

For the fourth day of the trial, Thatcher arrived dressed in a blue banker's suit with white shirt and blue tie. He looked older and greyer.

The courtroom was chilled as Dr. John Vetters, the pathologist, described in clinical, dispassionate detail the damage inflicted on the victim. There were no fewer than twenty well-defined cuts to the skull, each caused by a separate blow. "These blows were caused by a sharp instrument with some weight or heft to it," said the pathologist. "Because of the short length of each of the cuts, I believe it likely that the implement had a curved blade." He also described severe injuries to the hands, including the near severing of the left baby finger. And he said her face had been bruised, probably when she fell to the ground. The most serious wound, of course, had been caused by a gunshot wound at the base of her right ear, and the official cause of death was reported as disruption of the brain by the passage of the bullet. The pathologist was not able to say whether the blows would have caused her death, so great had been the damage done by the bullet.

Dr. Vetters's presentation was appropriately dry and technical. Indeed, the one element that was missing during the entire trial, as so often happens in murder trials, was any presence, any sense, of the victim. JoAnn's personality, her joys and miseries, her accomplishments and mistakes, would emerge not at all—only her final anguish and defeat, and they would emerge all too vividly.

The only forensic evidence presented during the trial was given by Staff Sergeant Arnold Somers, a firearms and ammunition expert with the RCMP in Regina. By the time his two and a half hours of testimony were completed, most heads in the courtroom were swimming with incomprehensible and contradictory facts.

The evidence elicited by the Crown was fairly straightforward. After Somers was given the fourteen tiny fragments of bullet found in JoAnn's skull, he was assigned three specific tasks: to find the calibre of the bullet, the make and type of ammunition, and the make and type of firearm used. He determined readily that the calibre of the bullet was .357 and that the bullet jacket was unusual in that it was made of aluminum. "It is made by only one company in the U.S., that being Winchester." He also decided that the bullet was probably a 95-grain hollow-point. On further investigation, he concluded that that particular weight was loaded only in the Winchester .38 ammunition. In other words the type of ammunition used was likely a Winchester .38 Special Plus P, aluminum-jacketed 95-grain. "Definitely it would not be available in the retail market in Canada as an over-the-counter item for just anyone," he said. Somers also said the gun would likely be a Ruger in either .38 special cartridge or .357 Magnum cartridge. "But," he added, "I wouldn't rule out other possibilities such as Smith and Wesson or possibly Colt."

The staff sergeant was a large, low-voiced placid witness. During cross-examination Allbright, the scrappy terrier, grabbed hold of Somers, the slow-moving mastiff, and gave him a good shake. Somers had, at one point, weighed the bullet fragments but had failed to record what he had found. Allbright made much of this. "I can't believe that you can't tell me what these weigh. Is that—is that what you're telling me?" he asked. Somers replied that it was. How could the sergeant possibly know it was a 95-grain bullet, then, Allbright indignantly demanded.

But that was only the beginning. Somers contended that the ammunition was only sold in Canada by police suppliers. "Under the explosives act, it is prohibited for use in a revolver." "I can buy that right here in Saskatchewan," barked Allbright, "and I can assure you I'm not a police officer; I can legally buy it, sir. . . . I'm going to show you the stuff that I can't buy in Saskatchewan, Witness. Take a look at that and you tell me if that isn't the same stuff, two boxes of that, that you've been talking about here this morning, that I can't buy in Saskatchewan, Witness?" Allbright then slammed down two boxes of 95-grain silver-tip hollow-point ammunition made by Winchester and produced an invoice made out to him from the Gun Rack of Drinkwater, Saskatchewan, dated October 11, 1984. It was a dramatic moment. But this piece of theatre would quickly come back to haunt the lawyer.

For the next hour or so calibres, velocities, and foot-pounds swirled around the room until the eyes of several of the jurors glazed over, one even appeared to fall asleep, and a couple of the policemen in attendance admitted that even they were completely lost.

After lunch there was some suspense as Sergeant Somers arrived with his scales. The bullet fragments were found to weigh 83.6 grains, although there were some very small pieces that had proved impossible to dislodge from the skull. "I think it would be quite logical that they might weigh the difference between what we have here and 95 grains," said Somers. "I would say the most logical bullet for it to be would be the 95-grain Silvertip Hollow Point manufactured by Winchester." The evidence appeared to have gone full circle, back to where Sergeant Somers had started.

The next witness was the burly ex-cop Ron Williams, who said that he sold Thatcher the Ruger Security-Six, calibre .357 Magnum, in Palm Springs on January 29, 1982. He also testified that Thatcher bought two boxes of Winchester Western .38 Special Plus P Silvertip Hollow Point. Williams revealed that this was highly potent ammunition. "It is designed specifically for police work, which is the reason for the Plus P designation. . . . It's commonly referred to as a dumdum or a hollow point, and it's designed upon entry into a medium such as human flesh to expand and open up, thereby causing a greater shock to the system, greater trauma, greater blood loss." Allbright emphasized through cross-examination that Thatcher made no attempt to hide the fact that he was buying the gun, that he had gone through all the necessary registration processes. Williams admitted that in California it would have been easy to buy a gun under the counter.

* * *

Tony Wilson, the murdered woman's husband, arrived dressed entirely in blue—blue suit, blue vest, blue shirt, and blue tie—and indeed he remained very cool and controlled on the stand. During the preliminary hearing, Wilson's raw hatred of Thatcher had been so evident and it had been so difficult to keep his evidence contained within legal niceties that Kujawa had actually considered not calling him for the trial. The Crown attorney finally decided that Tony could still best describe the motive Thatcher had for killing JoAnn, but on the stand he kept him under tight rein. Very briefly, in his clipped English accent, Wilson outlined the Thatcher's marital battles, including the fight for the custody of Regan. He pointed out that under the terms of the matrimonial property agreement, Thatcher got a year's moratorium on the $87,000 payment that was due February 1, 1984, because of JoAnn's death. What made his testimony haunting was what he was not allowed to say, rather than what he did say. None of the threats that Thatcher had made emerged, nor did the anger or fear JoAnn felt towards him, primarily because of the rules of evidence.

Allbright's cross-examination shocked almost everyone in court. What he was obviously attempting to do was implant in the jury's minds the possibility that Tony Wilson himself might have been responsible for the murder. Allbright began by asking Wilson about the first shooting.

ALLBRIGHT: Did he [Thatcher] have some concerns about some of the people that were associated with you possibly being involved?

WILSON: No, he did not.

ALLBRIGHT: No sons or step-sons of yours being considered?

WILSON: I don't have any step-sons.

ALLBRIGHT: Adopted children? Do you have sons?

WILSON: I have two sons, yes.

ALLBRIGHT: . . . Was there not a suggestion by someone, perhaps you or Mr. Thatcher, raising the possibility of them being—one of them being the assailants.

WILSON: Not that I'm aware of.

ALLBRIGHT: Not that you're aware of. You didn't admit—you didn't have anything to do with that, did you, that first shooting, or the second one, I want to be clear on that; you had nothing to do with that, did you?

WILSON: No, of course not.

ALLBRIGHT: Do you know an individual by the name of Garry Anderson?

WILSON: No.

Of course Wilson would have needed to have a motive, and the defence lawyer hinted at several. Allbright began by asking him who lived in his house, and Wilson responded that the other residents were his younger son and the former housekeeper, Marja Lahtinen, who was twenty-three.

ALLBRIGHT: Mr. Wilson, I'll ask it as directly as I can and I'm sure you'll answer it as directly as you can. Were you and JoAnn having some marital problems?

WILSON: No, definitely not.

ALLBRIGHT: So if I were to suggest to you that perhaps the presence of the housekeeper on an ongoing basis was the source of some friction between you and JoAnn, what would your answer to that be?

WILSON: I would say that that is nonsense, because JoAnn hired her and JoAnn was very happy to have her there because it permitted JoAnn to travel.

ALLBRIGHT: What is the purpose then today of having this particular individual remain in your house? What duties does this person perform?

WILSON: She doesn't perform any duties. She's a student.

ALLBRIGHT: She's a student. I take it...

WILSON: We have a large house.

ALLBRIGHT: Right.

WILSON: And there is no reason to throw her out.

The defence lawyer then asked Wilson questions that revealed that the lights in his garage were not working on the day of the murder in his garage. He then elicited from Tony the fact that he had been suffering from flu that day and had come home at noon.

ALLBRIGHT: You didn't go and see a doctor, sir.

WILSON: No.

ALLBRIGHT: You didn't go and seek a prescription?

WILSON: No.

ALLBRIGHT: Just went home and went to bed?

WILSON: Yes. Flu isn't a particularly serious disease.

ALLBRIGHT: Serious enough apparently to keep you home, is that the case?

WILSON: A precaution.

ALLBRIGHT: . . . Who was home when you went home at noon?

WILSON: Stephanie and Marja.

ALLBRIGHT: Marja, the housekeeper and the young girl. At the time, how old was Stephanie?

WILSON: Eight.

ALLBRIGHT: All right. She would have been school age, and I presume would have gone to school . . .

WILSON: Yes.

ALLBRIGHT: . . . Friday afternoon, is that correct?

WILSON: That's right.

ALLBRIGHT: Okay. So in the afternoon, from say 1:30 to 5:00 o'clock, who was at home?

WILSON: I was at home. I can't remember whether Marja was home. She could have been at university because she was going part-time.

ALLBRIGHT: She was home for part of that afternoon, wasn't she.

WILSON: I don't remember.

ALLBRIGHT: . . . And you were upstairs with your—you were laying in bed at the time that you were aroused.

WILSON: Yes.

ALLBRIGHT: . . . You didn't hear anything at all in the garage?

WILSON: No.

ALLBRIGHT: Never heard a shot?

WILSON: No.

ALLBRIGHT: Never heard cries or screams?

WILSON: No. The bedroom is on the front of the house and it's on Albert Street, and at that time of day there is a fair amount of traffic noise.

ALLBRIGHT: And there is no doubt that you'd been in bed prior to being summoned? I take it you recall that fairly clearly, do you?

WILSON: Yes.

Allbright then emphasized that Wilson was a beneficiary under JoAnn's will. Of the $350,000 owed to the dead woman's estate by Colin Thatcher, Stephanie would get $250,000, Tony, $70,000 and JoAnn's parents, $30,000. "Isn't the reason that you're taking foreclosure proceedings . . . is pure and sheer spite that you have against Mr. Thatcher? Isn't that the motivation?" he asked Wilson. Tony said he was only following JoAnn's wishes by taking these proceedings against Thatcher.

Finally Wilson was able to convey some of the terror JoAnn must have lived with constantly—Kujawa would later call it a textbook case of what not to do when cross-examining a witness. Allbright was implying that Thatcher would not have wanted to kill his wife in May of 1981, when she was shot in the shoulder, because he would have owed the estate far more than was eventually negotiated.

ALLBRIGHT: Did it occur to you, Mr. Wilson, that when you finally reached an agreement of $500,000 that it was three hundred and some thousand dollars less than $800,000?

WILSON: Yes, because we were, or JoAnn was, extremely frightened [for] her life.

ALLBRIGHT: Oh, that's very convenient, Mr. Wilson, and she was, of course, frightened, had every right to be, but I suggest to you that you're making the judgment call that she was frightened—what, of this man . . . ?

WILSON: Yes.

ALLBRIGHT: Not someone else, but this man?

WILSON: That man there.

ALLBRIGHT: Was that her reaction, or yours, Witness?

WILSON: Hers.

ALLBRIGHT: I see. And, of course, she shared this with you many times?

WILSON: Yes.

ALLBRIGHT: You don't like Colin Thatcher at all, do you?

WILSON: No.

ALLBRIGHT: Would I be correct in saying that you wouldn't mind seeing Colin Thatcher be convicted for this, would you?

WILSON: I wouldn't mind.

On that note, the trial concluded for the day.

FRIDAY, OCTOBER 19

This was to be a day full of surprises. First, there was a formal admission by Allbright. It involved those packages of bullets he had so dramatically produced to disprove the ammunition expert's assertion that the Winchester .38 special hollow-tip were not readily available in Saskatchewan. The admission read, "The Crown alleges and the accused, W. Colin Thatcher, admits the following: that Clint Sandborn, the owner and registered gun dealer at The Gun Rack, Drinkwater, Saskatchewan, attended the Red Rock Sporting Goods Store at Miles City, Montana, on October 10, 1984, and purchased three boxes of Winchester .38 Special Silver Tip Hollow Point Ammunition, together with a number of other boxes of ammunition. That Clint Sandborn then returned the ammunition to Drinkwater, Saskatchewan, after declaring all of it at the Canada Customs Office and that he subsequently sold two boxes of that ammunition to Gerald Allbright." In other words, the day before Allbright had purchased the bullets in Drinkwater, the gun shop owner had bought them in the United States. Not only that, but David Nederhoff, the reeve of Rouleau and Thatcher's close friend—he would sit in the family seats many days during the trial—had gone with Sandborn specifically to purchase the ammunition in Miles City, Montana.

The police had discovered through a telephone tap that David Nederhoff, Nederhoff's brother, and Clint Sandborn were going to buy the bullets. A pre-warned official phoned Inspector Swayze when the trio came through Customs. The next day Sergeant Murton went to Miles City, Montana, and received statements from the gun shop owner that he had sold this specific ammunition to the Nederhoffs and Sandborn.

It was an extremely embarrassing moment for Allbright. But he now feels the whole thing was overplayed, and gives this version of events. At the preliminary he had taken Sergeant Somers's word that these bullets weren't available in Canada. But Allbright ran into Lyle Stewart, a good friend and political supporter of Colin Thatcher. Stewart had been talking to David Nederhoff, and he told him that an American gun dealer had said that these bullets were easy to obtain in Canada. Allbright then asked a friend who worked at the Saskatoon Gun Works about the bullets. "He said, 'Of course they're available. Anything that can be shot out of a handgun or a rifle you can use.'" And he showed him two boxes of .358 silver-tip hollow-point bullets. Nederhoff then asked Allbright if he wanted him to get some of the ammunition. "If you can get them legitimately, I'll take them. But it's got to be legitimate because if it isn't I don't need them. I can get them from the Saskatoon Gun Works," the lawyer said.

"Well, you shouldn't trust amateurs. I got these bullets and I thumped them down in court, and then of course the world erupted. Serge called me into the back room and he and Johnson were mad. It was the first time I had ever seen Johnson mad. He said, 'We're going to bring in the Customs guy.' I said fine. But then that's when I got mad and that's when I sent my partner over to the Saskatoon Gun Works." Allbright submitted an invoice from the Saskatoon Gun Works for a box of .357 Magnum ammunition.

The whole thing seemed like a tempest in a teapot. Allbright probably made his point that the specific bullets could indeed be obtained in Saskatchewan. But the evidence remained that Thatcher himself had purchased that type of ammunition in Palm Springs. And since Allbright didn't have the opportunity to tell his side of the story in the courtroom, the jurors must have been influenced by what looked like sleight of hand on the part of the defence.

Immediately after this set-to, there was another surprising development. Kujawa announced to the court that the next witness, Garry Anderson, was not available to testify that day. He asked that proceedings be adjourned until Monday. He knew—and the police knew—that the Crown's case was collapsing about their ears.

CHAPTER TWENTY
DENY, DENY, DENY

The disaster had started to take shape the first day of the trial. At about 1:30 p.m. Jack Janzen, the Caron service station owner, Craig Dotson, and a few police officers, including Bob Murton, were waiting their turn in the courthouse witness room. They were chatting about this and that and Janzen said to Murton, "Do you think I'll get on today?" Murton replied that he wasn't sure but he hoped so. "Well, I guess Garry Anderson won't be on today?" said Janzen. "Oh, why's that?" said the policeman. "Because on my way here, I saw him heading south on the highway." "Oh," said Murton and then quickly, "Anybody like a cup of coffee? I've got to go out for a few minutes."

Actually Anderson had driven to Saskatoon earlier that day, arriving just before court started. It had been arranged that he would stay at the Ramada Renaissance, under the watchful eyes of the police officers who were also in residence there, until he had completed testifying. The police were already nervous about their prime witness and they were anxiously waiting for him. "We thought we'd hear his truck coming, but it was a car and he kinda slouched down in it. He saw that I saw him," says Swayze. Anderson then called the sheriff's office and spoke to the deputy chief (Swayze had been promoted from inspector). He said he was angry at the Regina police and the RCMP and he "threatened to do me in," says Swayze. "If you want me, you can damn well come to the farm and get me," Anderson said and headed back for Caron; along the way Janzen, who was going in the opposite direction, spotted his truck.

Thus began a week of trying to keep track of and soothe the emotionally overwrought and nearly suicidal Garry Anderson. "We knew he was going to be upset, he was always upset," says Swayze. "I would have put people with him, or even stayed with him myself, talked him down, kept him loose. But he was hiding out at his mother's place, and he didn't have anybody to talk to."

Things had not gone well for Anderson for several months, although the Regina police had tried to help him. Sergeants Street and Murton were ordered to go to his farm at one o'clock one morning to help him pack furniture into a rented van. He was moving to Edmonton to assume the new identity and the new life that had been promised if he agreed to testify. The RCMP was in charge of this operation. Unfortunately the Mounties were not quite as sensitive to his demands as the Regina police, and Anderson felt he was caught up in a bureaucratic nightmare. He complained bitterly that he had trouble getting a driver's licence, a job, and a social insurance number and that he was not receiving the amount of relocation money he thought he would be getting. In his words, "It was my opinion that the RCMP in Regina really didn't give a shit about me, the people who were in charge of it." By early September he was miserable, lonely, and depressed, and decided to move back to his mother's farm in Caron. It was obvious to everybody that he was emotionally worked up even at this point. And soon he was mad at the Regina police and Ed Swayze in particular.

After his anger reached the boiling point, Anderson phoned Serge Kujawa. "I want to see you. Don't phone, 'cause I won't answer the phone. And you had better not bring any goddamn cops. Come alone!" he barked. Kujawa wasn't about to do that, so he and Swayze drove to Caron in an unmarked police car.

They waited for a while outside the ramshackle old farmhouse. "My basic reason for not going to the door was fear," says Kujawa. They waited and waited and finally drove up close to the house, pointed the car right at the door and waited some more. Anderson, who stands six-foot-two and weighs 235 pounds, finally came out and Kujawa jumped out of the car to join him. "All I can remember is him roaring, 'I told you not to bring any blankety-blank cops. I hate 'em.' Then he came very close to me and said, 'Why do you have that blankety-blank smirk on your face?' I hadn't realized that I had a smirk on my face but I answered, 'I wish you were eighty pounds lighter'—'cause I thought at that weight I

could handle him until help came. He burst out laughing."
After that Anderson, Kujawa, and Swayze had a good long
talk.

By the time the trial started, however, Anderson was again
in an emotional frenzy. On Monday, after he had made his
frantic trip to Saskatoon and back, he developed severe
headaches and began taking larger and larger doses of Tylenol.
"During the last few and preceding weeks, and especially in
the last week, I had one—I had a very, very hell of a
headache, and I originally took Tylenol to keep it down, and
the headache got worse and I just kept taking more," he said.
On Thursday he swallowed twelve before supper and twenty-
four afterwards, which plunged him into an emotional abyss.

Meanwhile Swayze and company were desperately trying
to figure out what to do about the Crown's chief witness. It
was Sergeant Jim Street who volunteered to go to Caron and
talk to Anderson. Swayze didn't like the idea at first because
they knew that Anderson would be armed, as well as emotional, but then it began to make sense. "Street is a hunter
and a fisherman and a backwoodsman. He loves that kind of
stuff," says Swayze. "So does Garry Anderson and they had
talked about stuff like that. Street used to be a SWAT leader
so he knows how to handle himself." Street says he wasn't
frightened of Anderson at all. "I took him for a drive across
the country once that scared the shit out of him," says Street,
"and I gained a certain amount of respect. I'm a farm boy too
and if he wants to drive on gravel roads and chase deer, I've
done that as much as he has. And he knows it. So I wasn't
scared of him, not at all."

Still, Swayze wanted to be sure that Street was able to
approach Anderson's house in daylight, so the two men and
Bob Murton flew to Regina early Thursday afternoon in an
RCMP plane. Street wanted to make his point emphatically,
so he started kicking and banging on Anderson's door. Garry
in turn began hollering and screaming for Street to goddamn
fuck off, he didn't want to talk to no cop. He was waving a
long-barrelled rifle around. "He's carrying it in a way that
he's menacing me but he's making a point of not pointing it
right at me," remembers Street. Anderson's girlfriend, who
had been holed up inside the creaky farmhouse with Garry,
led Street into the front porch. The sergeant tried to settle
the raving man down and tried to talk sense with him. "He

was upset with us because he figured he was gonna get a whole bunch of relocation money. And of course he hadn't got it yet, he hadn't testified. He wasn't gonna get nothing till he testified, I told him."

Street says Anderson's girlfriend made him more nervous than Garry did. "There were times when he would take a step forward, and she'd jump back. She was between us. I got the impression that she thought he was gonna shoot both of us." Anderson continued to rant and rave and Street, realizing that he wasn't getting anywhere, gave up and left.

After that the RCMP surrounded the place. At about 3 a.m. they detonated an explosive out in the yard which, as Swayze says, "probably sounded like the whole house blew up." Thereupon Anderson and his girlfriend gave themselves up and Garry handed over his guns. The RCMP were amazed that at that point he was "as calm and cool as a cucumber." Anderson was arrested for failing to respond to a subpoena and threatening a police officer. The police had already made arrangements for him to see a psychiatrist in Regina. After that, he was flown to Saskatoon and admitted to the psychiatric wing of the city hospital. By that time he had contacted a Moose Jaw lawyer, William Gardner, who was negotiating for him with the police.

MONDAY, OCTOBER 22

Anderson arrived at the courthouse in the back seat of a police car, hidden under a blanket. While big-name national photographers were running around like chickens, a greenhorn from the Saskatoon *Star-Phoenix* who had shrewdly brought a small ladder with him placed it near the courthouse garage windows. It was the only photos anyone would get of Anderson, but they were published and broadcast across the country.

Colin Thatcher's elegance—he was dressed in an ultra-suede royal blue jacket and a light blue shirt, with dark blue-and-grey striped tie—was in marked contrast with Garry Anderson's jeans, navy blue quilted vest, and the great scraggly beard he had grown to hide his identity. He was more paunchy than he was at the preliminary hearing and there was a look of desperation in his eyes. And yet his testimony was surprisingly straightforward and devoid of erratic emotions. At the preliminary he had taken so long to respond to questions that his delivery had often been embarrassing, to the point that he seemed slow-witted, which apparently wasn't the case at all. Swayze claimed that it was his dire warning that Anderson would be charged with conspiracy to murder if he made one false statement that caused him to be so careful. During the trial, however, although Anderson answered questions with as few words as possible, and though the words were unimaginative, his testimony was not as wooden or slow.

Under Kujawa's careful questioning, Anderson told the sorry story of his involvement with Thatcher. In the fall of 1980 Thatcher had offered to pay him $50,000 on an instalment plan if he would murder JoAnn. Anderson said he refused the deal but promised Colin that he would try to find somebody who might be interested. Some months after, he met with Charlie Wilde and Cody Crutcher in a bar, got an undertaking from Crutcher that he would kill JoAnn, and then gave him $7,500 of Thatcher's money. On a Regina street a few days later he delivered to Wilde another $7,000, a set of Thunderbird car keys, and a picture of Thatcher's ex-wife. When nothing happened, Thatcher again approached Anderson, who arranged a meeting with him and Charlie Wilde at the abandoned farm. Wilde and Thatcher talked about killing JoAnn in the United States during Easter of 1981. Thatcher later told Anderson that he had given yet more money to Charlie but nothing had come of it. Shortly after that, Thatcher asked Anderson to buy him a rifle and ammunition and he duly purchased a .303 Lee Enfield. As well, on two occasions Anderson went with Thatcher to Regina to survey the Wilson property. He also rented a car from Scott Ford and left it two or three blocks west of Thatcher's residence. After Garry had heard that JoAnn had been shot on May 17, 1981, he picked up the rental car and returned it to the dealer.

Anderson then saw nothing of Thatcher until the fall of 1982, when they met 'at the abandoned farm, where Colin gave Anderson a .357 Magnum and asked him to make a silencer for it. He made six, test-fired them, and eventually threw three of them into the field of his brother's farm and disposed of another three at the garbage dump.

On January 20, Anderson, on a visit to Caron from La Ronge, accidentally met Colin at a gas station near his mother's farm. Thatcher mentioned that he had been stalking his wife and asked Anderson if he could lend him his car and if he still had the .357 Magnum. When Anderson replied yes to both questions, Thatcher asked to meet him the next day in Moose Jaw. Anderson picked Thatcher up a couple of blocks from his Redland home in his 1974 Mercury, and the two drove to the bus station. At that point Anderson handed the car over to Colin and then went to the dentist. The next day Anderson read that JoAnn Wilson had been murdered, and as arranged he picked up the Mercury, noticing once again that the licence plates were smeared with mud. He found left on the passenger seat a black ski jacket, a pair of blue jeans, grey work socks, a credit card receipt, and a pair of sunglasses, while on the floor there were tufts of hair that seemed to be out of a wig. Anderson took all of these things and burned them in a barrel at his mother's farm.

Once the bare bones of the story had been put before the jury, Kujawa quickly moved to the tape recording between Anderson and Thatcher. In law it was necessary to establish that Anderson had not been coerced to make the recording. During a *voir dire*, Anderson stated that he consented both to being involved in the recording session and also to the tape's being played in court. A very hostile Allbright asked him, "Do you mean to tell me, Mr. Anderson, and I want to make sure I understand, that if, in April of 1984, you had refused to participate in the body pack, you're telling me that you don't believe that would have had any effect on your immunity agreement?" Anderson replied, "I believe it would have had no effect on it." After legal argument, Justice Maher ruled that the tape was admissible.

It proved to be a bombshell. Besides what the actual words revealed, what was astonishing about the tape was Thatcher's tone of voice. Unlike Garry Anderson, who sounded as though he were frightened for his life, Thatcher was not quite relaxed—the subject matter made that unlikely—but comfortable and in control. His conversation sounded conspiratorial; like that of a man participating in a deadly secret cabal. The code language that was used, however, was a sinister version of cowboy vernacular, rather than that of high-level political intrigue. Thatcher's forceful personality was obvious throughout; he dominated the discussion, and his tone of voice revealed that he was used to manipulating and controlling the other man. It was ironic in the extreme that throughout the conversation Garry Anderson was the one who was really in control, aware of the microphones, the command posts, and the camouflaged SWAT team members crouching nearby with their guns.

The jury listened intently as the tape was played.

Thatcher began the conversation by telling Anderson that he had been having truck trouble and suggested that the two get in his car and go for a ride. Anderson declined, whereupon Thatcher said, "Have to be awful cautious, one never knows." The two men talked about Thatcher's farming operation for a while, but soon got down to business.

THATCHER: . . . Well, everything is—let's walk over this way. Everything is—there's no problem, have you been hassled?

ANDERSON: Well, they came once and talked to me and just asked me about the Chevy car, and that was about it. Other than that, nothing at all. How about you?

THATCHER: Just the once, the day after, and that was—they— no question, there's been some attempts to put us together and we should not be seen together.

ANDERSON: Okay.

Thatcher then described what he termed "cheap stunts" pulled by the police in their investigation of the murder. Abruptly changing the subject, Anderson talked about his work in north Saskatchewan and Thatcher commented that the police had tried to prove that he had got Anderson that job. The police had also talked to Jane Graham in California, Thatcher reported, and they might even be trying to "hang something onto Ron Graham." Wally Beaton had been to see Graham in Calgary on April 11, 1984, said Thatcher, adding, "I can't figure it out." Once again Anderson steered the conversation onto another track.

ANDERSON: I got rid of the stuff out of the car.

THATCHER: Good.

ANDERSON: You kind of give me a scare there with—I found the stuff lying in there and then I wondered what the

hell—I didn't know where the hell you—what the hell
you'd done with the gun?

THATCHER: Don't even talk like that, don't—don't even—walk
out this way a little, away from the car. Now, there are no
loose ends, at all, and, you know, they've gone—every which
direction. Was there any way a loose end from a couple of
years ago can ever resurface, from some of the guys
that—discussing some business with, is there any way
there'd ever be a problem surface from them?

ANDERSON: You mean from Vancouver and Winnipeg? I located one of them.

THATCHER: The one that I met, or the other one?

ANDERSON: The other one.

THATCHER: Son of a bitch.

ANDERSON: Well, it's up to you.

THATCHER: Is he is—he's not in jail now, is he, or in any
trouble?

ANDERSON: Not to my knowledge.

THATCHER: Is he about to cause any problems?

ANDERSON: I don't know. He didn't exactly recognize me.

THATCHER: Oh, okay.

ANDERSON: Like, I know who he is, but I don't think he
has—knows who I am or has connected me.

THATCHER: Okay, I'll—I'm going to tell you something my
lawyer told me, and he had heard this on a real rumour
basis. There's just a rumour, and of course, there's been
fifty thousand rumours. I heard this oh, almost a year ago,
and this is from Merchant.

ANDERSON: Mhmm.

Thatcher related how Eddie Johnson, on a plea bargain, had
told the story of a meeting involving Thatcher and one or two
others including an unidentified killer, which was supposed to
have taken place at a local hotel. "I mean, everybody laughed
at the story, including me, but does any of that have any
familiarity to you at all?" Thatcher asked. "Nothing at all,"
responded Anderson.

THATCHER: I think there's been some crap. Like what gets
them going, I think somebody gets made for something...

ANDERSON: Mhmm.

THATCHER: And then I think, you know, as they say, "I know

what happened," and he'll make up some sort of a fabrication and they'll, you know, start running around. Do you need some bread?

ANDERSON: Yeah, I can use some. I can use some for that car.

THATCHER: Okay.

ANDERSON: How about Friday, in the afternoon?

THATCHER: Yeah.

ANDERSON: Pick a time, later in the afternoon the better.

Thatcher then said he and Anderson should not be seen talking again because there was at least one person in the Caronport area who might tell the police. Anderson suggested that Thatcher wrap the money in a plastic bag and throw it in the coulee. Thatcher sad he would leave it near where they were talking. At that point, his anxiety about being bugged once again surfaced. "I always have a real fear of those parabolic mikes that they have," he said. "There is no question my phones are bugged."

The conversation once again returned to the question of whether either man had been hassled by the police. Thatcher said, "Well, remember you don't—remember your rights. You don't even have to talk to them." Anderson replied that he was worried because he had no money and didn't want to have to rely on a legal aid lawyer—"There isn't any good ones," he claimed—if anything should happen.

THATCHER: Oh, well, don't worry about that, but I mean, it ain't coming to that. It ain't coming to that. It ain't coming to that 'cause they have no way of—there's only two places to put the connection together, and they got zero else. They've got zero else, and I mean you know what there is to put together and it ain't possible, and it ain't coming from me. I mean, just always remember that if you were ever to say that I said this or that, it's a crock of garbage. It's just always deny, deny, deny.

ANDERSON: Mhmm.

THATCHER: Because no matter what it was, you know. And, you know, I was just lucky that night, I was home with four people. Four people, pretty solid, and that's pretty hard. What about you, are you covered at the time?

ANDERSON: Yup.

THATCHER: Well, then there's you know, that's—I didn't know
about you, but—

ANDERSON: Yeah, but, under questioning or if something ever
happens, would they ever crack those—your witnesses?

THATCHER: No. Never.

Thatcher continued to discuss the police investigation—how
they had "worked on" Sandra Silversides, how they had
shown a variety of photographs around to people in the
Caronport area, how they used a particular trick—". . . their
style is, 'Well, listen, we know that he did it, and we're close
to it, and we know that you know.' They're just fishing,"
Thatcher concluded. Once again, however, Anderson abruptly
changed the subject.

ANDERSON: Oh, I had a hell of a time to clean the car out.

THATCHER: Is that right?

ANDERSON: Yeah. I had a bitch of a time getting the blood and
stuff off.

THATCHER: Yeah. Is there no chance that it can ever surface?
There is a chance it can surface?

ANDERSON: No, I don't—no.

THATCHER: Okay.

ANDERSON: The car was cleaned.

THATCHER: Okay.

ANDERSON: I didn't burn it, but it was cleaned.

THATCHER: All right. They—as I say, the only—the only link
that they've got—when you want to see me just—like this
again—just give me that—I'd have gone right up there. I
was out of gas.

The two men agreed that if they ever had to get together
again, they'd meet at another abandoned farm.

THATCHER: Okay, okay. Are we—is that the only—that is the
only connection and the only one is those ones we're
talking business with over two—almost two years ago.
Unless one of those—the other guy, the one was here, is he
still in—is he still in Manitoba?

ANDERSON: I'm assuming. I'm close to coming to that, but I
haven't had the opportunity to really get into it. I just
happened to run into the other one by very, very—quite

by accident. I was asking some people and just sort of checking around and I found him. He doesn't know me.

THATCHER: You know, should go just visit that son of a bitch some day, but not right now, not right. Now, there is no problem, there are no other loose ends, eh, I mean, you know what the ends were and obviously I ain't a loose end and you're not, and there's nothing—there's nothing to come to.

Thatcher again began discussing the police investigation, again mentioning that they had talked to Ron Graham. Thatcher confided that he thought Wally Beaton was a "nice guy," but that he didn't trust any of them. He then said that he would drop the "stuff," meaning the money, some time on Friday. Thatcher told Anderson that if he needed to contact him again he should wave at him and he would meet him right away.

THATCHER: If I'm by myself, I'll go right there. But, you know, there's no problem unless something stupid's done, now, and I'll put what I safely can, and, but I just don't want to do something stupid in this stage of the game. But, next time slip back, give me that—don't drive in my yard again, though. There's no problem. I know. I know. I saw you and I couldn't come because I thought I was going to run out of gas any minute.

ANDERSON: Oh.

THATCHER: And, I would have.

ANDERSON: That's—I didn't stick around, I just—in and out.

THATCHER: Okay, and just remember there are no—there's no problems and there won't be unless they trip over something and I got no intention of giving them anything to trip on. There are no loose ends like, you know, there's nothing for them to find, you know.

ANDERSON: It's all been taken care of.

THATCHER: All, sure. Heavens yes, heavens yes. I still don't trust the bastards for bugs. I mean, I don't know whether there's any possibility that that—that's why when we talk, just assume the bastards are listening.

ANDERSON: Okay.

THATCHER: Don't give them any information. You taught me that. Remember, they got that one guy three years later.

ANDERSON: Mhmm.
THATCHER: And certainly never call, okay, on the telephone. But no question, no question, I'm bugged.

The conversation then took a sharp turn as Anderson asked Thatcher if he was planning to switch political parties. Thatcher said he wasn't, but informed Anderson that Devine was in trouble and that the premier had called him in California: "All of a sudden Devine likes to talk to an old pro again there.... I'm falling back into favour again, even though I really don't care one way or the other."

The discussion then veered back to the police investigation. Anderson wondered, if he had to get a lawyer, whether Merchant would represent him.

THATCHER: Oh, I think so.
ANDERSON: Is he familiar on...
THATCHER: Nope.
ANDERSON: No?
THATCHER: Zero. Knows zero. But it ain't coming to that.
ANDERSON: Well...
THATCHER: Do you have some feeling it is?
ANDERSON: Not really, but it's like everything else. We went second—well, basically one step further, you know, really
THATCHER: Well, it ain't coming to that because, you know, you're covered that night. No question. Like they're not...As long as you're covered that night there's not a hell of a lot they can do. Are you covered good?
ANDERSON: Mhmm.
THATCHER: Well, then...
ANDERSON: I was...Well, I'm covered.
THATCHER: Don't even tell me. But if you're covered good that night, there isn't anything. And they got no interest in you anyway. It's me.
ANDERSON: Mhmm.

Thatcher then told Anderson that even if he didn't have any money he could still get a "hell of a lawyer."

THATCHER: You can almost name who it is. Oh yeah, that is the least of your problems. But just remember, it's you know deny, deny, deny. Sure you know me as a constituent. Sure, you've rented some land. Now they've never asked about me, but, you know, sure, I've rented some land from him and yeah, sure, they did ask my office about, like, that you had a government job. They pedalled to Royden and he said, "Well, you know, we know he got him a government job." I didn't get you any DNS one. Of course I'd given your name to SMDC.

ANDERSON: Mhmm.

THATCHER: But, you know, they were just pulling through everything. But, you know, if they ever come up to you, sure, you know, just tell them the general stuff.

ANDERSON: Mhmm.

THATCHER: Well, there's . . . If nothing's happening with you, you would have the feeling, because nothing is happening with me. Like I say, I think they get in . . . I think some guy that's bucked to go up the river makes a cock and bull story up to get them running again . . .

ANDERSON: Mhmm.

THATCHER: . . . running around. But if they ain't hassling you then there's nothing going on. I didn't know how heavy they'd leaned on you.

ANDERSON: What . . . Okay. Well, I'm glad it went down.

THATCHER: Yeah. If they ain't leaned on you, then they, well, then they're . . .

ANDERSON: I'm glad it's over.

THATCHER: Yeah.

ANDERSON: You know.

THATCHER: So am I. Well, if they like, if they haven't been leaning on you and they were in Alberta two weeks ago, I mean, what's that tell you?

ANDERSON: They're still fishing.

THATCHER: Sure they are. Totally. Totally. Totally. In fact, it sounds, Janie thought they were looking hard at her husband. Couldn't care less.

ANDERSON: Still got visions of him?

THATCHER: Not particularly.

ANDERSON: How's your feelings with your old buddy Gerry . . .

At this point Thatcher laughed.

ANDERSON: . . . Gerry Gerrand.

THATCHER: Well . . .

ANDERSON: Kind of mellow to him?

THATCHER: No. A guy I could do. That guy I could do.

The conversation then once again turned to the police investigation. "They've tried every goddamn gimmick in the world on me," said Thatcher. "However, let's not push it."

ANDERSON: Okay.

THATCHER: Well, I'll tell you what, I'll put her in a garbage bag and I'll dump her there. Next time I see you, just give me that same sign and there is no problem unless you do something stupid.

ANDERSON: Okay.

THATCHER: Okay?

ANDERSON: Yeah. I'm glad you got her.

THATCHER: Okay.

ANDERSON: See you.

THATCHER: You bet.

When the tape was finished playing there were few in the charged courtroom atmosphere who would have described the conversation they had just heard as an innocent discussion between two law-abiding citizens.

At Kujawa's request, Anderson then explained that Thatcher was referring to Cody Crutcher and Charlie Wilde when he said, "Was there any way a loose end from a couple of years ago can ever resurface, from some of the guys that—discussing some business with, is there any way there'd ever be a problem surface from them?" Crutcher was the person Anderson referred to as coming from Vancouver, and Wilde was from Manitoba.

After Anderson had explained his ordeal over the last week, how he had taken an overdose of Tylenol and had finally surrendered to the RCMP, Justice Maher adjourned until the next morning.

Peggy and Greg Thatcher had been joined this day by Diane Stoner, a highly respected nurse at the Plains Health Centre and Thatcher's most recent girlfriend, who moved into the Redland home when he was arrested. She was very tastefully and traditionally dressed in a wine-coloured jersey, a grey flowered shawl, and gold jewellery. A long-time friend of the Thatchers who was attending the trial remarked that there was a quality about Diane that reminded her of some-one else. "Diane has class, just like JoAnn used to," she said.

TUESDAY, OCTOBER 23

This day the Thatcher ranks in court swelled impressively. In attendance were Greg, Regan, now fifteen, the faithful house-keeper Sandra Silversides and her brother, Pat Hammond, Peggy Thatcher, and Diane Stoner. Courtroom heads turned in amazement to see ten-year-old Stephanie Thatcher in attendance for the first time; she was wearing a smart blue cap, the one that Lynne Mendell had picked out for her in Paris during her trip with Colin. Obviously the Thatchers were anticipating that Gerry Allbright would devastate Garry Anderson in the course of the day, and indeed the lawyer's cross-examination of this most damning witness would prove to be his finest hour during the trial. He began aggressively by asking Anderson if he believed in the commandment "Thou shalt not kill." Anderson replied that he did.

ALLBRIGHT: From what you told us yesterday, if what you said yesterday was true, Mr. Anderson, isn't your interpretation of that commandment from Exodus this, that "Thou shalt not kill yourself, but it's okay to help someone else," is that your personal interpretation, Mr. Anderson?

ANDERSON: . . . It is not.

ALLBRIGHT: If what you told us yesterday is true, Mr. Anderson, what kind of a man does what you did. If what you tell us is true, what kind of a man helps in the way that you helped to take the life of another person?

ANDERSON: I would say someone who is a fool.

ALLBRIGHT: Were you a fool, Mr. Anderson?

ANDERSON: Yes, I was.

But Allbright did not dwell on weaknesses in Garry's charac-ter as he had with Lynne Mendell—perhaps the old adage that you don't ask the village preacher to murder your wife came into play. What he did instead was concentrate on the tape recording. Anderson admitted to Allbright that he had gone to meet Thatcher that May day for one reason only—to obtain a confession of murder. Over and over again Allbright, often in mocking and sarcastic terms, hammered home that Anderson had "failed miserably" to do any such thing.

ALLBRIGHT: By a, may I suggest, a clever bit of work on your part, you got the following unequivocal admission out of Colin Thatcher, no question about it. Mr. Anderson says the very brilliant statement, "Mhmm." Mr. Thatcher says, "'Cause no matter what it was, y'know. And ah, y'know, I was just lucky that night. I was home with four people. Four people. Pretty, pretty solid and that's pretty hard." . . . He said that to you, didn't he, Mr. Anderson?

ANDERSON: Yes, he did.

ALLBRIGHT: Good job, Mr. Anderson. . . . I suggest you come up with another one that you elicit from him. Very skillfully you lead into it this way, Mr. Anderson says, "Yup." Mr. Thatcher says, "Well, then they're y'know. That's ahh, I, I didn't know about you but ah." Good job, Mr. Anderson. You got Mr. Thatcher to admit he didn't know where you were that night.

Allbright continued in that vein for a good two hours, emphasizing the "golden opportunities" that Anderson had missed to elicit a confession from Thatcher.

ALLBRIGHT: You also make the statement, "The car was cleaned." And Thatcher says, "Okay." You say, "I didn't burn it but it was clean." Why don't you put the nail in a little more and say, "The car that you used the night you killed JoAnn Wilson," or "The car that you took to Regina to do the murder," or "The car that you used to do the killing." Why didn't you use some of that phraseology and put the nail in?

ANDERSON: I don't know. I guess I just didn't.

Of course there had to be a reason why Anderson would ask such "oblique" questions, and a reason he would get involved in the tape recording in the first place. Allbright did not hesitate to put forward his theory. Garry Anderson knew that the police were investigating him, and to take the heat off he made up a story connecting Colin Thatcher to the murder. Because of that, during the tape recording he had to be very careful not to say anything that would blow his tall tale. "I'm suggesting to you that you were walking a tightrope because if you asked the wrong question of Thatcher, I suggest you were going to get an answer that showed he had nothing to do with this matter, and that was an answer you couldn't afford the police to hear." Anderson denied that this was the case. And so it went on all day, with Allbright never tiring, banging away at Anderson's motives and ridiculing his "pathetic" attempt to elicit a confession from Colin Thatcher.

There was great rejoicing among the Thatchers and their friends that night. Allbright had "demolished" Anderson, they were sure. Diane Stoner decided to buy two tickets to Palm Springs and a magnum of very good champagne to celebrate the "not guilty" verdict and the release of Colin Thatcher that was sure to follow.

On the other side, however, Kujawa and Johnson were not downcast. Although Anderson had been subjected to Allbright's rough questioning for the entire day, he had stood up pretty well, even if his answers never were very imaginative or clever. In the afternoon Allbright had questioned him in great detail about his part in the murder plot and had caught one contradiction. Ron Williams, the gun dealer, had said the gun Thatcher had bought had a nickel-type finish and Anderson had said the gun had a blue finish. But that was not major. Most of the other details seemed to them to mesh neatly, like strands of a spider web, with the story of Lynne Mendell, as they would with the testimony of the last Crown witness, Charlie Wilde.

WEDNESDAY, OCTOBER 24

The first five witnesses were all police officers testifying that Thatcher was at the abandoned farm when Anderson said he was. Fred Waelz and Robert Britton were the two RCMP officers who were added to the list at the last minute because Kujawa suspected that Thatcher was going to deny the authenticity of the tape recording. Allbright had said before the trial had begun that he would object to their evidence. Not only did he not do that, but he did not even cross-examine them. It left the two Crown attorneys wondering how on earth the accused was going to explain the tape away.

On the stand Sergeant Street described how two days after

the tape-recorded conversation took place, he picked up $550, which had been placed in a green garbage bag and hidden under an old two-by-six plank located at the rear of the Quonset hut at the abandoned farm.

Street also told of an interesting driving feat that he had recently performed. Three days before the trial began, he and Sergeant Bing Forbes parked an unmarked police car on Angus Street at five-thirty in the evening. Street ran from the Wilson garage into the lane, and through a backyard to the parked car. He then drove through Regina, onto the Trans-Canada Highway and into Moose Jaw at about 110 miles per hour. He parked two and a half blocks from Redland Avenue and ran to the back of Thatcher's home. The entire exercise took twenty-eight minutes and nineteen seconds. What he intended to prove was that Thatcher could have murdered JoAnn shortly before six o'clock and arrived back in Moose Jaw in time to make the 6:24 telephone call to Palm Springs. In cross-examination, Allbright brought out the facts that Anderson's Mercury was nine years older than the police car used, that there had been no snow on the ground when Street had performed his feat, and that to get out of Regina, the sergeant had driven along the Lewvan Expressway, which had not been completed at the time of the murder.

Charlie Wilde was listed as the Crown's last witness. He was somewhat chubbier than he had been at the preliminary hearing but his curly head bore evidence of the recent attentions of a stylist and he wore a smart brown-and-white tweed jacket with a white shirt. He admitted to having criminal convictions starting in 1968 that stretched fairly continuously to 1980, with "the odd break in between." Almost all his crimes were related to drug abuse, he said, and then added that he was currently receiving methadone treatment at St. Boniface Hospital in Winnipeg.

Wilde related the story of how he had met Garry Anderson in jail in the summer of 1980 and how in November Anderson had approached him about murdering someone. Wilde said no, but then talked to his friend Cody Crutcher and the two decided to take Thatcher's money and run. They met Anderson at the Fireside Lounge at the Sheraton, where Anderson gave Cody Crutcher $7,500. He split it with Charlie Wilde, who then met Anderson a few days later and received another

$7,000 plus a set of car keys and a picture of a woman. The "hit" was supposed to take place during the Christmas holidays when Thatcher would be safely in Palm Springs. When this failed to happen, Anderson reached Wilde again and the two men met Thatcher at the abandoned farmhouse. Thatcher expressed concern that Crutcher had disappeared with JoAnn's car keys, and Charlie Wilde promised he'd try to get them back. Thatcher then asked Wilde if *he* would be interested in killing his former wife. Charlie said he would, and one evening met the MLA outside the legislature. They went for a ride in Colin's yellow Corvette, and Thatcher gave Charlie $3,000 in Canadian money and $1,500 in American. He told Wilde that he wanted him to kill JoAnn at Easter in Ames while the Wilsons were visiting her parents. Thatcher gave Charlie the Geigers' address and described where their house was located. Wilde had no intention of killing the woman and at Easter was arrested in Brandon, Manitoba, for using a phoney medical card to obtain drugs, a misdeed for which he had received thirty months in Stony Mountain Penitentiary. Finally in March of 1984 he was picked up once again by Winnipeg police after, as Kujawa pointed out, he was found in "somebody else's drugstore about three hours after it had closed for business."

Rising to cross-examine, Allbright realized that his only recourse, once again, was to discredit the witness as thoroughly as possible. One of the high points of the preliminary hearing had occurred after Allbright had tried to establish that Charlie's brain must have been "pickled" from all the drugs he had consumed over the years and Wilde had responded by reciting his criminal record chapter and verse, a feat many non-dopers would have found very difficult. The defence lawyer took the same approach.

ALLBRIGHT: Those drugs do anything to you when you were using them?

WILDE: Yes, they did.

ALLBRIGHT: What did they do to you?

WILDE: They got me into trouble.

ALLBRIGHT: I suppose that everything I'm going to ask you about, the only problem with it is that it got you into a little trouble?

WILDE: That's my opinion, yes.

ALLBRIGHT: Yes. Didn't fry your mind, Witness, at all.
WILDE: I don't think so.

Charlie turned out to be an excellent witness for the Crown, calm, cool, and something of a match for Allbright. The defence lawyer tried hard to punch holes in Wilde's testimony: had he told anybody besides Cody about his escapade with Thatcher? Why couldn't he remember the Geigers' exact address in Ames? Wasn't it a fact that he was only making up the story to get a portion of the $50,000 reward? Allbright further suggested that if Crutcher and Wilde truly had received the car keys and the picture of JoAnn, they would have seized the chance to blackmail Thatcher. "And you guys strike me, from what you've told me about you and Crutcher . . . you strike me as being prepared to do that kind of thing?" Wilde: "I don't know. What do I say? I don't know how I strike you, really, you know."

By the end of the cross-examination, courtroom observers felt that Allbright had not been able to crack Charlie Wilde's story open one inch.

At that point Kujawa, impressive in his black gown, announced, "That's the case for the Crown, My Lord." He had no idea that the very next day he would find a witness who would eventually prove to be as important to his case as any heard from thus far.

CHAPTER TWENTY-ONE
THE ALIBI

THURSDAY, OCTOBER 26

"Do you think Daddy will wear the lucky tie I gave him?"
Stephanie Thatcher whispered to her grandmother and brother, as the courtroom awaited the arrival of the accused. Even
hardened courtroom observers found it shocking and almost
unbelieveable that the ten-year-old girl sat there day after
day listening to the sordid details linking her father to the
murder of her mother. (Fifteen-year-old Regan was in the
courtroom only occasionally.) The hungry eyes of journalists
and spectators had watched Stephanie hug and kiss her daddy
during breaks or at adjournment. Indeed Thatcher had been
so keen to have his family there that he insisted that the
entire front row of the courtroom be reserved for the Thatchers
and guests. Court officials flatly refused; the first two rows
were reserved for the media while the Thatchers got half a
dozen seats in the third row.

Tony Wilson had foreseen that Stephanie might be served
up as a curiosity at the trial, and during the summer he had
applied to the courts for temporary custody, arguing that the
child would be better off staying with her grandparents in
Iowa during the trial. A nasty custody battle ensued. In
August Mr. Justice A.L. Sirois turned down Wilson's request,
saying he had been persuaded by a psychiatrist. The persuasive physician was Dr. Peter Matthews, the same psychiatrist
who four years ago had recommended that Thatcher be given
custody of Regan. "I think Stephanie's bright enough to be
able to express her opinion and I accept it," he said, and the
judge accepted his conclusion.

The child seemed to cope with the situation by retreating
into her own little world. As the legal proceedings droned on,

Stephanie sat reading *The Ghost Rock Mystery;* when she had devoured that, she turned to a Nancy Drew thriller.

Gerry Allbright opened the case for the defence by dealing with those troublesome bullets. As his first witness he produced Wayne Mantyka, a CKTV news reporter, who had gone into the Saskatoon Gun Works with a camera crew to ascertain whether he could obtain the disputed ammunition himself; he was able to buy a box of silver-tip hollow-point Winchester. This was a point for the defence—until it turned out that he had purchased .357 Magnum, not .38 special, which was a much rarer type of ammunition. His testimony served only to further complicate the bullet controversy.

The defence's first major witness was Tony Merchant, looking a little like a puckered Peter Lawford in a broad-shouldered blue suit and stark white shirt. The witness and the accused had been through so many legal battles together that they were like two old war veterans, their scars visible, but their sense of mission still intact. Their most recent legal skirmish, however, threatened to cause serious injury to the lawyer. After Merchant and Thatcher had been charged with abducting Stephanie, the day after her mother's murder, it took a year and a half for the matter to be brought to the preliminary hearing stage because of legal complications, mostly introduced by the defence. When the preliminary was finally heard on May 4, three days before Colin was arrested for murder, provincial court judge R.H. Allan ruled that there was not enough evidence to commit the two men to trial on the abduction charge. He did decide, however, that they would have to stand trial on the nuisance charge. This was still hanging over Merchant's head (and remains so at the time of this writing), and since it was a criminal offence, the lawyer faced the possibility of being disbarred if he was found guilty.

Still, Merchant remained a prominent officer in Thatcher's army. Under Allbright's questioning, he began now by reciting in great detail the life and times of Tony Merchant, which obviously was meant to contrast sharply with the life and crimes of Charlie Wilde. He talked about his grandfather the judge, his father the lawyer, who died during the war, his mother Sally, his sister Adrian, all the schools he had attended, all the provincial bars to which he belonged. He described his legal practice, the university courses he had taken, his business holdings—two concrete companies with sales of about $5 million, a large service station complex with sales of slightly less than $3 million, parts of three different shopping centres, part of a professional building, three or four different land developments in Phoenix, portions of twelve or thirteen apartment buildings, a company that erects electronic signs, a farm, a couple of videotape rental outlets—and he did not neglect his political career, nor his community activities—the Legion, the Naval Reserve, the Catholic Church, Cubs, the United Appeal.

(Serge Kujawa would sarcastically begin his cross-examination: "Mr. Merchant, tell me, I don't think it was in. Was your father an Eagle Scout?" Merchant: "Actually, I think he was, amazingly he went to England on a scouting something or other." Kujawa: "I'm absolutely amazed that you left that out because you put in everything else.")

Merchant was there to provide alibis for Thatcher for both the first shooting and the murder.

He testified that during the weekend of May 17, 1981, he and his wife, Pana, had supervised a Cub camp. "And I had only slept two or three hours and I had done some physical work, which I never do, so I was, we were very tired. And I think my wife and I went to bed about 8:30 or 9 p.m." The nanny woke them up and said the police were downstairs. "I came to know that the reason that they had come to my home was that my home was close to the Wilson home and that Mrs. Wilson had been shot ten or twelve minutes earlier and they wanted to know whether Mr. Thatcher was in our home." Merchant said he phoned Moose Jaw immediately and talked to Thatcher. He expected that the police would go immediately to Colin's house so he told his client not to say anything until he got there. Merchant said he drove to Moose Jaw at speeds of 97 or 98 miles an hour. "I went by two or three police cars clearly marked, and when I went by the first one I thought, oh, you know, great, for certain I'm going to be stopped for speeding." He was not stopped, however, and about thirty-five minutes later he arrived at the Redland house.

Merchant claimed that he stayed at the Thatcher residence "for quite a while" but the police never showed. He also maintained that he had not called the police that night. Some time later, satisfied that nothing was going to happen, he drove back to Regina.

On the night of the murder, he had gone home from his law office at about 5 p.m. A law partner phoned at about 6:10 or 6:15 and told Merchant that the Wilson residence was surrounded by police, the street was blockaded, and there appeared to have been another shooting. Merchant said that he immediately called Thatcher in Moose Jaw and told him that it appeared to be more serious than the shooting in 1981, that JoAnn might even be dead. Thatcher responded, "You've got to be kidding." Between thirty and forty-five minutes later, Merchant said, a CBC employee came to his door; they also had heard that JoAnn had probably been killed, and Merchant stated that he made another phone call to Thatcher just after seven, giving him this news. On the way to a Regina restaurant where he was going with his family and friends, Merchant was told by a police officer that indeed JoAnn was dead. Tony said he made a third call to Moose Jaw about 7:20 p.m., giving Thatcher this information.

Serge Kujawa and Tony Merchant did not like each other, and the Crown prosecutor's cross-examination of the lawyer clearly revealed this. After his sarcastic opening, Kujawa was a little like a sinister black cat toying mercilessly with a squeaky mouse.

If Merchant's testimony during direct examination regarding the first shooting had been entirely accurate, the timing would have been thus: JoAnn was shot at 10:10 p.m.; the police informed Merchant at 10:20; he talked to Thatcher immediately by phone in Moose Jaw; he reached the Redland home half an hour to thirty-five minutes later, at about 10:55. Through cross-examination, Kujawa revealed that Merchant's own telephone records revealed that his call that night to Moose Jaw was made not around 10:25, as Merchant claimed, but in the twenty-third hour, in other words between 11 and 12 p.m. Further, he could not have arrived at the Redland home at 10:55 as he estimated, because a Moose Jaw policeman had seen him enter the Redland home at 12:45 a.m. Finally, Merchant said that after he got to the Redland home, he had not contacted the Regina police on behalf of Thatcher. Yet Kujawa revealed that Merchant phoned Sergeant Jeannotte in Regina at 1:30 a.m. Merchant did not deny this; in fact his recollection of events that evening was hazy. For example, he said that he had never known the exact time of the shooting. "The only information I had as to the time of the first shooting was what was relayed to me by the police officer," said Merchant. But, as Kujawa pointed out, despite this limited and inexact information, Merchant felt quite free to sign an affidavit providing an alibi for Thatcher.

Kujawa also drilled Merchant about the telephone call the night of the murder. In his original affidavit, Merchant had said that his partner had made the call informing him that there may have been a shooting at the Wilsons' at "some time prior to 6:30 p.m." He had not mentioned the specific time of 6:10 or 6:15. Kujawa pounced on this discrepancy: "How did you shave about twenty minutes off that today?" Merchant: "I would have preferred to have said 6:10 or 6:15 and in discussion with counsel it was decided that it would be preferable to not specify because I was just going by recollection at that time."

The strangest part of Merchant's testimony, however, was his accusation that police had broken into his law office and stolen telephone records. "We had three very mysterious break-ins, mysterious in the sense that they were very well done and virtually nothing was taken. No money was taken, no liquor was taken, even though the room of the break-ins was through a room with [clearly visible] money and liquor." Merchant explained why he thought the police were responsible. After the bail hearing in May of 1984, he had filed an affidavit claiming that he phoned Thatcher the night of the murder and that he had telephone records that would back this claim. Since the Saskatchewan Telephone Company kept these records for only three months, the police would not have had access to them. And Merchant's client's records would be considered privileged, so that the police could not have legally obtained them. Since the thief had ignored money and liquor, and taken only the telephone bills, Merchant felt sure the police must be the culprits.

Kujawa wanted to know what the police would gain from doing such an outrageous thing. The telephone bill did not show specifically when a call was made, only the hour in which it occurred. Merchant's records, therefore, showed only that he telephoned Moose Jaw on January 21, 1984, in the eighteenth hour, in other words some time between 6 and 7 p.m.

KUJAWA: . . . That is your affidavit?

MERCHANT: I swore that affidavit.

KUJAWA: Right. And in there, to make it look good, having phoned the telephone company knowing that three months have elapsed, you said you could back this with your phone bills?

MERCHANT: Yes.

KUJAWA: You knew you couldn't.

MERCHANT: I knew I could.

KUJAWA: In spite of knowing there is a 59-minute spread on them.

MERCHANT: I, I see, I see what you are saying. I, it, it didn't back them in terms of the specifics of the time, but it, but it, but it, backed, it backed the, it backed them in general and the people involved who corroborate what, corroborate the approximate time, were questioned by the police.

Kujawa's questioning of Merchant at this point was so heavily laced with sarcasm and ridicule that some people in the courtroom were embarrassed. And indeed the lawyer visibly became more and more nervous under the onslaught. Allbright didn't like it one bit, but he didn't interfere.

Kujawa believed it important to show the nature of the relationship that existed between Merchant and Thatcher.

KUJAWA: Now, we're talking about your friendship and I suggest that there might be considerably more than friendship between you and the accused. I understand that one of the first acts when he became a Minister was to give a great job of doing legal work for the Department that he was Minister of?

MERCHANT: My law firm, that's correct.

KUJAWA: That's right. Did that strike you as a bit strange?

MERCHANT: Yes.

KUJAWA: Why was it strange?

MERCHANT: I'm not a Conservative.

KUJAWA: Right . . . That is most unusual isn't it?

MERCHANT: Yes, I think that's unusual. It is not unheard of, but it is unusual.

KUJAWA: Quite unusual. And it caused some considerable difficulty within the Government itself, didn't it?

MERCHANT: You would know better than I do what goes on within the Government. I don't know.

KUJAWA: . . . And wasn't that one of the major reasons for Colin Thatcher being fired from the Cabinet?

MERCHANT: I don't know.

Merchant's testimony would come back to haunt the defence the next day.

Barbara Wright, twenty-seven, the wife of Wayne Wright, who lived and worked on Thatcher's ranch, testified next for the defence. She remembered that she made it home to the Thatcher ranch in Caron from her job in the physiotherapy department of the Providence Hospital in Moose Jaw at about 4:35 on January 21, 1983. She was making the supper at about five when she saw Colin Thatcher drive into the yard in his truck. He stayed around the ranch yard for about twenty minutes, checking the cattle in the corral. He left, she said, somewhere between 5:20 and 5:30.

Under the probing cross-examination of Kujawa, Wright admitted that, yes, she had received four phone calls from Tony Merchant and Allbright the day before she signed the affidavit with its relevant information in May of 1984. "Some of those phone calls took a long time, didn't it?" asked Kujawa. "No, ten minutes, fifteen minutes," said Wright. "To refresh your memory?" ". . . Well, no, they had asked me what had happened and I told them. . . ."

Kujawa then referred to the fact that Wally Beaton and Constable Affie of the Regina police had talked to her on March 7, 1983: "And did you on that occasion tell them that you had not seen Colin Thatcher for months?" Wright replied, "No, I did not."

Pat Hammond, Sandra Silversides's brother, was next up. A short, stocky young fellow, he seemed very self-confident while giving evidence, punching his answers home with great determination. He told the court that he was twenty-four, a brakeman with the Canadian Pacific Railway, and married, with two children. Hammond said he did body work and mechanics on the side and had worked on many of Thatcher's vehicles. He claimed that on January 21, 1983, he had picked up paint at the Great West Auto Electric in Moose Jaw just before the store closed at 5:30 p.m. Five minutes later he caught sight of Colin Thatcher in his truck at the intersection of Saskatchewan Street and Redland in Moose Jaw, and the two men waved at each other.

Hammond said that the police approached him a few days after the murder, but he had not mentioned to them that he had seen Colin Thatcher the evening of January 21. "At the time they showed me the [composite] drawing, they said this is the man they believed to have committed the crime, so I had no reason to believe that it was Colin Thatcher, so I didn't think that the information was relevant at the time."

But under Kujawa's cross-examination, it was revealed that Hammond had been visited by the Regina police twice, once a few days after the murder and once in February. Hammond admitted he had not been shown the composite drawing during the second visit. The judge intervened to ask the young man: "Your evidence is that on that occasion, too, they didn't ask you about the whereabouts of Colin Thatcher on the 21st of January?" Hammond responded, "I don't recall them asking."

KUJAWA: I suggest to you that Murton and Street, a couple of policemen, came to you on February 11, 1983 and interviewed you? Is that right?

HAMMOND: That could be right, yes.

KUJAWA: And you told them that you didn't know anything about this matter at all. You had nothing relevant to give them.

HAMMOND: That's correct.

KUJAWA: You also called JoAnn Wilson a few nasty names?

HAMMOND: I did not like the woman.

KUJAWA: And you made that extremely clear?

HAMMOND: I don't pull any punches, no.

Kujawa revealed that in his affidavit signed in May of 1984, Hammond stated that he had met Thatcher "sometime between 5 and 5:30 p.m." Referring to the revised version that had him waving at Thatcher at about 5:35, Kujawa asked him,

"How did you gain the twenty-five minutes today?" Hammond responded, "I guess I should have been more accurate on the affidavit." What he had said, under Allbright's questioning, was that he had been at the paint store just as it was closing at 5:30 and then had driven for five minutes before he had encountered Thatcher. These were all small details, but they could possibly weigh heavily when the jury was deciding whom they were going to believe, and whether Colin Thatcher could have been in Moose Jaw at 6 p.m.

Pale-skinned, plump, and already matronly at twenty-two, Sandra Silversides, the ever-faithful housekeeper, now took the stand. She spoke in a very soft, very gentle voice, indeed it was difficult for people in the hushed courtroom to hear her, and several times during her testimony she appeared to be on the edge of tears. She was most sincere, almost melodramatically so. She told the court that she had graduated from Central Collegiate in Moose Jaw in 1980, attended two years at Saskatchewan Technical Institute in business administration, and now worked for the provincial government's Department of Tourism and Small Business, "mostly doing secretarial work but also consulting with businesses." Sandra said that she was also paid in her capacity as Colin's constituency secretary and still babysat and regularly cooked meals for the family.

Sandra remembered that on January 21, 1983, she took the day off work; she wasn't feeling well so she slept most of the afternoon. She went over to the Thatchers to make a supper of Hamburger Helper at about 5 p.m. and noticed that Greg and Regan were there. She did not see Thatcher and did not know he was there until he sat down for supper. "It would be around six because we always eat just about 6 o'clock. . . . We normally sit down at the table about five to six or six o'clock because we're all fast eaters and we can be done by ten after six." After dinner she told the Thatchers that it was their turn to clean up, and went home. She was in the bathtub when her brother came running to tell her that JoAnn had been murdered. She went back to the Redland house immediately and noticed that Colin was "just sitting at the kitchen table, staring at the wall. . . . I didn't notice anything about Greg, but Regan was very subdued and he didn't want to talk about it. . . . I really didn't know what to do for them and I mean I can't console Mr. Thatcher so I phoned Mr. Thatcher's executive, the president, and I just told them what happened." After that, said Sandra, several of Thatcher's friends arrived at the Redland residence. She picked up some soft drinks at the store for the guests and then went home.

On May 7, 1984, the day Thatcher was arrested, Greg came dashing over to her office to tell her that his dad had been arrested and that he was taking Regan and Stephanie to their grandmother's place in Regina. "I just about passed out," said Silversides. Greg asked if she wanted to come with them but she replied, "Well, maybe I'll be more help here." The people she worked with then drove her home. She was there with her mother, her fiancé, and a friend of her mother's (Ann Jenner, whose husband, Fred, would play a most interesting role in the Thatcher saga after the trial) when at about 11 p.m. Sergeants Murton and Street appeared at the house and arrested her. They told her she was being charged with accessory before and after the fact of murder. Her reaction was one of "disbelief." The two detectives escorted the terrified young woman to the Regina police station where she was fingerprinted and photographed. She said, "I waited in the waiting room and they never came and then some constable came and took me back and he said that I would not be going on until the next day. And they put me in a back cell because they said they didn't want me to get any publicity. And I waited there and two policemen came and told me they wanted to talk to me and they took me into a room and they talked to me and then they let me go."

Explaining this strange episode, Swayze says that he had an order from the Department of Justice instructing him to release Sandra before she had been properly questioned. She was released at 3:15 without ever being charged.

On the advice of her lawyer, John Epp (who worked in Tony Merchant's firm), she sued Murton, Street, Swayze, and Police Chief New for false arrest. The court documents claimed that the police had been "high-handed, arrogant and acting in such a manner as to display a reckless disregard for the right of the Plaintiff." Sandra said she had suffered "a great deal of mental suffering and frustraton," and she wanted "punitive and exemplary damages." In defence, the Regina police said, "At some time before the murder of JoAnn Wilson, the Plaintiff agreed with Wilbert Colin Thatcher to fabricate matters of fact with a view to attempting to provide Thatcher with an alibi during the period that JoAnn was being murdered." In spite of this extraordinary statement, no such charges have been laid.

In his cross-examination of Silversides, Kujawa was careful not to be too harsh. "I very deliberately set out to not be rough on Sandra. She was too close to great tears coming out of her great, innocent-looking eyes onto her beautiful blue dress. She just came in there looking like Little Miss Chastity. And very young, and she is very young, and to pick on her, I didn't think would do the case any good."

He did ask her about a series of cheques amounting to over $10,000 that were cashed during November and December of 1980 and January of 1981, the period of time that Thatcher was supposed to have been handing out money to Charlie Wilde and Cody Crutcher. Sandra explained that she had done some banking for Thatcher. He would leave her a cheque to cash when he left his house in the morning. If it was for a large amount, she would not have enough to cover it in her bank account so that the cheque would sit overnight until it cleared Thatcher's bank. Kujawa pointed out that she had cashed cheques for $1,500 in November, 1980, $1,500 in December, $1,500 and $2,200 in January. He also asked her if she had seen a Mustang with a rifle in it in Thatcher's garage around the time of the first shooting. She denied that she had.

What Kujawa was most interested in, however, was a certain telephone call on the night of the murder.

KUJAWA: You are playing a bit of a role here, aren't you?
SILVERSIDES: I don't think so.
KUJAWA: You are playing it very well. You have always told the police everything you know. And yet when you told the whole story in your affidavit of how you went there at five o'clock or shortly thereafter and prepared this food and everyone was there milling around and sat down to eat shortly before six, you left out a very important part, didn't you?
SILVERSIDES: I don't think so.

Kujawa then proceeded to elicit the information from Sandra

that there was a telephone in Thatcher's office, which was located on the other side of the house from the kitchen.

KUJAWA: And I suggest to you that for most of that time you were in that office talking on a telephone to your boyfriend [Blaine Mathieson] on long distance. I'll use the name. I'd rather not, but I will if it will refresh your memory.

SILVERSIDES: Go ahead.

KUJAWA: Do you know the name, do you know who I am referring to?

SILVERSIDES: You mean my old boyfriend, Blaine Mathieson?

KUJAWA: Right.

SILVERSIDES: Well, I don't remember the call, but I'm not saying it didn't happen. I could have very well talked to him because we were still friends...

KUJAWA: ... And you just didn't remember about that phone call?

SILVERSIDES: No, I didn't because I make a lot of phone calls.

KUJAWA: I suggest to you that that phone call started at precisely 5:32 p.m. and lasted until two minutes to six. Would you deny that?

SILVERSIDES: No. I don't remember if it happened but I wouldn't deny it, no.

Since obviously Sandra could not be making Hamburger Helper and talking for a half-hour on the telephone with her boyfriend at exactly the same time, Kujawa had managed to cast grave doubt on her testimony, as well as that of many of the witnesses who would follow.

FRIDAY, OCTOBER 26

Allbright made a surprise announcement to a hushed courtroom before calling his first witness. While in the barristers' lounge that morning he had received a surprise phone call from Tony Merchant about the dramatic matter of the alleged police break-in to steal his telephone records. Allbright said that in the phone call Merchant "advised me that he had checked with his partners in Regina and that the break-in occurred before, and I think this is very important, and I want to clarify it, the break-ins occurred before Mr. Thatcher was arrested and of course that certainly wasn't what he indicated to us in his cross-examination to us yesterday." Embarrassing as Merchant's admission was for the defence, that wasn't the end of it. In his charge to the jury at the conclusion of the trial, Mr. Justice Maher said, "I find it incredible that Mr. Merchant would make the suggestion that the police may have been involved in criminal activities when he was in possession of no evidence to support such a suggestion and when it later transpired that his ill-founded suspicions were based on statements he made to this court that were inaccurate and in error. So much for the evidence of Mr. Merchant."

Allbright admits now that this episode didn't help his case much, but he maintains to this day that Merchant was right the first time about the break-ins. He makes the astonishing statement: "During the trial, I saw the original telephone bills, and they weren't on my side of the room."

Regan Thatcher, dressed in a subtle blue-grey plaid suit, a blue shirt, and dark-blue tie, took the stand. At fifteen he still possessed the ungainliness and the passions of adolescence; collegiate football was what he loved most in the world. His physique and features were not as handsomely refined as his brother's, yet a soft, sensitive side to the boy's nature was evident. A friend had found him crying in the garage at his Redland home after he had listened to the tape recording between his father and Anderson at the preliminary. And it did seem cruelly ironic that the child who had been so bitterly fought over during the Thatcher marital wars should now be called upon to protect his father from his mother's ultimate revenge.

Regan gave his evidence in a calm, matter-of-fact manner, proving more sure of himself than Greg would be when his turn came. After his year's sojourn in California, Regan testified that he returned to Moose Jaw in the spring of 1981, just two weeks before his mother was shot and wounded. Regan said that on May 17, 1981, he spent most of the day hanging around the house, watching television. He recalled that his father opened the pool that day and was getting the pumps and other apparatus ready. He said that he and his father were home the entire evening. He remembered getting a phone call "in the early evening." "I was supposed to screen his [Thatcher's] phone calls 'cause there's a lot of phone calls for him. And at first I said he wasn't home until I found who it was." It was Tony Merchant informing Colin Thatcher that JoAnn had been wounded. Regan remembered that the lawyer arrived in Moose Jaw shortly after.

On the day of the murder, Regan recalled that when he got home from school only Greg was there. Sandra arrived soon after, and his father had come home from the ranch at about 5:30 p.m. "Do you recall what she cooked for supper that evening?" Allbright asked. "Hamburger Helper," said Regan. "Is that one of your favourites?" said the lawyer. "Not mine. . . . We started at six o'clock for sure, I know that . . . because every time we had supper my dad would always take his supper down to the T.V. room and watch the news." Regan said he answered the telephone "between ten after six and quarter after six." It was Tony Merchant telling Thatcher that something was going on at the Wilson house. "My dad seemed shaken up," said Regan.

In his cross-examination, Kujawa was gentle with the teenaged boy.

KUJAWA: Do you remember that Tony phoned that particular night of the [first] shooting?

REGAN: Yes, he did.

KUJAWA: And you remember how long after the phone call that he got out to the house?

REGAN: I'm told that, like, right after he phoned.

KUJAWA: Don't go by what you were told. Go by your own memory.

REGAN: Okay. Well, I don't remember how long it was, but I remember it was maybe an hour, little over an hour at most.

KUJAWA: And he arrived there when?

REGAN: I don't remember.

KUJAWA: If I said a quarter to, a quarter to one a.m. would that sound about right? [This was the time of Merchant's arrival according to the Moose Jaw police officer watching the house.]

REGAN: No.

KUJAWA: Pardon?

REGAN: No, it wouldn't.

KUJAWA: It wouldn't?

REGAN: No.

KUJAWA: All right. How long did he stay?

REGAN: I believe he was there right up until I went to bed.

KUJAWA: When was that?

REGAN: Roughly ten o'clock. Nine thirty, ten o'clock.

KUJAWA: And he was still there?

REGAN: Yes, I believe so. But I'm not sure.

KUJAWA: I'd say you were not sure, yeah. You knew or do you know now that the shooting took place at nine minutes after ten?

REGAN: I never knew what time it took place.

In May of 1984, Regan had signed an affidavit referring to the night of the murder. It stated: "That I initially received a telephone call from Mr. Tony Merchant to my father when we were advised of the shooting, and I further state that I remained at the residence throughout that evening." Kujawa pointed out that Regan had not given the specific time Merchant had called.

KUJAWA: Didn't you know at that time that the phone call came precisely between 6:10 and 6:15?

REGAN: You mean from phone records?

KUJAWA: No, no, from your memory.

REGAN: Yes, I did.

KUJAWA: So you knew it then?

REGAN: Yes, I did.

KUJAWA: Just as clearly as you know it today?

REGAN: Yes, I do.

KUJAWA: And much more clearly than Tony Merchant knew it because his affidavit said shortly before six-thirty.

REGAN: Well, I don't know how clearly he remembers it...

As the young man left the stand he seemed not at all shaken or nervous.

Greg Thatcher was the subject of much gossip during the trial. A beautiful young blonde woman had been seen on his arm, and the rumour was that she had stayed with him at the

Ramada Renaissance for a while, and that Dad was very displeased. Greg had the body and grace of an Italian racing cyclist; his casual clothes had a European look to them. Today on the stand, however, looking handsome and very mature for nineteen, he wore a smart blue suit, a white shirt and blue-and-red striped tie.

After pointing out that his grandmother and sister were in the courtroom, Greg said he had graduated from Central Collegiate in 1983–84. He had taken an arts course with a political science major, and he had planned to go into law afterwards. He revealed, however, that he was not going to university this year because "I stayed home to help take care of the family and the farm."

He said that during the Sunday evening of the first shooting in May of 1981, he had been home for supper but at 7 p.m. went to the house of a friend, Matt Lindsay. He got back to Redland, he said, at about 10 p.m. His father was cleaning the pool and Regan was there as well. Greg said he thought Merchant phoned later that evening. The lawyer arrived in Moose Jaw and arranged for Colin and Greg to give a statement to the Moose Jaw police, which they did the next day.

On the day of the murder, Greg had been at Central Collegiate. He finished school at about 3:30, and since he didn't have sports practice after school, he reached home at about 3:45. His father was there but left soon afterwards to check things at the farm. Sandra arrived at about 5 p.m. and his father returned somewhere between 5:15 and 5:30. "What did you have for dinner that night?" Allbright asked him. "Hamburger Helper," replied Greg. "I remember it was about six o'clock when we ate because that's when the news comes on and sports comes on right first. And I was getting up to go and see it and plus... there's a clock in our kitchen." Greg recalled that Merchant phoned twice and the second time told them that JoAnn had been murdered. "I had to get out of the house. I was very jumpy," said Greg. At nine he went to a friend's place and about 11 p.m. another friend gave him a ride. They stopped at a store for a pop and then Greg went home.

As usual Kujawa got right to the point, questioning Greg about the night of the first shooting. Greg seemed nervous and uncomfortable responding to the prosecutor's questions.

* * *

KUJAWA: And if I suggested to you that he [Matt Lindsay] drove you home at 10:45, you wouldn't quarrel with that?

GREG: Yes, I would.

KUJAWA: You would, eh?

GREG: It was ten o'clock.

KUJAWA: At ten o'clock.

GREG: Yes, it was.

KUJAWA: I want to refer you to a statement that you gave to the police shortly after.

GREG: Okay.

KUJAWA: On that statement what time did you say that you got home?

GREG: It says ten-thirty.

KUJAWA: This says ten-thirty.

GREG: M'hm.

KUJAWA: And your memory today says that you got home at ten?

GREG: Yes, that's the way I remember it.

KUJAWA: I have trouble with that. Could you explain how you remember it so much better now than you did right after it happened?

GREG: I'm just saying that's the way I remember it happened now. I'm not arguing. I'm not arguing with that I may have said the time was ten-thirty. As I remember now it was ten o'clock.

Kujawa then asked a series of questions about a certain trip to Phoenix, Arizona, that the Thatchers as well as Sandra and Blaine Mathieson had taken one Christmas. He asked about a credit card belonging to Ron Graham, and about Sandra encouraging the Thatcher children to refer to their mother as "that bitch." This entire line of questioning was confusing to people in the courtroom at the time but it would become crystal-clear all too soon.

Kujawa closed his cross-examination with the famous Hamburger Helper dinner episode.

KUJAWA: Did you know that Sandra was on a telephone at the far end of the house away from the kitchen for almost half an hour, ending at 5:58?

GREG: I don't remember her being on it, but I'm not going to say she wasn't. I don't remember her being on it, but I'm not going to argue with you about it. I don't know or remember.

KUJAWA: . . . Was she in the kitchen making and serving a meal on the 21st of January, just before six?

GREG: Yeah. She, she is there. She served it up at six and we had Hamburger Helper.

KUJAWA: She was also on the telephone at the same time?

GREG: She may have been. I don't know.

KUJAWA: Like I said, she's good. I'm impressed. I have no further questions.

The cynical media wags had started to dub the ongoing spectacle "The Hamburger Helper Trial." Indeed, souvenir T-shirts cropped up, with "DENY, DENY, DENY" on the front and "THE HAMBURGER HELPER TRIAL, SUNNY SASKATOON, OCTOBER–NOVEMBER, 1984" on the back. After the trial, these were worn as proud badges by correspondents as far away as Beijing, China.

MONDAY, OCTOBER 29

Although a rumour persisted—and was even reported by a radio station—that a British Columbia criminal was going to take the stand and admit he had murdered JoAnn, it quickly became obvious that the defence's main witness was Colin Thatcher himself.

There are always great risks in allowing the accused to give evidence and the defence had to weigh the pros and cons very carefully. Rumours spread that Allbright did not want Thatcher to take the stand, that he even made him sign a letter exonerating the defence lawyer from any repercussions that might result from Thatcher testifying. Allbright denies that such a letter existed, but does admit he was in a dilemma. "It was really a no-win situation from a lawyer's point of view, and I laugh to myself from time to time. Every major high-profile murder trial—the Demeter case, the Alberta law professor—where the accused hasn't testified, he'd been convicted. I say to myself, if he's called and he's convicted, everybody will say, 'Why would you call the guy?' If he's not called, they're going to say, 'You know that they're all convicted if they're not called.'" There were many rumours, as well, that Thatcher dominated Allbright to the degree that he was actually running his own trial. Allbright denies this; he says his client was most cooperative. By the trial, Thatcher was a devoted born-again Christian. Since Gerry Allbright shared these beliefs, it added an extra dimension to their relationship. "We had an excellent relationship, still do," says Allbright, "I saw a side of Colin that I very much liked. He displayed, throughout, faith in me."

CHAPTER TWENTY-TWO

BAD LUCK

During his day in court, Colin Thatcher obviously intended to emphasize to the jurors his prestige in the community, his respectability and his accomplishments. He was dressed in a highly businesslike way, in a grey pin-striped suit, white shirt, and Stephanie's "lucky" brown-and-cream tie. As he spoke, he was extremely articulate, self-confident, and quick-thinking—all those years of debating in the Legislature, managing a vast ranch and taking command in his family had left their mark. He was sure he could convince the twelve men and women judging him that someone like him could not possibly have brutally murdered his former wife.

Allbright began by asking Thatcher his age. "Forty-six, unfortunately," he replied. Thatcher then began an exposition of his family's background—the hardware store, the ranch, his father's political career. He explained that he met JoAnn while at university in Ames, Iowa, when she was twenty and he was twenty-one. He described their courtship and their wedding and their early married life. He outlined the thriving farm-ranch operation and his promising political career. He described the difficult times JoAnn had carrying her babies and the birth of their three "very fine" children. "I think we had an excellent relationship and an excellent marriage," he said. He maintained this was the case for sixteen of the seventeen years they lived together.

Why then did such an excellent marriage fail? "I thought she was going through, oh, just this syndrome or whatever they call it, when somebody approached forty. You see it or hear about it on television. I guess you read about it in magazines, but when suddenly it is happening in your family, you really don't know what to do about it. And I didn't know what to do about it. I thought it was something that would pass." Thatcher said that when JoAnn opened up her design business, he thought that would help. Colin's closest friend was Ron Graham and when JoAnn asked him if he would mind if she travelled with Graham on business, Thatcher said, "Go ahead, don't even talk about it." "To this day I don't know what took place on that trip, but I think it was a foolish... thing to have agreed to in retrospect. I think it led to developments down the road.... I was shocked at some of the things [about the relationship between JoAnn and Ron] that came out in court that I had no idea of."

Thatcher continued to describe how his marriage was crumbling before his eyes during 1979. "JoAnn was very troubled. I didn't know why.... She wasn't sleeping. She was losing weight. I would wake up in the middle of the night. She wouldn't be there. She would be downstairs doing some strange things.... She was a very troubled person. It wasn't unusual to find her crying or sobbing or just generally being very down through 1979." Thatcher said he had no idea what was wrong. "I'm not trying to convey the impression to you that I was the perfect husband over seventeen years because I have the same frailties that anybody else does that's married. But for that particular time frame, I put more effort into our marriage than, I put everything in it that was possible to put." At that moment, it wasn't difficult to feel sorry indeed for this cuckolded husband.

Thatcher then related how in August of 1979, after returning from his annual "golf trip" to southern California with Ron Graham, he discovered that JoAnn and the two youngest children were missing. He described in some detail how he had searched for JoAnn, how he went with Sandra Hammond to Brampton to Moose Jaw. He related the custody battles that ensued and how, although JoAnn had been awarded custody of Regan and Stephanie, the young boy refused to stay with her. "The only option was to send him away. And it was, it was a terrible decision to make.... That is what he wanted and he then went into exile."

Thatcher also mentioned the property settlement and how his ex-wife had been awarded some $820,000. He recalled that he had had two or three meetings with JoAnn and her new husband Tony Wilson before the first shooting. "They were in the same state of mind I was. They were sick of lawyers, they were sick of courts, they were sick of being bled financially and they wanted to make a deal." Thatcher insisted that they had worked out a property settlement in principle before JoAnn was wounded. (This, of course, directly contradicted Tony Wilson, who had claimed that negotiations on the property settlement hadn't started until several months after JoAnn was shot the first time.)

Thatcher said he spent the evening of May 17, 1981, opening his pool for the season. "It's a pretty major job by the time you do the filter and the pumps and close valves." Regan was with him for the entire evening, and Greg was at a friend's until about 10:15 or 10:30. He related how Merchant phoned, and then came to Moose Jaw. The next day, he said, he and Greg gave a statement to police.

He told the poignant story of how he visited JoAnn in the hospital and how she showed him her wound. He said their relationship at that point "was quite cordial."

Describing how he fought for his "political life" and lost during January of 1983, Thatcher said he spent the week leading up to JoAnn's death "licking my political wounds." He said he attended a funeral in Regina on Monday but did not return to that city for the rest of the week. On January 21, the day of the murder, Thatcher went to his ranch in the afternoon—he didn't see Barbara Wright—and returned at about 5:30. In Moose Jaw he waved to Pat Hammond. At 6 p.m., he insisted, he was having dinner with Regan, Greg, and Sandra Hammond. He received the first telephone call from Tony Merchant somewhere between 6:15 and 6:20. After Merchant phoned back to confirm that JoAnn was dead, Thatcher felt "shock," and was very concerned about Stephanie. Thatcher said that when Sandra returned he "put on a jogging suit and I went around a few blocks and came back. . . . I just wanted to think, or I just maybe wanted some fresh air. I just had to move." Thatcher admitted that when friends came to console him that night, he had "quite a bit" to drink. 'It had been one blazes of a week."

He explained how he had met Lynne Dally in Palm Springs, "which has been my playground ever since I became single." "Lynne had led a very unique life in the late '60s. She is a—one of these Vietnam war protesters. She's been in the front lines when the police had been there swinging their sticks, etcetera. She has had some very unique experiences with soft drugs.... Maybe that was partly a part of the fascination for her, too, that I had for some time, but she had reached that stage where she had just decided she wanted to get married."

That his divorce with JoAnn had not been finalized was an excuse he used to put off Lynne and because of that Thatcher said, "I believe Lynne became rather bitter towards JoAnn without ever knowing her." When he phoned the night of the first shooting to tell her that JoAnn had been shot, Thatcher said Lynne asked him, "Is she alive?" When he said yes, she replied, "Oh, shit."

"There were times when I cared for her, but I never trusted her.... I had no confidence in Lynne in many respects, would be the best way I could think to answer it. I didn't have enough confidence in her to allow her to live in my condominium as she wanted to do on many occasions. I didn't have enough confidence in her to drive my car. And it sounds like a contradiction; I cared for her in a certain way, but I did not have confidence in her and I did not totally trust her."

Colin said that after receiving the seven roses and threatening phone calls in January of 1982, he bought the .357 Ruger Security-Six. Of course, he had to account for what had happened to the gun. "I noticed it was gone in mid-1982. I believed that it was, rightly or wrongly, I came to the conclusion that my cleaning woman had taken it." He had fired the woman because of his suspicions, he added.

Thatcher said he phoned Lynne at 6:24 the night of the murder, after Merchant called him to break the news. He said that when he had first talked to police after the murder, he hadn't recalled when Merchant had actually telephoned him. But then at a bail hearing he had seen an affidavit signed by Sergeant Beaton that said he had made a phone call to Palm Springs at 6:24. "And then that, of course, put a lot of things into direct perspective. Until that time, I could not put a direct, to the minute on the phone call from Tony Merchant."

After Thatcher visited Palm Springs a week or so later, he claimed he and Lynne were still on friendly terms. "We were in bed, and she asked very quietly, 'Did you blow her away?'

and I said, 'I cannot imagine what a strange feeling that would be. No, of course not.'"

The last time he had sexual relations with Lynne was in the last part of February or first part of March, 1983, but after that they maintained a friendship and saw each other often, said Thatcher. She had set him up with a date once, he had congratulated her on her upcoming marriage, and he had introduced her to (her successor) Diane Stoner.

Discussing Thatcher's conversations with Lynne Mendell, Allbright asked him, "Did you ever, Mr. Thatcher, say to her that you had killed JoAnn?"

THATCHER: No, certainly not.

ALLBRIGHT: Was there ever a discussion that was in any way similar to a discussion about JoAnn shot and beaten? Was there ever a discussion between you, stemmed from a newspaper article?

THATCHER: Well, only in this context. Her parents had received volumes of press clippings on the incident from Canadians; people they knew as Canadians and knew that their daughter was seeing me. And of course, they had things from all over Canada. And she said to me once something to the effect, and I may not—I'm probably not quoting verbatim, but said—and this is the way Lynne talks, she said, "Christ, why would they beat her and then shoot her?" and I said, "I have no idea. Whoever was in there was an animal anyway.... Nobody could do that to another human being."

With that the trial adjourned for the day.

TUESDAY, OCTOBER 30

Many of those in the courtroom who had watched Thatcher give evidence the previous day considered that he had done well; he had remained cool and collected, assertive but soft-spoken. The assistant Crown prosecutor, Al Johnson, felt that he had glimpsed the compelling attraction that Thatcher held for so many people. "He was confident, talked forcefully, and lied very convincingly," says Johnson. Still, the accused man had yet to explain away the troublesome tape, and at this point his testimony began to strike many courtroom observers as highly imaginative. In order to present his interpretation, it was necessary that Thatcher give a detailed account of his involvement with Garry Anderson.

Thatcher said he had known Anderson for about ten years. "He is a person that it is easier to be nice to, it is easier to get along with than it is to have trouble with him, as some people have. He's, he's a very volatile, irrational individual and someone you just don't need any trouble with."

Thatcher admitted that he had met with Anderson in the fall of 1980 but he simply told Garry, he explained, that he would be interested in leasing or buying some land Garry's mother owned near the Thatcher ranch. The two men met again in early 1981 and Anderson told him his mother was going to lease it to somebody else and there was nothing he could do. At that point, Thatcher said, Anderson asked him how he felt about Ron Graham. "And I told him I still had some fairly strong feelings towards Ron Graham. He said, 'I hear that Graham has some problems in the construction business over some work which he did. It has something to do with cutting some corners on a construction project.' I asked him where he had heard that. And he said, 'I heard it from one of his employees out of the Calgary office.' He said, 'Are you interested in pursuing it?'" Thatcher, who had heard similar rumours, said he was and agreed to cover Anderson's expenses.

In the spring of 1981, Thatcher claimed he met Anderson on the road near Caron. "Two fellows from Calgary are coming through tomorrow, where are you gong to be?" Anderson asked. Thatcher told him he'd be at the Bergren farm and Anderson appeared there with one other person. Thatcher said he had the same hair colour as Charlie Wilde but he remembered him as being taller, "more my height. I don't believe it was Charlie Wilde." "What have you got?" Thatcher asked him. "And what he had was not at all what I had been led to believe. . . . What he had was that his friend knows a girl that Graham was seeing. And the scheme they had in mind was setting Graham up with this girl and before they had even finished with the scheme I told him, 'Forget it. I'm not even remotely interested.'" According to Thatcher the blond-haired man then said, "We could lay a good licking on him or we can go even further than that if you want." "I have no interest at all," Thatcher said he responded.

Thatcher then told the jury that he had seen Anderson a few days later. "I told him that I hadn't been happy. And he said, 'Well, you are going to be even unhappier. You owe me five hundred dollars for arranging this meeting.' I was upset with myself. I knew I was being ripped off but I wasn't going to argue. I, I was disgusted with myself that I had even taken part in a meeting like that. . . . I said, 'You'll have to wait because I haven't got five hundred dollars on me.'" He did not see Anderson for a while after that.

Thatcher said that in the winter of 1982, just before the election, he got a call from someone who said he knew Garry Anderson. The caller remarked on the Tories' growing popularity and then made an attempt at what Thatcher said was "crude blackmail." "With things going as well as they are, you certainly don't need any difficulties and we're sorry that we couldn't do business last year." "I told him what he could do with himself in the strongest language," Thatcher said.

During the fall of 1982, Thatcher informed the court, Anderson left a letter at his ranch saying he had applied for employment with the Saskatchewan Mining Development Corporation in the La Ronge area but hadn't been given the job. Thatcher claimed he gave the letter to Chuck Guillaume, his executive assistant, and said, "This is a sort of a constituent. If you can place him with SMDC without any problem or any difficulties in that area, go ahead, but don't do anything out of the ordinary." Then Thatcher said he forgot about it.

In late 1982, Thatcher said he was driving into the Legislature grounds when he spotted Anderson standing on the corner. "I stopped and yelled across at him, 'Are you lost?'" "No, I've been waiting for you. I've got a problem," Anderson shouted back. Thatcher claims he pulled into his parking spot and Anderson and some other person pulled up beside him. Thatcher got into the back seat of their car. "You won't believe this," said Anderson, "but we left a car here and it's gone." Thatcher replied, "You're right, I wouldn't believe it. What have you been up to?" Anderson explained that the car was left in one place too long and so was towed away. Thatcher said he then went into the Legislative Buildings to call the Wascana Authority. "I went out and I waved to him, said it will be back shortly." When he was about to leave his office later in the day, Thatcher realized he had left his topcoat, gloves, and scarf in Anderson's car. The topcoat, he said, had his name in it.

Thatcher recalled that after the murder, rumours were rampant around the Caron area that he had hired Anderson to murder JoAnn and that he had arranged to get Garry a government job in northern Saskatchewan. "I was very concerned about it because the rumour was all over the area. The police had been putting tremendous pressure on people that were close to me, particularly Sandra. They had come down very heavily on some people that had known me and made, I think, some very inappropriate suggestions to some of them."

With this background information neatly laid out, Thatcher could set about interpreting the tape to demonstrate his innocence.

Thatcher said he went to the abandoned farm with Anderson on May 1, 1984, for two reasons. "I wanted to know what was happening with Anderson and the Regina police. I knew the rumours. I knew what they were trying to do. Then on top of that Anderson felt that I owed him five hundred dollars and I don't need Garry Anderson on my neck. I didn't need any haystacks burning or any outlying granaries on fire or something like that. So I didn't need any trouble with him so I certainly went."

According to Thatcher, much of what was on the tape was related to his fear the police were out to link him with the murder. At one point on tape Anderson asked how he could get a good lawyer it if became necessary. Thatcher responded: "Oh well, don't worry about that, but I mean, it ain't coming to that. It ain't coming to that 'cause they have no way of—there's only two places to put the connection together, and they got zero else. They've got zero else, and I mean you know what there is to put together and it ain't possible, and it ain't coming from me. I mean, just always remember that if you were ever to say that I said this or that, it's a crock of garbage. It's just always deny, deny, deny."

Thatcher translated for the jury the meaning of this little speech as follows. "Well, in my Caron slang I guess what I'm saying is that we have done nothing wrong and nothing is going to happen. There's only two places that they, that they can go to make, do anything to make their story wash and one of those is Anderson and the other one is me. I'm again suggesting in slang that we have done nothing wrong... When you have done nothing wrong, I see nothing wrong with denying it."

Not everything on the tape, however, could be linked to the police campaign to pin the murder of JoAnn on Thatcher, through Anderson.

In a most significant part of the tape Anderson says, "I got rid of the stuff out of the car."

THATCHER: Good.

ANDERSON: You kind of give me a scare there with—I found the stuff lying in there and then I wondered what the hell—I didn't know where the hell you—what the hell you'd done with the gun?

THATCHER: Don't even talk like that, don't—don't even—walk out this way a little, away from the car. Now, there are no loose ends, at all, and, you know, they've gone—every which direction. Was there any way a loose end from a couple of years ago can ever resurface, from some of the guys that—discussing some business with, is there any way there'd ever be a problem surface from them?

ANDERSON: You mean from Vancouver and Winnipeg? I located one of them.

THATCHER: The one that I met, or the other one?

ANDERSON: The other one.

THATCHER: Son of a bitch.

Thatcher's explanation of this portion of the tape struck the spectators in court as ingenious. The stuff out of the car, he said, referred to the coat, scarf, and gloves that, ignoring the cold weather, he left in Anderson's Dodge that winter day in 1982. As to the mention of the gun, Thatcher explained "He [Anderson] said that with a smile on his face. I took it to be a very ill attempt at humour, a very poor attempt at humour. I guess the look on my face and what I said ended that line of questioning." Thatcher wanted to walk away from the car while the conversation was going on, not because the conversation was especially sensitive and he was afraid of police bugs but because "I was scratching around looking for moisture and checking the weeds." What about the loose end from a couple of years ago? Thatcher admitted that loose end was a poor choice of words but he was referring to the "ridiculous meeting" that had taken place three years before when Thatcher had been open to information about Ron Graham. One of the people he was referring to was the man who had attempted to "crudely blackmail" Thatcher.

One of the great moments of the trial came when Thatcher attempted to explain away his "son of a bitch" expletive. He was not in any way referring to the two men from Vancouver and Winnipeg, not at all. Thatcher said that at the time he was down scratching in the dirt and when he found some unwelcome tansy mustard there, he let loose with, "Son of a bitch." "I wanted to find out if the wild oats are coming," he offered. Thatcher was deadly serious when he gave this explanation, so that no one laughed outright—many in the courtroom couldn't help but snicker under their breath, however.

At one point in the tape, Thatcher asked Anderson, "Do you need some bread?" Anderson replied, "Yeah, I can use some. I can use some for that car." Thatcher explained, "When Anderson told me that I owed him five hundred dollars for his expenses for arranging that meeting, I knew that I was being ripped off. He gave me a story which I didn't pay much attention to that he had some difficulties with his car and that was a major part of it and somehow this tied into it." Thatcher admitted that he did agree to leave the money for Anderson at the abandoned farm.

The remainder of Allbright's examination continued in a similar manner. He would ask questions about the tape and Thatcher would methodically interpret what had seemed such damaging revelations. To many observers, some of his explanations seemed pretty implausible.

Anderson had asked him if he planned to change political parties, and Thatcher replied that the Tories were in trouble. "All of a sudden Devine likes to talk to an old pro again there.... He called me in California.... Things are slipping away from him and I think he's starting to know it," Thatcher had said. He admitted now, however, that the premier had not called him. He had been in Palm Springs, he said, with his daughter and her girlfriend. "I had missed some time in the Legislature and the girls used to tease me, they would come running outside and say, 'The premier is calling and wants to know where you are.' It was just a private joke that I passed on to Anderson." For those in the courtroom who had acquired the hobby of analyzing Thatcher's personality, this was another example of his habit of creating reality as he wished it. It reminded the police of all those telephone conversations with women about the imaginary important people he had encountered and important places he had been.

On the tape the two men parted with these words.

ANDERSON: I'm glad you got her.
THATCHER: Yeah.
ANDERSON: See you.
THATCHER: You bet.

According to Thatcher, while Anderson was talking, he was also extending his hand out at waist level as if indicating that he were talking about a small person. Thatcher explained that he thought Anderson was referring to the fact that he had obtained custody of Stephanie some months before.

Thatcher had taken a big chance gambling that the jury would believe his interpretation of the tape. Many onlookers in the courtroom believed that he had been so convincingly indignant at what he considered police harassment and so self-confident in relating his story that he had scored a coup. He still had to face Kujawa, however, who was considered one of the mightiest bruisers around. It would prove to be a titanic clash between two formidable personalities.

Kujawa had been itching for some time to take on Colin Thatcher. He had watched his performance on the stand with both fascination and disgust. "His mother, his little daughter, his boys, the world is watching him, he is on trial for his life, and he has to resort to cheap, stupid, really stupid, macho theatrics." Unlike Allbright, who sailed about the room while he was examining a witness, Kujawa remained rooted in one spot—squarely in front of the witness box, which enabled him to look his victim directly in the eye. His large, gnarled peasant hands often gripped the lapels of his court gown but at a critical point he would extend his left hand, which lacked the two middle fingers, adding great drama to his questioning. With his flowing black robes, he looked like a huge, hostile bald eagle, and in his attack on Thatcher he did indeed resemble a frightening bird of prey. For his part, Thatcher chose to fight back defiantly and aggressively. The opening round set the tone for this heavyweight bout that was to run for a fascinating and exhausting five hours.

KUJAWA: Mr. Thatcher, you gave us a great long story on how happy and great a marriage you had for some sixteen and a half years, right?

THATCHER: That is your description.

KUJAWA: Let's have yours. We've heard it about four times but tell it again if you disagree with my summary, tell it again.

THATCHER: It's very difficult to summarize sixteen and a half years into a few moments. What aspect would you like?

KUJAWA: You told us that for sixteen and a half years it was a pretty happy, pretty good marriage, you were very much in love with your wife and she with you, so far as you knew.

THATCHER: I think I said that we had a very good marriage by any standards. We had our . . .

KUJAWA: You did admit—you did admit to some human frailties, and I commend you for that.

THATCHER: I had many human frailties. I obviously—I obviously failed as a husband. Our marriage broke up.

KUJAWA: You've pulled a wonderful switch to humility this afternoon. I'm pleased with that as well, sir.

THATCHER: I'm glad you're pleased.

KUJAWA: We'll deal with it. You pointed out that when you realized that something was going wrong in your marriage that you, for the last eight months, nobody could have tried harder to be a good husband.

THATCHER: I tried harder. I also had my failings there also.

KUJAWA: Right.

THATCHER: As you know, Mr. Kujawa, the breakdown of a marriage is a two-way street. You heard one version of it yesterday.

KUJAWA: We're going to hear some more from the same person, I assure you. While you were trying this hard to make the marriage work, you and your dear friend Ron Graham went on a golfing trip to California.

THATCHER: Yes.

KUJAWA: And you told us how you trusted this man, how he betrayed you.

THATCHER: Yes.

KUJAWA: And it tore you apart.

THATCHER: Yes.

KUJAWA: You didn't expect anything like that from him at all. And, of course, you didn't expect your wife to take off either, did you?

THATCHER: If I had been anticipating that, obviously I would not have been away.

KUJAWA: What were you doing on that golfing trip besides golfing?

THATCHER: We were over in Palm Springs. We...

KUJAWA: I didn't ask you where you were. I asked you what you were doing besides golfing?

THATCHER: Would you be more specific?

KUJAWA: I suggest to you that you were doing one [Janis] Gardiner at the same time as 'you were golfing, or in between?

THATCHER: Yes, we were joined—both of us were joined by company, yes.

KUJAWA: I suggest you were having intercourse with her?

THATCHER: Yes.

KUJAWA: This is while you were trying so hard to be a good husband?

THATCHER: I think I suggested to you that I had my frailties also.

Kujawa asked Thatcher if he had reported the fact of his stolen gun to the authorities. Thatcher responded that he had telephoned a description and serial number to the sheriff's department in Indio, California, but unfortunately no record had been kept of this call. "So you just had bad luck with that gun loss report not being registered anywhere in the State of California," said Kujawa. As for the Ruger holster that had been found in the car he had signed out from the Saskatchewan government, Thatcher simply stated that it was not his; he had written his name on the one he had purchased from Ron Williams. "Then do you have an explanation for why it was there?" Kujawa asked. Thatcher responded, "I have no idea.' "Bad luck, right?" asked the Crown attorney mockingly.

There was more bad luck, said Kujawa, when the police found the Cindy Shower box filled with the crumpled *L.A. Times* in Thatcher's bedroom. "More extremely bad luck, your credit card found this far from the body," said Kujawa. "That's what I understand," Thatcher responded. Bad luck again, suggested Kujawa, when a government car with its licence plate smeared in mud and ending in the number 292 had been signed out to Thatcher. "I had a car checked out to me. I did not have the car that you suggest was stalking JoAnn the week before," insisted Thatcher. "You've taken 'deny, deny, deny' to new heights already and we haven't even got going good yet," said the prosecutor, his voice laden with sarcasm.

Before the trial had started, Kujawa had told colleagues in the Crown attorney's office that he was determined to get Thatcher roaring mad during his cross-examination. "I'm going to get him angry 'cause, you see, I am the perfect example of a nobody to Colin. All I have to do is be disrespectful and if necessary, a little contemptuous, and he will blow his top. He has to. There is no way his ego can tolerate a guy like me being totally disrespectful, nasty, even, to the great Colin. He assumes that I know my place and I'm afraid, etc. It's going to come as a hell of a shock when he finds out that I don't." Kujawa didn't have to wait long for the explosion.

Kujawa had been suggesting that the evidence of Thatcher's defence witnesses was almost invariably different from the affidavits they had signed. Thatcher was quick to react. "And if you think that they did not tell the truth, Mr. Kujawa, then why don't you take appropriate action, rather than asking me about it?"

KUJAWA: Because right now I've got a more interesting case than a little perjury trial.

THATCHER: Why don't you . . . if you're accusing them of perjury, why don't you do something about it? Why tell me about it? They testified. They're vulnerable. They didn't have immunity like your witnesses.

KUJAWA: Mr. Thatcher, keep calm. As long as you're telling the truth, the whole truth, and nothing but the truth, nothing can hurt you.

* * *

In a flash of rage, that scornful mouth taut with fury, his eyes flashing, Thatcher thundered, "It's very easy to say that my sons have lied. Why don't you step out of the courthouse and say that." In a lower voice he added, "Where you don't have immunity," but few people in the courtroom heard that part. They had visions of these two large and powerful men determining justice through an old-fashioned, bloody, single combat on the courthouse stairs. It was a shocking, frightening performance by Thatcher. A seventy-year-old lady, a habituée of the trial from day one, said in a rather loud whisper, "I wouldn't want that man to get mad at me." The jurors might have felt the same way.

Allbright bristled when the Crown attorney flung back at Thatcher, "How about the fourth green on the golf course?" referring to Thatcher's threat to Ron Graham while playing golf. "Look, Charlie Bronson you're not," Kujawa snarled at the accused man.

Now that his strategem had worked, Kujawa took advantage of Thatcher's outburst.

KUJAWA: I suggest to you that your wife lived in great fear of you, physical fear.

THATCHER: I do not agree with that at all.

KUJAWA: You do admit that you got into fights with her?

THATCHER: No more than simple civil disagreements, typical of any marriage. If you mean, were they physical? The answer is no.

KUJAWA: She blackened eyes by falling off ladders and such quite a lot?

THATCHER: No, about eleven years before our break-up, I was hanging wallpaper from the ceiling and the stepladder collapsed. On my way down my elbow caught her eye and I heard about it in court eleven years later.

KUJAWA: And during these arguments would you talk to her the way you talked to me, or do you reserve that...?

THATCHER: I reserve it for people that may be making misrepresentations. Generally she did not make misrepresentations. That's the only way I can answer that question.

KUJAWA: I'm suggesting to you, sir, that when you get mad, you get wild, like you did a while ago?

THATCHER: I don't think that was getting wild. On the other hand, Mr. Kujawa, perhaps if you had spent six months where I have and the source and the reason for that comes up, you may tend to get just a trifle emotional yourself.

Kujawa continued to pound at Thatcher for the rest of the afternoon. When the trial adjourned for the day, he had finished less than half his cross-examination.

By this stage, the trial had stirred people's interest so much that each day's events grabbed headlines in Canadian papers from coast to coast. More often than not, the trial was the lead item on the national television news. In Saskatoon, the fascination with the drama being played out right there in the city was such that some people actually camped on the courthouse steps overnight to grab a seat the next morning. It was below freezing, windy, and snowy. These hardy souls wrapped themselves in blankets, scarves, and shawls before they crept into their sleeping bags, to think about the next round between Serge Kujawa and Colin Thatcher.

WEDNESDAY, OCTOBER 31

The remainder of Kujawa's cross-examination was a meticulous analysis of the tape and Thatcher's interpretation of it. The Crown attorney was unrelenting in his sarcasm, pointing out sentence by sentence the illogic and inconsistencies in Thatcher's responses. As the morning progressed, Thatcher's version became more and more tattered. Kujawa's questioning on the bloody car was a good example.

On the tape Anderson had said, "Oh, I had a hell of a time to clean the car out."

THATCHER: Is that right?
ANDERSON: Yeah. I had a bitch of a time getting the blood and stuff off.
THATCHER: Yeah. Is there no chance that it can ever surface? There is a chance it can surface?
ANDERSON: No, I don't—no.
THATCHER: Okay. . . .
ANDERSON: I didn't burn it, but it was cleaned.
THATCHER: All right.

Thatcher explained that he had no idea what Anderson was talking about when he said, "I had a hell of a time to clean the car out," so he responded, "Is that right?" As to Anderson having a hard time getting the "blood and stuff" off, Thatcher accounted for that by saying, "I think if you had had a camera there, I think the look on my face would have told you my reaction to that. . . . As he said that he had a smirk on his face. I did not consider it funny. . . . I think the look on my face told it all and that was the end of it." Kujawa had that portion of the tape played back to the silent courtroom. The prosecutor pointed out that Anderson sounded as if he was breathing very heavily, as if in fright, while he spoke. He asked Thatcher how Anderson could be joking and hyperventilating at the same time. "He still had a smirk on his face," answered Thatcher, "smirk that I didn't appreciate and I suggest to you that I probably had a . . . a piercing look which told him everything." Kujawa had the tape played back again. Kujawa asked Thatcher if he noticed the great concern, even fear, in his voice, when he immediately asked, "Is there no chance that it can ever surface? There is a chance it can surface?" Thatcher replied, "I don't believe there is at all. I believe there is just a secondary question and nothing else." Thatcher maintained that he was worrying about the car surfacing because he had left his coat and gloves in it. "I was concerned that perhaps that coat could surface in his car and something could be misconstrued out of something that was in fact very innocent." Finally Kujawa asked what Anderson's remark "I didn't burn it, but it was cleaned" meant. "Why wouldn't you say, 'What the hell do you mean, burn it? What for? Why do you burn a car?" To that, Thatcher's reply was "I had no idea why he would want to burn it and I really didn't care."

There was one portion of the tape that Thatcher said proved his innocence. It began with his saying to Anderson, "I mean, just always remember that if you were ever to say that I said this or that, it's a crock of garbage. It's just always deny, deny, deny."

ANDERSON: Mhmm.

THATCHER: Because no matter what it was, you know. And you know, I was just lucky that night, I was home with four people. Four people, pretty solid, and that's pretty hard. What about you, are you covered at the time? . . .

ANDERSON: Yeah, but, under questioning or if something ever happens, would they ever crack those—your witnesses?

THATCHER: No. Never.

Kujawa, however, maintained that when Thatcher talked about the four people being "pretty solid, and that's pretty hard" he was illustrating to Anderson how to deny, deny, deny. Thatcher went on the attack, saying, "May I suggest, Mr. Kujawa, you are reaching pretty far on that one."

There had been one exchange between the two men that revealed the undercurrent of bitterness prevailing in the courtroom. On this occasion, Thatcher was visibly squirming in his seat. Kujawa asked Thatcher, "You were very, very, very concerned about the safety of Stephanie the night your wife was shot by some animal, as you described the beast?"

THATCHER: Yes.

KUJAWA: Who did you phone to inquire about her safety?

THATCHER: Tony Merchant was finding out what the situation was for me.

KUJAWA: Did you say one specific word to Tony Merchant

THATCHER: I phoned—I . . .

KUJAWA: Nobody.

THATCHER: No, I did not. It was being done for me.

KUJAWA: Did you say one specific word to Tony Merchant about that?

THATCHER: Of course. Well, one of the things that Tony was going to find out is if Stephanie was safe. And on the second phone call, he—he gave me as much as he knew.

KUJAWA: You didn't tell us that before, did you?

THATCHER: I think I did.

KUJAWA: You are still extremely concerned about your children?

THATCHER: Yes.

KUJAWA: Yes. You, when you brought in that little girl, Stephanie, pushed hard to get her and the other members of the family into the front row of this courtroom, didn't you?

Thatcher said he personally hadn't asked that his family be positioned front row and centre, but he eventually admitted that Greg had made the request.

The cross-examination finaly concluded at 2:29 p.m. Everyone in the courtroom felt exhausted.

With Thatcher's testimony concluded, the defense rested its case.

There had been much controversy among the prosecution team about whether rebuttal evidence should be called. Thatcher had flatly denied that he had seen Garry Anderson at any time during the week before the murder. Sergeant Hagerty of the Moose Jaw police had spotted the two men talking together at a gas station near Caron the day before the murder. Hagerty was on alert in the event that Kujawa wanted him to testify. There was also Blaine Mathieson, Sandra's old boyfriend, who could give evidence about the rented Mustang with the gun in it that he had seen in Thatcher's garage just before the first shooting, after being warned about it by Sandra. Sandra and Colin, under questioning by Kujawa, had both denied any knowledge of this car. And the Crown prosecutor also considered calling police officers who had interviewed Barbara Wright shortly after the murder. On the stand, Wright had said she had seen Thatcher in the ranch yard that evening, but according to the police she had told them that she had not seen the accused man at all on that day. Kujawa decided he would call none of these people. He was going after the one big fish that had unexpectedly plopped into his lap.

The previous Wednesday, after the Crown's case had concluded, Kujawa and Al Johnson were riding the elevator at the Ramada Renaissance Hotel. They were joined by a middle-aged couple who had planned to go down but found themselves going up instead. Looking at Kujawa, the man joked, "Well, we don't mind since we're riding with a celebrity." Kujawa was chatting away about something, and only glanced at the speaker. But when they got off on the nineteenth floor, Johnson exclaimed, "You know who that was? Dick Collver!"

The two men were joined by Ed Swayze and others for a few drinks and Johnson mentioned that they had seen Collver. "Wonder what he's doing in Saskatoon?" Ed Swayze asked. Kujawa noticed that the policeman's "antennae started to quiver." Swayze immediately went to the desk and discovered that Collver was staying in room 1705 in the same hotel. That evening, however, he was out visiting his daughter.

After Collver had stepped down as leader of the Saskatchewan Progressive Conservative party in 1979, his political career had taken a strange twist. Angered at the liberal tendencies in his old party, he began his own fringe group called the Unionist Party, which basically advocated throwing in the towel on Canada and joining with the United States. After some dreadful donnybrooks in the Legislature, the Unionist Party died a merciful death, and Collver did not run in the 1982 election. He moved to Arizona, eventually sold his dude ranch at Wickenburg, and began a successful health insurance billing company. By the fall of 1984, he was living in a palatial Spanish-style house set on a golf course in Phoenix, Arizona. His daughter, meanwhile, had married and remained in Saskatoon. At the time of the trial, Dick and Eleanor were visiting her because she had just had a baby girl, their first grandchild.

Early the next morning Swayze knocked on the Collvers' door. Eleanor said that Dick had already gone to the YMCA for a workout and massage. Wally Beaton and Ed Swayze tracked him down at the Y's health club. "He was lying naked on the rubdown table," remembers Swayze. "I said, 'Mr. Collver? Can we talk to you in private?' Collver said, 'Can I get dressed first?' We said sure and he was just great."

Collver's lawyer Ron Barclay had told him that he did not have a legal obligation to come forward but if he was ever questioned by police he would have to tell them what he knew or he could be charged with obstructing justice. "Had I not come forward at that point and Thatcher had got off, I don't think I could have lived with myself," says Collver. Barclay would accompany Collver as he told his story from the witness stand.

Because it would impose strict limitations on what could be asked, Kujawa did not want to call Collver as rebuttal evidence; instead he wanted the Crown's case to be reopened. He told Justice Maher, "At this point, I am stating that in my opinion this is significant, not trivial evidence, and I didn't know about it before, had no way of knowing about it before. I don't think it was in the existence of the police or anybody. It was sort of an act of God that brought the man here."

Allbright argued against this, but not very strenuously, and Maher ruled that Collver could be called as a Crown witness.

Dick Collver was less hirsute and a little pudgier than when he was the gung-ho leader of the newly rejuvenated Saskatchewan Progressive Conservatives, but he was just as self-confident and just as convincing. On the stand, he related that in the fall of 1979, Thatcher had asked if he and his wife, Eleanor, would meet with JoAnn and talk to her about a reconciliation. They had taken JoAnn out for dinner but she refused to go back to Colin because "she was afraid for herself and she was afraid for her children." She had been so nervous and upset that evening that she had been ill.

Collver then recounted how just after Christmas of 1979, Thatcher had taken Collver up on his invitation to bring his family to the Wickenburg dude ranch. Thatcher arrived before New Year's with the three children, Sandra Hammond, and Sandra's boyfriend, Blaine Mathieson. Collver testified that during the entire time the group was at his home, "I never heard Colin or the babysitter [Sandra] refer to JoAnn as anything but 'the bitch'." According to Collver, Sandra and Colin taught the children to play a get-even game against Ron Graham by using his telephone credit card to make calls around the world. Collver said he was told this by a laughing Sandra and Colin. "I said, 'This is nonsense, absolute nonsense, and it's wrong.'"

The morning after Thatcher arrived, he and Collver were having a little chat about Colin's matrimonial problems when Thatcher said there was "only one solution for the bitch.... I've got to hire someone to kill her." Collver knew Calgary lawyers who had some pretty unsavoury clients. "Will you please call them and find out who would do it?" Colin asked him. Although Collver asked Thatcher not to discuss the matter further, Colin brought the subject up again on two other occasions during the day. Finally Collver told him that until he got rid of this awful obsession, he did not want him in his house. The group left the next day.

Finally Collver related how in the spring of 1980, Thatcher asked him to negotiate with JoAnn. Dick said that he worked out a settlement whereby Colin would have had custody of the two boys, and JoAnn of Stephanie. As well, JoAnn agreed to settle the matrimonial property question for $230,000. Collver was delighted with this arrangement and phoned

Thatcher immediately. "The bitch isn't going to get anything," was his curt reply. Collver said, "Colin, that is the last time I ever want to be involved with your personal life."

It was shocking testimony. For one thing, it cast Sandra Silversides in a very different light than the one that she had presented in court. And it cast doubt on the credibility of several defence witnesses. The day after Swayze had come upon Collver had been the day Greg Thatcher testified and Kujawa had questioned him about the Collver ranch incident. Greg had admitted that Graham's credit card had been used, but said it was Blaine Mathieson who had used it, not Sandra or any of the Thatchers. This line of questioning naturally tipped off Allbright that this damaging evidence might be coming, and during his examination of Thatcher, he queried him about the Arizona visit. Thatcher, of course, had a very different version.

Thatcher said that they had been there for New Year's Eve. The two families had gone out for dinner and alcohol was consumed "freely." "Collver is the cheapest drunk in the world. And what I mean by that is Dick cannot drink," Thatcher said. The next morning Collver was in "that never-never land when you are still half drunk and hung over". They started talking about the upcoming divorce and according to Thatcher, Collver said, "You can be bled to death financially. Or you can settle before it gets into the hands of the lawyers. . . . Or you can kill her." Thatcher said Collver didn't really mean that the last option was a possibility; he was trying to persuade his friend to settle out of court. Colin said that he would have to give up his two kids to get any kind of negotiated settlement, which he was not prepared to do. "Dick would sort of lurch, 'Go to La Costa, then. Get a hit man. Lots of them over there.'"

Now, in cross-examination, Allbright attempted to discredit Collver as a witness, suggesting he had been too drunk at the time to remember details and suggesting that he was making the whole thing up. "I'm a great believer in friendship and loyalty," Collver replied. "I don't have flights of the imagination. I wish I did not have to be sitting in this chair."

The cases for both the defence and Crown concluded at 4:49 after eighteen full days of evidence. It was Hallowe'en night and ten-year-old Stephanie, who was staying at the Ramada Renaissance Hotel with Peggy, was disappointed because she couldn't get dressed up and go trick-or-treating. Duane Smith, the courtroom guard, felt sorry for the young girl and offered to take her along with his eight-year-old daughter. The Smiths dressed Stephanie as a punk rocker, hair dyed and all, and she had a marvellous time. It was a gratifyingly warm, human gesture during an ordeal that to the child must have seemed very inhuman indeed.

THURSDAY, NOVEMBER 1

Gerry Allbright gave a closing address to the jury that was six times longer than the one Kujawa would give. There were no dramatics here, just words upon words pouring over the jury like syrup. Emphasizing that the country's very system of justice was on trial, he began by giving a long lecture on the serious responsibility facing the jurors, and underscored their duty to judge Thatcher on the evidence presented, not on news reports or gossip.

Much more interesting was his analysis of the evidence. "I don't believe for one moment that there is a shade of doubt in anyone's mind that Colin Thatcher was in Moose Jaw at 6 p.m., January 21, 1983," the defence lawyer said. And, he added, this could be proven in four different ways. If you accept Craig Dotson's testimony, said Allbright, Thatcher was not the killer coming out of the Wilson garage. The phone call that was made from Moose Jaw at 6:24 also proved he couldn't have been in Regina at the time of the murder; it was "utter folly" to suggest that anyone could drive the sixty-four kilometres between the cities in twenty or so minutes. On the infamous tape itself, Allbright stressed, Thatcher himself says, "I was just lucky that night. I was home with four people." Finally, there was the testimony of no fewer than six people who put him in Moose Jaw near the time the crime was committed. "How many people do you know would lie on a first-degree murder charge?" Allbright asked the jurors.

What about the theory that Thatcher could have hired someone to kill JoAnn? A simple piece of evidence, a small slip of paper, showed absolutely that Thatcher had not hired a hit man, said Allbright. "Whoever killed JoAnn Wilson planted a credit card slip, I suggest to you, eight feet from the corner of the garage so that Colin Thatcher would become the accused in these proceedings." Obviously a killer hired by Thatcher was not going to drop the "calling card."

Allbright then claimed that there were five witnesses who were conspicuous by their very absence. Where was Danny Doyle, the man who supposedly helped Garry Anderson make the silencers, the defence lawyer asked. Where was Cody Crutcher, Charlie Wilde's confrère? Where was Garry Anderson's brother-in-law, who drove Garry to pick up his Mercury from the Moose Jaw location where Thatcher supposedly left it after the murder? And finally why hadn't Wally Beaton and Ed Swayze, the two senior police officers in the investigation, been called? "You decide whether you've had all the evidence fairly put before you that the law says you should have," the defence lawyer challenged the jury.

About Tony Wilson's evidence, Allbright said, "I don't suggest to you for one minute that Tony Wilson's a suspect. That's not my job." But, said Allbright, if you wanted to make somebody look like a suspect, he would be a good example. He was home in the afternoon; hadn't seen a doctor, though he said he had the flu; the young housekeeper was there—and there may be a problem there or not—and he stood to gain financially if a death occurred. "My purpose is to say that if you want somebody to look guilty, you don't have to be particularly imaginative to do it."

Finally, he took on the Crown's four main witnesses. Lynne Mendell: What was her motive for coming all the way to Saskatoon to testify? Allbright had a suggestion: "If I can't have your name in marriage, if I can't use you name that way, I'll use it some other way." As for Charlie Wilde, he would do anything for a dollar, especially if a $50,000 reward was hung out as a carrot. And, added the lawyer, could the jury believe a drug addict? Dick Collver was a "fine, fine salesman," said Allbright. "Did he come here because he thought it was the right thing to do, or did he come here to salve a conscience?" Allbright also asked the jury, "You decide if, in fact, the Crown maybe thought it was slipping away a little bit on them... and decided to call Dick Collver." And Garry Anderson? "His evidence isn't worth the paper that we're ultimately going to record it on. A guy who'd do what he says he'd do for a thousand bucks, ... what would he do for $50,000?"

Allbright then turned to the defence witnesses. Of Sandra Hammond Silversides, he said, "You decide whether, in fact.

this is a scheming, devious type of person, or whether she's just a twenty-two-year-old girl on the stand, doing her best, who gave you her recollection?" As for Regan and Greg Thatcher, Allbright asked the jury a very tough, very provocative question; would any child lie to protect a father who had murdered his mother?

Allbright concluded his remarks by emphasizing that police, prosecutors, and jurors often make honest mistakes. "Many, many years ago there was a man who got up in the morning, looked in the mirror, had a shave, I suppose that everything looked fine, his world was all where it should be and it was in place. The next day that man is arrested. He wakes up in a cell, he shaves in a cell, and he spends over ten years, getting up every morning of every week of every year looking in the mirror, but he's got a problem because he knows he doesn't belong there. Nobody else believes it, but he believes it." That man, said Allbright, was Donald Marshall, a young man who was falsely imprisoned for eleven years "because honest policemen, honest prosecutors, honest people were wrong." Allbright also mentioned a Mr. W. in Vancouver who had been wrongly convicted by a jury of raping a woman. Finally he pointed to Susan Nelles, the unfortunate nurse who had been charged with causing mysterious deaths of babies at the Hospital for Sick Children in Toronto, but had been released at the preliminary hearing.

Finally, Allbright ended his plea in a theatrical fashion. After gazing for a few seconds at Colin Thatcher, he said almost mournfully, "A verdict on the evidence will be a verdict that ends a long night for this man. Six months of agony, six months of incarceration."

Kujawa's blood was boiling by the end of Allbright's address. "I have never seen Serge so mad in my life," says Al Johnson. After the jury had left the room, the Crown attorney, barely able to control himself, pointed out what he considered were misrepresentations of the facts in Allbright's address. Kujawa argued that the telephone call from Moose Jaw to Palm Springs at 6:24 had never been made evidence and therefore should not have been referred to by Allbright. He stated that the Crown didn't call Cody Crutcher, Danny Doyle, or Anderson's brother-in-law because "I know of no way on earth that their evidence is admissible. I'm sure Mr. Allbright doesn't either." Kujawa denounced the references to

Donald Marshall, Mr. W., and Susan Nelles as totally inappropriate. He was furious that Allbright would suggest that "the Crown called Dick Collver out of the clear blue sky to bolster a crumpling case, which he [Allbright] knows is not the case." Mr. Justice Maher felt the same way: He told the jury that Collver had not simply appeared on a "whim," but that he himself had made the decision to allow Collver's evidence. "I wanted to clarify it, in case you were left with the wrong impression, that the Crown simply went out and found another witness, because that is not actually what happened", the judge said.

And finally, Kujawa was upset at what he termed was the giving of evidence by Allbright—the references to publicity and other court procedures that were not part of the evidence presented in that courtroom. Justice Maher again agreed with the Crown attorney and said to Allbright, "I told the jury they must only decide this case on what they heard in this courtroom. You introduced things that just came from your own mind, or your own reading, and what you did, without any regard to their admissibilty or their being before the jury."

Despite the indignation of both the Crown and the judge that Allbright had knowingly ignored a number of legal conventions, the feeling in the courtroom was that his address had been a powerful, effective, sobering one.

Kujawa's address, by contrast, was economical to the point of seeming almost skeletal. First he referred to Allbright's summation, particularly his theory that the killer had planted Thatcher's credit card slip, and then set about discrediting the theory. "For what reason we don't really know. But if it is planted, just look at what had to have happened. He would have had to go in and come up with a brutal beating, because that would make it look like Colin, with his great hate; he would have to get Colin's credit card to begin with; he would have to get Colin's car; he would have to have someone put a holster a year before in Colin's other car; he would have to have some experts come along and say the bullet in her head is the same or similar to the bullet that was sold to Colin by Williams some considerable time ago. This fellow had a pretty, pretty impossible task, I suggest to you."

For the Crown, the tape recording was the convincing evidence. "The tape fits the rest of the evidence like a transparency put over the top that fits everything underneath, and there isn't one part anywhere that it doesn't fit," said Kujawa. "On top of the other evidence, this amounts to a complete, plain, ordinary English confession of the murder by the accused." Kujawa spoke in a very matter-of-fact, unemotional but emphatic manner. He did not dramatize at all but, gazing steadily at the jurors, concluded, "I believe that you have the courage to bring in the only verdict that the evidence will support and that is guilty as charged."

This would be the last evening the jury would be free. After Justice Maher gave his charge the next morning, they would be sequestered in the antique surroundings of the Bessborough Hotel until they reached a verdict.

FRIDAY, NOVEMBER 2

Mr. Justice Maher began his charge to the jury by reprimanding Gerry Allbright for remarks made in his closing address. First Allbright had mentioned that the jurors were obliged to hold the Crown attorney to the remarks made in his opening address. Mr. Maher refuted this, saying, "It is clear from what I told you at the outset and what counsel for the Crown, Mr. Kujawa, said, that the opening statement made by counsel on behalf of the Crown is not evidence and you will ignore any comments that counsel made regarding its effect on you or on your findings." But what had particularly incensed the judge was Allbright's reference to Donald Marshall, Mr. W., and Susan Nelles. "To raise matters such as this is highly improper," said Maher. His admonishments could not have helped Thatcher's cause with the jury.

Justice Maher then went on to give the standard instructions on credibility of witnesses, circumstantial evidence, and reasonable doubt. His charge on the law was extremely important for this particular trial, however. He ruled that the jury must find Thatcher guilty of first-degree murder whether he committed the crime himself or "if acts done or performed by the accused resulted in the death of JoAnn Wilson." Allbright would hotly challenge his interpretation of the law, which drastically widened the chances of the jury finding his client guilty.

Justice Maher proceeded to sketch the evidence represented during the trial. He found some of Lynne Mendell's testimony, if the jury were to find it to be true, of vital importance. "In the event you accept the portion of Garry Anderson's evidence where he says he rented an automobile from Scott Ford in Moose Jaw and gave it to Thatcher to drive into Regina to do the shooting in May 1981, it is difficult to determine how Mrs. Mendell could obtain this information from anyone but Thatcher," the judge said.

He found Charlie Wilde's evidence of significance as well. "If he had not talked to Thatcher, is it not more than just coincidence that he should know that the parents of JoAnn Wilson lived in Ames, Iowa and that her father was a professor at the university in Ames? Is it likely that he would have picked up this information from media reports that followed the first shooting when at the time he was serving a term of imprisonment in Stony Mountain Penitentiary?" he asked.

Maher spent far less time outlining the evidence presented by the defence, a fact that upset both Allbright and his client. Indeed, Thatcher looked as though he was about to burst into tears after Justice Maher completed his address. Judging from his anguished tone of voice, his lawyer was obviously terribly upset as well. In his objections to the judge's charge, Allbright claimed that the comments made by Maher "have been prejudicial to Mr. Thatcher." The court had therefore "pointed a judicial finger at Colin Thatcher." "My Lord spent a great deal of time pointing out the highlights of the Crown's case that in my view, very respectfully my view, stress in fact the suggestion of implication and guilt. . . . There was almost no comment whatever, My Lord, on the evidence of the six witnesses testifying, taking the stand, giving direct evidence to this court about Mr. Thatcher being in Moose Jaw at the time. And may I respectfully suggest, My Lord, that the manner in which the charge dealt with the defence witnesses I think was highly detrimental to the defence." Mr. Justice Maher's reply was short and to the point, "You are entitled to your opinions, Mr. Allbright."

And after the jury finally began deliberations at 12:20 p.m. an informal poll was taken of the media attending the trial. Of the thirty-six reporters asked, thirty-four thought Colin Thatcher would be convicted of first-degree murder, while two thought the jury would be hung—that is, they would not arrive at a unanimous verdict so that a new trial would have to be held.

At 8:14 that night the word went out that the jury was returning to the courthouse. All the players scurried to their

seats, only to discover that the jury had produced not a
verdict but a list of eleven questions. Since many of these
required the court reporters to read evidence from their
shorthand notes, it was decided to wait until the next morning to answer them. The jury of seven men and five women,
so varied in ages and personalities, walked across the slushy
street under the watchful eyes of the court attendants to their
rooms in the Bessborough Hotel. How much sleep they
managed as they pondered Colin Thatcher's fate was never
revealed.

SATURDAY, NOVEMBER 3

The questions that had been posed indicated that the jury
was a notably careful and perceptive one, for they touched on
a number of the contradictions in the trial. What colour was
the gun allegedly given by Thatcher to Anderson for him to
attach a silencer, they asked; Anderson had said blue, but
Ron Williams, the gun dealer, had said nickel. What time
was the meeting between Anderson and Thatcher on Thursday, January 20? Allbright had hoped to pry out of Anderson
testimony that it occurred between 3 and 3:30 p.m. so that
Thatcher could not have been the man Joan Hasz had spotted
sitting in the car near the Wilson house at that time. Anderson,
however, had said he had met Thatcher between 2 and 3
p.m. Where was Anderson on the afternoon and evening of
the murder? The court reported read Anderson's evidence
that he had gone to the dentist, had his hair cut, talked to
some friends. When was the gun handed over on the day of
the murder? Anderson said at 1 p.m., that afternoon. The
jurors wanted to hear again the section of Charlie Wilde's
evidence that pertained to his meetings with Anderson and
Crutcher. When was Lynne Mendell in Moose Jaw in the
summer of 1982? they asked. Her testimony was read again.
But one question threw the defence for a loop. The jurors
asked, "When did Mrs. Hasz testify to seeing Colin Thatcher
on Thursday, January 20th?" Of course, Mrs. Hasz did not say
she had seen Thatcher himself but only a mysterious stalker.
The phrasing of the question seemed to indicate that all was
not going well for the accused.

The jury also asked a question about some puzzling evidence given by Thatcher. Thatcher had admitted that after he had met with Anderson on May 1, 1984, he had dropped $550 off in a green garbage bag at the abandoned farm. But he had lied about the time he had done so. He had said that he left the money on Thursday evening, "just before dark and dark is around nine-thirty that time of year." He also described in great detail his whereabouts on the Friday. This seemed odd because once Thatcher had dropped the money off, his comings and goings the next day were not relevant to his explanation of the tape or to the evidence at the trial. The jury heard this portion of Thatcher's testimony read, as well as the evidence of RCMP Constables Waelz and Britton, the two witnesses Kujawa had added at the last moment. Their evidence detailed how they had followed him by truck and plane, beginning at 7:30 a.m. on Friday, to the Bergren farmhouse, where he had dropped off the money.

Clearly Thatcher wasn't telling the truth when he swore that he had left the money on Thursday evening. The big question was why Thatcher would lie at this point. Since he had admitted to leaving the money for Anderson, the lie was of no benefit to him; indeed it did him great harm by showing the jury that Thatcher's word could not be trusted, and perhaps raised their suspicions that he lived in his own world. Why then would he do it? Serge Kujawa thought he had the right answer; it was called the tail-on-the-dog theory. "I think he was preparing the story that he was going to deny that the tape was authentic, and therefore he had to deny the dropping-off of the money. So, he had to give a very detailed story of where he was Friday. . . . I think he changed his story in midstream but he got tired and forgot to change the ending." Allbright's claim at the pre-trial conference that he was going to call experts to deny the authenticity of the tape was another indication to Kujawa that his theory was correct.

Yet as he was leaving the courtroom, when the jury retired into the November dusk at 5 p.m., young Greg Thatcher was overheard to say, "Well, now at least we've got a chance."

SUNDAY, NOVEMBER 4

Irony of ironies, on this of all weekends the provincial Liberals were holding their annual meeting at the grandiose

Bessborough Hotel, across the street from the courthouse. Pictures of old man Thatcher were mounted in the hallways—now that the party has fallen on such hard times, he is glorified as the leader who knew how to capture power. That his son was being tried for murder across the street and that their hotel was being shared by his jurors was almost too much for some of the dedicated older members to bear. Some simply refused to consider that the son of the Great Ross could possibly be guilty. Others who knew the family more intimately were not so sure. One sixty-year-old man who had been an important fundraiser for the party when Ross Thatcher was leader, and who had lived in Moose Jaw and watched the boy Colin grown into a man, believed that he was guilty. His reasons were compelling, based on the theory that Colin really believed in a Thatcher dynasty. "JoAnn took away from Colin his money, his family, his political prestige, but most important, his date with destiny. He believed that as Bill [Bennett] followed Wacky [W.A.X. Bennett, former premier of British Columbia], Colin should follow Ross. JoAnn denied him his manifest destiny."

Nothing was heard from the jury the entire day. The betting among the media had shifted; there were many more hung-jury votes, but still few would wager that Thatcher would be acquitted.

Both the prosecution team and the Thatcher family were staying at the luxurious nineteen-story Ramada Renaissance, which overlooked the courthouse. None of the group took much advantage of its saunas and pools and its famed indoor water slide. They were all too busy brooding about Thatcher's fate.

Thatcher's surroundings, of course, were not nearly so comfortable. He spent some of the weekend with Ray Mathieson, the preacher who first converted him to evangelism. Mathieson had travelled to Saskatoon especially to console and shore up the accused man.

MONDAY, NOVEMBER 5

A message from the sequestered jury brought everyone scrambling to the courtroom at ten in the morning, only to discover that the jurors wanted Craig Dotson's evidence read again.

By this time, hopes were high in the Thatcher camp. Allbright was sure either that Thatcher would be acquitted or that the jury would be hung and a new trial would be held. Thatcher himself seemed happy and remarkably relaxed, chatting to the RCMP officer guarding him and examining the pictures that were exhibits in the trial. Serge Kujawa, on the other hand, seemed like some brooding fatalistic hero in a Dostoyevsky novel. He was worried. Later he would say, "Speculating on what a jury is doing and why is a total waste of time. So I spent much of my time speculating." Ed Swayze was also, in his cool way, concerned; he wondered how his cops were going to be able to protect all the witnesses who had testified against Thatcher.

As the court reporter read Dotson's evidence, Colin Thatcher sat stoically, almost motionless, as he had through all of the trial. There was only one sign of nervousness. His hands, surprisingly slender and sensitive for so big a man, had never ceased playing with his pen. That distinctive, unfortunate downward thrust of his mouth, which made him look as though he was sneering even when he was in repose, seemed to be more pronounced each day of the trial.

When by that evening nothing had been heard from the jury, Justice Maher sent word in to the foreman suggesting that perhaps the jury might want him to provide some further interpretation of the law for them. The foreman indignantly answered that if they wanted further information they would ask for it. They were systematically poring over the evidence and they would not be rushed into a verdict. As the jurors walked back and forth from the courthouse to the Bessborough Hotel in the city slush to eat or sleep, everybody watched carefully for signs of strife or emotion in the ranks. There never seemed to be any. They all simply looked tired.

TUESDAY, NOVEMBER 6, 10:53 a.m.

Word spread quickly that a verdict had been reached and everyone rushed to the courtroom, where the excitement was almost overwhelming. Some of the media people had been sick to their stomachs from the terrible tension; in comparison, the torture the Thatcher family must have been enduring was unimaginable. They all grimly filed in, Greg, Regan,

Peggy, Diane Stoner—not, thank God, Stephanie. Thatcher himself looked old and grey and very frightened. Allbright glanced at the jury and immediately knew the verdict. Kujawa refused to look at the accused at all. The end was as sharp and short as a pistol shot.

COURT CLERK: Ladies and gentlemen of the jury, have you agreed upon your verdict?
JURY FOREMAN: Yes, we have.
COURT CLERK: How say you, do you find the accused guilty or not guilty on the charge of first-degree murder?
JURY FOREMAN: We find the accused guilty.

Colin Thatcher's body snapped back as if he had been hit in the face. That was the only emotion he showed publicly.

Poor Peggy Thatcher had not heard the verdict and had to ask her grandson, "What did they say? What did they say?" Greg growled painfully, "He's found guilty."

Mr. Justice Maher responded immediately. He asked Thatcher to stand and then sentenced him to life imprisonment in a federal penitentiary without eligibility for parole for twenty-five years.

The family of the former premier did not break down in public. They filed out quietly, as if in shock, and were allowed into the cells in the basement to comfort the convicted man. Gerry Allbright was there too. They all cried together for many minutes and then a little prayer was said.

Bedlam reigned everywhere else. Kujawa was left to deal with the frantic media. "It was not a happy moment for anybody," he told them, paying tribute to Colin Thatcher's undoubted talents. During the day other defence lawyers, police officers, and Crown prosecutors dropped into the Crown's nineteenth-floor gathering room to pursue every detail of the case. Thatcher's personality dominated the conversation. How could a man who possessed everything—health, intellect, wealth, an important name, three beautiful children, an occupation, ranching, that he both liked and was successful at, a political career that might have gone anywhere— how could he fall so low? Surely only a deranged man would do so much damage to himself and to all the other unfortunates—the victim herself, of course, but also his mother, his children, his friends, the people who remained devoted to the name of Ross Thatcher—who were caught up in the tragedy.

Serge Kujawa attempted an answer. He told a colleague, "What you have to understand about Colin Thatcher is that he isn't crazy. He's evil."

EPILOGUE

NOVEMBER 6, 1984

As he was being led, handcuffed, into the provincial jail in Saskatoon after his conviction for the first-degree murder of his former wife, Colin Thatcher yelled to the assembled throng of reporters, "No, I am not going to appeal—it doesn't matter now. I am innocent, I did not do it. But it [an acquittal] wasn't in the cards." And dressed as he was in jeans, a sports shirt, and a kangaroo-pocketed pullover, he seemed already to have stepped into another world, where baby-blue ultra-suede jackets were not appropriate.

NOVEMBER 7, 1984

When Thatcher discovered that he had been assigned to the prison's security wing, which meant he was released from his cell only two hours a day, he promptly went on a hunger strike. Terry Youngman, the director of the Saskatoon Correctional Institute, said that Thatcher may not like the security wing, but he didn't have any say in the matter.

That same day, Premier Grant Devine formally asked his former political colleague to resign his seat in the Legislative Assembly. Thatcher did not reply.

NOVEMBER 9, 1984

Gerry Allbright went to see Thatcher, who was still in a state of shock and depression, as he did almost every day. It did not take the defence lawyer long to change his client's mind;

he must not give up at this point, Allbright insisted. The defence lawyer felt strongly that Mr. Justice Maher's charge to the jury had been so heavily slanted in favour of the Crown that an appeal court might very well order a new trial. Three days after the Thatcher conviction, Allbright announced that his client would appeal.

That same evening about a hundred people, mostly ranchers and farmers, crowded into Caron's tiny Legion Hall to formally set up the Colin Thatcher Defence Fund. Rick Wildfong, a farmer who had driven some eighty kilometres to attend the meeting, summed up why many people were there. "I think Colin got a bad deal. What was he supposed to have done? If it takes four days for the jury to make up its mind, something stinks."

The people who were the mainspring behind this organization were notable. One was Bernice Crosbie, the woman who had nominated Colin Thatcher thirteen years before, when, after his father died, he had tried to wrest the Liberal nomination away from Jack Wiebe. Another was Sandra Sparks, the clerk of the rural municipality of Caron, and the woman who had lent Thatcher her car the day the tape recording between Garry Anderson and Colin Thatcher took place. Greg Thatcher was the featured speaker at the meeting. He explained why his father had first decided not to appeal. "After the first day, Dad thought there was nobody there. When he first said he wasn't going to launch an appeal, he felt the world had deserted him and nobody cared." Looking out over the crowd he said, "This kind of support is important to him. It means very much [to him]."

Sandra Sparks said the group did not want to "hurt" Thatcher in any way. Greg responded, "I talked to Dad and we decided there's not a lot that can be done to hurt him any more." Young Thatcher emphasized that Allbright should have nothing to do with the Defence Fund. 'It's you people doing this, not Allbright. Neither the family nor I had anything to do with this meeting and when I was told about it, I had no idea how much support would be there."

The group then enthusiastically talked about what they could do to help Colin Thatcher, and it was quickly agreed that their main objective would be to raise money, perhaps $100,000, to pay for Thatcher's legal bills arising out of the appeal process. The charter members of the Colin Thatcher

Defence Fund decided they would hold a meeting the following week, and at that point details would be worked out as to how the $100,000 could be raised.

NOVEMBER 15, 1984

The huge Exhibition Building in Moose Jaw was packed, mostly with people in windbreakers and cowboy hats, for the second meeting of the Colin Thatcher Defence Fund. There was an odd assortment of people gathered. The leader of the Western Canada Concept party, a political organization that advocated the separation of the western provinces from the rest of Canada, was there proselytizing. There was a man who said that he too had been "badly burned" by the Married Persons' Property Act and could see that he might do the same thing—that is, murder his wife. "I ended up as the garbage patch king," he said. There was a woman there who advocated the castration of "hateful men" like Colin Thatcher. There were also supporters and friends of the convicted man. But most of the crowd consisted of the merely curious.

The formal portion of the meeting was disappointingly short and dull. It lasted only fourteen minutes. Bernice Crosbie told the throng that, despite what the media had reported, Thatcher had been a model prisoner. "He's been most cooperative. There have been no complaints from the guards. I've talked to his family and they wish to assure us that Colin never said he was on a hunger strike." It had all been a misunderstanding, said Crosbie. Thatcher hadn't been able to hold down solid food after his conviction, and just didn't feel like eating.

Most of her speech, however, consisted of an attack on journalists. "Some media have questioned our motives and we say this: If the roles were reversed and one of us were in trouble, Colin would do the same thing for us." After her speech, a persistent reporter asked her, "Do you mean, Mrs. Crosbie, if you murdered your husband, Colin Thatcher would help you?" "That's not what I mean. Colin Thatcher didn't murder anybody," she spluttered and made her escape. That a jury had deliberated long and hard before finding the accused guilty of first-degree murder seemed simply irrelevant to the pro-Thatcher contingent.

The main purpose of the gathering was to raise money, and two tables manned with receipt-signers had been set up. While some people did pull out bills, often fifty or a hundred dollars, and wrote cheques, the lines were surprisingly short. Obviously most people were there to offer their sympathy, not their cash—or perhaps they were there merely to watch the event unfold.

Despite the sizeable amount of publicity the defence fund generated, a third meeting held a few weeks later at a Legion Hall in Regina was a complete flop. Only two dozen people showed up, and most of them were reporters or members of the family. It was an indication that the people of Saskatchewan were certainly not rushing to Colin Thatcher's support. Indeed by the time of the appeal in May, 1985, a little over $17,000 had been raised; while it helped pay Thatcher's legal fees, it was a far cry from the $100,000 originally planned.

The Thatcher family's spirits were revived, however, at the end of November when Fred Jenner, a sixty-three-year-old well-digger from Moose Jaw, told Gerry Allbright that he had seen Colin Thatcher just outside Moose Jaw at 5:45 on the night of the murder. That meant, of course, that Thatcher himself could not have committed the terrible crime. Jenner said that on January 21, 1983, he had been working on a pump in the Boharm area, about ten kilometres west of Moose Jaw. When he pulled onto Number 1 highway, he saw a two-tone Chevy or GMC truck, driven by Colin Thatcher. "Then I followed the vehicle in question to the overpass of Moose Jaw, at which time the vehicle turned into Moose Jaw. This would be about eighteen minutes to six."

Jenner emphasized that he was not a personal friend of Thatcher's. He did admit, however, that Bev Hammond, the mother of Sandra Hammond Silversides, had come to his house on January 21, 1983, to tell him and his wife, Ann, about the murder of JoAnn Wilson. Ann was also at the Hammond house the day Sandra was arrested by the police and charged with being an accessory to murder. But Fred Jenner insisted, "I'm not a great friend of Bev Hammond because of the stories she used to spread when Colin Thatcher and JoAnn first split up. The gossip she used to spread upset me, so I even told her to leave my house one time. Bev Hammond always had a police scanner as well, so that she would report to everyone what happened."

Jenner said that three days after Thatcher was arrested, at about 10 a.m., he phoned the Regina police either from his office or his home. "I first spoke to a female person and I asked her who was handling the case, and then a male person came on the phone and I told him that I had information of where Colin Thatcher was between 5 and 6 p.m. that night. He sounded like he wrote it all down. He thanked me for calling and stated he would get back to me." But, added Jenner, no police officer ever contacted him again. While Thatcher's trial was under way, he expected that he would be called as a witness. When this didn't happen, he decided to come forward after the trial was over.

Some people in the Moose Jaw area found Jenner's bombshell news somewhat suspect. During the summer of 1984, Jenner had spent a week digging a well and fence posts at one farm. He was there almost every day for lunch and talked so much about the Thatcher case that the farmer and his wife thought the man was obsessed with the subject. Yet not once did he mention that he had seen Colin Thatcher on the night of the murder.

Naturally Jenner's information thrilled Thatcher—it would be very helpful at his appeal, he felt, and at a new trial. As he was boarding a plane to fly to the Edmonton Federal Correctional Institute, where he would serve his sentence, he told reporters to phone Gerry Allbright in about a week and the lawyer would reveal sensational new evidence. Jenner's information, however, was kept under wraps by Allbright until many months later, then revealed just before Thatcher's appeal.

NOVEMBER 20, 1984

Gerry Allbright released a statement on Thatcher's behalf that said that his client would not resign his seat until the appeal process had been dealt with. Saskatchewan Liberal leader Ralph Goodale accused the Conservatives of moving with "unusual and unseemly haste" when they ordered Thatcher to resign the day after his conviction. "It is difficult weighing proper representation against proper decorum," Goodale said. But the government's handling of the affair was neither "tactful nor tasteful."

NOVEMBER 22, 1984

The Conservative government decided that the Speech from the Throne, opening a new session of the Saskatchewan Legislature, should be postponed for one week to allow a full discussion of the Colin Thatcher affair. But if the Tories expected the debate to be a polite, calm one, they were in for a rude shock. Opposition leader Allan Blakeney had found copies of the Ottawa *Citizen* and the Montreal *Gazette* that revealed some astonishing information. Southam News correspondent Peter Calamai indirectly quoted Colin Thatcher as saying at a cabinet meeting, "Why do I have to pay the [$819,000 property] settlement when a bullet only costs a dollar?" If the newspaper quote was accurate, Blakeney demanded, why hadn't Devine or any of his cabinet ministers gone to the authorities with information that may have prevented the murder of JoAnn Wilson? But, despite the uproar in the House around him, Devine would not confirm whether the quote was accurate or not. "What is said in cabinet is confidential. It always has been. We are sworn to an oath of office," he said.

Justice minister Gary Lane, Thatcher's old friend and colleague, then put forth a motion that would have expelled Thatcher from the Legislature, vacating his seat. The motion needed unanimous consent, however, and it was blocked by the lone Liberal in the House, Bill Sveinson. He needed more time to study it, he said, and asked, "Why all the haste to get the bill through the House?" It didn't seem to matter to him that for sixteen days the good people of Thunder Creek had been represented by a convicted murderer.

NOVEMBER 23, 1984

It was Premier Grant Devine's turn to go on the attack. He said that ex-premier Blakeney's questions the previous day about references Thatcher made in a cabinet meeting to killing his wife were "disgusting." It was disappointing "that a former premier would stoop to something like this. . . . The man [Blakeney] has gone down an awful lot in the eyes of an awful lot of people." His sting must have hurt because the NDP faint-heartedly gave up that line of questioning. Lonely Bill Sveinson didn't back down, however. Not only did he block the legislation pushing Thatcher out of his seat that day, but he continued to do so for the next three days that the Legislature sat.

NOVEMBER 28, 1984

Finally the forty Progressive Conservatives who were in the Legislature—Grant Devine and fourteen other Tories were absent at the time—voted for the bill expelling Colin Thatcher from his seat. Sveinson and the eight-member NDP caucus opposed the resolution because they felt that Thatcher should not have been expelled from the Legislature; they believed that he should have been suspended, at least until all his avenues of appeal were exhausted. It was interesting to note that his old arch-enemies, the socialists, were more humane in their attitude towards Thatcher than his former colleagues.

Ironically, though, it was the Tories who saved the Thatcher family from immediate financial ruin. In May of 1984 Tony Wilson had started foreclosure proceedings against Thatcher for the remaining $350,000 owed JoAnn's estate, which with interest and default penalties totalled $470,600. Nothing was done while Thatcher was on trial for murder. Then in December of 1984, the PCs brought down a bill that effectively imposed a moratorium on farm foreclosures in the province until the end of 1985. This meant that Thatcher's empire was safe from Wilson's clutches for at least a year.

Eleven-year-old Stephanie Thatcher is the chief beneficiary of her dead mother's estate; the amount owed to her by her father is now over $225,000. On May 2, 1985, Greg Thatcher asked the Court of Queen's Bench to appoint him guardian of Stephanie's considerable estate. He put forth the argument that he was a very mature nineteen-year-old capable of managing Stephanie's financial affairs, pointing out in an affidavit that since his father's arrest he has managed the family farm and the ranch. "In consultation with my father, Colin Thatcher, I make decisions which affect our employees, our business and our creditors. . . . I am willing and able to look after her [Stephanie's] affairs, to ensure that her best interests are protected, and I will account to this Court from time to time as required." Armand J. Bachelu, the deputy public trustee for Saskatchewan, was not impressed. "It is my belief that, as a beneficiary of the estate of JoAnn Kay Wilson, Stephanie Thatcher has a substantial interest in the assets of Wilbert Colin Thatcher through his indebtedness to the estate. As Greg Ross Thatcher deposes . . . in his affidavit he runs the farm and ranch operation and deals with creditors, it appears he would have a conflict between the interest of Stephanie Thatcher in the estate and the interests of Wilbert Colin Thatcher as a creditor of the estate." The issue remains to be decided by the courts.

The Wilson estate, however, is not Thatcher's main creditor, not by any means. In the spring of 1983, the Moose Jaw Credit Union started foreclosure proceedings against 1,920 acres of Thatcher land on which it held mortgages of $375,500. The amount in arrears at that point was almost $30,000. In November, 1983, however, Thatcher was able to consolidate four outstanding debts by negotiating a $750,000 mortgage with the credit union. And that is not the end of Thatcher's debts. In May of 1984, the Toronto-Dominion Bank in Moose Jaw registered a caveat on three quarter-sections of property that were used as security for a $440,000 loan taken out in April, 1983. As well, Thatcher borrowed $147,500 from the Bank of Montreal in February, 1980, using two quarter-sections as surety. And the Royal Bank in Moose Jaw has caveats on just under a thousand acres. This means that in managing the farm, Greg must service a debt of over $1.4 million. And the Thatchers remain adamant that they will not sell land; they will do anything to keep the empire from crumbling.

FEBRUARY 20, 1985

When the Thunder Creek Progressive Conservatives held their nomination meeting for the forthcoming by-election, it was Colin Thatcher's last opportunity to retain political control of his riding. His good friend and disciple Lyle Stewart, who had sat with the Thatcher family throughout the trial, tried very hard to capture the nomination, and nineteen-year-old Greg Thatcher assisted him. Despite opposition from powerful members of the Saskatchewan Progressive Conservative party, Stewart came remarkably close to capturing the nomination.

In fact the campaign to wrest control from the Thatcher forces had begun two months before. "Colin was still trying to pull strings from Edmonton," says Don Hill, who had himself attempted to take the nomination away from Thatcher in 1982. "The last official thing I had to do with the party was with the last annual meeting in December, 1984. We were going to get people elected [to the executive] who weren't Colin's people." The meeting was held at Rouleau, in the far southerly part of the riding. "That's where Thatcher's support was, so we had to truck 175 people to the meeting to make sure Colin didn't put his people in again. We knew who they were running and what their support was, so we just made sure we had enough people to put other people in place.

"And they [Thatcher's people] were all ready to have another nominating meeting immediately after the annual meeting. After they were elected, they were going to stand up and say, 'We're having the nominating meeting, and Lyle Stewart's our candidate, and too bad for the rest of you.'" Hill said that the idea put forward was that Stewart would be elected as an interim candidate, until the appeal was over and Thatcher could step back into his "rightful place."

On the night of the nomination meeting, an overflowing crowd of 1,500 packed the ballroom of a Moose Jaw hotel. It was a loud, old-fashioned political rally, with bands, balloons, and buttons. Premier Grant Devine and several Tory cabinet ministers and MLAs were there. Although Colin Thatcher's name was never once mentioned, his presence loomed large. Most people felt that voting for Lyle Stewart was in effect voting for Colin Thatcher, although Stewart kept insisting, over and over, that there was no connection—despite the fact that Gregory Thatcher was sitting in his cheering section. Stewart was well ahead on the first two ballots. But as other candidates dropped off, their support went elsewhere. On the third ballot, Rick Swenson, a thirty-two-year-old farmer, captured the nomination with 471 votes to Stewart's 407. Swenson went on to win the March 27 by-election handily.

The nomination had ushered into the limelight people who had been connected with Thatcher's political affairs in Thunder Creek for years. One of the candidates was Neil Seaman, the former president of the Thunder Creek P.C. Association, the man who had discovered Thatcher's phoney count of the ballots during the meeting to elect delegates to the 1979 leadership race. Rick Swenson was the son of Don Swenson, who had run against Thatcher, then a Liberal, in the 1975 election campaign, and then had fought him for the 1978 Conservative nomination in Thunder Creek. There must have been some glee among the anti-Thatcher faction in Thunder Creek when Colin Thatcher's grip on the seat was finally torn away.

And what about the other key players in the Thatcher drama—have they fared better since the trial? Charlie Wilde certainly got a big break. In February of 1985, a Manitoba Crown attorney stayed charges of breaking and entering against Wilde. The charges had been laid after he broke into a Winnipeg drugstore during the spring of 1984. Serge Kujawa admitted that he had talked to senior Manitoba Crown attorney Wayne Myshkowsky following Thatcher's trial. "We told him we were through and Charlie had done everything he'd undertaken to do." But, said Kujawa, he was surprised at the decision to drop the charges against Wilde; he insisted he had made no deal with his witness.

Charlie, as well as Garry Anderson, Lynne Mendell, Cody Crutcher, and even the anonymous informer who tipped the police off to the role Crutcher and Wilde played in the Thatcher affair could all take a share of the $50,000 reward. The decision as to who will get what will not be made until after the entire appeal process, including any hearing before the Supreme Court of Canada, is over. So the division of the spoils might have to wait for several years.

Garry Anderson never did take up the new identity offered him by the police, although many in the Caron area disapproved of his role in the murder. He travels between Prince Albert and his mother's farm in Caron, praying that nobody will challenge him, at least in public, about the part he played. Lynne Mendell continues with her artwork, intricate fantasy montages. For the moment at least, she and her husband have separated, and she is living with her parents. And the star of the show, Colin Thatcher, seems to have adjusted quite well to life in prison.

On December 6, 1984, he was transferred from the Saskatoon provincial jail to what is referred to simply as the Edmonton Institute. The newest prison in Canada, it was opened in 1978 to accommodate 195 prisoners, although another unit was quickly constructed, so that the present population is between 240 and 250. Most of the prisoners are considered security risks; they range from forgers who have a propensity to violence, to violent armed robbers and recently convicted murderers. Someone like Colin Thatcher, who has been convicted of murdering his wife or some other relative, is not considered a hardened criminal. Depending on such factors as behaviour in prison and length of sentence, this type of prisoner might spend only four or five years here before being transferred to a medium-security prison.

Edmonton Institute has a skating rink in winter and a multipurpose sports area; it is also the only prison in Canada to boast a rodeo. Plans are in the works for a miniature golf course. Thatcher has taken advantage of these facilities, getting in shape by running, skating, and playing golf. He spends a great deal of his time, however, preaching to his fellow inmates. His born-again Christian faith has become so pronounced that even his children are a little aghast. During the trial Stephanie Thatcher said to an old friend of the family, "I don't know how we're going to handle the situation when Daddy gets home because he's religious now." "Well, everybody's religious," the friend said. "No, this is different with our dad. He's talking different than other people. There's something different about him. Something happened to him."

Thatcher continued to tell anyone who visited him in Edmonton that he would be out of prison by the spring; he was positive that the Court of Appeal would decide in his favour.

MAY 27, 1985

Colin Thatcher arrived at the Regina courthouse looking surprisingly fit and tanned. He later quipped to Gerry Allbright that he had missed a prison golf tournament by attending his appeal hearing. He arrived in blue jeans and a casual shirt and jacket, but the clothes that had become his insignia—a blue ultra-suede sports jacket, white shirt, and striped tie—were neatly folded in a green garbage bag that an RCMP officer dutifully carried in. As he was led into the courtroom in handcuffs, Thatcher did not say a word to the crowding media although they asked him, "Mr. Thatcher, do you think you'll be exonerated now?"

Although for weeks the media had been predicting huge line-ups to get into the smallish appeal courtroom, and old Ted Bourree, the fixture from the original Saskatoon trial, was again on hand to organize the proceedings, few of the public showed up. Probably they realized that the complicated legal interpretations would not exactly be thrilling, Saturday-night-at-the-movies material.

Greg and Peggy Thatcher and Diane Stoner, Thatcher's ever-faithful girlfriend, walked into the courtroom like good soldiers and seated themselves behind Gerry Allbright. As usual Thatcher was given permission to sit at his lawyer's side. At closer range, Thatcher did look older and greyer. Throughout the entire day and a half of the appeal, he sat, as usual, passive and still and utterly emotionless.

The five appeal justices—William Vancise, forty-seven, Calvin Tallis, fifty-five, Roy Hill, sixty-four, Russell Brownridge, seventy, and Chief Justice Edward Bayda, fifty-three—were imposing, sitting on a raised platform in their huge stuffed chairs. Stacked near each of the judges was the ten-volume transcript of the Thatcher trial. Each was carefully annotated—an indication of how much work the justices had done in preparation for the appeal.

Gerry Allbright first dealt with Fred Jenner's startling evidence that he had seen Colin Thatcher on the night of the murder, at about 5:40. There were four criteria in law that had to be met before the appeal court would hear fresh evidence—Allbright had to show that the information was not accessible at the time of the trial; it was relevant; it was credible; and, if believed, it could reasonably affect the outcome of the trial. Allbright said that Jenner's evidence fitted all four categories. It was "credible, highly persuasive and very cogent evidence," and if the judges agreed with Allbright, that in itself should result in a new trial for Thatcher.

Serge Kujawa agreed that Jenner's evidence met the first two criteria. But he disagreed entirely that his evidence was credible, and the Crown attorney presented some concrete arguments to back up his claim. Jenner had said very specifically that at 10 a.m. on May 10, 1984, six days after Thatcher's arrest, he had phoned the Regina police either from his office or from home, he couldn't remember which. But the Regina police had obtained Saskatchewan telephone records for the period that showed plainly that no such call had been made. As well, Sergeant Bob Murton had questioned everybody in the Regina police department who could possibly have talked to Jenner that day, and nobody could remember anything about him.

Several other aspects of Jenner's testimony troubled Kujawa. Was it possible on a dark winter's night to be able to spot somebody ahead of you in a truck? he asked. And, Kujawa emphasized, why did Jenner go to such pains to illustrate that he was not a friend of Colin Thatcher's, even to the point of casting aspersions on Bev Hammond? Finally, the Crown argued that even if Jenner's story could be believed, it probably would not have any effect on the jury's final decision since six defence witnesses had already given similar alibi evidence at the trial.

The five judges adjourned to consider the matter, but returned quickly. They had decided to reserve their judgment on whether they would hear Mr. Jenner's evidence at some later date.

Gerry Allbright then got down to the nuts and bolts of Thatcher's appeal. Although he had put forward nine grounds of appeal, Allbright's argument could be roughly divided into two parts—the legal error he felt that Mr. Justice Maher, the trial judge, had committed in the course of the trial, and the gross unfairness to the defence of Justice Maher's charge to the jury.

The judge had told the jury that under Section 21 of the Criminal Code, Thatcher could be found guilty of murder if he committed the act himself or if he had assisted or encouraged someone else to do so. This was completely erroneous, according to Allbright, since there was "no evidence whatsoever" that Thatcher had hired a hit man. Allbright pointed out that the Crown had strongly suggested that Thatcher himself had committed the crime; it was unfair to suddenly throw into the pot the idea that Thatcher might have hired someone to do it. "The Crown had two half-baked theories and they couldn't prove either one, so they threw them together," reasoned Allbright. Chief Justice Bayda challenged the lawyer, pointing out that the law states that there need be only "some evidence" that Thatcher hired a hit man for Section 21 to apply. And surely Allbright would agree that there was some evidence of that? The lawyer replied that the testimony of Dick Collver and Charlie Wilde linked Thatcher with a hit man a good three years before the murder, and that was, he argued, not strong enough evidence for the judge to charge the jury under Section 21.

Allbright pointed out what he considered to be other legal errors. The jurors should have been told by the judge that they had to be unanimous in finding Thatcher guilty either of having committed the murder himself or of hiring someone to do it. There was a distinct possibility that the jury "concluded a unanimous verdict of guilty by a split vote on a combination of the two methods of committing the offence," and this was patently unfair, he said. Allbright also felt that Collver's evidence should not have been permitted. "The evidence of such a witness in law was inadmissible, and, in fact, inflammatory against the accused," he insisted. In addition, Allbright held that Mr. Justice Maher had not explained the principle of circumstantial evidence adequately.

But what Allbright termed "the essence" of the appeal revolved around the fact that the trial judge "in detail and in length" had been unfair to the defence in his charge to the jury. "There is no more powerful figure in the courtroom than the trial judge," said Allbright. And in their "extraordinary long deliberation" the jurors, while wrestling with issues, could well have looked to the judge's charge for assistance in arriving at their final conclusion. Allbright insisted that in his charge to the jury, Justice Maher had "at every turn of the road favoured the Crown, away from impartiality." Mr. Justice Maher, he said, "had impugned the theory, impugned the witnesses and impugned the counsel for the defence."

These were very tough charges and Allbright was quick to back them up with facts. In the judge's sixty-page charge to the jury, the only reference to the defence witnesses who provided an alibi for Thatcher was as follows:

> Two friends of Mr. Thatcher, one the wife of his farm manager and the other a railroad employee who did mechanical work on Thatcher's vehicle, both testi-fied that they had seen Mr. Thatcher, one at the

farm and the other in the City of Moose Jaw, in the
area of about 5:30 p.m. on January 21st, 1983, the
day JoAnn Wilson was killed. His housekeeper,
Sandra Silversides, and his two sons, Greg and
Regan, both gave evidence that they sat down at
supper at 6:00 p.m. with their father that evening.
Mr. Thatcher testified to the same effect.

Three days of evidence from Thatcher himself was treated in
a similarly summary fashion.

The final witness for the defence was the accused,
Colin Thatcher. Both his examination-in-chief and
cross-examination were very lengthy. I have been
talking almost too long as it is and I do not propose
to review his evidence in detail. Much of it related
to the tape recording to which he admitted he was a
party and you will determine whether you accept
his version of the meaning to be attributed to the
conversation he had with Garry Anderson.

Thatcher denies that he had anything to do with
either of the two shootings of his wife and you will
weigh his testimony against the other evidence of
Lynne Mendell and Anderson and Wilde.

The evidence of Thatcher is also in direct contradiction to that of Dick Collver with respect to the
hiring of the hit man and it will be up to you to
decide whose evidence you accept.

These brief references to the defence's case were totally
inadequate, Allbright insisted, especially since so much emphasis had been placed on the Crown's evidence. The lawyer
also pointed to several other examples of what he considered
was gross unfairness to Thatcher's case. Why hadn't the
Crown introduced the records that showed that there had
been a phone call from Moose Jaw to Palm Springs at 6:24 on
the night of the murder? Why did not Ed Swayze and Wally
Beaton, the two senior police officers investigating the murder, give evidence? Finally, Allbright made reference to the
fact that Mr. Justice Maher had reprimanded him on two
occasions, once after Allbright had concluded his address to
the jury and again during his own charge to the jury. Allbright

said these criticisms could not help but detract from "the credibility a defence lawyer tries to build throughout the trial." There was the overall flavour, or tone, of Maher's address that was so detrimental to Thatcher that "it had to be devastating against him."

At 4:50 p.m. Gerry Allbright concluded his arguments. He had talked almost non-stop for five hours. The general feeling in the courtroom was that although he had been wordy, the young defence counsel had been sincere and emphatic in his appeal to the court, and many of his arguments had made a great deal of sense.

MAY 28, 1985

As Thatcher was walking into the courthouse, this time without handcuffs, a CBC reporter yelled, "Have you been ordered not to talk to us, Mr. Thatcher?" That inspired a response in the following words: "I would just like to say thank you to everybody who has written me in my situation. Anybody who has helped me in so many ways, I am very grateful. I wish I could thank them in some other way. Perhaps later."

Crown attorney Kujawa began his rebuttal of Allbright's argument by discussing Section 21 of the Criminal Code, tackling the question of whether the jury should have been told to find the accused guilty whether he committed murder himself or whether he hired somebody to do it. Kujawa pointed to the Peter Demeter case in Ontario. "There was an amazing parallel in both the evidence at trial and points of appeal," said Kujawa. The same motive, the long history of trying to arrange for someone to kill his wife, the indulging of his motive, a tape recording, and a possible accomplice. "But," added Kujawa, "this was a stronger case than Demeter."

One appeal court judge quickly pointed out, however, that no one had ever suggested that Demeter had committed the crime himself. Several of the justices posed very tough questions to Kujawa on this point. The essence of their concern was that during the trial and in his address to the jury, Kujawa had emphasized that Thatcher probably committed the crime himself. The existence of the credit card receipt near the body particularly pointed in that direction. Wasn't it inconsistent, they asked, to also suggest to a jury that he could have hired somebody to carry out the crime? "Are you not in danger of blowing hot and cold?" asked Mr. Justice Vancise. Kujawa could only point to the evidence—the descriptions by Joan Hasz, Duane Adams, and Craig Dotson— and the testimony of the defence witnesses as indicating that someone other than Thatcher could have committed the crime.

Kujawa then addressed the question of the fairness of the judge's charge to the jury. It was only natural that Mr. Justice Maher would spend a great deal more time on the Crown evidence, Kujawa argued, because it was far more complicated, and there was much more of it, than the defence evidence. "The judge had to weave a web or a net," said Kujawa. But there was another important point he made to the appeal court judges. Kujawa pointed out that the trial judge had spent more time on the defence witnesses in his charge than Gerry Allbright had in his own address to the jury; there simply wasn't much about these witnesses that would have promoted the defence's cause, he insisted. As to Thatcher's own evidence, Kujawa maintained that his story regarding the tape was so far-fetched that the more the judge analyzed it for the jury, the worse it would have seemed. Therefore, it was to the defence's benefit for the judge to avoid going into too much detail in summarizing Thatcher's evidence.

Finally Kujawa got to the evidence that Allbright claimed should have been brought forward but wasn't—the 6:24 phone call and the testimony of Swayze and Beaton. "There is no way that I know of that that evidence is admissible," was Kujawa's only remark.

In keeping with his style of presenting his case in as short and sharp a manner as possible, Kujawa completed his presentation in one hour and twenty minutes.

The judges naturally reserved their decision.

As Colin Thatcher left the courtroom he was, as always, impassive.

While the workings of an appeal court judge's mind remain as mysterious to most laymen as a fairy godmother's magic, the impression many who walked out of the courtroom were left with was that Colin Thatcher might indeed be given another chance, that a new trial might be ordered. One reporter shouted to Sergeant Bob Murton, who had been sitting in the courtroom, "You had better start being nice to Garry Anderson again!" At the press conference that immediately followed the adjournment, a journalist asked Kujawa if it would be easy to round up Crown witnesses for a retrial. The wily Crown attorney groaned. "You've just spoiled my day. I don't want to gather any witnesses." Gerry Allbright, who had grown far plumper since the trial, said little at the press conference. But he looked pleased.

The Saskatchewan summer was a dry one, bringing back to many old-timers alarming memories of the dust-bowl conditions of the Dirty Thirties. Like everyone else in the rural-based province, the lawyers in the case discussed the weather and its effect on the crops in casual conversations, and at work immersed themselves in new cases. There were always other cases, other important cases, to work on, but still the uncertainty of the appeal court's secret deliberations on the Thatcher trial hung over them, as well as over the Thatcher family, and JoAnn's friends and relatives.

In these circumstances rumours ran wild. Someone knew a judge who knew that the court was going to rule four-to-one against Thatcher. Someone else heard that because the court frequently took a year to make its decisions, a quick decision on this case would offend the others in the line-up, so the judges planned to take their time. And someone else heard in the courtroom corridors that, yes, Colin Thatcher was indeed going to get a new trial.

All this time Colin Thatcher was ensconced in prison in Edmonton. He whiled away the time putting the finishing touches to a book, due to be published in the fall. Entitled *Backrooms,* it purported to tell all about the dirty business of politics from the inside. To the publishers' surprise it had been written, in prison, from Colin Thatcher's impressive memory.

In the interim, in July, something happened in a courtroom in Peterborough, Ontario, that must have seemed a most encouraging omen to Serge Kujawa. In his argument before the appeal court he had introduced the parallel between

Colin Thatcher's case and the case of Peter Demeter, convicted of arranging his wife's 1973 murder "by a person or persons unknown." Now Demeter, still serving that controversial sentence but under only light supervision, had been accused of trying to arrange another murder. This time the intended victim was his cousin's 19-year-old son, Stuart Demeter. It was a bizarre case, involving an initial mistrial, but on July 2, Peter Demeter was convicted of the crime.

As summer gave way to fall and the appeal court remained silent the lawyers, police, witnesses and jurors whose lives had briefly centred on that Saskatoon courtroom tried to put the case out of their minds and get on with their lives. That process was a little harder, of course, for the members of the Thatcher family and for JoAnn's friends. For Colin Thatcher in his Edmonton cell, it must have been impossible. At any moment he might hear that his appeal had been successful, and that his case would be re-tried in open court, with a fighting chance of freedom at the end of it. Or the news could be disastrous, with the appeal denied; that would leave him only the faint hope of a successful appeal to the Supreme Court of Canada. Without success there, he knew that he would not be eligible for parole until the year 2009. But even if the worst happened, and the Damoclean sword did fall, it seemed unlikely he or his remarkable story—with all of the alarming elements of Greek tragedy—would soon be forgotten.

Meanwhile, late-season visitors to the pristine Legislative Building, an impressive monument to Edwardian hopes for the province and its distinguished lawmakers, could turn from the manicured lawns to look across Albert Street. There, on the corner, stood the house where JoAnn was murdered. The house was for sale.

ABOUT THE AUTHOR

Widely experienced in television, radio, and print journalism, Maggie Siggins is a former Max Bell Professor of Journalism at the University of Regina. She is the author of five previous books, including *Bassett*, a biography, and *Brian and the Boys* the study of a controversial Ontario trial.

Since 1983 she has lived in Regina, which allowed her to research this book exhaustively over many months. She reported every day on the Thatcher trial for *As It Happens* on CBC national radio. She is now working in China.